D0204659

BUSINESS HISTORY
OF THE WORLD

BUSINESS HISTORY OF THE WORLD

A Chronology

Compiled by
Richard Robinson

GREENWOOD PRESS
Westport, Connecticut • London

Library of Congress Cataloging-in-Publication Data

Robinson, Richard.
  Business history of the world : a chronology / compiled by Richard
Robinson.
    p. cm.
  Includes bibliographical references and indexes.
  ISBN 0-313-26094-X
  1. Economic history—Chronology. 2. Business—History—
Chronology. 3. Industry—History—Chronology. 4. Business
enterprises—History—Chronology. I. Title.
  HC51.R615   1993
  330.9—dc20   93-25476

British Library Cataloguing in Publication Data is available.

Library of Congress Catalog Card Number: 93-25476
ISBN: 0-313-26094-X

First published in 1993

Greenwood Press, 88 Post Road West, Westport, CT 06881
An imprint of Greenwood Publishing Group, Inc.

Printed in the United States of America

The paper used in this book complies with the
Permanent Paper Standard issued by the National
Information Standards Organization (Z39.48-1984).

10 9 8 7 6 5 4 3 2 1

For the pleasure of their company along the way,

Thomas Bossort
John Mee

Margaret Fenn
Wendell French
Joseph McGuire

William Boore
Donald Parker
John Rian

Contents

Preface

Business History of the World was compiled to complement my earlier chronology, United States Business History, 1602-1988. Together, the books present an overall picture of the evolution of business through time. This volume gives a basic timeline for business activity in the world for the years from 10,000 B.C. to the 1980s. Where possible, business events are extended into the 1990s as their stories unfold.

By identifying the documented entrepreneurs, managers and enterprises, this chronology records representative events in the evolution of business throughout the world. One aim is to give a general sense of what transpired as business evolved and thus to provide a general understanding of the diversity and pervasiveness of business activity. Of course, no chronology could presume to list all of the business events in worldwide history or to recount the innumerable stories of individuals succeeding and failing in economic activity. This volume makes no such claim.

In addition, the chronology seeks to provide information about the environment surrounding business activity. This data will illustrate the background for business transactions, identifying the dimensions of the marketplace and the external factors influencing the success or failure of any particular business enterprise at a given time and place. Then, too, the work endeavors to contribute to the understanding of business behavior by classifying cross-cultural data by time and place. Perhaps, in time, similar chronologies will be prepared for each country, helping us to reach a better understanding of the role that business plays in our life today.

The chronology begins by recording environmental and business events that show the development of economic activity from ancient times through the Middle Ages. Starting with the 1600s, the historical material is divided into two sections: General Events and Business Events.

The sections on General Events provide material on the environmental infrastructure, such as events occurring in agriculture, education and construction which contribute to the conduct and growth of business activity. Other events represent those factors influencing the demand and supply for the products and/or services provided by enterprises. Statistical indicators, including population figures, are given at times to show the dimensions and changes in economic activity. Discoveries in science are noted for their contributions to the development of technology and business enterprises.

Social trends, such as fashion, entertainment and sports, are also included in the General Events sections to show their evolution as business activities. Guild and union activities are given to indicate the reactions of workers to business practices. Governmental actions, including decrees, laws and judicial decisions, help to define the arena in which business takes place. Major social and political events, such as wars, catastrophes and rulers, are given as historical markers to show the passage of time.

Moreover, military events related to technological and organizational innovations and management activities are identified. In many cases, these events were precursors for techniques adopted later by business firms, particularly in organizational planning and structure. For example, the staff unit evolved in military organization long before appearing in business. In another illustration, during and after the Long March of 1934-35 in China, Mao Tse-Tung and fellow Communists developed a rankless army; the cadre was basically one of leaders, followers and specialists. This planned organizational change predates Organization Development (OD), the methodology stressing harmonious teamwork, designed and utilized by American and British business enterprises in the 1940s and 1950s. By studying such events, one can consider how the problems of dissimilar organizations lead to similar responses and what factors, external and internal, shape organizational behavior.

Although the primary focus of the study is on the evolution of business, the General Events also cover some non-business organizations engaged in commercial activity, i.e., the Kirov Ballet, the Vatican Bank, Spain's National Organization for the Blind and Le Cirque du Soleil. For a specific illustration, England's Salisbury Cathedral signed a sponsorship deal with McDonald's. All church visitors during a two-month period in 1992 received a scroll on the history of the building, which served as a voucher for a free sandwich with every sandwich bought. The cathedral received a share of the profits to help defray its $6,000 daily cost for maintenance.

The sections on Business Events seek to identify both the pivotal and the commonplace occurrences in business. The continua of activity ranges from legal to illegal enterprises, governmental businesses to private firms, corporate conglomerates to simple proprietorships, and local concerns to transnational organizations. This date gives some sense as to the ever-changing complexity and diversity of business activity in world history.

The Business Events sections are also concerned with the rise and fall of various business activities - from producers of goods and/or services to wholesalers and retailers. The areas covered include manufacturing, transportation, insurance, banking, construction, communications, advertising, real estate and personal services, such as consulting. Further citations document the changes in distribution, as the markets evolve from peddlers and hawkers to market stalls, shops, department stores and grand shopping centers. One might see from this chronology how the supply and demand for goods and services interact to satisfy the needs of a society.

The chronology also records events in the technical areas of accounting, financing, marketing and manufacturing, as well as items related to the universal practice of management, covering the functions of directing, planning, organizing, staffing and controlling. Such practices show the problems businesses have had to resolve at certain times and places.

This chronology includes as many business people as possible. While many heads of state and public figures are identified for their impact on business activity, the hoi polloi of the business world deserve at least equal attention. After all, the entrepreneur is the wellspring of economic activity in a society. Innovators are of special concern for the key roles they have played in breaking the web of tradition. Brief biographies of various individuals are occasionally given to enrich the fabric of business history.

Furthermore, the chronology endeavors to present all events in a descriptive manner. The compiler has tried to withhold normative judgments. Thus, readers are free to reach their own conclusions as to why certain events took place when they did and the significance of these events. Such thoughts should enable one to develop a clearer understanding of what is taking place today in the world of business, and provide a more logical basis for detecting the future direction of business activity.

A selected bibliography of primary references follows the chronology. Then, three indexes - names, places and subjects - have been prepared to aid in locating specific data. Notes for using the indexes are given on page 440.

Since this work is the first such chronology for world business, the research can only be viewed as exploratory. In this sense, the volume only begins the study so others later may more completely identify and describe what took place in business. Then, scholars can begin to formulate and test hypotheses on what happened, what didn't happen, and why.

The events recorded here have been identified in common references on world history. The selection of events was not so much a matter of personal choice, but was based on those events cited as distinct occurrences in the available references. Availability was the major criterion for the years prior to 1600. For the modern era (particularly since World War II when historical data became almost overwhelming in the annual publications of Facts on File and in various business magazines), events were chosen for their display of innovation, such as those that pioneered a new technology or procedure, or for their representativeness, such as those that illustrated the common practice or highlighted a trend. When space permitted, atypical events were included for those curious about the more unusual activities of business endeavor.

Unfortunately, the recorded events are skewed toward business activities in Europe. This reporting was not by design, but instead resulted from the limitations of the references available in English on the history of business. Perhaps with this start, more research on the growth of business in other countries will be forthcoming. Until then, this chronology endeavors to provide an overview as to that the general picture might be.

As already mentioned, the chronology does not pretend to cover all, or even most, of the business events occurring throughout history, a task that is obviously impossible. This record tries, instead, to contribute to the quest for more knowledge about what has evolved in world business by reporting events that illustrate the highlights of what transpired.

The compiler has endeavored to list events within a specified time period in the actual order of their occurrence, but this has proved to be most difficult, as the references do not always give specific months and days. Then, too, the sources do not always agree on which year a particular event took place. In such instances, events are cited as occurring circa a specific year, or during a time span ranging from five years to a decade or fifty years to a century.

Regrettably, some events worthy of inclusion became apparent only after the chronological record was compiled. For example, Yvon Chouinard, college dropout and noted rock climber, started a climbing-equipment business with a partner in 1966. After incorporating in 1972, he spun off the Patagonia climbing clothes business as a separate venture in 1976, and it eventually became one of the most successful firms in the United States, with branches worldwide, achieving sales of $120 million in 1990-91. Chouinard started donating part of the pre-tax profits to environmental causes in 1984. After four lawsuits resulting from climbing accidents, he was forced to declare bankruptcy for the equipment business in 1989. Perhaps, as other such business experiences become known, they can be included in ensuing historical records.

In addition to lacking data on some events, the chronology is unable to give in-depth coverage to many of the giant enterprises currently dominating international commerce. Such business organizations are too complex for this volume. Indeed, each would warrant its own individual timeline. For example, the mighty Mitsubishi, Japan's largest industrial group, or <u>keiretso</u>, with total revenues of $176 billion by 1990, operates with an interlocking complex of 25 core member firms surrounding a nucleus composed of Mitsubishi Corp., Mitsubishi Bank and Mitsubishi Heavy Industries. Hundreds of related companies are interwoven with the core group. The elegant intricacy of this organization defies a simple accounting. Moreover, Mitsubishi is just one of many Japanese firms so constructed. The Dai-Ichi Kangin Group has 47 core members, Fuyo has 29, Mitsui has 24, Sanwa has 44, and Sumitomo has 20 member firms.

Then, of course, there are the many giant enterprises existing in Europe, such as Nestle, Unilever, Royal Dutch Shell, N.V. Philips and Daimler-Benz.

Because of this overwhelming complexity, the chronology only records the dates when these firms appeared on the scene and some of their most noteworthy events. Thus, the reader should realize that what has been covered in this account is but the tip of the iceberg. Nevertheless, the chronology does try to identify the major and representative contestants in the global market. Again, additional research in the future will be able to offer a more detailed picture of world business.

History ever continues on its way to whatever destiny awaits. In this sense, history is a seamless continuum of time, as the past flows through the present into the future. Dievole vineyard near Chianti, Italy, is just one example. After appearing c. 1090, it was sold to Germany's Schwenn family in the mid-1980s, and it continues to evolve. However, for practical reasons, the chronology must stop at some point for publication. Due to time constraints, it was necessary to conclude the formal chronology with 1988. Nevertheless, where possible, attempts were made to update the material by including parenthetical information about events in the 1990s. For instance, the listing for Hanson Trust in 1986 covers its activities to 1990, and the account for BAT Industries in 1987 continues to 1991. However, as history continues to reveal itself faster than it can be recorded, one can only conclude that the accounts of many reported events, such as the story of Sweden's Stora Kopporberg of 1228 which still evolves, remain to be completed, and may not be finished by the year 2000 or even in the next century.

Acknowledgments are due to those who helped me with this research. Patty Taylor's efforts in recording the material helped me to start the project. Besides letting me enjoy their camaraderie through the ups and downs of compiling the chronology, Edith and David Park played a critical role in organizing and preparing the work for publication. The assistance of Joan Dalton in correcting my material was a major contribution. All mentioned merit a hearty "well done" in appreciation of their support and encouragement.

Chronology

10,000-9001 B.C.

Last glacial age gradually ends (-7000 B.C., leads to rise in summer temperatures and less rain, migration of nomads to river valleys in India, Middle East, Egypt and Central America)... Dogs are domesticated, cats by Egypt in 2500-2401... Pottery appears in Japan, China in 6000.

9000-8001

Sheep are domesticated in areas of Iraq, Romania... People in Zagros foothills of Mesopotamia cultivate grains, domesticate animals... Sumerians, possibly from Caspian Sea area, appear in Tigris-Euphrates Valley, disappear with destruction of Ur c. 1950, B.C.

8000-7001

Crude written symbols are used in Mesopotamia to keep records (follows use of pebbles, notches on sticks, scratches on rock and charcoal marks on cave walls)... Walled City of Jericho covers some 10 acres, world's "first" settlement... Potatoes, beans are cultivated in Peru.

7000-6001

People in Zagros foothills of Mesopotamia build crude mud huts... Pigs, chickens and water buffalo are domesticated... Durum wheat for macaroni is grown in Anatolia... Sugar cane is cultivated in New Guinea... Yams, bananas and coconuts are grown in Indonesia... Cloth weaving appears in Anatolia, woven mats in Jordan... Clay pottery appears in Near East and flax in Southwestern Asia... Ovens for bread appear in Middle East, raised bread in Egypt in 3000 and China bakes bread in 1400.

6000-5001

Cows, last major food animal, are domesticated in Turkey, Macedonia... First definite traces of agrarian settlers in Europe appear in Balkans, mining pits seen in Poland... Mesopotamia's Hassuna society uses irrigation, fine pottery, permanent dwellings (brews beer, seen in China by 2300, for sacrificial rites - 16 types from barley, wheat and honey by 4000)... Wheel evolves, follows use of rollers under platforms to transport heavy objects... Picture of Egyptian vessel shows first sail... Wheat, lentils appear in Southwestern Asia, citrus fruit in Indochina.

5000-4001

After noting cycle of rise and fall of Nile, irrigation is used along river (leads to canals and bureaucratic "water provinces," 3000-2501, to regulate supply of irrigation water to fields and to pay bailiffs tending canals with harvest of farmers)... Rice is cultivated... Mesopotamian villages cluster along rivers flowing into Persian Gulf, dominance by Halafian society trading in sailing vessels from Persian Gulf to Mediterranean... First known calendar is devised in Egypt, year with 12 months, 360 days... Climate of Africa changes from dry to wet, turning upper half into fertile region, new dry period around 2000... Basket weaving appears in Middle East, Egypt... Egyptians mine, smelt copper ores, produce tons of copper from Sinai mines c. 3200... Cotton is grown in Mexico... Llamas, alpacas are domesticated in Andes... Farmers at head of Persian Gulf use crude irrigation for fields.

4400

Looms are used to weave cloth.

4000-3501

Bronze Age appears in Mesopotamia and Egypt, widespread by 3000 and reaches Europe by 2000... In Mesopotamia Ubaidians use division of labor to build villages and religious shrines, use cylinder seals to show ownership of documents, vessels... Sumerians settle Babylon, use copper alloys... Russian-made ceramics are seen in China... Vineyards are planted, Egypt, to make wine... Egyptian stone cutters leave marks, used also to brand livestock, on buildings, perhaps evidence for wage claims... Seen since 5000 copper metallurgy appears in Balkan villages, mines in 2500 B.C... Wine, domesticated grapes appear in Turkestan, olives in Crete... Ard, primitive plow, appears in China... Egypt, Sumeria smelt gold, silver... Cattle pull plows in Northern Mesopotamia... Ur appears in Mesopotamia.

3600

Sand table, earliest known form of abacus, is used to make calculations.

3560

Sumerians in Erech use pictograms, 2,000 signs, on soft clay tablets to keep temple records, used later for business transactions.

3500-3001

In Egypt simple scratch plow is used on farmlands along Nile, numbers are developed, upper and lower Egypt are unified by King Menes, and hieroglyphics are changed with use of characters in writing of hieratics by Egyptian priests... Bronze weapons, potter's wheel appear in Mesopotamia... Sumerians use wheeled vehicles, build reed huts with prefabricated parts for assembly... Amber appears as currency throughout Europe, reaches Greece by 1500... Sumerians use draft animals, usually oxen... Sledge appears in Erech... Cooking steamers are seen in China... Sumerians use clay tokens to represent numbers of animals or measures of grain, new tokens for finished clothing, jars of olive oil, loaves of bread and metal objects... Egyptians write on papyrus and use metal mirrors... Candles appear... Sumerians use columns, domes, arches and vaults building Ziggurat in Ur.

3000-2701

Vegetable tanning is used in Egypt to make leather... Linen is made in Middle East... Sumerians use factories, royal and private, and temples to make goods (use temples to collect taxes, oil lamps for illumination, coins for legal tender instead of barley)... Chinese warlords play war games with stones on stylized maps to practice their craft... Egypt builds sea trade with Byblos, Tyre and Dison... Wrestling evolves as sport... Weaving loom appears in Europe... Wooden ships are used in Mediterranean for trading... Glass appears in Egypt... Flax is grown in Babylonia, Egypt... Sumerians develop cuneiform writing... Donkeys, mules appear in Canaan, camels in Iran and Arabia and elephants in India... India cultivates cotton... Egyptian traders barter knowledge, seeds, tools, domesticated animals with Eritrea, Somalia for frankincense, myrrh... Byblos, perhaps Middle East's first major port, cites copper imports, later exports cedars of Lebanon... Sumerians trade, donkey caravans and boats, with Asia Minor, Syria, Elam and Persian Gulf islands (barter agricultural surplus, 40% of grain to brewers, for raw materials, exotic goods).

2800

Chief minister and architect Imhotep, served by cabinet of advisers and civil service, builds step pyramid of Saqqarah, oldest known stone structure, for King Djoser, founder of Dynasty III, Egypt... District governors in Old Kingdom, Egypt, designate Diggers of Canals for irrigation... Chinese make hempen ropes.

2750

Gilgamesh rules Uruk (develops Uruk as city of 10-15,000).

2700-2601

Book of instructions on arts of leadership, communications is prepared by vizer for son of King Issi, Egypt (covers planning, counselors, authority and responsibility, job descriptions, performance evaluations, trade specialization)... Wife of Chinese Emperor Huang-ti "discovers" winding of silk (travels to West over Silk Road 200s B.C., industry goes to Japan 300s A.D. and Constantinople 530 A.D.)... Chinese use vertical pole to estimate time.

2600-2501

Calculating frame, early abacus, appears in China, Japan... Cheops Pyramid is built at Gizeh,

Egypt (needs 2.5 million blocks to build structure to height of 481 feet in 20 years, requires astronomical measurements, surveying techniques and 30,000-100,000 free and conscripted peasants in specialized craft units, by tradition sons required to practice trade of fathers to avoid distraction of political activity)... Xue clan, China, uses wheeled vehicles, mineral oil lubrication in 400s A.D.

2500-2001

Civil engineering, astronomical measurements, water-lifting devices, mathematics and crude metallurgy appear in Egypt, Mesopotamia... Ard replaces hoe as primary agricultural tool, yoke, ox-traction and sled seen... Map of Babylonia is made, chickens domesticated in area... Pottery is made, China... Sumerian priests operate Houses of Wisdom (use libraries, develop mathematical tables for improving calculations used in trade)... Sumerians use weights, shekel and mina, in trading, Egypt c. 1500... Bronze sickles appear, seed drills in Babylonia and skis in Scandinavia... Egypt imports olive oil from eastern Mediterranean... Sumerians use chariots... Flint is mined in Europe... Chaldeans in Ur solder sheets of gold... Mesopotamia sets legal units for weight, length and capacity... Sumerians are first to use soap.

2400

Farmers in area of Peru irrigate fields.

2364

"Compass" may have been used by military, China, to advance through enemy's fog screen.

2360

Sargon is ruler of Akkadians (-2305, leads expedition northward to aid his merchants in City of Puruskhanda in 2350, develops compound bow, uses maps for land taxation).

2350

Advisory staff appears during rule of Emperor Yao, China.

2300

Ebla, follows farming settlement around 3000, evolves as commercial city near Aleppo, Turkey, of 30,000, some 300,000 in local area, with traders, may have used gold and silver for exchange, farmers, artisans and scribes, destroyed by Hittites in 1600... Trade between Harappans in Indus Valley and Sumerians reaches height.

2255

Emperor Shun rules in China (-2206), strategy game of weigi or Go appears (is carried to Japan by Japanese Ambassador in 754 A.D., played by samurai in 1200s).

2205

Yu the Great tames Yellow River with dikes, drainage canals.

2160

In this time (-1788) Egyptian government decentralizes, new centralization by pharaohs, military in 1600.

2100

Sumer's government uses a "civil service".

2000-1501

Study of astrology to predict future develops in Babylonia, used for individual horoscopes in 600s-200s B.C... Butter is known... Decimal system is seen in Crete... Stonehenge is built, England, perhaps an astronomical instrument... Mercury, contraceptives are used in Egypt... Horses are used to pull vehicles... Trade routes evolve from Eastern Mediterranean throughout Europe... Chalybes tribe, Hittite Empire, works iron (-1200s, appears in Egypt, Levant, Mycenaen Greece and Crete in 1500-1200 and in Europe 800- 500)... Cotton is grown in Indus Valley, spreads to Mesopotamia... Chinese potters use kaolin clay... Asian steppe people use war horses, Hyksos uses horses to conquer Egypt in 1700... Earliest Chinese script appears... Alfalfa is grown, Persia... Cretan palace of Minos provides water to interior bathrooms... First zoo, Park of Intelligence, appears in China... Physicians in Babylon, Syria form professional group, base practice on astrology and belief in dreams... Ard plow appears in Uruk, iron plowshares in Canaan... Rice paddies appear in China... Spoke wheels appear in Asia Minor, Persia... Seafaring Minoans build maritime empire on Crete by controlling Eastern Mediterranean trade routes.

1900

Assyria uses iron to forge tools, weapons... Akkadian code of Eshunna sets price controls.

1844

Ammenemes III rules Egypt (-1797, builds irrigation projects, opens copper mines on Sinai peninsula, governs with viser to oversee royal residence, public works, military, police, royal artisans, high court, royal farms and tax collection, chancellor and provincial governors).

1818

Kieh Kwei reigns as provincial ruler in China (-1767), vassal Wu devises playing cards.

1800

Minoan vessels sail throughout Eastern Mediterranean and to Sicily... Primitive bayonets appear in Mesopotamia, sword evolves 1000-901.

1766

Shang dynasty appears in China (-1754, during rule delegates authority to ministers to manage functional departments).

1728

Hammurabi is ruler of Babylonia (-1686, requires students preparing to be scribes to study languages, mathematics, early forms of algebra and geometry, law, medicine, and divination or astrology, formulates Code of Hammurabi to designate places for safekeeping of valuables, to legalize contracts for selling, leasing and bartering, to allow women in business, to create social classes of aristocrats, freemen and slaves, to permit private ownership of land, to require all business transactions to be recorded and signed - execution a penalty for failure, to set conditions for employment of workers - specifies wages for tanners, to provide government insurance to those robbed by brigands, to allow temples, as done in Egypt, to charge interest on loans, to set standards for beer in condemning understrength and over-pricing, and to levy stiff penalties on wine shops for violations).

1700

Phoenicians use 22-letter alphabet (-1651).

1600

During Egyptian rule of Thothmes I staff units are used by army, apparently for gathering intelligence... Core-molded opaque glass is developed, Mesopotamia, to make small vials for unguents and perfumes, Egypt in 1500-1400 (-1500)... Bellows are used in glass manufacture, metallurgy.

1500-1001

Egypt regulates sale of beer... Labor strikes are seen in Thebes... First known treatise on horse breeding, training is written... Corinth appears in Greece... Olmec society appears in Central America... Hinduism evolves in India (flourishes 500s B.C.-300s A.D.)... Moses leads Israelites from Egypt (shows use of planning, delegation, organization, personnel selection and training in Old Testament)... Saddle, bridle harness appear in Cossack villages... Silk fabrics appear in China... Maize is grown in America... Assyrians use simple pulleys... Shaduf, pole with balanced bucket, is used in Egypt for irrigation, possibly endless chain of buckets in 600s-500s B.C. to water Hanging Gardens of Babylon... Sundial appears in Egypt... Liquor is distilled in Asia... Soybeans are grown in Manchuria... Water clocks appear in Egypt (1450-1401)... Swedish traders visit Western Europe, Britain and Ireland to barter amber, etc., for gold, copper, tin... Amphora, invented by Canaanites, appears in Egypt.

1483

Mycenaean states evolve in Greece with chiefdoms within revenue states (-1200)... Thutmose III is sole ruler of Egypt (-c. 1450, erects "Needle of Cleopatra" obelisk in Heliopolis to calculate time).

1450

Imported cinnamon from Malaya, Indonesia is known in Egypt.

1385

Rule of Amenhotep IV, Nefertiti starts in Egypt (-1358, try to use military as civil servants, replace traditional worship with one universal God).

1334

Egypt's King Tutankhamen plays game of Senet in this time.

1300

Hittites establish code to regulate prices... Goods from China are identified by trademarks, used also to identify Chinese porcelain, Greek and Roman pottery... Decimals appear in China, first cited in Spain in 976 A.D.

1292

Rameses II rules Egypt (-1225, builds obelisk, shows man astride horizontal bar on two wheels).

1200

England is settled by branch of Celts from Gaul... Egyptian symbols are used in Phoenicia to create alphabet of written characters (-876 B.C.)... In this time, Chinese Queen Fu Hao is buried in lacquered, a plastic varnish, coffin - first artificial plastic, celluloid, in 1869 by J. W. Hyatt... Aegean seafarers start Philistine civilization in Levant area between Israelite tribes and Egypt (-600s B.C.)... Alquerque, ancestor to game of checkers, appears in Egypt (appears in France c. 1720).

1167

Merchants of Rhodes write pioneering maritime code (evolves with every ship having owner or hirer distinct from captain, with merchant always traveling with goods, with captain in command after departure, with crew of petty officers, mate carpenter and helmsman, sailors and cook, and with specified wages: captain at twice the rate for sailors, officers at 75% of captain's rate and cook at 50% of sailors' pay).

1122

In this time, Chou Dynasty appears in Western Chinese kingdom (-271 B.C., uses systematic irrigation, fertilization, field rotation, and animal-drawn plows in farming, uses iron tools in farming and mining, smelts and casts iron, uses cowry shells, silk, grain, jade, pearls, leather and pieces of metal as money in trading, uses job descriptions for all civil servants from ministers to servants, uses organization with ministers, great officials and warrior- officials in governing, and uses I Ching to make court decisions by considering five elements of water, metal, wood, fire and earth as systems and two forces of Yin and Yang in changing from flux to reflux).

1100

Phoenicia founds Cadiz on Atlantic Coast of Spain, ruled by Carthage in 500 B.C., Rome 200 B.C., Moors 711 A.D., Castile 1262.

1050

Duke of Chou, China, builds (-1001) "South-pointing carriage" with differential gears.

1000-901

In Mesopotamia Chaldeans use water-filled cubes to measure time, weight, length... Saul is first King of Israel (conquers Jerusalem, reconquered some 37 times in next 4 millenniums)... Iron tools replace those of copper, bronze... Phoenicians create purple dye... After being evicted from Greece by Dorians, Ionians settle West Coast of Asia Minor... Professional musicians appear in religious ceremonies in Israel... Game of As, forerunner of poker, is played in Persia, introduced to Europe by Crusaders... Camel-riding appears in Arabia... Iron-tipped plow appears... Lock, keys are devised in Egypt... Knitted fabrics are seen... Mesopotamia uses pack camels... Oats are grown in central Europe.

900-801

Iron, steel production appears in Indo-Caucasian culture... Natural gas wells are drilled in China... First known arched bridge appears in Smyrna.

876

Zero symbol appears in Indian inscription.

814

Phoenician traders found Carthage on North Africa, use early form of Greek alphabet in commerce.

800-701

Phoenicians take Malaga in Spain, mining base from 1000 B.C... Etruscan settlements appear in Italy, evolve as loose confederation of cities ruled by princes... Royal palace of Nineveh is built, library with some 20,000 clay tablets on history, medicine, astronomy, astrology... Babylonians use silver shekel unit for exchange... Phoenicia uses Tripoli as port on East Mediterranean Coast... Sparta forbids citizens to engage in economic activity, handled by underclass of non-citizens... First diamonds are found, India.

776

After starting as early as 1300s, regular athletic games are held at Olympia, site for shrine of Zeus and treasuries of city states (-394 A.D. when banned as pagan ritual).

775

Greek colonists on Pithecusae, Bay of Naples, trade with Etruscans, spurs production of metals in Etruria.

753

Rome is founded (after joint rule by Romulus and Titus Tatius of Sabines, rotates kingship between men of Sabine and Latin extraction until rule of Etruscan Tarquin I in 616-579 B.C., uses council of 100 elders as senate to advise King, develops salt marshes at mouth of Tiber, source of wealth for Etruscan city of Veii, for commerce via Salt Road).

722

Alphabet with vowels, consonants appears in Greece (-481 B.C.).

715

Numa Pompilius is King of Rome (-673, "legalizes" collegia of flute players, goldsmiths, coppersmiths, fullers, shoemakers, potters, dyers, carpenters, actors as mutual-benefit societies).

700-601

Water clocks appear in Assyria (uses military force of some 50,000 men with archers, spearmen, cavalry and charioteers with specialists in siegecraft, supply)... Nineveh evolves in Mesopotamia as trading center (shows use of sales, money exchanges, rentals, leases, interest on loans, mortgages)... Light horseshoes are seen in Mediterranean area, use of heavy horseshoes in Europe during 800s-900s A.D... Ornamental weaving evolves in Greece... Glaucus of Chios discovers soldering of iron... Greek alphabet is acquired from Etruria by Romans... Bireme with oars and sails replaces monoreme vessel with 50 oars... Spoke wheels appear in Europe... Phoenicians use oar-propelled galleys as first war vessels (use drum to set rowing tempo, later flute and pipe music used in Greece to pace standardized motions for those doing monotonous, repetitive tasks)... Arab merchants use monsoon winds to trade along East African coast... Lydia mints "first" coins of gold and silver alloy, possibly to pay mercenaries, while nearby states of Miletus, Ephesus mint coins with state emblems (leads to mints by 600 in most Greek cities and by 300 in Middle Europe).

685

Touchstone is used in Lydia to determine purity of gold, previously gold and silver ingots valued by weight in Egypt, Mesopotamia.

657

Greek colonists found Byzantium, evolves as Nova Roma, Constantinople, and Istanbul (is populated by some 50,000 in 337 A.D., 400,000 by 400 A.D., 1 million by 500 A.D.).

630

Samos ship, Colacus, is driven by storm through Pillars of Hercules to land on Atlantic Coast of Spain.

610

Phoenicians from Carthage voyage around Africa (-595)... Necho fails to build canal from Nile to Red Sea.

605

Nebuchadnezzar II is King of Babylonia (-561, builds "Tower of Babel", uses color coding in textile mills for production control of different yarns, in granaries for storage of grains by age and in payments, based on amount of production, for women spinners, weavers).

603

Babylonians destroy Philistine town near Jerusalem, Ekron, over 6000 people, a major olive oil center with 100-200 processors (shows distinct industrial section, with crude factories apart from living and public areas).

600-501

Theater is built at Delphi... Sundials appear in Greece, China... Mayan civilization appears in

Central America... Round-cast coins are used for exchange in China... Theodorus of Samos devises ore smelting and casting, water level, lock-and-key, carpenter's square, and lathe... Some 250 Greek colonies appear on Coast of Aegean and Black Seas, Cypress, Libya, Sicily, Southern Italy, Corsica, Spain and France, Marseilles oldest French community (becomes trading center with interior)... Roman numerals appear... Thales of Miletus observes static electricity by rubbing ore magnetite to attract metallic iron and amber, Elekton in Greek, to attract light objects... Iron plow appears in China, frame-plow in 400s B.C. (appears in Europe in 1784)... Corinth builds 3-mile slipway to transport vessels over Isthmus, used to 800s A.D... Chinese states employ educated bureaucrats... Phoenicians develop soap, cited by Galen of Pergamon, c. 130 A.D.-200 A.D., as cleansing agent... Iron weapons replace those of bronze in China... Salt trade develops... Chinese fumigate houses to eliminate pests... Assyria builds 50-mile canal to link Nineveh, Bavia... Celts work salt mines at Hallstatt, Austria... Merchant class appears in China.

598

King Chao of Yen may have used whale-oil lamps, possibly 308 B.C. by king similarly named.

594

Solon starts governmental reforms in Athens (repeals bondage of debtors, grants limited land ownership, forms class system for military service and taxes, designs governance by 9 archons from elite class with advice by council of 400 from 3rd class, forbids export of any agricultural produce except olive oil, standardizes coinage, increases trade).

590

Pythian games appear at Delphi in this time.

588

In this time (-484 B.C.) Olympic games are dominated by athletes of Kroton, prosperous Greek colony on instep of Italian boot (develops medical school to provide training advice).

585

Thales of Miletus predicts eclipse of sun, first known explanation of earth, sky by logic (uses knowledge of meteorology later to forecast bumper crop of olives, buys olive oil presses in Miletus to control supply, retires in one year after becoming wealthy).

578

Servius Tullis rules Rome (-534, forms each legion with 6 tribunes as board of governors, is reorganized by Caius, Roman Consul, in 102 B.C., and Julius Caesar in 1st Century B.C.).

575

Igibi Bank operates in Babylon (acts as buying agent, loans money on crops, signatures and tangible goods, and pays interest on deposits).

561

Croesus rules Lydia (-547, issues first Imperial gold and silver coins in 550, follows use of coins in India c. 2900 B.C., Assyria c. 700 B.C.).

560

Tyrant Peisistratus rules Athens (-527, promotes industry and exports, extends loans to small farmers, confirms rights of artisans).

550

Cyrus the Great rules Persian Empire, started 559 (-530, divides land into 20 provinces, forms local military garrisons to report to king's general, starts regular courier service - first such messengers introduced by Assyria in 745-728, and recognizes need for planning, motivating subordinates, using teamwork, dividing work by specialization, and using orderly work methods)... Merchant class appears in India.

549

Hecataeus of Miletus, historian (draws map of known world to show Europe, Asia linked with Northern Africa divided, bounded by water), is born (-486).

539

Persia's Cyrus captures Babylon, world's greatest commercial trading center of Middle East with some 200,000 people.

534

Peisistratus sponsors Dionysian festivals to satisfy popular demand (recognizes Thespis as winner of 1st prize for tragedy).

530

Greek architect, engineer Eupalinus builds aqueduct, water system for Megara.

521

Hanno of Carthage explores, first known, interior Africa... Himilco of Carthage explores England (becomes source of tin), Ireland and Scandinavia... Darius I rules Persian Empire (-486, governs with special group of ad hoc advisers instead of permanent body used earlier by Assyrian kings, decentralizes land into 20-22 provinces for collecting taxes and raising military forces, establishes permanent board of judges, codifies laws, follows Egyptian custom in granting patents with privileges to temples, appoints head treasurer over regional treasuries to make clothing, tapestries, furniture, metalcraft and leather goods, standardizes currency, gold darics with emperor's image, to replace barter, forbids coining of gold by anyone but royal mints, builds pontoon bridge across Bosphorus and canal from Red Sea to Nile, provides awards to inventors, starts Houses of Life in major temples as colleges for study of priesthood and medicine, recognizes unity of authority, proper placement of individuals, need for planning, motivation and teamwork, and specialization of work with uniform methods in practice of management, builds royal road from Susa, Persian capitol, to Anatolia's Sardis).

518

Darius I sends Skylax down Indus River and around Arabia to Red Sea canal.

513

Iron is used in China to make agricultural implements, weapons (appears in Scandinavia in 750-800

A.D. and widespread in Europe in 1300s)... Darius I of Persia mints gold, silver coins.

509

After Etruscan Tarquin is overthrown, Rome becomes a republic with collegiate magistracy of two elected consuls.

500-451

Confucius, Minister of Justice in China (496), prepares detailed plan for daily conduct of all citizens to develop harmonious, stable state... Chinese farmers plant crops in rows, hoe weeds and apply manure, not seen in West until 1700s... Corinth develops trireme vessel... Treasury of Delian league in Greece is moved from Delos to Athens, used as safe depository (allows priests to charge interest on loans)... Athens forbids exports of all agricultural products except olive oil (-462, pays city soldiers, judges regular salaries)... Rome's senate sets maximum rate of interest (develops banking system with accounts, receipts of deposit, bills of exchange, letters of credit, loans, mortgages)... African settlements slowly appear in area of Ethiopia... People south of Sahara gradually develop mining, refining, working of metal (-100s B.C.)... Hanno of Carthage explores West Coast of Africa... First iron saw appears, augers and planes by 50 B.C... Anonymous treatise on art of war describes uniform methods to perform tasks... Steel is made in India.

499

After defeating Etruscans, new Latin league forms, Rome dominant member.

494

After withholding labor from Patricians in Rome, debt-burdened Plebeians win concessions in first known strike (institute first "ombudsman" to protect rights of Plebeians).

490

Athens opens treasury at Delphi for those seeing Pythian games.

484

State-owned mines of Athens find silver (uses funds for navy).

480

Xerxes' Persian forces invade Greece (-479, uses 6 marshals, 29 nobles to command largest army, some 200,000-300,000 men, of its time).

461

Pericles governs Athens, state of some 300,000 as largest importer of grain from Black Sea area (-430, rebuilds public areas with marketplaces, introduces policy of state pay for public service).

450-401

Hippodamus of Miletus builds town, port of Rhodes... Rome assigns administration of treasury to magistrates and establishes Code of Twelve Tables, basic law for some 900 years (sets maximum rate of interest with penalties for any rates over limit, protects property rights, specifies rights of creditors in collecting debts, requires fines to be paid in weights of bronze, allows prices to be determined by market conditions instead of by custom).

430

Athens is decimated by a plague (-427)... Optical telegraph with torches is used in China (-421).

423

When Athens invokes trade embargo against Sparta's ally Megara, Peloponnesian War begins (-404, leads to Athens' use of 10 strategoi, generals, as communal command system).

406

Dionysius the Elder, ruler of Syracuse, introduces forerunner of catapult, builds quadriremes.

403

Period of Warring States evolves in China (-221, shows use of cart with two shafts, merchant entrepreneurs, industrial activity with iron mines and foundries, use of coal firing to make cast iron)... Greek alphabet, adapted from letters used by Phoenician traders since 800s, is officially adopted by Athens.

400-351

China builds first wall to keep out invaders... Etruscans build first true arch in Italy... Etruscan actors give first theatrical performances in Rome... Terra cotta lamps, using sesame, flaxseed or olive oil, are made by regional pottery manufacturers in Asia Minor, Greece, Sicily, parts of Italy and elsewhere around Mediterranean... Criers, tracing heritage to Hermes the god of commerce and theft, appear in Greek cities to announce commercial matters... Process for casting, cutting and polishing glass appears in Mediterranean area, glass blowing in 1st century B.C... China uses petroleum, natural gas as fuel... Zeros, negative numbers in 100s B.C., appear in China, Cambodia and Sumatra in 683 A.D.... The Book of the Devil Valley Master, China, cites use of compass device by jade miners searching for mineral, first cited in Europe by Neckam in 1190 A.D... Xenophon, Greek historian (holds mechanical arts have bad repute for their injury to health of workers), prepares treatise, Oeconomicus, on estate management (discusses universality of management in commerce and military, specialization, inventory control, incentives, planning and budgeting).

387

Plato opens an academy in Athens (-525 A.D.).

383

Rome establishes two colonies, City's first in Italy, as protection against Etruria.

380

Plato "invents" water clock with alarm (-371).

370

Plato, Greek philosopher (attributes invention of dice to Egyptian god Thot, god of knowledge and magic formulation), writes Republic (-360, holds that commerce and industry are debasing occupation, that war is an inevitable result of economic growth and that specialization is required to supply needs of citizens).

367

Rome reforms law allowing debtors, their inheritors to be put in virtual slavery.

359

Philip II rules Macedonia (-336, devises phalanx infantry information, prototype for field artillery, to conquer most of Greece by 338, uses engineers, surgeons and training officers in military force).

352

Rome institutes commission, commissioners called bankers, with extensive powers to lend state funds, adjust mortgages, settle bankruptcies and to discharge debts (oversees financial activities of money lenders, cooperative loans to reduce risks of individual lenders, money-changers, loans with land and crops for security, government contracts, a monopoly of joint-stock companies with public shares, and bonds).

350-301

Greek explorer Pytheas of Massilla reaches Britain.

350

Mencius, Chinese philosopher (proposes that benevolent government is one by self interest and that craft specialization is a required for hereditary lifetime career), explains need for system approach in any activity.

348

Carthage, Rome sign commercial treaty to establish trading areas and rights.

340

Daimachus, Greek historian (identifies three categories of steel in works: tools, razors and swords, files and chisels), is born (-?).

338

Rome uses first copper coins, replaces bronze tokens and cattle as units of exchange (mints silver coins in 269 B.C., gold coins in 217 B.C.).

336

Alexander the Great starts rule (-323, is advised by informal council with specialists from supply, engineering and provost-marshal on matters of military administration and organization, uses voice trumpets, spear movements, smoke signals, fire beacons and messengers to command troops).

335

Aristotle, Greek philosopher (views commerce as ignoble in <u>De anima</u>, first great treatise in psychology, discusses role of chance in life and poverty as parent of revolution in <u>Politics</u>, and happiness, not wealth, as indispensable to virtuous life in <u>Nichomachean Ethics</u>, and cites use of glass mirror in work), opens Lyceum as school of philosophy.

331

Alexander the Great locates Alexandria at mouth of the Nile (in 307 B.C. is base for museum and library, some 700,000 manuscripts by time of Julius Caesar, as world's first state-supported research institution).

329

Alexander the Great conquers Samarkand on ancient trade route between Middle East and China, dotted with caravansaries to provide lodgings for traders.

321

Brahman Kautilya: <u>Arthasastra</u> (discusses organization and management of trade and commerce, analyzes those practices that result in success in order to identify principles).

312

Work is started in Italy to build Appian Way between Rome and Capua, extended to Brindisi with spur in 109 A.D... Rome builds its first aqueduct, Aqua Appia, to bring spring water 10 miles to City.

310

Aristarchus of Samos, Greek astronomer (views sun as center of universe), is born (-230)... Chinese invent double-acting piston bellows, not known in West until 1500s.

306

Epicurus, Greek philosopher (advocates materialism, hedonism), opens School of Philosophy in Athens.

301

Zeno opens School of "Stoic" Philosophy in Athens.

300-251

China exports silk to India... Sun Tzu: <u>The Art of War</u> (discusses evaluating terrain, analyzing offensive and defensive strategies in making decisions, maintaining logistical services, waging psychological warfare)... Rotary hand-mills are used in Mediterranean area to mill grains (leads to growth of professional millers)... Trace harness for horses appears in China to replace throat harness, collar harness c. 100 B.C. (appears in Europe in 568 A.D. with Avars).

300

Antioch is founded in Syria... Euclid opens School of Geometry in Alexandria.

298

Third Samnite war of Etruscans and Rome is started (-290, makes Rome a power in Italy).

280

Mechanical Problems is written, possibly by Aristotle (cites various devices required to move weights against nature)... Ptolemy Philadelphus builds canal, started 610 B.C. by Necho, to link Nile with Red Sea.

273

Egypt, Rome exchange embassies.

272

With fall of Tarentum, Rome governs all of Italy.

270

Ctesibios, son of Greek barber, is cited working in Alexandria (-247, devises air gun, mechanical toys, water clocks, precursors of automata and cuckoo clocks, hydraulic organ, adjustable mirror, air pump with valves and force pump for water, designs catapults worked by springs or compressed air).

269

Rome issues silver money for foreign trade (uses copper coins in domestic trade)... Asoka is first ruler in India, Mauryan empire covers all of India but three small kingdoms in south (-232, puts to death anyone causing artisan to lose eye or hand, builds roads with rest houses for communications and commerce, trades spices, precious gems and metals, silks and ivory for linen, glass vessels, metals and medicinal herbs).

264

First Punic War is started between Rome and Italian allies with Carthage when Sicilian Greeks, traditional enemy of Rome, are attacked by Syracuse, ally of Rome (-201, establishes Rome as major power in Mediterranean)... Rome holds first public combats of gladiators (-325 A.D.).

260

Philo of Byzantium designs chain drive for loading a catapult (-241).

252

Wells for salt, natural gas are drilled in China, basis for salt industry and government monopoly.

250-201

Construction continues in China to build Great Wall, completed in 1368-1644 A.D. to range over some 1,500 miles... Magic Canal, first contour canal, is built in China, completes 20-mile link for inland navigation of 1,250 miles from Peking to Canton... Koreans start first agricultural community in Japan... Parchment or vellum for writing appears, Pergamum.

248

After revolting against Seleucid authority, Parthia becomes State in Mesopotamia, Persia.

242

Rome forms Peregrine Court to promote foreign trade.

240

Erathosthenes is head of Alexandria's library (theorizes sun circles earth, calculates first known scientific measurements of earth's circumference).

234

Inventions of salt-making, carts and carriages, plow, rotary millstone, computations are described in record of Chinese lore (-228).

230

Oil lamps appear in China and Greece... Chinese state of Qi develops federal bureaucratic system (-221, lasts 2,000 years).

221

Divided feudal Warring States in China are unified (-1911) for first time by King Cheng from western state of Ch'in (with Mandate of Heaven centralizes land under his unlimited authority as Son of Heaven to be ruler, administrator, military leader, judge, manager of the economy, priest, educator and moral exemplar, uses ministers, two chief counselors, one left and one right, grand marshal, censor-in-chief to evaluate governmental performance, and other officials selected by qualifications and evaluated by merit, establishes common written language and law, standardizes weights and measures, and builds imperial road system).

220

Rome builds Via Flaminia north to Rimini.

218

Second Punic War between Rome, Carthage is started (-201, causes Rome to contract for supplies from corporations of knights)... Roman forces gradually conquer Spain (-24 B.C., leads to formations of corporations by knights, men of property, to operate mines with winches, windlasses and chain-buckets).

212

To defend itself against naval siege of Rome, Syracuse hires Archimedes, Greek mathematician best known for Archimedean screw as efficient means to raise water, to devise methods to break the attack (in early use of science for military activity devises cranes and rock-throwing slings).

210

Rome ordinance regulates private bankers, public fish markets (supervises public markets in cattle, vegetables)... Chinese emperor uses division of labor to form crossbow regiments.

202

Han dynasty appears in China (-220 A.D., provides governmental model for future governments with emperor over grand marshal, chief counselor supervises 9 ministers administering imperial household and 13 government departments, and censor-in-chief to audit governmental performance).

200-151

Ox-powered water wheel with gears is used for irrigation... Romans use concrete as building material... Archimedean screw is used in Rome's Spanish mines to pump water from lower levels... Philon of Byzantium: <u>Pneumatics</u> (shows design for vertical water wheel with mechanical apparatus)... Paper technology appears in China as well as rotary winnowing fan, first seen in Europe in 1700-20, multi-tube seed drill, follows single tube by Sumerians in 1500 B.C., gimbals - first cited in Europe in 1550, and crank handle on winnowing machine, seen in West in 830 A.D... Chinese merchant Los Kass operates chain of stores... State foundries appear in most provinces of China... Hopewell society appears in Ohio Valley, U.S. (-400 A.D., trades special flint for minerals, shells to fashion ornaments with people of Gulf Coast, Rocky Mountains, Lake Superior)... Cato the Elder, Roman politician (invests in marine insurance) and general: <u>On Agriculture</u> discusses use of slaves, instead of peasants, as base for large-scale farming estates, need for a farmer to provide overseer with yearly written work plan, and need for crops to be sown in three successive plantings, specifies 13 people as required to operate medium-size estate).

199

Chinese merchants (acquire wealth from agricultural enterprises in cereals and/or rice, cattle, fish-farming, cloth mills, private foundries, lacquer factories, shops and/or money lending) are forbidden to wear silk garments, to ride horses, to carry arms and to own farms, taxed on sales and inventory, limited to certain locations and types of business, and disqualified, including sons and grandsons, from official appointments.

196

Local officials in China are asked to recommend worthy men for imperial appointments.

195

Cato the Elder is Roman consul (despite bans on nobility engaging in commerce, uses freedman Quinto as frontman for running prosperous shipping company).

193

Warehouse is built in Rome with multiple barrel-vaults.

189

Insurrections against high taxes are seen in upper Egypt.

175

China authorizes private minting of coins.

170

First paved streets appear in Rome... Greek slave is Rome's first professional baker.

168

After three Macedonian wars (215-), Rome rules Greece to build empire.

167

Rome makes Delos a free port (leads to decline of Rhodes as commercial center in Eastern Mediterranean).

166

In this time Chinese use signal communications for rapid transmission of coded messages between frontier posts (use flags and smoke in daytime, fires on tall poles at night).

165

China uses first official written examinations to select qualified civil servants for governmental appointments.

160

China gives first reference to soy sauce.

159

First water clock in Rome is made.

152

Cordoba appears in Spain.

150-101

Rome grants public contracts to corporations, joint-stock companies, for collection of taxes and construction of public buildings... Mayan community of El Mirador, one of largest in Americas, flourishes in Guatemala area (as trading center for region provides market stalls for merchants in jade beads, ceramic pots, obsidian blades, etc.).

146

Roman forces destroy Carthage, trading city of 500,000-700,000, rebuilt 123 B.C.

144

China prohibits coining of false gold.

141

Wu-ti, Han dynasty, rules China, some 10% of population live in some 1,500 towns with few hundreds to 300,000-650,000 for Chang'an, perhaps world's largest with nine walled markets with stalls grouped by products (-87, levies inventory taxes on merchants to suppress their power from wealth acquired from iron, salt and liquor businesses, grain speculations and mortgage foreclosures, bars merchants, as well as grain bakers, manufacturers and money-lenders, from holding office, owning land and riding horses, forms civil service, includes imperial concubines, with 14 grades, gives entrance exams on understanding of Confucius - later quota of one candidate for bureaucracy for every 200,000 citizens, gives one year probation and performance reviews every three years, pays generous salaries, top level gets 20 times more than bottom, gives exemptions from military and labor service, provides some pensions).

140

China issues parchment money for economic transactions, prepares first book on alchemy... Crates of Mallus devises first globe of the world... Chinese make paper for personal hygiene and stuffing for clothes, not for writing.

138

China's Zhang Qian leads party to Tibet, opens Silk Road as East-West trade route.

129

Rome forms province of Asia and passes laws to protect wine, oil monopolies... China builds canal from Shensi to Honan.

128

First appearance of wine vines in China, seeds from Persia, is cited.

124

Local governments in China are asked to recommend promising youths to study with scholars, each a specialist in one of Five Classics and advisor to imperial government, in forming "university" to prepare men for administrative careers.

123

With cost-of-living in Rome soaring, all citizens are allowed to buy grain from public granaries below market prices (by 71 B.C. grants free grain to some 40,000 citizens).

121

Chinese magician Shao Ong projects moving images on a screen (leads to, although known as early as 207 B.C., magic lantern in 100s A.D)... Optimum is marketed in Rome as first great Italian wine... China nationalizes salt and iron industries, uses 46 bureaus to supervise mass production (-117 B.C., shows 48 foundries in operation with 100-1,000 workers at each)... Chinese forces defeat raiding Huns to open He-xi Corridor, west of Yellow River at southern edge of Gobi Desert, for trade, emperor wants to swap treasured silk for Heavenly Western Horses, along Silk Road.

118

Narbonne is founded in Gaul as first Roman colony outside Italy.

109

Milvian Bridge is built near Rome with arch, seen earlier in Egypt in 500s B.C., Greece 200s B.C.

105

Mathematician Hero starts College of Technology, world's first in Alexandria.

102

Caius Marius, General and Consul of Republic, reorganizes Roman Army into legions of 6,000 men each, each legion with 6 centuries and each century with 10 cohorts (drafts citizens with property to staff forces, later recruits poor, unemployed as volunteers for rewards of campaign prizes, land allotments and free equipment).

100-51

Roman lawmakers legalize corporate organizational structure as voluntary association to pool financial resources of its members, own property and to litigate... Guilds of cooks, tanners, builders, bronze workers, ironworkers, rope makers and weavers exist in Rome as social, mutual-benefit societies... Deep drilling is used in China for salt brine, reaches 4,800 feet to find gas... Retail bakeries appear in Rome, established by millers, owners of large rotary mills powered by animals, as form of vertical integration... Silk Road from China is extended through Samarkand to Tyre, India... Glass-blowing is invented, possibly in Levant... Water wheels appear throughout Roman world... Rhodian vessel is wrecked off Antikythera (uses cogwheel device, first known analog computer, to calculate relative movements of sun, moon and five known planets)... Caius Sergius Orata devises underfloor heating of rooms... Water-powered mills are used in area of Yugoslavia to grind corn... First Chinese ships reach India.

98

China establishes state monopoly on alcohol.

90

Marius Vitruvius, Roman engineer: De Architectura (lists 13 kinds of sun dials, discusses architecture, describes water-lifting machines: vertical water wheel with Hellenistic gearing system, bucket-chain, scoop-wheels and wheels with paddles, shows designs for undershot and overshot water wheels, and describes "large-scale" production of 2 factories making pigments, processing papyrus as paper).

89

Chao Kuo develops new agricultural implements and new system of crop rotation in China.

82

Tullius Tiro, former slave of Cicero, devises system of shorthand.

81

Cornelian laws of Sulla become constitution for Rome (permits partnerships only for private business)... Chinese book discusses use of hydraulic engineering and irrigation... 60 scholars throughout China are summoned to Imperial Court to debate merits, demerits of governmental monopolies and other issues.

80

Greek engineers invent differential gear.

75

Crassus operates Rome's first fire brigade (acquires wealth by letting fires burn when house owners refuse to pay high charges and buying remains at fire-sale prices).

73

Thracian Spartacus leads revolt of gladiators, slaves in Rome (-71).

62

Florence appears in Italy.

60

Pompey, Julius Caesar and Crassus (acquired wealth as businessmen from real estate, mines) form First Triumvirate to rule Rome.

59

Rome's <u>Arta diurnau</u> with news is posted daily during this time in public places.

58

Roman forces of Julius Caesar start conquest of Gaul (-50, invade Britain in 54 B.C.).

55

Pompey builds Rome's first permanent stone theater, 17,500 seats.

52

Julius Caesar captures small fishing village on Seine, evolves as Paris.

50-01

Roman law discourages formation of joint-stock companies with limited liability for business ventures... Auctions, foreign currency exchanges, deposits with no interest, loans on securities, real estate transactions, investments and foreign drafts are seen in Rome (shows factory activities in spinning and weaving, pottery and pigments, records guilds of bronze workers, ringmakers and goldsmiths)... Tower of Winds is built in Athens with water clock and dial, 9 sundials and windvane.

50

North Africa's Cyrene mints silver coins in this time, stamped with leaf of plant grown in city and marketed throughout ancient world as medicine, condiment.

49

Crude paper of hemp, ramie is used in Shangsi province, China.

47

Library of Ptolemy I in Alexandria is destroyed by fire.

46

Julius Caesar becomes dictator of Rome for 10 years (-44, orders census for purposes of taxation and administration, starts public works program to build library, dikes, harbor improvements at Ostia and canal at Corinth, grants Italian citizens status as freemen, reduces provincial taxes, plans municipal charters for Italian cities, sponsors expeditions to Black Sea, Germany for riches to end economic depression).

44

Cicero, Roman orator and writer (cites use of tradesman sign for advertising and views mechanics as mean employment, manual labor as degrading, trades as vulgar, arts as skillful, and agriculture as worthy work in writings): De officiis (writes "Business on a small scale is despicable; but if it is extensive and imports commodities in large quantities from all over the world, and distributes them honestly, it is not very discreditable; nay, if the merchant satiated, or rather satisfied, with the fortune he has made, retires from the harbor and steps into an estate, as once he returned to harbor from the sea, he deserves, I think, the highest respect.").

40

First public library in Rome is started with donation of manuscripts by Asinus Pollio.

38

Horace: Ars Poetica (-8, describes advertising notices of booksellers).

36

Marcus Terentius Varro: De Re Rustica (recommends agricultural methods for rich landlords with 100-200 acres and gives specifications for hiring farm works, also writes Nine Books of Disciplines on Greco-Roman curriculum of medicine, architecture, grammar, dialectic, rhetoric, geometry, arithmetic, astronomy, and music as basis, except for first two studies, for Seven Liberal Arts studied in church schools in 900s A.D.).

32

Twenty ranks of government officials in China are reduced to sixteen, basis for status, salary, clothing, carriage, privileges.

30

Principate of Caius Octavius, named Augustus in 27, over Roman Empire begins (-14 A.D., acquires governmental revenues from leases of public lands, court fines, taxes on bequests, auctions, sales of slaves, imports and water, and from state monopolies in mines, quarries, fisheries, salt works, timber mills and arsenals, moves Treasury of Egypt to Rome, cancels tax debts of property owners, guarantees property rights, starts public post based on earlier Persian system, takes City census to discover some 50% of City's population of 400,000 are slaves, centralizes administration of provinces, creates Imperial Civil Service, appoints businessmen to fixed-salaried positions in government, uses civil service to audit performances of appointments, starts construction on Pantheon - finished 124 A.D., appoints Marcus Agrippa as surveyor - prepares practical map of routes in Roman world, bans investments of senatorial class in commerce and industry - circumvented by use of freemen, bans workers' organizations - prohibited by Trajan in 98-116 A.D. and tolerated by Marcus Aurelius in 161-180 A.D.).

29

Virgil: Georgics (discusses estate management of slave labor).

18

Chinese government sells official titles.

15

Yang Hsiung: Dictionary of Local Expressions (cites belt-drive, seen in Europe in 1430).

07

Strabo: Geography (cites use of water mill with no gears).

04

Jesus of Nazareth is born in this time (-c. 30 A.D.)... During Han Dynasty (202 B.C. - 220 A.D.) guild of master bowyers requires applicants to submit to 7-day test by Examining Commission of nine Master Bowyers: 1st day applicant submits bow and takes oral test on knowledge of craft, 2nd, bow is studied, 3rd, bow tested by use, 4th, bow tested by destruction, 5th, parts dissected, 6th, all tests evaluated and 7th, acceptance into guild, failure means 5-year wait for next examination.

01-99 A.D.

Hero of Alexandria: Mechanike (shows use of levers, valves, gears, cylinders and pistons, cogwheels and pulleys in designs of 78 mechanical objects, such as pressure engine operated by steam, screw-cutting machine, holy-water dispenser, automatic temple door-opener and automated puppet theaters and toys), and Pneumatika (shows tiny windmill to blow organ, shows steam-operated toy)... Abacus is used in India... Early horse-powered mechanical harvester appears in France... Chinese vessels appear with rudders, masts and sails, first evidence of rudders in West in 1180 and lateen sails in Europe around 1304... Christians flee to Pella, one of ten cities in Decapolis commercial league, to escape persecution in Jerusalem.

01

Chinese government workshop makes rice bowl, inscribed with tasks of lacquer preparation, lacquer laying, bronze rim-making, polishing, painting and finishing, and departments of bookkeeping, production, security... Tea is grown in China... Ko Yu invents wheelbarrow, seen in West by 1220... Adjustable calipers appear in China.

02

China takes first known national population census, records 57,671,400 taxable individuals.

09

Wang Mang is Emperor of China (-23, repeals nationalization of estates and manumission of slaves, levies taxes on slaves and mining profits, forms state wine monopoly, provides free and low-interest loans to curb usury, forms regional commissions to set prices on staple goods, builds granaries to hold surplus grain in good years for distribution in bad times).

10

Thaddeus of Florence: De Virtutibus Aquae vitae (-19, describes medical use of alcohol).

14

Tiberius is ruler of Rome (-37, continues policies of Augustus, reforms taxes, after determining no one knows of discovery of unbreakable glass executes inventor to avoid potential effects of technological unemployment).

20

Water powers batteries of pestles in China.

25

Eastern Han dynasty evolves in China (-220, cites magnetic polarity).

31

Hydraulic power is used, China, to operate bellows of blast furnace used in casting iron.

33

Inflation and resulting economic panic in Rome bankrupt several banking houses, usually operated by Greeks or Syrians.

41

Claudius starts rule in Rome (-54, forms Cabinet with Secretary of State, Treasurer, Secretary and Attorney General, uses Civil Service, reforms courts, tries to change alphabet, grants concessions to shippers of grain, approves trade guilds, primarily fraternal societies with some business interests, in grains, wine and oil, and craft guilds of shipbuilders, warehousemen, stevedores, salvage divers, and grain measurers, and overseas large factories processing papyrus and Spanish red-lead).

42

With Rome's Port of Ostia inoperative by silt from Tiber River, construction is started to build largest man-made harbor of ancient world at Portus to handle imports of Arabian incense, Chinese silk, cattle, slaves, geese and tin from Britain, amber from Germany, cereals, woolens, hides, fish, vegetables, poultry, flax and glass from Gaul, minerals and agricultural produce from Spain, marble from Greece, copper and bronze from Cyprus, timber from Black Sea, ebony, animals, and slaves from North Africa, and grains from Egypt).

43

Rome conquers Britain (-407, founds London and Aquae Sulis, named Bath later, at natural hot springs, establishes towns which evolve as villa-system in 300s).

50

Romans use soap, custom from Gaul... Cologne, military garrison, becomes Roman colony and main distribution center for Western Provinces... In this time (-70) molded oil lamps are produced in Northern Italy, one factory at Modena (is called "factory lamp" for manufacturer by semi- skilled workers on assembly line, dominates market for over two centuries)... Italian glassworkers migrate to Gaul to start workshops at Arles and Lyons, like most large towns with jewelers, goldsmiths and silversmiths on their own streets (by 100 evolves with some 100 glassworks at Namur, Trier, Worms and Cologne).

57

China receives Japanese Embassy, initiates first direct contact of two countries.

58

Ming-Ti, new Emperor of China, introduces Buddhism to land.

59

Pompeii amphitheater is scene of riot between spectators from rural cities at gladiatorial contest (results in ban on all such contests in Pompeii for 10 years).

60

Gospels are written to prepare followers of Christianity for Kingdom of justice, kindness, simplicity (-120).

64

Great fire destroys most of Nero's Rome, uses brick in reconstruction (leads to Domitii family, 22 freedmen and 53 slaves at works, gaining near monopoly of brickyards in Italy with 46 foremen).

69

Vitellius is ruler of Roman Empire (-79, starts first system of State education - schools for physicians, refuses use of hoisting machine in construction for its adverse impact on unemployment, levies tax on animal urine - other taxes of Empire at one time or another on children, slaves, doors, acts of prostitution, pleasures of matrimony).

75

Glass factory is operated in Britain in this time, joins those of metalworking, potteries, tileries, brick, salt-works, textiles... Rome builds Colosseum, world's largest amphitheater until Yale Bowl in 1914).

77

Caius Plinius Secundus: <u>Historia Naturalis</u> (discusses medicine and industry, cites use of coal and petroleum).

79

Pompeii, flourishing port and prosperous resort (shows use of business signs by cloth merchant, woolen manufacturers with various operations, and shopkeepers, shows use of placard on statue to advertise political candidates), is buried with eruption of Mt. Vesuvius.

83

Wang Ch'ung: <u>Discourses weighed in the balance</u> (gives first known reference to chain pump for raising water, appears in West in 1500s).

88

China abolishes state monopolies in iron, salt.

89

China receives India Embassy (-105, receives Parthia in 101, Japan in 107, Burma in 120, Rome in 166, Byzantium in 643).

92

St. Clement is Pope (-101, becomes Patron Saint of Hatters for, according to tradition, inventing felt).

97

Frontinus, former military governor of Britain, is put in charge of Rome's water supply (commands workforce of 700 to tend 250 miles of piping).

100-199

Alexandria becomes major manufacturing and trading center in Mediterranean area, Rome center for finance... Parchment manuscripts are folded, sewn together as books... Hinduism is codified in Laws of Manu (establishes social castes, based on Aryan classes of priests, noble warriors, farmers and artisans, of brahmans, kings and warriors, farmers and merchants, and serfs with subcastes of banyan as moneylenders and kayastha as scribes)... Places on public square of Ostia are reserved for meetings of merchants and shipowners (pioneers informal business exchanges)... Chinese discover insecticide... Greek merchant Alexander reaches south of China by sea (-109).

105

Government official reports to Chinese Emperor on paper-making process using pulp of tree bark, hemp and rags... Roman engineers devise iron-frame torsion catapult.

110

Earliest known piece of paper is used for writing, China.

117

Hadrian rules Roman Empire (-138, codifies Roman Law, establishes postal system, insists shippers must use bulk of capital for state duties to qualify for privileges).

121

Spinning wheel is first cited in China, first noted in West at Speyer in 1280... Marcus Aurelius rules Roman Empire (-180, declares no one should belong to two collegia of craftsmen).

129

Claudius Ptolemy: Almagest (-149, summarizes geographical and astronomical knowledge of day in 13 volumes, rejects theory of Aristarchus that earth revolves around the sun, and establishes time divisions of minutes and seconds in standard reference until Middle Ages, provides crude tables for determining latitude, longitude in Geographical Outline).

130

In this time 20 high schools in Rome provide studies in grammar, Greek language and literature, music, astronomy, history, mythology, philosophy.

170

Claudius Ptolemy prepares 26 maps of various countries.

172

Lyons, France, holds a fair.

175

Water organ is replaced by bellows organ (-199).

180

First writings in alchemy appear in Egypt.

193

Septimius Severus rules Roman Empire (-211, grants concessions to individuals for services but not guildsmen).

200-299

Rome builds Imperial grain mill complex at Barbegal, France (uses 16 water wheels to power 16 mills in grinding flour from as far away as Egypt, produces as much as 24 tons of meal in 24 hours)... Gaius Julius Solinus: Polyhistor (in geography tells of monstrous beasts and strange races, is source for rumors, myths through ages)... Knitting appears, probably Middle East (is disseminated by sailors, traders)... Rome starts military "fabrica" to make iron weapons at Bath, England... Five collegia of shippers in Arles strike for higher rates... Shippers in corn trade, smiths, oil merchants, 'corn- measurers,' bakers, and swine merchants are privileged guilds in Rome.

213

Rome builds elegant baths around hot springs of Baden-Baden.

219

China changes selection for civil service so applicants are classified by impartial judge into nine different grades by ability, knowledge, experience and character (is replaced in 606 by governmental examinations when judges are deemed partial).

220

Han Dynasty ends in China (cites State's silk-weaving workshops with up to several thousand employees in each).

222

Wu Dynasty rules in China (-280, establishes tea as substitute for wine)... Roman Emperor approves collegia or guilds of wine merchants, dealers in lupins, and makers of soldiers' shoes (requires all craftsmen to have legal advisers, law courts).

226

After overthrow of Parthia, Sassanid Empire appears in area of Persia (-651, uses swords of Damask steel, based on steelmaking processes of India and China, to win battles with Rome, contributes to European development of metallurgy in 1800s with research on damask process).

240

Liu Shao: The Study of Human Abilities (-250).

250

China's first cybernetic device with feedback uses differential gears.

260

Zenobia of Palmyra wears "first" known diamond jewelry... Roman Empire is devastated by plague (-265, cites death in almost every family).

271

Crude compass may have been used in China.

275

Julius Africanus cites shooting substance, perhaps form of gunpowder (is "used" at siege of Constantinople in 668, by Arabs in 690, and by Chinese in 700s).

280

Jewish scholars compile Talmud (-500, covers Jewish history, theology, ritual, medicine, folklore, agriculture, industry, professions, commerce, and finance, includes provisions against false weights and measures, adulteration, speculation, and monopoly, advocates virtues of self-control, hard work, moderation, sobriety, charity, education and thrift).

284

Diocletian rules Roman Empire (-305, shifts Capitol from Rome to Asia Minor, decentralizes Empire with three other emperors over districts into 101 provinces with each having 13 dioceses, establishes sound currency with state mints to end provincial currencies - fixed value of gold coins lasts to 1453, puts many voluntary guilds in industries under state control - members tied to trade and to pass on obligations to sons).

285

Pappus of Alexandria describes five machines of cogwheel, lever, pulley, screw, and wedge in work.... Diocletian makes General Maximian head of western provinces (makes Milan Italian headquarters, oversees Trier, a base in Gaul which evolves as manufacturing, mining, largest producer of gold and silver in western sector, and agricultural center with mint).

290

Tu Shih, Prefect of Nanyang: History of the Three Kingdoms (cites a superintendent of metallurgical production c. 230 A.D.)... Trip hammers are used, China, by water-powered mills to hull rice.

296

Rome operates mints at Carthage and London (-324).

298

Baths of Diocletian are built in Rome.

300-399

De Rebos Bellicis shows design for animal-powered war ship, converts oxen power by capstan to paddle-wheel... Silk is made in Japan... In China helicopter rotor is used in tops... Greek writer is first in West to describe abacus... Zosimas of Alexandria is recognized as first alchemist of note... Iron smelters are used to forge tools, weapons in area of Nigeria... Classical period of Aztec civilization evolves in Mexico (-900s, shows formation of association of long-distant traders with hereditary membership and professional status with rights, codes, and courts to judge fair-trading practices in handling exports of slaves, garments, ornaments, and imports of feathers, stones, cacao, gold, and materials, uses cotton cloth, gold dust in quills, quetzal feathers and cacao as money)... Umbrella, seen earlier as chariot cover of silk, appears in China... Memoirs on Neglected Matters cites use of oil-and-wick lamps in China, large-scale production in 800s... Chinese use coal instead of wood to make cast iron.

301

To ensure adequate pay for soldiers Diocletian's decree sets maximum prices for goods and labor (lists 84 different articles of wool, over 2,000 linen items made by five linen centers).

306

Constantine rules Roman Empire (-337, divides Empire in 313-323, is baptized as Christian in 337).

313

Christianity is legalized with Constantine the Great's Edict of Milan (exempts Christian clergy from municipal offices and some taxes).

320

Gupta Dynasty evolves in Northern India (-467, cites subcaste of kayastha as scribes - later used as secretaries by Mogul rulers c. 1550 and as clerks by English East India Co. in 1800s).

321

Roman Empire declares Sunday a statutory holiday.

325

Council of Nicaea is held, first ecumenical council to settle religious dispute on nature of Christ, God (in discussion prohibits clergy to lend money for grain)... Pachomius starts monastic community, model for those following, in Egypt (establishes order with minute regulations for collective praying, working, eating, sleeping).

326

Constantine the Great gives ship owners immunity from all fiscal charges, reaffirmed 334 and 337.

330

Constantine the Great dedicates Constantinople as new capitol of Roman Empire, built with public forums, great avenues lined with arcades and shops, and areas for related trades (evolves as major commercial center)... Itinerary from Bordeaux to Jerusalem provides pilgrims with directions for traveling to the Holy Land.

365

By Imperial edict anyone in Roman Empire can leave occupation to prospect for gold on condition of annual payment of gold to Treasury.

369

Roman Empire makes purple dyeing a state monopoly.

370

Design for ox-powered boat with paddlewheel is submitted to Roman Emperor in this time.

372

For first time Eastern Roman Empire levies special 5-year tax in gold on any occupation for gain (covers traders, moneylenders, innkeepers, and brothel- keepers, exempts rural craftsmen, doctors, teachers, painters, and lower clergy).

379

In this time Chandra Gupta II rules area across North India from Bengal to Arabian Sea (-415, oversees growth of guilds, written constitutions to preserve traditions, trade secrets and special techniques, to adjudicate disputes, determine marriages and expulsion, establish work rules, fix wages and prices, and provide benefits for widows and orphans, with each having own insignia for holiday parades, religious festivals).

383

London mint re-opens (-388).

392

Theodosius the Great is last ruler of united Roman Empire (-395, outlaws paganism).

394

Theodosius I ends Olympic Games when athletes show displeasure with insufficient prizes of olive-wreaths, revived 1896.

395

Western Roman Empire forbids collegiati to leave guilds... Notitia-Dignitatum cites departments of Western Imperial bureaucracy (shows existence of potteries, weaving mills, dye works, linen mills, embroidery works and ordinance factories in Gaul, Spain, Germany and Italy to supplement work of private enterprise and state arsenals).

397

Roman Emperor bans wear of barbarian trousers, another edict in 416... King Kuk I is Mayan ruler (starts Maya classic period in Central America lasting to 1799, shows use of dikes, irrigation ditches, terraces, raised fields, slash-and-burn farming, trade and grand architecture).

399

Chinese Buddhist monk travels to India, Central Asia, Siam and Sumatra.

400-499

Harness with padded horse collar appears in China... First fair in Champagne region of France is held at Troyes (by 1066 sponsors six fairs/year for European merchants)... Fusion process for making steel is used in China, Siemen's process in 1863... Cloaks for Imperial Roman Army are made at Tournai on English Channel (uses fleece of sheep in area known for quality, is basis for woolen industry of Flanders)... Buddhist priest Huishen may have sailed from China to North America... First true porcelain, use of kaolin clay since 200s A.D., is made in China (perfects process by 900s)... Martianus Cappella: On the Marriage of Philology and Mercury (drops medicine, architecture from Varro's disciplines as being too practical)... Teotihuacan, holiest spot in Mexico with most of its 150,000 people living in compounds, nears its zenith (as seat of empire hosts some 400 workshops making obsidian tools and weapons, over 200 potters, some mass-production in reusable molds, other artisans make, trade goods for jade, ornamental shells, cacao beans, used for chocolate and money, or Quetzal feathers, and state religious bureaucracy, builds holy structures, as principal employers).

400

Chinese Buddhist pilgrim Fa Xian travels 766-mile Silk Road across Himalayas from Kashgar,

China, to Islamabad, India... Japan adopts Chinese-style of script (-424).

405

For first time, Roman troops are paid wages to maintain long siege of Veii.

418

Paddle-wheel boat is first cited in China, by 1100s up to 300 feet.

421

By tradition Venice evolves as Padua trading post on islands of Rialto.

425

Constantinople University is founded by Byzantium to specialize in study of literature, other institutions later with medicine at Alexandria, philosophy at Athens, rhetoric at Antioch.

476

Roman Emperor Romulus Augustulus is forced to abdicate by Odoacer in forming Germanic kingdom in Italy (ends Western Roman Empire, starts Dark Ages to 814 and death of Charlemagne).

477

Chinese text cites use of stirrup to ride horses.

481

Clovis' Franks invade Gaul (gives rules for agriculture, handicrafts in laws).

496

Clovis, ruler of Franks, converts to Christianity.

500-599

Jujitsu first appears at Shaolin Temple, China (appears in 1400s in Japan at various academies, evolves with yellow, green, blue, brown and black belts to show levels of ability)... New plow appears in Central Europe with wheels, vertical iron knife and curved-board at rear, horse harness in 900s-1000s... Open-hearth process for making steel is cited in China, first produced in 100s B.C... Taliesin, Aneurin are recognized as bards, poetic-clerical caste in Wales... Craft society of bakers, formed as monopolistic and fraternal group with work regulations and quality standards, is cited in Ravenna, followed by notaries, merchants in 800s and fishermen in 900s... Irish monk Brendan and crew "discover" Westward Island on voyage from Ireland, seen on maps for next 1,200 years... Flourishing trade of Yemen in frankincense is blocked when dams become silted, turns to drugs to forget plight... Law of Debts, The Institutes of Vishnu, gives rules for charging interest... Abacus appears in Europe, follows use of counting boards by ancient Greeks and Romans.

520

Monastery at St. Gall, Switzerland, builds brew house.

525

Chinese Buddhists encourage drinking of tea, substitute for alcohol (-549).

527

Justinian the Great rules Byzantine Empire (-565, considers design for war vessel with paddle-wheels powered by six pairs of oxen).

529

Code of Justinian is basis for Byzantine law... Justinian the Great closes 1,000-year-old School of Philosophy in Athens (forces many Greek scholars to flee to Persian college of Jundi-i-Shapur)... St. Benedict of Nursia, founder of Benedictine Order, establishes monastery of Monte Cassino, Italy (advocates to work is to pray, leads to evolution of European monasteries as self- contained economic operations with farm lands, workshops, libraries, hospitals, schools).

530

China's Description of the Buddhists' Temples and Monasteries of Loyang shows basics of steam engine, lacks only crankshaft, and piston in water-powered flour and shaking machine.

531

Anushirwan the Just is Sassanian King of Persia (develops college of Juni-i-Shapur, founded in 300s-400s, as center of learning, decentralizes government into 4 great satrapies, fixes land taxes, improves irrigation and communications, reforms army, encourages agriculture, trade and "guilds," grants limited monopolies, enjoys pastimes of period: music, dancing, chess, hunting).

533

Code of Justinian is revised with regulations on rates of interest.

535

Cosmas Indicopleustes, geographer at Alexandria: Topographia Christiana (describes travels to Red Sea, East Africa, Persian Gulf with accounts of India, Ceylon).

537

Ostrogoths besiege Rome (forces Byzantine General Belisarius to use floating mills on Tiber River to process grain).

540

Luan's Book of the Golden Hall Master cites Chinese wind-powered vehicles carrying up to 30 people.

541

World's first epidemic, kills about 50% of Europe's population, is started in Constantinople by rats from Egypt and Syria, first of 14 by 767 (-594, forces Justinian to use wage, price controls to stabilize economy).

550

Augsburg is established in Germany as Bishop's See, evolves as trading center... Decimal notation evolves in India (-574).

552

Emperor Justinian sends missionaries to China to smuggle out silk worms, mulberry leaves (makes silk industry a state monopoly in 553).

565

Reign of Justinian I over Byzantine Empire ends (evolves by 1095 with state supervision of docks and ports, regulation of insurance and loans, adoption of Rural Code to check feudalism, stable currency, prohibition of certain exports and imports, taxation on sales, regulation of interest rates, organization of commercial "factories" for foreign merchants, and operation of extensive credit system).

568

Avars invade Hungary from East, bring trace harness and stirrup from China.

569

Leovigild is King of Visigoths (-586, unifies Spain, formulates law code, issues new coinage, grants charters to confirm ownership of land).

577

China cites use of sulfur matches for cooking and heating, first noted in West in 1530.

584

Byzantine Empire recognizes Venice as independent state.

589

Early reference to paper cites use as toilet tissue, China.

590

Gregory the Great becomes Pope (-604, establishes rule of papacy in Europe, develops Church's first filing system, in letters cites corporations of silk makers in Naples and bakers in Otranto, saves last silversmith in Rome doing business as banker from bankruptcy).

597

St. Augustine starts Benedictine monastery at Canterbury, England, Christian by 700s (uses land grants and charters with title deeds for recognition of church property by 616).

600-699

Watermill appears in England... Transport workers in Rome form an association... Man-powered boat with paddle-wheel appears in China... Abbey of St. Denis is founded outside Paris, site for annual international fairs... Brandy is developed in China, in West in 1100s... Viking ships use keel, mast... Windmills appear in Persia... Cahokia, city of some 10,000 in 900-1100, appears near juncture of Mississippi, Ohio Rivers to farm bottomlands, becomes trade center... Merchants of 27 lands meet at Zhang-ye, on Silk Road west of Yellow River, to discuss trade.

604

Cambodian Sanskrit inscription shows use of decimal.

615

"Burning water," petroleum, is used in Japan.

618

China's 1,000-mile Grand Canal, longest in world, links Yellow, Yangtze Rivers (400s B.C.-, is used by thousands of commercial craft))... T'ang Dynasty begins in China (-907, adopts Confucianism for governing, forms centralized government, basically unchanged to 1912, with functions of state affairs over public administration, finances, rites, army, justice and public works, chancellery to issue Imperial decrees, grand secretariat to issue official publications, grand council over advisory secretariat, and censorate to ensure compliance of governmental performance with plans, forms national militia, uses receipts of deposits for exchange in commercial transactions, ignores earlier restrictions on business activities, recognizes middle-class over peasants, cites 26 of largest provinces with populations over 500,000 each - largest over 1 million).

619

China establishes new tax system for grain, cloth.

622

Muhammed flees Mecca to Medina after his philosophy of generosity, charity is rejected by populace as attack on commercial profits... Issadore of Seville writes encyclopedia on arts and sciences (includes world map of Asia, Paradise, Europe, Africa).

624

China establishes first complete legal code (allots cropland on lifetime tenure).

630

Cotton may have been cultivated in Arab lands... Dagobert I rules Austrasia, France (-639, cites guilds in legal code, seen in capitularies of Charlemagne in 779-789, ordinances of Archbishop of Rheims in 852).

631

Nestorians from Persia introduce Gospel to China.

633

Moslem forces conquer Iraq, take Damascus in 635, Jerusalem in 637, and Persia in 640 (starts Zoroastrian migration to India to become merchant class of Parsee) to extend realm from Lisbon to China by 716.

636

Rotharsis is King of Lombardy (-652, cites guilds of master masons in Como, bakers in Otranto in legal code).

639

Moslems invade Egypt (found Cairo in 641 on ruins of Memphis, open canal in 641 between Nile and Red Sea - abandoned in 723).

645

Taika Reform begins in Japan (-1156, nationalizes estates, grants land tenure to peasants to break hereditary power of provincial clans, ranks court nobles in hierarchy, fills governmental positions by ancestry, levies stiff taxes on new landowners and all adult males - peasants flee).

650

Art of weaving is developed in Byzantine Empire in this time... Artists in China use wood blocks to print their works... Caliphs start first organized news service... Sun Ssu-Mo: Methods of the Various Schools of Magical Elixir Preparations (gives some Chinese recipes with sulfur and saltpeter, followed by 808 work to cite gunpowder and first true formula in 1044 text)... Official version of Koran, first written in 633, is recognized (advocates faith, prayer, alms, fasting and pilgrimage, stipulates sources of ruler's wealth in Sharia law: tax on agricultural produce, tax on non-Moslems, 20% of booty from battle, and tax on Moslems for general good of society, recommends tradition be used if no answers available from Koran, promises worldly success in business to good Moslems, denounces cheating merchants, monopolists, and speculators, prohibits use of interest, expects wills to leave contributions for poor).

670

Moslems found Tunis on coast of North Africa.

673

Kailinikas, Syrian-Greek engineer, devises "Greek Fire," missile weapon with petroleum, for use by Byzantine forces against Moslem siege of Constantinople.

675

First English sundial is at Newcastle.

687

Visigothic King Egiza rules Spain (-702, forbids Jews to approach docks or trade with Christians).

688

Ine, King of Wessex, takes Essex (-726, in evolution of England's guild system cites in laws a gegildan as an association of people to help each other to pay any weregild assessed against them, guild becomes Anglo-Saxon word to mean contribution to common fund and then to mean society that administers the mutual fund)... Empress Wo Tse, China, builds cast iron pagoda, 294 ft. in height.

690

English monk undertakes mission to convert Germans to Christianity.

694

Egiza issues royal decree in Spain to enslave Jews (confiscates properties in order to replenish treasury, exercises royal patronage as forerunner of medieval Europe).

695

First Arab coinage is minted.

698

Moslem forces take Carthage.

700-799

Monk at Chartres, France, is credited for inventing sand hourglass... Arab vessels use lateen sail, permits sailing into wind... Mills throughout Europe use water wheels... Horse collar, perhaps from camel harness in Bactria, appears in Europe (increases pulling power of horses by factor of 4 or 5, allows use of horses to replace oxen in plowing)... Ghana Empire evolves as first great trading center in Africa (-1200s)... Tapestry weaving evolves in Peru... Large estates are formed in Europe, forces peasants to become serfs... Wallibord is first Christian missionary sent to Scandinavia... Japanese swordsmiths make world's finest blades by folding, hammering metal into 10,000 microlayers of steel... Soap makers appear in Spain, by 1700 make renowned Castile soap with monopoly for being pure, mild and gentle.

702

After years of study, Japan issues code of Taiho (shows two major branches of government: Department of State over Mediate Office and ministries of Aristocratic Affairs, Popular Affairs, Ceremonies and Personnel, War, Justice, Treasury and Imperial Household, and Department of Religion).

704

Earliest printed text, using woodblocks, is Buddhist charm scroll, China (-751).

706

Hospital opens in Damascus, 24 physicians in 978.

710

Sugar cane is planted in Egypt... First Japanese capitol is located at Nara.

711

Moslems start conquest of Spain (-715, grant Spanish-Jews freedom, develop Moslem Spain as center for study of astronomy, mathematics, optics and chemistry, ends in 1492 with fall of Granada).

712

Moslem forces take Samarkand on silk route between China, Asia Minor (acquire secret of paper-making from captured Chinese, seen at Baghdad in 794, Egypt in 800, Spain in 955, Italy in 1154, Germany in 1190, England in 1304)... Charles Martel rules Austrasia, France (-741, recognizes vassalage as system of mutual obligations, based on Roman institution of clients exchanging patronage for service, whereby vassals fight for king in return for cattle, office, land).

717

Leo III rules Byzantine Empire (-741, formulates Maritime Code, based on ancient nautical regulations of Rhodes, as first body of commercial law in medieval Christendom).

720

Abu Masa Dshaffar, noted Arab chemist, "invents" sulfuric acid, nitric acid, aqua regia, and nitrate of silver (-800).

721

Li Yuan-Hung destroys number of water mills in China as they are jeopardizing irrigation projects (razes 70 in 764 belonging to wealthy merchants and Buddhist abbeys, destroys 80 more in 778).

725

Chinese Buddhist monk, I-Hsing, and Chinese engineer build water clock with escapement device to power astronomical devices.

726

Byzantium's Constantine V bans use of images in religious worship, opposed by monks who obtain income from such paintings.

727

King Ine of Wessex, England, opens hostel for Saxon pilgrims in Rome.

731

Venerable Bede compiles Ecclesiastical History (describes London as "an emporium of many people coming by land and sea").

732

Advancement of Moslem forces in Europe is blocked in Battle of Tours by army of Charles Martel with use of stirrups by knights, previously used in India during 100s B.C. and China in 477-523 A.D. (secularizes Church property to reward faithful followers with land for military service).

733

Chinese court employs some 18,000 civil servants, over 57,000 by local governments.

748

Peking publishes first printed newspaper... Irish monk St. Fergil suggests in this time the possibilities of another world and men under the earth.

749

English landowners are required to help build bridges and fortifications, usually given land in return.

750

Arabs found Granada in Spain during this time... Beds are seen in France, Germany... Hanlin Academy for arts and sciences opens in China (-1900s)... Wind organs replace water organs in Europe, technology from Byzantium... Lombard King Aistulf lists class of landed proprietors and three classes of merchants who owe military service relative to wealth, allowed to redeem obligations in cash... Paper factory at Samarkand is first outside China.

757

Offa is first ruler of England to use title of "King of the English" (-796, although first coinage in use earlier by East Anglian ruler introduces beautiful pennies to eliminate circulation of foreign gold coins).

758

Chinese government forms salt monopoly, gets over 50% of revenues from salt in 778.

760

Arabic numerals of Indian origin are used in Baghdad, Spain by 976.

762

Baghdad is founded as capitol of Caliphs, soon distribution center for India's coconuts, China's rhubarb and cinnamon, Bactria's grapes, Isfahan's honey, fruit, saffron and salt, Mosul's quail and Hulwan's figs, pomegranates, vinegar sauces.

764

Japanese Buddhists print 1 million copies of charm scroll, oldest work dated.

765

Caliph Al-Mansur persuades Jirjis Bukhtu Yishu and monks to move their monastery and library (contains rare copy of Ptolemy's Almagest and copies of works destroyed at Library of Alexandria) in Southern Persia to Baghdad (becomes center to translate classical Greek and Persian texts, including manual of stars, into Arabic).

768

Use of hops to make beer is first cited in Europe (contributes to development of brewing by European monasteries).

771

Charlemagne rules in France (-814, is crowned Emperor by Pope in 800, protects fairs, standardizes weights and measures, moderates tolls, reduces speculations on future, builds roads and bridges, stabilizes value of currency - interest forbidden by canon law, establishes poor relief, advocates formation of schools in cathedrals and monasteries).

774

Euclid's Elements is translated from Greek into Arabic.

779

Boso is King of Provence (-887, grants Church of Arles right to collect tolls from Greeks, other strangers).

780

Tax on family units in China is replaced by taxation on land (results in fewer families, growth of large agricultural enterprises).

781

Nestorian Christian community is cited at Changan, China.

782

Arab scientist Jabir starts study of chemistry as distinct area from alchemy (develops chemical apparatus and techniques for refining metals, making glass, and distilling alcohol, based on Greek process to make perfume)... Li Kao describes Chinese warship propelled by two treadmill paddle-wheels.

786

Haroun Al-Rashid is ruler of Abbasid Caliphate (-809, presents water clock to Charlemagne, hears tales of Sinbad in "A Thousand and One Nights" in questing on spice routes from Oman to India, Ceylon, Sumatra, Singapore, and Canton)... Public market operates at Canterbury, England.

787

Church council of Byzantium rules that artists are to paint only those subjects ordained by clergy... Charlemagne closes Frankish ports to English traders in dispute with Offa... England puts compulsory tax on householders for papacy (-1534).

790

Blast furnaces for cast iron appear in Scandinavia.

793

China taxes tea... Vikings plunder island monastery of Lindisfarne, England, raid Jarrow in 794 and Iona in 795 (leads to raid in Kent in 835, landing of Danish "Great Army" in 865, acquisition of East Anglia in 870 by Danes, creation of North Kingdom of York in 919, Danish invasion by King Swein in 1003 - King by Danelaw in 1013, recognition of Cnut as King of all England in 1016).

794

Baghdad establishes state-owned paper mills... Charlemagne signs commercial agreement with Offa... Japanese emperor moves capital from Nara to newly built, boulevards and wards for similar artisans, Heian-kyo, now Kyoto (-1185 as Heian period governs with Emperor, Great Council of State with prime minister, ministers, left most powerful, right and center least powerful, counselors, major, middle and minor, imperial advisers and officers of left, right boards over 8 ministries, central affairs, ceremonial affairs, civil administration, popular affairs, justice, war, treasury and imperial household, over individual bureaus, i.e., medicine, court university and divination until overshadowed by extralegal regent, chancellor when Fujiwara clan gains power... Court posts, top five with access to emperor and other four for clerks, scribes and functionaries, and attendant status determined mostly by lineage).

797

France establishes horse-changing posts for royal messengers.

800-899

Ibn-Firnas "invents" spectacles and chronometer... China replaces conscripted armies with professional mercenaries (selects recruits in 1000s-1200s by physical ability, height)... Orange tree is brought from India to Arabia... Bruges appears in Flanders... Form of gunpowder is cited in Chinese works, shows knowledge of saltpeter in 500s A.D. by using smoke and incense for yearly fumigations of dwellings... New harness, rigid horse collar connected to wagon by traces, appears in Europe for hitching horses with heavy horseshoes in tandem... Scheldt basin uses 3-field system of farming... Arabs perfect astrolabe, basic instrument for astronomers and navigators for some 700 years... Trading empire of Kanem-Bornu evolves in mid-interior of Africa (-1800s)... Islamic technology develops apparatus to lift objects out of water and maintain water levels... Vikings use knarr, designed as single-masted, square-sailed vessel with overlapping planking, to discover Faroe Islands (evolves by 1200s for European commerce with shorter, higher and broader hull, stern-rudder and bow and stern castles to compete with Mediterranean vessels with lateen sails and fitted planking, evolves c. 1350 as carrack with joint features)... In earliest known use fore-and-aft sails are seen on Hindu vessels sailing to Java, used by 990s on Greek one-masters and by 1200s with lateen sails on Portuguese, Italian boats... Japanese government adds new audit bureau, in time usurps original audit and revenue offices (adds bureau of archivists in 810, gradually controls palace affairs and issues imperial decrees)... Trading towns of Hedeby, Denmark (hosts open market places, temporary stalls or tents used during trading season, where Franks hawk glass and Germans barter basalt millstones, pottery jars of oil or wine for smelted iron, cast bronze, carved combs, knives with reindeer-horn handles), and Birka, Sweden (puts trading posts at Staraya Ladoga, Novgorod, Kiev for trade with Constantinople via Volga, Dnieper Rivers), appear.

801

Charlemagne bans prostitution.

806

China circulates first bills of exchange, 'flying money' used mostly by tea merchants (-820).

808

Idrisid Dynasty, 789-974, founds Fez as capitol of Morocco (opens oldest Arab university in 859).

810

Persian scientist Muhammad ibn Musal Chwarazmi writes book on equations (coins term "algebra," introduces Hindu numerals to Moslem mathematics, is translated into English by Adelard of Bath in 1145).

811

In treaty with Franks, Byzantium renounces all territorial claims to Province of Venetia.

812

Charlemagne's Capitulare de Villis Imperialibus lists brewers among artisans, laborers employed by public administrators... China takes over merchant using paper certificates as cash (authorizes 16 private businesses to issue notes in early 1000s).

813

Caliph al-Mamun begins reign in Baghdad (-833, opens House of Wisdom in 830 with observatory, library, school and translation office for rendering Greek, Persian, and Sanskrit works into Arabic)... Hindu numerals are used in astronomical tables of al-Khwarizmi... Charlemagne's treaty with Byzantium grants all subjects access to highways, waterways, and State-controlled markets.

815

Marshallah, Jewish scholar dies after writing On Prices.

819

Piacenza, Italy, holds 1-day fair, 3 fairs of 8 days each in 872-873 and 5 fairs of 17 days each in 896 (needs no charters for weekly markets).

820

St. Gaul Monastery uses water power to mill grain (runs trip-hammers to crush malt for beer mash).

822

Abd al-Rahman II is ruler of Spain (-852, introduces asparagus, underarm deodorant to Europe).

825

Old English word work, originally weorc and worc, is first cited in this time, followed by first use of apprentice in 1362, worker in 1382, foreman in 1574, management in 1589, factory in 1618, manufacture in 1653, workman in 1683, homemade in 1689, strike in 1768, factory goods in 1793, scab as worker replacement in 1806, working class in 1813, labor in 1830, union in 1833, labor movement in 1870s... Council of Churchmen in Rome advocates establishment of cathedral schools, observed by every European cathedral by 1050... London Mint is founded... University of Pavia is founded, probably school of law (provides general studies in 1361), as first secular institution in Europe.

828

Remains of St. Mark are stolen from Alexandria and taken to Venice for veneration, Apostolic patronage (builds St. Mark's in 976-1004)... Ptolemy's Astronomical System is translated into Arabic as Almagest.

830

Utrecht Psalter shows earliest use of crankhandle in Europe.

831

Hamburg becomes center for missionary work in North (leads to conversion of Sweden 993-1024, of Denmark 1014-1034, of Norway 1016-1028).

840

Danish settlers found Dublin and Limerick.

841

Northmen plunder Rouen... Moslem forces take Italy's Bari, conquer Corsica in 809, Sardinia in 810, Crete in 823, Palermo in 831, and Malta in 870.

843

Treaty of Verdun divides Carolingian Empire into three parts.

844

In first Spanish raid Vikings sack Seville.

845

Northmen levy general tax, Danegeld, on French in payment for no raids, introduce tax to England in 865... China declares bankruptcy, caused by inflationary use of paper money... Monastery of Montier-en-Der operates 11 water mills on different French rivers.

850

Northmen destroy Ghent, re-built in 900s... Jewish settlements appear in Germany, genesis for language of Yiddish... Salerno University is founded... Beauties of Commerce is written in Damascus with advice to merchants.

851

Anonymous writer describes trade journey of Sulieman to China.

852

In this time great fiefs are formed, France, for protection against raids of Northmen (-886).

856

Bardas is Emperor of Byzantium (-866, founds great university in Constantinople for age's great thinkers).

857

Thousands in Rhine Valley die from fungus contaminated bread.

859

Bjorn Ironside leads Viking raid into Mediterranean (-862).

860

Al-Kindi: Book of Artifices (describes some 100 technical devices, such as water clock)... Northmen locate Iceland, visited by Irish Monks in early 800s and followed by Viking settlements after 874... First Russians appear at Constantinople during raid.

861

Northmen raid Paris, Toulouse, Cologne and Worms.

862

Charles the Bald of France grants Flanders to son-in-law Baldwin Iron-Arm... Northman Rurik founds Novgorod (starts Varangian or Rus Dynasty) at junction of trade routes into Russia to compete with Polotsk, Vitebsk, Smolensk and Pskov (is visited by Bremen merchants in 1158, declines after St. Petersburg is built in 1703)... Monks Cyril and Methodius, developers of Slavonic alphabet, undertake mission to convert Slavs to Christianity.

868

Buddhist Diamond sutra is oldest complete printed work, China.

870

English monasteries use calibrated candles in this time to measure time.

871

Alfred the Great is King of Wessex (-899, after repulsing Danes institutes code of laws, sponsors foreign scholarships in schools to train sons of nobles as administrators, uses candle clock for prayers, develops Wessex with network of public strongholds, some like Winchester with regular grid of streets, as first evidence of town planning in England).

875

In this time Cordoba physician Abbas ibn-Firnas is cited to have flown with wings attached to his body, injured in failing to have fashioned a tail.

877

Edict of Quierzy makes fiefs hereditary in France.

880

Arab chemists, physicians prepare alcohol by distilling wine (-909).

882

Oleg, Rurik's successor, seizes control of Kiev, commercial city on Dnieper River since 400s (makes Kiev new capitol of Russia, sends yearly trading expeditions to Byzantium to ensure realm's prosperity).

886

Vikings besiege Paris, protected by town walls... Leo IV rules Byzantine Empire (-913, issues Book of the Perfect with commercial regulations for organizations, corporations, and guilds of linen merchants, wine merchants, tanners, jewelers, wax chandlers, saddlers, notaries, perfumers - absorbed by apothecaries by 900s, grocers, goldsmiths, money lenders, and bakers - not required to perform public service, for selection of guild members, for trade, building and manufacturing activities, for imports and exports, for location of shops in designated areas, for supervision of weights, measures and coinage, and for prices, profits, and competition - disputes handled by Perfect's Bureau).

890

St. Gaul Monastery uses cam with water wheel, developed by Greeks in 300-200s B.C., as tripping mechanism on rotating shaft to trigger hammers in crushing malt to make beer (provides first clear evidence that water power is used for other purposes than milling cereals, evolves by 990 with water-powered hammers in use by hemp mills in Southern France, in 1000s with forge hammers used in Bavarian and Italian oil and silk mills, in 1200s hammers used in Sicily to crush sugar cane, in France to pound leather, in Normandy to sharpen and polish weapons, in Austria to crush ore, and in textile mills throughout Europe, later water-powered hammers used to ring carillon bells of Mechelen).

894

Japan severs relations with China (-1300s, allows informal commercial visits by private traders with luxury goods).

900-999

European nobility build castles... Constantinople becomes commercial, cultural center for Near East... Monastic schools are replaced by cathedral schools at Paris, Chartres, Tours, Cologne, Rheims and Liege to teach Seven Liberal Arts of grammar, rhetoric, dialectic, geometry, arithmetic, astronomy and music... Commerce in Moslem world is transported by camel caravans, up to 4,700 animals, on trails between Persia (textiles), Syria (textiles), Egypt (textiles), Mosul (cotton), Damascus (linen, steel), Sidon and Tyre (glass), and Baghdad (glass, pottery)... Transport workers form association in Worms... Nailed horseshoes are used in Northern Europe... All water mills in China are placed under control of a commission with responsibility for water conservation programs... Viking vessel blown off course by a storm sights Greenland... Al-Farabi cites ideal traits for ruler, intelligence, memory, honesty, and temperance, in work... Real paper money appears in Szechuan Province, China.

905

Fire lance, bamboo tube to discharge explosive shells, is devised during this time in China (evolves as Chinese cannon in 1280, first seen in Europe in 1396, and bronze handgun in 1288).

907

Prince Oleg of Kiev attacks Constantinople (forces city to sign trade treaties to allow Russian traders, given free accommodations and food, to import goods duty-free, gets Russian quarter in city by 1000).

912

Abd-al-Rahman III rules Cordoba (-961, starts City's role as center of learning with library - many manuscripts survive purges in 975-1002 when moved to Toledo).

919

China uses gunpowder to ignite flame-thrower in this time, follows fireworks from 200 B.C. (uses gunpowder in simple bombs, rockets, and grenades by 1000s-1100s).

925

Athelstan is King of England (-939, establishes earliest regulations for coining money)... Vertical-axle windmills are seen in Persia (-949).

930

Althing is established in Iceland as world's first parliament.

931

Baghdad licenses some 860 physicians to practice medicine (requires doctors, druggists, barbers to have state diplomas).

934

Moslem navy sacks Genoa, community of fishermen (forces Genoa to develop fleet for protection and commerce).

940

In this time stern-post rudder is first cited in Chinese text.

942

Caliphate uses some 1,000 stations for postal and news service... Linens and woolens are manufactured in Flanders.

945

Churchman Gerbert, Pope Sylvester in 999, introduces abacus and Hindu-Arabic numerals to Europe, fail to catch on.

960

Northern Sung Dynasty begins at K'ai-feng, city of some 1 million with broad streets, wide canals, markets open from dawn to after midnight, eateries - grand restaurants with over 100 rooms, merchants, vendors and entertainers of all kinds (-1127, cites invention of gunpowder, navigational compasses, astronomical instruments, celestial globes, water-driven mechanical clocks, blast furnace using coke, and spinning wheels, prints government promissory notes, uses civil servants to manage state monopolies, institutes public health services, recognizes associations of merchants and artisans and "chambers of commerce," shows use of silk-working machinery and specialization in making pottery, cultivates major crops of tea, cotton)... Earliest known Moslem tide mill is operated on canal at Basra, Persia.

962

Otto I, King of Germany since 936, is crowned first ruler of Holy Roman Empire by Pope John XII (-1806).

963

Nicephorus II rules Byzantine Empire (-969, with shortage of whole wheat corners supply and sells to bakers' guild for profit).

964

Silver, gold mines are worked at Goslar in Harz Mountains, Germany (-969, finances German trade with Elbe Slavs and Poland, faces end in 1980s with loss of ores and environmental pollution).

966

Holy Roman Empire grants Bremen authority to hold public markets.

968

Arabs found Cordoba University as center of learning in science, library evolves with some 600,000 Moslem manuscripts.

969

China replaces military personnel administering provincial governments with civil officials... "Sheet-dice," playing cards, are block-printed in China (appear in Germany and Spain by 1377, Italy and Belgium by 1379, and France by 1381).

970

China uses eccentric, crankshaft and piston rod, to convert rotary actions into alternating movements, seen in Europe around 1450.

972

Cairo University is founded, Egypt.

973

Sung Dynasty holds recruitment competition for selection of civil servants.

975

Magyars, conquerors of Hungary and other lands, accept Christianity... Ibn Hagal describes use of promissory note by Moroccan merchants, Arabic word "sakk" becomes term "check"... In this time (-999) Arab traders start settlements at Mogadishu, Mombasa and Zanzibar, blocked in expanding throughout Africa by Tsetse fly... Hurdy-gurdy musical instrument appears in Europe (-999, shows one of first applications of crankhandle to turn a wheel).. Norse mint first coins, previously used as bullion, in quantity.

976

Muhammad ibn Ahmad: Keys of the Sciences (uses Arabic numeral zero)... Ali ibn Hasan captures East Africa from Persia (-1016, develops Mombasa, Kilwa as trade centers for gold, ivory, slaves, copper, brass)... Chain-drive appears in Chinese mechanical clock, in Europe in 1770 in silk reeling device of de Vaucanson and in 1869 with bicycle of Tretz).

979

First astronomical clock in China is designed.

980

China's Simple Discourses on the Investigation of Things cites use of fumigation to reduce infection.

983

China's government establishes three departments of state monopolies, agrarian taxes and budgets to oversee economic activities... Otto II grants City of Lazise right to levy tolls, dues.

984

To prevent theft of cargos from boats wrecked being hauled over spillways, Ch'iao Wei-Yo invents first canal lock, seen in Holland in 1200s.

986

Eric the Red starts colony of some 400 in Greenland, disappears... Herjolfsson from Norway undertakes trip to Greenland, sights North America after losing way in fog.

987

Saint-Saudeur Monastery uses water-powered mill with camshaft in this time to make beer (-996, followed by use of water-driven hammers in Oberpfalz mill in Germany in 1010, Normandy fulling mill in 1086, Paris tanning mill in 1138, Spanish paper mill in 1238, and French paper mill near Ambert, still extant, in 1326).

988

Prince Vladimir of Kiev adopts Christianity.

990

Venice starts municipal mint to issue coinage... Chinese geomancy work cites a compass, noted in 1044 text and used on boat in 1090 with first European reference in 1190... France operates earliest known water-powered hemp mill.

991

Witenagemot, assembly of wisemen, is formed in England, genesis for Parliament.

992

Constantinople grants Venetian goods lower tariffs than other foreign merchandise... Poland becomes state with rule of Boleslav I (-1025, evolves with system of production and services around castles with craftsmen in up to 40 different trades).

993

Sung Dynasty of China forms salt, tea commissariats (issues transferable exchange certificates redeemable in cash or goods).

996

Alexandria ships sugar cane to Venice... Byzantium grants seller of property the right to redeem land at any time for original price... Holy Roman Empire grants Venice rights for warehouses, trading posts, and tax exemptions.

998

China's Sung Dynasty produces 125,000 tons of iron (-1078), not achieved by Europe until 1530-40 and England, Wales in 1540-1620.

1000-1099

Loom with horizontal frame instead of vertical appears in Europe, probably from China via Moslem Spain (promotes fame of wool products from Flanders with speed of weaving and quality of cloth)... Mahona, a share-holding company, is formed in Genoa for privateering... Coffee appears in Ethiopia (follows myth of discovery by Arab goatherd c. 850)... Water power is used in France to drive hemp, fulling mills... Panic is widespread in Europe with fear for End of the World... Merchant guilds appear in Flanders and France, Paris Company for the Transit of Merchandise by Water with near monopoly for Seine River traffic... Dikes are built along Meuse, Rhine rivers... Crude ovens are used in Saar for smelting iron, site for water wheels using bellows and hammers during 1000-1100s... In China a large-scale iron and steel complex, uses blast furnaces and employs some 3,000 workers, evolves in North near Hopei with bituminous coal fields, coke used for cooking and heating since 800s (-1194 when area's canal system is destroyed by Yellow River flood)... Industrial complex is built, China, to mass-produce ceramics for Imperial Court... German traders appear in London and on Swedish island of Gotland, evolves in 1100s-1200s as Company of Gotland Travelers at Visby as forerunner of Hanseatic League... Bailiffs evolve in England as estate managers... Knights Hospitallers evolves as military religious order in Holy Land, known in 1310 as Knights of Rhodes and 1530s as Knights of Malta... Persians or merchants introduce 7-day week to Chinese, previously used week of 10 days.

1001

On returning to Greenland from Norway, Leif Ericsson's vessel is driven off-course by a storm to North American coast, discovers Newfoundland.

1002

Bishop of Liege grants mortgage loan to abbot of St. Riquier.

1008

Earliest known water-powered fulling mill is operated at Ludi near Milan (appears in England by 1185, some 130 in operation by 1327).

1012

To maintain their standing armies Danish rulers levy "Danegeld," a tribute based on assessing value of land in hides, on English (-1051, is continued by Norman kings for nearly a century after 1066 Conquest).

1014

King Ethelred, England, requires compulsory tithes to aid the poor.

1015

Municipal self-government of Benvento, Italy, is first recognized as "Communitas"... Moslems are driven from Corsica, Sardinia by Pisans, Genoese (-1016).

1016

Church makes a boy an archbishop in return for due payment and services, frequency of such transactions discussed at Church Council in 1099... King Cnute's reign starts in England (-1035, with towns unable to pay levied Danegeld collects tax from lords to force most freemen into servile status in manors, uses first known royal writs to notify shire-earl, sheriff or bishop of land grants).

1020

Leon is first city in Spain chartered by King of Castile.

1023

China forms official government agency to print bank notes, Sweden in 1661, Amsterdam 1690, France 1720, England 1779, and Germany 1806.

1024

First bank notes in China are issued in Szechwan as promissory notes... Venice takes over glass industry (moves glass workers to Murano in 1278 for safety and secrecy, passes ordinances later to forbid travel of glassmakers and disclosure of techniques)... Tolls are placed on wool, dyestuff and teasels at Arras fairs.

1025

Mantled fireplace appears in Western Europe (-1029).

1030

Vienna appears as a community.

1033

Castile is formed as separate kingdom, ruled by Ferdinand I in 1036.

1035

Chinese painting shows a spinning wheel.

1037

Conrad II makes (May 28) fiefs hereditary in Italy... Seljuk Turks seize Ghaznavid city of Merv, ancient trading site in Middle East.

1038

Ibn al-Haitham: Optical Thesaurus (cites existence of lens, spectacles).

1040

Cantle at back of saddle is raised to support riding knight (-1120)... Chinese treatise on art of war describes magnetism... Scotland's King Malcolm Canmore stages foot race up Creag Choinnich to select winner as his "running footman" (evolves as modern fell racing in Britain, Europe)... Lady Godiva, opponent of high taxes in Coventry, is born (-1080).

1041

China's Bi Sheng devises world's first movable-type printing system with clay characters, woodblock printing known since 700s (-1048, is little used due to vast size of alphabet).

1042

Edward is King of England (-1066, uses secretariat of clerical staff of priests, headed by chief clerk as early chancellor, to maintain records of land-tenure and tax obligations in number of hides - may have handled fiscal matters, gives evidence of tradesmen in Winchester doing business in stalls, shops).

1044

Tseng Kung-liang: General Principals of the Classics on War (describes paraffin flame-thrower, toxic smokes, repeating crossbows, crude tanks, grenades and formula for making gunpowder)... Venice uses tide mills (-1078, appear in Southern France in 1124-33, in Brittany by 1182, in Britain - 38 by 1300 and 89 by 1600)... Chinese military encyclopedia gives first description of floating compass... Chinese Wu Ching Tsao gives first recipe for saltpeter, main ingredient of gunpowder.

1045

Tokdor of Senegal are first people south of Sahara to adopt Islam (-1049)... School for European scholars opens at Abbey of Bec, Normandy.

1050

Nuremberg, chartered 1219, Oslo and Delhi appear as communities... Anasazi center evolves in Chaco Canyon, NM (-1150, erects Great Houses up to five stories tall, builds irrigation system and network of hard-surfaced roads, 30' in width, to serve prosperous commercial trade of pottery, turquoise, jewelry and produce for cotton, buffalo meat from Plains' Indians and copper bells, macaws from Mexico)... Arabs bring decimal system to Spain... Some Chinese books are printed with movable type.

1052

Countess Matilda rules Tuscany (-1115, allows guild societies to govern Florence).

1059

Philip I is King of France (-1108, starts formation of monarchy).

1062

Marrakesh is founded in North Africa.

1065

For first time in Chinese history government's cash revenues are greater than commodity revenues (uses paper money later to ease chronic shortages of coins)... Genoa sends commercial convoy to Levant.

1066

After winning Battle of Hastings (shows use of lance, kite-shaped shield, crossbow and bugles and/or flags to coordinate units in attack), William the Conqueror is first Norman King of England (-1087, introduces European feudalism, sees during rule formation of associations, called firthgilds, by Saxon families for mutual protection against Normans, adopted in 1100s as device by townspeople to form guilds to protect their trading interests)... Al-Bakri of Cordoba: Book of Roads and Kingdoms (discusses geography of Africa)... Bishop of Liege grants first town charter north of Alps to Huy.

1067

Bayeux tapestry is woven (shows use of horse-collar instead of traditional yoke).

1068

Shen Tsung is Emperor of China (-1085, appoints finance minister who substitutes provincial money taxes for labor obligations to reduce dependence of peasants on moneylenders, forms financial bureau to reduce budget by 40%, raises salaries of civil servants so they will not be dependent on outsiders for funds, and loans cash or grain to poor families as protection against usury on crop loans)... William the Conqueror appoints town crier for Lyme Regis, England.

1070

In this time William of Champeaux is master of Cathedral School of Notre Dame, Paris (-1121, initiates intellectual movement in 1100s for formation of University of Paris)... Newcastle is founded, England... In this time Church loans funds to lords in exchange for shares of their land revenues (leads to use of Jewish moneylender by Abbey of St. Andre, France, to manage its finances).

1071

New Greek wife of Doge introduces bathing, two-tined fork and other customs to Venice...

Guilhelm, first troubadour of note, is born (-1127).

1072

State banking and barter offices are used in China to stabilize prices.

1073

When drought in China dries up wells used for water clocks, an incense stick is devised to measure time... China mints 6 billion copper coins, string of 1,000 official unit of exchange, with stamp "Circulating Treasure of Sung" (are supplemented with credit instruments as merchants put coins in deposit houses, use receipts as security for commercial transactions).

1074

Worms receives (January 18) imperial charter.

1075

Glasgow appears on River Clyde, Scotland.

1077

Weavers, fullers of Cambrai join forces with fellow citizens to win freedom from Bishop... After his agreement to certain conditions Pope Gregory VII repeals excommunication of Emperor Henry IV to establish supremacy.

1079

London is chartered as a city, some 300 borough charters by 1216.

1080

After other French towns fail to gain their freedom as communities, St. Quentin is recognized as a commune, followed by Marseilles in 1100 and Amiens in 1113.

1081

Celestial globe is made in Valencia, cited as first in Europe since Greeks... Byzantine Emperor Alexius I grants Venice commercial privileges, renewed 1126.

1082

Alexius I asks help from Venice to repel Norman invasion (grants Venetian merchants special area in Constantinople for commercial activities, issues Golden Bull in 1092 to repay loan, allows Venetians to trade in Imperial cities without interference from customs officials and exempts traders from 10% duty paid by other foreign merchants).

1083

China monopolizes successful industries of iron, agricultural implements.

1085

Christian forces recapture Toledo from Moslems, later site for "School of Translation" of

Archbishop Raymond... William the Conqueror orders Doomsday survey to determine productive capacity of each manor for taxation (-1087, cites use of 5,624 water mills in England to produce grain - some 60,000 in France by 1500s, 10,000-20,000 in England by 1700s, and around 500,000 in Europe before Industrial Revolution in 1800s).

1086

China's Emperor appoints Su Sung to form team of officials, craftsmen, technicians to build water-powered astronomical clock, uses oldest known chain drive, escapement wheel and three automatic rotating instruments (-1094, is abandoned with parts carried off by Chin Tartars in 1126)... First cited, next 1145, fulling mill operates at St. Wandrille, Normandy, 29 in Northern France by late 1100s... Chinese scientist Shen Kua gives first known account of use of magnetic compass for navigation.

1087

Merchant shipping office opens at Ch'uan-chou, China.

1088

Mahdiyah, located near Tunis, North Africa, grants commercial privileges to Genoa.

1091

Walcher of Lorraine observes lunar eclipse with astrolab in Italy, cited as first study of astronomy in Europe... Soon after conquering Sicily, Norman rulers use translators for transcribing Arabic, Greek works on mathematics, astronomy into Latin.

1092

Nizam al-Mulk: Book on the Art of Rule.

1093

Chinese study describes Moslem use of magnetic needle... Trade guilds are first cited in England, guilds of weavers noted in London, Lincoln and Oxford in 1099.

1094

Venice holds a carnival, first known use of gondolas... China installs new emperor (declares previous emperor's calendar faulty, ignores Su Sung's Heavenly Clockwork).

1096

First Crusade is undertaken (-1099).

1097

Genoese ships carry horses for First Crusade to Near East, continued assistance in later crusades wins extensive territorial, commercial privileges in Holy Land.

1098

Robert of Molesme, followers establish religious order of Cistercians in Burgundy (expands with St. Bernard in 1112, attempts to become independent of outside world by developing self-contained economic order with centralized administration over some 530 monasteries, each a medieval factory with water-powered foundries, corn and sawmills, wine presses, etc., throughout Europe in 1100s).

1099

Guild of weavers operates in Maintz... After seeing profits gained by Genoa, Pisa from First Crusade, Venice supports Crusaders in return for trading concessions, land... Crusaders form Kingdom of Jerusalem (-1143).

1100-1199

In addition to other mills, some 150 fulling mills are built in England during next 200 years, contribute to land's "first" industrial revolution... As trip from Canterbury, England, to Rome might take 29 days, Church forms religious fraternities to repair, build bridges to improve travel for its dignitaries... Lombard Street, London, evolves as banking center for merchants from North Italy... Provins, France, is site for major fairs, visited by traveling groups of entertainers, such as acrobats, and pack caravans of merchant companies (evolves from word com-panis to mean breadshare as genesis for company of merchants, at first vagabonds, adventurers, brigands and/or thieves who rob and pillage as they traded, in sharing mutual perils of brigands, robber barons and armies of warlike monks in visiting fairs, such as at St. Denis, Ypres, Lille, Bruges, Ghent, Bar, Troyes, Lagny, Champagne and Cambrai, to buy and sell goods by gross, thus called grossers, grocers later, as small amounts of goods provided too little profit for risk of leftovers, with protection from passes by local lords to provide traders with safe travel to and from fairs, to guarantee no merchant could be held for debts contracted outside fairs and to grant them the right to play cards, roll dice on saints' days)... Arabic numerals appear in Europe to keep records, make calculations... Treadle loom, padded horse-collar, wood cuts for initial letters of manuscripts, and heavy-wheeled plows are seen in Europe... Intaglio printing, China, is used in making bank notes to avoid counterfeiting, seen first in Europe at Holland, Northern Italy in 1440... Ghazali advises kings in manuscript to have justice, intelligence, patience, and modesty... Medieval communes form in Europe for self-government in order to set tariffs, mint currency, supervise public works, arrange food supplies, regulate commerce, establish weights and measures, regulate prices for essential foods and beer, and to grant some monopolies, i.e., salt in Basel, Genoa and beer in Nuremberg... Bruges banking house provides insurance on goods, City charters insurance company in 1310... Henry I of England designates yard as length of his arm... In Florence some washers, fullers, sorters, spinners, weavers, inspectors and clerks work in one-roof buildings, use materials and tools supplied by cloth merchants in Wool Guild... Wangko, poor peasant, starts iron works, eventually employs some 500 workers, in South China (is executed in 1181 after dispute with government officials)... Textiles of Flanders are sold at fairs in England, Germany... Carthusian monks in Alps may have devised process for making cast iron... Italians distill wine to make brandy... French monks develop sport of court tennis, banned by Church with so many monks, priests playing and betting (evolves by 1600 with over 1,800 courts in Paris alone)... Cistercian monasteries revive vineyards of Burgundy.

1100

Henry I is King of England (-1135, starts centralized administration of offices, finances and justice)... In this time a payment is recorded being made to weaver's guild of London, earliest certain reference in England to fraternity, company or corporation of merchants.

1102

Crusaders grant Venice trading rights in Sidon, rights for Tyre in 1123... Roger is Bishop of

Salisbury (establishes Exchequer for Henry I, 1100-35, and Stephen 1135-54).

1104

Work is started in Venice to build first basin of Arsenal (evolves by 1423 with some 16,000 craftsmen, workers building galleys on assembly line).

1106

Worms records guild of fishmongers.

1107

European Jews seek refuge in Old Cairo from tribulations, commercial and religious, at home... Using wood blocks China prints paper money in three colors to prevent counterfeiting.

1111

Byzantium grants Pisa trading rights (reduces duties to 4%, allows factory in Constantinople)... Moneychangers meet informally near St. Martin's church in Lucca, echoed by other such meetings on cathedral steps in Seville, on Rua Nova in Lisbon, on Calle Nueva in Cadiz, under Venice's Rialto and on wooden benches in Venice's city square - banca rotta basis for word bankrupt as angry creditors would put a merchant out of business for loss of capital by breaking his bench.

1113

Craftsmen, in separate quarter of Kiev, protest nonpayment for services, Novgorod in 1209... English wool is exported to Flanders, first record.

1114

Champagne fairs are held regularly at Troyes, Provins, Lagny, and Bar-sur- Aube, France (provide meeting places for merchants at intersection of European trading routes).

1115

Cistercian monastery at Clairvaux is established (evolves to operate olive oil mill, water wheels and cornmill, uses canals to provide water in conduit for washing and latrines)... City-State of Florence becomes a commune, ruled by association of nobles for the people.

1118

Byzantium withdraws Venice's commercial privileges, renews 1126... Band of nine knights forms order of Knights Templars in this time to protect pilgrims in Holy Land (moves to Cyprus in 1291 to become bankers to European nobility, ends in 1307 when charged with heresy, immorality).

1119

Guild of students organizes Bologna University, revives study of Roman law (is founded 1158).

1120

Duke of Zahringen, 24 prominent merchants found Freibury-im-Breisgau, Germany... During these years Lambert of Ardres prepares Liber Floridus map (shows Europe, Africa each a quarter of the earth with Asia the remaining half)... Walcher of Malvern calculates differences in degrees, minutes and seconds.

1125

Gerbert builds organ at Rheims, inflated by air and compressed by "heated water"... Account books of Ramsey Abbey record 40 oxen and 2 horses, 24 oxen and 8 horses after 1160.

1126

Boats with paddles operated by crank or connecting-rods are seen in China, perhaps used in 700s (are used in 1130, 1161 naval battles on rivers and canals, appear in Europe in 1543).

1127

Flanders notes first visit of Italian merchants... Count of Flanders grants town rights to Bruges, Arras in 1224... Prisbislav Henry, Prince of Stodorans, mints first coins in Slavonic lands of Elbe.

1128

Wurzburg cites guild of shoemakers.

1130

Evolving from financial reports by sheriffs to Exchequer, oldest surviving financial account is compiled by clerks of treasury to show rents, leases and other royal revenues (cites payments by guilds of weavers in London, Winchester, Lincoln, Oxford and Nottingham, and fullers of Winchester)... Aymery de Picaud, French Clerk: The Way of St. James (provides travel guide, one of many, to show pilgrims roads, hostels for visiting tomb of St. James, first discovered in 812, at Spain's Santiago de Compostela).

1132

Experiments are made, China, to test gunpowder as propellant for rockets, tests first mortars c. 1280... Henry I of France grants charters to incorporate towns (gives protection for commerce, industry)... London is authorized to appoint a sheriff, derived from "Shire Reeve" or county justice, to create City's oldest office, replaced by mayoralty in 1192.

1133

Following creation of other English fairs after 1066, Royal Charter for London's Bartholomew fair at Smithfield is granted to Rahere, court jester to Henry I, to raise funds for the Priory and Hospice he dedicated to St. Bartholomew in 1102 (evolves as country's greatest cloth fair, is acquired by Corporation of London in 1604, becomes center of entertainment in 1600s-1700s, is replaced by Smithfield's Market in 1866)... Construction is started to build France's Church of St. Denis, spurs business activity in area (-1144, signals era of Gothic architecture).

1135

John of Seville at Toledo translates Arabic texts on mathematics, astronomy, and philosophy into Latin (-1153)... Vertical water wheel is used in Italy for ore-stamping, used for tanning in France in 1138, for grinding and polishing cutlery in France in 1204, for sawing lumber in France in 1204, for mechanical bellows in Styria in 1214, for making paper in Italy in 1276, for pumping water in Moravian mine in Germany in 1315, for turning a lathe in France in 1347, for boring pipe in Germany in 1480, and for polishing gems in France in 1534.

1136

Traders carrying rock salt from Halle to Bohemia discover silver vein in Saxony region of Freiberg (attracts many adventurers to beginning mining industry)... Market square of Paris is moved from Place de Greve to area of Les Halles (-1969 when replaced by modern museum)... Metal trades are first cited in Poland... Kloster Eberbach is founded by monks of St. Bernard, center for some 200 monasteries along Rhine between Worms and Cologne (is world's largest wine-growing establishment in 1100s-1200s).

1137

Some 20% of South China's income is derived from excise taxes on maritime trade.

1138

First use of Arabic, originally Indian, numerals in Europe is on coins minted by Roger II of Sicily.

1140

Norman King Roger II decrees only licensed physicians may practice medicine.

1141

Twelve town criers in French province of Berry form a company, chartered by Louis VII with exclusive rights to give commercial announcements in province... Ricasoli family produces Chianti wine, officially standardized by Duke of Tuscany in 1716.

1143

In this time Lubeck becomes Baltic seaport, chartered 1226.

1145

Rouen, France, is chartered.

1147

Moscow is first cited... Second Crusade begins (-1149)... Lisbon is liberated from Moslems.

1148

Grafian, monk of Bologna, compiles laws of Roman Church (includes sections on usury, just price and regulations for schools, universities).

1150

University of Paris appears in this time, guild of masters granted freedom later from royal courts by king (is founded 1170, obtains first charter 1213, forms first endowed college, Sorbonne, in 1257)... Silk cultures are imported into Sicily... Bologna University forms medical faculty... Abbey of Fontenay, Burgundy, operates workshop, forge and grain-mill with water power (-1199)... Cahokia, 900-1300 A.D., evolves as settlement of some 40,000 Indians near St. Louis (becomes trade center for Dakota, Gulf Coast, Appalachian, Great Lakes Indians)... Polders are built in this time in Flanders with participation of Benedictine, Cistercian monasteries... Magister Salernus gives first clear reference on distillation of alcohol... Makhzumi, senior financial official in Egypt: Kitab al-Minhaj (-1200, reports on taxes levied on agriculture and trade of linen, cotton, spices, fish, chickens, salt, dates, grain, alum, condiments, silk, wool, coral, oil, saffron)... Company of Gothard Travelers at Visby opens St. Peter's Yard at Novgorod (-1199)... Troubadour music becomes organized in Southern France.

1151

Twenty physicians, Salerno, form "Civitas Hippocratica"... First known fire and plaque insurance are issued in Iceland... Chess, originated in India, is first played in England.

1152

Sea-laws of Oleron describe regulations governing shares for co-owners of trading vessels, space for goods, and duties of traders-proprietors and valets in joint-ventures.

1153

A chicken bucket restaurant, world's oldest continuing eatery, opens in K'ai-feng, China.

1154

Chin rulers of China issue paper money, secured by cash reserve... Henry II rules England (-1189, develops English common law, issues silver coinage, subdues barons, centralizes power to restore war-ravaged land, puts royal treasury in order, restores and extends Henry I's system to assess, collect revenues from royal domain and vassals, requires sheriffs, local administrators, to present accounts twice/year to Royal Exchequer).

1155

Frederick Barbarossa is German Emperor (-1190, claims regalian rights to mines)... Bristol receives city charter, England (is designated staple town in 1353 as export center for European trade in wine, wool)... Genoese notary G. Scriba: Notularium (records joint venture for Mediterranean voyage, some 400 in City by 1164)... Weavers' Company, existence cited in 1130, is chartered, London... England's Henry II abolishes fiscal earldoms, resumes royal demesnes... Map of Western China is oldest known printed map.

1156

When Fujiwara clan loses political power in Japan, Minamoto and Taira clans struggle for dominance (begins militaristic feudal age).

1157

To raise funds for war with Constantinople, Bank of Venice, formed by merchants as City's first institution to exchange and deposit money, issues first government bonds... Despite little acceptance of regalian rights elsewhere in Europe Barbarossa grants Rammelsborg mines, Germany, to three monasteries and town of Gosler... England grants German merchants privileges, again 1194... Kurenberg is first famous German minnesinger.

1158

Duke Henry of Saxony founds Munich on site of former monastery, evolves as European center for salt trade (is ruled by Bavarian kings from 1180 on)... Rabbi Benjamin of Tudela travels through Persia, Central Asia to China.

1161

Chinese use catapults in battle to hurl explosive grenades.

1163

Paris builds Notre Dame (-1235)... Synagogue is built in China's Kaifeng, follows appearance of Jews in China in 200s B.C. and Jewish settlers among cotton traders in 900s.

1164

Yorkshire weavers are granted monopoly to make dyed cloth.

1165

Maimonides, famed Jewish scholar, moves to old Cairo to write (-1204, formulates 12 rules for ethical conduct in moneylending, approves usury when making loans to heathens).

1166

England levies its first personal property taxes.

1167

16 cities in Northern Italy form Lombard League... Monks at Cathedral Priory of Canterbury develop elaborate underground system of pipes to distribute water to infirmary hall, fish tank, latrines, refectory, scullery, kitchen, baker's house, brewer's house, guest hall and bath house... Alcohol is distilled from wine at Salerno, first recorded use of chemical process in Europe... Absalm, Archbishop of Lund, founds Copenhagen as commercial port, Denmark's capitol in 1443... Student dissidents from University of Paris form University of Oxford, perhaps lectures as early as 1133 (evolves in 1200s to provide male students with practical instruction in conveyancing, administration and elementary legal procedure, unveils M.B.A. program for business in 1990).

1169

Manuscript shows waterwheel with succession of diminishing gears, first cited in England in 1185.

1170

Windmills with horizontal axles are seen in Low Countries (-1174).

1171

Byzantine Emperor Manuel I confiscates (March 12) goods of Venetian traders... Bank of Venice arranges bookkeeping exchanges in accounts for clients.

1172

Milanese looking for wool are first Italians at Champagne fairs, France (devise commenda, contract between investors and traveling merchants selling goods, to grant merchants carte blanche to sell goods and require fair statements of profit and loss to investors)... Exchequer, financial and accounting office in royal households of Norman kings, is organized at Westminster (-1833, becomes treasury office in 1558-1603 with permanent staff in 1660)... Bad Ems spa, Germany, opens for business.

1173

Smithfield Market, later London's largest for distribution of meat, is first cited as a field for selling horses (evolves as Royal cattle market in 1638)... England's first fulling mill is operated... Moslem Saladin rules Egypt (-1193, in leveraged strategy uses riches of Egypt to take Syria, riches of Syria to take Mesopotamia, and riches of Mesopotamia to take Palestine, dies with empty treasuries).

1174

Earliest known English horse races are held.

1175

Gerard of Cremona translates Ptolemy's Almagest from Arabic into Latin... Rich veins of copper, silver and gold are found in Erz Gebirge, Germany.

1176

Sugar mills are seen in Norman Sicily.

1177

Bazacle Dam is first cited, France (is built by Company Le Bazacle formed by citizens of Toulouse to operate 12 mills on Garonne River, divides ownership into shares which are freely traded with fluctuating values, becomes limited company in 1370s, considers merger with similar limited company in 1374, substitutes first cash dividends for grain in 1840, is nationalized by France after WW II).

1178

Richard Fitznigel: Dialogus de Saccario (discusses financial administration of English government).

1180

Windmill is used in England, originally from Persia or Afghanistan... Glass windows are seen in English private houses... First windmills with vertical-sails, horizontal-shafts appear in Normandy... Livery companies, liverymen are employers of craft workers, are first cited in London (are operated as guilds or mysteries, derived from Italian word for trade, with master, usually two Wardens, and later a Court of Assistance, use banners in 1200s in City processions of guilds for identification, mint medals with guild signs and portraits of patron saints as early trademarks)... Traveling English monk Alexander Neckham brings news to Paris of mysterious needle that always points in the same direction (is used in 1269 experiments with pointer by Peter of Maricort, is cited in 1270 decree of Alphonso the Wise that all ships must carry the needle, evolves in 1300s, according to tradition, with compass card and frame at Italian Republic of Amalfi)... When main harbor gradually fills with silt, Bruges builds new outer harbor with deeper moorings for Hanseatic shipping... Carving shows earliest Western use of rudder.

1181

Assize of Arms authorizes militia in England (requires every freeman, according to income, to do his share in national defense)... Jayavarman VII rules Cambodia (restores Khmer empire with roads, bridges, rest houses for travelers, over 100 state hospitals, improved rice production, and great capitol city of Angkor Thom).

1182

France banishes Jews... Samson is Abbot of Bury St. Edmonds (-1211, appoints bailiffs and reeves to run estate and sell any surpluses on open market, maintains yearly records so auditors can compare performances of manors to detect fraud and plan decisions for next year)... In Florence consuls of cloth guild of dyers and finishers, Arte di Calimala, are appointed as City's consuls of commerce (becomes City's most important guild over rival Arte della Lania in wool cloth).

1183

Famous London public cookshop, follows those in days of Nebuchadnezzar and medieval years of Middle East, offers array of cooked meats for sale while bakers handle baking needs of housewives.

1185

Earliest example of chimney with flue in England is built in Conisborough Keep, Yorkshire, follows use of chimney stacks in 800s at monastery of St. Gall which used such stacks to vent fumes, for heating... Paris paves streets with stones, followed by Florence in 1240, London in 1280... Yoritomo, Minamoto leader, is Japan's Shogun (allows arts and trades to flourish, sponsors samurai as warrior class)... Bishop of Trent establishes first code, Germany, for miners, King of Bohemia c. 1249 for Iglau miners.

1186

Great Mosque of Damascus uses water clock in this time.

1187

Instead of leading military forces in battle, Saladin directs troops from hill near Hattin.

1189

Paper is made in Southern France... Third Crusade begins (-1193)... Florence mints silver florin... Novgorod, German merchants sign commercial treaty... Henry Fitzaylwin, London's first Lord Mayor, is installed in guildhall, first cited in 1128 (-1212)... Barbarossa grants seaport of Hamburg freedom of trade, exemption from custom duties (leads to sailors devising spicy meat concoction called hamburger).

1190

Monk Theophilus discusses medieval crafts in manuscripts... Alexander Neckam: De Naturis Rerum (gives first sure evidence of mariner's compass in Europe)... Notary Guglielmo Cassinese, Genoa, registers local payments transferred between accounts in same bank, between different banks.

1191

Chinese tea is popular in Japan... Merchant guilds win control of London's government (offer annual payment to King John to suppress weavers' guild, accepted 1200)... Celestine III is new pope (-1198, levies tax on windmills).

1192

Venice mints silver groat coins.

1193

England imports indigo, brazilwood from India to dye cloth.

1194

Work is started in rebuilding Cathedral of Chartres, France, in dedication to the Virgin (-1260, uses tread-wheel hoist, winch in construction)... Richard I charters London agents for German merchants (eliminates rents, grants them freedom to trade throughout country).

1196

English crown sets standards for size, quality of woolen cloth.

1197

England's Assize of Measures decrees production of dyed cloth for markets only in cities and capitol boroughs (sets uniform standards for size, quality)... Water-powered iron mill is operated in Southern Scandinavia (-1224).

1198

Papal ban exempts Venice from trading with Infidel as commerce is required for City's survival... Benedictine monastery and church at Bury St. Edmunds uses water clocks in this time to signal times for prayers, cited as first use in England... Order of the Knights of the Hospital of St. Mary of Teutons is formed in Jerusalem by German merchants of Lubeck, Bremen (founds Riga in 1201 as missionary center for Teutonic Knights, is organized 1226 to crusade for Church, funds from customs dues by Emperor Frederick II, with grand master, general chapter, and five chief officers to report to pope and emperor, gains Prussia in 1229, forms union with Livonian Brothers in 1237, obtains Papal permission in 1263 to engage in non-profit trade, circumvented to become commercial and military corporation, with other areas, locates headquarters at Marienburg in 1309, after declining in 1400s from wars survives to 1809, is revived in 1840 by Hapsburgs)... Byzantium exempts Venetian merchants from customs duties.

1199

Liverpool is founded (obtains charter in 1207, evolves as port for pottery, textile industries)... King John rules England (-1216, sees demonstration of bear and bull baiting given by visiting Italians, evolves as sport with operation of Bear Gardens in 1546 - banned by law in 1835, sees fairs, which developed in England with pilgrims assembling at abbeys, cathedrals on feast days of their enshrined saints)... King John's chancery clerks start to make parchment copies of all important documents.

1200-1299

Tidal mills are seen at Suffolk, England, and Bayonne, France... Moslem world uses alcohol for medicinal purposes... Engagement rings are fashionable... Paris is recognized as capitol of France... Constantinople is trading center for some 60,000 Italian merchants... Arabs develop macrame, reaches Europe by 1300s... Mali trading empire absorbs Ghana in extending its territory to Atlantic Coast (-1500s)... China uses first windmill, idea from Afghanistan... Wrought iron is used in England instead of cast iron... In sailing southward with monsoon winds Moslem merchants develop East African coast as trading area... Coal is mined in Liege... Commercial guild evolves as hanse of "The Seventeen Towns," France, grows to over 24 towns... Some 19 toll stations operate along Rhine River, some 35 by 1300, 50 by 1400, and over 65 by 1500 - also seen on European roads... Number of Flemish towns, headed by Bruges, form Hansa in London... Holland completes diking system (develops agriculture, cattle and industry in 1300s, cloth and salted herring industries in 1400s - Leyden a world center by 1450)... Inca Empire evolves in South America (-1493, develops irrigation canals, bridges, and roads, produces textiles, uses governmental planning for farming)... Imitation Persian tapestries are made at Arras... Weavers, fullers of Beverley, England, are required by law to foreswear craft in joining ranks of burgess... Moslem engineer Jazari devises irrigation machine with donkey power... Friar records some 6,000 public fountains, 300 public ovens, 10 hospitals, 1,500 lawyers, 40 copyists, 10,000 monks and 100 armorers in Milan... Hoop and Grapes opens in London, claims to be City's oldest licensed house... Bakewell Hall appears in London as weekly marketplace for woolen cloth... In early years, cloth guild forms in Florence to import wool, export finished fabric (operates some 300 textile factories by 1306, employs some 30,000 textile workers by 1336)... Professional "bards" appear in Ireland.

1201

Patent rolls are started in England to record royal grants for privileges, offices, lands, etc... Cambridge petitions King John of England for communal rights... Riga is seat of Livonian Brothers of the Sword, German military order to Christianize Baltics (joins Hanseatic League in 1282).

1202

Fourth Crusade begins (-1204)... Jesters are seen in European courts... Leonardo Fibonacci: Liber Abaci, first serious examination in Europe of Hindu mathematics.

1203

Corn market operates in Toulouse.

1204

Crusaders, Venetians sack Constantinople to found Latin Kingdom of Romania (rewards Venetians with booty, lands for developing trading routes in spices, textiles, silver, slaves)... Amsterdam appears on Amstel River... Wealthy families in Florence form guild of bankers (allow no Florentine to provide banking services unless a guild member)... Traders smuggle secret silk process of Constantinople to Genoa, Venice... In earliest reference water-powered sawmill is operated in Eureux, Normandy, seen in Northern France and Switzerland during 1200s... According to legend, Donnybrook, a section of Dublin, is granted royal permission to hold an annual 2-week fair, exuberant revels evolve as Donnybrooks.

1205

Regulations are established to protect woods belonging to monks of Chelles from use as fuel for local furnaces.

1206

At Karakorum Jenghiz Khan is ruler of Mongols (-1227, invades China in 1215- 18, Central Asia in 1218-21 with army of 150,000-240,000 calvary, 60% light and 40% heavy, with support troops, organizes force with one corp of 3 Toumans, 1 Touman of 10 regiments, 1 regiment of 10 squadrons, 1 squadron of 10 troops and 1 troop of 10 men, uses intelligence data in campaigns to prepare centralized strategy with decentralized tactics, disciplines men for precise and quick deployment, selects officers by merit and valor, uses psychological warfare, communicates with troops by couriers, signal flags, and flaming arrows).

1207

Leeds is chartered (evolves as English wool center until replaced by local iron industry in 1800s).

1208

Artisans, journeymen miners in Central Europe form Tridentiner Bergwerkgebrauche as a mining enterprise.

1209

Valencia University is founded... In protest against hanging of students by townsfolk, students and faculty of Oxford University form Cambridge University (considers students eligible for rank of master after 7-year apprenticeship, plans business school in 1989)... Merchant house of Buonsignori begins as family enterprise, Siena.

1210

Pope Innocent III approves teachers' guilds at University of Paris... St. Frances of Assisi, merchant's son, founds Franciscan Order of Friars (teaches poverty and repentance).

1211

Word capital, from Latin word for head, is used in Italy to mean assets in form of funds, merchandise (leads to use of word capitalist by 1633-1654, capitalism by 1753).

1212

London requires tile roofs to replace those of thatch.

1213

Bishop of Sarum plans English community of Salisbury as textile town (-1220, is developed as source for revenues, provides marketplace, church and guildhall, center for shopkeepers, serves as model for other new towns in Europe).

1214

Monastic iron mill at Trent, Northern Italy, uses water-powered bellows... Mongul forces of Jenghiz Khan capture Peking (conquers Persia in 1219 and invades Russia in 1223 before death in 1227).

1215

King John and barons sign Magna Carta to establish rule of law in England (stipulates in commercial provisions all merchants to have safe, secure conduct in leaving, entering country for buying, selling without unjust tolls, protects citizens for payment of interest on debts owed to Jews).

1216

First known artesian well for water is at Artois, French province... Some 700 religious houses with about 13,000 monks, nuns operate in England, around 50 houses in 1066 with nearly 1,000 members (leads to almost 900 houses with some 17,500 members by 1300)... Henry III is King of England (-1272, forms wardrobe department in household to handle financial needs during travels).

1218

Fifth Crusade begins (-1221).

1220

Mongols capture trading center of Samarkand, junction of trade routes between Asia Minor and China... Berthold of Regensburg describes in book different forms of cheating used in various trades and tricks played on country folk by merchants at fairs... Corn mill of St. Ame, Douai, claims damages for up-river waste by dyers.

1221

Castle of Covey, Picardy, is built (-1230, uses 800 stone masons, 800 other craftsmen: carpenters, roofers, iron and lead masons, painters, wood-carvers, etc.)... Due to economic conditions, work is stopped on building Bologna Cathedral, followed by work stoppages on Siena Cathedral in 1265, Santa Maria del Fiore of Florence in 1301-1302... Chinese use bombs with shrapnel, follows use of bombs for just loud explosions.

1222

Scholars from Bologna University start University of Padua... Dyers organize guild in Genoa.

1224

King of France sponsors wine tasting, 70 samples.

1225

Cotton is manufactured in Spain... Town government of Valenciennes, North France, is deposed and rich looted by weavers, fullers to form commune.

1226

Russia, Bulgar sign 6-year treaty (requires Bulgarian merchants to show appropriate sealed documents and to trade only in towns, allows Russian merchants to live and trade in Bulgar).

1227

After traveling four years in China, Toshiro starts making porcelain in Japan... Church condemns "Goliardi," guild of wandering students formed as early as 900s, for parodies of sacred songs... Church council at Narbonne forbids laymen to possess any portion of scriptures... Gregory IX is new Pope (-1241, directs every parish church to have parochial school)... By 1350, 1,200 new markets appear in England... Marseilles resumes gold coinage.

1228

Sixth Crusade begins (-1229)... In Flanders, Douai carders of wool are allowed to petition for wage increases so long cost of living and market conditions warrant raises... Toulouse University is founded.

1229

System of postal relays is started from Mongolia to Eastern Europe (-1237)... German merchants, Grand Duke of Smolensk sign first commercial treaty... Douai devises sliding wage scale to settle disputes between employers, employees.

1230

England imports first shipments of Norwegian fir, needed to replace deforestation... Hansa of 17-23 textile towns appears in Flanders... Bartholomew Anglicus: <u>On the Property of Things</u> (cites world as round)... Berlin appears, consolidates two trading villages... Lubeck, Hamburg sign a treaty to establish free trade between two cities (guarantees safe passage from Baltic to North Sea)... Hall, Swabia, mints first Heller.

1231

Holy Roman Empire coins gold Augustales... Pope Gregory IX recognizes rights of several faculties at University of Paris to administer their own activities.

1232

Islamic work cites mariners' compass, first in Arab world.

1233

First coal is mined at Newcastle, England.

1234

Avignon is first town to require a red lantern over doors of brothels.

1235

Earliest buttons to be seen are illustrated in cathedral near Hamburg... Villard le Honnecourt, architect of Picard: <u>Bauhuttenbuch</u> (provides designs of machines, such as wheel with uneven hammers and water-powered sawmill, and of Gothic buttresses)... England's statue of Merton upholds right of lord of manor to enclose common lands.

1236

With decline of fresh water London uses lead pipes to provide City with water supply (uses first pump in 1581 to replace gravity conduits, steam power in 1712 and sand filtration in 1929)... Castile takes Cordoba from Moslems... Mongol realm of China issues paper money.

1237

St. Gotthard pass opens for traffic between Italy, Europe... Company of Gotland Travelers of Visby gets trading rights from England, later Flanders.

1239

Humiliation monks bring technology of Flemish textile production to Florence.

1240

Public market opens, Bruges, 3 days/week to sell cloth, 2nd market in 1300s... Arabic <u>The Book of the Assembly of Medical Simples</u> gives formula for gunpowder... Benedetto Zaccaria is born in this time in Genoa (-?, besides being admiral, pirate, port governor and diplomat, trades in spices, cutlery, cloth, linen, furs, salt, grain and other wares, speculates in foreign exchange, shares in public loans and real estate, oversees fiefs of Chios, only source of aromatic herb, and Phocaea, mines source for alum in dyeing).

1241

Lubeck, Hamburg form commercial alliance to protect their Baltic trade (evolves as Hanseatic League, first cited as such in 1344)... After defeating German forces in Silesia, Mongols invade Poland and Hungary before withdrawing from Europe with death of leader Ughetai... Mongols may have used gunpowder explosives at Battle of Sajo, Hungary.

1242

City seal of Ebling, Baltic port, shows sternpost rudder, probably devised in 1100s by Northern European shipwrights to replace steering oar (is used by Basque pirates in Mediterranean in 1300s)... The Bear, oldest pub in Oxford by 1980s, opens.

1244

Campagina della Misericordia is founded, Florence, to care for sick.

1245

Strike, earliest recorded in Medieval time, is called by Douai cottage weavers of Flanders against cloth merchants, followed by strike of Ghent weavers, fullers in 1274... Water-driven sawmill operates in Germany... Pope sends Friar John to Karakorum to propose alliance with Mongols against Moslems (-1247, fails).

1247

Arles, Avignon and Marseilles form a league... Sheriff Simon Fitz Mary founds Priory of St. Mary Bethlehem, London (evolves as hospital from 1329 on, is re-established as lunatic asylum, Bedlam, in 1547).

1248

Seventh Crusade begins (-1254)... Ferdinand III of Castile takes Seville from Berbers to acquire port on Atlantic Coast (permits settlement of Genoese colony which operates some 100 major banking houses by 1573)... English merchants create Brotherhood of St. Thomas Becket of Canterbury, granted special trading privileges by Duke of Brabant... Andalusian botanist Ibn al-Baytar dies in Damascus, provided possible means in works for European acquisition of knowledge of Chinese saltpeter... Chaine des Rotisseurs is formed, France, by gourmands (-1950).

1250

Hats are fashionable... Goose quills are used for writing... Annuity loans are used in Flanders to provide credit to borrowers... Genoese reach Atlantic Coast of Morocco, explore Sahara Desert, interior of Africa, Canary Islands by 1300s... Pueblo Indians use sun-clock calendar... Joint partnerships are formed with non-family entrepreneurs in Flanders, common practice of Italian families in Bologna, Rome, Tuscany, etc... Loans are made in Bruges to princes in return for public appointments, tax receipts and/or toll fees... Walter of Henley writes treatise in this time to encourage experimental use of techniques to improve farming (discusses operations of estates with efficient organization, accurate methods of bookkeeping and yearly audits)... University of Oxford prohibits masked students appearing in ribald dramas in churches (starts gradual movement of religious drama out of church to courtyards, marketplaces or various sites)... Florence becomes major center for commerce, industry (-1299, by law allows only nobles in government as guild members in Great Guilds of judges and notaries, cloth importers and refinishers, cloth manufacturers, leading retailers and silk merchants, furriers, moneychangers, physicians and apothecaries or Lesser Guilds of butchers, shoemakers, blacksmiths, secondhand dealers, wine dealers, innkeepers, sellers of salt, oil and cheese dealers, tanners, armorers, ironmakers, girdlemakers, wood workers, bakers)... Douai employs seven inspectors, three at fairs and four at Douai (gives inspectors right of entry to premises at any time to see that rules are enforced, authority to settle disputes)... China starts making guns (-1280).

1251

Oppressed peasantry in France, Flanders organize rebellions against secular, ecclesiastical landlords.

1252

Following lead of other areas in Low Countries as early as 1158, Flanders abolishes serfdom... Florence mints first gold florin, becomes standard gold coin throughout Europe... Alfonse X establishes House of Castile (-1504)... England's Henry III acquires fir wood from Norway for wainscotting and paneling to replace colored plaster walls (leads to tapestries, chiefly from French town of Arras, for wall insulation by 1400s)... New Round Table tournament appears in England as social event, evolves from tournaments brought to land in 1100s from France (during social festivities of several days provides all kinds of sports, such as wrestling, casting the stone, and high and long jumping, in addition to usual jousts)... Bruges grants common rights for trade to Lubeck and Hamburg, exempted from usual brokerage fees in 1309 (evolves as most important commercial city in Northern Europe in 1200s-1300s)... Brothers Nicolo, Maffeo Polo leave Venice for Cathay (-1265/66, return to Venice in 1269, travel to Cathay with Marco in 1271).

1253

Linen is manufactured in England, first record... Franciscan Friar William Ruysbroecke returns to England from China, tells of fire-crackers.

1254

Cologne, Mainz, Speyer, Worms, Strasbourg, Basel form Rhenish League... Eleanor of Castile goes to England as bride for future Edward I (uses carpets, a Spanish custom, to cover floors of her apartment)... English iron center in Sussex, Kent, makes some 30,000 horseshoes, 60,000 nails (uses crude form of large-scale production).

1255

Prague, Stockholm appear as towns... As early evidence of city planning, Venice moves heavy industry, glass works, and Arsenal in preparing for economic growth... Coppersmiths in Dinant protest for better working conditions, followed by weavers of Tournai in 1281, all crafts of Ghent in 1274... Teutonic Knights found Konigsberg on Eastern Baltic Coast as fortress, joins Hanseatic League in 1340... With control of alum production in Seljuk Anatolia, Genoa and Venice raise prices of dyeing agent... Five Wendish towns form alliance, Lubeck becomes dominant member.

1256

French law bans gambling with dice... English government establishes central office of works at Westminster (evolves with large technical and administrative staff).

1257

Henry III, England, issues first gold penny... Queen of England leaves Nottingham Castle to avoid coal fumes from local industry.

1258

House of Commons is formed in England, first session 1265... Paris recognizes a guild of embroiderers.

1259

Lubeck, Rostock, Wismar sign agreement for mutual protection... Explosive weapons appear in China during conflicts of Mongols, forces of Sung Dynasty (-1273).

1260

Chinese document cites reading glasses (-1300)... By 1347 some 80 banking ventures are recorded in Florence... Mamluks defeat Mongols in Egypt to preserve Moslem culture of illuminated manuscripts, metal work, rugs, tapestries of woven silk, and ceramics until rule by Ottoman Turks in 1517... Abingdon Abbey, England, establishes accounting office... First Mastersinger school appears at Mainz... Kublai Khan rules Mongol empire covering Golden Horde of Russia, Khanate of Persia, Khanate of Central Asia, and Great Khanate of North China and Mongolia (-1294, is advised by Chinese Buddhist monk and two counselors on Confucianism for virtues and duties of ruler, drops Chancellery and Department of State, retains State monopolies on salt and iron, opposes revival of civil service examinations for free hand in selecting officials from Mongols and aliens, mostly Moslems, from West and Central Asia, Northern Chinese and Southern Chinese - least trustworthy, adopts three types of paper currency - one based on silk and two on silver, adopts fixed tax, drops extraordinary levies of Sung Dynasty, governs in North China with subsidiary administration at Khara Khorum, uses Prime Ministers on Left and Right over six functional ministries, including Bureau of Imperial Manufacturers, to implement policy, forms Central Secretariat with provincial branches in 1260, formulates policy for civilian matters and supervises six ministries, Privy Council in 1263 for military matters, Censorate to evaluate officials in 1269 and offices of personnel, revenue, rites, war, justice and public works in 1273, develops postal system with 1,400 stations, sees use of banners to advertise wine, pawn shops).

1261

Will of Henry III banishes Jews and Lombards from Brabant for usury on loans in securities... Etienne Boileau: <u>Book of Crafts</u> (cites regulations, rules for 101 Paris guilds with supervision by Provost of Merchants)... Kublai Khan puts Moslems in positions of authority, exempted from regular taxes and granted monopoly for tax collection (waives taxes on Huaimeng, Honan facing economic difficulties, also area around Peking in 1262, forms office for Stimulation of Agriculture).

1262

Venice funds public debt, followed by Florence in 1345... Kublai Khan names Moslem Ahmad Finance Minister, Vice Chancellor of Central Secretariat (establishes state monopolies on tea, liquor, vinegar, gold and silver to generate funds to run government and finance military activities, dies 1282 after controversial charges of embezzlement, favoritism, profiteering)... Kublai Khan forms General Administration for Supervision to loan funds to traders (uses Moslem merchants as intermediaries in overland trade with imports of camels, horses, carpets, medicines, and spices for exports of textiles, ceramics, lacquerware, ginger and cassia)... Adam de la Italle, French composer, writes first operetta.

1264

Merton College is founded at Oxford University (becomes center for scientific investigations of Bacon, others)... Leicester weavers are accused for making provisions against guild merchants.

1265

Group of North German towns accepts code "Law of Lubeck," based on sea laws of Vikings (in 1272 acquires Novgorod, closed 1494, as member to link league with East, South trade routes in Russia, evolves by 1300s-1400s as Hanseatic League with 52-70 towns, holds last assembly of 6 towns in 1669, maintains agents in Bergen to 1775, in London to 1852, and in Augsburg to 1863)... Linen market opens in Mons, France... Pera, across Golden Horn from Constantinople, becomes Genoese trade center... Clement IV is Pope (-1268, is petitioned by Bacon for approval to add experimental sciences to university curriculum)... Sienese merchant in Troyes warns others in Lombardy to watch for fall in value of French currency in Italy as Charles of Anjou prepares for military expedition.

1266

English law requires bakers to put their mark on every loaf of bread sold, also required of goldsmiths and silversmiths... Bacon: Opus Maius (observes world as a sphere)... Louis IX reforms French coinage... Hamburg is chartered (-1267).

1267

Guilds of Goldsmiths and Tailors, joined by Clothworkers and Cordwainers, fight pitched battle in London (results in hanging of ringleaders, is followed by 1340 melee between Fishmongers, Skinners)... Bacon makes first European reference to gunpowder, devises formula in 1285... Cologne Confederation is formed by 77 towns in Southern Germany.

1268

Crown's Foulques du Temple supervises societies of masons (regulates wages), carpenters... Perhaps existing since rule of King John in 1199-1216, Charlton Fair, London, obtains its first charter (-1872)... In essay on vision Roger Bacon, English scientist (develops experimental science, ideas for flying machines and powered carriages, and devices to copy, walk on water and lift weights), describes magnifying power of lenses, precedes development of spectacles in 1300s and telescope in 1604 (dies 1292, perhaps from exposure after testing methods to freeze food).

1269

First toll roads appear in England... Peter the Pilgrim: Epistola de Magnete (pens first original scientific study in Europe, devises pivotal floating compass)... Petrus Peregrinus de Maricourt, France, devises first complete compass... Magnetic clock is proposed for measuring time, abandoned as unworkable.

1270

Eighth Crusade begins (-1271)... Etienne Boileau: Book of Trades (describes open markets of period)... France mints gold coins, regular coinage in 1303... Marcus Graecus: Book of Fires for Burning Enemies (provides recipe for gunpowder)... Peter of St. Omer: Liber de colorbius faciendis (gives formulas for pigments)... Mariners' chart is used during Crusade... Alfonso the Wise orders all sailors to carry magnetic needle... In this time Robert of England states theory for pendulum clock, followed by Galileo's design in 1630s and construction by Huygens in 1656.

1271

Nicolo Polo, brother Maffeo and son Marco undertake journey to Orient (-1295)... Kublai Khan forms Institute of Moslem Astronomy... Henry III decrees all woolen workers of Flanders free to come to England (grants them freedom from taxation for five years).

1272

Marco Polo visits Baku, sees burning of petroleum gas at fire-temple... Kublai Khan sponsors hospitals, also starts charitable relief program for aged scholars, orphans and sick... Edward I is King of England (-1307, levies first custom duties on wools and leather, restricts fairs, usually licensed with monopoly for area within a day's travel, because of damage caused to church grounds and property, establishes courts by law merchants at fairs - abolished 1971, sees use of pipes for waste disposal)... Fishmongers' Company of London, cited as guild in 1154, gets its first charter, City's 4th oldest... London ordinance cites Cordwainers' Company, chartered 1439... Process for reeling fine silk from cocoons is mechanized at Bologna.

1273

Kublai Khan names Nepalese craftsman to head Directorate-General for Management of Artisans with 30 branches in country... Thomas Aquinas: <u>Summa Theologica</u> (attacks advertising for not being factual, maintains merchant's activities to be subordinate to commonwealth, recognizes certain monopolies as acceptable - those to support and help unfortunate, and views credit as necessary and investors as legitimate in sharing the gain for taking the risks)... Sons of Arrigo Sandonis, Bonaccorso Bianchi form limited liability partnership in Lucca, Italy... During hostilities with Flanders, England puts royal embargo on wool exports (controls trade with export licenses).

1274

Bergen enacts maritime laws... Mongols make first attempt to invade Japan, use gunpowder explosives (fail in second invasion when destroyed by Kamikaze typhoon in 1281)... English monastery of St. Albans confiscates cloth of those tenants not using its fulling mill (forces obedience despite resistance, defense funds)... In this time (-1291) Franciscan Fidenzo of Padua prepares complete plan for reconquest of Holy Land for Pope Nicholas IV... England, France sign commercial treaty... Paris Provost of Merchants forbids cottage spinsters to pawn, sell or exchange silk given them for work by mercers.

1275

Leicester fullers are accused of holding illegal meeting without guild merchants... Oldest extant nautical map is made in Pisa in this time.... Richard of Haldingham prepares Hereford map (views earth as circular disk with Jerusalem at center, shows mythical creatures, strange races of Europe, Asia, and Africa, and well-traveled routes)... Edward I levies tariffs on imports, exports as first duties by England... Flanders grants special moneylending license for specific locality, grants 15-20 by 1300s... Statute of Westminster I grants duty on wool to king.

1276

Alfonse the Wise of Castile and Leon orders new addition of star tables to review works of Ptolemy, Arabs (publishes <u>Alphonsine Tables</u>, standard astronomical reference for some three centuries)... Water-powered paper mill, uses trip hammers to beat rags to pulp, is operated at Fabriano, Italy, to undercut price of Moslem paper (provides first clear evidence of process in Europe, appears in France in 1300s, in Germany by 1390).

1277

Genoese galley visits France, Flanders, England... Marco Polo is appointed agent to Imperial Council in China.

1279

England mints first half-penny, abandoned as legal tender in 1984 as too costly to mint for its value... Edward I's Household Ordinance establishes royal organization for governance, first known description in 1136 (covers political, domestic, military and administrative activities, creates Chancellor with chancery clerks and treasurer with chamberlains for handling money and valuables)... Statute of Mortmain forbids grants of land to corporations.

1280

Monks devise verge and foliot system as clock timing mechanism to determine when to pray (-1290)... Textile workers in Flanders rebel against cloth merchants... Archbishop charters London's Surrey Street Market (-1289)... Spinning wheel, Chinese invention, is demonstrated in Speyer, Germany (is first cord drive device in Europe)... Glass mirror is invented... German merchants from Cologne in London form Hansa, English word for right of merchants to form trading association (evolves as Hanse of the Steelyard for nearly all German traders in City, other yards at York, Bristol, Yarmouth, Lynn, Boston, and Sturbridge Fair, to trade raw materials, timber pitch, tar, turpentine, iron, and copper, livestock, salt fish, leather, hides, wool and some textiles, grain, beer and drugs, gets full title in 1474, is revoked 1551 by Edward VI after pressure by English guilds jealous of their privileges, is closed by Queen Elizabeth in 1598, guildhall destroyed by 1666 Great Fire).

1281

Textile workers in Rouen rebel against monopolistic merchant drapers... Pawnshop, operated by Lombards, in Bruges is licensed by count... Venetians are forbidden to work in woolen industries of Padua, Treviso.

1282

Fullers develop detailed schedule of rates, Brussels... Merchants, cloth makers and other guilds acquire control of Florence's government to rule City with six guild foremen (-1301)... Brussels declares 1/3 price of fulling cloth to master, 2/3 to journeymen... Lubeck, Riga, and Visby form alliance to safeguard Baltic trade... According to legend, Mafia appears in Sicily with revolt against French rulers (evolves with uprising against persecutors when drunken French soldier attacks, kills young girl on her wedding day)... Edward I conquers Wales (-1284, forms union with England in 1536)... Catalan Company of mercenaries with crossbows defeats French army, mostly knights, in Sicily.

1283

Rudolph von Hapsburg grants privilege of brewing beer to Furstenberg family, extant to 1900s... Venice orders its merchants to form cartels to buy cotton, pepper in Alexandria.

1284

Venice issues first sequins, ducats as money... Crude blunderbuss is used at Forli, Italy.

1285

Philip IV reigns in France (-1314, taxes and regulates fairs into penury)... Parliament passes law to authorize auditors to imprison any estate officers defrauding their lords... Statute of Winchester requires all landowners in England to maintain highways through their manors, allowed to charge strangers toll for their use... England's Statute of Merchants expedites payment of debts (sentences debtors to prison and forfeiture of property) and encourages trade of foreign merchants in England, repealed 1863... James II rules Aragon (-1291, employs alchemist Arnold of Villanova, first European to prepare alcohol, derived from Arabic word for liquefaction and solidification of kohl, a cosmetic powder, as personal physician).

1286

Bartholomew, Orologist of St. Paul's, notes use of some clockwork in cathedrals.

1287

To cope with catastrophic inflation Kublai Khan replaces paper money with new currency.

1288

Cochio, 4-wheeled coach with 2-horse team, appears in Italy... Stock certificate, first known, in Sweden's Stora Kopparberg is issued to Bishop Petrus of Vasteras (after 100-200 years of individual miners digging ore at Falun, is formed by master miners as world's oldest industrial corporation in 1200s, evolves as Europe's largest supplier of copper, diversifies into electrical power, wood pulp, steel, chemicals, agricultural produce by 1980s)... First known cannon appears in China, first use cited 1332.

1289

Pope sends friar to Peking to establish Archbishopric (-1328)... City of Bologna offers to pay salaries of university professors to replace salaries paid by student guild... Block printing is used at Ravenna... Sandra di Popozo: Traite di conduite de la famille (describes use of spectacles by elderly).

1290

Salvino d'Amarto makes spectacles... Lisbon University is founded... Thugee, secret guild of assassins and robbers in India, is first cited, discovered and suppressed by Bengal army of British Raj in 1830s-1840s... King Edward expels Jews from England, followed by Cologne in 1425, Augsburg in 1439, Spain and Sicily in 1492, Nuremberg in 1498, Ulm in 1499, Naples in 1540, Genoa and Venice in 1550.

1291

Cantons in Alpine valleys form league for mutual protection against feudal lords, starts evolution of Switzerland... Vivaldi brothers undertake Genoese expedition to India via Atlantic, disappear... After fall of Acre to Christians, sugar cane cultivation is started on Cyprus, originally from Bengal Coast and exported to China in 700s A.D., Egypt in 900s, Brazil in 1520.

1293

Norwich fullers are accused of having an illegal guild... Florence makes enrollment in one commercial, industrial or professional guild a requirement for holding public office... Hansa towns recognize Lubeck as capitol of Hanseatic League (-1295).

1294

More than 36,000 of almost 50,000 inhabitants of Bologna are listed as members of a guild or relatives of members... French law regulates a citizen's expenditure on wardrobe in accordance with fortune and class... Peace of Tonsberg gives German Hanse economic control of Norway... In need of funds for war, Edward I creates staple of wool merchants for trade with Dordrecht (shifts from one town to another on continent in 1316-1326, after 1350 evolves as monopoly of English Company of the Staple by 1361, is established in Calais in 1399).

1295

Thirty-nine cities in Castile form brotherhood... England's Edward I borrows 2.5 million gold lire from Frescobaldi family of Florence, charged interest rate of 260%... Marco Polo regales Doge of Venice with tales of China, describes customs of salt coins with seal of Great Khan, pasta and sherbet... Philip the Fair dissolves Paris workers' organization in belief they are plotting a revolution.

1296

Pope Boniface forbids clergy to pay taxes to any lay ruler... England's Edward I establishes wool staple of English merchants in Antwerp, grants them monopoly for trade with England (are granted privileges from Duke of Brabant to operate their companies, are granted right in 1305 to elect their own governing officials)... Genoa forms tribunal to hear claims of foreign merchants.

1297

England, Flanders become allies (results in France arresting all Flemish merchants, confiscating goods and credits, and seizing their halls)... After winning concessions, weavers of Speyer accept use of spinning wheel... Coal mining appears in Charleroi Basin... Venice closes rolls of merchant 'nobility'... Parliament is granted the right to approve taxation.

1298

Lubeck merchants obtain right from Prince of Pomerania to operate a trade agency... Last major source of silver in Europe is found in Bohemia... Buonsignori firm, Europe's largest credit institution as Magna Tavola, is ruined by discord among partners (is replaced by Florentine banks of Bardi, Peruzzi and Acciaiuola)... Geoffrey de Norton, London's senior law officer, is its first known Recorder... Marco Polo: Book of Various Experiences (is written by Rusticciano de Pisa after chance meeting with Polo in Genoese jail).

1299

England passes act to repress bad coinage... Venice develops "Great Galley" as new merchant vessel, leased in 1350s by government to merchants... Frescobaldi, Florentine financiers and merchants, lease Devon Mines of the Crown (-1300)... Florence bans use of Arabic numerals.

1300-1399

Municipal establishments for refining, assaying of silver appear in Bruges, other cities in Flanders... Windmills are used in Europe to mill grain... "Jongleurs," professional musical entertainers, appear in France... Apothecaries appear in Germany... Trade fairs are held at Bruges, Antwerp, Lyons, Geneva... Eyeglasses are common sight in Europe... Wholesalers appear in Germany as distinct business activity... Secular education is started, Florence, for children (after primary schooling provides facilities for merchant apprentices to study arithmetic, record-keeping)... England recruits journeymen weavers of Flanders with promises of good beer, good food, good bed, and good bedfellow... Ownership of Toulouse textile mills is divided into shares, traded like real estate... In India governmental agricultural department is formed as response to widespread famine and banking networks are established in urban centers, dominated by Hindu sub-caste of Banyans... Gautier de Metz: Image du Monde (notes world as round as an apple)... Some 4,000 are recorded living in London, some four times more than any other English town... Taureg founds Timbuktu in North Africa, becomes culture center for Mali empire with gold trade...

Paradis des Femmes, bazaar of many shops, opens in Paris... Pisan Chart is prepared by cosmographers with data from sailors on incoming ships, oldest map of sailing directions for Mediterranean... Cog, single-masted and square-rigged vessel, becomes major merchant ship in Mediterranean (in mid-1400s is transformed into the carrack, a full-rigged, 3-masted ship for more maneuverability into winds)... Compass is used for accurate sailing in Mediterranean and Bay of Biscay, followed by use of magnetic needle and major compass points by 1380... Whirlicote, 4-wheeled wagon pulled by 5 horses in tandem, is used in England by women of rank... Deposits of alum, necessary ingredient to dye textiles, are discovered in Syria... Marriage fair for singles appears in Europe (still extant)... Italian dairy farmers in countryside of Parma develop Parmigiano - Reggiano cheese (leads to some 1,000 cheese-making establishments, controlled by consortium of producers, churning out some 3 million cheeses per year in 1980s)... Homowa yearly harvest festival evolves in Ghana (still extant).

1300

Giovanni Villani, Florentine banker: Chronicles... England's Privy Council is established... Venice imports art of clear glassmaking from Syria for island of Murano in this time.

1301

London bans use of coal as smoke is poisoning the air... Guilds appear in Barcelona, considered last European area to have guilds.

1302

Workers revolt for better working conditions in Ypres, Douai, Ghent, and Lille... Flemish artisans, mostly pikemen, defeat patrician forces of France, mostly knights, at Battle of Courtrai... Venice, Egypt reestablish formal relationships, approved by Pope in 1334... Boniface VIII: Unam Sanctam (asserts papal supremacy in temporal affairs)... France creates Estates-General of clergy, nobility, and wealthy citizens to support Philip IV against the Pope... Led by weavers and fullers, workers in Brussels, Louvain and Antwerp drive patricians from cities, seize power and abolish guilds (are suppressed 1306)... To pay father's wine bill, England's Edward I exempts Gascons from regulations for overseas merchants (grants Gascons in London right to form association, later known as Mystery of Vintners and incorporated by royal charter in 1345 as Vintners' Co.).

1303

Rome University is founded... Bernard of Gordon gives first medical reference to spectacles...

English Crown hires four German miners to search for minerals in Wales, fail... England places first export duty on cloth, first tax on domestic merchants in 1347... Artisans of Liege, Brabant are admitted to magistracy... Edward I, England, grants privileges (provides freedom of entry, stipulates disputes with local merchants be settled by law merchants, jury) to foreign merchants with Carta Mercatoria.

1304

Genoese forces seize Chios as base for Black Sea trade, re-taken by Turks in 1556... Dauphin orders all sawmills in or near forests of Premol Mountains be removed to stop deforestation... Holzschuher Co., Nuremberg, sells 2/3 of business with 445 clients to nobility, clergy.... Ypres finishes building its Drapers' Hall.

1305

German business book, 3rd oldest, is written... House of Taxis operates messenger service with couriers in Europe for princes, generals, merchants, and moneylenders (-early 1800s, employs some 20,000 men in 1628)... England's Edward I standardizes measurements for yard, acre.

1306

Baltic Sea freezes over during "Little Ice Age"... France expels Jews... Giotto completes Frescoes for Areana Chapel in Padua, signals Renaissance era to mid-1600s.

1307

Church condemns alchemy as diabolical act... Because of air pollution Royal Proclamation bans use of sea coal in Southwark, Wapping, and East Smithfield... York forbids members of girdlers guild to work by night or to farm out surplus work and limits number of apprentices serving master craftsmen.

1308

Mercanzia, common court of City's guilds, is founded in Florence... Bruges records 52 guilds.

1309

Pope Clement V moves Papacy to Avignon (-1378)... Political exiles from Lucca start Venice's silk industry.

1310

Insurance company is chartered in Bruges, follows insurance on goods by banking house in 1200s.

1311

Catalan merchants capture Athens, flourishes with trade of goods through Mediterranean... Fraternity of Cooks forms in London, chartered as Livery Co. in 1482... Pietrus Vesconte signs earliest dated marine chart... Hugh Matfrey, London fishmonger, is convicted of forestalling or circumventing the market, England's common law with sanctions against engrossing or monopolizing and regrating or buying goods for resale at higher price in same market.

1312

Genoese re-discover Canary Islands, find Madeira Islands in 1330 and Azores in 1351... France incorporates Lyons... Khan Usbek is head of Golden Horde (-1340, moves capitol to Sarai-Berke, near present-day Volgograd, becomes trade center for Central Asia, Far and Near East)... Mansa Musa rules Mali on Africa's Atlantic coast (-1337, encourages Islamic cultural and commercial practices, obtains virtual monopoly on gold trade, establishes Timbuktu as terminus for one of main trans-Saharan trade routes, levies toll on all commodities passing through city).

1313

Water mill is used at Douai, France, to make edged tools... Raschid al-Din writes book on Chinese medicine, mentions first use of engraved wood blocks for printing... German friar Berthold Schwartz claims to have invented gunpowder.

1314

Ghent bans sale of any cloth within radius of three miles from City... England bans football for being too violent, followed by some 30 or more bans by monarchs, local magistrates to 1617... Gunpowder weapons may have been used in this time in Flanders, used at Metz in 1324, Florence in 1326, Scotland in 1327, 1331 siege of Friuli, perhaps at Algeciras in 1342 and Crecy in 1346 (becomes major weapon with ironshot for stone in 1494 Italian campaign of Charles VIII).

1315

Italian immigrants start silk industry of Lyons... Swiss pikemen defeat Austrian cavalry at Mortgarten, leads to formation of Swiss Confederation... King Louis X liberates all serfs in France... Due to incessant rains and crop failures, famine occurs throughout Europe (-1316)... Verge and pallment escapement, necessary for mechanical clock, is invented in Europe (-1319)... Mongol government of China gives first doctoral examinations and reinstates examinations, based on Confucian texts, for civil service positions (sets quotas for Mongols, non-Chinese officials)... English ordinances makes barons administrators of royal revenues, repealed 1322.

1317

Venetian fleet of galleys, world's first known convoy, makes first of annual trade trips to Northern Europe, by 1400s establishes factories in Bruges, London... Pope John XXII bans practice of alchemy.

1318

Edward II makes land grant on London's Lombard Street to Florentine colony, composed of goldsmiths, silversmiths, moneylenders, and pawn brokers, for establishing banking services to the City (use sign for trade of three golden purses or balls)... Laws of Verona show forward market for stocks... Bardi, Florence, insures risks on overland assignments of cloth.

1320

Major gold deposits are found in Hungary.

1321

Missionary Oderic of Pordenone visits India, China... Roger de Stoke starts building a tower clock with astronomical dial for England's Norwich Cathedral, followed by another mechanical clock with pulleys, weights, and gears of Richard of Wallingford at St. Albans in 1330s-1360 (takes some 400 years to make clocks accurate timepieces).

1322

London's Ordinance recognizes guild of Armourers, granted first charter as Livery Co. in 1453 (is absorbed by Blacksmiths in 1515 and by workers in brass, copper in 1708).

1323

First-known furnace in Europe to make iron with water-driven bellows is operated, first real blast-furnace in 1380... 13 floating mills are operated under Grand Pont of Paris... Abbot of St. Pierre authorizes Ghent fullers "to install a bell in the work house," followed by royal grant for bell tower to Amiens in 1335 for signaling hours of work... Weavers, fullers of Ypres and Bruges join peasants in revolt against rich, suppressed by France in 1328 (banishes 500 weavers, 500 fullers from Ypres).

1325

Flemish manuscript, first known example, shows an illustration of a helicopter... Ibn Battuta of Tangiers travels to Egypt, Mecca, Persia, Arabia, Syria, Black Sea, Central Asia, Northern India, Ceylon, Sumatra, Java, and China (-1349, observes Chinese use of hydraulic machines, paper money, coal, boat construction, manufacture of porcelain)... Aztecs start building Great Temple at Tenochtitlan (-1390, divide City's population of some 200,000 by quadrants to symbolize world's corners, use merchants, artisans, public markets, fairs, and contracts)... Flanders mints gold coins, followed by Brabant in 1330, Liege in 1350, Holland in 1388... Venice builds Central Basin of its Arsenal... Small cannon, ribaud, is reported in France.

1326

Ottoman Turks capture Byzantium's Bursa in Anatolia (as capitol becomes commercial center for east-west, north-south trade routes, uses Greeks in administrative positions).

1327

In this time 43 branches of Italian banking houses operate in Avignon to collect revenues for Church from sales of offices, indulgences... London charters Skinners' Co... London charters Merchant Taylor's Co., evolved from medieval times as maker of tents and tunics... London charters Goldsmiths' Co., cited as guild in 1180... Edward III is King of England (-1377, recruits military forces from those obliged by feudal services, those by volunteering and those raised by commission levies - commissioners to equip, pay and deliver men to place of assembly, borrows from Peruzzi in 1336 to finance war, Bardi in 1337-40, uses taxes, mostly wool customs, as collateral, defaults on loans in 1343).

1328

Venice shifts from silver standard to one of gold... Rotterdam is chartered as city (acquires access to ocean shipping with New Waterway in 1866-1890)... Ivan I, Grand Duke of Russia, makes Moscow his capitol... Sawmill is invented... Stocks in state loans are traded in Florence during this period, used also for such purposes by Venice and Genoa and at Leipzig fairs in 1400s for trading ownership in German mines... Insurance contract for shipping is signed in Marseilles.

1329

Korea's Department of Books uses foundry to print books with metal type instead of wood.

1330

Gottingen, Germany, establishes street-cleaning regulations... Musicians' Guild forms in Paris (-1773).

1331

Wine merchants of Bordeaux, Libourne and La Rochelle unite to dictate terms to Count of Flanders... Ibn Battuta visits Kilwa, inland trading city near Africa's East Coast with monopoly of interior gold trade from Zimbabwe.

1332

Ibn-Khaidun, last of great Moslem philosophers, is born (-1404)... Bubonic Plague begins in India... Company of Mastersingers, German musical and poetical guild (requires candidates for rank of master be judged in public contests), forms at Toulouse.

1333

Ordinances of London recognize Carpenters' Co., granted first charter in 1477.

1334

Some English merchants get royal licenses to export grain to Bordeaux.

1335

Italian Guido da Viegerano, personal physician to Queen of France, devises crankshaft, sketches also a submarine, propelled by paddle-wheels turned by manually-operated crankshaft, and possible automobile, to move siege towers from the inside (is used by royal engineers to operate theatrical machinery for court pageants)... Church of St. Gothard, Milan, installs first clock recorded striking equal hours, followed by clock installations at Genoa in 1353, Florence in 1354, Bologna in 1356, Ferrara in 1362, Paris in 1370.

1336

Avignon branch of Florentine Acciali House gets order from Pope to ship grain to starving Armenians (sends orders to branches in Naples, Bari to ship over 7,000 tons by end of month)... Peruzzi financial-trading house operates 15 branches from Cyprus to London with six partners to share in profits, one share reserved for Lord God representing poor, and losses (manages business with nine salaried factors and nine clerks)... Mints of Flanders, Brabant, Cambrai, and Guelders issue gold coins... After Count of Flanders bans commerce with England, Edward III prohibits exports of wool to Flanders (moves staple from Bruges to Antwerp, England 1353 and Calais 1362)... Paris University decrees no student can graduate without knowing some mathematics... Japan's Ashikaga shogun period starts (-1568, encourages foreign trade, industries, trade guilds - usually with patronage of religious institution, controls ash trade to dyers' guild by agent - later by private wholesalers).

1337

Korea prints book with moveable type... William Merlee, Oxford University, tries to make first scientific weather forecasts... English weavers of Lincoln are given "liberty" to prohibit any weaver not of their guild from working within 12 leagues of City... England's Edward III cancels all debts of makers of yew bows, arrows (bans all sports, except archery, with death sentence for violators)... England, France begin Hundred Years War (-1453, severs economic links: England needs salt from Brittany and Bordeaux wine while France needs wool from England for weavers in Flanders).

1338

England signs commercial treaty with Ghent weavers... <u>Mary of Tudor</u> carries cannon, seen on most English vessels by 1373.

1339

Four London carpenters are charged for intimidating "foreign" carpenters willing to work for less money... Frankfort mints gold coins.

1340

In this time French forces, commanded by constable and two marshals with decisions made jointly, are reviewed monthly to determine if the appropriate quantity, quality of troops are mustered for their fixed-rate wages... England's Edward III agrees that new taxation requires Parliamentary consent... Illuminated manuscript of Flanders illustrates medieval entertainers... Philippe VI of France establishes salt monopoly... Francisco Pegolotti, agent for Florentine Banking family: <u>Merchants' Handbook</u>, used by traders as travel guide.

1341

Water power is used in Bologna to make silk thread... Acciaiuola banking family operates with 43 factors at branches in other countries (closes with Black Death in 1348).

1342

Japanese Zen monks sponsor trading expedition to China, return with weapons, fans, screens, lacquerware, books... England's Edward III starts first campaign on French soil, financed by Bardi, Peruzzi in return for monopolistic licenses on wool (are forced to declare bankruptcy in 1345 when king defaults on loans)... Cross-staff, used by ancient Greeks and Arabs, is used in Europe to measure latitude (is developed as backstaff by England's John Davis in 1595).

1343

Nao or carrack, fairly large and wide-bodied cargo vessel, is first cited in Spanish royal chronicle... Magnus of Norway gives privileges to German merchants at Bergen... Florence's constitution is changed to favor lesser guilds.

1344

Dover Castle clock is built, England, with balance wheel... Astronomical clock, designed by Jacopo de Dondi with first dial, is installed on tower of Padua's Palazzo Capitano... Edward III mints first English gold coins, last European country to do so.

1345

Ghent fullers break manufacturing monopoly of Jacques van Artevelde with master weavers in Flanders... Florence rebuilds Ponte Vecchio, bridge space for shops and viewing... Florence consolidates all of City's outstanding debts into Monte (pays 5% to bondholders, allows holders to buy, sell shares)... Clifford's Inn opens, London (is Inn of Chancery for lawyers in 1618)... Florentine wool carder Cinto Brandini is arrested and hanged, despite protest strike of woolcombers and carders, for holding public meeting to organize workers... English merchants, led by William de la Pole, form consortium to help finance, wool customs as security, siege of Calais, monopoly collapses by 1349... Master of the Works, York, issues report on working practices (reveals absenteeism, stolen materials, quarreling workers, refusals to work, unfit workers, building defects, rusting machinery)... London poulterers, enraged by competition of out-of-town henwives selling poultry on streets, insist City pass ordinance to require all sales at Leadenhall market.

1346

Association, possibly joint stock company, is formed by shareholders in Genoa to colonize Chios... Bristol, England, bans local weavers in fulling their cloth outside City.

1347

When refused port privileges by Sicily, Genoese galley from Caffa, a Black Sea colony, is permitted to dock at Marseilles (starts bubonic plague throughout Europe, reaches Iceland by 1402, kills some 20 million by 1350, followed by other plagues: Spain 1647-1654, England 1666, Russia 1709 and 1720, Marseilles 1720, Italy 1743, India 1899)... Hanseatic merchants organize at Bruges... First evidence of gun, small cannon to fire arrows, in Europe is cited.

1348

Blast furnace with water-powered bellows is operated in Liege, first in Europe... Nuremberg patricians permit guilds to exist, banned during all other years... 1/3 of English population is killed by Black Death... Jews are persecuted in Germany in wake of Black Death, migrate to Poland... Giovanni de Dondi builds astrarium with dials for movements of planets, 24-hour clock, fixed feasts of Church, moveable feasts and nodes... Medical faculty, University of Paris, reports to Philip VI that the plague is a result of certain planets being in triple conjunction with each other.

1349

England's Royal Ordinance of Labourers requires all able-bodied men to work at previous wages (provides no relief to able-bodied beggars, sets price limits on goods).

1350

Woolen workshops, coordinated by merchant entrepreneurs, are seen in Flanders countryside, followed by dispersed metal-working near Cologne in 1400s, in Lyons in 1500s... Songhai trading empire gradually absorbs Mali territory in Africa in this time... Ayutthaya is founded as city-state in Siam on trade route between India, China... London Ordinance recognizes Worshipful Company of Musicians, incorporated 1500... In this time many men wear tight tunics instead of long robes, starts fashion cycle.

1351

French ordinances set hours for journeymen, fix wages and abolish guild regulations limiting apprentices, foreign workers - unsuccessful so laws in 1354, 1356... England's Statute of Labourers sets maximum wages (bans all almsgiving except for impotent poor, requires imprisonment for anyone refusing to work for wages prevailing before plague)... Water-powered wire puller may have been operated in Augsburg, 1489 watercolor of Durer is first specific evidence... Royal Ordinance raises military pay in France to make adjustments for inflation from Black Death, negates right of men to quit service... Parliament grants wool subsidies for three years in abolishing all wool monopolies.

1352

Strasbourg Cathedral is cited, first sure evidence, in having a striking time mechanism with automata operating movements of planets, figures.

1353

England taxes all cloth produced for sale.

1354

In Statute of the Staple, 15 English communities, such as Bristol, London, Newcastle, and Norwich, are designated as staple towns with monopolies for certain exports... Ottoman Turks take Gallipoli on Dardanelles, Constantinople in 1453.

1355

In this time nobles in Siena, governed by bankers and merchant-industrialists, are excluded from public affairs... France's Royal Ordinance sets maximum prices for goods and wages for workers.

1356

French forces of King John II are defeated at Poitiers by English army of Black Prince deploying dismounted knights without lances (leads to growth of Free Companies of mercenaries pillaging in France)... London adopts first regulations for masons, laws on hours and wages by 1500s (grants Arms in 1472, Livery in 1481 and charter in 1677)... Charles IV states in Golden Bull that regalian rights for mines goes with sovereign authority.

1357

Jacquerie revolt in Northern France to protest rents and services required by local lord, followed by uprisings of French peasants in 1358 and Ghent weavers in 1379... Francisco di Marco, Florence merchant (uses simple cost accounting), is born (-1412).

1358

London's first major sanitary act is passed to clean the streets... Hanseatic League puts embargo on Flanders (-1360, again 1388).

1359

Guilds revolt in Bruges to demand participation in government... Edward III grants self-government to English merchants in Holland.

1360

France issues first francs... By law Catalonia money-changer, unable to pay creditors, is beheaded in front of his bank... England establishes police-judges to administer price and labor regulations... After uprising Brussels bans hundred weavers and fullers... After boycott Bruges joins Hanseatic League.

1361

Denmark goes to war with Hanseatic League (sacks Visby center and defeats German fleet to curtail its monopolistic privileges, loses 2nd war in 1368- 70).

1362

In this time William Langland: <u>Piers Plowman</u> (features criers of wares in street scene in poem)... English staple goes to Calais, evolves as corporate Company of the Merchants of the Staple of Calais, as one of many companies of merchant adventurers (moves to Middleberg in 1558 and then to Bruges, is main conduit for exports to Continent by 1617 with ban on wool exports)... Florence starts credit fund to provide interest-free loans of public money to condottieri in financial straits (requires two constables to stand surety for knight borrowing funds).

1363

Florentine Francesco Datini starts business in armaments, banking, international commerce and cloth manufacturing and dyeing (-1410, evolves with branches in Avignon, Genoa, Barcelona, Valencia, Majorca, Pisa and agencies in Northern Europe, changes from single-entry to double-entry bookkeeping in account books)... Nuremberg lists 50 groups of handicraftsmen, 1,217 masters in industry... By English law merchant is entitled to same dress as worn by knight with 1/2 the wealth.

1364

First reference about arquebus firearm is recorded in Perugia, Italy... Clock with seven faces, shows movements of sun, moon and five planets, is installed in Padua... Drapers' Company, existed as association in 1100s, is chartered as London Livery Company... English adventurer John Hawkwood, son of tanner, is Captain-General of White Co. of mercenaries in service of Pisa (supervises administrative staff of treasurer, lawyers, diplomats, accountants, and paymaster, competes in marketplace with "Great Company" of freebooters governed by informally elected leader, council).

1365

England issues proclamation against time wasted in dicing, football, dancing, and playing games (ordains Sundays for praying, practicing archery)... Vienna University is founded.

1367

Towns meet in Cologne to form a confederation, merchants form 'Hanse' trading association by 1370.

1368

Freedom is granted to 22 towns, villages in French barony of Courcy in return for specific grants, revenues... Ming Dynasty begins in China (-1644, by 1398, suspecting conspiracy, abolishes chancellor office and secretariat coordinating lesser ministries to rule with Grand Secretariat, coordinates five military commissioners, six ministries, and censorate, and subordinate grand coordinator supervising regional and local governments, reserves silk for Imperial use, establishes nationwide tax system to replace corrupt tax collectors of Mongols, abolishes slavery, confiscates large estates, rents land to landless, levies high taxes on wealthy, restores civil service examinations, forms secret police, restricts contacts with foreigners, and develops elementary schools)... Guild of smiths appears in Augsburg, accepts first clockmaker member in 1441.

1369

Amsterdam joins Hanseatic League... Parish Guild of Holy Trinity forms, London (enrolls 530 men, 274 women as members from various occupations).

1370

Although Chinese had been using porcelain block-printing to put symbols on paper for centuries, Korea does first mechanical printing with interchangeable copper blocks... Steel crossbow is common weapon in this time... Heinrich von Wyck builds well-designed mechanical clock in Paris... By Royal decree all clocks in Paris are synchronized with palace clock... Charles V regulates use of bloodletting by barbers.

1373

Private company forms in Genoa to capture Cyprus in order to establish commercial monopoly for Egyptian trade (-1489 when Island is taken by Venice)... Guillaume Tirel, called Taillevent as chief cook to Charles IV: Le Viander (-1380, describes elaborate cuisine of upper classes with lower classes restricted to vegetables, dairy produce, potages and soups)... England sets tonnage, poundage standards for English, foreign merchants.

1374

France issues ordinance to pay military companies fixed rates for their services, fails as Free Companies continue their looting... Black Death returns to England (-1375).

1375

Cartographer Abraham Cresques of Palma: Catalan Atlas (shows "unknown continent")... Merchant-citizens of commercial cities of Ghent, Bruges fight Count of Flanders for independence (-1379).

1376

Hamburg cites some 1,000 brewmasters... Earliest known property deed in England is written, first will in 1387.

1377

Castle walls of Ardres are destroyed by cannon during siege... Edward III takes over House of Converted Jews in London for use by Keeper of the Rolls of the Chancery to keep records... Venice uses first known instance of specific quarantine to stop spread of plague... London permits foreigners, non- residents of City, to sell poultry, cheese and butter in Leadenhall Market... Richard II, England, borrows thousands of pounds from merchants... Playing cards are printed, Germany... Richard II, England, confirms Hanse privileges.

1378

Mass rising of wool carders in Florence is ruthlessly suppressed... Brewery is built near Pilsen, Austria-Hungary (until 1500s allows only Austrian military officers to brew beer)... Pope Gregory XI dies, succeeded by Urban VI in Rome to rule England, Italy and Germany and by Clement VII to oversee France, Scotland, Spain and Sicily from Avignon (-1408)... Nobles wrest control of Florence from merchants, supported by temporary workers who want guild status and unemployed (-1381 when merchants regain power)... In honor of visit by Holy Roman Emperor Charles VI, Paris presents spectacle with elaborate stagecraft on taking of Jerusalem by First Crusade... After inclusive wars during 1257-1355, commercial cities of Venice, Genoa begin War of Chioggia, sees use of handgun as forerunner of musket (-1381, enables Venice take over Genoa's Levantine trade).

1379

Weavers of Ypres, Ghent and Bruges rebel.

1380

Wyclif translates Bible into English... Grosse Ravensburger Gesellschaft, Magna Societas, is formed as Swabian trading company by three family firms to do business throughout Europe (-1530, apparently reorganizes every six years, shows at times membership with 300 individuals from 120 families, operates 21 foreign centers, including Bilbao, Pest, Venice and Bruges)... First rockets in Europe are used in battle between Genoese, Venetians... Cast iron is commonplace in Europe.

1381

England passes first Navigation Act to require goods to be carried in English ships (leads to others in 1485, 1540, 1650 to forbid foreign ships to trade with English colonies, 1651 to require shipment of colonial goods with crew 75% English, 1660 to require certain colonial goods to be shipped direct to England, 1663, 1672, and 1696 to ban shipments on Dutch vessels, are repealed in 1849 and 1854)... In opposition to use of landless labor by landlords due to labor shortages from 1337 war, 1348 Black Death, and King Richard II's poll tax (is resisted also in 1990), Peasant's Rebellion arises in England, led by Wat Tyler in London, to demand equitable rents and taxes, abolition of serfdom (is echoed in France, Holland, Italy)... English workers attack members of Hanseatic League.

1382

France auctions post of tax collector for salt, wine, etc., to highest bidder... Pratese Francisco di Marco starts business in Florence as merchant-banker (joins guild of silk merchants in 1388, shows in records of 1399 early use of double-entry bookkeeping)... Winchester is first public school in England, Eton in 1440... Venice admits first consortium of Jewish usurers (-1387).

1383

Compagnia dell'Arte della lana forms in Prato (operates with 12 workers in small shop, some 1,000 in countryside cottages)... Lowenbrau beer is first brewed in Munich, leader of 2,500 breweries in West Germany in 1980s... Accounts of Runtinger Co., Venice, show exports of goods to Levant (-1407).

1384

Fishmongers' Co. is formed in London... Water-powered blast furnace operates at Liege.

1385

Artisan-influenced governance of Re'formatori ends with expulsion of some 4,000 artisans (cripples growth of Siena textile industry)... First French court ball is held for wedding of Charles VI, Isabella of Bavaria.

1386

Heidelberg University is founded.

1388

Cologne University is founded... England passes first Poor Law (restricts movements of all beggars and laborers, provides relief to those unable to work, prohibits all 12-year-old common field workers to train for any trade, handicraft)... Parliament passes urban sanitary act... London holds first public executions at Tyburn, evolve as public entertainment (-1783)... Sieur de Coucy is made Grand Bouteiller to French Crown (is rewarded with permit to hold two annual fairs of three days each with sales of merchandise exempted from taxes)... By treaty with Hanseatic League English merchants are allowed to trade, settle in lands of Hanse and Prussia.

1389

England's governmental inquiry investigates affairs of all fraternal guilds, basically benevolent, religious and/or social groups, to determine if conspiracies exist to raise wages, prices.

1390

Ottoman sultan demands Byzantine emperor provide special quarter in Constantinople for Turkish merchants and judge to arbitrate affairs with Christian residents (is rejected).

1391

Group of English merchant adventurers gets permission to trade with Prussia, granted governmental privileges at Danzig by Grand Master of the Teutonic Order (is followed in 1408 by other English enterprises with trading rights for Norway, Sweden, Denmark)... Paper mill appears at Nuremberg.

1392

First unified in 668 A.D., Korea is ruled by Confucian Dynasty (-1910 when occupied by Japan to 1945)... England forbids foreigners to sell goods at retail... Malines stops minting silver, Florence in 1393, Louvain in 1394, Egypt in 1397 and Calais in 1439... After working in Rome's bank of Florence's Vieri di Cambio, Giovanni di Bicci de Medici acquires ownership of branch to start family banking dynasty (moves headquarters to Florence in 1397 - Rome a branch, opens branch bank in 1400 in Naples - discontinued 1426, Venice in 1401-26, and Geneva in 1426 as center for international trade fairs - moves to Lyons around 1464 as new center for international trade fairs, starts joint venture in wool manufacturing in 1403 - later others in silk and wool, retires in 1427)... German Hansa, Novgorod sign commercial treaty.

1393

French lawsuit rules it is not proper for a noble to be an innkeeper, allows nobles later to have a license to trade without loss of status... Construction is finished in building a money exchange in Barcelona... After a strike had been called in Burgundy by vineyard workers, temporary labor market appears in town square to hire replacements... China's Bureau of Imperial Supplies produces 720,000 sheets of toilet paper.

1394

London merchants charter Mercers' Co., cited in 1347... Fraternity and Guild of Corpus Christi is founded in London by salters, licensed in 1467 and chartered in 1559.

1395

Buxtehude altarpiece gives first illustration of knitting... Paris merchants open City's first theater to promote attendance at fairs... Jacques Coeur, French merchant (operates 7 merchant vessels under flag of Mother of God, operates number of bazaars, large shops selling variety of goods with bargains advertised by street heralds, with 2 places in Paris, 2 in Tours, 4 in Lyons, 6 in Bruges, 4 in Montpellier and 6 in other areas, employs staff of traveling salesmen) and financier (serves as banker to royalty, Master of the Mint in 1436), is born to a furrier (-1456, is employed by Royal Mint in 1428, gains acquaintance of Agnes Sorel, King's mistress, obtains royal charters for silver, copper, and lead mines, is ennobled 1441, is appointed French envoy to Genoa in 1446 and to Pope Nicholas V in 1447, loans funds in 1450 to France to win war with England over Brittany, acquires estates to live regally, is arrested by pressure of enemies in 1451 for murder of Sorel - charge dropped but banished, property confiscated for forging King's signature, debasing royal coinage)... Saddlers' Co. of London, perhaps chartered 1272, incorporates.

1396

Venice restricts exports of silver, Genoa in 1400 and Bruges in 1401... Paris fixes rates for hiring of common carts by neighborhoods to clean streets, followed by special tax in 1506 to finance public street cleaning... Doll, dressed in latest court fashion, is sent from Paris to English court, used as means to provide fashion information to 1700s when replaced by printed cardboard substitutes with latest in Paris styles... Milan statutes prevent merchants manufacturing fine wool to sell wares over a certain value except on short-term credit... Richard II licenses first London hackney coach, first note of London cab trade.

1398

Richard Whittington, orphan, merchant and moneylender, is Lord Mayor of London.

1399

Jacopo Gasco purchases bill of exchange from merchant-banking House of Bruges (issues order to Barcelona branch of merchant house to pay Domenico Sancio certain sum of money).

1400-1499

Rosaries are made in Lubeck for export to Italy, work by "putting out" system with product standardization... In Italy condottieri are employed as companies of mercenaries... Bank of deposit is founded in Rome... Como, Cremona, Venice are recognized as cloth towns, Lucca and Genoa as silk towns... Fairs in Genoa are meeting places for European merchants to trade and settle accounts, use law merchant to resolve disputes... Two silk merchants, Lucca, form company to contract work with cottage weavers, "putting out" system perhaps started in Ghent, Ypres, Florence or Milan... Great Hanseatic route evolves from Novgorod, Riga to Lubeck, Hamburg, Bruges, Gascony, Spain... Venice is home port for seven yearly convoys trading with Flanders and England, Barbary Coast, Northeast Africa, France, Spain, Italy, and Alexandria, Beirut, and Romania (serves as port city, population of some 150,000, for merchant fleet of some 3,300 vessels with 36,000 sailors, builds and maintains vessels at Arsenal which uses 1,000-2,000 skilled/unskilled workers on assembly line with standardized tasks, interchangeable parts and quality control, examinations for worker selection, evaluations of worker performance and "wine breaks")... Individual dish replaces bread trencher, square of wood with center circular depression, chair replaces bench, and fireplace replaces roof hole... John of Calabria, Italian immigrant to France, devises new loom to weave silk... Horses are used for plowing instead of oxen, France... Monomotaga Kingdom, Zimbabwe, acquires power in Central Africa (evolves as chief collection point for gold going to coast for Portuguese trade)... Dutch devise new techniques for barreling, pickling North Sea herring (operates some 1,000 fishing, factory ships by 1662).

1401

Scotland mints gold coins, followed by Hamburg in 1440, Denmark in 1490 and Poland in 1520... Catalan merchants, Barcelona, open public bank, Tavala de Cambis, to handle deposits, transfers, bills of exchange, and loans to manufacturers to purchase raw materials (opens branch in Valencia in 1407), followed by Banco di Rialto of Venice in 1587, Amsterdam bank in 1609, Bank Giro in Venice in 1619, Bank of England in 1694 to introduce loans, advances... Edward IV charters London's annual Southwark Fair (evolves with market stalls and variety of public amusements, is suppressed in 1763 by City after trouble with pickpockets, prostitutes)... Diet of the Hanse, Lubeck, forbids credit sales, purchases from non-members.

1402

France licenses group of citizens, craftsmen to give Mystery plays... Ethiopian embassy visits Venice... Malacca is founded, by 1500s trade center for spice trade, Chinese silk and porcelain, Borneo camphor, Burma teak, Indian cottons, and European woolens (is taken by Portuguese in 1511 and Dutch in 1641).

1403

Stationers' Co. is formed in England as book-trade guild of scriveners, limners, bookbinders, and stationers (gets charter in 1557 with practical monopoly for printing, publishing)... Korea uses movable type for mass production of government printing (-1484).

1404

Pier Paolo Vergerio: <u>De ingenuis moribus</u> (urges education to prepare children for life as well as to produce scholars)... England's King Henry IV borrows some 1,000 marks from merchants of Genoa (allows them to keep duties on their products imported, exported from London).

1405

Konrad Keyser von Eichstatt, German military engineer: <u>Bellifortis</u> (discusses vehicles, guns, lifting gear, pumps, pontoons, life-belts, and hot-air balloons, suggests idea for repeating gun)... Admiral Cheng Ho commands first Grand Treasure Fleet of Ming Dynasty (leads six more expeditions by 1433 to visit Annam, Borneo, Java, Sumatra, Malaysia, Siam, Ceylon, India, Persian Gulf, and East Coast of Africa to display splendor, gives gifts to countries acknowledging power of China)... After fire destroys nearly 75% of City, Bern grants nearby Fribourg the right for all time to hold a market in Bern for its aid (leads to annual Onion Market Day, some 300 stands in 1988 on 4th Monday, November).

1406

Florence gains access to sea by conquering Pisa... English merchants are chartered for Mediterranean trade.

1407

Genoa bank, Casa di San Giorgio, forms as joint-stock venture with stockholders to fund Commune's debt (issues notes for deposits)... England's Henry IV grants first charter to Merchant Adventurers' with members from various towns (lists grocers, drapers, haberdashers, mercers, skinners, etc., in London fellowship) to trade in Holland, Zeeland, Brabant, Flanders (operates first continental mart at Bruges, moves to Antwerp in 1446, to Calais in 1493, to Antwerp in 1496, and to Hamburg in 1567, after controlling 75% of English foreign trade in 1500s dissolves with canceled charter in 1689).

1408

Genoese ordinance permits agents to sign insurance contracts... In this time English merchants get trading privileges with towns in Norway, Sweden, Denmark... Holland uses windmill to pump inland water to sea.

1409

England, Teutonic Order sign commercial treaty... German refugees from Prague found Leipzig University... First Bourse, name from earlier informal meetings near Hotel des Bourse, opens in Bruges as regular meeting place for bankers and merchants, followed by Antwerp 1460, Lyons 1462, Toulouse 1469, Amsterdam 1530, London 1554, Rouen 1556, Hamburg 1558, Paris 1563, Bordeaux 1564, Cologne 1566, Danzig 1593, Leipzig 1635, Berlin 1716, Vienna 1771, and New York 1772... Johannes Fugger, son of country weaver, dies after becoming linen merchant in Augsburg (leaves estate of 3,000 golden florins to two sons: one to purchase patent of nobility, marry quality, and join rural gentry, other to enter banking business to build House of Fugger as financial empire with seven sons).

1410

Endorsement of bill of exchange is first recorded (follows use of Babylonia, Greek, and Roman traders, is re-discovered by Europe in 1200s)... Soranzo brothers, Venice, use journal entries, ledgers in recording business transactions... Italian architect Brunelleschi may have made a spring-driven clock.

1411

St. Andrews University is founded in Edinburgh... London Guildhall is built (-1426).

1413

Iceland uses dried fish for money... Royal Edict, France, makes it illegal for any lords to collect royalties on mining.

1414

Pope makes Medici of Florence Church's bankers (-1476).

1415

Portugal's Prince Henry the Navigator starts school of navigation and cartography at Sagres... Council of Constance ends Papal schism (-1417)... Portuguese forces capture Ceuta, Muslim center in North Africa for Saharan caravans (pass Cape Bojador 1433, reach Cape Verde in 1445, cross equator in 1471, discover Congo River in 1482, reach southern end of Africa in 1487)... Parliament grants Henry V customs on wool for life.

1416

Dutch fishermen are first to use drift nets... London law requires homemakers to hang light outside their houses during certain hours on dark nights, followed by attempt in 1685 to place oil lamps outside every 10th house and gas lighting in early 1800s... Master mason of Gerona guild, Spain, prepares plan to finish cathedral church... Cutlers' Company of London is chartered, formed in 1200s as craft guild.

1417

Hanse establishes principles that no man should buy grain before it has grown, cloth before it is woven, or herring before they are caught (prohibits advertising by members)... Charles d'Orleans gives aldermen in Chateaudun, France, right to inspect bakeries (-1602, sentences 3rd time offenders of standards to torture)... Camorra, secret society of criminals, forms in Naples... Battle plan is prepared for John the Pearless, Duke of Burgundy, for attacking Paris, uses another for attacking Pontoise in 1441... French edict allows crown to send experts to prospect for ore on private lands.

1418

Andrea Barbarigo, merchant of Venice (uses partnerships and joint-ventures to charter merchant galleys, employs commission agents, uses bookkeeping practices in determining expenses, profits on transactions), is born (-1499)... Portuguese ships visit Madeira Islands in first of almost annual expeditions of southward exploration by Prince Henry (sponsors last voyage in 1455-1457 to explore Senegal River and discover Cape Verde Islands before death in 1460).

1419

Philip II, the Good, rules Burgundy (-1467, during rule prohibits importation of English cloth, subsidizes fishing industry, develops fishing fleet as "infant-industry").

1420

With financial support from Genoa, Portuguese settle Madeira Islands during decade... Ming Navy shows 1,350 combat vessels, includes 400 large floating fortresses and 250 ships for long-range voyages... German Fireworkbook is written in this time to give directions to master gunsmiths...After Jews are expelled from France, Castilians take over some of their banking activities... Bit and brace appear in Flanders (-1424, first evidence of compound crank in Europe)... Lyons holds commercial fairs.

1421

Florence grants first recorded patent for an invention... Peking becomes major capitol of China, (places restrictions later on role of court eunuchs, hold power in supervising secret police and running imperial workshops employing some 27,000 craftsmen, in trade and foreign relations)... Vespaniano da Bisticci, Florentine publisher (develops business with large-scale reproduction of manuscripts), is born (-1498).

1423

Holy Roman Empire grants fair concession to Nuremberg... Guildhall Library, containing mostly theological books chained to shelves, is established in London in this time with money left by Lord Mayor Whittington... One of Castile's first wine ordinances regulates what wine could be brought into capitol.

1424

James I of Scotland bans golf as game takes troops away from archery training, fails... Master Franke paints St. Thomas' Altar for Hamburg merchants trading with England.

1425

Siena forbids women to wear silk clothes, train, or crepe lining which would reveal curves of their bodies.

1426

Marine insurance company operates in Genoa, followed by such specialists in Venice during early 1500s... Denmark levies Sound Toll (-1857).

1427

English bishops go to Iceland, start trade with license from Denmark... Diego de Sevilla of Portugal finds Azores in searching for mythical islands of St. Brendan shown on "Medicean Portolano" of 1351 (-1431)... Florence levies property tax... London appoints Commissioner of Sewers... Cosimo de Medici heads family bank in Florence (opens decentralized branches in Bruges in 1439, Pisa in 1442, London and Avignon in 1446, Milan in 1451-1453 and temporary branch at Basel for Church Council in 1433)... Some 38% of household heads in Florence are employed in textile industry (allows only men in knitting and hosiery guilds, requires 6-year apprenticeship for admission, requires applicant for master knitter to pass inspection on 4 projects made in 13 weeks: small original carpet, beret, wool skirt and hose with Spanish clocks).

1428

Grocers' Company, first cited as Pepperers in 1180 (evolves to deal in spices, drugs and tobacco as wholesale merchants), is chartered by London... Sultan of Egypt takes over pepper monopoly, raises prices (when Venetians refuse to pay for shipments in 1480 jails merchants until they pay)... Philip the Good grants Castilian merchants in Bruges guild status, get right in 1441 to elect their own council.

1430

German manuscript shows first crank and connecting rod in Europe... Libel of English Policie shows importance of commerce and sea power to England... Single-handed plow is used in France during these years... Brussels becomes center for dukes of Burgundy, used as seat in 1477 for Spanish governors... Burgundy clock is made with main spring (although idea usually credited to Peter Henlein in 1502, gives first evidence of device required for portable time pieces)... First European representation shows belt drive used to turn a grindstone.

1431

Masons' guild objects to council of York in having to stage a particular play during pageant of Corpus Christi Day, allowed to perform "Herod" play... China sends 62 ships, 28,000 men, to visit East Coast of Africa.

1432

After palace revolution in China, new government adopts anti-trade policies.

1433

After 10 years of repeated attempts, Diaz expedition finally passes Africa's Cape Bojador on Atlantic Coast (allows Portuguese to continue their explorations southward along the coastline).

1434

Spain cites first caravel vessel, usually under 50 tons with square sails on fore and main masts and lateen sail on mizzen for steering... Although not a prince, Cosimo de Medici, son of wool dealer and international banker, acquires indirect control of Florence's government... When Filippo Brunelleschi refuses to pay dues to guild of building workers, he is arrested and put into prison, released later by cathedral authorities.

1435

Italian trader Nicolo di Conti visits Burma in this time... John Fastolf submits planning advice for conducting Hundred Years War to Henry VI's government.

1436

After developing fleet of some 3,800 ships, Chinese government halts all naval construction of seagoing ships, bans ships over two masts later (starts Great Withdrawal from world scene by new emperor by 1449, bans foreign trade in 1452-57, circumvented by bribery as result of bureaucratic infighting between Confucian mandarins and court eunuchs).

1437

In treaty Danzig grants English merchants rights of entry, trade and residence (gives fiscal exemptions)... Ulrich Ellenbog: "On the Poisonous and Noxious Vapors and Fumes of Metal" (is published in 1524 to pioneer field of industrial medicine, followed in 1500s by Vernardino Ramazzini, Italian physician and professor, with first book on occupational diseases)... Brewers' Company, cited in 1292, is chartered by London.

1438

Holland breaks Hanseatic monopoly in trade-war.

1439

Portugal colonizes Azores.

1440

Laurens Jamszoom Koster, Holland, dies after trying to invent a printing press, followed by Pamifilo Castaldi of Italy and Albrecht Pfister of Bamberg... Platonic Academy opens in Florence... Oba Equare is King of Benin (-1481, leads West African Kingdom to greatest power with trade in ivory, pepper, cloth, metals and slaves, is revived in 1802 with palm products).

1441

Holland, Hanseatic League pledge freedom for all parties in Baltic trade... Voyage to African region of Rio de Outo, south of Cape Bojador, returns to Portugal with gold, slaves... Public dancing hall opens, Cologne (-1447).

1442

Parish Clerks' Company, existing as religious fraternity since 1274, is chartered by London.

1443

John II of Castile, Hansa sign commercial treaty.

1444

Portuguese ships reach Senegal River in Africa... Leather Sellers' Company of London, cited by City for dyeing of leather in 1372, is chartered, joined by Pouchmakers in 1573.

1445

Dinis Zias, Portugal, sights Cape Verde... Fraternity for Mariners forms in Bristol to trade with Irish, Gascony, Iberian, Mediterranean ports.

1446

By Act of Retainer English Co. of the Staple handles customs on wool (for subsidy on wool requires Staple to pay wages of Calais garrison).

1447

Genoa grants 29-year lease on Cyprus to City's Bank of St. George.

1448

Portuguese establish first European trading factory on African coast at Cape Blanco... Andrea Bianco shows location of land, in area of Brazil, on map... Haberdashers' Company, offshoot of Mercers, is chartered by London, cited in Ordinances of 1371... Trailok is King of Ayudhya, Siam (forms government with departments of capital, lands, treasury, palace and military, establishes duties, privileges in ranking all civil servants, and grants land to officials as salary).

1450

Mocha, Southwestern Arabia, evolves in this time as port for coffee exports, appears as drink in Cairo by 1510, Mecca 1511, Istanbul 1517, Venice 1615, Paris 1643, London 1651... Cardinal Nicholas makes statement at Cusa that scientific findings can solve technological problems... Ironworks is started near Liege (uses blast furnaces, charcoal)... Johann Gutenberg prints <u>Constant Mass Book</u> in this time (uses printing press with interchangeable type, devises printing ink)... In this time large hydropower dam is built near Cesena, Italy, followed by other dam projects by Germany in 1714-21, by Russia 1721-23, and Spain 1730-1747... During late 1400s, book with sailing directions for waters from Cadiz to Gulf of Finland is published with data gathered from experiences of Hanse ships... Spring-driven clock appears in portrait of Burgundian noble.

1451

Two galleys land at Valencia, fail to sell cargoes as no money available in City... Flanders, Burgundy start commercial war with Hansa (-1457)... Monopoly for coral fisheries on North African coasts is granted to Genoese joint-stock company... Hanseatic League opens Sound to English.

1452

Rome orders citizens to clean street in front of their houses every Saturday from May to August... Leon Battista Alberti: <u>De re edificatoria</u>, first modern work on architecture... First professional association of midwives forms in Regensburg.

1453

Genoa gives Bank of St. George control over Corsica, acquired by Milan in 1464 and Fregosi in

1478, re-acquired by Bank of St. George in 1485-1583, 1599-1700s)... In this time Gutenberg, Johann Fust print <u>Mazarin Bible</u> at Mainz, evolves as center of bookmaking until sacked in 1462 (is followed by use of printing press in Italy in 1464, Switzerland 1468, France and Venice 1470, Holland and Austria 1473, Poland and Spain 1474, England 1476, Mexico 1539, Russia 1563, North America 1640)... Charles VII of France confiscates three mining enterprises of Bruges merchant Coeur... Soranzo Bank, Venice, fails... Constantinople, last bastion of Byzantine empire, is taken by Ottoman Turks, forces scholars to flee with classical manuscripts to Europe, ends monopoly of Genoese and Venetians as middlemen, means higher prices for spices in Europe, and leads to major glassmaking industry in Turkey with colored strips (capture Belgrade in 1521, fail to take Vienna in 1529 and 1683, grant Greece independence in 1829)... Florence, governed by group of merchants, exporters, importers and wool manufacturers in guild of Arte de Calimala on Evil Street, is granted trading privileges for Golden Horn by Grand Turk... Barcelona passes laws to regulate marine insurance, used by Phoenicians and Greeks c. 1000 B.C. and coolies on Yangtze River... England, France end Hundred Years War with Calais only possession of England left on continent.

1454

France recruits German miners with lavish benefits of food, housing.

1455

Portugal petitions Pope for monopoly rights on trading, conquests along African Coast... Venetian in service of Prince Henry explores Senegal, Gambia Rivers (discovers Cape Verde Islands for Portugal)... Turks take Genoese mines of Focea, used to produce alum for manufacturing textiles.

1456

Thomas Douton employs 11 apprentices, 7 servants in pewter workshop, viewed as "largest" craft business in London... Madeira ships wine to England.

1457

King James II bans golf in Scotland... Fust, Peter Schoeffer print <u>Mainz Psalter</u>, first dated material in Europe (use Gutenberg's press, type when he fails to repay his loan to Fust).

1458

Benedict Kotrulic of Dubrovnik: <u>On Commerce and the Perfect Merchant</u> (praises determination of merchants to stay in business against all odds).

1459

Masons from such cities as Strasbourg, Vienna and Salzburg meet to codify their statues (agree not to reveal their secret of determining elevation from a plan, exposed in 1486 by German architect Mathias Roriczer)... Masons establish craft guild in Regensburg, confirmed by Crown in 1498, 1563... Russian merchant A. Nikitin of Tver travels to India, first European to visit land (-1472, sees no possibility of serious trade).

1460

Portuguese vessels reach Sierra Leone... As artists of Florence no longer view themselves as guild members, Cosimo de Medici grants them permission to form an academy (-1469).

1461

Louis XI rules France (-1483, installs silk loom at Tours)... Philip the Good of Burgundy forbids those able to work to beg... After John de Castro discovers alum, vital for dyeing, in Papal States, Societas Aluminum, first chemical trust, is formed by Church (produces 1,000 tons in 1471, uses 711 miners in 1557)... Louis XI diverts (October 20) French commerce from Genoa to Lyons fairs... Ivan the Great is first Czar of Russia (-1505, ends payment of tributes to Mongols)... Barbers' Company, first cited 1308, gets first charter from London to assist monks in surgery, joined by surgeons in 1540... Scholar Marsilio Ficino, his translation of Greek manuscripts for the de Medici family a stimulus to growth of science in Italy, is head of Platonic Academy.

1463

Monte di Pieta, Orvieto, loans money at low interest rates to poor people... Ironmongers' Company of London, cited as fellowship in 1200s and granted Arms in 1455, is chartered... Venice, Turkey start war (-1479).

1464

Medici Bank opens branch bank in Lyons to serve popular fairs of Louis XI (with death of Cosimo is succeeded by ineffectual administration of banking interests by Piero the Gouty, Lorenzo the Magnificent, and Piero the Unfortunate until 1494 when family's operations, on verge of bankruptcy, are confiscated and brothers expelled from Florence)... Louis XI starts French Royal Mail Service... Antonio Averlino Filarete: Architecture (describes use of pig iron furnace to produce molten iron).

1465

Edward IV coins first Angel-Noble coins... England's Edward IV issues edict to forbid "hustling of stones" and other sports... Louis XI of France is one of first men in Europe to have personal carriage, follows tradition of carriages used by only women in Persia c. 1440 B.C.

1466

Johann Mentel prints first German Bible in Strasbourg... De Medici bank, fiscal agents for Holy See, acquires control of Societas Aluminum in Papal States (following ban of Pope on importation of Turkish alum in all Christian lands becomes 25-year cartel in 1470 with other alum mines in Italy)... Louis XI establishes silk industry at Lyons to reduce France's reliance on imports.

1467

Scotland bans golf... Medici's London bank and Edward IV sign agreement to retire his debt (-1478 when branch is closed being unable to collect on debt with revival of War of Roses)... Onin War is started in Japan between lords in struggle for power (-1477, leads to decentralized feudal system and settlements of Japanese in Philippines, Formosa, Indonesia, Malaysia, Siam, Vietnam)... Merchant Adventurers of Bristol receive royal charter.

1469

Lorenzo de Medici is ruler of Florence... Fernao Gomes leases Guinea trade from Portugal for five years, required to continue annual explorations along coast... Pliny: Historia naturalis, first printed book on science... Spain is united with marriage of Ferdinand of Aragon and Isabella of Castile... Tommaso Portinari, Medici bank manager in Bruges and financial adviser to Dukes of Burgundy, signs new contract of service with Florence house (is required to put up a certain percent of branch's funds, is warned on granting more credit to Duke - bankruptcy with military defeats in

1476, 1477 as mercenaries leave field when Duke's money fails to arrive for pay).

1470

Sienese engineer sketches conical "parachute" as way to free his friend in prison tower, followed c.1480 by crude pyramidal parachute designed by da Vinci... Florentine merchant Benedetto Dei visits Timbuktu (cites City as metropolitan center for trading caravans)... Florence lists 32 separate banking houses.

1471

Louis XI issues edict that royal mining administration will either lease mines or work them if landlords fail to operate them... Black Book of the Household is compiled (-1472) to record expenditures for England's royal staff (specifies appropriate amounts for various ranks of peerage)... Josefa Barbaro, Venice, visits Persia... London charters Dyers' Company, first cited 1188... Portuguese discover Niger River... John Fortescue: The Governance of England.

1472

Dietrich Pining, German explorer in service of Denmark, claims to have discovered Newfoundland... Teutonic Order grants fair charter to Lwow... Florence lists 33 banchi grossi, merchant companies or partnerships, doing business in City, recognized as superior to banchi in mercato as moneychangers and banchi di pegni as pawnbrokers, an activity of Jews and citizens of Asti, Chieri in Piedmont who risk Church law outlawing such business to operate throughout Europe as Lombards... German engineer Jan Thurzo and citizens of Cracow start large lead works, partnership with Fuggers in 1495... Catalog is prepared for monastic libraries, England, first known subject catalog at Alexandria library in 300s B.C.

1473

Portuguese ship of Lopo Goncalves crosses equator in exploring African Coast... Pewters' Company of London, applied for articles in 1348, is chartered... Fuggers start business dealings with Hapsburgs (change family business into private company in 1474)... With shortages of gold and silver Venice mints some copper coins, Naples first in Europe... Venice builds north boat basin of Arsenal to extend overall site to some 60 acres, developed by 1480 with capacity to build 80 galleys at one time - 116 later (is administered by Lords and Commissioners, a supervisory body of patricians elected for 3-year terms and required to inspect yards every 3 days, Admiral of the Arsenal, plebeian appointed from craftsmen, and hereditary chief foremen supervising carpenters, sawyers, caulkers, mast and rudder workers, and oar craftsmen, produces 20 galleys in 6 months with 32 sawyers, 96 carpenters and 96 caulkers).

1474

Venice passes patent law... During a siege Charles the Bold, Duke of Burgundy, uses a machine, called "crane," to assault city's walls (prepares ideal battle plan for deploying forces in 1476)... Florentine physician-astrologer-cosmographer Paolo Toscanelli suggests to Portuguese king that there is a westward way to Spice Islands, contacted in 1480s by Columbus to obtain information, charts... Hansa, England sign (February 28) Peace of Utrecht.

1475

London mercers and grocers form Merchant Adventures in this time to trade with continent (-1809, when required by Crown in 1497 to enroll other merchants, accepts them on an inferior status)... Bartolomeo Sacchi: De Honesta Voluptate (signals end of medieval cookery of porridges and gravies, starts new trend of substantial meat dishes with careful preparation to bring out flavors)...

Cologne becomes a free imperial city, founded first century B.C... Rodericus Zamorensis: Speculum humane vite (describes The Seven Mechanical Arts as weaving, weapon forging, navigation, agriculture, hunting, medicine, acting).

1476

At battle of Grandson Swiss pikemen defeat Burgundian armored men-at-arms of Charles the Bold (upsets feudal system)... After printing first English book at Bruges in 1474, W. Caxton, textile merchant at Westminster, operates first English printing press (prints first advertisement in English of handbill to announce publication of book on religious services).

1477

Luca-Antonio Giunti of Florentine merchant family starts publishing house in Venice, followed by Florence press of brother in 1497... Louvain cites 72 breweries, 27 by 1520... Largest privileged company of sheepmen, Castile, runs two million sheep.

1478

Grand Duke Ivan III of Moscow subdues Novgorod (closes Hanse factory in 1494)... After leaving priesthood, Jakob Fugger the Elder (1459-1525) is employed in family business (trades in textiles, fruits, spices, drugs) in Augsburg (starts apprenticeship in Venice factory in 1484, enters metal trade of Tyrol in late 1480s - basis of family business with Hapsburgs, develops silver, copper monopolies in Hungary with Thurzo in 1490s)... Diamond cutters are employed in Antwerp, cited as first of their craft in City (move to Amsterdam in 1585 after City's capture by Spain)... Treviso Arithmetic is first popular textbook in mathematics.

1479

Mayor of Bristol makes Robert Ricard town clerk (-1500s)... Lodovico Sforza is ruler of Milan (-1500, develops experimental farm for growing rice, vines and mulberry trees, starts cattle breeding station)... After destruction of Arras, Brussels becomes center for European tapestry industry... University of Copenhagen opens, provides studies in divinity, law, medicine, arts... Treaty of Alcacovas recognizes Portugal's monopoly in West Africa and confirms Spain's claim to Canary Islands.

1480

Botticelli: "Birth of Venus" (pioneers oil-bound paints)... After voyaging westward for nine weeks, John Jay is forced to return to Bristol (fails to find western world)... Cardinal Pierre d'Ailly: Imago mundi (suggests possibility of westward passage to India, used by Columbus in supporting request to King Ferdinand)... In this time German clockmaker devises small lathe... Printing presses are operated in 111 European localities, over 238 by 1500... Pioneering labor market appears in Hamburg for hiring day-workers... Venetian printers Nickolas Jensen, Johannes de Colonia use pressmark of oval topped by double-barreled cross, used as trademark by Nabisco in 1900.

1481

English request Papal permission for trading in Africa... Papal bull awards new lands discovered south of Canary Islands to Portugal.

1482

Portuguese explore African Coast (-1484, reach Congo River, establish factory-fort on Gold

Coast).

1483

Thomas Rotherdam, Archbishop of York, starts school (provides instruction in accountancy as well as grammar)... Population of England is some 5 million, 9 million in 1760 and over 24 million by 1830.

1484

After pressure by merchants of Languedoc, Charles VIII bans fairs of Lyons, re-started bi-annually in 1494... Maximillian of Austria orders foreign merchants in Bruges to leave City, most go to Antwerp... Parliament passes reform acts on law, trade, tax-collection... England renews privileges of Hansa (limits imports of Bordeaux wine, permanent 1489)... In this time, Leonardo da Vinci sketches earliest form of camera, the camera obscura, followed by Gianbattista della Porta with improvements around 1553... London charters Wax Chandlers' Company, first collective action cited in 1330... Columbus proposes to Portugal's King John to sail westward to Spice Island (is reviewed, rejected by King's committee of experts, rejects also his 1488 proposal).

1485

Flemming Dulmo contracts with Portuguese King to discover fabled Isle of Seven Cities, project later dropped... King Henry VII is ruler of England (-1509, encourages raising of sheep to meet needs for wool exports, supports laws to authorize enclosures of common lands for grazing, develops system of financial, administrative checks to streamline government)... First printed cookbook, Kuchenmeisterey, is published in Nuremberg (is printed in 56 editions, followed in 1500 by first cookbook in English, This is the Bok of Cokery, for noble households).

1486

Worshipful Company of Bakers, cited as guild in 1155, is granted Royal Charter from Henry VII to make white bread, evolves as one of 94 livery companies of London (uses portrait of St. Michael, its patron saint, as early trademark on banners, medals and tokens, is followed in 1569 by charter for bakers of brown bread)... Portugal tries to establish trading relations with kingdom of Benin, discovered 1470s... Modern Watneys brewery business evolves in England.

1487

Coal miners of Liege are forbidden to leave their trade except in case of war, harvests... King John of Portugal sends Pero da Covilha overland to India to discover trade routes of Moslem spice ships to Africa (submits report in 1490)... Portugal sends Alfonso de Paiva to seek Prester John in area of Ethiopia... After surviving rough seas at Cape of Storms, later renamed Cape of Good Hope by King, Bartolemeu Dias of Portugal reaches Indian Ocean (-1488)... Russia, Hansa sign commercial treaty.

1488

Swabian League is formed by 26 cities (-1534)... Berlin's first apotheke opens... Parliament passes act to limit evils of land enclosures on Isle of Wight, followed by similar laws for England in 1515, 1516, 1533, 1535, 1552... Henry VII grants concessions to Italian merchants.

1489

Venice occupies Cyprus, acquires Island's sugar monopoly... Plus and minus symbols appear in this time... England, Spain sign commercial treaty.

1490

All crafts in the building and repair of ships organize in Genoa to resist demands of shipowners to lower wages, reorganize 1526... After serving on Council of Nautical Advisers to King John of Portugal, Martin Behaim builds terrestrial globe in Nuremberg, first since those of ancient Greece... Aldus Manutius starts Aldine Press in Venice, European center of printing since 1482 (prints hundreds of compact and inexpensive books, world's first pocket editions, from contemporary poetry to Greek classics, closes 1597 after printing some 908 works)... Anglo-Danish treaty permits English shipping to Iceland... Ballet appears at Italian courts.

1491

Portugal sends expedition to Angola... With port of Bruges blocked by silt, Antwerp becomes alum staple for Northern Europe... <u>Arithmetica</u> is printed in Italy (provides mathematics for merchants)... Duke of Medina Sidonia abolishes taxes on export of wine in Sanlucar in both Spanish, foreign ships (gives English merchants preferential status in 1517).

1492

After conquering Granada, last Moorish post from 711, Ferdinand and Isabella of Spain finance first voyage of Christopher Columbus to New World (after 33 days discovers Bahamas, Cuba and Haiti, finds best westward and eastward sea passages for winds, observes compass does not always point to Pole Star)... Da Vinci draws a flying machine, helicopter in 1500... Bishop declares Liege neutral in Spanish-Dutch conflict (encourages development of local armament industry, provides arms later to France, Sweden, Berlin, Russia)... When Spain recaptures Granada from Moors, some 200,000 Sephardi Jews are given 3 months to accept Christianity or leave (forces most Jews to North Africa, Eastern Mediterranean, Asia, Amsterdam, Hamburg)... Amerigo Vespucci goes to Seville to represent de Medici business interests (starts explorations in 1499)... Francisco Pellos: <u>Compendio de lo abaco</u> (covers commercial arithmetic, gives precursor for decimal point).

1493

Emperor Maximillian builds Hofkammer, King's treasury, at Innsbruck (establishes 2nd at Vienna in 1501, sponsors chairs later at universities to provide required knowledge for their administration)... Two Genoese merchants undertake commercial expedition to Middle East, Red Sea, Far East, Sumatra (fails)... During second voyage to New World Columbus discovers Puerto Rico, Jamaica, Dominica... Juan Rodriquez de Fonseca is de facto Spanish minister for trade with New World (-1503)... Pope Alexander VI issues bull to divide world between Spain, granted area west of Azores, and Portugal, granted lands east of demarcation line... Portugal establishes first port on east coast of Africa, followed by ports at Mozambique and Zanzibar in 1502, Mombasa in 1505... England, Flanders begin commercial war (-1496, leads to banishment of Flemings from England and move of Merchant Adventurers from Antwerp to Calais).

1494

Savonarola, Dominican friar seeking revival in religious faith, gains power in Florence (-1497, attacks business for its economic activities, expels Medici family)... Goods lottery is popular amusement in Germany in this time... Grand Duke Ivan III of Moscow closes Hanseatic trading post in Novgorod... Treaty of Tordesillas shifts territorial line for Spain, Portugal westward so Portugal can settle Brazil... Luca Pacioli: <u>Summa de Arithmetica, Geometria, Proporcioni et porporcionalita</u> (describes double-entry bookkeeping with journal, ledger, documents for transactions, periodic audits)... Spanish ships carry hens, roosters to West Indies (transports jacks, jennets, mares, cattle, pigs, sheep in 1495)... Player in religious drama at Hull, England, is paid for taking part of God... Burgos, Spain, establishes Consul for administering "university" of merchants, follows use of Consul of the Sea as port authority for traders in Pisa since 1200s (used by Toulouse in 1549, Rouen 1556, Paris 1563)... Leonardo da Vinci draws clock with pendulum... Spanish royal decree gives top officials of Burgos merchant guild, evolved in 1300s with royal exemption in paying tolls to towns or nobles (uses Medina del Campo fairs, twice/year, as clearing house for merchants, bankers), a monopoly in chartering ships, usually two fleets/year, to export Castilian wool to England, Flanders (makes Bruges, satellite of Spain, subordinate to Burgos merchant guild until commerce disrupted by Revolt of Netherlands in 1567).

1495

Portugal evicts Jews... Paper mill is started in England (-1507)... Aldo Manuzio starts Venetian publishing house at sign of the dolphin and anchor, becomes trademark (by 1515 issues some 130 editions in popular sizes of mostly Greek classics)... Thurzo builds Neusohl smelting and rolling mill in Hungary for Fugger-Thurzo Company (strengthens alliance with Fuggers through other partnerships and marriages, provides minerals, metals as basis for wealth amassed by House of Fugger).

1496

Ten leaders of miners and three company officials are executed to settle labor dispute at German mine, operated in feudal times by mostly mining guilds which often own shafts and pay tribute in metals to lord for subsoil rights and use referees to settle labor disputes, usually on number of working hours and/or value of work to be credited in foodstuffs... Columbus finds Santo Domingo in New World... Romano Payne, monk with Columbus, is first to describe tobacco plant... Da Vinci shows curiosity about number of machines required to make so many needles/hour (reflects on automatic sawmill, automatic file-cutting machine and other automatic devices, designs roller bearings, rolling mill)... Henry VII, England, grants royal patent, provides trade monopoly in return for 20% of all profits, to Cabots, John and son Sebastian, to establish post in West Indies (sail from Bristol, used as port for vessels searching for Atlantic Islands since 1480s, in 1497 to discover Grand Banks and reach east coast of North America, possibly sighting Newfoundland)... Cologne registers 42 craft guilds, 50 cited in Lubeck and 28 in Frankfort-on-Main.

1497

Vasco da Gama undertakes voyage from Portugal to Cape of Good Hope, Mozambique, Mombasa and Calicut, India (-1499, returns with cargo of spices)... Amerigo Vespucci, Florentine geographer and Medici agent at Seville, claims to have discovered Honduras, Mexico on voyage to New World... Russian peasants are legally bound to employers' land, permitted to leave only during two-week period in celebrating November holiday of St. George's Day... Common people in Low Countries are forbidden to wear silks, velvets, satins at insistence of cloth towns... Merchant Adventurers obtain English trade monopoly for Holland.

1498

On 3rd voyage to New World Columbus sights South American Coast, Trinidad... First German pawnshop opens in Nuremberg... First known toothbrush, uses hog bristles, appears in China... John Cabot fails to return from 2nd voyage to New World, no finds reported by remaining ship of 5 starting expedition... With 'Law of Magdeburg' Grand Duke Alexandria of Lithuania grants staple to Polotsk (cancels all rights of Hanseatic merchants).

1499

All but one of the great banks, including Garzoni and Lippomani, in Venice are forced into liquidation during monetary panic, caused by rumors of possible wars with Milan, Ottoman Empire... Giovanni Battista Danti tries to fly in Perugia, Italy, with wings attached to body... Spain grants licenses for New World exploration to Vicente Pinzon and Diego de Lepe for Coast of South America, Peralonso Nino and Cristobal Guerra for Orinoco River (find pearls), and Alonso de Ojeda, Juan de la Casa and Amerigo Vespucci to cover Northeast Coast of South America (discover Amazon River).

1500-1599

Paris is major center for making perfume in Europe... Waterwheel, one of some 60,000 in France during 1500s, is used in Paris to polish stones (later, after being confiscated by King, is used to make "milled" coins)... Spinning wheel, workman's bench appear throughout Europe... Attempts are made in Europe to restrict practice of medicine to qualified doctors... Protection is gradually established in Europe, particularly Holland and Saxony, to provide inventors with rights to their creations... Earthenware stove, pocket handkerchiefs are seen in Europe... Normans, Bretons start fishing off North American Coast, increases demand for salt... Some 100 million people live on Europe's 3.75 million square miles, about 24 acres/person - same ratio as 150 years earlier and later... Johann Kiefus, Germany, "invents" wheel lock, essential step in developing the pistol... Korporation Oberaegeri is formed, Switzerland, as farm cooperative (still extant)... Magna Societas controls almost half of Barcelona's international trade... Consul of Burgos regulates use of marine insurance... Antwerp port is enlarged to moor some 2,500 vessels, handles some 500 daily sailings... Some 9 million books are estimated to exist in Europe, perhaps 100,000 manuscripts in 1450... Spa evolves as mineral water resort, Belgium... Holland's fields are spread with mud, lime and peat ash, manure later... Leyden becomes textile center, produces 30,000 cloths yearly... German Count Philip Edward Fugger produces first documented newsletters to report on business news gathered by agents in trade centers throughout Europe, overseas... Agent for Florence's merchants at Bruges is appointed Consul of the Sea to represent concerns at port of all foreign merchants... Failing to repress coca chewing by South American natives, Spanish start selling the leaf to make fortunes... Chalk artists appear in Italian cities to draw pictures, usually secular images, on thoroughfares for delight, cash of pedestrians (still extant in Europe in 1990s).

1500

Diet of Augsburg forms Consul of Regency for administration of Holy Roman Empire... Gaspar de Corte Real, Portugal, visits Greenland, disappears at sea during 2nd expedition in 1501 to Labrador... Leonardo da Vinci devises treadle lathe to improve crank-powered grindstone used in 1400s... Catholic monarchs Isabella, Ferdinand prohibit loading of merchandise in foreign ships if Spanish ones are available... Pedro Cabral commands fleet of 13 Portuguese caravels sailing to India (passes Cape Verde Islands and Brazil, identified as Tierra de Vera Cruz, and Cape of Good Hope before visiting Calicut factory and Cochin (returns to Lisbon in 1501 with first significant cargo of spices by sea route, undercuts high prices of European spice trade controlled by Egypt, Venice)... Columbus, accused of mistreating natives in West Indies, is returned to Spain in chains... Wynken De Worde opens in this time a printing office on London's Fleet Street (-1535, starts development of area for printers, publishers)... Albrecht de Menningen publishes catalog listing 200 books for sale (advertises books with handbills)... China makes building of seagoing junks a capital offense (orders all such vessels to be destroyed by 1525 edict)... First commercial colleges appear in Venice... Regular postal service starts between Vienna and Brussels, extended to Madrid in 1504... Black-lead pencils appear in England... Silver guilders are coined in Germany, used in Austria to 1892... Hieronymus Brunschig publishes first illustrations of chemical apparatus and operations... England writes detailed statutes for new company of Merchant Adventurers, joins existing companies of Merchant Adventurers and Merchant Staplers... In this time Welser merchant house appears in Augsburg to finance large commercial enterprises (-1614)... Chinese scientist Wan Hu uses gunpowder rockets to power flying craft, killed during tests.

1501

Anglo-Portuguese syndicate makes first voyage to North America, 5th in 1505... Portugal sends caravels of Gonsolvo Coelho, Vespucci in crew to investigate sightings of Brazilian Coast by Cabral... Spain sends Alonso de Ojeda to New World for trading, raiding... Spain legalizes shipments of slaves to its colonies in New World... Ypres bans handicrafts in suburbs, other bans in 1512, 1545... Spain prohibits sale of its ships abroad... Girolamo Cardano, Milanese physician (invents vacuum device to provide even flow of oil to portable clock lamp), is born (-1576)... Juanelo Torriano, Cremona craftsmen (invents "first" gear-cutting machine), is born (-1575)... Spain's Juan de la Cosa, Rodrigo de Bastidas explore Darien Coast of Central America (report finding gold, abundant food, no outlet from Southern Caribbean)... Butchers' Hall is built, Antwerp,to provide space for sales and meetings of guild (-1503)... Coopers Co. of London, fraternity by 1422, is chartered... First Portuguese spice ship docks at Lisbon, starts branch of Casa de las Indies at Antwerp in 1508.

1502

Alberto Cantino shows islands discovered by Columbus on map as separated from Asia... Vespucci deems South America to be independent continent... Venice appoints Supervisor of Banks to audit any enterprise claiming bankruptcy... Peter Henlein, Nuremberg, uses iron parts and coiled springs to build portable timepiece, followed by pendulum clock in 1650s, electric clock in late 1800s, quartz clock in 1929, atomic clock in 1948... Michael de Corte Real disappears while exploring Coast of Newfoundland... Venice grants monopoly for italic type to Aldine Press.

1503

Casa de la Contratacion (is Council of the Indies in 1524, moves to Cadiz in 1717) forms in Seville (uses organizational structure based on Genoa's Officum Gazarie) with Juan Rodriguez de Fonseca as first minister to supervise New World commerce (requires all trade to go through Seville in 1522, starts navigation school for training - licenses by examination) and collect revenues... Julius II is Pope (-1513, is recognized for abilities as financier, administrator)... Raw sugar is refined... Del Gallo brothers petition Venice for rights to modern mirror.

1504

Venice proposes building Suez Canal to Sultan of Turkey... England's Henry VII places guilds, trade companies under Crown supervision... King of France grants contract to Franz von Taxis to provide postal service between courts of France, Netherlands, Spain... Amerigo Vespucci: <u>Mundus Novus</u>, first source book on New World discoveries... Portugal's King Manuel makes plans for pepper monopoly (establishes death penalty for anyone distributing charts of country's African explorations)... Hernando Cortes undertakes voyage to Santo Domingo (joins with Valaquez in 1515 conquest of Cuba, after ranching and mining there, forms partnership company to conquer Mexico in 1519-1521)... Mexican chocolate appears in Spain, seen in England, France c. 1657.

1505

On east coast of Africa, Kilwa (follows greatest influence in 1100-1400s, builds first mint in Africa, trades with Arabia, India and interior Africa in ivory, gold, salt) and Mombasa (is conquered by Moslems in 976 A.D.) are captured by Portugal (opens factories, annexes lands in 1515)... Franz von Taxis starts first regular mail between Vienna, Brussels... Portuguese spice trade is centralized at India House, Lisbon (distributes royal spices to Antwerp as exclusive distributor for Northern Europe, later forms Casa da Mina for supervising African trade)... Henry VII charters Merchant Adventurers of London... Portuguese traders begin New World slave trade (evolves with trading firms branding slaves).

1506

First map of New World is printed, shows area linked with Asia... Spain cultivates sugar in Greater Antilles... Royal factor of Portugal employs Italian trading houses to distribute spices at Antwerp (replaces Italians later with such German firms as Fuggers, Welsers)... Colmar merchants make first cited sales of brandy... Portugal puts fort at Cochin, India, to block Arab Red Sea spice trade, used as headquarters until Goa in 1510... England, Netherlands sign commercial treaty... Jakob Fugger imports spices from East Indies by sea.

1507

Holder of a bill payable in Antwerp is permitted to get his money back without having to show authorized deed... Martin Waldseemuller makes map of New World, labels region of Brazil as America for its "discoverer" Vespucci... Francisco de Almeida, first governor of Indies for Portugal, establishes forts at Calicut, Cananor on Malabar Coast.

1508

Holy Roman Empire, France, Papal States, and Spain form League of Cambrai to break power of Venice... Lyons becomes distribution center for Portuguese spices... In first of two voyages to North America to find Northwest Passage, Sebastian Cabot commands expedition with father's letters of patent (when rejected by England's Henry VII goes to Spain in 1512 to train navigators, develop navigation instruments, prepare charts in planning convoy routes to New World)... Spanish forces of Juan Ponce de Leon conquer Puerto Rico (-1509)... Syndicate is formed in Antwerp to buy all spices Portugal can obtain in Orient (starts City's rapid growth while Bruges declines with harbor too small for new vessels)... Portugal starts factory in Mozambique... Vasco Nunez de Balboa is discovered as stowaway on Spanish expedition to New World (gains command in Darien, explores Panama in 1511, locates source of gold artifacts in 1512 expedition, discovers Pacific Ocean on 1513 exploration along with gold, pearls, fisheries)... King Ferdinand of Spain calls meeting to plan for maritime discovery, territorial conquest, settlement in New World... Florian de Ocampo circumnavigates Cuba, colony in 1511 and conquest by Diego Valazquez in 1515... Vespucci is pilot-major of Spain's Casa de las Indies, granted authority to examine and test all pilots for expertise (is required to maintain maps)... Maximillian I makes Jakob Fugger the Elder an hereditary knight in Holy Roman Empire (loans funds in 1509 to Emperor to fight Venice).

1509

After proposal by Catholic bishop, Spanish settlers in New World use slave trade to obtain workers for plantations... Navy of Almeida destroys fleet of Arabs, Egyptians, and Venetians at Div... Portuguese emissary, Antonio Fernandes, is first white man to visit Zimbabwe... Afonso de Albuquerque commands Portuguese fleet to India (captures Goa in 1510 to develop permanent trading center, naval base and capitol, serves as Governor of Indies to 1515)... Duke of Saxony establishes comprehensive code for mining, basis for mining law in Germany... Henry VIII is ruler of England (-1547, introduces "enclosure system" to grant manorial lords right to fence public lands for sheep pasture, increases land rents)... Spanish colony is started in Jamaica, followed by capture of Island by English in 1655, abolition of slavery in 1838 - sugar production declines, and independence in 1962... English Merchant Adventurers, headquarters in Antwerp, are chartered... Henry VIII starts trend as first member of English royalty to wear silk stockings, gift from Spain... Of 139 vineyards in Bordeaux area, 11 are owned by noblemen and 52 by Church.

1510

Transatlantic trade increases eightfold by 1550, threefold 1550-1610... Leonardo da Vinci designs horizontal water wheel, basis for water turbine... Empson and Dudley, tax collectors of Henry VII, are executed... Holy Roman Empire makes Hamburg a Free City... Probiebdergbuchlein is printed in this time, first book on assaying, mining... Portugal annexes Goa as major trading port in India (-1961, follows with ports in Div in 1535, Bombay in 1661, and Malacca in 1511)... Parliament grants lifetime wool duties to Henry VIII.

1511

Lodovico de Varthema: Itinerary (describes travels to North Africa, Arabia, India, Ceylon, Siam, East Indies)... After obtaining chart for Indian Ocean, Albuquerque conquers Indonesia, Sumatra and Malacca for Portugal (surveys Java, sends envoy to Ayudhya in Siam)... England requires all physicians, surgeons to be university graduates or licensed by bishop after examination by experts... First road map of Europe is published, Germany... Genoa uses lottery, first cited, to select senators.

1512

Jakob Fugger the Younger heads House of Fugger in Augsburg (-1525, after family's wealth peaks in 1546 declines in 1575 with bankruptcy of Spain)... Portuguese discover Celebes... Ponce de Leon, governor of Puerto Rico, lands near St. Augustine, FL, in search of fabled Fountain of Youth, 2nd voyage in 1521... England starts building double-deck ships of 1,000 tons to carry 70 guns... Diet of Cologne issues acts against monopolies... Augsburg bans quack doctors... De Medici family regains royal power in Florence (-1527).

1513

C. de Haro, Fugger agent in Lisbon, tries to find strait around South America (-1514, reaches Brazil)... Portuguese vessels visit Canton, Moluccas... Niccolo Machiavelli: The Prince, published 1532 (advises ruler how to rule and stay in power, describes ideal prince as having "flexible disposition, varying as fortune and circumstance dictate")... Giovanni de Medici is Pope Leo X (-1521, in order to obtain funds to build St. Peter's grants archbishop chair in Mainz to Albrecht of Brandenberg who agrees to sell indulgences - half of proceeds to Pope and rest to pay bankers for loan of 24,000 gold pieces to purchase position).

1514

New World ships pineapples to Europe... House of Fugger secures right to sell Papal indulgences in Germany... Spain sends expedition of Pedrarias Davila with 1,500 members to Darien (relieves Balboa of command, after arrest by Francisco Pizarro for treason is beheaded in 1519)... Portugal sends ship to Canton to establish trade with Celestial Empire, followed by closure of Chinese ports to foreign traders later when China discovers children used as slaves... Genoese ships slaves from Africa to Hispanola... French guild of vinegar-makers is granted privilege to distill brandy... Venice' "Board of Trade" opens spice trade monopoly to all Venetians (grants right to buy pepper to Portugal in 1520)... Innholders' Company of London, cited as Hostellers in 1300s-1400s, is chartered... As result of plague England establishes national maximum wage... Werbucz Code establishes perpetual serfdom in Hungary after revolt of peasants... Henry VIII establishes Trinity House to train, license all English pilots, masters.

1515

Portuguese take Hormuz on Persian Gulf, annexed in 1543-1622 (starts other fortified trading posts in East Africa, Cochin and Goa, Malacca, Moluccas)... France nationalizes armaments, tapestry industries... Juan Bermudez is shipwrecked on unknown island in Atlantic... Valerius Cordus, physician and botanist (cites first preparation of sulfuric acid), is born (-1544)... England, Spain sign commercial treaty... Albrecht Durer, two German astronomers make first star charts for Northern Hemisphere in Nuremberg... Coffee from Arabia appears in Europe (-1519)... German gunsmiths develop wheel-lock rifles, used by sportsmen as too expensive for military who continue with smooth-bore matchlocks to 1600s... No qualified clockmakers are available in Geneva to repair cathedral clock, appear after 1550 with French persecution of Protestants (lists some 25 master clockmakers by 1600).

1516

Franz von Taxis is postmaster-general for Netherlands (extends Imperial mail service to Rome, Naples)... Dyestuff indigo is imported to Europe... Silver lode, one of world's greatest finds, is found in Harz Mountains of Northern Czechoslovakia (results in mint at town of Joachimsthal to coin silver joachimsthalers, thaler basis for term dollar, produces 3 million ounces by 1540)... Portugal gives Siamese guns, munitions for right to trade, settle... Duke William IV of Bavaria enacts law, world's first pure-food act, to specify that beer could only be brewed from malted barley, hops and water... Spanish missionary to Santo Domingo takes first bananas, first cultivated in jungles of Southeast Asia, to New World... Dutch devise large dragnet in this time to catch North Sea herring.

1517

Galleon ship appears in Mediterranean to combat Barbary pirates, use cited by Spain and Venice in 1526... Spanish concession for slave trade is granted to Flemish merchants... Portuguese start factory in Ceylon... After indignation over public selling of indulgences by Dominican John Tetzel, priced by social class, to raise money for Church and Hohenzollern family (owes money to Fuggers), Martin Luther posts 95 theses on door, used as public bulletin board, of Frederick's Castle Church in Wittenberg, excommunicated 1520... Archduke Charles grants monopoly for Negro slave trade to Florence merchants... England starts government postal service... Austrian mining code curbs private investors in mines, forges, mills... Spain grants privileges to English merchants in Andalusia... Troops suppress immense mob of apprentices, ruffians and disillusioned clerics on London's May Day after attacking houses and workshops of foreign merchants and craftsmen... Spanish expedition of Hernandez de Cordoba from Cuba explores Yucatan to seek slaves, riches.

1518

Barbary states of Algiers, Tunis are founded... Regular performances are given in this time at court theater of Ferrara... Royal College of Physicians is founded, London... Europe imports first Asian porcelain... License to ship 4,000 African slaves to Spanish colonies in New World is granted to Lorenz de Gominot... Spain sends expedition from Cuba to Cozumel Island, Yucatan, to find gold (discovers Mexico)... European illustration shows clerk using abacus as coin counter at "counting bench," term source for word "bank"... Byzantine custom of eating with a fork appears in Italy, adopted to simplify eating of long strands of pasta... Captured Moor tells Pope Leo X that Timbuktu has so many scholars that its merchants make greater profits from books than any other commodity... English merchants, Antwerp sign agreement.

1519

Burma grants trading privileges to Portugal... Charles V, Holy Roman Emperor, inherits Austria, Netherlands, Aragon, Sardinian, Naples and Sicily (develops Spain, Europe's major power to 1659, with wealth from sales taxes, taxes on Church property of Castile, customs duties, Church levies and 20% of gold and silver from America)... On directions of governor for Jamaica, Alvarez Pineda explores coast of Gulf of Mexico for northern route to Spice Islands (covers coast from Vera Cruz to Florida to prove existence of North America land mass)... Hernando Cortes undertakes conquest of Mexico (-1521, lands with 10 stallions and 6 mares, descendants captured by Pueblo Indians in 1680 revolt to introduce horses to North America)... With 5 ships and crew of 270 (carries 21 quadrants, 7 marine astrolabes, 18 sandglasses, 23 charts, 37 compass needles), Ferdinand Magellan undertakes to circumnavigate world (-1522 with return of 18 survivors to Spain which views voyage as pointless exercise)... Leonardo da Vinci dies, leaves some 7,000 manuscript pages on scientific and engineering matters... Ulrich Zwingli starts Reformation in Switzerland... England's John Winchcombe, "Jack of Newberry," dies (supposedly acquires fortune from textile factory employing 1,040 workers, mostly boys, girls and women, in dyehouse, fulling mill, and in workshops for sorting, carding, spinning, weaving, shearing).

1520

Henry VIII puts bowling lanes in Whitehall... England, Holy Roman Empire sign commercial treaty... Sultan Suleyman the Magnificent rules Ottoman Empire (-1566, develops system of artisans' guilds at Istanbul, invades Hungary in 1521 and Rhodes in 1522, attacks Austria in 1529 but fails to take Vienna, annexes Hungary in 1541 and Tripoli in 1551, destroys Spanish fleet in 1560)... August Kotter invents rifled barrel to improve on straight-grooved barrel of Austria's Gastard Kollner in 1490.

1521

Pamplona, Spain, holds first annual running of bulls... Francisco de Gordillo explores Atlantic Coast to South Carolina, followed by voyage of Pedro de Quexos in 1525... Proposal is made at Worms Reichstag to disband great companies, abolish monopolies... Ponce de Leon is unsuccessful in colonizing Florida... Cortes founds Mexico City... In response to French menace toward Portuguese lands in New World, Portugal's John III starts colonization of Brazil (-1530)... Portuguese reach Molucca Islands (are ousted by Dutch in 1605 who drive out English in 1623).

1522

With ships built in Panama, Gil Gonzalez explores Pacific Coast of Honduras and Nicaragua, followed by other expeditions by 1526 to explore Mexico's Pacific Coast... China expels Portuguese for pirating activities... Spain claims Philippines, Moluccas when Magellan's ship returns from voyage, gives areas to Portugal in 1529 Treaty of Saragossa... Durer designs flying machine for warfare... Municipal stocks are traded in Paris... Ludovico degli Arrighi's La Operina is first writing manual, followed by Spencerian style in mid-1800s... Pascul de Andagoya scouts Peruvian coast of South America, learns of Inca Empire... Turks take Rhodes to control trade in Eastern Mediterranean... An attempt is made at Schwaz mining center to replace buckets with water-driven pumping machine - success unknown... Seville merchants petition King for ships to guard merchant vessels to Americas (with tax on merchants provides Armada de la Guardia for escort duty - fleet evolves to use staffing/ton formula to employ captain-admiral, master of material and food, contramaster, guardian, chief pilot and others: fleet master of silver, House of Trade's notary, chaplain, carpenters, caulkers, divers, musicians, water bailiff, surgeon/barber, infantry, pages and sailors).

1523

Ypres subsidizes wool buying... Luther starts "Common Chest" to provide funds for church officials, schoolmasters, needy... Herman Schreiber, John Gottlieb publish first bookkeeping book in Germany, 2nd in 1531 and one by Hugh Oldcastle, England, in 1602... Anthony Fitzherbert: Book of Husbandry, first manual in English advocates enclosure of large areas for increasing agricultural production... Marine insurance policies appear in Florence... After assisting Sweden to win war with Denmark, Hansa merchants receive exclusive rights to trade with any citizen without paying any customs duties, to restrict travel by Swedish merchants to only Hansa cities... China expels Europeans.

1524

Esslingen regulations attempt to unify German monetary system... English see first turkeys from

South America... Spanish settlers develop City of Guatemala... After exploration of Carolina Coast by Lucas Vazquez de Ayllon, Portugal's Esteban Gomez surveys further north along Atlantic Coast (-1525)... France sends Giovanni de Verrazano, financed by silk merchants of Lyons, to explore coast of North America (notes Pacific Ocean to be on other side of Carolina's Outer Banks, discovers Hudson River)... Martin Luther: On Trade and Usury (discusses anti-trust movement in Germany)... At sound of trumpets at 9:00 each evening, Paris requires all inhabitants to put lighted candles in their windows... Cortes starts sugar cultivation and refining in Mexico along with cattle and horse ranches - exports in 1530 (operates plantations for wheat and silk, fails to grow olives commercially).

1525

Of seven Spanish ships tracing Magellan's route, only one is able to reach Moluccas, fails to return... Miners hold strikes in Hungary (-1526)... Spanish Square, first country in Europe to standardize size and fire-power of firearms, defeats Swiss formation of pikemen, employed by France, at Pavia... Florence passes law to regulate marine insurance contracts... Emperor Charles V estimates some 100,000 employed in mining, metallurgy in Europe... First publishing house in Holland is established, some 50 others by 1555... Rodrigo de Bastidas founds Santa Marta as first permanent settlement in New Granada... Marquis de Pescara, Spain, invents harquebus, first portable firearm... Rome employs first public street cleaners, paid by tax on artisans and tradespeople... Jean Fernel is first to measure degree of latitude using time difference... Ulrich Zwingli organizes distribution of money, food, and clothing to poor in Zurich... Albrecht Durer: Instructions concerning measurements with compasses and straight edge (uses geometry to solve practical problems)... Ypres starts governmental relief program.

1526

Spain requires merchant ships to travel in convoys, regulated by detailed ordinances in 1536, 1543... Spain starts colony at Santee River, Carolina, abandoned 1528 with loss of supplies and 200 dead... Scotland grants some Germans a mining lease for gold, silver and other metals, follows discovery of gold during reign of James IV in 1488-1513... Bruges forms single charitable fund for all needy groups, followed by Lille 1527, Paris 1533... Spain forms Audiencia to govern Santo Domingo, lesser officials to govern West Indies... Babar starts Mogul Empire in Northern India with Mongols from Russian Turkistan (-1857)... City Post is started in London for King's Letters, followed in 1619 by Foreign Post for overseas letters and General Post for public in 1635... Sigismondo Fanti: Triompho de fortune (discusses cycles of changes in human affairs with peaks, valleys)... Venice builds its first galleon, a combination of carvel and nao (-1530)... Portuguese vessels explore coastline of New Guinea.

1527

After overthrow of Medici family Florence forms a republic... Moluccas is reached by one of ships built by Cortes on Pacific Coast of Mexico, fails to return... Spain forms Audiencia to govern New Spain (replaces royal patents to governors and captain-generals, is adopted for Guatemala in 1542, New Galicia in 1548)... John Rut tries to find Northwest Passage... Austria reorganizes its administration (-1848)... Bleaching-guild monopoly appears in Germany's Wupper Valley (starts industrial development along Rhine, leads to water-powered mill in 1783, machine-spinning mills by 1799 and steam-powered cotton mill in 1821)... Emperor Charles V grants territory of Venezuela to Welsers (sends colonists in 1529, loses concession 1546-1556)... First Protestant university appears in Marburg... Sweden adopts Lutheran religion... Altes Presshaus, claims to be Vienna's oldest wine tavern (evolves by 1990s as fancy restaurant), opens in Grinzing, city's famed wine village where growers still sell their vintages.

1528

Spain arrests English merchants in Spain, Flanders to protest Wolsey's policy on wool trade... When England's wool staple is shifted from Antwerp to Calais by Cardinal Wolsey, Kent weavers riot... Henry VIII appoints principal surveyor to find, work mines of gold, silver, copper and lead in England, Wales, Ireland... After forming partnership company with contractual arrangements with Spanish Crown, Pizarro, brothers start search to find fabled Inca Empire (-1533)... Guilds of Fullers, 1480, and Shearmen, 1508, merge to form company... Narvaez expedition of 300 from Cuba lands on Florida's West Coast, four survivors go overland to Mexico in 1536 via Mississippi, Colorado Rivers.

1529

Hochstetters are ruined in trying to form mercury cartel... Spain appoints viceroy to represent King in government of New Spain (receives ruling authority in 1535, appoints viceroys for New Granada in 1549, Philippines in 1538-1593).

1530

Portugal founds Sao Vicente in Brazil... Fuggers try to colonize West Coast of South America... Antwerp Exchange is built... English merchants in Spain form company... Emperor Charles V cedes Malta to Knights of St. John (repel Ottoman Turks in Great Siege of 1565, develop towns, palaces, forts and churches in 1566-1798, develop Island as financial center in 1600s-1700s, is taken over by Malta in 1798)... England's first formal horse racing is seen at York... In this time Paracelsus prepares tincture of opium, known as laudanum, as a pain reliever... Holy Roman Empire establishes criminal code, police regulations... Matches appear in Europe, some thousand years after creation in China.

1531

Paris requires every house to have a latrine... Fuggers opens branch in Chile (-1535)... Francois de la Nove, military theorist (discusses strategy, tactics of warfare), is born (-1591).

1532

Sugar cane from Madeira is first cultivated in Brazil, followed by plantations in 1550s, first sugar cane in West Indies in 1680... Spain orders all ships to New World to carry seeds, plants, domestic animals... Venice cancels annual trading convoys to North Africa, cancels convoys to Northern Europe by 1535 and Egypt 1654... Portugal forms organization with religious, financial powers to govern South American colonies.

1533

Spain founds Cartagena in New World... Manual for making paints, inks is published in Augsburg... Catherine de Medici is married to future Henry II of France (brings fork, pasta, sherbet and ices to French Court, little or no impact on French cuisine or dining habits)... Hernando Cortes is first Viceroy for New Spain... Ivan the Terrible is Grand Duke of Moscow (-1584, if they can take it promises Siberia to Stroganov family, evolved from Christian tartar and fur-trader named Spiridion and succeeded by three sons, develop enterprises in salt, furs and mining with aid of German craftsmen and bookkeepers, and grandson, seizes granted land with Cossacks and rules area to time of Peter the Great, 1689-1725)... Reiner Gemma Frisius: De principis astronomiae et cosmographie (shows use of mechanical clock to determine longitude).

1534

Cortes orders vineyards planted in Mexico with grapes from Spain (predicts winemaking will be leading New World industry)... English farmers are prohibited in owning more than 2,000-sheep... French explorer Jacques Cartier makes voyage of discovery to New World (searches Labrador Coast and St. Lawrence River, sees French fishing vessel in Labrador Harbor, takes 2nd voyage in 1335 to find rich kingdom of Saquenay, locates sites for Quebec and Mont Real instead, launches 3rd venture in 1541)... Francis I of France issues edict to suppress printers as menace to calligraphers' guild, never enforced... Adopting Genoese colonial organizational structure Portugal divides Brazil into 15 captaincies, each with fiscal, political privileges for land development... Spain settles Lima in Peru, founds Valparaiso in Chile in 1536... Luther translates Bible into German... Ignatius de Loyola organizes Society of Jesus, Jesuits, as vanguard of Counter Reformation.

1535

Spain sends vessels to explore, conquer Chile (-1553)... Spain sends expedition of 11 ships, 1,200-1,500 colonists, to settle South America (starts Buenos Aires in 1536, abandoned in 1541 and re-founded in 1580, and establishes fort at Asuncion, Paraguay, in 1537)... Coverdale's Bible, first complete Bible in English, is printed (-1536)... Antonia de Mendoza replaces Cortes as Viceroy of New Spain... In this time Spanish cultivate tobacco in Haiti and operate New World's first printing press in Mexico.

1536

When Parliament declares authority of Pope to be void, Henry VIII appoints Court of Augmentation to confiscate Church property of 578 monasteries, 130 convents (after takeover makes parishes responsible with Poor Law to aid destitute, followed by 1572 act to levy tax for poor, 1576 and 1597 acts to start reformatories, and 1601 Poor Act to consolidate all laws)... Gonzalo Jimenez de Quesada explores Colombia, founds Santa Fe de Bogota (-1538)... Giolito Press is started, Venice, to print vernacular literature (-1599)... Ottoman Empire grants merchants in Marseilles liberty of commerce on parity with those of Venice, gain virtual monopoly by 1569... Lyons develops silk-weaving industry (obtains raw silk from Spain, Italy)... Italian clock maker Bolori dies after trying to fly from cathedral tower in Troyes, France... John Calvin: Institutes of the Christian Religion (proclaims "The man who performs efficiently is fulfilling God's mission for him", advocates thrift, not poverty, as prime virtue in life of hard work, piety and diligence in order to be saved now).

1537

John Herford, St. Albans, writes first book in English on arithmetic (gives calculations to determine payments for hired men)... New World ships potatoes to Europe, cultivated by Incas in 200s B.C... Formerly The Fraternity or Guilds of Artillery of Longbows, Crossbows and Handguns, "The Honourable Artillery Company," England's oldest regiment, incorporates... Hanseatic League, Sweden sign treaty for free trade in Baltic.

1538

Geographer Mercator uses America designation for first time... Flemish artist Marinus van Romerwael paints St. Matthew (shows wrath of public against tax collectors)... France's Francis I orders flat plates for eating from Antwerp goldsmith... Turkish navy defeats combined fleet of Genoa, Spain, Venice in Ionian Sea... Wisbech shoemakers organize embryo trade union in England, combination of London saddlers in 1560.

1539

France holds public lottery... Spain annexes Cuba... First Christmas tree is seen at Strasbourg Cathedral... Hernando De Sota explores Southeast U.S. from Florida to Mississippi (-1542)... Traditional trading monopolies of Japanese guilds, temples, shrines, and nobles are broken by Sasaki family in fief near Osaka to establish free trade market... Venice requires most craftsmen to be guild members... Some 100 printing presses are operated in Lyons when printing workers hold City's first big strike to protest long hours, 2:00 a.m. to 11:00 p.m. with 40-minute meal break, excessive profits by masters, and poor working conditions... England grants merchants free trade for seven years... Brandenberg, Pomerania start trade war (-1592)... Franciscan friar Marcos de Niza leads Spanish expedition to explore Southwestern U.S. (returns with tale of fabled Seven Cities of Cibola)... Banco di Napoli is founded (after acting as central bank for Kingdom of the Two Sicilies, minting coins in capitol of Naples, and raising funds for royal wars against invaders and Italy unification in 1860, runs 500 branches, 400 in South, in Italy by 1989).

1540

Charles V limits Lombard bankers to an interest rate of 33%, 21% maximum in 1600s... In peace treaty with Ottoman Empire, Venice is forced to give reparations, territories (is forced out of Cyprus in 1573)... Van der Molen operates commission business in Antwerp... England forms Privy Council to assist King in governing, evolves from King's Council in 1530s... Astronomical clock is installed at Royal Palace at Hampton Court, London... Francisco Vazquez de Coronado leads expedition of some 300, 800 Indians to find Seven Cities of Cibola (-1542, discovers Grand Canyon, explores Texas, Oklahoma and Kansas, introduces longhorn cattle and sheep to Navajo)... Ether is produced from alcohol, sulfuric acid... Hartmann of Nuremberg devises method to calibrate firearms, leads to standardization in making muskets... Vannoccio Biringuccio: Work on Fire, first practical text on metallurgy (describes practical methods for iron foundry and mass production of common objects, discusses metal, glass and chemical industries)... Companies of Surgeons and Barbers are united, divided with formation of Royal College of Surgeons in 1800s... First Finnish weaving establishment appears in Abo... France's first commercial theater company is licensed by Lyons... In this time Nicaragua's ladies of pleasure charge 10 cacao beans for services.

1541

Santiago is founded in Chile... Cartier undertakes 3rd voyage to New World, fails to settle Quebec... Orellano undertakes transcontinental journey across South America from Quito, emerges at mouth of Amazon later in year... Spain issues edict on debt repayment for Low Countries (makes previous purchasers of promissory notes liable if final owner defaults on promised payment)... Venetian starts mirror factory in Antwerp... Bruges opens training school for poor children.

1542

Juan Cabrillo explores Pacific Coast of Lower California, followed by search along California Coast to Oregon by Bartolome Ferrelo in 1542-1543... A brewery operates in Seville... Spain bans enslavement of Amerindians... Small Portuguese vessel trading with China is driven off course by typhoon to a strange island in the East (makes Antonio da Mota first European to land in Japan, introduces muskets).

1543

Nicolaus Copernicus: Revolutionibus Orbium Coesestium proscribed in Church Index from 1616 to 1822... Navigator Blasco de Garay submits steamboat design to Charles V, Holy Roman Empire... Using technology of clergyman William Levett, England makes cast iron cannons in Sussex for war with France, some 50 other ironworks by 1550... W. Stumpe acquires unused buildings of Malmesbury Abbey for looms, followed by unsuccessful 1546 plan to employ 200 textile workers in vacant Osney Abbey... France sends Sieur de Roberval to find strait to Asia... Spain starts annual convoys to New Spain, Peru.

1544

In this time Antwerp schoolmaster Jan Ympyrn publishes bookkeeping manual in English, based on 1494 treatise of Luca Pacioli... Guild of Clockmakers forms in Paris, followed by Nuremberg 1565, Bois 1600, Geneva 1601, London 1631, Copenhagen 1755.

1545

England's Henry VIII confiscates property of guilds... Hansa moves post at Bruges to Antwerp... Spain's Pedro de Medina writes pioneering book for pilots... First silver in Cerro Rico do Potosi is discovered in Upper Peru, acquired by Bolivia later (produces almost 50% of world's silver in 1570-1620, operates mines with some 13,000 workers by 1650)... Cosmo I starts tapestry factory in Florence... Copper is made in Cuba... England passes usury law to set 10% as maximum legal rate of interest, followed by 10 more laws by 1850 and repealed in 1854... Geronimo Cardano: De subtilitate rerum (describes first universal joint)... Bremen founds world's oldest continuing charity for benefit of sailors.

1546

English government forms Navy Board, replaced by Board of Admiralty in 1832-1964... Florentine geographer Mercator holds that earth has magnetic poles... Attempts to find El Dorado in Venezuela fail... Niccolo Tartaglia: Quesiti (uses mathematics to resolve practical problems)... Lyons, Toulouse form exchanges.

1547

French replaces Latin as official language of France... Revolts are seen in Genoa, Augsburg by populace, artisans against banking plutocracies, fail... Ivan IV, the Terrible, is Czar of Russia (-1584, decrees anyone found selling breeding stock to foreigners will be beheaded)... Edward VI rules England (-1553, approves Weavers Act to restrict entry, set standards and regulate work methods, confiscates properties of monasteries and guilds - transferred to court favorites, courtiers for investment of their new wealth in commercial undertakings).

1548

First roofed theater opens in Paris... Royal edict bans performance of "mysteries" in Paris... Portugal closes silver factory in Antwerp (ships new silver supply from Peru to India instead of Northern Europe)... Portugal appoints commissioner of finances, chief justice for Brazil... Thomas Gresham establishes seven professorships in London (leads to formation of University of London in 1828)... England's Chantries Act abolishes religious guilds... Portugal's new commissioner for finance ships silver from Peru to India instead of Northern Europe.

1549

England legalizes enclosures... Thomas Smith: Discourse of the Common Weal of this Realm of England (discusses favorable balance of trade)... When feudal hereditary captaincies prove unsuccessful in governing Brazil, Portugal appoints Thome de Souza as first governor-general (founds Sao Salvador, renamed Bahia later)... Spain creates New Granada, South America, with Santa Fe (Bogota) as capitol... Riots against land enclosures are seen in several English counties, results in some 3,500 killed... Court jesters appear in Europe... England recruits Venetian glassmakers, ordered to return by Venice in 1550.

1550

Beretta family's arms business of Brescia, founded late 1520s to make crossbows, gets order from Venice for blunderbusses (evolves as Fabberica d'Armi by 1980s as world's oldest family business with 13-generation dynasty, sues GM in 1988 for $250 million for trademark infraction in use of name)... Acapulco appears on Pacific Coast of Mexico, becomes port for exchanging annual ships with Manila... Alsatian mine uses wooden rails in this time for hauling ore by horse or man in heavy trucks... Water garden is built at Tivoli outside Rome (uses ideas of Hero of Alexandria to operate automata powered by water and air pressure)... Sealing wax appears in this period... Spain sets standard weights and sizes for common items carried on Indies run, average turnabout of fleets is 14-15 months... South American rubber is shipped to Europe (-1600)... G.D. Rhaeticus prepares trigonometric tables... In this time (-1559) 4-wheeled carriage of Europe appears in London... German mining engineers in Harz Mountains build complex set of dams, water reservoirs and canals to generate power for deeper mines... African slaves are shipped to Brazil to work sugar plantations of Bahia, used generally by estates as work force of 60-100 - over 200 slaves the exception... Dutch develop boyer ships, sturdy, lighter and cheaper with less crew, for commerce, replaced by fluyts in 1590s... Castile merchant house of Ruiz of Medina del Campo is formed (after trade in Breton linens, diversifies in spices, grains by 1597 for acquisition of wealth)... Russia's Ivan IV issues decrees in this time to forbid peasants, traders, artisans in moving from their residences (issues ban to prevent serfs leaving estates to earn more money from boyers, monasteries)... Some 12,000 professionals, 500-600 workers are employed in Tyrol mines of Schwaz, Falkenstein in this time... Tobacco is grown in Spain... Brazil hosts five sugar plantations, 350 by 1623.

1551

Some 200 German miners are employed to reopen silver and lead mine in Spain... For first time England licenses ale houses, taverns... National University of Mexico is founded, first in New World... Bank of Palermo opens... Pope Julius III gives Portuguese Crown complete spiritual jurisdiction over its conquests... 1447 London Grammar School, one of oldest in City, is acquired by Mercers' Company as school for poor boys (-1859, in 1804 provides commercial education for professionals, middle classes)... First large shipments of Mexican silver are sent to Spain... Codorniu, claims to be world's largest sparkling wine producer in 1980s, is founded (produces Spain's first sparkling wine in 1872)... John Dee, mathematician, alchemist and astrologer, begins to train English navigators (-1580s).

1552

Spain grants charter for trade with Portugal to Bristol's Society of Merchant Ventures... Church officially prohibits practice of usury... Parliament forbids use of gig mill to make fabrics... Gilbert van Schoonbeke starts brewery in Antwerp, grows to operate 24... French company is formed, Marseilles, to trade with Barbary Coast... English wood stove is used in this time as brazier for burning fuel, follows use in China since 600 B.C. and first wood-burning cast-iron stove in France in 1475 (evolves with first colonial stove in 1642, MA, and development of enclosed fireplace by 1702)... Golf is played at St. Andrews, Scotland.

1553

Mary I is Queen of England (-1558, sponsors new Book of Rules in 1558 to increase customs receipts by 75%, initiates financial reforms and reorganization of Exchequer)... Company of Merchant Adventurers, later renamed Muscovy or Russia Company, is formed by Duke of Northumberland, some 200 London merchants with monopoly to explore North, Northeast and Northwest for passage to India (is created as regulated enterprise with activities of members prescribed by rules and each free to invest own capital, makes S. Cabot first governor, sponsors 1st voyages of Hugh Willoughby to Northeast, lost at sea, and Richard Chancelor who reaches

Archangel, Moscow before returning to England in 1555 after acquiring previous monopoly of Hanseatic League from Ivan IV to trade in arms, woolens, and manufactured goods for Russia's furs, hemp and tallow, issues shares in 1564, continues in business to 1917 after monopoly ends in 1698).

1554

Saxony puts mines under state supervision... Spain's king engages factor Francisco Duarte to make arrangements for royal fleet to take King to England, required to account for all sums spent (evolves by 1600 with purveyors provisioning royal armadas)... Portuguese found Sao Paulo, Brazil (open first school in Brazil)... Schoonbeke invents new water pump for brewery, chased from Antwerp by irate citizens when local businesses lose water supply... Constantinople's first coffee house opens, seen in Italy in 1580, England in 1650, Marseilles in 1671 and Paris 1672.

1555

English expedition completes voyage to Africa (returns to London with 400 pounds of gold and 250 ivory tusks, leads to investments in African trade by Queen Elizabeth in 1561)... Spanish navigator Juan Gaetano sights Hawaiian Islands, neglected until Cook's landing in 1778... England charters Muscovy Company... France, Turkey sign commercial treaty... Spain starts two annual convoys to New Spain, South America... French colony settles at Rio de Janeiro, taken over by Portugal 1565-67... Cargo shipped from Portuguese India to Europe is insured in London... New World ships first tobacco to Spain... Parliament passes Weaver's Act (allows clothiers to work only in towns and places where clothing had been made for 10 years, prevents county clothiers to use more than one loom, to hire out looms to others)... Parliament founds Watermen and Lightermen of the River Thames Company to license all boat operators on the river.

1556

Stationers' Company of London gets monopoly for printing in England, incorporates 1557... Ferdinand I forms military council for German possessions of Hapsburgs... Muscovy Company sends Stephen Burrough, crew of 8 to find Northeast Passage... Akbar is ruler of Mogul Empire in Northern India (-1605, forms imperial service with officials ranked by number of imaginary horsemen they command, uses no rules for selection, promotion and functions, finances government by rents from peasants - no ownership as peasants only inherit right to till the soil, centralizes collection of revenues - single tax on 1/3 of farm's output)... After abdication of Charles I, Philip II rules Spain, Netherlands (-1598, considers proposal by Baltasar de Rios to build large cannon that can be dismantled, transported in parts)... George Bauer (physician in mining area of Saxony): De re metallica (covers mining, metallurgy and diseases of miners, identifies water as one of main reasons for abandoning mines, describes series of suction pumps used to raise water from 600 feet when force pumps and Archimedes' screws are ineffective, illustrates machines, methods to hoist, crush and transport ore and shore walls).

1557

Spain repudiates its debts, again 1560, 1575, 1576 and 1596... England passes laws to protect artisans, evolve as tenants to rent use of tools to others, work in their own houses because of unfair competition by textile manufacturers who employ journeymen, unskilled workers doing specialized tasks in workshops... China allows Portuguese to start colony and factories with warehouses and offices on Macao (-1597, restricts Portuguese to foreign compound in 1573)... Cardan: De Rerum Natura (mentions power of steam, method to produce vacuum by condensing steam - also cited by Matthesius in 1571)... Muscovy Co. opens rope house in Russia with English craftsmen to make cordage.

1558

Hamburg Exchange opens... Portugal introduces snuff to England... Anthony Jenkenson, chief factor for Muscovy Company, takes overland trip from Moscow to Cathay (visits Bokhara, Samarkand on trip, ventures down Volga in 1562 to visit Persia)... Lorenz Meder: Handelsbuch (cites Nuremberg's growth as European trading center)... Venetian Nicolo Zeno draws map of New World, based supposedly on ventures of ancestors in 1380 (is used by later expeditions of Forbisher, Davis)... Giambattista Della Porta: Magia Naturalis (discusses magnetism, optics of magnifying glasses and camera obscura, hydraulics, statics, pneumatics)... Elizabeth I is Queen of England (-1603, issues grants for special industrial privileges to partnerships, companies to start formation of joint stock organizations as legal entities, appoints William Cecil as Secretary of State, later Lord Treasurer, to encourage entrepreneurs to make capital investments and manufacture munitions, grants monopolies in iron, oil, vinegar, coal, lead, saltpeter, starch, yarns, skins, leather and glass, recruits foreign workers in metallurgical trades to work in England, preserves forests for shipbuilding industry, promotes cultivation of flax, hemp for making canvas, and insists Protestant England eat fish on Fridays).

1559

Spain regulates insurance in Low Countries, codified in 1569... London poster advertises fares for public transport between City, Gravesend... Spain attempts to start garrison at Pensacola, FL (-1561 when rescued)... Ferdinand I tries to standardize coinage in Holy Roman Empire.

1560

Puritanism appears in England (-1660)... In this time hiring-fairs appear in small towns, villages of Lower Normandy... Porta suggests use of steam to create vacuum so air pressure will force water in mines up a pipe, used in 1615 by de Caus for steam-driven fountain to operate like steam kettle in removing water from mine shaft... Academia Secretorum Naturae, Europe's first scientific society, forms in Naples, followed by others in Rome 1603, Florence 1657, London 1662, Paris 1666 from informal meetings in 1631-38, Berlin 1700, Uppsala 1710... Porta devises camera obscura... Pieter Breughel: "Children's Games" (shows members of painting in some 80 activities: dolls, jacks, masks, swings, marbles, king-of-the-mountain, mumbledy-peg, leapfrog, etc.)... England reforms currency with gold's value based on value of silver... Gene Nicot, France, imports tobacco... In this time (-1569) Huron mystic Degangwida, Mohawk disciple Hiawatha create Iroquois Confederacy with vision to establish "Great Peace" by combining warring Five Nations of Oneida, Mohawk, Onondaga, Seneca, Cayuga (-1700s)... Thomas Gresham warns England's Queen Elizabeth that bad money drives out the good... France, Portugal repudiate their debts.

1561

Philip II of Spain orders no further attempts colonize Florida... England hires German to instruct subjects in art of making saltpeter... Near East exports first tulips to Europe... After existing in corporate form since 1376, Borderers' Company of London receives first charter... Madrid is Capitol of Spain.

1562

France sends Jene Ribaut to start colony in Florida, fails... French Catholics in Vassy massacre Huguenots, starts religious wars in France (-1598 with Edict of Nantes)... France starts Charlesfort, SC, abandoned... Parliament's act on apprenticeship sets term of service as 7 years, ratios of journeymen to apprentices and qualifications for apprenticeship... John Dowland, Irish composer (pioneers popular songs), is born (-1626)... W. Kendall receives 20-year monopoly to mine alum in England (develops Isle of Wight mine in 1566)... Scotland grants Italian exclusive rights to make salt... Peking law allows compulsory labor of craftsmen to be redeemed by payment of money...

England makes witchcraft a capital offense.

1563

French Protestants start Ft. Caroline in North America, visited in 1565 by John Hawkins to pick up first tobacco from North America (is destroyed by Spanish in 1565)... To reduce English dependence on French imports, Lord Cecil invites German financier from Augsburg to England to develop manufacturer of white salt... Venice petitions Portugal for right to trade with East via Red Sea... Holland codifies maritime laws (covers ships using shares for joint ownership, discusses use of managing director and bookkeeper in handling ship's enterprise)... Italian Protestant Acontius moves to England (introduces idea of patents for monopolies, used at first to require users of foreign inventions to hire, train number of English workers)... England enacts Statute of Artificers to set regulations for all workers between 12 and 60, not otherwise employed, as servants in husbandry (allows impressment of youths refusing apprenticeship, allows only sons of weavers, freeholders to be apprentice weavers, prevents anyone below rank of yeoman to withdraw from agricultural work, requires 7-year apprenticeship for practicing trades, provides regulation of wages by local magistrates - penalties for employers paying higher rates)... Book cites first known use of word "architect" in English instead of master mason... Plague sweeps Europe, some 20,000 deaths in London alone... Russia uses first printing presses, first printed book in 1564.

1564

Horse-drawn coach appears in Holland... Work is started in building Tuileries in Paris... Spain starts conquest of Philippines (-1575, founds Manila)... Armed fleet is sent to Spain with gold bullion from Mexico, Panama (is first of two annual convoys)... Newcastle exports less than 33,000 tons of coal, over 450,000 tons by 1634... In trade war with England, Spain confiscates English ships, each embargo the other... England starts factory at Emden... Merchant Adventurers get new charter... Lord Cecil invites some Germans from Tyrol, one a partner in Augsberg firm of merchant financiers, to prospect for copper (recruits 30-40 German miners in 1565 to work discovered mine)... With available iron ore and wood for charcoal, George Talbot, 6th Earl of Shrewsbury, starts blast furnace on vast estates in West Midlands, followed by steel plant in 1590s at Sheffield as 3rd recorded in England... England grants Royal Charter to Society of Merchant Venturers to export cloth to Netherlands, follows organization of Merchants of the Staple exporting raw wool to Calais in Middle Ages, cloth merchants exporting to Antwerp since 1442, and regulated company of merchants in 1515... Augsburg allows clockmakers to form their own guild, granted authority to select apprentices and inspect quality of work of members... Graphite is discovered in Cumberland area of England, used in invention of graphite pencils and erasers in 1700s.

1565

Spanish expedition founds St. Augustine in Florida, then captures France's Ft. Caroline - San Mateo recaptured by France 1568 (becomes first permanent settlement of Europeans in North America - burned by Drake in 1586, is used as base for locating forts and missions along Atlantic Coast to Carolinas)... Antwerp magistrates claim that only they are capable of writing contracts, notaries the custom in Italy... Violent winds in Labrador's Red Bay, site of industrial complex for Basque fishermen hunting whales 1540-1610, capsize Basque galleon, perhaps the San Juan (is built with prefabricated frames for faster, stronger construction)... In order to develop England's brass industry, Lord Cecil authorizes search for colamine ore, discovered by foreign miners in 1566 (forms Mineral and Battery Works in 1568 to work the mine, is attacked by local inhabitants in 1576 for using too many trees for charcoal)... John Hawkins introduces sweet potatoes, tobacco to England... Dutch establish trading posts on Russia's Kola Peninsula, start Archangel post in 1578... Spanish expedition visits Monterey, CA... In this time bachelor Georg Roll opens clock shop in area of Augsburg, opposed by Augsburg clockmakers as guild rules stipulate only married men can enter business and train apprentices... Guild of cutlery engravers is granted English monopoly for making mathematical instruments, disputed by foundry guild when brass is used... Pencils are manufactured in Europe.

1566

Spain makes Santa Elena capitol of La Florida (-1587 when abandoned for St. Augustine after Drake's raid)... Vienna publishes newspaper, one of first in Europe... When their complaints against taxation, religious restrictions are rejected by Spain, Dutch nobles form an association of Sea Beggars (starts independence movement, achieves de facto freedom in 1609 - de jure 1648)... Muscovy Co. establishes trade route through Persia to Orient... Parliament approves Lords of the Salt Privilege... In this time (-1571) Gresham erects Royal Exchange, large building with many shops, as meeting place for merchants, bankers (is modeled on Antwerp's Bourse)... Rouen, Cologne open exchanges... Camillo Torello patents first European seed drill in Venice, some 1,700 years after use in China.

1567

Immigrants Jean Carre from Arras, associate from Antwerp start glass-furnaces in England with 21-year patent... Alvaro ve Mendana de Neyra is first to explore Pacific Ocean from Peru (discovers Solomon Islands, assumed apart of Terra Australia as location of fabled mines)... Spanish reach Tennessee area... Catholic Church sells last indulgences... Despite opposition of Hanseatic League, England is granted 10-year commercial concession by Hamburg, breaks Hansa trade monopoly... John Weddington, England, publishes first bookkeeping text with Hindu-Arabic numerals... Old Curiosity Shop opens in London (still extant)... In this time Antwerp holds four annual major fairs... Queen Elizabeth grants Ralph Hogge sole right to export iron cannon... Some 30,000 people live in Amsterdam, 105,000 by 1622, 115,000 by 1630... Diego de Losada founds Caracas in Venezuela.

1568

Madrid sees its first public theater presentation... Bottled beer is invented in London... Company of London Bricklayers and Tylers incorporates... Jean Bodin: Reply to the Paradoxes of M. Malestroit (explains rise in prices)... Mercator devises cylindrical projection for charts... When English traders are killed in West Indies by Spanish, Queen Elizabeth impounds Spain's silver treasure safeguarded in England, borrowed by King Philip from Genoa banking houses for payment of troops in Holland... Charters are granted to Society of Mines, created to develop copper mines, and Mineral and Battery Works, created to operate copper and brass works, as first industrial joint-stock companies in England... Swiss artisan lists 90 different crafts, 826 listed by London firm of Pigot in 1826... Spain forbids captains-general of fleets to trade for themselves or others.

1569

Lyons registers some 552 merchants (indicates 10% import 30% of all goods, mostly raw materials for textile manufacturing)... Craftsmen at Venice's Arsenal strike to demand pay for work on Saturday afternoons... First English public lottery is held in London's St. Paul's Cathedral to finance port repairs... Mercator publishes world map.

1570

Jean de Beauchesne: Book Containing Divers Sorts of Hands (is first English book on handwriting for scriveners, scribes, clerks)... Earliest known music festival is held in Normandy... Nuremberg starts postal service... Ottoman Empire declares war on Venice... In this time Antoinne, Gilles Hermite form trading partnership in Marseilles (operate City's first business with Levant, trade with Barbary Coast to raise funds to issue maritime loans to shipowners, buy real estate)... Abraham Ortelius: Theatrum Orbis (is first modern atlas with 70 maps, shows Terra Australia with

New Guinea, New Zealand, Australia and Kingdom of Lokak to be northwest from Strait of Magellan)... Japan allows foreign ships to visit, Nagasaki named as port of entry... By this time some 60 sugar mills operate in Brazil, some 120 in 1585 and 350 in 1630... Water-powered paper mill operates in this time in China (uses water-power for sawmills in 1627, silk mills in 1780)... Thomas Sutton is Surveyor of the Ordinance for North England (acquires coal lease in 1583 as basis for acquired fortune - perhaps richest commoner in England on death)... Local lord Omura opens fishing village of Nagasaki to foreign trade, becomes Japan's greatest commercial port.

1571

Francis Willoughby starts iron works, England (is modernized 1590)... House of Commons forms first standing committees... First permanent London gallows are built at Tyburn, site for hawkers, vendors serving viewers of entertainment (-1783)... At Gulf of Lepanto in Adriatic Sea, Venice, Spain, Papal States defeat naval forces of Ottoman Empire (with disappearance of national fleets in Mediterranean, gives control of sea to Barbary corsairs, Italian and Dalmatian pirates, and privateers of Holland, England, Knights of St. John)... England promotes exports of grain, bans exports of wool... Spanish Netherlands puts trade embargo on England... Roman Catholic Church permits individuals to charge interest, maximum rate of 10%... Blacksmiths' and Joiners' Companies of London incorporate... Spanish missionaries settle Jamestown area, VA, massacred by Indians... Portugal starts trading factory at Nagasaki... Florence opens public library... Francis Drake starts first voyage of privateering against Spanish ships in Americas.

1572

After serving as Secretary of State (1550-), William Cecil is Lord Treasurer (-1598)... Philip Sidney of England makes grand tour of European capitols with Italian tutor and servants... Parliament forms governmental agency to administer poor relief program... Dutch use pigeons to carry messages during Spanish siege of Haarlem... Catholics slay over 10,000 French Protestants in massacre of St. Bartholomew... University of Bologna drops instruction of astrology, study denounced by Spanish Inquisition in 1582... Brandenburg allows great land-owners to expropriate their peasants.

1573

First German cane-sugar refinery is built at Augsburg... Spanish engineers build series of dams, 32 by 1621, and reservoirs at Potosi mines, Bolivian Andes, to supply power for stamping mills... Philip II of Spain issues Royal Ordinances for laying out of new towns in New World (requires grid system with main square for celebrations, market-place)... Port of Sakai is first in Japan opened as free market (encourages growth of craft guilds and merchant associations - official recognition in 1721)... Humphry Cole "devises" ship's log in this time to measure vessel's speed.

1574

Henry III of France visits Venice (sees Arsenal assemble, launch, equip one galley within one hour)... Portugal starts settlement of Angola (-1975)... Lazarus Ercker publishes book on mining techniques.

1575

Venice, Florence make first European imitations of Chinese porcelain... Georg Obrecht is professor of law at Strasbourg (advocates Kammeralism, economic philosophy which generally opposes guild monopolies and favors dense population, governmental regulations, efficient government administration)... William of Orange founds University of Leyden (uses first external board to oversee university, appoint faculty)... England builds Revenge, 450-ton model for future ships of Royal Navy after 1578, with lower lines (reduces fore-and-aft castles) and longer hull for speed, maneuverability... Paris, London and Cologne are estimated to have 300,000, 180,000 and 35,000 inhabitants respectively... Philip II repudiates rising debts of Spain to bankers of Nuremberg, Antwerp and Augsburg, forces Portugal, France and Spanish Netherlands into bankruptcy (is survived by Tucher family bank, Nuremberg, to present, leads to decline of House of Fugger and sack of Antwerp in 1576 by Spanish soldiers in mutiny over loss of pay)... Flemish Jan Sanders paints Christ chasing moneylenders from the temple... Child labor is abolished in Hungarian mines.

1576

James Burbage builds England's first permanent playhouse, joined by two other London theaters... Parliament prevents clothiers in several shires in acquiring more than 20 acres for their operations... Forestry regulations are established to protect trees in Harz Mountains for use as fuel in local charcoal furnaces... Martin Frobisher, Cathay Co., tries to find Northwest Passage (reaches Baffin Island and entrance to Hudson Bay, follows with 2nd attempt in 1577 to reach Hudson Strait)... Seville's House of Trade appoints chief gunner to train gunners for armadas... Denmark's King Frederick II builds observatory, Europe's first real science institute, for astronomer Tycho Brahe (uses tested precision instruments for observations, after King's death leaves Denmark in 1588 for Prague to become protege of Rudolph II, Holy Roman Emperor, selects Johannes Kepler, mystic, mathematician, astrologer and astronomer, as aide in 1600)... Oda Nobunaga builds Japan's first great castle, starts development of castle cities... Humphrey Gilbert: Discourse of a Discovery for a New Passage to Cathay, first written in 1566 on Northwest Passage as route to Asia.

1577

Portugal abolishes state monopoly of colonial trade... Queen Elizabeth charters Spanish Company with 20-year trade monopoly with Spain, Portugal... Government survey records some 24,000 alehouse-keepers, one for about every 142 inhabitants, in England... Hispano-Portuguese expedition goes to Africa with crew of 1.5 men/ton (-1578)... Drake in Golden Hind raids Spanish treasure ships in Pacific (-1580, explores California Coast, obtains spice cargo in Moluccas, returns with profits of 4,500% on investment).

1578

When Martin Forbisher's 3rd voyage with 15 ships fails due to weather in starting mining colony in area of Hudson Bay, patrons are forced to declare bankruptcy (discourages further attempts for a time to find Northwest Passage)... Queen Elizabeth grants Humphrey Gilbert a general patent "to inhabit and possess at his choice all remote and even lands not in the possession of any Christian prince" (flounders during storm on first voyage, fails in 1579 to start West Indies colony, fails to start small fishing colony on Newfoundland in 1582)... Walter Raleigh, half-brother to Gilbert, proposes two projects for colonization, Virginia and Guinea for precious metals, to England... Matteo Ricci starts mission to Asia (after stops at Goa, India, to 1582 and at Macao and Canton to 1589, arrives at Peking in early 1600s)... Russians cross Urals to start conquest of Siberia in 1581.

1579

Portuguese start trading post in Bengal... Thomas Gresham's will establishes Gresham College in London to provide public lectures on divinity, music, astronomy, geometry, physics, law and rhetoric (is site for development of Royal Society for the Advancement of Natural Sciences in 1645)... English Eastland Co. is chartered for trade with Scandinavian countries (exports cloth for naval stores)... Four annual fairs are started at Piacenza near Genoa, used as European clearing house for bills of exchange (-1622)... Surveyor Christopher Saxon publishes atlas with first accurate maps of England, John Norden's atlas is first with principle roads... Union of Utrecht establishes basis for Dutch Republic... William of Hesse hires Swiss clockmaker to build clock with hands for minutes and seconds, accurate within one minute/day... England withdraws privileges to Hansa merchants.

1580

Swedish law sentences any clergyman to death if caught three times in trading... England, Turkey sign first commercial treaty... Crowns of Portugal, Castile are united under one king (results in spread of Portuguese traders, merchants throughout Spanish America in years to 1640)... Raleigh introduces potatoes to England (despite some resistance to strange food are seen in France by 1660, Flanders by 1680)... Spain's Armada de Mar Oceano, usually 40-60 ships owned or leased by Crown, is divided into 3 squadrons to protect North Coast, Atlantic Gateway, Strait of Gibraltar... John Dee of England fails to find Northwest Passage... Venice imports Turkish coffee to Europe... Michel de Montaigne: Essais (describes fashion as "a mania which turns the head and makes a baboon of even the wisest")... To prevent over-crowding, London prohibits building new houses where none existed before within three miles of City gates... Private theater is built, Vicenza (-1584).

1581

In this time James VI of Scotland recruits skilled workmen from Low Countries to start textile manufacturing... Sedan chairs appear in England... Robert Norman, London compass-maker: The New Attractive (experiments with magnetized, unmagnetized needles to find errors of compass needles)... Galileo devises pendulum, first used in clocks in 1641... With rising use of wood by glassmakers, Parliament bans selling of trees within 22 miles of Thames, 4 miles of Sussex forest, and 3 miles of any coastline (passes laws in 1500s to restrict use of forests for Royal Navy shipyards)... William Strafford: Compendious or Brief Examination of Certain Ordinary Complaints of our Countrymen, pioneering work of English mercantilism... France, Turkey renew commercial treaty... Apothecaries' Chamber is created in Moscow to provide medical care by foreign doctors, evolves as Medical Chancellery of Peter the Great in 1689-1725... English merchant-adventurers form Levant Co. in this time in Aleppo to export spices to England (when English East India Co. provides cheaper spices in 1600s, imports London spices to Middle East, by 1626 makes greater profits on new trade route)... Spain forbids Portugal, source for spices to Northern Europe, to trade with Holland (results in Dutch trade with Turkey in 1590, East Indies in 1595, Japan in 1610, Siam in 1613).

1582

Royal Navy allots pay on basis of rank... Tour d'Argent is Paris' first hostelry... University of Edinburgh is chartered (grants town council right to govern institution)... After death of John the Elder and replacement with partnership by non-family associates, family firm of della Failles, Antwerp, operates on 10-year contract in accordance with stated interests... General Hideyoshi is new ruler of Japan, unifies country by 1590... Gilbert proposes to Crown to colonize millions of North American acres with feudal form of proprietorship, rejected by indifferent London merchants... London builds City's first waterworks.

1583

Gilbert claims Newfoundland for England with first colony... Toyotomi Hideyoshi takes Osaka (develops town as capitol and commercial center with free fairs, markets, no business taxes and licenses for foreign traders, becomes site for rice exchange)... First recorded life insurance policy is issued, England, on life of William Gibbons by 16 individuals... Elzevir family starts publishing business in Holland (-1712, is recognized as Europe's greatest publisher of inexpensive books with presses in Leyden, Amsterdam, Utrecht, the Hague and with agencies in major cities from Denmark to Italy)... Muscovy Co. sends Anthony Jenkinson on trade mission to India (-1591)... Ralph Fitch (returns with valuable information for English East India Co. to compete with Dutch in spice trade), John Eldred are sent by Levant Co. on trading expeditions to Mesopotamia, India and Persian Gulf (-1591)... Queen's Company of Players is formed in London... Thomas Smith: De republica Anglorum (discusses governmental administration in England).

1584

Richard Hakluyt: Discourse Concerning Western Planting (argues colony in North America would block Spanish West Indian trade, eliminate middlemen in West Indies, provide base for starting slave revolts in Spanish areas)... After death of Gilbert, Raleigh takes over 1578 patent (sponsors first voyage to explore Virginia Coast in 1584 - annexes Virginia, 2nd in 1585-86 with colonists to reconnoiter coast south of Chesapeake Bay - no settlement)... Portugal proposes forming a European pepper cartel to Venice, rejected... Dutch trading post opens at Archangel, Russia... Holland publishes The Mariners Mirrour, atlas of 45 charts for European coastlines.

1585

John Davis discovers Cumberland Sound in seeking Northwest Passage, follows with 2nd voyage in 1586 and 3rd in 1587... Bartholomew Newsam builds first English traveling and standing clocks... Maurice of Nassau, Prince of Orange, is captain-general of Holland, Zeeland (-1625, introduces discipline of drills to prepare troops for obedience and efficiency, forms forces in smaller tactical units for flexibility, and trains officers as professionals)... Amsterdam Exchange lists commodity prices ... Mendoza describes, first time in Europe, Chinese "system of examinations" for governmental offices, leads to use of recruitment competitions by France in 1791... Amsterdam publishes weekly price lists, used as commercial indices throughout Europe... After siege, capture of Antwerp, Spanish forces close port (results in Amsterdam evolving as new center for spice trade in Northern Europe and immigration of cotton workers from Antwerp to re-start industry in England)... Drake pillages Spanish cities in Caribbean, including Cartagena (causes Spain's credit rating to drop so low that money cannot be raised to pay Spanish troops in Flanders)... Allegorical German print portrays merchant in quest of profit, shows "Lady Luck" as determining factor in fate of all ventures (shows specialists of bookkeepers, cashiers, middlemen)... First fashion magazine appears in this time in Frankfort... Oxford University Press is established, commercial success after 1672... By law Japanese are ranked as samurai, farmers, artisans, merchants (-1587).

1586

Pope Sixtus V forbids practice of usury... Engineer Domenico Fontana oversees erection of Obelisk of 327 tons at Vatican, uses 40 capstans, 140 horses, and 800 workers... Reorganization of Muscovy Co. fails (forms new enterprise in 1593, is united later with East India Co.)... In this time Kabuki theater is started, Japan, when shrine maiden O-Kuni takes temple dancers on tour for profit (results in ban on women performers in 1692 when prostitutes imitate dancers, becomes popular in 1600s when commoners are denied access to No dramas for nobility)... England's Davis explores Western Greenland, fails to find signs of earlier Vikings.

1587

Diego Garcia de Palacio publishes first complete treatment of ship construction and design in Europe (gives detailed mathematical proportions for hull, rigging)... Hideyoshi issues edict for expulsion of Portuguese Jesuit missionaries, not enforced... Banco della Piazza di Rialto is founded, Venice... Drake captures Portuguese vessel San Felipe in Azores (finds fortune in Asian spices, silks, calico, indigo, ivory, gold, and silver)... Fuggers, Welsers send agent to Cochin, India, to represent their business interests (-1619)... Spain founds Quito in Peru... Krupp family history begins when bubonic plague refugee Arndt Krupe is granted membership by merchant guild of Essende (acquires real estate from those fleeing City for safety from plague, is followed by son Anton who becomes wine merchant and marries into wealthy family of gunsmiths - sold armaments during Thirty Years War of 1618-48, by Anton's grandson Matthias, as town clerk in 1648 acquires fortune from tax collections, by Matthias' grandson Friedrich, marries heiress in 1726, dies early, to become merchant of groceries and spices, by widow Helen in 1757 who develops fortune of some $1 million by acquiring coal mines, real estate and two iron works and supplying munitions in 1802 to Prussia in fighting French forces of Napoleon, and by her grandson Peter who starts iron foundry in 1811 but is bilked of fortune by two British investors offering to sell him British secret for making steel, closes works in 1815 after quarrels with partner, reopens in 1816, gets subsidy from Berlin in 1817 after threat to build plant in Russia, leaves business in 1824 after family feud, is replaced by son Alfred Krupp in 1826 to build modern enterprise)... Raleigh gets land and wine monopolies in New World (as advised by Hakluyts sends three ships with 112 colonists to settle Chesapeake area, lands at Roanoke Island instead, no trace of existence when Governor White returns in 1590 with supplies).

1588

Agostino Ramelli: Le Diverse et Artificiose Machine (shows drawings on pumps, mills, cranes, dams, automata, military bridges and machines)... Shah Abbas the Great rules Persia (-1629, builds new Capitol of Isfahan for one million people with covered bazaar, tradesmen in own quarters, with maze of shops, workshops, royal mint, royal caravansary, mosques, schools, baths and warehouses with revenues from silk trade and customs duties, lets Armenians dominate overland trade in luxury goods, i.e., raw silk)... English Guinea Co. is chartered... Spanish Armada, 20 great galleons, 44 armed merchant ships, 23 transports and 43 others with 8,500 seamen and 19,000 troops, is defeated by North Sea storms and English naval forces, 4 squadrons of 121 vessels plus 50 others, in first naval battle by only ships, guns... Timothy Bright: An Arte of Shorte, Swifte, and Secrete Writings by Character (is shorthand manual)... Venice rebuilds Rialto Bridge with shops.

1589

Richard Hakluyt: The Principle Navigations, Voyages, and Discoveries of the English Nation... John Browne, Bristol merchant: The Merchants Avizo (gives advice for business career)... Henry IV is King of France (-1610, stabilizes currency, reorganizes bureaucracy, builds roads, bridges, and canals, improves farming with science, protects industries with tariffs, sponsors 40 of 47 new manufactories, particularly those in pottery, glass and silk, reorganizes industry in corporate form with employers and employees, opposes restrictive policies of guilds)... Queen Elizabeth gives her jeweler a 10-year monopoly for making paper... Christopher Marlowe: "The Jew of Malta" (shows greed for wealth in drama)... Medici family gives festival with masquerade for wedding of Grand Duke Francisco to Joanna of Austria, carnivals by festive societies popular entertainment of time... Indians are replaced in Chile's mines by African slaves... London merchants petition Queen Elizabeth to send trading fleet to India, approved 1591... Nottingham clergyman William Lee invents semi-automatic "stocking frame" for knitting, denied patent by Queen Elizabeth I for fear of unemployment among hand-knitters (takes invention to Rouen, flees to Paris as textile workers view him as Protestant foreigner with dangerous device, after death is used in England by associates to develop nation's machine knitting industry, leads to 1758 hosiery frame of Jedediah Strutt, 1864 by machine of William Cotton to knit heels and toes).

1590

France grants fur monopolies to develop New France... John Hawkins, Lord Howard and Drake sponsor Chalham Chest, fund collected from seamen's wages, to provide care for injured sailors (-1814 when replaced by Greenwich Hospital Fund)... Horse-drawn trucks are pulled on rails in British coal mines (-1599)... Spanish book is first to describe game of draughts, first English book in 1756... First English paper mill is started, Dartford... Commedia dell' arte troupe appears in Northern Italy... Coal mining begins in Ruhr area... Stagenkunst system evolves in Europe to transmit power of water wheels over several miles to mine heads by network of pivoted field - rods (-1599)... Hideyoshi forbids peasants to bear arms and samurai to change masters (-1598, creates rigid classification of Japanese society with nobility, samurai, artisans, peasants and fishermen, and merchants at bottom)... English start trading post at Calcutta... William Segar: Book of Honor and Armes (notes: "Who without learning can conceive the ordering and disposing of men in marching, encamping, or fighting without arithmetic?")... Braunschweig's oldest guild, tailors, builds Garment House, Germany.

1591

Hardwick Hall is built with prolific use of glass in Derbyshire (-1597)... Trinity College opens in Dublin... F. Carletti finances his world voyage by trading goods from country to country... Edo's first commercial public bath opens... James Lancaster's trading expedition goes to East Indies to break Portugal's monopoly on spice trade, survived by only 25 on three vessels (-1594).

1592

Holland issues marine insurance policy, oldest in existence... Jan Huyghen van Linschoten, former clerk for five years to Goa's archbishop: Itinerary (reveals secret sea routes and sailing directions of Portugal to Indonesia)... Lucien Motte, provincial French merchant (obtains fortune from cloth trade, land mortgages with lesser nobility), is born (-1645)... New Levant Co. is formed by merger of Turkey Co. (1581) with Venice Co. (1583) to exercise trading monopoly with Ottoman Empire (-1821, exports tin, cloth for currents, wine, cotton, silk, spices)... Richard Johnson: The Nine Worthies of London (discusses proper conduct for new tradesmen)... Galileo devises crude instrument to measure temperature (-1596)... Portugal starts colony at Mombasa... Juan de Fuca discovers British Columbia... Holland uses windmills in this period to power mechanical saws (-1599)... English capture Madre de Deus, Portuguese carrack returning from India (astounds all by rich cargo, perhaps worth nearly 50% of all money in Exchequer, of gold and silver coins, diamond jewelry, pearls, amber, musk, ebony, tapestries, calico and valuable spices of pepper, cloves, mace, cinnamon and nutmeg).

1593

Sant' Ambrogio Bank opens, Milan... Earliest dated illustrated poster advertises a fire pump for sale.

1594

John Davis: Seamans Secrets (reports on existence of Northeast Passage)... Willem Barents, Cornelius Nay start first of 3 voyages to find Northeast Passage, search basis for lucrative Dutch whale, seal fisheries in 1600s-1700s (-1596)... Company of Far Lands is formed in Amsterdam by nine merchants to finance expeditions to Spice Islands, followed by five other trading companies sponsored by different Dutch towns in 1597-1602... England reaps poor harvests.

1595

First Dutch fleet, commanded by Cornelius van Houtman for Company of Far Lands, sails to Java (signs trade agreements with Bantam, starts colony, returns with 89 of original crew of 249 to break even on spice cargo)... Spain grants first Asiento to Portuguese contractor Reynel to supply 38,000 slaves to Indies in nine years, uses Asientos as patents to 1640... Spain sends 2nd expedition from South America to explore Pacific Ocean (discovers Marquesas Islands, is survived by only 100 of 378 members)... First new Dutch fluyts, efficient merchant ships with long hulls and flat bottoms, are built at Hoorn to replace bulky galleons (launches 80 by 1603 to make commercial vessels of England and Spain obsolete, develops highly mechanized ship-building industry in 1600s with wind-powered sawmills, wind-powered feeders for saws, blocks and tackles, and cranes, needs some 2,000 oak trees from 50 acres of woodland to build one ship)... John Davis devises back-staff as new navigational instrument to replace traditional cross-staff in measuring latitude, replaced by John Hadley's quadrant in 1740s... Holland starts first colony on Guinea Coast (establishes Gold Coast fort in 1637)... Holland discovers whaling fishery off Spitzbergen (-1599, learns harpooning from Basque fishermen, grants whaling monopoly to Northern Co. for 1614-1645).

1596

Robert Dudley finances voyage to Cathay via Straits of Magellan, all 3 ships disappear... Philip II repudiates debts of France in 3rd bankruptcy (bankrupts Bank of Genoa)... Dutch factory starts in Sumatra... Juan de Onate leads expedition from Mexico City to Santa Fe, Arkansas River, Colorado River (-1605, brings first sheep to area)... First water closets, invented by John Harrington, are installed in Queen's Richmond Palace... Tomatoes are introduced to England, considered at first to be poisonous... William Shakespeare: "Merchant of Venice"... Korean Admiral Visunsin builds world's first ironclad warship.

1597

Holland founds Batavia on Java... Buonaiuto Lorini, military engineer for Florence and Venice: Della fortificationi (shows use of cable railway to build fortress)... With pressure from Hansa, Holy Roman Empire bans English merchants, goods for treatment of Hanseatic League in London... Duke of Sully is superintendent of finance for France (-1610, stabilizes currency, balances budget, reforms taxation, economic policy, foreign trade, and agriculture, reorganizes bureaucracy, forces officials to return stolen goods, builds roads and bridges, plans canals, encourages business)... Printed bills of exchange appear in Amsterdam... English Muscovy Co. charters Dutch vessels, again 1598... English law permits transportation of convicted criminals to colonies... Francis Bacon: Bacon's Essays (discusses "Of Negociating")... Grand Duke of Florence grants permission to printer Gigli to publish weekly commercial bulletins (prints first regular newspaper advertising)... England convicts two goldsmiths for putting false marks on wares, nailed to pillory by their ears... Marrano Jews from Spain, Portugal start synagogue in Amsterdam.

1598

Philip III of Spain exercises closer control over building industry to bring private construction in line with public needs (revives ailing industry)... Holland sends, every year on average, 25 ships to West Africa, 20 to Brazil, 10 to East Indies, 150 to Caribbean (-1605)... To end religious wars King Henry IV of France issues Edict of Nantes (grants political equality to Protestant Huguenots, revoked in 1685)... Peter Paul Rubens joins Antwerp painters' guild... Hanseatic League closes London Steelyard... After Dutch fleet is dispersed by storm, one ship, navigated by Will Adams of England, lands on Japan (after settling there, provides knowledge of shipbuilding, navigation to Japanese)... Company of Far Lands sends 2nd fleet of eight ships to Bantam on Java, Spice Islands (shows profits of 100-400%)... Dutch take Mauritius... Chamber of Assurance forms in Amsterdam to register insurance policies... Mechanical sawmill, invented in late 1500s, is operated in Amsterdam with 20-year monopoly... Onate conquers New Mexico under royal patent (-1608, establishes base for expeditions to explore from Kansas to Gulf of California, is re-conquered 1696 after Indians revolt in 1680)... Spain, Siam sign treaty of amity, commerce... Spain's Philip III offers princely reward to "discover the longitude," no winners... Cornelius Drebbel, Holland, patents timepiece using barometric pressure.

1599

Shakespeare, others of Lord Chamberlain's Men form syndicate to build, operate Globe Theater in London (-1613, reopens 1614-42, is destroyed by Puritans in 1644)... Disgusted with high prices of Portuguese pepper monopoly, 80 London merchants meet to raise funds for voyage to East Indies (receive charter in 1600 with 15-year trade monopoly, fund first expedition in 1601 to Table Bay, Madagascar, Sumatra to net 95% on investment, greater profits on voyages in 1604, 1607)... Germany sets first postal rates... Scottish Convention decides that a burgess of any town can sell goods to a freeman of any borough without having to make first offer to fellow townsmen... First cited Chamber of Commerce appears in Marseilles, U.S.' first by New York in 1768... Hideyoshi dies after completing unification of Japan.

1600-1699

General Events

Punch & Judy shows, derived from masques, are popular entertainment in Europe... Gunpowder is used in mining... Yakuza, modern Japan's Mafia of 3,100 clans with 86,000 members, evolves as young men form gangs to protect hamlets, villages from unemployed samurai roaming the countryside... Adding, subtracting are done as vertical calculations... Croquet appears as lawn game in France... Wigs, dress trains are European fashions... Chinese use rickshaws for transportation... Maurice of Nassau reduces massive military formations to 8-10 ranks (-1625), 4-5 ranks by Duke of Marlborough in early 1700s and 2 ranks, sometimes, by Napoleon in early 1800s... Quartermaster, formerly petty naval officer to load and unload ships, appears as army position, starts formal growth of military staff (evolves as rank of "quartermaster general" by 1701 to select, prepare camp sites with staff for marching army)... Pressgangs, used since medieval times, are used by English military to get recruits (-1815 for army and 1830s for navy)... Alkmaar cheese market appears in Holland, commercial buyers buy by Dutch auction (still extant)... France taxes distilled spirits (determines proof that liquid is at least 50% alcohol by mixing in and igniting it with gunpowder to produce steady blue flame).

1600

General Events

William Gilbert, physician to Queen Elizabeth: De Magnete (discusses magnetism, electricity)... After death of Hideyoshi and defeating rivals, Ieyasu Tokugawa rules Japan, starts Tokugawa period of centralized feudalism to 1867 (is shogun in 1603, expels missionaries in 1603, moves Capitol to Edo in 1603, establishes Ginza area for mint in 1612-1800, provides free business sites to develop City as commercial center - bills of exchange used between Osaka and Edo, is succeeded by son after "retirement" in 1605)... Some 400,000 live in Paris, 500,000 in 1700 and 550,000 in 1800, while London has 200,000, 575,000 and 900,000... Queen Elizabeth charters (December 31) The Governor and Company of Merchants of London Trading into the East Indies, known as East India Co. (-1858 when dissolved by Britain after 1857 Indian Mutiny)... A discovery is made in this time that fruit can be preserved in sugar, used to make jam before 1730.

Business Events

Amsterdam Bank opens... First endorsed bill of exchange appears, Naples... English, Dutch East India companies destroy Portuguese forts in Malaysia (-1602)... Sweden recruits Belgian workers prosecuted for religious beliefs (-1607).

1601

General Events

Dutch fleet circumnavigates world... Japan adopts official monetary system (bans Chinese copper coins in 1608, adopts standard coinage in 1636)... Germany, France sign postal agreement... Parliament's Poor Law, basis for relief programs in England, U.S. for over 200 years, covers recipients, employment of able-bodied poor, almshouses for unemployables, apprentice programs for children, taxes for funding, localities responsible for needy... Henry IV of France borrows factory of Gobelin family of dyers to weave tapestries (recruits some 200 weavers from Flanders)... Battista Porta: I Tre Libri de Spiritali (describes machine to raise column of water by steam pressure)... England passes first insurance law... John Wheeler, secretary of Merchant Adventurers, notes merchant should be aloof, not aggressive in treatise on commerce... Itakura Katsushige is magistrate of Kyoto, responsible for order in city (oversees licensed quarter with sake shops and brothels, some with branches in Edo).

Business Events

Dutch vessels visit Siam, start pepper factory in 1602... John Lancaster leads first expedition of English East India Co. to Spice Islands (-1603, returns from Moluccas with 1 million pounds of pepper)... London gentlemen get monopoly to make pipes and sell tobacco, some six retail outlets in city by 1610.

1602

General Events

Spanish traders are admitted to Japan... Sebastian Viscaino, Martin Aguilar explore Pacific Coast of North America to San Francisco in seeking fabled City of Quivira (plan to settle Monterey Bay, never implemented)... Venetian Board of Trade's report cites undesirable control of shipping in area by foreigners... Portugal hangs two Dutch traders trying to start trading post at Surat... John Willie: The Art of Stenographie.

Business Events

Holland's United East India Co. is formed by Dutch Protestant grain dealers, "Old Sea-Beggars," to eliminate competition among themselves and finance stronger competition with England, Portugal as an amalgamation of companies of various cities, Amsterdam last in 1595 (is "first" public joint stock company, gets 21-year monopoly for Asian trade, averages dividends of 18% in 1605-1614 and 3-75% before 1792 bankruptcy, operates with 17 directors, Amsterdam dominates, from six cities - each responsible for its share of costs and supplies, gets political, commercial and military powers, provides limited liability to subscribers of shares, puts posts at Bantam 1602, Macassar 1613, Sumatra 1615, and Persia 1616, seizes Malacca in 1641, expels Portuguese from Ceylon 1638-58, operates by 1669 with 150 ships, 40 warships, and 10,000 soldiers)... Dutch, English trading posts appear in Siam, England out in 1623 (leads to Dutch monopoly in 1664-1680s when displaced by French)... English trading post opens at Bantam, Northwest Java... Amsterdam starts exchange market... Newspaper appears in Germany, Holland 1616 and France 1631.. Amsterdam chamber of United East India Co. uses four committees to sign crews, buy supplies, procure ships and get merchandise (forms Court of Directors in 1602, committee in 1606 to process financial data, and correspondence committee in 1649).

1603

General Events

Go Academy appears in Japan to teach students Chinese game of strategy (still extant)... James VI of Scotland is James I of England (-1625, fails in 1610 to reform royal finance with Great Contract to rationalize revenues)... Accademia dei Lineei, early scientific society, appears as informal group in Rome (collapses after Galileo's persecution by Inquisition in 1632)... In this time Armenian merchants in Persia are confined to Julfa, suburb of Isfahan, by Shah (spurs extensive world traveling by Armenian traders)... Henry IV of France sends expedition, Samuel de Champlain cartographer, to explore St. Lawrence, New England coast (-1607, returns with beaver skins, tales of vast lakes)... Galileo uses principles of Hero of Alexandria in this time to invent the thermometer... Court of the King's Bench: Darcy, Queen Elizabeth's groom granted sole privilege to make and import playing cards, v. Allen, London merchant who ignores monopoly (voids patent as encroachment upon freedom of Englishman to engage in trade of own choice)... Hugh Platt makes coke by heating coal.

1604

General Events

James I, England, condemns use of tobacco... Holland's Johann Lippersley, maker of spectacles (used in Pisa, Venice in 1300s for clerks transcribing manuscripts), invents telescope by 1608 (offers "looker" to Holland in 1608 for battlefield use, is used by Galileo in 1610), claim by Zacharias Janssen for 1604... Russia founds Tomsk in Siberia, reaches Pacific Ocean in 1638 with settlement at Okhotsk... Portugal forms Council of the Indies to govern Brazilian colonies (establishes centralized rule with feudal grants to nobles, appoints first viceroy in 1640, changes Council in early 1700s to Transmarine Council with religious, military authority over 9 provinces)... Holland captures Portuguese carrack, Catharina (introduces Chinese porcelain to Europe)... England, Portugal sign truce, no recognition given to England's claim to Asian commerce... France's Henry IV sells official positions to applicants to increase Royal revenues, buyers get tax payments for investments... England petitions Venice for trading rights, denied and Holland denied 1610... China denies trading privileges to Holland, again in 1607.

Business Events

Henry Middleton leads 2nd voyage of English East India Co. to Java, Moluccas... Dutch East India Co. drives Portuguese out of Tidore, Amboina islands in Moluccas (continues with attacks on Malacca, repulsed by Portuguese in 1605, and on Portuguese clove port in Moluccas in 1607, repulsed by Spanish ships)... Company of Musicians incorporates in London.

1605

General Events

Spain sends 3rd expedition from South America to explore Pacific Ocean, discovers Northern New Hebrides in 1606... First public library in Rome opens... First permanent theater in Germany appears... England colonizes Barbados, West Indies... Willem Janszoom from Bantam, Java, explores New Guinea (sights coast of New Holland, Australia, in 1606)... Franciscan friars, some 50 friars in 90 villages by 1630, and Mexican settlers, seen in Tucson 1700, Albuquerque 1706, San Antonio 1718, and San Diego 1769, start Santa Fe in Southwest America... George Weymouth leads English expedition to Maine coast to start Catholic colony (spurs formation of Plymouth, Virginia Companies in 1606).

Business Events

London charters companies of Pinmakers', Shipwrights'... London's Butchers' Co., first cited 1179 as guild and regulated in 1331, is chartered... First newspaper with regular editions, twice/month, appears in Amsterdam... Fruiterers Co., first cited in 1292, is chartered to inspect all fruit entering London, levy duties.

1606

General Events

England, France sign commercial treaty... Duke of Bouillon opens Academie des Exercises, early training school for military officers (follows those of Italy in 1500s)... Despite strong opposition from Portuguese, Kingdom of Golconda, just south of Mogul Empire, grants permission to Dutch to trade at Coromandel ports, permission to England in 1611... France starts extensive road building program... First Portuguese Jesuits visit Siam.

Business Events

Bank of St. George, Venice, uses bank notes payable in gold and silver... Society of Apothecaries and Grocers forms in London.

1607

General Events

Spain puts wage scale for shipwrights in ship regulations (in first rules for shipbuilding substitutes science for traditional art to build faster ships)... Emperor Rudolph II approves English factory at Stade... Jacob de Gheyn: The Exercise of Arms (in early motion study shows each sequential, standardized steps of military drill for arquesbusiers, musketeers, pikemen)... Spanish expedition of Luis Vaz Torres visits Philippines, a continuation of 1605 voyage by Queiros.

Business Events

Henry Hudson undertakes voyage to find Northeast Passage for Muscovy Co. (discovers Spitsbergen fisheries on 2nd voyage in 1608, becomes monopoly of Muscovy Co. in 1612 - lost in competition with Dutch, Danish fleets)... Bank of Genoa goes bankrupt after Spain's 4th bankruptcy... London Co. makes Thomas Studley its "Cape-Merchant," London agent for Virginia Colony's pitch, soap, iron ore, lumber and glass items... Beaune reforms courtier-gourmet to establish profession of wine masters, six masters by 1615.

1608

General Events

Ryther's London map shows Petticoat Lane street market... Society of Blackheath Golfers forms in London... Isaac van de Luck paints allegory of Danzig trade on Hanse Hall ceiling (shows grain being ferried up Vistula via connecting canal to Baltic port)... English traveler Thomas Coryate is cited for bringing fork from Italy to England.

Business Events

Champlain starts trading post at Quebec, opens fur trade route to Georgian Bay... "Cash Letters" are used in Holland for exchange of money... New bourse opens in Amsterdam, bourse for grains in 1616... Dutch start factory at Ayudhya, Siam... Hector, commanded by Captain William Hawkins for English East India Co., is first English vessel to reach India (lands at Mogul port near Bombay, is received by Emperor Jehangir despite strong protests of Portuguese, gets its first trading concession in India)... Bushmills whiskey, world's oldest, is distilled in Ireland... New exchange, named 'Britain's Bourse' by King James I, is built in London (-1609)... Livery Companies of London are virtually forced to finance plantations of English and Scottish workers in Ulster, pressured to support Virginia scheme in 1610.

1609

General Events

Lippershey and Janssen, perhaps in 1590, independently invent compound microscope... Holland is first in Europe to receive Siamese embassy... Hugo Grotius: Mare liberum (urges freedom of sea for Holland, pioneers international law)... France builds Briare Canal to Loire and Seine Rivers

(-1642).

Business Events

First weekly news sheet appears in Augsburg, irregular handout in Germany in 1505 (is followed by Vienna in 1610, Basel in 1611)... Cockpit Theater opens, London, for cockfighting... Amsterdam's exchange bank, Wisselbank, is first public bank in North Europe, appears to aid merchants to do business with each other, modeled on Bank of Venice (issues receipts for deposits to 708 depositors in 1611, 2,698 by 1701, is City's leading bank by 1614, gives credit in 1683 and loans to individuals in 1685 for 3-5%, 6% or more the rate in England)... Dutch trading post appears on India's East Coast, Ceylon in 1639 and Cochin in 1663... Japanese cinnabar guild gets monopoly for manufacturing, selling the mineral... English East India Co. lands at Surat, trading rights in 1612 (puts posts at Madras in 1639, Bombay in 1661, Calcutta in 1690)... Dutch open trading post in Japan... England renews charter of East India Co.

1610

General Events

One account puts invention of bagel in Cracow, Poland, another puts creation in 1683 by Austrian baker to honor King of Poland for defeating Turkish invaders... Jean Begin writes first chemistry textbook... Roland Vaughn: His Booke (describes artisan community to be formed in England)... Hudson leads English voyage to find Northwest Passage (-1611, reaches Hudson Bay, is exiled on raft by mutineers, tales of promised passage by returning mutineers leads to formation of Northwest Co., further expeditions)... Several hundred Marranen families, Jews of Portuguese and Spanish origin, live in Amsterdam (acquire wealth during 1609-1621 truce with Spain and in 1640s with Dutch West India Co. in Brazil).

Business Events

English farmer Robert Loder keeps account book (-1620, uses mathematical calculations to analyze results for different courses of action)... Isaac Le Maire, wealthy Amsterdam pearl merchant, starts Australian Co. to compete with Dutch East India Co... Dutch East India Co. is first to use term "share"... First cargo of Oriental tea to Europe lands in Amsterdam, France c. 1635 (although Dutch prefer stronger coffee drink tea after 1641 when Nicholas Tulpe, Amsterdam physician, states tea is remedy for almost all ills, import 20,000 lbs/year by 1685)... England charters Newfoundland Co... London's Spring Gardens with archery butts, bathing pond and pheasant yard is first cited for public pleasures (adds bowling green in 1629, garden house later).

1611

General Events

Seville is site of Spain's royal arms factory... Edward Zouch, partners patent English process to make glass without using wood (use furnace, probably designed by Thomas Percival, with coal as fuel)... Palermo vendor is sent to galley after selling goods over fixed prices... Gustavus Adolphus is King of Sweden (-1632, establishes free schools and universities, grants monopolies for foreign trade, encourages developments in metallurgy and mining industries, stabilizes government finances, reorganizes courts, postal service, hospitals, and poor relief, innovates in military field with transportation, training, discipline, regimental organization, integrated chain of command for infantry, calvary and artillery, chaplain and headquarters staff, uses linear tactics)... Dutch navigator discovers constant Westerly winds below Cape of Good Hope.

Business Events

Merchant Adventurers start post at Hamburg... With patent, follows idea in Montaigne's Of A Defect in our Policies in 1595, Georges Gorges and Walter Coke start "The Publicke Register for General Commerce" as bureau to advertise transactions in buying, selling, borrowing and hiring (-1612 when fails, leads to another patent to Captain R. Innys in 1637)... Plumbers' Co. of London, first cited 1365, is chartered... English East India Co. starts trading post on India's East Coast... English East India Co. petitions England for aid against Dutch after their insistence that its commerce in former Portugal territories was their exclusive right.

1612

General Events

Dutch build fort in Ceylon... Amsterdam encourages development of industries of silk finishing, cloth making, cloth dressing, leather gilding, glass blowing, salt refining, mirror making, shipbuilding (-1623, recruits foreign craftsmen, many French Protestants, as workers)... Simon Sturtevant: The Treatise of Mettallica (discusses art of invention and entrepreneurship, working of metal with coal)... English ships defeat Portuguese fleet at Surat, key port of Mogul empire (lets English East India Co. start trading station, first exports of cotton, indigo in 1614)... Serra: A Brief Treatise on the Causes Which Make Gold and Silver Abound in Kingdoms Where There Are No Mines, (is first systematic explanation of Mercantilism, genesis in 1500s)... Guild of Feltmakers forms in England... Hamburg State Lottery appears in this time, still extant.

Business Events

Sturtevant, German immigrant, gets exclusive rights from England to smelt iron ore with coal, patent voided for lack of use and rights go to protege of Prince of Wales who fails to develop process... Some 300 adventurers form Company of Merchants of London (sponsors 1612-13 voyage of Thomas Bulton to find route to Orient by Northwest Passage)... Somers Islands Co. forms to colonize Bermuda... Northern Co. is formed, each Dutch city represented by different chamber, with monopoly for whaling between Novaya Zemlya, Davis Strait... English East India Co. establishes formal relations with Ayudhya (starts British factory)... John Woodall is first surgeon general for English East Co.

1613

General Events

Denmark abolishes guilds for monopolistic tendencies, allowed 1621, regulated 1800 and abolished 1857-62... Seville's Seafarers Guild, shipwrights, owners and merchants, ask Spanish Crown to exempt current ships from 1613 regulations making merchant ships safer... Dutch settle Western Timor.

Business Events

Amsterdam Exchange opens... English buy cloves at Moluccan island of Ceram at much higher prices than offered by Dutch monopoly (within few years leads to Dutch factories on Malay Peninsula, Sumatra, Java, and Celebes).

1614

General Events

To stop export of undyed cloth to Holland for finishing, England bans export of white cloth (when

Holland prohibits export of finished cloth to England, ends ban in 1617)... To reduce air pollution Amsterdam forbids sugar refineries to use coal... In this time some 400 different currencies are circulated in Holland, 82 in France.

Business Events

Merchant Adventurers' Charter is revoked (-1617), replaced by King's Merchant Adventurers with members of Eastland, Levant companies... Two Dutchmen charter Danish East India Co. for expedition to Ceylon (leases port of Tranquebar on India's Coromandel Coast in 1620, sold to England in 1845, reorganizes in 1670)... Welser banking house declares bankruptcy.

1615

General Events

French gunsmith Le Bourgeoys invents flintlock musket, (is adopted by French Army around 1660, standard weapon of European armies by 1699)... King James I, England, bans use of wood to make glass... Holland makes Batavia, Java, headquarters for Dutch East India Co., renamed Djakarta with independence in 1949... Salomon de Caus: Raisons des Forces Mouvantes, first practical discussion of steam (builds steam device somewhat like Hero's invention)... Rubber appears in Europe, used successfully as commercial solvent in 1765... Guild of Pewterers forms, England, to regulate selling activities of members... Inigo Jones is King's surveyor of works, early English architect... English defeat Portuguese fleet off coast of Bombay... Holland seizes Moluccas from Portugal... William Baffin leads English expedition to find Northwest Passage, 2nd in 1616... Galileo is called before the Inquisition, prohibited in 1616 to continue scientific work.

Business Events

Merchants Adventurers Co. gets monopoly to export English cloth... Bank of Amsterdam grants commercial credit to Dutch East India Co... Three Liege merchants (leads to one, De Greer, to operate Swedish copper mines in 1619 - basis for Swedish munitions industry, and to get patent in 1627 to make iron cannon) start Amsterdam munitions business in this time.

1616

General Events

Holland, Japan sign commercial treaty... Portuguese Gaspar Boccaro travels up Zambezi River, early exploration of interior Africa... China expels Portuguese Jesuits to Macao, gradually return... Raleigh is released from Tower of London to lead expedition to Guiana in search of El Dorado (-1617)... Dutch are first Europeans to land on Australia in briefly stopping at westernmost part... Guild of pinmakers forms in England... Tired of Portuguese, Turkish domination of its silk trade, Persia welcomes first English East India vessel (leads to withdrawal of Portuguese in 1622)...

Business Events

Privy Council approves Company of Drapers, Herfordshire, to raise funds to make draperies (collapses when investors demand repayment of funds regardless of project's success).

1617

General Events

John Matier: Rabdologia (shows use of 'Napier's Bones,' devised 1614, to make logarithmic calculations)... Edo feudal lord petitions Tokugawa government to create area, known as happy field, in City for prostitutes (-1958, evolves as site for geisha guild).

Business Events

Apothecaries' Society of London, former members of Livery Co. of Grocers, gets its own charter... Rakoczi family acquires Transylvania estate to monopolize wines of area (acquires Tokaji castle in 1647 to develop Tokay wine as best in Hapsburg Empire.)

1618

General Events

Gian-Battista Aleotti builds Teatro Farnese at Parma, starts development of modern theater... Robert Fludd, English astrologer and alchemist, describes single-acting water-pressure engine, described by two French inventors in 1731, built successfully c. 1750 and used in Slovakia mines... England's James I issues Declaration of Sports (bans specific village pastimes, merriments and parish feasts for reasons of Puritanism)... David Ramsay suggests use of steam power to power ships (gets 30 patents)... Protestant Bohemians revolt against Catholic Emperor Ferdinand in Prague, starts Thirty Years War... Jean Tardin: Histoire naturelle de la fontaine qui brule pres de Grenoble (studies gas with distillation of coal)... English defeat Portuguese again to control trade with Mogul empire.

Business Events

Dutch West African Co. forms... Kawamura Zuiken, Edo coolie and entrepreneur (plans transportation network, builds canals, develops commercial trade business), is born (-1700)... English West Africa Co. occupies Gambia, Gold Coast.

1619

General Events

Adolphus forms Swedish Trading Co. with monopoly to market copper (-1627)... Duke of Saxe-Weimar proclaims universal education for all children from 6-12, universal education in Germany by 1719... Denmark sponsors expedition to find Northwest Passage.

Business Events

Copenhagen builds Bourse (-1625)... English Amazon Co. is chartered (-1623)... Giro-Bank is founded, Hamburg, to improve "desolate state of currency"... Dud Dudley, son of Lord Dudley, makes "good quality" iron with pitcoal (patents process in 1621, works ruined by flood and attacks by local iron makers)... Factory is built at Mortlake, England to encourage development of foreign industry, tapestries first introduced in area in 1560s by Flemish weavers... After years of skirmishing, Dutch and English East India Companies end hostilities (grants England 33% of Moluccan spice trade and 50% of Java pepper trade, provides expenses for Dutch forts and aid to Holland against Portuguese, Spanish)... For reasons of mismanagement, deficits and criticism by settlers, Thomas Smyth is replaced as head merchant of Virginia Colony by Edward Sandys.

1620

General Events

Currency inflation appears in Germany (-1623)... England's Privy Council orders study of land enclosures, 2nd in 1633... Oliver Cromwell is denounced for playing disreputable game of cricket... Francis Bacon: Novum organum scientarium (proposes idea for Royal Society, formed

1662)... John Evelyn pioneers new agricultural methods in Holland, is born (-1706)... Kingdoms of Upper Senegal, Upper Niger use salt as money in this time, other monetary forms in Africa: cotton cloth, copper bracelets, horses, coral, chickens, sea shells... Dutch-born Cornelius J. Drebbel tests submarine, cruises 15 feet under the Thames.

Business Events

Drebbel devises process to dye wool, silk... Liege ironworkers build new blast furnace in Sweden to increase iron production... Rotterdam's Beyerman is oldest foreign wine broker in Bordeaux... After family flees Omi Province in 1568 to escape victorious shogun, Sokubei Mitsui, unemployed samurai of noble Fujiwara heritage, opens provincial shop in decade to make saki and shoyu sauce, success with wife's pawn shop (is succeeded on death, 1633, by wife, Shuho, who trains sons; oldest goes to Edo to start drygoods shop - fails; Hachirobei, after training with older brother and opposing his loans to samurai, returns to home town in 1650 to become a moneylender).

1621

General Events

Philip IV of Spain licenses privateers... First potatoes are planted in Germany... Adolphus designs military system of court martial... Thomas Mun, director of English East India Co.: <u>A Discourse of Trade from England Into the East Indies</u>... Treatise on mechanics for weaving silk is published in Padua (describes weaving machine, secret stolen by England's John Lombe in 1716).

Business Events

English, Dutch East India Companies renew conflict... London's first periodical with news is published... Dutch West India Co. forms with 25-year monopoly for trade with Americas, West Africa (-1791, seizes Pernamubuco in 1623, battles Portugal for Brazil 1624-54, starts Fort Amsterdam on Manhattan Island in 1626, colonizes islands of St. Eustace, Curacao in 1634-35, Saba in 1640, St. Martin in 1648)... Englishman estimates 3,000 tons of spice bought for $227 in West Indies would sell for some $2 million in Alleppo.

1622

General Events

Some 56% of Holland's 670,000 live in medium-sized towns... Hamburg issues Mark Banko currency... Work ends in building Bruges-Dunkirk Canal... Papacy adopts January 1st as start of new year, replaces March 25th... Kyoto bans all merchant combinations, leads to regulations in 1629, 1657, 1684 to allow certain trade associations by artisans, traders, merchants, moneylenders, etc., for mutual protection and solidarity (admit members by inheritance, vacancy, bankruptcy of member, and apprenticeship, regulate prices, quality, credit and transfer of funds)... Nicholas Bourne, Thomas Archer publish <u>The Weekly News</u>, first newspaper in English (print first known ad, another in 1624)... Wealthy Liege foundry owner builds cannon factory on contract near Santander, Spain.

1623

General Events

English, French settlements appear on St. Kitts, English island in 1626... Professor Wilhem Schickard, University of Heidelberg, invents mechanical calculator (-1624)... England abandons East Indies after colonists at Amboina are slain (February) by Dutch... Consuls of Marseilles complain to French King about Armenian silk traders... Collegium Indicum is started, Leyden, to give Dutch students knowledge of Malay, Oriental religions... Cornelius de Witt, Dutch administrator (uses life-table sell annuities), is born (-1672)... Holland, Persia sign commercial treaty... England's Royal Proclamation forbids use of needle-making machine.... England starts fishing base at Gloucester, MA.

1624

General Events

England's Statute of Monopolies cancels all Royal monopolies, exempts patents for inventions, customary monopolies of towns or guilds, and legislative monopolies (establishes modern patent law in providing rights for limited period to inventor for new process or for substantial improvement of existing process)... Submarine is tested in Thames River, travels 2 miles... Home for destitute children opens, Stockholm, to train youth for work in textile mills, supervised by German master craftsmen... Louis XIII makes Cardinal Richelieu Minister of France (-1642, establishes trading companies, develops merchant marine)... English start first settlement in Eastern India.

Business Events

Dutch trading post appears on Formosa (-1625)... After Virginia Colony enters receivership, Crown takes control.

1625

General Events

Parliament grants taxes on tunnage, poundage to Charles I for one year... After periodic censuses in 1500s Spain requires registration of mariners... England forms Colonial Office to administer overseas activities... French settlement appears on St. Christopher, West Indies (forms Company of St. Christopher in 1626, forms Compagnie des Iles d'Amerique in 1635 to settle Martinique, Guadeloupe and govern West Indies colonies)... First fire engines in England are seen... France takes over Dahomey, inland kingdom in West Africa (-1892, uses coastal freeport in 1727 for palm oil and European slave traders, access to interior market of Africa controlled by tollhouses)... English colonists settle Barbados, Nevis in 1628, Antigua and Montserrat in 1632... By ordinance guilds of drapers, grocers, moneychangers, goldsmiths, haberdashers and furriers are formed in Paris (-1776)... Charles I is King of England (-1649, stops land enclosures in 5 counties, raises wages for textile workers, orders local magistrates to exercise better price controls, appoints commissioners to protect wage scales, supervises poor relief and coal monopoly, grants monopolies in soap, salt, starch, beer, wine and hides, balances budget, streamlines administration, reorganizes Privy Council with judicial and executive powers, advisory only by 1641).

Business Events

Danish West India Co. is formed with Dutch capital... Martin de Arana, Bilbao, signs contract with Spain to build six galleons (-1628)... Seville merchants offer Spanish Crown one-time subsidy in lieu of tax.

1626

General Events

England grants knighthoods to raise revenues for government... When Genoese bankers refuse aid for impending financial crisis, Hapsburgs arrange loan with syndicate of Portuguese Jewish bankers.

Business Events

Upholders' Co. of London, first cited in 1360, is chartered.

1627

General Events

Japan bans all foreigners (-1852)... English occupy Nova Scotia... Spain declares bankruptcy (suspends payments to creditors, issues devalued state bonds for short-term loans)... Spain inspects galleons being made by Arana for conformance to regulations... English students at Charterhouse are taught 'to cypher and cast an account' in preparation for trades... To prevent private merchandise being smuggled on English East Indiamen by crew, passengers for trading, Charles I lists allowed imports and exports... Richelieu forms Company of New France, given fur trading monopoly with title to all lands from Florida to Arctic... Charles I charters Guiana Co.

Business Events

Swedish South Sea Co. is formed... Haig & Haig distillery appears, Scotland, to make whisky.

1628

General Events

Richelieu forms Canada and Senegal Companies... Dutch take Java, Malacca... Shah Jahan is Great Mogul in Northern India (-1658)... British seize Acadia and Quebec, returned to France in 1632... Chinese Emperor abolishes country-wide postal service over post roads, begun by Mongols in 1200s, to save money.

Business Events

London's Makers of Playing Cards' Co. is chartered... After Dutch opposition, English East India Co. abandons factory at Batavia (moves spice trade to Macassar, Sumatra).

1629

General Events

Spain bases advancement for pilots (join with captains, masters to form nautical guild) on meritorious service, follows apprenticeship program in 1500s... French buccaneers start base at Tortuga off Hispaniola, soon used by pirates of all nationalities... Huguenots revolt in France, ends with Peace of Alais... Charles I dissolves Parliament (-1660, spurs immigration to colonies, some 65,000 to North America, West Indies in next decade and some 2.5 million, about 25% of population, by 1776)... Dr. Giovanni Branca: Le Machine (describes crude steam turbine to crush medicines).

Business Events

Portuguese send slave-raiding parties into Brazil's interior to get native workers for cotton, sugar cane and coffee plantations... Amsterdam company with monopoly for maritime insurance fails, opposed by merchants as proposed premiums more than expected profits (fails again in 1634)... Scotland makes William Claiborne agent for New England, Nova Scotia (trades in corn, furs, etc., starts Virginia trading post in 1631)... Worshipful Co. of Spectacle Makers forms, London (sets strict apprenticeship regulations, imposes fines for "illegally" made spectacles, smashes inferior glasses in public display on large stone).

1630

General Events

Total number of paid public officials of English Crown is under 2,000, some 50% are private domestic servants of King (-1639)... Benedetti Castelli proposes basic law for hydraulics, follows crude analysis of raw water power by da Vinci c. 1500 (leads to works by Evangelista Torricelli in 1640s, Christiaan Huggens and Edme Mariotte in 1666-70)... Jesuit priests discover Cinchoma plant, bark a source for quinine... Game of cribbage appears in England... Labor-exchange charity organization forms, Paris... Shah Jahan builds Taj Mahal, Agra (-1648)... Charles I grants patent to Ramsay for invention of steam engine to raise water from low places.

Business Events

Richard Dafforne opens London bookkeeping school... Public advertising appears in Paris... Abo merchant builds Finland's first private foundry, Antskog Iron Works (leads to land's 8 furnaces, 15 forges, 6 iron works by 1695, all destroyed in 1713-14 conflict with Russia)... In this time Masatomo Sumitomo, Buddhist priest, opens medicine shop/bookstore when sect dissolves while colleague Riemon Soga uses western technology to improve copper mining in Japan, genesis of modern Sumitomo Group (by 1693, with Soga's son in charge after marrying Sumitomo's daughter to combine interests, evolves as land's dominant copper enterprise, prospers with Besshi mine until mid-1800s when output declines).

1631

General Events

William Petty: Political Arithmetic (urges state regulation of economic policy)... P. Vernier, France, devises scale for precise measurements, caliper by U.S.' J. Brown in 1851... English mathematician, clergyman Oughtred devises multiplication sign... England sends two expeditions, London and Bristol, to find Northwest Passage... Hasan al-Din, Moslem, rules Celebes in East Indies (-1670, develops island as center for spice trade).

Business Events

After breaking away from Blacksmith Company, Clockmakers' Co. of London forms, Ramsay first guildmaster... Gazette de France appears.

1632

General Events

William Oughtred, Richard Delamain devise crude slide rule, modern slide rule in 1850 by French artillery officer A. Mannheim... Holland builds waterway with towpath, starts land's canal system... England bans export of grain without Royal License... Siena holds (July, August) bizarre horse race, each horse represents city district in public spectacle... English drive Portuguese out of Bengal... Jean Rey, French doctor, devises first liquid thermometer... Russian fur trade post appears at Yakutsk, Pacific Coast of Siberia... Nicholas Sanson publishes first systematic illustrations of roads on large-scale maps, first map with roads by John Morden in 1592, in French post-road atlas... Galileo Galilei: Dialogue Concerning the Two Chief Systems of the World, the Ptolemaic and the Copernican, first scientific treatise in modern Italian (is on Index of Prohibited Books until 1822).

Business Events

Dutch merchants Andries Winius and Peter Marselis (starts Russia's copper industry later while Swedes start paper, glass industries and Dutch start Moscow woolen mill - required to sell output to State at cost) start Russian iron foundries at Tula, eventually some 700 workers, and Kashira (leads to 4 others by 1640s, 14 between 1637-62 - 10 by Dutchmen, 3 by Russian nobles and 1 by State).

1633

General Events

Father Vincent de Paul trains first social workers in Paris... China regulates merchants to restrict modernization... Japan's shogunate eliminates all contacts with other nations (closes all ports in 1635 to foreign vessels by Ordinance of National Isolation, only two Dutch vessels licensed to visit Nagasaki yearly)... Galileo is required by Inquisition to reject theories of Copernicus... Plague devastates Bavaria (makes people of Oberammergau vow to stage passion play every 10 years for protection, first in 1634, is seen by some 460,000 visitors, spend near $5 million, in 1990).

Business Events

English East India Co. starts Bengal trading post... Wind-powered mechanical sawmill appears in London, demolished by order of Charles I for unemployment of too many sawyers... London Ironmongers' Co. forms to sell cutlery and ironware, general merchandise later... Private contractor, Spain, takes over manufacture of gunpowder from Royal monopoly.

1634

General Events

John Bate: <u>Mysteryes of Nature and Art</u> (covers magic lantern, cited in China in 100s A.D.)... In seeking route to China and Japan, France's Jean Nicolet explores land to Lake Superior.

1635

General Events

English colonize Virgin Islands... Dutch settle Formosa... With creation of General Post in London, Royal postal system is available to public (charges postage for distance carried)... Franco-Swedish alliance forms, introduces Sweden's headquarters staff to French military in late 1630s... France limits sale of tobacco to doctors' prescriptions... London sets speed limit for hackney coaches at 3 mph... First inland postal service in England starts between London, Edinburgh... Schwenteer suggests idea for electric telegraph.

Business Events

Freebooter Henry Morgan starts buccaneer base at Port Royal, destroyed by 1692 earthquake (leads last raid in 1670-71 on Panama City, is Jamaica's Lt.-Governor in 1671)... Captain Bailey forms London's first cab company with four hackneys, uniformed drivers.

1636

General Events

Regiment of superstitious Croats visits Paris, wear silk kerchiefs at throat as talismans (leads to use of "cravat," French for Croat, by Louis XIV)... First tea is sold in Paris... Dutch start settlement in Ceylon, expel Portuguese in 1638-58... Japan stops building seagoing vessels (forbids subjects to sail high seas).

Business Events

Company of Saltmakers of South and North Shield is chartered in England... Markets appear throughout Holland for speculators in buying, selling rare Oriental tulip bulbs (within year causes "tulipmania" and voiding of all contracts).

1637

General Events

Dutch oust Portuguese from Africa's Gold Coast... Japan forbids practice of Christianity, expels Portuguese... Venice's Teatro di San Cossiano is first public opera house, followed by Paris' 1669, Rome's 1671, Hamburg's 1678 and London's Covent Garden 1732... Galileo designs pendulum clock, built by Huygens in 1656... England's Star Chamber lets only four persons at a time operate type-foundries or printing presses... Rene Descartes: On Method (develops deductive thinking, believes, as world is a mechanical system, mathematics can describe its behavior).

Business Events

French trading post appears on Senegal River... First English factory appears at Canton... Theophraste Renaudot opens first pawnshop, follows those run by Italian monks in 1400s, in Paris (leads to first government pawnshop in 1777 by King Louis XVI to protect poor from exploitation by dishonest or greedy pawnbrokers, establishment of city-operated monopoly of all pawnbroking business in Paris in 1804, at one time with 26 branches, and creation of 21 other Credit Municipals throughout France).

1638

General Events

Lewes Roberts: The Merchands Mappe of Commerce (advises merchants on international business, cites distilled Cognac wine)... China's imperial commission issues report on government's administration... After leaving masters in London Company of Leathersellers, journeymen glovers form guild.

Business Events

After years of financial struggle and Spanish raids, England's Guiana Co. declares bankruptcy... Distillers' Co. of London is chartered... Venice's first casino opens for gambling... London's Glaziers' Co., first cited in 1328, is chartered.

1639

General Events

London charters Corporation of Coachmen to drive hackney coaches for hire (licenses some 700 drivers in 1694, 1,000 in 1768)... Chinese book criticizes Christianity for corrupting morals, destroying statues, plotting with Japanese and coastal pirates, and forming secret associations... Japan finally expels all Europeans on suspicion they urged revolt of Christian peasants, kills almost all Portuguese protesting expulsion... William Gascoigne invents micrometer... Ryukoku University opens in Kyoto.

Business Events

Drury Lane Theater is patented as London playhouse.

1640

General Events

Frederick William, the Great Elector, rules Brandenburg, Prussia (-1688, creates and maintains standing army of some 30,000 - some 40,000 by Frederick I of Prussia in 1701-13, 83,000 by Frederick William I in 1713-40 and 200,000 by Frederick the Great in 1740-86, adopts staff activities from Swedish model with positions of quartermaster-general, first noted in 1657, commissary-general, two adjutants-general, provender master-general, wagonmaster-general, master of ordinance, chaplain, apothecary, surgeon, provost marshal and general for miliary justice, genesis for Prussian general staff in 1800s)... Dutch destroy Malacca, Portuguese surrender 1641... England operates eight postal lines in this time... For first time in England, coke is made from coal... English settlers found Fort St. George, Bengal... Holland wins trading monopoly with Japan.

Business Events

Nicholas Sauvage starts first public taxi business in Paris with 20 coaches, leads to City's first regulation in 1703 to require registration of drivers... Leyden workshop employs some 30 weavers, four the average, in this time... First European "cafe" opens in Venice... English East India Co. leases land from Hindu ruler to build a post, factory and fort, for trading in cotton, muslin, indigo and saltpeter (evolves as Madras, captured by France in 1746 and returned in 1748 treaty).

1641

General Events

Dutch forces capture Moluccas from Portuguese... Renaudot prepares plan for free medical treatment of needy in Paris (is forbidden to practice medicine in 1644 by University of Paris faculty)... Galileo's son designs, uses concept of father, clock with pendulum... Grand Duke of Tuscany, Ferdinand II, invents liquid thermometer.

Business Events

Cotton goods are manufactured in Manchester, England... Dutch East India Co. starts saltpeter plant in Bengal, a textile print works, over 4,000 silk spinners, in 1671.

1642

General Events

Blaise Pascal, France, invents Pascaline, world's first calculating machine, to ease bookkeeping drudgery of tax-collector father, no buyers as too complicated and would idle bookkeepers, clerks... England enacts income, property taxes... Dutch expedition, Abel Tasman pilot, discovers Tasmania, Staten Island (is renamed New Zeeland, then New Zealand), Tonga and Fiji (explores Australia North Coast in 1644 expedition)... France authorizes privateers to prey on English shipping off India... Osaka recognizes association of pawn shops, Edo in 1692... Montreal appears in Canada... Portugal cedes Africa's Gold Coast to Holland.

Business Events

Group of wealthy merchants corners Edo rice market, wealth confiscated, individuals exiled, and government officials executed... Portugal, English East India Co. form alliance to counter power of Holland in East Indies.

1643

General Events

France builds first fort on Madagascar (transfers post to Societe des Indes Orientales in 1664, annexes land in 1686, is French protectorate in 1882 and colony in 1896)... Italian physicist Torricelli, student of Galileo, devises first mercury barometer in this time... Austria devises first subscription loans... Parcel post service appears in France.

Business Events

Moliere forms "Illustre Theatre" in Paris, basis for "Theatre de la Comedie Francaise" in 1680... Cuper's Garden evolves in London as popular public amusement park (-1760)... Levantine opens Paris coffee house, fails (leads to some 300 by 1716, 1,800 by 1788, and 4,000 by 1807)... Joseph Bejart, head of French family of actors in touring company, joins Moliere.

1644

General Events

Sweden tries copper-based currency, abandoned when fall in price of copper leads to coin weighing 20 lbs... Denmark, Sweden go to war (-1645 with both navies chartering Dutch vessels)... China's Ming government, Canton as city of merchants and richest trading center is last to fall, is overthrown by Manchu Dynasty (-1912 when overthrown, rules with bureaucracy of Emperor over Imperial Household, consists of six departments, and state government, consists of censorate to audit performance, grand secretariat, coordinates seven offices, and grand council with six subordinate boards to supervise provincial administration of director-general of river conservation, governor- general and director-general of grain transport, restricts foreign trade to licensed brokers, called hong merchants, develops coal and iron complex at Hopei with 1,700 miners, 1,000 furnace workers to produce some 14,000 tons of pig iron yearly)... Floodgate Fraternity, called Green Gang by foreigners, appears as secret society to resist Manchu invaders (supports Sun Yat-sen's overthrow in 1911, evolves as criminal group ruling Shanghai in 1900s).

1645

General Events

Manchu emperor requires Chinese to wear pigtails... Portuguese begin to overthrow rule of Dutch in Brazil (-1654, grant country independence in 1822)... Chinese supporters of ousted Ming Dynasty resist new Manchu government by forming Society of the Triad or Society of Heaven in Earth and Society of Elders, evolved from Han period, 202 B.C. - 220 A.D., as religious group, and White Lotus Society, formed during Ming period, 1368-1644, as militant, messianic Buddhist order (evolve as modern criminal societies with Red Pole as enforcer, White Paper Fan as financial adviser)... Capuchin monks explore Congo River... Scientists, philosophers hold informal meetings at London's Gresham College to exchange information... German mathematician A. Kircher invents projection "magic" lantern, improved by Pieter van Musschenbroek in 1736... England forms first standing army, reformed 1685-88 (-1660, operates with headquarters units of chief of staff, three commissary generals, judge advocate general, a civilian, physician, apothecary, chaplain, secretary to Council of War, army messenger service).

1646

General Events

English settle Bahamas... Russian edict makes serfs part of land they inhabit, 1682 edict allows serfs to be sold with land.

1647

General Events

London ordinance punishes all persons acting in playhouses as rogues.

Business Events

Swedish African Co. is formed, mostly Dutch capital... Newspaper advertisements appear in England.

1648

General Events

Arabs take Muscat from Portuguese... Public strikes, France, against poll taxes, sales of offices... George Fox forms Society of Friends, Quakers, in England... Spain grants Holland trading privileges with West Indies in Treaty of Munster... Peace of Westphalia ends Thirty Years War in Europe (recognizes independence of Holland)... John Wilkens: Mathematical Magic (discusses aviation theories)... Perier, brother-in-law of Pascal, devises crude barometer (gets information of Torricelli's experiments from Friar Merin Mersenne, head of informal clearing house of science information at Paris monastery)... Semjon Deshnjov's voyage proves America, Asia not connected.

Business Events

Mirrors, chandeliers are manufactured in Murano, Venice, in this time.

1649

General Events

England builds first frigate... England grants state support to free enterprise... Russia abolishes trading privileges of Muscovy Co... Russia's Collection of Law divides society into three closed, hereditary classes of service, urban, includes merchants in three guilds, and peasants (gives each class specific duties, obligations)... To deter use of seditious material, Paris bans posting of any bill which has not first been read, distributed by criers and city provosts.

Business Events

Commercial Co. of Brazil forms in Portugal, monopoly abolished in early 1700s... Members of trading, artisan communities in Russian cities are given exclusive rights to produce articles for sale and maintain shops, leads to competition from serfs on estates and workshops of clergy.

1650

General Events

England forms Council of Trade to oversee international commerce, replaced by Commission for

Foreign Plantations in 1660, independent Commission on Trade and Plantations, called Lords of Trade, in 1675 to advise Privy Council and enforce navigation acts for maximum returns to Crown, and Board of Trade in 1696 with paid officials... Tea appears in England, first official purchase by English East India Co.in 1664... Walter Charleton coins term "electricity"... Henry Robinson: The Office of Addresses and Encounters (shows use of private employment offices, hiring halls used by mostly domestic servants, shop assistants and clerks, while artisans and craftsmen visit public houses, "houses of call," where landlords maintain lists of available jobs and provide meeting places for box clubs which provide benefits to those unable to work)... Italian Count Montecuccoli views 30,000 men as maximum number that can be managed by one commander (leads to 50,000 limit of French Marshal Turenne in late 1600s and 100,000 of General Saint Cyr in early 1800s)... Science-fiction writer Cyrano de Bergerac suggests use of rockets for man to reach moon... In this time, engineer Otto von Guericke, Mayor of Magdeburg, invents air pump (gives public demonstration of vacuum for emperor in 1652)... Holland has world's largest merchant fleet with some 10,000 vessels.

Business Events

Fukagawa porcelain is first made in Japan, modern family company in 1894... Turkish Jew opens first English coffee house in Oxford, 82 by 1663 and some 3,000 in 1700s... Edo approves association of public bathhouses in this time... Some 10 workshops in Delft, Holland, make pottery, about 30 in 1670... Successful dye business, started by Astrakhan traders in Persian trade, gets Russian Crown monopoly, other joint ventures appear later in leather, flax, meerschaum, beef fat... "Several Proceedings in Parliament" prints early newspaper ad, offers reward for return of 12 stolen horses... London's Marylebone Garden opens to provide public with dog-fights, cock-fights, bear and bull-baiting, bowling greens, and boxing matches (-1778)... Leipzig's Einkommenden Zeitungen is first daily newspaper... J. M. Rivero starts oldest foreign sherry firm in Spain, C. Z. perhaps oldest brand of any wine.

1651

General Events

Thomas Hobbes: Leviathan (urges need for strong central leadership by state)... England's Navigation Act limits European imports in only British or colonial ships (specifies that colonial exports of sugar, tobacco and indigo must be shipped only to England, leads to wars with Holland in 1652-54, 1665-67, and 1672-78 over restrictions).

Business Events

Division of publisher, printer appears in book trade.

1652

General Events

Holland starts colony at Cape of Good Hope as supply station for ships of Dutch East India Co. going to Spice Islands (gets slaves for farm labor from West Africa, Asia in 1657 to replace native Hottentots, evolves with settlements of French Huguenots from Holland in 1688-94, is seized by British 1795, possession in 1814)... Minuet is fashionable dance at French Court... Russia abolishes official drink shops, 25 in Moscow in 1626 (are replaced by off-license pot houses, one/town, and forbidden to serve more than one cup/customer, no credit, drunkards, dicers, and clerics allowed).

Business Events

Tuscan registry shows trading links for Florence's Samininati firm (-1658, trades with Venice,

Smyrna, Tripoli in Syria and Barbary, Messina, Genoa, Marseilles, Constantinople, Alexandria, Algiers, Lyons, Amsterdam, London, Hamburg, Vienna)... First wooden pencils appear in Bavaria... Bowman's Coffee House is London's first... Coffee is advertised in England as cure for gout, scurvy.

1653

General Events

First network of weather stations appears in Italy... England, Portugal sign (March 10) commercial treaty... England's Walter Blith pens first treatise on plow construction... Following postal systems of Cyrus the Great, 558-528 B.C., Augustus, 27 B.C.-14 A.D., and monasteries in Middle Ages, four post offices link Paris (uses first mail boxes) with provinces (leads to Paris' first city directory in 1785).

1654

General Events

London bans cock-fighting... Pascal, Pierre de Fermat formulate theory of probability... England, Sweden sign (April 11) commercial treaty... England, Denmark sign (September 14) commercial treaty... Medard Chouart, Pierre Radisson lead French expedition to explore Lake Michigan (-1656, make fur-trading agreements with local Indians).

1655

General Events

England, France sign commercial treaty... A call is issued in West Midland for nailers to cooperate in strike against ironmongers for holding them in debt and controlling sales... Pascal devises game of roulette... England seizes Jamaica from Spain (imports slaves in 1700s to work sugar plantations)... English scientist Robert Hooke tests model ornithopters.

Business Events

In this time, Palmstruck Bank is founded in Stockholm, modeled on banks in Amsterdam, Hamburg (is Bank of The Estates of the Realm in 1668).

1656

General Events

After ban of 366 years, England allows Jews to return... Holland starts trade with China... England, Sweden sign (June) commercial treaty... Italian Lorenzo Tonti proposes insurance scheme to raise revenue for Crown to Cardinal Mazarin, "advisor" to Louis XIV (begins tontine as form of life insurance)... Combination of hospital, poorhouse and factory opens in Paris... Dutch forces take Colombo, Ceylon, from Portugal.

Business Events

After lending money to lord in Osaka, House of Konoike, former samurai and brewer of sake, starts money exchange... Dutch painter Rembrandt declares bankruptcy... Covent Garden, London's fruit and vegetable market, evolves when temporary stalls appear in Bedford House garden... Stockings are first manufactured in Paris.

1657

General Events

Accadema del Cimento appears in Florence (-1667, continues Galileo tradition in performing scientific experiments)... Regular "penny post" stagecoach service runs in England, scheduled passenger service in 1658... Montmor Academy forms in France to discuss science.

Business Events

English East India Co. forms permanent headquarters with board and officers (-1857)... England holds first public tea sale... Fountain pens are made in Paris... Public Advisor, England, prints first classified ads... Chocolate House opens in London, drink appears in France c. 1660.

1658

General Events

Hooke designs first marine clock with balance wheel, regulator, and balance spring, no patent (is followed by Huygens' watch with balance spring in 1674)... Holland takes last Portuguese possession in Ceylon.

Business Events

Smith & Co. of Nottingham is England's oldest country bank... Ahasuerus Fromanteel, English entrepreneur, sells pendulum clocks (evolve as "Grandfather" clocks, made by guild's Clockmakers Co. despite opposition of Blacksmiths' Co. claim of traditional guild rights).

1659

General Events

Tokugawa shogunate requires merchants in Edo to be licensed.

Business Events

Edo approves associations of peddlers, hairdressers.

1660

General Events

London theaters, closed 1642 by Puritans, reopen, actresses replace boys in female roles... Sweden, Denmark end war with Peace of Copenhagen (opens Baltic Sea to foreign ships)... Robert May: The Accomplish't Cook, or the Art and Mystery of Cooking, pioneering work to advise professional chefs... Richard Alestree: The Gentlemen's Calling (notes "Every Rich Man is God's Steward")... Robert Boyle, Hooke develop improved air-pump... Guericke devises rotating globe as generator, basic electrical machine (emits sparks from friction)... England mines some half-a-million tons of coal/year, more than five times all other countries... Table napkins are fashionable in France in this time... Charles II is King of England (-1685, gets Tangier and Bombay as dowry from Portugal in marriage to Catherine of Braganza, sponsors naval academies to train professional officers, sponsors mathematics course to prepare sailors in determining longitude, makes George Monk, former staff aide to Cromwell, army commander, keeps palace at Newmarket, center of flat racing with 40 breeding farms, 52 racing stables by 1990)... Sweden makes tobacco a government monopoly, private ownership with government protection in 1685...

Men of science at Gresham College form academy, chartered as Royal Society in 1662 (issues first specific science publication in 1665, general journal in France in 1665-68)... Brandenburg postal service serves Cleves to Memel... England's Navigation Act requires all goods to and from England to be shipped in English-manned, English-built vessels (requires all colonial shipments of sugar, tobacco, cotton, wood and indigo go to England, extends list to rice in 1705, naval stores in 1706, copper ore and furs in 1721, molasses in 1733, and whale fins, hides, iron, lumber, and raw silk in 1764)... In this time military units wear gaudy uniforms to identify troops in battle.

Business Events

Syndicate of 80 pipe makers forms, Gouda, to set prices... Sicilian Francisco Procopio opens Cafe Procope, City's first, in Paris, Vienna's first in 1683 by Kolschitzky... First pencil factory appears in Nuremberg... French water closets are introduced to England... Company of Printers is formed, London, by 11 leading printers... New Spring Gardens, renamed Vauxhall Gardens in 1785, opens near London for public entertainment with exhibitions, performances and balls (-1859, builds Rotunda, circular building with great central fireplace, orchestra, circuit of supper boxes, and space for promenading, model for Vauxhalls in Paris in 1760s and London's Pantheonian in 1772)... London's Mercurius Politius advertises dentifrice... Royal Africa Co. is chartered (December 18) to supply English sugar colonies with 3,000 slaves/year, one slave valued at one ton of sugar... Haut-Brion is first Bordeaux wine marketed as distinct brand.

1661

General Events

Robert Boyle: Sceptical Chemist (substitutes elements for matter of fire, water, earth and air of alchemists to launch modern chemistry)... Rembrandt: "The Syndics of the Cloth Guild"... Holland gives England's Charles II a yacht, sails in first known yacht race... John Evelyn pens treatise on London's air pollution... France's Louis XIV begins personal rule (-1715, replaces previous bureaucracy of hereditary nobles with advisors from middle class, increases governmental employees from 600 to some 10,000, and organizes army as structure of authority, responsibility with inspector-general, experts and professional soldiers).

Business Events

After devaluation of Swedish currency, Stockholm's Palmstruch Bank issues first bank notes backed by government (starts branch operation at Abo, Finland, in 1663)... Takanoshi family starts soy sauce factory with 20 workers, 15 by contract, in Noda near Edo, first Japanese soy sauce in 1200s and first at Noda in 1560 (evolves as 1980 international Kikkoman Corp. from guild of Noda brewers in 1781)... Following proposal of Pascal for Paris public transport system with coaches, Marquis de Sourches and Marquis de Crenan start project, abandoned 1677 as too slow on crooked, crowded medieval streets.

1662

General Events

Italy's Punch and Judy show of slapstick comedy is first noted in England... England forbids exports of leather, skins and wool and imports of laces, embroideries, linen and curtains in 1663... After seeing Finance Minister Fouquet's opulent chateau, Louis XIV builds Versailles Palace (-1680s, uses some 36,000 workers, craftsmen)... English inventor William Petty launches twin-hulled catamaran Invention... Parliament authorizes transportation of "incorrigible roads, vagabonds, and sturdy beggars" to North America... England's Printing Act limits field to 20 master printers, 2 universities, and Archbishop of York... John Graunt: Remarks on the Bills of Mortality, pioneers study of demographics... Jean Baptiste Colbert is Controller-General of

Finances, "A banker is a soldier in the service of the state" (-1683, starts some 400 new enterprises - 300 in textiles and others in paper, iron, metals, glass, furniture, and shipbuilding, shows "first" battleship in <u>Atlas de Colbert</u>, bible of French shipwrights, institutes bookkeeping and audit activities, establishes uniform commercial code, requires merchants to pass tests in accounting and commercial law, builds roads, bridges and canals, provides subsidies to industries, increases royal manufacturers from 68 to 113, nationalizes Gobelins factory, originally dyeworks in 1400s, in Paris with 800 artisans in tapestry, fine textiles, woodwork, silver work, metalwork, and glass as model for other royal enterprises, limits guilds to regulations of quality, bans immigration of skilled French workers, starts workshops to train apprentices, opposes use of machinery causing unemployment, and issues regulations for manufacturing methods, working conditions and quality standards)... British fort is built at mouth of Gambia River, Africa... England revives hearth tax (-1689, is replaced by window tax in 1696-1851)... Parliament declares Kenelm Digby, courtier, alchemist and part-time pirate, had indeed invented modern wine bottle in 1633... Charles II forms board of commissioners to regulate fares of London hackneys.

Business Events

English Guinea Co. is formed.

1663

General Events

England excludes Irish shipping from colonial trade... Minister Colbert establishes North American colony of New France, Quebec the Capitol... England's Turnpike Act institutes tolls, 1750 law for Scotland (uses some 8,000 tollgates for about 22,000 miles by 1830s, most of system abolished by 1864)... Edward Somerset gets 99-year monopoly for engine to pump water from depth of about 40 feet (dies before plans for London waterworks can be implemented)... English workers, employers in frame-work knitting form guild... England mints first guinea coin... Marquis of Worcester claims to have used steam to raise water from wells.

Business Events

Olde Wine Shades, claims to be oldest such shop in London in 1900s, opens... Kings Co. builds Drury Lane Theater, one of London's two patent theaters... Company of Royal Adventurers into Africa is chartered for slave trading (-1698, is succeeded by Royal Africa Co. in 1672)... Leyden drapers use looms to compete with lower labor costs of textile mills in Tilburg, Germany.

1664

General Events

Holland buys Swedish colonies on Gold Coast (-1667)... France builds Canal Du Midi to link Atlantic Coast with Mediterranean at Toulouse (-1681)... Louis XIV hosts one-week extravaganza, "The Pleasure of the Enchanted Isle," with tournaments, ballets, operas, concerts, plays and feasts... Richard Baxter: <u>Christian Directory</u> (gives practical ethics for Puritans as strenuous life, hard work)... Holland gets monopoly to administer Siam's trade with China... French colonies in New World are put under direct control of Crown, previously administered by various merchant companies... Colbert charters French East India Co. (puts posts at Madagascar, Mauritius, East Africa, and India with Pondichery as Capitol, reorganizes in 1682 after financial difficulties, after some 20 East Indiamen take yearly trips to India is liquidated in 1769 by Louis XV for bankruptcy)... Colbert establishes special tariff areas, "Five Great Farms," in center of France to stimulate free trade (abolishes land duties)... Cast iron pipes are used at Versailles to supply palace with water... Colbert forms French West India Co. (-1674 when assets, liabilities of bankrupt company are assumed by Crown).

Business Events

Robert L'Estrange publishes London's <u>The Publick Advertiser</u> to carry public, private messages.

1665

General Events

Louis XIV creates La Compagnie de Saint-Gobain to make glass (evolves by 1980 with sales over $41 billion, 88,000 employees and 350 plants worldwide, from glass, chemicals, plastics, paper, insulating materials, petroleum products, atomic power, television, acquires U.S.' Norton, sales of $1.5 billion, abrasives, engineering and ceramic materials, with 16,000 employees and 113 plants, in 1990 for $1.8 billion to block hostile takeover of British conglomerate)... Isaac Newton experiments with gravitation (devises differential calculus in this time)... Colbert establishes port, shipyard of Lorient... French mission starts at Lake Superior... First known Western census, China's census the model, is taken in French Canada, Sweden in 1749... Magic lantern device is shown in Lyn, France, by Dane... Great Plague kills over 68,000 in London, some 1,500/day at height... Royal cloth manufactory, Colbert is sponsor, is started at Abbeville by Dutch-born Van Robais (sees worker protest in 1686 and strike in 1716, uses some 18,000 workers in 1780s, 1,800 in factory and 16,000 in homes, closes 1804)... Dud Dudley: <u>McHalum martis</u> (claims to have made iron with coal instead of charcoal).

Business Events

First French journal is seen (-1791)... Royal African Co. drives out Dutch vessels trading with British islands in West Indies... <u>London Gazette</u> appears... Britain's <u>The Journal des squants</u> is issued for intellectuals, others in Rome in 1668, Venice in 1671, Leipzig in 1682 and Rotterdam in 1684.

1666

General Events

To replace "Napier's Bones" with discs, Samuel Morland devises workable multiplier... England bans imports of Irish cattle, sheep, and swine... France captures Antigua, Montserrat, St. Christopher... Holland captures Surinam... England's first cheddar cheese appears in this time... Almost 66% of London is destroyed (September 2-7) by Great Fire (leads to first use of brick construction by major city in re-building, builds Leadenhall as new public market, perhaps largest in Europe)... Academie Royal des Sciences, sponsored by Louis XIV, forms in Paris, previous informal meetings of French scientists as early as 1620 at Aix-en-Provence house of wealthy lawyer... Louis XIV makes Marquis de Louvois French Minister of War (-1691, innovates, uses Swedish model, in hierarchy of command with permanent classification of officers by rank, in military supply system)... Huygens proposes to Colbert to use gunpowder, steam to pump water from flooded mines.

Business Events

First violin with Stradivarius mark is made... Robert Cavalier Sieur de La Salle starts trading post near Montreal (sells holdings in 1669 to explore Great Lakes, forms business association with Governor Frontenac to develop Western fur trade, starts Fort Crevecoeur near Peoria, IL, in 1680 and Fort St. Louis in 1682, explores Mississippi River to mouth in 1684).

1667

General Events

France passes protectionist tariff... Brandenburg, Saxony, Hanover and Brunswick hold monetary convention... After Great Fire of London, Parliament passes Rebuilding Act (shifts authority from companies of Carpenters and Bricklayers to King's Bench to regulate prices, wages, quality of building materials)... Paris uses some 6,500 candle-lanterns to light streets... Hooke proposes systematic weather reading... Trading Statute forbids all foreign merchants to trade in Russia... Treaties are signed at Breda between England (gets Antigua, Montserrat, St. Kitts from France and keeps New York, considered taking Spice Island in East Indies instead of colony, and New Jersey), Holland (retains Surinam), France (retains Acadia), and Denmark... Colbert forms Manufacture Royale des Meubles de la Couronne (forms three classes of industrial enterprises: state factories to produce luxury goods, mainly for Royal family, manufacturers royals, owned by individuals and controlled by Crown, to make consumer goods, and those private firms with special privileges to make, sell certain goods)... Holland captures Sumatra... Margaret Cavendish, Duchess of Newcastle, is first woman member of Royal Society, 2nd 1945... Holland assumes control of Celebes, East Indies center for European spice trade.

Business Events

After London's Great Fire of 1666, Nicholas Barbon, physician and real estate speculator, starts office to insure houses, commercial property against loss by fire (-1680).

1668

General Events

Joshua Child: Brief Observations Concerning Trade and the Interest of Money (notes social role of wages: high a sign of wealth, low evidence of poverty)... Bank of Sweden is created... England builds Fort William near Calcutta... Colbert introduces use of depots to provision troops... Chain-of-buckets engine powered by water wheel is invented, France... France starts first trading station in India... Ft. Charles trading post is built on Hudson's Bay... Colbert builds Grand Canal at Versailles to test model war ships, provides water festivals for Louis XIV (-1680)... Bombay, acquired in dowry of Catherine of Braganza, is leased by Charles II to English East India Co., headquarters until company's dissolution in 1858... Sweden forms manufacturing commission to promote industry (recruits foreign workers, buys raw materials, provides advice and funds, grants free sites, tax exemptions, and freedom from import duties on raw materials, machinery)... Francesco Redi pioneers use of controlled experiments in science... Dom Perignon is Treasurer of Abbey of Hautvillers with 25 acres of vineyards (becomes cellar-master).

Business Events

First Italian periodical appears... Samuel Pepys visits Chatelain's, famous French ordinary in London serving meals at fixed prices... Separated from Woodmongers, London Carmen form Livery Company for those in transport, chartered 1946.

1669

General Events

Venice's colonial empire ends with loss of Crete to Ottoman Empire... Josiah Child, director of East India Co.: A New Discourse of Trade (gives new view of Mercantilism)... Hanseatic League holds last meeting... France grants Royal patent to Pierre Perrin to form Academie Royales des Operas... German alchemist Hennig Brand is first to prepare phosphorus, keeps discovery secret...

French nobles are allowed to engage in sea-born commerce without loss of status, allowed to enter large-scale commerce in 1701, to enter mining and glass-making, and metallurgy in 1727... Oder-Spree Canal opens in Prussia... England bans export of woolen cloth from one colony to another... France forms Compagnie du Nord, a fiasco... Turkish ambassador introduces coffee to Paris.

Business Events

Garraway's Coffee House opens in London (-1872, becomes one of City's chief auction houses).

1670

General Events

Richard Lasser: <u>Voyage of Italy</u>, first to use phrase "Grand Tour"... Italian scientist Giobanni Borelli tries to fly with artificial wings... France cultivates vines in Languedoc area... Roger Coke: <u>Discourse on Trade</u>, on expansion of commerce... Franesco Lana: <u>Prodomo</u> (shows design for lighter-than-air flying ship)... Austria forms tobacco monopoly... Ashanti, West African chiefdom, evolves with trade of cola nuts, gold, slaves.

Business Events

First Italian "Commedia del arte" companies appear in Germany... Charles II charters Governor and Company of Adventurers of England's Trading into Hudson's Bay to Prince Rupert and London associates, genesis from French traders, Pierre-Esprit Radisson, Medard Chouart and Sieur des Groseillers in 1668-69, who had their furs from Sioux land confiscated by French governor (adopts coat of arms symbolic of New World fur trade, opens York Factory in 1682 as overseas headquarters - closed 1957, starts Westward exploration in 1689, opens first inland post, Cumberland House, in 1774 - 498 employees in 1799 at chain of posts to North West's 1,276, uses "beaver" tokens as medium of exchange, after bitter competition takes over rival North West Co. in 1821, loses trading license in 1859, transfers all land, keeps seven million acres, to Canada in 1869, organizes by business interests, such as retailing in 1930, is acquired in 1979 by Kenneth Thomson for $640 million in cash, after losing over $250 million after 1981 sells 178 outlets in North in 1987 to run 404 retail stores and Markborough Properties, one of Canada's largest retail firms with 32 shopping centers, 23 warehouses and factories, 11 office buildings, one hotel, two apartment towers in U.S., Canada and Britain).

1671

General Events

Academie de l'Architecture is formed, France... Ruling is made in English case of <u>Dr. Salmon v. The Hamborough Co.</u> that a creditor can find remedy in equity against personal effects of members of assetless corporation... Crown assumes control of England's customs, franchised since 1605... William Carter: <u>England's Interest by Trade Asserted</u>... After reaching Sault Ste. Marie, French explorers claim interior of North America for France.

Business Events

French Senegal Co. forms in this time... Buccaneers raid Panama.

1672

General Events

Germany's Gottfried Wilhelm Leibniz devises mechanical calculator to add, subtract, divide and multiply... Otto von Guericke: Experimenta Nova Magdeburgica (studies strange force of electricity)... England's Exchequer stops (January 2) payments for 12 months, bankrupts thousands of businesses... First known teacher training class is held in Lyons, France... Count de Frontenac is governor of Canada (-1682, is recalled for advocating representative assembly, approving brandy as barter for furs)... Oxford University founds Clarendon Press (still extant)... Holland starts war with England (-1674, yields New York to England for sugar lands of Surinam) and France (-1678)... Jean Baptiste Lully, court composer of ballet, orchestra, minuet music, founds Royal Academy of Music with monopoly to produce operas.

Business Events

First French fashion magazine appears... Testing-bench is used in Liege to ensure quality of firearms... Violinist John Bannister gives first public concert by musician at London inn, first concert hall at Oxford in 1748... Danish West India-Guinea Co. is founded... Baltic monopoly of Eastland Trading Co., formed during rule of Henry IV in 1399-1413, is canceled... After merger with English Guinea Co., Royal African Co. is chartered with monopoly for English slave trade (-1698 when monopoly is abolished after protests from independent traders)... Richard Hoare, goldsmith and banker, opens Hoare & Co., London's oldest continuing banking house for gentry with Toye, Kenning and Spencer following in 1685 (focuses on banking in 1690s, only private U.K. deposit bank left in 1988)... Coffee stall opens in Paris market.

1673

General Events

Christiaan Huygens: De Horologium Osccillatorium (shows design for chronometer)... French start post on Ganges River, India... Wilhelm von Schroeder: Manufakturhaus... Italian Ordinance du Commerce codifies regulations for merchants (establishes modern mercantile law)... Colbert tries to control guilds, finally abolished with French Revolution... G.B. Cardinale di Luca: Il Dottore Vulgare, an investor's guide... French ordinance creates societies generales, known as "free firms" or "joint liability" firms... Dutch scientist Christiaan Huygens builds engine with piston powered by explosion of gunpowder (views engine as power for possible flying machines).

Business Events

Water-coach service operates on Loire River in this time, one on Rhone in 1728... After 20 years as provincial moneylender, Hachirobei Mitsui starts family trading and banking house, 2nd largest Sogo Shosha with 1987 sales of $113.3 billion, with drygoods store in Kyoto (innovates with cash payments, single prices, and cloth in any length, later opens branch store and warehouse in Edo with over 1,000 employees, innovates with wood-block handbill advertisements, free umbrellas on rainy days, and commercials inserted in stage dramas, uses Grandmother, mother to train six sons for six main branches, operates large network of wholesale associations, courier service between Edo and Osaka, and "chain" of drug stores to W.W. II... Contemporary entrepreneur composes popular song to advertise expected shipment of oranges).

1674

General Events

France makes tobacco a state monopoly... England uses grain bounties to achieve self-sufficiency in food production... Earl of Danby, Lord Treasurer, reorganizes England's finances... John Mayow: <u>Tractatus quinque medico physici</u>, on nature of combustion... Compagnie des Indes Orientals starts settlement at Pondichery, India's Coromandel Coast (-1954)... Portugal settles Manaus on the Amazon.

Business Events

English East India Co. sets shipping limits on what privileged goods can be privately traded by super cargo in India, some captains wealthy from trade of private goods on one 2-year voyage to India.

1675

General Events

Jacques Savary: <u>Le Parfait Negociant</u> (advises merchants on banking, counting, exchange, bankruptcy, foreign commercial practices)... Royal Observatory, designed by Christopher Wren, is built at Greenwich to advance science of navigation, naval astronomy... Mongols ask Father Verbiest to cast European-style cannon... Huygens makes claim to Royal Society for inventing balance wheel spring, contested by Hooke for his design in 1658 and construction in 1675... George Ravenscroft develops flint and lead glass, England, in this time, basis for lead crystal... English silk workers attack immigrant French weavers in London for using ribbon-looms, device to weave 10-12 ribbons at one time... Leibniz invents differential calculus independent of Newton... England's king issues proclamation to close popular coffee houses as many tradesmen and others waste too much time in such evil places, later canceled... Samuel Morlund, master mechanic to Charles II, invents plunger pump.

Business Events

Procopio opens Paris coffee house (opens 2nd in 1686 to sell coffee, Italian ices, and candy).

1676

General Events

Barlow invents repeating clock... England grants legal protection for observance of the Sabbath... Johann Kunckel: <u>Ars Vitraria Experimentalis</u> (uses experiment, reason to develop technology for glass manufacture)... Ice cream is popular dessert in Paris in this time... After five trips to Turkey, Persia and India seeking diamonds for Louis XIV of France, Jean-Baptist Tavernier, Europe's greatest gem and diamond trader, begins new journey (disappears on 1687 trip)... William Petty: <u>Political Arithmetic</u> (discusses quantitative measurements)... Hooke invents universal joint.

Business Events

Check, one England's first, is submitted to Hoare & Co... Exeter Change is built on London's Strand to house small shops of hosiers, millers and drapers (-1829, is site in 1773-1829 for Edward Cross' animal menagerie).

1677

General Events

England prohibits French imports (-1685)... Thomas Grosvenor's 12-year-old bride brings London cabbage patch as dowry, basis for family wealth, some $4 billion, by 1990.

Business Events

German-born Blauenstein builds blast furnace in England to make iron with coal (although previously tried in Sweden fails as iron deteriorates from sulphurous vapors of furnace)... Persia's Shiraz ships bottled wine to Gulf Coast for export.

1678

General Events

English patent to use coal-burning furnace to smelt lead, make glass is granted to Grandison, use of idea later to work copper... France's Besnier tries to fly with flappers, first detailed description of actual flying machine in account of unsuccessful attempt.

1679

General Events

William Petty: A Treatise on Taxes and Contributions... Leibniz invents binary system of calculations used in modern computers... Renaudot dies in Paris after running free clinic for Paris poor and providing facilities for scientific meetings, publishing house and employment agency... France's Denis Papin invents safety valve for pressure-cooker, demonstrated 1680 (leads to first controlled pressure-cooker by French engineer Hautier in 1927)... In tariff squabble England bans all French wine, settled by 1697 treaty with England charging duty on French wines (at twice the rate for Spanish and Portuguese wines makes French wine a luxury, status symbol).

Business Events

First German coffee house opens in Hamburg... Blind moneylenders in Edo form association to set common rules for monopoly... Turkish merchants open Royal Bagnio, London's first Turkish bath... London shipbroker James Whiston issues first company journal to give quotations on imported goods, copied by coffee houses in 1680s with news-sheets to increase clientele.

1680

General Events

Isaac Newton devises jet-propelled 'horseless carriage' powered by steam, a failure... Hunckwitz makes first phosphorous matches... Chinese emperor starts factories to develop art industries... Louis XIV combines two acting companies to form Comedie-Francaise, reorganized by Napoleon in 1803... Sweden is Europe's major exporter of iron... Giovanni Borelli: De Mot Amimialium (views human muscle power inadequate for ornithopter flight)... Manchu forces capture Amoy, Formosa only trading center left for England in area (is costly because of endless bribes to local officials)... Clocks appear with minute hands, second hands in 1690s.

Business Events

London merchant Dockwra starts penny post... Sadler Wells Co. presents musical entertainment in London... Some 450,000 textile workers are employed in Languedoc region of France... Brandenburg Co. is formed for trade with Guinea, Angola (gets capital, ships, navigators and factors from Holland, sends first German expedition to West Africa)... France builds first factory in Siam.

1681

General Events

Boyle devises first matches of sulphur, phosphorous (leads to phosphorous matches of France's Charles Sauria, after commercialization in 1836 are perfected in 1844 by Sweden's Carl F. Lundstrom)... Samuel Richard: The New Businessman... City of London provides fire insurance (-1683)... Academy of Sciences forms in Moscow... Large waterworks, 14 water-wheels for 221 pumps, is built on Seine to provide water for fountains of Versailles (-1685)... Corkscrew is first cited, word not coined until 1720.

Business Events

Checks are circulated in England.

1682

General Events

Windmill is built to pump water from flooded mines at Matinmas, Germany, uses 1676 idea of Peter Harzingk... After treatment by secret medicine, local lord of Toyama lets seller distribute medicine throughout Japan via itinerant peddlers (is current with another practice: money lent to feudal lord for privilege to place branches of commercial firm in other provinces)... Peter the Great rules Russia (-1725, plans campaigns with military and naval "games," forms College of Manufacturing and Mining, transforms industrial sector of 21 "manufacturies", 4 state operated, into some 178 factories, nearly 50% started by state, with 40 in armaments and iron, first developed in 1630s by foreigners, 15 in non-ferrous metallurgy, 23 sawmills, 15 woolen-cloth plants and 13 tanneries, grants privately-owned factories privileges and loans, leads to some 25,000 at work in Perm mines and 1,000 in sailcloth factory, requires merchants to start woolen-cloth factory in 1698, sponsors first newspaper in 1703, sponsors silk factory in 1717 - some 1,500 workers at mill of Evreinob & Co. by 1728, rules in 1721 that merchants have right to buy villages for factories, mills)... Danish settle Africa's Gold Coast... William Petty: Quantolumcunque, or a Tract concerning money... Acta Eruditorum is first German scholarly journal (-1776)... Amsterdam builds recreational area with flower gardens, walks, inn, bowling green, tennis court and open-air theater (is model for other European cities: Bordeaux in 1746, Nancy 1765-72, Berlin's Tiergarten in 1772, Vienna in 1775 - its Prater Park in 1780s, and Munich in 1791)... Charles II licenses London's Spitalfields Market to sell vegetables in bulk.

Business Events

Pierre Baille starts weaving mill, 100 looms, at Amsterdam... Maranhao Co. is formed in Portugal to conduct trade with Brazil, monopoly canceled in early 1700s.

1683

General Events

Manchus conquer Formosa (-1895)... Brandenburg puts factories on Africa's Gold Coast (-1720)... European plantation families in Trinidad hold carnival (after abolition of slavery in 1833, becomes Afro-West Indian festival)... Dutch traders are admitted to Canton... Francesco Marziolli: Precetti Militri (shows movements required for precise military drill)... Siege of Vienna by Ottoman Turks spurs development of Viennese cafes.

Business Events

During harsh cold winter public market appears on London's frozen Thames River... Bank of Amsterdam accepts coins as security for negotiable receipts, ingots after 1763 (when Bank of Amsterdam's conversions decline in use, leads to "cashier" of private banks substituting cash for "bank money")... Friendly Society forms in London to write fire insurance for home owners (leads to Contributors for Insuring Houses, Chambers or Rooms from Loss by Fire by Amicable Contributions)... London's Nag's Head tavern finances bills of credit... After studying in Italy, Mathias Klotz returns to Mittenwald, Germany, to craft violins, by 1800s over 30% of community in industry and six left by 1980s... Hachirobei Mitsui starts currency exchange, basis for Mitsui Bank in 1876 (is Osaka's official money changer in 1691, innovates with money orders, dies 1694 after establishing nontraditional succession to pass control to those qualified in related families instead of eldest son).

1684

General Events

Dutch conquer island of Java in East Indies... London makes first attempt to light its streets... German explorer Kampfer visits Persian Gulf, Java and Japan... Allain M. Mallet: Les Travaux de Marsov l'Art de la Guerre (shows motions required to tend, fire siege guns)... Portugal bans imports of woolen goods.

Business Events

Boyle develops London's Islington Spa with gardens, amusements for fashionable society... Dutch entrepreneurs start Moscow Woolen Manufacture to supply cloth to Russian army (after displeasure with high costs and low quality leads to formation of Commercial Co., first chartered business in Russia, by Peter the Great, makes leading merchants supervise operations)... English East India Co. closes factory in Siam.

1685

General Events

France sends embassy to Siam... London gives Edward Hemming a monopoly to put oil lamps outside every 10th house... The Discovered Gold Mine describes large-scale woolen manufacturing... When colony of Canada lacks money, De Meulle issues requisitioned playing cards as currency with assigned values... Louis XIV revokes (October 18) Edict of Nantes (renews persecution of French Protestants, thousands flee to England, Holland, Brandenburg to start new industries)... Glasgow's James Lewis Robertson proposes idea for steam power, ruined struggling for acceptance of idea (is proved successful in 1789)... China opens all ports to foreign trade... Samuel Morlund, master mechanic to Charles II of England, gives first accurate description on expansive power of steam... Miyamoto Musashi, renowned samurai: A Book of Five Rings, popular in 1980s with samurai guidelines for entrepreneurship.

Business Events

British factory appears in Sumatra... English East India Co. sends China Merchant to Amoy to open a factory... Ambrose Crowley's English iron works employs some 1,000 workers in this time (provides workers with doctor, clergymen, 3 teachers, poor relief, pension and funeral plans)... French Guinea Co. forms... In this period, Geneva watch industry employs some 100 masters, 300 workers (evolves by 1740s with 550 masters, by 1760 with some 800 masters, 4,000 workers in City and unknown number in rural cottages)... Simon van der Stel, Dutch East India Co., develops estate of Constantia near Stellenbosch (evolves to produce South Africa's finest wine).

1686

General Events

Abraham Theuart, France, casts first plate-glass (replaces work of skilled glass blowers)... English astronomer Edmund Halley draws first known weather map... France bans printed calicoes, other bans by 1759 from pressure of guilds (leads to protective bans by England in 1700, 1720).

Business Events

Barbon, associates start Fire Office, England's first stock company to write fire insurance (-1720, is renamed Phoenix Office later, insures 5,650 buildings by 1693)... Job Charnock starts India trading post, genesis for Calcutta in 1690s.

1687

General Events

Brandenburg starts colony in Guinea... Coffee grinder is invented, first electrical model in 1937 by Kitchen Aid... French Huguenots settle Cape of Good Hope.

Business Events

English East India Co. moves headquarters from Surat to Bombay... After joining English East India Co. as bookkeeper in 1672 and becoming Madras Governor, Elihu Yale retires (returns to England in 1699 with private fortune, supposedly acquired during service as merchant adventurer but not proved, from cloth, spices and precious gems).

1688

General Events

Dom Pierre Perignon invents champagne (devises cork stopper, c.1690, to hold gaseous pressure)... Commercial centers evolve in Japan at castle towns during "The Great Peace" of Genroko era (-1703, leads to cycles of economic activity: expansion 1751-86 and 1804-29 to feudal retrenchment in 1600-87, 1716-35, 1787-83, 1841-43)... Joseph de la Vega: Confusion de Confusiones, on operations of Amsterdam stock market.

Business Events

Some 15 stock companies operate in London, first seen in mid-1500s... Edward Lloyd opens London coffee shop where shipping insurance is bought, sold (is office for marine insurance in 1692, publishes lists in 1700 to classify ships by risk).

1689

General Events

England's Corn Law subsidizes those who ship grain abroad when prices are below designated levels... Natal is Dutch Colony in South Africa... England abolishes Royal right to grant monopolies... Parliament's Declaration of Rights provides Bill of Rights, establishes budgetary system for government.

Business Events

First modern European trade fair is held at Leyden... First caravan of Russian merchants travels to Peking, 49 more by 1727.

1690

General Events

England drops export duties on corn... Mathematical academy appears at Bologna... Water power is used in Silesia to etch glass... Aging Louis XIV of France wears wig to cover baldness (starts fashion when copied by courtiers)... Placer gold is found in Brazil's interior, biggest discovery in South America... Nizam Al-Mulk, vizer to sultan of Safavid Dynasty in Persia: The Book of Government... Papin, engineer and former assistant to Huygens, describes all of components and principles for practical steam engine as mechanism to drive boat (tests paddlewheel boat on Germany's Fulda River in 1707 - wrecked and further development discouraged for fear of causing unemployment, leads to first patent by England's J. Allen in 1729 and tugboat test in 1730s by Jonathan Hulls).

Business Events

English East India Co. starts factory at Calcutta... Worcester Postman is England's first provincial paper, world's oldest in continuous publication... Calico printing of France is introduced to England... Hudson's Bay Co. sends Henry Kelsey to establish fur trade with Indians of Western interior (-1691, visits Sioux, Cheyenne and Crow tribes).

1691

General Events

England patents washing machine, U.S. patent in 1846... John Clayton demonstrates lighting capability of coal gas... Silver is discovered at Nerchinsk in Siberia, developed by Greek entrepreneurs... Paris prints first directory of street addresses to aid firefighters... Louis XIV forms office to set prices, arrange purchases and take commissions for regular commerce of Champagne... William Petty: Essays in Political Arithmetick (views land, labor as real sources of wealth).

Business Events

New East India Co., forms to compete with established company... English Copper Co. incorporates (-1800s).

1692

General Events

China's Edict of Toleration grants religious freedom to Christians... English Crown authorizes 50 privateers to attack merchant shipping of trading rivals... Greenwich Hospital opens for wounded soldiers, sailors.

Business Events

England's John Houghton: Collection for the Improvement of Husbandry and Trade, pioneering trade publication... Goldsmith John Campbell starts one of London's oldest banks, known as Coutts & Co. after 1822.

1693

General Events

Britain uses national debt to fund war with France... Zimbabwe expels Portuguese settlers.

Business Events

London's <u>The Ladies Mercury</u> is pioneering periodical for women... White's Chocolate House opens in London (-1755, spawns White's Club in 1736 with amenities for gentlemen members, is known for high stakes gambling in late 1700s, early 1800s)... First English East India Co. is re-chartered.

1694

General Events

England doubles its salt tax... Leibniz builds first general-purpose calculating device for bookkeepers, mathematicians... City of London declares bankruptcy after overspending on rebuilding after 1666 Great Fire (auctions city services, such as City Marshal, to raise money)... In need of funds to finance war with French and Dutch, Bank of England is created with funds from 1,268 shareholders in return for payments from shipping duties, liquor taxes (issues counters in granting credit, gets monopoly to issue money in 1844)... Royal Laboratory is built in Woolwich Warren of London, Royal Arsenal in 1805.

Business Events

G.G. Careri leaves Naples on world trip (finances journey by trading goods at each port)... Merchants of Glasgow, Edinburgh form Scottish Africa Co., abandoned when unable to raise capital in London, Hamburg, Amsterdam... France's Vauban estimates windmills, water wheels power 80,000 flour mills, 15,000 industrial mills, fulling, oil, hemp, paper, and salt, and 500 iron mills, metallurgical works.

1695

General Events

France levies first universal tax... Academy of Science forms, Naples... Hapsburg Empire takes first public census in Europe... England's state censorship ends with lapse of Licensing Act... France starts Royal mirror manufactory at Saint-Gobain with Venetian glassworkers (still extant)... Royal Bank of Scotland is established... French Academy of Sciences begins comprehensive study of manufacturing processes and technical equipment, <u>Description of the Arts and Crafts</u> in 1761-89... Marquis de Louvois, French War Minister, starts military reforms in this time (forms first military supply system, establishes pay scales)... English law, first, bans exports of textile machinery, blueprints (bans on artisans in 1781-86, creates licensing system in 1825)... Papin uses 1654 vacuum pump of Guericke and steam in trying to operate piston pump to raise water from mine.

1696

General Events

Journeymen hatters strike in England... Austrian Empress Maria Theresa builds baroque Schonbrunn Palace with park, formal gardens, chapel, coach house and zoo (-1730)... Pierre Giffart: <u>L'Art Militaire</u> (shows specializations of French soldiers)... Joshua Child, governor of

East India Co.: <u>A Discourse on Trade</u> (urges low interest rates so enterprises will borrow for commercial activities)... England contracts with manufacturers to operate work houses for unemployed and paupers, no relief to anyone not in a work house... Chinese book shows sequential steps for silk production in series of woodblock prints... Peter the Great sends 50 nobles abroad, England, Holland and Venice, to study shipbuilding, seamanship, navigation.

Business Events

Royal Africa Company loses monopoly to transport slaves (spurs New England slave trade)... Fire insurance office, first real mutual fund, is started in London as The Amicable Contributorship, known later as Hand-In-Hand (is absorbed in 1905 by Commercial Union Assurance Co. of London)... Lloyd's Coffee House issues <u>Lloyd's News</u> with shipping information... First English property insurance company appears.

1697

General Events

Peter the Great takes "The Great Embassy" to study technology and recruit experts in Prussia, Austria, England and Holland (-1698)... Sedan-chair is popular transportation in major European cities... Daniel Defoe proposes income tax... France tries to colonize West Africa (-1702, 1714-20)... English law requires all hawkers, peddlers be licensed... After inquiry of disreputable practices of stock jobbers, Parliament law regulates market (requires all brokers, limited to 100, to be licensed, restricts commissions to 10%, issues first listing of stocks in 1698)... B.F. de Belidor, French engineer (applies theory of mechanics to machine design), is born (-1761).

1698

General Events

<u>The Merchants' Companion</u> covers maritime insurance (shows policies at rates of 30-50% depending on season of voyage)... Russia taxes beards... Thomas Savery patents atmospheric 'fire-engine,' first practical steam engine, to pump water from mines (gets 14-year monopoly in 1699, fails as metal work does not hold pressure)... French government leases rights to individuals to collect indirect taxes for six years... Parliament declares Billingsgate Market for fish, first cited 1016, to be free and open (breaks monopoly of local fishmongers, closes 1982 for move to new site)... English salt workers strike to protest rates for piece work (form union in 1768, hold regular meetings by 1777).

Business Events

After eight years of lobbying and bribes, New East India Co. is chartered, causes scandal as largest single shareholder is an officer of the Honourable English East India Co. (leads to merger of first, New enterprises in 1708 as United Company of Merchants of England trading to the East Indies, known as "John Company")... Charnock, English East India Co., gets permission to start factories in Bengal.

1699

General Events

Statutes of French Academy of Sciences specify official role of savants in certifying efficiency of new machines... Parliament's Wool Act limits production in Ireland, bans export of wool from American colonies... Manchu mandarin issues trading permits in Macao to Europeans... England's Board of Trade urges Parliament to prohibit wool workers leaving country.

Business Events

Society of Assurance for widows and orphans forms in England... London's Berry Bros. & Rudd business forms to sell wine (evolves by 1980s as City's premier purveyor)... English East India Co. is allowed to start Canton factory.

1700-1799

General Events

Many towns in Germany are lit by oil lamps... Many European houses have commodes... Europe's population is some 118 million, around 187 million by 1801.

Business Events

Cotton mills south of Shanghai employ some 200,000 workers... Some 34 distilleries operate in Rotterdam, 121 by 1730... London's Worshipful Company of Cooks, evolved from medieval companies of cookshop proprietors, pie makers and confectioners, tries to enforce its right to require anyone practicing as a cook in the city to be a guild freeman... Calixto Valenti goldsmith firm appears in Spain's Catalonia area (still extant as global business).

1700

General Events

Charles Eyre organizes administration of Bengal... In this time a trade union appears in London as confederation of five box clubs of journeymen tailors (evolves as City's most powerful by 1764 with executive committee over 42 affiliated clubs)... English woolcombers of Tiverton form friendly society for mutual economic aid... Parliament bans imported cotton fabrics from India, Persia, China... Peter the Great starts School of Navigation and Mathematics, Moscow (moves to St. Petersburg in 1715 to become Naval Academy)... Berlin taxes unmarried women... Parliament's Piracy Act mandates colonial courts to try, sentence those suspected of piracy... Peter the Great orders all courtiers, officials in Russia to adopt Western dress... Savery submits steamboat design to England's Navy Board (is rejected after demonstration of model on the Thames).

Business Events

Glasgow textile factory employs some 1,400 workers in this time... Dunkirk forms chamber of commerce, Venice in 1763 and Florence 1770... In this time, Sweden's Polhem tries to make iron products with mechanized processes that do not require skilled craftsmen (also devises measuring rods to establish precision required for interchangeable parts, uses water to power rolling mill).

1701

General Events

Captain Kidd is hanged (May 23) in London for piracy (after commission as privateer in 1695 to guard English ships in Red Sea and India Ocean, becomes entrepreneur for treasure), murder... Henry Martyn: Considerations on the East India Trade (links division of labor to market and technical change, argues trade strategies, technologies necessary for manufacturing development)... Daniel Defoe: The Villany of Stockjobbers Detected... Jethro Tull devises first horse-drawn mechanical drill to plant seeds in rows... Leyden weavers strike, 14 ring leaders hanged and 6 flogged... Royal charters are granted to weavers in Axminister, Wilton to make carpets... Music publisher Henry Playford presents series of weekly concerts at Oxford... War of Spanish Succession begins (-1714, results in Blenheim campaign of 1704 where victorious English forces are commanded by Duke of Marlborough, assisted by William Cadogan as quartermaster-general, writes strategic plan, and by civilian Adam Cardonnel as personal secretary, handles correspondence to pioneer development of command secretariat)... Engineer Christopher Polhem, associate build experimental apparatus to test water wheels in Sweden, follows use of models by Fontana in 1500s with replica of Vatican obelisk in order to determine how to move, lift real one and by Riquet in 1600s to determine feasibility of a canal to link Atlantic, Mediterranean.

Business Events

Hotel Pupp opens in Karlovy Vary, Western Bohemia, for wealthy enjoying mineral-rich waters of Carlsbad... Bordeaux wholesalers, retailers of fats form 'secret society' to charge high prices for goods during war, fraud exposed 1708.

1702

General Events

England's Queen Anne approves horse racing... Earliest known pantomime in England appears at Drury Lane Theater... Denmark abolishes serfdom... Thomas Savery: The Miners' Friend, discusses 1698 steam engine.

Business Events

Asiento Guinea Co. is chartered to ship slaves to North America... The Daily Courant is London's first daily newspaper.

1703

General Events

Peter the Great plans, founds St. Petersburg, Russia's Capitol in 1712 (-1922)... Queen Anne charters London's leather industry... St. Petersburg Exchange, modeled on those of London and Amsterdam, opens, followed by Kremenchog in 1834, Moscow in 1839, Odessa and Nizhnyi Novgorod in 1848.

1704

General Events

In use since 1200s, Peter the Great starts routine minting of rubles... England offers bounties to encourage colonial production of tar, pitch, hemp, mass, yards, and flax, followed by bounties for indigo in 1749, potash in 1751, and silk in 1770... First known subscription library appears in Germany... Swiss Nicolas Facio seeks English patent to put jeweled bearings in watch movements (gets grant, rejected when Clockmakers' Co. opposes innovation for putting watchmakers in servitude, weakening monopoly)... France builds Fort Miami at Maumee, Wabash Rivers to protect trade route from Lake Erie to Mississippi River... Duke of Marlborough directs military forces at Blenheim from rear position, uses messengers to carry orders.

Business Events

Three enterprises in Wales merge to form London Lead Co. (-1905)... Quaker Abraham Darby goes to Holland to recruit skilled workers for his Bristol Brass Wire Co. (gets idea in 1707 from apprentice John Thomas to cast iron like brass)... Vossiche Zeitung paper is published in Berlin (-1933)... First forge of Wendel family is contracted by France to supply bullets to army of Louis XIV (escapes Robespierre's Reign of Terror, returns to France under Napoleon to prosper, contributes to France's industrial revolution with steel mills, is revitalized by new family head in 1978 after partial nationalization and collapse of steel market - only 30 small, unprofitable companies remaining of family's steel empire, prospers by eliminating firms and jobs, reorganizing makers of tin cans and plastic bottles as profit centers, cutting costs, using management incentives, and expanding into computer software)... Thomas Tompion, noted maker of timepieces,is master of Clockmakers' Co., London.

1705

General Events

Yodoya merchant house, most prominent in Osaka, is accused by government bureaucrats of ostentatious luxury (confiscate its wealth and cancel debts of local lord to house, other prosperous merchants so penalized)... Paris establishes commissioner for transportation (supervises innkeepers as commission agents for haulers).

Business Events

With operating losses, Dutch close factories at Ayudhya, Siam.. Richard "Beau" Nash is master of ceremonies at Bath Assembly Rooms, revives declining spa as fashionable resort.

1706

General Events

Francis Hauksbee devises Influence Machine (produces glow of electricity)... England classifies navy's men-of-war from "first rate," 100 guns or more, to "sixth-rate," under 30 guns, to standardize vessels... English blacksmith Thomas Newcomen, aided by plumber John Calley, develops first practical "atmospheric machine" to pump water from colliery, introduced 1711 and perfected by 1720 (forms firm in 1711 to build and sell "fire engines")... English inventor Henry Mill devises carriage springs... Steering wheel for sailing vessels is developed in England in this time... Peter the Great starts medical school in Moscow... Dick Turpin, English highwayman, is born (-1739)... Hotel des Invalides is built in Paris (1675-).

Business Events

London company provides fire insurance (after being absorbed by another firm, evolves as Sun Fire Office in 1709, still extant)... The Evening Post, London's first evening paper, is published... Thomas Twining starts family tea business with London coffee house, serves tea as specialty (with success opens Golden Lyon tea parlor, gets Royal Warrant as tea purveyor in 1837, takes over Edmond Antrobus' tea and coffee business in 1872, opens branch in 1874).

1707

General Events

Emperor Aurangzeb, last of great Mogul Moslem rulers, dies (causes disintegration of empire and formation of mercenary armies in Bombay, Madras and Calcutta by English East India Co.)... Great Britain is formed by union of England, Scotland and Wales, becomes Europe's largest free-trade area... Papin tests paddlewheel steam boat on Germany's Fulda River, destroyed by mob... Mitchman Cricket Club forms in London... Papin devises high-pressure boiler... Game of billiards evolves at Berlin coffee house... Patent for cast iron pots, idea from Dutch smelters, is granted to Quakers Darby, founder of family dynasty of ironmasters, and John Thomas, Bristol business becomes world famous for black kettles (moves Darby Works to Coalbrookdale in 1709 for coal and water, forms Coalbrookdale Co. with Quakers Thomas Goldney, investor, and ironmaster Richard Reynolds).

Business Events

After arriving in London in 1705, William Fortnum, footman in Queen Anne's household, is allowed to keep and sell used Palace candles (forms business with grocer Hugh Mason to serve specialty foods to Palace and aristocracy, imports fancy foods through English East India Co. to acquire reputation for exotic delicacies, evolves by 1788 to handle many potted foods, provides victuals to Duke of Wellington's staff during Spanish campaign, develops ready-to-eat dishes in 1800s, imports newly invented canned food from U.S.' H. J. Heinz in 1886)... English ironmonger, Ambrose Crowley, runs Europe's largest iron enterprise, sponsors model village for workers.

1708

General Events

Peter the Great divides Russia into eight governmental districts to centralize administration after Cossack uprising... Augustus the Strong of Saxony orders alchemist Johann F. Bottger to develop first European Chinese-type porcelain (after finding right clay, starts factory at Meissen in 1710 to make first European porcelain, employs 378 workers in 1750)... Seeking development funds, Papin submits specifications for vacuum engine to Royal Society of London, no money granted unless success assured... Parliament passes first of many acts to establish standards, regulations for woolen industry (uses government officials, supervised by Justices of the Peace, to inspect woolen goods)... Britain's Currency Act fines those guilty in offering illegal exchange rates for foreign coins.

1709

General Events

Bad harvests appear in Europe (causes in bread riots in Britain and famine in France)... Britain passes first copyright act... Postage rates in England are determined by mileage... Liverpool improves harbor to handle increased trade, first dock in 1715... Portuguese priest, Laurenco de Gusmao, builds and "flies" bird-shaped model glider... Italian harpsichord maker Bartolomew Cristfori, curator of musical instruments for Medici family, creates Pianoforte... Queen Anne's first act encloses open and common fields (follows fencing in 1500s, suspended in 1630 by Charles I as pasturage more profitable than tillage).

Business Events

Joseph Addison, Richard Steele publish The Tattler (reports imaginary trial of brewers adulterating wine), issue The Spectator in 1711... Italian Farina family in Cologne are credited for creating eau de Cologne... In this time, Darby invents blast furnace (is first to produce iron with coke, leads to four iron masters by late 1700s: Darby at Coalbrookdale, Wilkinson brothers at New Willey and Bersham - closes 1795, and Roebuck at Carron).

1710

General Events

London stocking-knitters strike masters for unemployment caused by employment of workhouse children, destroy knitting frames... Paris council of commerce refuses permission to two Avignon peddlers to sell silk, woolen goods in City because they don't have a shop... A report is made to French Controller-General on failures to block imports of fashionable printed calicoes from India when food is expensive, money scarce (leads to attempts to control calicoes by inspections, confiscations, imprisonments, fines - proposal by Paris merchant that women on the street be stripped of Indian fabrics)... German engraver Jakob le Bon devises 3-color printing... Hoop skirt is fashionable in London (fades away in high society by 1780s)... Tattler cites use of umbrella, noted by Jonathan Swift in 1704 and John Gay in 1716... Russia prepares first budget... Private science society forms in Uppsala, Sweden.

Business Events

Charles Povey, London, runs same ad for 6 months, pioneers advertising campaigns.

1711

General Events

Coffee is produced in Dutch East Indies... Peter the Great abolishes most trading monopolies, retains those in grain, vodka, salt and tobacco... Queen Anne sponsors first Ascot horse races... Sedan chair appears in London, competes in public transport with hackney coach... Partels invents first ventilator... Peter the Great replaces council of boyars with Senate to coordinate central, local governments in handling revenues.

Business Events

Mrs. Salmon's Waxworks moves to London's Fleet Street... To pay for Marlborough's Continental campaigns, English politicians, Harley Earl of Oxford as principal, form The Governor and Company of Merchants of Great Britain trading to the South Seas and other parts of America, incorporated by Tory Government with monopoly of trade with South America and power to issue stock to fund public debt (assumes debt of certain government debentures in return for guaranteed 6% from duties on wines, vinegar, India goods, silks, whale-fins, etc., gets monopoly for Spanish slave-trade and share in "rich" South American market for European goods in 1713 Anglo-Spanish Treaty, devises speculative scheme in 1719 to revive its fortunes, leads to speculative frenzy and panic after 1720 act converts outstanding debt to stock in South Sea Co., despite bribes to public officials and loans to investors to reinvest ruins many investors in collapse of South Sea Bubble, dissolved in 1854 with all debts paid).

1712

General Events

Savery supplies steam engine to London water works to pump water from the Thames (-1853)... Britain levies stamp tax on publications (-1853), forces many newspapers to close... Four naval dockyards, England's largest employer, employ over 2,000 workers (rises to over 2,900 in 1754, some 4,300 in 1761 and 2,300 in 1783)... Jan Kruse starts farming East Friesland's moorlands... England holds last execution for witchcraft.

Business Events

Antoine Crozat gets monopoly for French trade from Illinois to Pacific Coast, gives rights to Compagnie d'Occident in 1717 and Law's Compagnie des Indes Orientales in 1719.

1713

Business Events

Some 3,000 coffee houses do business in London... In contrast to 1553 Muscovy Co. as regulated company, Royal Africa Co. is a partnership.

1714

General Events

Spanish Academy of Science forms... Prussia abolishes witch trials... Spain creates Honduras Co. to colonize Central America (forms Caracas Co. in 1728, Havana Co. in 1740, Santo Domingo Co. in 1757)... England's Henry Mills is first known to patent a typewriting machine - never built, 112 others by 1874 (leads to machines in 1808 by Italy's Pellegrini Turri for blind friend - no details, in 1833 by Xavier Progin, Marseilles, to help blind - few sold, in 1870 by Danish pastor Malling Hansen - marketed as Skrivekugle, and in U.S. by Christopher Sholes, James Densmore - acquired by Remington in 1874)... Russia holds last witch trial... Bernard de Mandeville, Dutch physician in England: Fable of the Bees (-1719, notes multiplicity of wants by individuals seeking private interests, makes first reference to division of labor)... In this time (-1717) German instrument-maker Gabriel V. Fahrenheit devises first practical mercury thermometer, scale... Peter the Great puts Russian civil servants on salaries, previously allowed to get what money they could from public so long as state received its fixed share... After losing of four naval vessels and some 2,000 men due to uncertain navigation in 1707, Parliament forms Board of Longitude with scientists, admirals to determine a more precise measurement (awards Great Prize for marine chronometer to clockmaker John Harrison in 1761, similar prize by France in 1716).

1715

General Events

Essex weavers revolt against use of technical innovations... George Graham devises compensating pendulum for clocks... France issues rules to regulate guilds, some 300 by 1789... Venice holds government lottery.

Business Events

English East India Co. starts factory at Canton... Jean Martell leaves Jersey island, smugglers' headquarters, to make brandy in Cognac, Ranson and Delamain in 1723, England's Hine in 1763, and Ireland's Richard Hennessy in 1765... Count Waldstein starts wool mill in Czech territory (plans to put workshops under one roof, builds special settlements for serfs, workers)... L'Opera-Comique appears in Paris, vaudeville and musical comedies popular amusements of time...First installation of Newcomen engine is at a colliery, 135 in use by 1778, one runs from 1750-1900, when first Boulton and Watt engine is made.

1716

General Events

For first time, Russia is net exporter of iron, by 1800 world's largest iron producer... Emmanuel Swedenborg, Swedish philosopher, draws detailed sketch for flying machine... Thomas Watts: An Essay on the Proper Method for Forming the Man of Business (notes control value of double-entry bookkeeping)... Japan's Shogun bans cartels, still function in secret... Corps des Ponts et Chausses builds French roads in this time (leads to differentiation in civil and military engineering, technical school in 1747)... Peter the Great, using Swedish and German models, reorganizes Russian military organization... J.N. de la Hire invents double-acting pump to deliver continuous stream of water.

Business Events

After participating in Scotland's ill-fated Darien expedition in 1695-1701, Scottish economist John Law forms joint-stock Banque Generale, approved by regent Duke of Orleans, with authority to issue paper money (leads to paper inflation in dubious securities)... England's John Lombe, aided by priest, smuggles plans for silk-weaving machine out of Italy (starts first English factory in 1717 with 300 workers, water power, automatic tools, continuous production, specialization of labor)... Claude Moet starts making champagne in Epernay.

1717

General Events

Silver is found in Taxco, Mexico, when horse of Jose de la Borde stumbles and dislodges a stone, site for church in gratitude for accident... First Masonic Grand Lodge, based on guild practices of medieval stone masons, appears in London (evolves with worldwide membership of some 6 million by 1980s)... Some 900 weavers going from town to town smashing looms are dispersed by English troops at Devon... Louis XV grants trade monopoly to Law for Louisiana Territory, forms Compagnie de la Louisiane ou d'Occident (issues shares in 1718 based on "holdings" in government securities, gets tobacco monopoly in 1718, combines French East India Co., Guinea Co., Company of Santo Domingo, China Co. and Africa Co. as Company of the Indies in 1719 with privileges to collect taxes, mint coins)... Henry Beighton, Newcastle, invents safety valve for steam boilers of Newcomen's engines... Newton, Master of the Mint, issues England's first gold-backed currency... Robert Walpole starts first governmental sinking fund to redeem Britain's national debt... Mogul Emperor exempts English East India Co. from duties (grants concessions).

Business Events

60 charcoal furnaces operate in area of Coalbrookdale, Britain with 31 coke furnaces in 1774, 81 coke and 25 charcoal in 1790... Anglo-Irish landlords raise land rents in Ireland (spurs emigration of Irish to colonies).

1718

General Events

Peter the Great forms nine "colleges" as ministries, modeled on Sweden... London's Haymarket Opera House sponsors masquerades, basically masked assemblies (continues to 1730s when moved to larger facilities)... After French tax collectors are ordered in 1717 by Louis XV to accept notes from Law's private bank and exchange them for coins, Banque Royale is established, branches in five major towns, with King as sole stockholder (despite low earnings from loans by bank to Mississippi Co., appoints Law, viewed as financial wizard, Superintendent of Finance in 1719, merges Banque Royale with 1717 Mississippi Co. in 1720, leads to burst of Mississippi bubble in 1720 when bull market speculation collapses with company's inability to pay promised dividends)... Eliminating land and household taxes, Peter the Great adopts soul tax for all males, except clergy and nobility (-1887, after census lists 5.79 million taxable, collects first tax in 1724).

Business Events

Dutch start first coffee plantation at Surinam... London ships bound for Turkey are delayed in port for 10 months (raises prices for English exports, Turkish imports).

1719

General Events

Russia's Peter the Great decrees all women, girls held in jails in Moscow, other provinces are to be sent to linen mills of Andrei Turchaninov as punishment for misdeeds... England makes meetings of working people in public houses illegal.

Business Events

Bartholomew Roberts, perhaps greatest pirate of 1619-1723 period, begins career as Black Bart (-1722 after taking over 400 ships in waters of Caribbean, Atlantic and African Coast, as captain of pirate commune on Royal Fortune requires all to swear on Bible to obey articles - Article I gives all hands equal vote in affairs, divides loot, captain and quartermaster with two shares, master gunner and boatswain with 1.5 shares, other officers with 1.25 shares)... Oriental Co. is formed in Vienna to trade with the East... Champion James Figg opens London's first boxing school... Claude Innocent du Pacquier starts Royal Vienna porcelain factory (-1864, gets secret formula from friend of Bottger at Meissen - later process stolen by beau of director's daughter, despite exquisite workmanship is sold in 1744 to Archduchess Maria Theresa to resolve financial problems, is run by Queen, State to 1784 when Konrad von Sorgenthal takes over to his death in 1805, quality deteriorates).

1720

General Events

Law is Controller-General of France (merges Company of the Indies and Bank of France, flees to Venice when France goes bankrupt after paper money loses value)... Some 7,000 journeymen tailors hold London meeting to demand higher wages, reduction in work hours from masters (results in all-London strike, tentative "settlement" of struggle in 1745 after imprisonment of several journeymen and after masters form committee to start new houses of call, hire strike-breakers from provinces)... Parliament forbids unionization of tailors, other acts for weavers and woolmakers in 1725, hatters in 1777, and papermakers in 1796 (starts period of informal collective bargaining to settle labor disputes by various workers almost every year - some 383 by 1800 with 119 in London and 64 by woolcombers, weavers and spinners)... Secret of chimney draft is discovered in this time... First continental Newcomen "fire pump" is installed at coal field near Liege, first Boulton-Watt engine there in 1785... De La Jonchere, France, writes book on governmental reform... Marseilles is last European city to experience the plague... After wild two-year speculation in stock of South Sea Co. in anticipation of riches from slave trade to Spanish-American ports, frenzy in forming other joint-stock companies, i.e., to make gold from seawater, to make square cannonballs (promoter flees to Europe with funds), and to deliver fire from hell, and collapse of Bubble when investigation finds directors had "borrowed" from funds of South Sea Co., Parliament's Bubble Act forbids funding of stock companies without legislative approval (is followed by another public infatuation with commercial gambling in England's Great Railway mania of 1845)... Wallpaper is fashionable in England... First "yacht club" appears at Cork Harbor, Ireland... China authorizes Co-Hong merchant company to compete against European traders (-1771)... In this time, Protestant exiles are allowed to return to France, basis for increased trade at ports and growth of large-scale capitalistic enterprises... Rene Antoine Ferchault de Reumer builds cupola furnace to melt iron.

Business Events

In this time, Shimonura family opens secondhand clothing store in Nagoya, (expands later to Kyoto, Edo, Osaka in developing modern Daimaru department stores)... Foreign-owned linen mill is started in Russia, model for textile operation later in industrial village of Ivanovo.

1721

General Events

Holland buys Prussia's last factories in Africa... Regular postal service begins between London, New England... Robert Walpole is Chancellor of the Exchequer (-1742, abolishes over 100 duties, tariffs on imports of raw materials, semifinished goods)... As demanded by woolen industry, England's Calico Act bans importation of calicoes... Japan's shogunate gives control for distribution, sales of all commercial goods to Edo stalls, shops to 10 guilds of licensed middlemen.

Business Events

Russian merchants are allowed to buy villages to acquire workers for industrial mining enterprises, serfs bonded in 1736 in perpetuity to factories, mines... Elihu Yale, former American-born official for John Co., dies (1648-, leaves estate of souvenirs from India to be auctioned, first of importance in time, for funds for New Haven university).

1722

General Events

Prussia forms General Directory of War, Finance and Domains... Russian Imperial Decree forbids Russian factory owners to sell at retail... Work is started to build Norfolk residence, separate quarters for living and working, for Earl of Orford (-1735, some 84 other such residences in 1700s)... Hyacinthe Rigard, French painter: Grand Tour, guide for traveling... First Danish playhouse opens, features ballet previously seen only at court... France's Rene de Reaumur pens treatise on making steel (discovers secret of Chalybes, Caucasus, used in 1500-1400s B.C. to mix malleable iron, pig iron in crucible, discovery ignored)... Peter the Great establishes administrative grades with Table of Rank's Decree (forms three classes of state employees, military, civil and judicial, each with 14 levels for promotion, based on merit and service).

Business Events

Austrian East India Co. is formed (-1727)... After South Sea Bubble scandal, club of respectable brokers forms at Jonathan's Coffee House (leads to stock exchange on Threadneedle Street in 1773 with management by group of brokers, is replaced by new exchange in 1801-02 with 550 members managed by Committee of Proprietors, issues first rule book in 1812).

1723

General Events

Jacob Leupold, German engineer: Theatrum Machinarium Generale, first systematic study of mechanical engineering (-1739, shows design for noncondensing, high-pressure steam engine, built in early 1800s)... Basic law defining functions, obligations of Russian merchants is enacted (are permitted to purchase populated villages if attached permanently to factories, allows individuals of any class to establish factories and engage in town trade if a resident)... Three Choirs Festival, Britain's oldest musical festival, is started... England's Ambrose Godfrey devises crude sprinkler system for putting out fires, followed by improvements of Colonel S. William Congreve of England in 1809, U.S.' Philip W. Pratty in 1872 and U.S.' Henry S. Parmlee in 1884 with first system to be manufactured, sold... Chelsea Water Works Company of London incorporates, introduces first sand filtration process in 1829... Parliament establishes workhouses for poor... Spanish colonists settle Montevideo... Middlesex grand jury declares The Fable of the Bees as a public nuisance... M.P.L. Savary: Dictionnaire Universel de Commerce.

Business Events

Longman's, Britain's oldest continuing publishing house, appears... Jonas Alstromer goes to Sweden (smuggles workers into land to build textile looms).

1724

General Events

Daniel Defoe: Tour Thro' the Whole Island of Great Britain (-1726, notes new discoveries in metals, mines and minerals, new undertakings in trade, engines and manufacturers, and new developments in spa towns, cites mop fair, also called living fair, in Oxfordshire village for men, women seeking work)... Russia forms Manufacturing College to grant approval and privileges to new industrial enterprises (-1727, is re-started 1727, leads to commercial and mining colleges in 1731-41, is abolished 1779 with rivalry between merchant-manufacturers, merchant-traders)... Peter the Great establishes Russia's first comprehensive tariff system (requires all merchants, manufacturers to be licensed)... Nearly 20% of Russia's total tax revenue comes from state control of alcohol trade, over 30% by 1769.

Business Events

French Bourse opens in Paris, reorganized in 1816.

1725

General Events

Peter the Great commissions Danish Captain Vitus Bering to explore Northeastern Coast of Siberia (1728-41, discovers Bering Strait)... Catherine I opens Russian Academy of Science in St. Petersburg, first commissioned by Peter the Great with advice of Leibniz... Paris holds its first public concert... Sweden's Erik Salander writes book on animal husbandry, agriculture... Giambattista Vico pens treatise on possibility of cyclical changes in history... French organ maker Basil Bouchon devises mechanism for automated silk loom guided by pegs, punched paper roll (is improved in 1741 by automata maker Vaucanson).

Business Events

Seventy-six Russian ironworks operate in Urals... Swedish iron makers reopen Spain's Rio Tinto iron mines.

1726

General Events

Japan adopts money economy... Britain's first circulating library opens in Edinburgh... General George Wade starts building roads in Scotland (-1737, launches Britain's road system)... Manufacturers' Loan Fund is established in Sweden.

Business Events

Wealthy in France form Ferme generale with near monopoly to levy taxes on salt, tobacco, corn, etc... Lloyd's List is issued during this time in London as biweekly publication of shipping news, Lloyd's Register of Shipping in 1760.

1727

General Events

Humphrey Bland: <u>Treatise on Military Discipline</u> (becomes leading English manual on tactics)... Scottish goldsmith invents stereotype... Defoe identifies entertainment places for tea, coffee, cards and conversation as assemblies, first seen in France (evolve as central feature in many English towns)... Stephen Hales: <u>Vegetable Staticks</u>, quantitative analysis of biological phenomena... Brazil plants first coffee... Daniel Defoe: <u>The Complete English Tradesman</u>... Britain hires first Hessian mercenaries... French manufacturing inspectors tell Saintonge villages to make products in conformance with guild regulations... Johann Schulze finds silver nitrate darkens with exposure to light (leads to first photogram by Wedgwood and Davey, first negative by Niepce in 1816, and first known photograph in 1827)... Chinese emperor abolishes all hereditary servile groups.

Business Events

After helping to perfect Newcomen engine in England, Marten Triewald builds one for Swedish mine, replaced by Boulton and Watt engine in 1804... Fur trader Pierre Gaultier de Varennes builds trading post in Central Canada, first in chain by 1738... First Moslem press appears in Constantinople... British wine shippers, Oporto, form association to deal with growers.

1728

General Events

Prussia forms Foreign Ministry... Dr. Black, originator of pneumatic revolution, is born (-1799)... Holland grants tax privileges to brickworks.

Business Events

Caracas Co. is formed, Venezuela, to operate cocoa plantations.

1729

General Events

Holland starts direct voyages to China... China bans opium smoking (warns John Co. to stop drug trade or lose all commercial privileges, is ignored by Chinese officials and Western traders until 1830s)... Stephen Gray, English scientist, discovers some materials are conductors, non-conductors of electricity... China's government forms Grand Council, advisory body to provide policy guidelines for current operations of grand secretariat... Russia makes promissory notes legal tender.

1730

General Events

J.J. Wolrab: <u>Military Exercises</u> (shows motion study of specific steps to fire a musket)... German A. Ketterer invents cuckoo clock in this time... Parliament passes enclosure acts for various localities, some 3,500 other acts by 1820... Process of zinc-smelting is started in Britain... After retiring from politics, Lord Townshend devises four-course system, uses clover and turnips, of agriculture to revive his unproductive estate, used by nearby landowners to increase value of lands around Norfolk by tenfold... Lillo: <u>London Merchant</u>... Bernard Forest de Belidor: <u>Architecture hydraulique</u>, early engineering handbook (-1739)... Britain develops nationwide turnpike system... Diamonds are found in Brazil, replaces India as world's leading producer by 1800 with 300,000 carats/year until South Africa's discovery in 1866... Richard Cantillon, inside trader during

Mississippi scheme: Essai sur la Nature du Commerce en Generale, published 1755 (notes role of entrepreneur to balance rewards, risks).

Business Events

Spanish-born Juan Floris opens London perfumery (attracts fashionable clientele with individual scents, gets Royal Warrant in 1821, still extant)... Agent of English wine merchant, Pedro Domecq starts to make sherry in Jerez, Spain, still extant... Some 240,000 firearms are made in Liege region.

1731

General Events

Parliament prohibits English factory workers to migrate to U.S. colonies... Jethro Tull: The New Horse-Hoeing Husbandry, or an Essay On the Principles of Tillage and Vegetation (describes methods used by farmers in France, Germany and Holland to start England's agricultural revolution)... Holy Roman Empire restricts guild activities to economic interests, eliminates judicial powers and political activities (is adopted by Prussia in 1734-36, Saxony and Baden in 1760, Austria in 1770, Bavaria in 1764)... John Hadley presents paper on sea-octant with two mirrors to Royal Society, tested 1732 (leads to 1734 claim by U.S. inventor Thomas Godfrey for developing instrument in 1730, leads to invention of sextant for navigation by Captain John Campbell in 1757)... Edward Thurlow, Lord Chancellor of Britain (raises issue in a judgment: "did you ever expect a corporation to have a conscience, when it has no soul to be damned and no body to be kicked?"), is born (-1806)... Britain patents triangular plow for one man and two horses, replaces rectangular plow needing driver, plowman and 6-8 oxen (is not used until around 1870s).

Business Events

Swedish East India Co. is founded... Emperor Charles VI charters Ostend Co... First Finnish tobacco factory is started at Abo, by royal decree all towns to allot acreage for growing tobacco.

1732

General Events

Prussia places strict state controls on guilds (-1735)... Russia grants privileges to English merchants to trade with Persia via Kazan... London's Covent Garden Opera House opens... Russia bans weaving of broadcloth by peasants, bans on hats in 1747, gold and silver work in 1753... Russian government starts survey of Siberia Coast (-1743).

Business Events

After unsuccessful try in 1729, Danish Asiatic Co. forms, holds trade monopoly to 1839.

1733

General Events

France adopts compulsory service for roads, bridges and public works... To fight mechanization, North Essex cloth town petitions Parliament for help to revive lost trade (leads to dissolution of Cloth Workers Co. in early 1790s)... Britain uses term "budget" for compilation of government accounts, subjected to Parliamentary review in early 1800s... Prussia starts military conscription... Britain's John Kay invents flying shuttle to improve productivity of hand looms in weaving wider cloth (although rejected by wool manufacturers and house attacked by mobs, is used by cotton manufactories in 1760)... Hungary's Schemnitz Mining Academy is world's first technical college.

1734

General Events

Pierre Rameau: Le Maitre a Danser (shows sequence of steps required for dancing a minuet)... Denmark bans strikes by workers... With support of guilds, England bans handbills to advertise goods by wholesalers, retailers... England, Russia sign commercial treaty... John T. Desaquliers: A Course of Experimental Philosophy, Vol. I (discusses use of science for technology)... Society forms at sign of Three Tulips, London, to raise funds for suing outsiders practicing "Art of Mystery of Plaisterers."

Business Events

Irbit fair for traders appears in Siberia, others in period at Tobol'sk, Omsk, Tomsk, Irkutsk and Kyakhta... Famous prize-fighter James Figg dies, presented such entertainments as female-fighting, bear and tiger-baiting, cock-and-bull fights at Figg's House.

1735

General Events

Johannes Beyer designs water-powered threshing machine... Bathing machines appear on Scarborough seaside... King Louis XV sets specifications for classic champagne bottle, required to withstand internal pressure for wine's second fermentation.

Business Events

French East India Co. starts sugar industry on Indian Ocean islands of Mauritius, Reunion... Don Manuel Maria Gonzales starts making Tio Pepe sherry in Jerez... Blancpain is oldest Swiss watch company by 1990.

1736

General Events

Robert Phillips: Dissertation Concerning the Present State of the High Roads of England, Especially of Those Near London (deplores conditions for travel)... "India rubber" appears in England... Venice starts making Murano glass... Jonathan Hulls, English clock-repairer, patents steam towboat with Newcomen engine, no data on any tests... Russian serfs, their descendants are bonded in perpetuity to their factories, mines... George II founds University of Gottingen in Hanover for study of science... Leonhard Euler: Mechanica sive motus analytice exposita, first systematic study of mechanics.

Business Events

Some 600 looms, 3,000 cottage workers are employed by two brothers in English textile enterprise... Samuel Whitbread is apprenticed to London brewer (starts family brewery with partners in 1742, closes 1976).

1737

General Events

Britain's licensing act restricts number of London theaters (requires all public plays to be censored by Lord Chamberlain)... Mob of women in Macclesfield burn looms to force release of arrested leaders... General plan for country-wide road system in France is prepared, initial construction 1740-80.

1738

General Events

France uses British technical assistance during this time to modernize its cotton industry (-1800s)... Patent for first spinning machine, doubles output of weaver and improves quality, for cotton is granted to Lewis Paul, John Wyatt (go bankrupt in 1742, sell invention to Edward Cave, editor of Gentleman's Magazine, for use in his workshop - one of first cotton-spinning mills in England, leads to purchase of marginal mill in 1764 by Richard Arkwright)... English woolen workers riot to protest low piecework rate... Automata maker Jacques de Vaucanson designs wind-up flute player... Britain's Whitehaven Colliery introduces first iron rails.

Business Events

Request is made to French government for permission to start copper wire factory near Essonne... Swedish Levantine Co. forms (-1757)... Private porcelain factory is started at Chateau de Vincennes, acquired by king in 1756 (is moved, encouraged by Madame de Pompadour, to Sevres)... Finnish textile mill is started in Abo with 12-year monopoly, 3 looms by 1740, 4 in 1742, 5 and 62 workers in 1744.

1739

General Events

During war of Austrian Succession, Britain borrows large sums at 3-4%, half the rate of early 1700s (-1747)... Swedish Scientific Academy forms... Yorkshire clockmaker Henry Hindley devises clock-wheel cutter to make equal divisions for sextants... George Louis de Buffon is Keeper of Jardin du Roi (develops facility as research institute for French biologists, chemists)... Francois Marin: The Gift of Comus, first French cookbook with provincial recipes.

1740

General Events

Frederick the Great rules Prussia (-1786, introduces freedom of press and worship, founds Berlin Academy of Science, encourages use of credit societies to promote growth of agriculture, abolishes internal tolls, builds roads and canals, and provides public relief, to build economy fosters commercial ventures with privileges, opens mines, recruits foreign farmers and artisans, i.e., dairymen, silk weavers, metal workers and porcelain-makers, opens royal bank and stock exchange in Berlin, forms overseas trading firm - plagued by corruption, starts new industries, i.e., porcelain and cutlery, gets revenues from peasant "contribution" tax, rents on estates, profits from royal mint, Crown factories, and salt works, land taxes, tolls on roads and bridges, levies on town dwellers, customs, and excise duties, i.e., grain, leather, sugar, beer and firewood, maintains standing army of 200,000, during war of Austrian Succession, 1740-48, uses quartermaster-general and aides as staff and during Seven Years War of 1756-63, military victories leads to first mass production of toy soldiers)... Wood's Grand Parade, first so-called, is built in Bath as promenade for visiting society at spa (-1748)... Baron Von Stein starts canal construction on Ruhr River to improve transportation of coal (-1870)... Prussian Royal Warehouse in Berlin employs some 1,400 outworkers to supply cloth to army... Liege employs some 15,000 out-working nail workers.

Business Events

Doncaster clockmaker, Benjamin Huntsman develops high-quality steel at Sheffield with secret process to provide cutting edge for shaping other metals (when rejected by local cutters sends crucible steel to French cutlers, popularity forces Sheffield cutlers to use steel).

1741

General Events

Russian vessels explore Northern Pacific (-1742, discover Aleutian Islands and Alaska's shore)... Russian navigator, Alexi Cherikov, visits California... Britain's Highway Act is passed to improve roads... Britain founds Royal Military Academy... Anders Berch is first professor of economics in Uppsala, Sweden... Parliament declares issue of private paper-money is illegal... Vaucanson invents automated silk loom with notched cylinder to regulate weaving pattern (abandons loom after riots by silk weavers in Lyons, is reintroduced with endless chain of punch cards in 1801 by Jacquard)... Britain is first to use wrought iron in bridge construction.

Business Events

French clockmaker devises "fusee machine" to make large number of clocks for commercial market, automatic fusee in 1763 by Swiss clockmaker Ferdinand Berthoud.

1742

General Events

Edmund Hoyle: A Short Treatise On the Game of Whist, popularizes game of late 1600s throughout Europe - called "bridge" in 1880s... French chemist Jean Malouin discovers method to galvanize iron... Pope Benedict XIV directs commission of three mathematicians to do static examination of St. Peter's Dome, shows use of science to resolve practical problem... Swiss astronomer Anders Celsius invents centigrade thermometer... Thomas Bosover devises process to make Sheffield plate, thin layer of sterling silver over copper.

Business Events

Sweden's oldest glass works is started at Kosta, named Orrefors during World War I... Cotton factories appear in Birmingham, Northampton.

1743

General Events

William Champion, Bristol, is "first" in Europe to make zinc, used in Chinese coins in 1402... First known elevator, uses counterweights, is installed at Versailles palace for Louis XV to see mistress, followed by first public elevator, hand drawn, in 1829 at Regent's Park Coliseum, London, for tourists and first hydraulic elevator of France's Leon Edoux... Joseph Balsămo, Cagliostro the alchemist (is rumored he could turn pebbles into diamonds and crows into maidens, "transmutes" metals, tells fortunes, sells elixirs throughout Europe), is born in Sicily (-1790).

Business Events

Moet and Chandon wine business appears (grows in 1770s with stronger bottles devised by glass makers for Dom Perignon champagne)... Company of Nail Makers forms in Liege... Meyer Rothschild, founder of family dynasty (after distributing flyers to nobility to sell old coins and rare metals, is made court factor by Prince William of Hanau in 1769 - financial adviser when prince becomes Landgrave of Hesse-Cassel in 1785, starts branches with five sons at Frankfort, London, Paris, Vienna, and Naples), is born as Bauer to Frankfort ghetto moneychanger (-1812).

1744

General Events

Honourable Company of Edinburgh Golfers forms... England's first recorded cricket match is played, legal sport in 1748... Cesar Cassini undertakes first national land survey of France (-1792).

Business Events

First cotton factory in Berlin is built, City's first silk factory in 1748... Name of London's Maryland Coffee House, which provided facilities for merchants trading with Baltic area, is changed to Virginia and Baltrick Coffee House (evolves as Baltic Exchange, arranges most of world's chartering of ocean shipping by 1980s)... Samuel Baker, London book seller and auctioneer of literary works, starts Sotheby's auction house (after moving to new location in 1913 starts auctioning art).

1745

General Events

John Cary: <u>An Essay on the State of England</u> (covers wages, productivity, new manufacturers and technical change, notes reduction of costs in various industries, sugar refinery, distilling, tobacco manufacture, wood working and lead smelting, from technical changes)... W. Cooke invents steam heating... Robert Bakewell starts experiments, Leicester, to improve breeding of sheep... Trip from London to Edinburgh usually takes a fortnight (takes about 2.5 days in 1796, some 36 hours by coach or steamer in 1830)... Sweden is unsuccessful in forming West India Co... Ewald Jurgen von Kleist, Pomerania, and Musschenbroek, Holland, independently discover storage of electricity in bottles, called Leyden jars... Parliament offers reward to any British subject discovering passage westward from Hudson Bay to Pacific.

Business Events

Leaving Siberia for insufficient game, Russian fur traders start post on Attu Island in this time as base for hunting abundant sea otters, hunters reach eastern end of Aleutians by 1759.

1746

General Events

Christopher Polhem: <u>Patriotic Testament</u> (discusses theory and use of machines to make Sweden technically independent of England)... Book on science of shipbuilding is written, shows practical applications.

Business Events

John Roebuck opens Birmingham plant to make sulphuric acid, opens Scottish plant in 1749 to pioneer industrial chemistry in Britain.

1747

General Events

Sweden organizes Iron Office to provide low interest loans to iron works... William Hogarth: "Industry and Idleness," 12 engravings on trials and rewards of apprenticeship... Julien Offroy de la Mettrie: Man a Machine (discusses philosophy of materialism)... German chemist, A.S. Marggraf, isolates sugar from beets, first sugar plant in Silesia in 1801-02... Britain taxes carriages... France's School of Bridges and Highways is first civil engineering school, School of Engineering in 1749, School of Mines in 1783, first technical school in 1806... First clinical drug testing occurs in treating 12 British sailors for scurvy.

Business Events

Mimic Samuel Foote re-opens London's Haymarket Theater with patent for summer months, becomes Theater Royal... Glenlivet distillery is founded to make Scotch whisky... General Trading Co. forms in Denmark to trade with Faroe Islands, Iceland, Greenland, Finmarken (-1774)... Actor David Garrick is manager of London's Drury Lane Theater (-1776).

1748

General Events

Joseph Bramah, English master mechanic (trains Henry Maudslay) and inventor (devises spring-winding machine, modern water closet in 1778, tumbler-lock in 1784, hydraulic press in 1796, beer-pump in 1797, wood-planing machine in 1802), is born (-1814)... John Tuberville Needham finds micro-organisms in sealed flasks of broth... First South American platinum is shipped to Europe... In this time, Britain hosts 160 turnpike trusts, 530 by 1760... Sweden compiles reliable reports on population, starts study of demographics... Paul invents wool-carding machine... English writer, Henry Fielding, is appointed Justice of the Peace for Westminster, later Middlesex (publishes Covent Garden Journal with advertising for work, runs employment agency)... Ironmaster John Wilkinson builds Britain's first blast furnace... French engineer Francois Fresneau delivers paper to Academy of Science on coating boots, coats with latex soap for waterproofing.

Business Events

After discovering Huntsman's secret process for making steel by covert methods, Samuel Walker starts steel plant at Potherham, basis for fortune... Fry family starts Bristol apothecary, makes chocolate as sideline (acquires 1728 Churchman's patent for industrial manufacture of chocolate in 1759, buys Adolphe Lafont Chocolate business in 1863 to enter continental market, introduces famous chocolate cream bar in 1866, adds seven factories in 1869-1907).

1749

General Events

French nobility are required to pay direct taxes... Spanish Crown forms office of tax collector, ends practice of contracting collection of revenues... Dr. Russell: A Dissertation on the Use of Sea Water in the Diseases of the Land (promotes development of English seaside resorts, such as Brighton, by 1790s)... French sugar planters found Port-au-Prince, Haiti... Philip Vaughan patents ball bearings for carriage axles... David Hartley: Observations on Man (launches modern psychology).

Business Events

Swedish entrepreneur starts first Finnish glass works (employs bookkeeper in 1749 and pastor in 1763 to handle employee benefits, runs 3 furnaces and 18 workshops in 1806)... J & B Scotch whisky is blended, Scotland (still extant).

1750

General Events

By 1850, operational decisions for military tactical movements evolve from oral messages to written orders... Britain's Jockey Club forms to oversee horse racing... Europe produces 23.2% of world's manufacturing output, China with 32.8% and India with 24.5%, while Britain produces 1.9%, Hapsburg Empire 2.9%, France 4.0%, Germany 2.9%, Italy 2.4%, Russia 5%, Japan 3.8%, and U.S. 0.1%... By 1759, theater and assembly hall, provides space for cards, tea and social activities, opens in Norwich, copied by other British town centers... Andrew Meikle devises automatic turning gear to improve efficiency of windmills... Textiles are over 50% of England's exports, 60% by 1800... By 1800, 69 new scientific journals appear in Europe... Cesar Francois, son develop first complete topographical map of France (-1789)... English carding machines appear in France, spinning-jennies around 1770... Britain's John Spilsbury devises "first" jigsaw puzzles in this time... France's Bureau of Commerce limits grants of monopoly to encourage competition... Britain creates "tied house" system whereby breweries can own some 55% of pubs, faces end in 1989 with six breweries owning some 22,000 pubs of 82,000... Britain's first Stilton cheese appears... Parliament bans erection of slitting mills for hats... In this time Magistrates' Court at Bow Street, London, develops system of unarmed uniformed 'runners' to catch criminals, evolves as Metropolitan Police Force in 1829... Marquis de Pombal, title in 1770, heads Portuguese government of Joseph I (-1777, reforms finances, encourages industry and trade, forms trade companies with monopolistic powers, tries to revive agriculture with silk-raising, founds Aulo de Commercio, as Europe's first business school is destroyed by Lisbon's 1755 earthquake).

Business Events

20 banks operate in London, 50 in 1770 and 70 in 1800, with 12 outside, some 400 by 1793... Some 360 workers, 177 permanent and 183 part-time, are employed in teams of 15 or more on patrician farm of Trons near Venice (is an agricultural factory with steward, foremen)... Spain's ceramic production industrializes around Valencia, major center for tile in 1980s... John Fielding publishes Public Advertiser in this time (-1780).

1751

General Events

Frederick II founds Emden Trading Co... By 1760, France's Dohamel du Monceau publishes information on new agricultural machines, methods used in England... Abbe Galiani writes book on money (views high prices a sign of countries with greatest wealth)... Ecole Superieure de Guerre is founded, Paris... Denis Diderot: Encyclopedie, 28 volumes by 1772 (sells all of 4,000 printed, describes 18 stages in manufacturing pins).

Business Events

Robert Clive of English East India Co. takes French post at Arcot (starts demise of France in India)... During year 35 French ships, owned by merchants of Nantes, carry 10,003 slaves to West Indies, soon slave-trading companies appear in France for profitable business... Cannon factory appears in Denmark (trains peasants as craftsmen)... As a result of Meissen porcelain works, British porcelain factory is started in Worcester by 15 partners (after number of partnerships, becomes Royal Worcester Porcelain Co. in 1860)... Britain's John Holkes starts cloth factory with latest machinery in Rouen.

1752

General Events

Britain adopts Gregorian calendar (causes to riots by those wanting back 11 days lost on turnover).

Business Events

First known steam engine-water wheel combination is built at Bristol brass works.

1753

General Events

France declares 2nd bankruptcy... Scottish surgeon, Charles Morrison, suggests idea for electric telegraph in Scots Magazine, developed by Francisco Salva in 1804, S.T. von Sommering in 1812, Baron Schilling in 1832, and Cooke, Wheatstone with patent in 1837... British Museum is founded, opens 1759... Small-wear weavers form union, Britain... Frederick the Great sponsors Royal Iron Works in Upper Silesia (is technical source for development of coke blast furnace in 1796)... James Lind, Scottish naval surgeon, publishes research on use of citrus fruit to prevent scurvy.

Business Events

Vienna Bourse opens as stock exchange.

1754

General Events

Britain's Marriage Act bans clandestine weddings in taverns or private houses... Society for the Encouragement of Arts, Manufacturers and Commerce forms in Britain to discuss applied technology (devises scheme to bring fish from coast to London by road to break monopoly of Thames fish dealers), is model later for groups in France, Holland and Russia... French envoy to Holland seeks good mechanic (wants to get Dutch secrets on mills, engines)... Society of St. Andrews Golfers forms, known later as Royal and Ancient Golf Club of St. Andrews... Coach trip from London to Bristol is scheduled as two- day event, by 1780s fastest coach in 16 hours with drivers carrying locked clocks to maintain schedules... Britain's Joseph Blake experiments with specific and latent heat, results from doctoral thesis on finding remedy for common ailment of heavy drinkers... Thomas Chippendale: The Gentlemen and Cabinet Makers' Directory, dedicated to fashion arbiter Earl of Northumberland (runs several workshops for wealthy clients).

Business Events

Merchant Bank opens in St. Petersburg... Charles Cusin, Burgundy, opens small clock factory in Geneva (although craft flourished in past, starts development of Swiss watch industry with use of rural outworkers)... Darby operates blast furnaces, air by bellows powered by water wheel, at Coalbrookdale (replaces bellows with compressed-air pump of John Smeaton in 1760)... Henry Cort builds Britain's first iron-rolling mill at Fareham.

1755

General Events

Sankey Canal is built to carry coal from St. Helen's to Liverpool (-1757, is Britain's first modern canal)... Russia abolishes internal tolls (destroys virtual monopoly of local retail merchants by exposing them to ruinous competition from trading peasants)... Andre Morellet: Code de la Nature (proposes "from each according to his ability, to each according to his need")... During All Saints' Day in Lisbon, some 30,000 are killed by earthquake (leads to formation of Compagnie Royale to operate English vineyards making port wine and to recruitment of craftsmen from France, Italy and Germany to revive local industries, efforts fail)... Jean-Jacques Rousseau: Discourse on the Origin of Inequality (denounces private property as source of evils for civilization)... Richard Cantillon, French businessman: Upon the Nature of Commerce in General (covers production, distribution of wealth)... Jean Maritz is inspector-general of French gun foundries (devises cannon-boring machine similar to Wilkinson's in 1774)... Moscow University is founded, Bolshoi dancing school in 1773... Bernard Forest: Engineer's Handbook... Rangoon appears in Burma... Scottish chemist Joseph Black discovers carbon dioxide.

Business Events

Bank Lev appears in Zurich (still extant).

1756

General Events

Seven Years War between Britain, joined by Prussia, and France, joined by Austria, Russia and Spain, begins over boundary disputes in North America (-1763, leads to formation of Europe's first military division by Prussia's de Broglie, takes some 40 years for effective utilization)... Mogul forces capture Calcutta, imprison British in "Black Hole" (is re-captured 1757 by forces of East English Co.)... Royal funding for survey of France is discontinued (is continued by private investors for rights to publish map of France, work available in 1793).

Business Events

First European chocolate factory appears in Germany... Williamson's Liverpool Advertiser covers union activities of tailors, shoemakers... Douro Wine Co. is formed to control Portugal's wine exports, monopoly in 1761 for sale of brandy to fortify wines.

1757

General Events

Government orders some French cities to abandon pursuits of runaway workers as a waste of public money... All Western trade to China is restricted to Canton, Kiakhta opened for Russia in 1737.

Business Events

Italian pastry-cook opens Gunter's Tea Shop, London (-1956)... Cinzano family starts distillery in Italy, still extant... French, Hindu troops are beaten at Plassey, Bengal, by East English forces of Robert Clive, former Madras clerk in 1744 (drives French fleet from Indian waters in 1758, takes surrender of France's Pondichery in 1761, leads to British supremacy in India by 1765).

1758

General Events

Britain's Jedediah Strutt invents ribbing machine to make hose... Fitzgerald proposes to Royal Society to make Newcomen's engine into driving machine by connecting beam with some transmitting apparatus... Francois Quesnay: Tableau economique (notes agriculture source of wealth, goods and wealth circulated and regulated by natural laws, and country's economic policy should be one of Laisser faire)... English commission sets "imperial standards" for measurements.

Business Events

Bagnigge Wells opens, London, to provide customers with gardens, waters, banquet hall, bowling green, grotto, skittles, alley and bun house (-1841)... Johann Geigy begins Basel chemical business with organic merchandise, spices and dyes (makes new dyes in 1859, joins Basel AG cartel in 1918 to compete with Germans, in 1929 merges with I.G. Farben to join French, British interests, lasts until 1939).

1759

General Events

Frederick the Great leases Prussian coinage to Jewish firm of Ephraim and Itzig... Bavaria Academy of Science forms... First Danish-Norwegian economic journal appears... Charles III rules Spain (-1788, forms Sociedades Economicas de los Amigos del Pais in Madrid - other centers later to promote education, science, industry, and commerce, considers craft occupations as not compatible for nobles, establishes model factories in textiles, hats, silks, glass, tapestry).

Business Events

Modern Guinness brewery business appears in Dublin... Dr. Samuel Johnson denounces advertisements as being over-exaggerated, false... Duke of Bridgewater, owner of coal deposits in Worsely, hires James Brindley, practical engineer, to build canal from Liverpool to Leeds (opens 1761 to deliver coal to cotton mills)... After working for father, Birmingham silver stamper and piercer, in manufacturing and marketing, Matthew Boulton inherits fortune on death of father (forms partnership with John Fothesgill, knowledge of foreign markets, in 1762 to handle commercial activities, makes various metal products at Soho Manufactory, by 1769 employs 700-800 and sells throughout Europe, forms new partnership with Watt in 1775, builds first Boulton & Watt steam engine in 1776 - in first 7 years provides consulting engineers, drawings and cylinders to build engines at mines and water works, adopts policy in 1780 to sell engines on monthly payments, gets sufficient volume by 1782 to pay debts, produces rotary engines in 1782, tests steam power for corn mill, suggests use of pattern cards to Watt in 1782, takes son and Watt's son in partnership - ends 1850, after patent infringement cases in 1790s wins in 1799, patent expires 1800).

1760

General Events

Count Henri Claude de Rouvroy de Saint-Simon, French utopian socialist (thinks workers should receive just share of country's wealth), is born (-1825)... In this time, San Blas evolves as Spanish port on Mexico's Pacific Coast, base for Northern expeditions to California... Belgian-born Joseph Merlin devises roller skates by replacing blades of ice skates with wheels (during demonstration at elegant ball crashes into crystal mirror, spurs rumors that novel creation is unsafe, is European, U.S. fad in 1860s)... Britain imports 2.5 million pounds of raw cotton for countryside textile industry (imports 22 million tons in 1787)... James Watt, instrument maker at Glasgow University, is asked to repair model of Newcomen engine (after noting inefficiencies, conceives idea for separate condenser in 1765, with funds in 1768 from Roebuck, gets 2/3 interest in invention, develops steam engine)... By 1810, Parliament passes 2,438 acts, 246 since 1702 to remove 400 acres from planting, to remove enclosures on some 5 million acres.

Business Events

Finch's Grotto Gardens opens, London, with public amusements (-1773)... Dr. John Roebuck builds Carron Iron Works near Firth of Forth, world's first planned factory is prototype for others (hires Smeaton as consulting engineer, uses first Watt steam engine in 1769, declares bankruptcy in 1773, is revived by English and Scottish capitalists to develop Europe's largest munitions works by 1800)... First machine-made lace is woven in Europe in 1760s... 38 soap plants in Marseilles employ some 1,000 workers... William Hamley opens toy shop in Holborn, London, leads to 1881 branch, advertised as world's largest in 1990s, on Regent Street.

1761

General Events

Europe is ravaged by influenza epidemic... Prussia, Turkey sign trade treaty... In reversal of custom, English governor of Ft. William, India, grants Nawab of Bengal an audience... Osaka merchants are required to give "loans" to government bureaucrats for losing money on rice sales... Smeaton devises water-powered bellows to lower price of iron (also improves Newcomen's engine, designs bridges, harbors and canals)... Johann Sussmilch develops study of statistics, demography in treatise... Denmark-Norway restricts guild privileges, Sweden in 1773... Mersey Navigation Co. completes canal from Manchester to Mersey River, first phase in James Brindley's plan to develop Grand Trunk Canal to link major cities by 1770... First veterinary school of medicine appears in France, 2nd 1765... Danish expedition explores Arabia, Palestine, Syria, Asia Minor and Persia... Thomas Mortimer: Every Man His Broker, 13 editions by 1810 (protests activities of brokers)... London holds first exhibition of agricultural machines.

Business Events

Cuba's first tobacco factory opens in Pinar del Rio province west of Havana.

1762

General Events

London regulates tradesmen's signs, first used by Romans... France's Dumas devises jig-saw puzzles by selling cut-up geography maps for students to reassemble... Russian merchants are not allowed to buy serfs, landed estates... Chinese census counts some 200 million people, 361 million in 1812, over 421 million in 1846 and over 1 billion by 1990... Despommiers: How To Get Rich Quick in Farming... Jean-Jacques Rousseau: The Social Contract (notes "Man is born free and is everywhere in chains")... British gambler John Montague, Fourth Earl of Sandwich, creates sandwich in this time... Denmark- Norway puts tariffs on 150 commodities... French Academy of Science publishes first volume of Description of the Arts and Crafts (-1789, shows illustrations of ingenious and powerful machines, presents study by engineer J.R. Perronet on how division of labor would increase production of pins and on evaluating manual operations for required times)... Catherine the Great rules Russia (-1796, acquires land of church, monasteries - clergy to be supported by state, abolishes most commercial and manufacturing monopolies, transforms business sector from some 650 factories employing some 81,780 workers into over 2,000 enterprises, mostly in textiles, paper and leather, with over 200,000 workers - over 4,000 plants, 170,000 workers in mines, munitions and textiles, by 1815, some 9,000 plants, over 500,000 workers, by 1850, and about 14,000 plants over 520,000 workers, by 1861)... France abolishes private ownership of companies in military.

Business Events

Boodle's Club opens in London for smart set (gets reputation for high-stakes gambling, good food)... Society of Equitable Assurance on Lives and Survivorship, first important insurance enterprise in England and still extant as oldest life insurance firm, is formed, others in France in 1819, Germany in 1827, and U.S. in 1843... Carron Iron Works is first to convert cast iron into malleable iron, anticipates puddling process... Jean-Rodolphe's Swiss manufactory of printed cottons employs 600 in workshops (closes 1802).

1763

General Events

Charles III starts Christmas lottery in Spain, still extant... Paris holds first exhibition of industrial arts... Treaty of Paris is signed by Britain (gets Senegal, India settlements, not Pondichery and Chandernager, from France and Florida from Spain), France (abandons Canada to Britain for sugar island of Guadeloupe), Spain (re-acquires Cuba).

Business Events

Hosier Francis Beadsley of Bromscote, owner of 112 frames in Nottingham knitters' houses and 25 in area villages, dies... English pits use ponies to haul mined ore... Baring Brothers & Co., London's oldest mercantile merchant bank, is started to make serge cloth (expands into imports and exports, serves governments of U.S. in 1803, Argentina in 1824 and Russia in 1846 to enter field of international finance)... British potter, Josiah Wedgwood, patents cream-colored earthenware, becomes standard domestic ware.

1764

General Events

Catherine the Great promotes all civil servants with minimum of 7 years in rank to next level... German Melchior Bauer designs fixed-wing monoplane... Danish land is sold by Crown in small parcels to develop grain agriculture... Watt invents steam condenser, first step in developing steam engine... London numbers houses for identification, 75% of buildings by 1770... Hargreaves invents spinning-jenny, appears in France in 1770s (is patented 1770 to spin 8 threads, later 120 threads)... During strike of English journeymen tailors, 23 master tailors hire some 800 strike-breakers from provinces and 230 from continent to break strike... Britain's Sugar Act imposes higher duties on Colonial imports in order to raise money for war debt.

Business Events

First Finnish paper mill, supervised by Swedish master craftsman, is started at Abo.

1765

General Events

During experiments (-1769) Joseph Priestly, former preacher and scientific dabbler, discovers soda water... After jealously keeping Merino sheep, noted for fine wool, from export, Spanish king ships 92 rams and 128 ewes to Saxony, 300 more in 1774... Eberhard puts erasers on pencils... Watt patents a condenser for Newcomen's low-pressure steam engine, cast cylinders lack accuracy for precision (devises steam engine in 1766 - patent 1769, forms partnership in 1775 with Boulton after previous partner, Roebuck, declares bankruptcy in 1773, builds double-acting engine in 1783, devises centrifugal governor in 1785)... Clive is Governor of Bengal, commander-in-chief of English East India army (-1767, accepts, first time, land revenues of Bengal to establish political control over area, starts governmental and military reforms, returns to England in 1767 when accused by Parliament for having unlawfully enriched himself, after acquittal in 1773 commits suicide in 1774)... Frederick the Great founds Academie des Nobles to train young noblemen for military, diplomatic careers... Saxony starts school of mines, model for French school in 1783... Provincial scientific societies form in Birmingham and Manchester, others by 1780... Frederick the Great founds Bank of Prussia... London silk-weavers march to protest importation of French silk goods... French General de Bourcet starts training school to prepare aides-de-camp for planning, organizing troop movements with topographical maps (-1771 and 1783-90, forms French general staff in 1766)... Spain opens trade with West Indies to all Spaniards... Britain's Stamp Act taxes all Colonial legal and official documents, newspapers, dice and cards, repealed 1766... Spallanzan suggests food can be prepared by hermetic sealing... Smeaton designs cylinder-boring machine... After being convinced by Bishop of Metz to start glass factory to reduce flow of gold for imported Bohemian glass, Louis XV charters La Compagnie des Cristalleries de Baccarat (goes out of business during Revolution, is revived in 1822)... Jean Baptiste de Gribeauval reforms French artillery forces (lightens pieces, standardizes calibers of guns, mounts cannoneers on horses or gun carriages, replaces civilian teamsters with soldiers and improves accuracy of fire, gets funds in 1786-89 to produce standardized weapons, parts for production by Honore Blanc at Vincennes armory - unsuccessfully petitions National Assembly in 1790s to continue efforts to make uniform musket locks).

Business Events

Iron mine concession in Wales is granted to Anthony Bacon, former chief supplier of food and equipment to British military (after building Methyr canal, develops site as great iron center, provides artillery to British forces during Revolution, employs some 2,000 workers during Napoleonic period)... Boulanger, former soup vendor of bouillon, opens restaurant, first known use of term for public eating place, in Paris, first U.S. restaurant in 1827 (is sued in French court by guild of those selling meat dishes for violating their monopoly, wins when new law exempts his products from monopoly)... To compete with Mrs. Cornely's Assembly Rooms in Soho, Almack's Assembly Room opens in London to provide weekly balls, entry regulated by ladies of high rank (-1863, declines in 1833 when lesser nobles are admitted as guests).

1766

General Events

Prussia forms tobacco monopoly... J.A. de Serionne: <u>Les Interets des Nations d'Europe</u> (discusses speculation in public stock as means for England to maintain credit)... Britain sends Samuel Wallace, Philip Carteret to find Terra Australias (-1767, re-discover Tahiti, explore Solomon Islands)... London lays first paved sidewalks... Henry Cavendish isolates hydrogen, identified in 1670 by Boyle (is discovered independently by Sweden's Karl Scheele in 1770)... Boulton, others form Lunar Society to promote arts, sciences.

Business Events

Richard Tattersall, former groom to second Duke of Kingston, starts London horse auction business, still extant... After working for Covent Garden auctioneer, James Christie starts London auction business to sell whatever (handles paintings around 1800, still extant)... Wedgwood builds Etruria pottery on Grand Trunk Canal (gets commission from Catherine the Great in 1766, starts London art school in 1769 to train artisans, invents pyrometer in 1782 to measure kiln temperatures, uses business practices: international advertising, art to style pottery, large scale production, cost accounting, time clock system, product and price differentiation, money-back policy, product research - proposed cooperative research organization).

1767

General Events

Russian Legislative Commission reports on attitudes of merchants (notes top grievance as competition from nobles, peasants)... France's Louis de Bougainville voyages to Pacific (-1769, explores Tahiti, Samoa, New Hebrides)... Jesuits, their Instructions to the Jesuit Brothers Who Manage Haciendas discusses business practices, are expelled from New Spain... World's first public piano concert is held in London... James Steuart: An Inquiry Into the Principles of Political Economy (discusses authority, division of labor, work methods, threat of machines)... Parliament amends Malicious Injuries to Property Act to proscribe destruction of property by union members, follows violence by Northern miners in 1765... Francois Quesnay: Despotisme de la Chine (thinks king should have council of mandarins like Chinese emperor)... Joseph Priestly: The History and Present State of Electricity (notes electrical machines of glass as current European fad).

Business Events

In this time, Polzunov uses atmospheric pressure engine to work iron in Russia... Warmley Co., brassworking and coppersmithing, employs 800 mill workers, 2,000 out-workers... In this time, Reynolds, ironmaster of Coalbrookdale Iron Co., replaces wooden rails, connect mines and blast furnaces, with iron rails for horse-drawn trucks, followed by Watt's first efficient steam engine in 1769, first steam locomotive of Trevithick in 1804.

1768

General Events

Commercial academy opens in Hamburg to teach languages, arithmetic, accounting and modern history, English business schools cover reading, English, Latin and Greek, writing, navigation, shorthand, bookkeeping and gauging (-1771 when revived from near bankruptcy by Johann G. Bosch who continues operation for students throughout Europe until death in 1800)... Britain's London Tailors Act establishes penalties, up to two months in prison, for journeymen who demands more than legal maximum wage and employer who pays it... Frederick the Great: Military Testament (notes value of quartermaster-general unit as staff activity)... London silk-weavers riot when wages are reduced (-1769 when put down by troops to maintain order)... Captain James Cook in Endeavor explores Pacific (-1771 in visiting New Zealand and Australia's East Coast, takes 2nd voyage in 1772-75)... Geneva permits Geneva-born children of immigrants to sell goods they make as guild members, 1769 edict prevents them in selling other merchandise or bartering goods...French mathematician thinks Archimedean screw can power human flight, string- pull top existed in 1300s with principles of helicopter... British sailors refuse to work when grievances, 1481 word, are denied by ship owners... Charles III approves exploration, colonization of California, first of 21 Franciscan missions at San Diego by Father Junipero Serra in 1769 to start El Camino Real in linking missions by 1786 a day apart to Yerba Buena - San Carlos in 1770, San Antonio in 1771, San Louis Obispo in 1772, Los Angeles in 1781, Santa Barbara in 1786... Vaucanson develops drill, lathe (-1780)... French state factory at Sevres makes porcelain, formula stolen from Meissen works... Arkwright, English barber, perfects water frame in this time to make stronger cotton thread, "invention" similar to one by Wyatt in 1733 and improved later by Paul... Watt crafts first working model for practical steam engine, patent in 1769 and practical use in 1776 (is commercial success in 1785 with Boulton, adds epicyclic gear in 1781 and reciprocal piston action in 1782).

Business Events

Horse-riding act tours England, revives circus tradition of Roman times.

1769

General Events

Under orders of Minister of War, French artillery officer, Nicholas Joseph Cugnot, builds steam-powered, three-wheeled carriage to haul cannon, demonstrated 1770 for Gribeauval (follows moving "cars" discussed by Bacon in 1200s, design of military vehicle, analogous to tank, by da Vinci in 1500s)... Parliament passes First Act to prevent workers in destroying plants, machinery (makes destruction of machinery a capital crime)... Catherine the Great sponsors first Russian periodical... Spain's Gaspar de Portola explores Pacific Coast to San Francisco... English posts appear in Northern Borneo... Baron Wolfgang don Kempelen builds Terrible Turk, "robot" chess player, for Empress Maria Theresa, secret of automation, midget, revealed in 1834... Patent for water frame is granted to Arkwright, 2nd patent in 1775 with exclusive ownership of it and accessory inventions... Abbe Morellet publishes research to show 55 joint-stock trading firms had been chartered throughout Europe since 1600s, all failed for mismanagement.

Business Events

First Danish iron foundry is built... English East India Co. extends district supervision over Bengal (starts development of Indian Civil Service)... Prussian Herring Co. forms at Emden.

1770

General Events

In 1770s, London yachtsmen form Cumberland Fleet, evolves as Royal Yacht Club... Cook discovers Australia's Botany Bay, first convicts land in 1788 and last 1867... Chain-drive appears in Europe, seen in China 976 A.D. and in silk reeling of Vaucanson's loom (is used by J.F. Tretz in 1869 bicycle)... Empress Maria Theresa approves commercial school, modeled on Hamburg academy of 1768... French glass makers devise bottle in this time to withstand pressure of fermentation (leads to widespread use of champagne)... Patent is granted to James Hargreaves for 1765 spinning-jenny, ruled by court that Hargreaves lost rights to compensation from users because of use prior to patent (applies for patent on water-powered jenny in 1775)... By this time, Austria has lifted most of privileges of Church, government of Florence in governing business (eases taxes, other regulations to encourage industry, commerce)... Anne Robert Jacques Turgot: Reflections on the Formation and Distribution of Wages (covers   direction and control of organization, identifies ownership and screw-cutting lathe... Work is started in Paris to build a steamboat (-1774 when sinks on launching, leads to 2nd in 1775, too slow)... Finland issues industrial regulations (-1868, fines employers who raise wages and workers who demand higher wages)... English patent is granted to Thomas Saint for machine to sew leather, French patent in 1830 to Thimmier... Mission appears at Monterey, CA, first seen 1602... Swedish chemist Bergman produces first artificial carbonated or mineral water, dispensed by soda fountains in 1830s.

Business Events

During 1770s, Boulton employs 800-1,000 workers organized in departments at Soho factory, Birmingham (uses machinery but not mass production, sells directly to customers and through agents)... French East India Co. dissolves... Highbury Barn, cited in 1740 as cakes-and-ale house, is run in London by Willoughby family (provides customers with bowling green, tea gardens)... After discovery of Koalin clay in area, porcelain factory appears in Limoges (leads to purchase by Louis XVI, some 30 local works by 1840, and plant in 1842 by U.S.' David Haviland)... Josiah

Spode starts small earthenware pottery works at Stoke-On-Trent (develops bone china after 1797, is Royal Potter in 1806,is acquired in 1976 by Royal Worcester)... French-born Frederic Japy opens clock shop in Switzerland's Jura region, site for 464 watch makers in 1752, 686 in 1762 and 3,458 in 1792 (uses assortment of machines and unskilled workers in 1776 to mass produce standardized, reliable movements for sale to watch manufacturers)... In this time the Right Honorable Countess Dowagers of Jersey and Spencer are paid to advocate use of British skin cream, "first" personal endorsements... In decade, Kyoto clothing merchants form cartel to trade in other Japanese provinces (after dissolution for trade violations is revived in 1832)... Day and Martin, blacking manufacturer, is founded, pioneers English advertising... Wilkinson launches iron barge in Severn (builds iron bridge for London in 1801)... England's John Woodhouse develops (-1779) vineyards, Sicily, to produce Marsala wine.

1771

General Events

Jorge Juan y Santacilia: Examen maritimo (in first European treatise on shipbuilding gives results of controlled experiments)... London engineers form Smeatonian Club.

Business Events

Arkwright, two rich hosiers start spinning mill at Cromford, modeled on nearby Lombe's factory (runs continuously with hundreds of workers working at machines in shifts, is first factory with centralization, coordination of activities under one roof)... Nantes' merchant house, shareholders and creditors divided into those of privilege, first priority on assets, and those with secondary privileges, declares bankruptcy.

1772

General Events

Joseph Wright: "The Iron Forge," pioneering painting of industrial revolution... Priestly gives results on charging water with carbon dioxide (is used in 1800 by Richard Bewley to make money, mixes soda water with lemonade, selling "mephitic juleps")... Watt devises first dial measuring indicator... Jacques-Antoine Hypolite de Guilbert's military book states that 50,000 men is ideal size for army and 70,000 is maximum for effectiveness while Maurice de Saxe views 40,000 as most effective due to constraints of communications, supply, accurate maps, and proprietary rights in recruitment, selection, and promotion of soldiers... France abolishes Inquisition... Frederick the Great forms Overseas Trading Corp. to encourage industrial development of state-owned ironworks, coal and lead mines, genesis of Prussian State Bank... Some 116,000 square miles of Central Canada are sold by Hudson's Bay Co. to Earl of Selkirk, major stockholder, to start agricultural colony for Scottish peasants displaced in highland clearances, Rupert's Land acquired by Canada in 1869... Warren Hastings, employed by East India Co. as clerk in 1750, is governor of Bengal (-1785, initiates governmental reforms, simplifies revenue system, stabilizes coinage system, and supervises salt and opium manufacturing to establish British rule, is forced to resign after making English East India Co. solvent)... Daniel Rutherford, Priestly, Scheele, Cavendish independently discover nitrogen.

Business Events

English East India Co. forbids all employees except those in commercial section to engage in private trade... James Boswell visits Cox's Museum in London, exhibits mechanical works and art in precious semi-precious stones... London gunsmith, Henry Nock, starts business, operated after 1805 by partner James Wilkinson (is Wilkinson sword business in 1887,sells gardening tools, razors in 1920s)... Arkwright's first Nottingham mill employs 300 workers, some 200 at Cormford mill (employs 800 at 2nd Cromford mill by 1783 and 600 by 1780 at Manchester mill)... Morning Post appears in London (-1937)... Robert Peale, future member of Parliament and Baron, forms partnership to operate English textile mill with two former partners of his father, started his own textile business in 1750 after hawking goods door-to-door in countryside... With widespread reduction of credit, British banking system is forced into financial distress (requires liquidation of inventories by many colonial merchants, revival of business by Revolution)... After winning court case Haurie bodega, started 1724 by Ireland's Timothy O'Neale, is first in Spain to control wine at every stage of production.

1773

General Events

Russia's Manufacturing College lists 320 operating factories, 66 operated by gentry and 46 by foreigners... Regulation Act establishes government control of English East India Company's political activities... Samuel Crompton designs spinning wheel to produce fine yarn... To aid near-bankrupt English East India Co., Tea Act grants firm special monopoly to sell tea to colonies... Institute for veterinary science appears in Denmark, Sweden in 1784... Silk weavers of Spitalfields petition Parliament for wage regulations... British monopoly for smuggling opium into China, banned 1729, is granted to English East India Co., first shipment in 1773 for medicinal purposes (leads to ban by China in 1800 with strict enforcement in 1816-29, results in auctions by East India Co. to independent British and U.S. merchants, including Astor, Girard and prominent Boston houses, and massive imports in 1830s)... French commission sends military officer de la Houlier to England to determine why French cannons explode when fired (visits iron foundry of John, William Wilkinson in Coalbrookdale)... Spitalfields Act establishes standard rules, wages for weavers (leads to formation of unions of weavers to ensure implementation).

Business Events

London clearing house appears in this time to handle inter-bank check payments... Some 264 French boats, about 10,000 fishermen, fish for cod off of Newfoundland, in 1775 400 English vessels with 2,000 sailors and 665 American boats with 25,000... Zeniya Gohei, Japanese provincial merchant (starts with secondhand clothing store in pawnshop, uses forfeited boats to make fortune in shipping, warehouses, stores), is born (-1852)... After 1772's severe commercial depression, Roebuck sells interest in Watt's steam engine to Matthew Boulton... Philip Astley, wife present acrobatics of Veronese family, Polish and Spanish gymnasts and equestrian act in London (with canvas-covered ring, present dancing horses in 1779 with fox hunts, fireworks, waterworks, ventriloquist, conjurors, sword fights and melodramas).

1774

General Events

Parliament bans export of cotton machinery... William Howe standardizes training procedures for all British regiments in American colonies (stresses drill to maneuver soldiers with muskets and units for mass fire power)... John Wilkinson perfects drill to bore cannon, used to bore precise cylinders for Watt's steam engine... Priestly, at laboratory provided by Lord Shelburne, and Scheele independently discover oxygen (is observed, named by Lavoisier in 1772)... Ramsden, using work of Hindley, devises machine to mark sextants to win government's prize money... J.G. Gahn identifies manganese... Spanish expedition explores coast north of California (reaches 54th parallel, fails to reach 65th in 1775 expedition)... England adopts gold coin as sole legal monetary standard... Scheele discovers chlorine, used for bleach by Berthollet in 1784 as suggested by Watt... A.R.J. Turgot, French philosopher, is Controller-General of Finance (-1776, abolishes Six Guilds of Paris as work an "inalienable right of humanity," abolishes internal tariffs and monopolies, and establishes tax reforms, is dismissed after advocating taxation for all land owners).

Business Events

Wedgwood innovates with London showroom for pottery... Manchester Committee for the Protection and Encouragement of Trade forms in England, a chamber of commerce by 1820.

1775

General Events

France finishes last of four great canals, builds only 630 miles of canals by 1800... Prussia, Poland sign commercial treaty... Viceroyalty of Rio de la Plata consolidates administration of Portugal's South American empire in Rio de Janeiro... French fail with steamboat on Seine, successful in 1783... Alexander Cumming, Scottish mathematician who had watchmaker's business in London, gets patent for water-closet, improved by Bramah in 1778 (is popular in 1800s)... After unsuccessful attempts by others in late 1600s-early 1700s, Scottish Major Patrick Ferguson of British Army patents technically-advanced breechloading rifle (is tested successfully for accuracy, rapid fire in 1776 field trials and 1778 Battle of Brandywine, is rejected for adoption during Revolutionary War by Howe after Ferguson had formed, approved by King George III, special corps of riflemen without his approval, muzzleloading rifle used in Mexican and Civil Wars)... German lands of Hapsburg Empire form single customs union... French clockmaker A.L. Perrelet invents self-winding clock, first patented self-winding wristwatch by H. Cutte, J. Harwood in 1924... Royal Copenhagen Manufactory operates in Denmark, awarded Grand Prix by 1889 Paris Exposition... Pierre de Bourcet: <u>Principes de la Guerre des Montagnes</u> (describes staff role of quartermaster-general to reconnoiter ahead of marching army, to find suitable campsite, to gather intelligence, to coordinate all army correspondence to commanding general, to prepare marching and battle orders, and to inform sutlers of logistic requirements)... French Royal Plate Glass Co. employs some 1,200-1,400 workers in this time... Pierre- Simon Girard invents water turbine... Priestly discovers hydrochloric, sulphuric acids... Antoine Lavoisier is appointed to France's Gunpowder Committee (establishes best laboratory of time at Arsenal)... Britain hires some 29,000 German mercenaries for service in North America (recruits 2,000 Hessians from Duke of Wurttemburg, needs funds for ballets of Jean Gorges Noverre)... Catherine the Great ends government-sanctioned monopolies in Russia... Spanish expedition explores area of Puget Sound, Vancouver Island.

Business Events

Scottish merchants in Montreal form North West Co. (sends first fur expedition in 1775, builds fort, trading post on Slave River in 1778, joins Hudson's Bay Co. in 1821)... Wilkinson orders steam engine from Boulton & Watt, first to be used for purposes other than pumping water (manages three iron works with brother by 1770, establishes iron works in France near Nantes in 1777).

1776

General Events

Curr perfects construction of iron rails... Mob destroys spinning-jenny in Shepton Mallet... Cook starts 3rd expedition to Pacific (visits Tahiti, re-discovers Sandwich Islands, carries sauerkraut and grain malt to prevent scurvy, while seeking Northwest Passage visits Oregon Coast and Nootka Sound in Vancouver Island, fur trading center of West Coast for Spanish, French, U.S., and British vessels until Spanish leave in 1795, returns to Sandwich Islands in 1779, is killed by natives, expedition continues to Canton, Macao to sell otter furs)... Alessandro Volta devises glass pistol as portable electricity maker, used at Lake Maggiore to discover methane... Spanish mission appears at Yerba Buena, named San Francisco in 1849... Caisse d'Escompte is established in France, modeled on Bank of England... Patent for steam engine is granted to Watt, appears in

France in 1779, Germany 1788, and Italy 1816... La Scala Opera House opens in Milan... Norway holds military ski competition... Adam Smith: <u>An Inquiry Into the Nature and Causes of the Wealth of Nations</u> (discusses role of labor as source of nation's wealth, use of division of labor to improve productivity, exchange value in purchasing goods, supply and demand in determining wages, profits, interest and rent, and laissez faire role of government in competitive market).

Business Events

Wilkinson uses steam engine to improve efficiency of blast furnace, 24 steam-powered blast furnaces in England by 1800.

1777

General Events

English Magistrates of Middlesex propose masters, journeymen should determine the proper wages with "representative associations on both sides"... First known hot-water heating system is installed in castle near Paris... Circular saw, first seen in Holland c. 1700, is improved by English inventor, Samuel Miller (leads to band saw by William Newberry in 1808)... Jacques Necker is Director-General of Finance for France (is dismissed for reforms in 1781 and recalled in 1788, is dismissed in 1789, basis for storming of Bastille)... Liege arms makers are invited to Berlin, follows transfer of metallurgical techniques from Liege to Sweden in 1600s.

Business Events

Birmingham tailors form cooperative workshop... Grey Poupon makes Dijon mustard in France, still extant... Millwright William Murdock is hired by Bulton & Watt (as consulting engineer advises customers on erecting steam engines in 1779, Boulton & Watt supplies drawings, ready-made parts and materials for engines).

1778

General Events

Parliament requires keepers of lotteries to be licensed... France, U.S. sign commercial treaty... Thomas Coke, Norfolk, starts experiments to improve agricultural production.

Business Events

Some 200 zielverkoopers, "soul sellers" or crimps, operate in Amsterdam (recruit sailors by whatever means for ships of the Dutch East India Co).

1779

General Events

Richard Brinsley Sheridan: "The Critic" (presents Mr. Puff in play as very model of a public relations man)... Parliament permits newcomers to work as bakers without serving 7-year apprenticeship (breaks monopoly of Bakers Co.)... Proposal for business school at Dijon is made to Academie des Sciences et Belles Lettres, no action (is followed by similar proposal in 1800 by Lyons merchants, no response)... In this time, Crompton develops spinning mule to combine features of water frame (uses rollers to draw strong, coarse thread) and spinning-jenny (uses moving carriage to produce fine, weak thread), as no patent seems possible, only modifications of other inventions, gives device to public... Some 8,000 workers destroy English mill to protest use of machinery, Arkwright's factory saved by troops... World's first cast-iron bridge is erected over

Severn River by Coalbrookdale Co., Abraham Darby III ironmaster (demonstrates iron technology).

Business Events

Gun foundry is started at The Hague.

1780

General Events

Bohemia, Hungary abolish serfdom... Scheller devises first fountain pen... Felice Fontana produces water gas... Royal Anchor Smithy, Denmark, imports Newcomen engine... Ruhr River opens for boat traffic (leads to deep coal mining in 1840s, first furnace in 1848-1849, and industrial growth in mid-1800s)... National School of Bakery appears in France... Watt invents letter-copying press, standard office equipment until typewriters in late 1800s, in this time to handle his voluminous business correspondence (forms James Watt & Co. with Boulton to make machines)... Britain, Holland start war over trade with U.S., France... Duc de Chartres, needing funds for extravagant pleasures, develops land behind Palais Royal as public garden (-1784, opens with covered arcade of shops around garden with sunken area in center for concerts, balls and shows, replaces Palais Merchand as fashionable rendezvous in Paris, evolves as perpetual fair with theater, puppet-shows, silhouette-shows, waxworks, auction rooms, concert rooms, chess salon, gambling clubs, social clubs, Turkish bath, apartments, several small hotels, cafes, restaurants, picture collection, and elegant shops: tailors, prints and pictures, jewelers, glass, luxury goods and Magasin des Effets Precieux, first goods at fixed prices)... Harrison invents steel pen... James Graham operates London's Temple of Health with 'celestial or magnetico-electrico' bed for childless couples... Helwig, Master of Pages for Duke of Brunswick, invents war game of 1,666 squares, improved in 1795 by military writer Georg Vinturinus for play on map of actual terrain... With favorable monsoon winds, Englishman makes record trip from London to Calcutta, via Marseilles and Alexandria, in 72 days... James Pickard patents steam engine.

Business Events

John Jameson starts distillery in Dublin to make Irish whiskey (still extant)... Double-entry bookkeeping appears in Russia... Engraver Thomas Menton designs first English "willow" pattern for china, based on cobalt blue decorations of Sung Dynasty, 1280-1368 (leads to first inexpensive, classic blue willow dinnerware in 1810 by Spode)... In 1780s, French textile mills use water-frame, mule-jenny.

1781

General Events

Adam's Place with semi-detached cottages is developed in London's Southwark for artisans... Following panoramas and peepshows, painter Philippe de Loutherbourg opens diorama for public entertainment in London... Prussia establishes coffee monopoly... Jean Pierre Balanchard designs Vaisseau Volant, flying ship run by pedals and levers (includes horn player to provide operator with musical inspiration)... Robert Owen opens infant school for children of working parents in Scotland... Jonathan Hornblower applies for patent on a steam engine, more complicated than Watt's (is sued, ruined by Boulton & Watt)... Austria abolishes serfdom, peasants allowed to own land after Revolution of 1848... Russia starts building road to Siberia... Sweden's Karl Scheele discovers composition of tungsten... British forces take Dutch settlement at Madras, also take Dutch posts on Sumatra's West Coast... William Bolt proposes to Venice to explore Pacific Northwest, rejected... Watt gets 2nd patent for steam engine (patents double-acting rotary engine in 1782, installs first steam engine for cotton mill in 1785)... Franciscan monks start mission at Los Angeles... Henry Lloyd: <u>History of the Late War in Germany</u> (notes lower military ranks as mechanical, learnable while higher ranks are an art, not teachable).

Business Events

Clarendon Press is started at Oxford (still extant)... Wholesale herb business is started in Japan, genesis of present Takeda Chemical Co. with 1982 sales of $2.1 billion... First bottled Claret wine is stored in cellars of Chateau Lafite... To revive Scotland estate, Archibald Cochran, 9th Earl of Dundonald, patents method to extract tar, pitch from pit coal to coat ship's hull, ruined when Admiralty uses copper for sheathing (discovers coal gas by accidental explosion, notes finding to Watt in 1782, leads to Murdock using new illumination gas in 1899, 50 lamps used by firm of cotton-spinners in 1805)... In industry since 1760s, Simonds family starts brewery (builds new plant, first with steam power by Boulton & Watt engine, in 1799, with pioneering laboratory invents new fermentation system in 1880s, operates 300-350 licensed houses around Reading in 1916, acquires Tamar Brewery, formed by five local breweries in 1935-39, in 1953 to operate four active breweries, 1,400 licensed houses)... A "building society," crude form in China c. 200 B.C., forms in Birmingham (pioneers modern evolution of building and loan associations, U.S.' first, Pennsylvania Oxford Provident Assn., in 1831).

1782

General Events

England abandons workhouse system (substitutes "guardians of the poor" to provide relief to needy in own homes)... China compiles Index to Grand Library in this time (cites European clocks as oddities, "designed for the pleasures of the senses. They fulfill no basic needs")... Bangkok is new Capitol of Siam, builds Grand Palace... Spain completes conquest of Florida... Man-operated paddle-wheel boat is used in China in this time... Banco de San Carlos opens in Spain, land's first national bank... C.P. Moritz: Travels in England in 1782 (notes English invention of toasted bread)... Bread riots appear in England... Germany's Johann H. von Mueller invents calculating machine, set by hand then cranked (gets idea for mechanical differencing in 1786)... British plumber, William Watts, gets patent to make perfect round balls with shot tower.

Business Events

Royal Circus and Equestrian Philharmonic Academy opens in London (promotes circuses throughout land)... By 1786, Beauvillers opens La Grande Taverne de Londres in Paris, one of City's first great restaurants... Phoenix Fire Office is organized under Deed of Settlement to sell protection against hazards of fire, in 30 years an industry leader by planning invasion of international markets, ensuring new risks, checking competition, and making prudent investments.

1783

General Events

At urging of patient Duc d'Orleans, physician Nicholas Leblanc wins France's prize, never paid, for process to make alkali from salt and sulphuric acid, landmark in industrial chemistry (after losing patent commits suicide)... After testing materials and gases, earlier efforts by Italian-born Tiberius Cavallo in Britain unsuccessful, brothers Joseph, Etienne Montgolfier test hot-air balloon in France, first manned flight later in year... Watt designs 20-pound steam hammer to work iron... Spain issues general rules to regulate peddlers, packman, traveling vendors... Marquis Claude de Jouffroy d'Abbans tests paddle-wheel steamboat on Saone River, world's first working paddle-steamer... Britain's Henry Bell invents copper cylinder press to print calico cloth, idea used to print books in 1790... Bank of Ireland is formed... U.S., Sweden sign Treaty of Amity and Commerce... After previous attempts by Roebuck in 1762 and Thomas, George Cranage at Coalbrookdale in 1766, process of puddling to make iron, basis for large-scale production of malleable steel, is independently devised by Peter Onions, patent ignored, and Cort, contractor seeking to lower price of naval cannon (after initial commercial success, is forced into bankruptcy by government because partner's father had embezzled funds from Admiralty).

Business Events

Samuel Oldknown operates mill and 59 outweavers, 300 weavers and 500 looms in 1786... Glasgow Chamber of Commerce is formed, followed by Edinburgh and Leeds in 1785, Manchester in 1794, and London in 1881 (evolves in Germany during rule of Emperor William II in 1888-1918)... Birmingham Commercial Committee forms in England... George, William Pimrose start first glass factory in county Waterford, Ireland, with English glassmakers, later individual output of area glassmakers known collectively as Waterford glass... Jamsitjee Jeebehoy, Parsee industrialist (when denied citizenship as refugee from Persia, joins business caste in India with values of thrift, hard work, and material success, class generally successful as Hindus believe in poverty, Mohammedans are unable to charge interest, and Brahmins are unable to travel for fear of contamination), is born (-1859)... Jacob Schweppe, former Swiss jeweler, starts world's 1st soft drink business with three Englishmen to sell artificial mineral water, Britain (adds lemonade in 1835, tonic water and ginger ale in 1880s, diversifies with food products in 1960, merges with Cadbury in 1969).

1784

General Events

Watt patents steam-driven carriage, designed by aide Murdock... James Small: <u>Treatise on Plough and Wheel Carriages</u> (gives detailed mathematical analysis of moldboards)... Britain's India Act makes directors of English East India Co. subservient to board of control of cabinet ministers (leads to Lord Cornwallis becoming governor general, divides company into commercial and political branches to begin civil service, financed by reform of Bengal's revenue, land system and monopoly on salt)... London forms City Day Police (gives night protection in 1824)... St. John's Church is built in Calcutta with lottery funds, used to raise money for town hall in 1813 and other city improvements... London's balloon craze takes off with first successful ascent of Lunardi, Dr. Moret's earlier attempt was blocked by fire (flees with gate receipts)... General J.B.M. Meusnier makes first powered balloon flight... Pioneering typewriter is devised in France to emboss characters for blind... Switzerland's Aime Argand designs oil burner... Andrew Meikle, Scotland, invents threshing machine, follows Michael Menzies in 1732... Bramah devises first patent lock... Crown Prince Frederich, Denmark, starts agricultural reforms (-1790, partitions open fields, abolishes compulsory service of peasants and hereditary tenantry)... Belgium abolishes guild system, guild reforms by Spain in 1760s, Northern Italy in 1770s-1780s... First German mechanical spinning mill appears near Ratingen... Naturalist Launoy, artisan Bienvenu demonstrate model flying apparatus, crude helicopter, for French Academy of Science... Murdock, foreman at Boulton & Watts Soho plant, tests model road locomotive (runs at 8 mph, further development discouraged by Watt)... Watt uses steam pipes to heat his office, early use of steam heat.

Business Events

Richard Arkwright, David Dale build New Lanark spinning mills on Scotland's Clyde River (features model village, employs pauper children as apprentices, guarantees constant employment)... Siberian merchant Shelekhov starts first permanent Russian settlement in North America at Kodiak Island (applies for fur monopoly in 1786 - rejected by Catherine the Great and granted in 1799 by Czar Paul I to form Russian-American Fur Co.)... First cases in England of "factory fever" appear near Manchester, soon spreads to other districts.

1785

General Events

Trowbridge workers riot to protest flying shuttle (-1785, 1810-13)... Berthollet invents chemical bleaching... Switzerland's B.I. de Rivaz experiments with steam carriages, runs one in 1802... Bramah patents first propeller... Jessup designs metal rails for railroad use, England (follows use in mid-1500s of wood rails in Alsatian mine)... For first time British cotton industry uses steam power... French workshop making muskets with interchangeable parts, idea discarded by France later as impractical and derided in England as visionary, is visited by Thomas Jefferson, U.S. Minister to France (describes visit later in letter to John Jay)... Blanchard, Jeffries are first to cross English Channel by balloon... First German steam engine is used in Mansfield mining district... Transportation of debtors in English ships for purpose of servitude is banned... After unsuccessful attempts by others in Germany, France during 1600s, English clergyman Edmund Cartwright patents power loom (builds factory in 1787 to use loom, replaces animals with steam power in 1789, invents wool-combing machine in 1790 - not used until 1825-40 after strong resistance of wool-combers, loses everything in 1791 when weavers destroy factory)... Catherine the Great's City Charter legalizes urban corporations... Meusnier designs revolutionary ellipsoidal dirigible... In Court of Common Pleas, jury declares Arkwright's patent for water frame to have lapsed and actions of competitors to be right and proper (follows suit by Thomas Highs, supported by clockmaker Kay employed by Arkwright in 1768, that Arkwright used ideas of his 1767 invention).

Business Events

General Chamber of Manufacturers forms in Britain... John Rennie builds steam- powered Albion Mills (-1788, is designed by Watt as "first" factory with all machines, is destroyed by "accidental" fire in 1791)... Daily Universal Register appears in London, becomes The Times in 1788... Baron Wendel and French bankers, advised by William Wilkinson, start smelting plant, start of modern French iron industry, of Le Creusat near coal field (use new industrial method of mass production to make armaments, use steam power by Watt engine and employ 1,000 workers, declare bankruptcy in 1787-88, is converted to munitions by Napoleon, is purchased by Schneider family in 1800s)... Frontons appear in Basque area of Spain for Jai Alai, imported to Cuba c. 1900 (leads to pari-mutuel betting by Florida in 1935).

1786

General Events

England, France sign commercial treaty, France lowers duties on English cloth, cotton, and iron goods and Britain lowers duties on French wines, silk, and olive oil... Russian explorer finds Pribilof Islands in Bering Sea near Alaska, base for seal hunters... First attempts to develop internal gas lighting are made in Germany, England... French ship, first non-Spanish vessel at California harbor, visits Monterey in search of Northwest Passage... Penang is granted to English East India Co., permanent in 1790... Ezekiel Reed invents machine to make nails.

Business Events

Maidstone Journal carries ad to sell advertising services of William Tayler, first such record... Merchant Bank opens in St. Petersburg... English East India Co. gets monopoly of trade with Canton (when exports of British cottons, woolens fail to sell, ships drugs to offset deficits from imports in tea, cloth)... English East India Co. sends expedition to Vancouver Island... India merchants form Bengal Fur Co. to trade with Pacific Northwest, sponsor voyage from Calcutta... Linz Royal Woolen Factory "employs" over 35,000 workers, 29,000 in cottages throughout Upper Austria, Bohemia, Moravia... J. Molson starts brewery in Montreal, oldest extant in North America (joins Canadian breweries with those of Elders IXL in 1989 to control 53% of market).

1787

General Events

Famine riots are seen in Edo, Japan (reduces population by some one million in 1780-86)... Frederick the Great forms Supreme War Council for advice on military matters (forms three departments of mobilization, provisionment and general army affairs, uniforms and equipment, and one for disabled, adds subordinate activities of adjutant-general and quartermaster-general, responsible for military maps, in 1796)... Ernest Chladni experiments to produce sound patterns on vibrating plates... Near bankruptcy Louis XVI forms council of notables to resolve France's financial crisis... After testing troop formation in War of Austrian Succession (1740-48), French Army is reorganized by divisions of 12,000, coordinated by staff subordinate to single commander (introduces new tactical manual with standardized regulations in 1791)... Scottish painter R. Barker devises new panorama device, vertical cylinder with inside screen for moving pictures... Several countries use copper, silver tokens with effigy of ironmaster Wilkinson (-1808).

Business Events

At Gravesend shipyard, <u>Nottingham</u> is launched, largest East Indiaman at 1,152 tons, 160 feet in length and 40 feet in beam (is built to settle dispute on ship size between Committee of Managing Directors, cartel with hereditary privileges chartering ships to English East India Co., and independent shipowners seeking to charter larger vessels).

1788

General Events

Parliament rejects motion to abolish slave trade... Scotland's Patrick Miller builds steamboat... Hamburg starts first municipal system of poor relief... Britain produces 68,000 tons of pig iron, 244,000 tons in 1806 and 325,000 in 1811... Denmark abolishes serfdom... Parliament's act protects chimney-sweeps from dangers of trade, brutality of masters... Watt devises first centrifugal automatic governor... After systematic testing in 1763-67, French Army organizes new mobile field artillery force (-1829, uses precision sights, standardized shot and powder, and specialists)... Spanish expedition sails from San Blas to Pacific Northwest to claim area for Spain, puts Ft. San Miguel on Vancouver Island in 1789-90... Bread riots are seen in France... Exchequer pays tellers fixed salaries... England employs 60,000 in factory spinning, almost none in power weaving and 108,000 in handloom weaving, 90,000 in factory spinning and 184,000 on handlooms in 1806 (shows 122,000 in factory spinning, 45,000 in power spinning and 210,000 on handlooms in 1824; 133,000, 73,000 and 213,000 in 1833)... First Fleet lands in Australia.

1789

General Events

France abolishes feudal system... Spanish attack English at Nootka Sound, Vancouver Island... Robert Ransome, English brass maker, devises first all- iron plow... French edict takes status from nobles when engaged in money- making activities... France passes general legislation for enclosure of common lands, provincial enclosures from 1762... Paris mob storms Bastille to start French Revolution (-1792)... Antoine Lavoisier: <u>Traite Elementaire de Chimie</u> (founds science of chemistry)... G.J.C. Kunth is employed in Prussian civil service (later, as general commissioner of commerce, starts trade schools, Berlin's Royal Commercial College, technical school, and Assn. for Promotion of Industrial Knowledge)... Fur trader Alexander Mackenzie explores northern areas of Canada from Arctic Ocean to Pacific in this time... American-born Benjamin Thompson, fled U.S. as a Tory, installs prototype modern kitchen range in Bavarian noble's house, later devises closed-top range with adjustable heat (leads to gas ovens in London in 1830s, iron ranges in 1860s, gas stoves in 1880s, and reliable electric ranges in 1920s)... William Fairbairn introduces riveting machine to make steam boilers... By 1792 Honore Blanc, superintendent of French Royal Arsenals, tries to make muskets with interchangeable parts, blocked by gunsmiths.

Business Events

England's first steam-powered cotton factory is built in Manchester, some 142 mills in area use water power... Orleans stocking factory, France, employs some 800 workers under one roof, some 1,600 on outside contract work... By 1800, Japanese provincial merchant Takadaya Kahei sponsors, instead of giving direct loans, 10 fisheries to help Ainu people... Henry Maudslay, age 18, is hired by Bramah (develops tools so locksmiths can improve accuracy and speed of work, starts own business in 1797 with Maudslay lathe)... London paper prints ad that animals, lions, leopards, lynx, etc., from Botany Bay, Australia, are available for public amusement... Pears family starts soap business in Soho barbershop, London (develops quality toilet soap, is A. & F. Pears in 1835, names Andrew head in 1875 after father retires, is first to adopt 38-hour work week, after intensive advertising to become industrial complex, goes public in 1893).

1790

General Events

England bans coalitions of employers and employees... In this time, permanent Prussian general staff, genesis from ad hoc quartermaster staff units in 1700s, evolves from Frederick the Great's Academie des Nobles (extends traditional quartermaster activities in establishing lines of march and camps to intelligence, war diary)... With idea from hobby-horse, first crude bicycle, Celeritere with elegant lines and lion's head on handlebars, appears in France, runs without peddles, steering mechanism or brakes... William Kelly, Scotland, devises automatic spinning mule, powered by water to run number of spindles... Thomas Gifford develops nail-making machine, one by S. Guppy in 1796... Spain, Britain sign first Nootka Convention, Spain returns captured ships and land on Vancouver Island... Various areas of Rhineland abolish guild rules, abolished by Westaphalia in 1808-10 and Prussia in 1806-10... England builds first steam-powered rolling mill... Work is started in England to build Firth-Clyde, Oxford-Birmingham Canals... Hawaii plants first pineapples, large-scale production in 1880s and J.D. Dole's Hawaiian Pineapple Co. in 1921... By 1870, some 276 joint-stock companies appear in Europe, 726 in 1871-73... France removes internal customs, follows previous tariff exemptions for coal in 1761, grain in 1763, and wine in 1776... Benjamin Thompson, Count Rumford of Holy Roman Empire, starts Poor Peoples' Institute in Munich as work house (provides poor with lodgings, food and work making clothing for Bavarian military)... Watt devises pressure gauge... Patronage of Prince Regent, later George IV, ensures social success of Brighton as resort.

Business Events

Textile mill at Morley, Yorkshire, is first powered by steam... Alexander Barnov manages Russian fur post at Kodiak (-1817, as first governor of territory develops Alaskan colony)... Highly complicated Bramah lock is made by mechanized production system, designed by master mechanic Maudslay (-1791)... In 1790s, despite ban by English law on migrating artisans, Breguet makes first jeweled assemblies for watches in Paris.

1791

General Events

French Academy of Science defines meter as unit of measurement... Johann M.F. Scholz opens Commercial High School in Dessau, Germany (-1806, offers private lessons to businessmen, is state-supported school in 1803)... Hamburg sees first general strike... London School of Veterinary

Surgery is founded... Captain George Vancouver, member of Cook's last expedition, sails to Pacific Northwest to claim area for Britain (-1794, leads to discovery of unique fir tree by naturalist Archibald Menzies, tree named for 1823 research by David Douglas)... Patent to protect ships' bottoms is granted to Murdock... France bans guilds as combinations of workers, modified by Napoleonic code of 1804 (allows strikes in 1864, recognizes unions in 1884)... After experiments by Watt in 1784, patent for steam-heating unit is granted to inventor in Halifax, Nova Scotia (leads to steam heating in British factories by 1822)... Violinist Niccol Paganini, age 9, makes debut (-1840, is idolized by women for technical virtuosity, showmanship and Mephistophelian appearance)... King of France abolishes tax on wine, smuggled wine sold in cabaret bars, entering Paris, city goes bankrupt... Leblanc patents industrial-scale process to produce soda (closes factory, world's first to make soda, in 1793 after execution of backer, Philippe, Duc d'Orleans).

Business Events

Girard-Perregaux business making fine watches is started, Switzerland... Charles Lamb, English essayist, is employed as clerk-accountant by South Sea House (works for English East India Co. in 1791-1825).

1792

General Events

Britain exports last surplus wheat... France declares bankruptcy, again 1797 (sets maximum prices)... Murdock experiments with coal to produce vapors that will ignite, used to light home in Cornwall (installs two gas burners in Soho plant by 1799, leads to 50 gas lamps in Manchester firm of cotton spinners in 1805 and London's first public display of gas lighting in 1805)... French Assembly provides each field army with chief of staff (as described in 1796 book by Marshal Berthier, sends orders, maintains war diary, analyzes situation reports, maintains situation map, keeps enrollment registers and holds inspections, is revised in 1805 to handle Napoleon's military correspondence, to prepare orders, to gather information, and to supervise daily routine)... Spinners in Oldham, Stockport start benefit clubs to provide mutual protection against unemployment, sickness... Parliament passes legislation to protect members of friendly or benefit societies... French engineer, Claude Chappe, invents visual mechanical semaphore signal system (takes 21 minutes to send messages from Paris to Berlin, in good weather sends messages over 150 miles/hour to beat pigeon post used by private traders)... Vancouver visits Hawaii to restore good relations after death of Cook (lands first cattle on Islands, leads to employment of three California Spanish- Mexican cowboys and cattle business in 1832)... English workers destroy Manchester textile factory for ruining their trade... In this time, some 80,000 weavers work in Barcelona, Spain, 2nd in production of cotton cloth to English Midlands... James Smith, founder of Norwich shoe business, introduces sized shoes, left and right shoes appear in mid-1800s... Denmark is first to ban slave trade.

Business Events

Sierra Leone Co. is chartered... W.H. Smith opens small London newsstand (opens branches in 1820 to develop City's fastest newspaper delivery service, opens bookstalls in railroad stations in 1848, evolves by 1980s as chain of retail shops and bookstalls)... Bank of England is heated by hot-water system, used earlier in France for greenhouse, chicken hatchery... Benjamin Gott starts English woolen mill (becomes largest mechanized operation of time with 744 workers in 1813, 1,019 by 1817, and 1,120 by 1829)... North West Co. employs Simon Fraser (explores territory of British Columbia in 1807)... Richard Durtnell, five years old, is sole heir of Kent building and development business, family in field since 1000s (still extant).

1793

General Events

British seize French settlements in India... Parliament requires all civil offices in India be filled by servants of English East India Co... English law legalizes free insurance companies for sickness, invalidity and old age, first legal recognition of friendly societies... Louis XIV is executed, Reign of Terror to 1794... Rotary planner is patented... Alexander Mackenzie is first to travel overland to reach Canada's Pacific Coast... Britain establishes first Board of Agriculture to gather data on agricultural methods in other countries (-1822, 1893-1955)... After studying painting in London since 1786, Robert Fulton visits Paris (designs workable submarine in 1800-01 and crude torpedoes, France not interested)... Some 3,000 furnaces are used in Kin-te-Chin, China, to bake porcelain... By law, English East India Co.'s charter is to be renewed every 20 years... France finishes building Canal du Centre (leads to major canal construction in 1800-25, steamers on canals by 1820s)... British delegation presents gifts, including clocks and watches, from England's George III to Chinese Emperor (hears Celestial Dynasty does not need manufacturers by virtue of lacking nothing)... New South Wales is formed in Australia, first free settlers in 1793 and sheep-raising in 1794... After establishing first political contact in 1727, Russia founds trading settlement in China.

Business Events

Thomas Minton starts small porcelain factory at Stoke-On-Trent (gains reputation at 1851 Great Exposition in London, merges with Royal Doulton in 1968)... Irish artist, Robert Baker, opens Panorama in London to show public realistic scenic paintings (starts mania of Dioramas, Cycloramas, Poeculoramas and Typoramas until appearance of illustrated weekly magazines in 1860s)... John Patteson starts Norwich brewery, absorbed by Watney Mann in 1963 as one of biggest brewers outside London.

1794

General Events

French Army forms Aerostatic Corps of the Artillery Service, world's first air force... France abolishes slavery in French colonies... Britain's John Street, uses turpentine as liquid fuel, makes explosive charge by mixing gas with air... Duke Karl Eugen of Wuttemberg sponsors business academy, abandoned after death... Paris Conservatoire des Arts et Metiers opens as research institute... France pioneers formation of army corps, used in Napoleon's 1805 campaign, to organize some 150,000 men in eight corps, each with separate staff unit... Samuel Bentham, patents designs for wood-working machinery in 1791 and 1793, is Inspector-General to British Navy (-1812, sponsors efforts of Maudslay, master mechanic, and Marc Brunel, French-born U.S. emigre and ex-naval officer, surveyor and gunsmith, to mechanize manufacture of ship blocks in 1800-08, a sequence of specialized operations by Brunel for 10 unskilled workers and 44 specialized machines in production line by Maudsley to make, assemble 130,000 wooden pulleys/year with interchangeable parts for sailing ships)... Small West Riding manufacturers petition Parliament for protection of cottage industry from competition of large factory mills... Wool-combers petition Parliament to prevent use of Cartwright's combing machine, unsuccessful... France founds Ecole Polytechnic to study mathematics, applied science (leads to technical college, Ecole Centrale des Arts et Manufactures, in 1829)... Catherine the Great founds Odessa on Black Sea (becomes grain port, mostly Greek shippers, for Russian wheat, oats to London, etc.)... Paris Museum of Science and Technology shows models of new inventions.

Business Events

The Gallery of Fashion Magazine appears in London, others of time: The Ladies' Magazine, The

Ladies' Monthly Museum and The Fashions of London and Paris... In this time, London's Crown & Anchor Tavern provides entertainment with glee club (leads to male song and supper rooms in 1830s for gentlemanly pleasures, leaving taverns for working class)... First German coal-fire blast furnace is built in Upper Silesia (-1796, 2nd in 1799)... German engineer August Friedrich Wilhelm Hotzhausen builds engines, atmospheric and steam, for use in mines, factories in Silesia (-1825)... Sons of Matthew Boulton, James Watt become partners in Birmingham business (-1848, start Soho Foundry in 1795-1985, use market research, forecasting, planned site location, machine layout studies, time studies, production standards, standardization of parts and processes, cost controls, employee specialization, and piece rates and bonuses, provide employee training, employee benefits of overtime pay, Christmas presents, housing, and insurance, Mutual Assurance Society first to cover all workers).

1795

General Events

Royal Navy adopts lime juice to prevent scurvy... France adopts metric system... First English settlements appear in New Zealand... Britain's Samuel Hershaw perfects corkscrew... Some 1,500,000 textile workers work in this time in French provinces of Hainaut, Flanders, Artois, Cambresis, Picardy... British capture Malacca, returned to Holland in 1803 (is retaken in 1811, is retaken by Dutch in 1818, ceded to Britain in 1824)... John Aidkin: Description of the Country from 30-40 Miles Around Manchester, on rapid development of area's cotton industry... After studying work of Galvani in 1780-86, Volta, Professor of Physics at Pavia, devises first electrical current battery... Birkshire magistrates establish Speenhamland Law, allows for changes in poor relief for changes in cost-of-living... Bramah invents hydraulic press... London's first horse-drawn railroad is started... Parliament passes acts for poor relief (supplements wages with dole)... Madrid, Royal summer palace are linked by semaphore line... British forces occupy Cape of Good Hope... France offers monetary prize to inventor who devises new method to preserve food, replaces dried foods of ancient times, for campaigning troops (is won in 1809 by Nicholas Appert, Paris brewer, inventor of bouillon cube, and confectionnaire, with 1804 process to store boiled food in champagne bottles (starts House of Appert as world's first commercial cannery in 1810, operates to 1900s).

Business Events

Poor citizens of Hall form British co-operative to build flour mill as protection against rising cost of bread... Thomas Raffles, age 14, is hired as clerk by English East India Co. (is governor of Malay Peninsula in 1811, starts trading factory on Singapore Island in 1819)... Grachev, calico manufacturer (employs 121 workers, 722 by 1807), is first serf in Ivanovo, textile center of Russia, to purchase freedom (joins First Guild of Merchants).

1796

General Events

Napoleon starts campaign to conquer Italy (-1797, shows use of strategy and tactics, used in Egyptian expedition campaign of 1798-99)... Wool workers in Northern England form "Community" or "Institution"... British troops are posted in certain Yorkshire spinning mills to prevent violence, destruction... Japan's Lord Hosokawa Yorinao designs mechanical doll, like other automata used by Japanese merchants to attract customers... Edict of Peking forbids importation of opium into China... Royal Technical College is founded in Glasgow... J.T. Lewitz is first to prepare ethyl alcohol... Denmark's Royal Commission declares industry an unnatural occupation... British take Ceylon from Holland (results in joint administration by Crown, English East India Co. to 1802, Crown after 1802)... Britain's George Cayley flies model helicopter, perhaps used in ancient Egypt, as prototype for subsequent helicopters (designs fixed-wing plane in 1799, tests model glider with modern configuration in 1804, designs unmanned, full-sized glider in 1809, publishes papers on aviation in 1809 to start serious study of aerodynamics, leads to Cayley's basic rotor mechanism in 1853, first flight by France's Jean-Marie Le Bris in 1856 and miniature aircraft, powered by rubber band, of France's Alphonse Penaud in 1871)... Geneva watchmaker, A. Favre, "invents" mechanical music box, uses pin-studded cylinder as did mechanical chimes in 1300s.

1797

General Events

Bank of England suspends cash payments... Italian hydraulics engineer Giovanni Battista Venturi discovers velocity of water increases going through constricted tube, adapted by Daimler, Maybach in developing carburetor in 1892... Polish typographer Aloys Senefelder invents lithography... Frederick Eden: The State of the Poor (complains poorest workers exist mostly on dry bread and cheese, meat perhaps once/week)... England ups stamp tax (forces newspapers to become "permanent advertisement fairs" to survive)... Copper coins are minted... Istituto de Scienze Lettere e Arte forms in Milan... England exports first iron... Britain grants contract to stamp coins to Watt, Boulton (use new steam press with accuracy never previously achieved, also stamp coins for France, Russia)... John MacArthur introduces Merino sheep to Australia... French chemist discovers chromium... Enlisted personnel in Royal Navy at Spithead mutiny to protest cruel discipline, lash, harsh living conditions, abusive captains, and low pay, followed by violent Nore mutiny at North Sea Fleet... Maudslay invents accurate metal-cutting lathe with slide rest, one of history's most significant inventions (leaves Bramah to start own firm, perfects lathe in 1800 with interchangeable gear-wheels, by 1808 makes calico-printing machinery, small engines, power-driven lathes and marine engines, starts world-famous Maudslay, Field & Co. in 1810 with draftsman Joshua Field as partner, trains many engineers).

Business Events

North West Co. starts fur post on Red River to serve traders, buffalo hunters in Central Canada... Spode starts making modern English porcelain with feldspar, boneash... Assn. of Wholesale Merchants forms in Copenhagen... Owen is manager of New Lanark factories (-1828, provides homes, streets, meal facilities, schooling, recreation center and sanitary working conditions, hires no children under age of 10, reduces working hours, improves training for workers, provides unemployment pay, sells employees provisions at wholesale, evaluates employees for work, conduct)... Saeva Morozov, Russian serf, starts small ribbon plant (purchases freedom in 1820, becomes one of Russia's largest industrialists)... Odeon Theater opens in Paris... Strand haberdasher, John Etherington, wears first top hat, summoned to court for disturbing the peace (leads to first tuxedo by Pierre Lorillard c. 1888).

1798

General Events

England abolishes free coinage of silver... With funds from traders, Thames Police Force is formed, London, to stop river piracy, followed in 1805 by Bow Street Horse Patrol and Metropolitan Police in 1829... Royal Agricultural Hall opens for annual agricultural, livestock exhibitions... Richard, Marquess of Wellesley, is governor-general of all British lands in India (-1805, expands rule of Bengal to cover almost all of India not governed as states)... France taxes doors, windows (-1917)... Swiss patent for optical glass is granted to P.L. Guinard, basis for German optical industry in 1800s... Count Rumford turns horsepower into heat... France abolishes feudalism... Quaker Joseph Lancaster opens elementary school in poor area of London (uses production methods to process large number of pupils inexpensively to read, write in two months with teacher and student instructors, used by U.S. schools in 1806- 53)... England adopts 10%

income tax to fund war with France, abolished 1802 and reinstated 1815-42.

Business Events

M.M. Warburg starts Hamburg banking business (evolves as one of first great Jewish banking families in Europe, handles mostly foreign exchange and commercial bills of large trading firms by 1890)... First modern fair is held in France, others in 1801, 1802 and 1806... Nathan Meyer Rothschild starts textile import business in Manchester (opens London bank in 1805, after quitting textile business in 1811 focuses on bullion dealing and government loans)... Lievin Bauwens starts first mechanical cotton spinning in Belgium at Ghent, extensive mechanization in area after 1830... Geneva private bank of Mobard Odier & Cie forms (still extant)... W. Cockerill introduces English textile machinery to Belgium (starts textile machinery plant in Liege in 1807 to supply equipment to France - some 2,000 workers by 1812, leads to son starting Belgium ironworks in 1817 and building land's first steam engine in 1818, some 200 by 1830).

1799

General Events

Charles Tennant invents bleaching powder... Phillipe Lebon patents gas lamp... Dublin Exchange is founded... A.C. Albert, Paris, files patent application for circular saw, not granted (is granted in 1816 to Auguste Brunet, Jean Baptiste Cochot of Paris)... France's Pochon invents first clothes dryer... To eliminate laborious handwork in making paper sheet by sheet, Nicholas Robert, former director of personnel for industrial relations at Didot St. Leger paper mill of 1355, seeks patent for automated machine to make paper in continuous strips... Napoleon is first Consul of France (centralizes government with 91 departments all responsible to Paris, establishes new tax system, forms civil service)... Dutch government takes direct control of Indonesia (-1949)... Parliament passes first, 2nd in 1800, Workman's Combination Bill to forbid two or more workers in certain industries to join together in conspiracy to obtain higher wages, better working conditions (-1824)... Benjamin Thompson founds Royal Institution, England, to promote practical application of science, introduce technology, sponsor research, and provide lectures.

1800

General Events

In early years Baden-Baden becomes fashionable summer resort for European rich, titled (follows use of hot springs there by Roman soldiers in 75 A.D. - 260 A.D.)... First iron trolley tracks in England are built... European fashion of pigtails for men is passe... University of Wurzburg offers commercial courses, rejected by University of Gottingen in 1789... Owen starts social reforms at New Lanark textile mills... Fichte: The Isolated Commercial State (advocates state-socialism)... Maudslay builds lathe with accuracy to 1/1000 of an inch... English journal, The Porcupine, carries one of first attacks on disreputable advertising... Europe has 28.1% relative share of world's manufacturing output, Britain with 4.3%, Hapsburg empire 3.2%, France 4.2%, German area 3.5%, Italian area 2.5%, Russia 5.6%, U.S. 0.8%, Japan 3.5%, China 33.3% and India 19.7%... England's Richard Trevithick builds low-pressure steam engine (uses steam engine in Cornwall in 1801 to haul mine carriages on rails, patents high-pressure steam engine in 1802)... In this time, Barberi "Invents" barrel organ for wandering musicians... Stockholm has 6,000 people, 250,000 by 1914 while Dusseldorf goes from 10,000 to 360,000 by 1910... James Finley builds suspension bridge with iron chains, construction if wire-suspension bridge in 1825 by Marc Sequin... British East India Co., Persia sign political, commercial treaty... Manchester, England, has 75,000 people, some 400,000 in 1850... Napoleon appoints commission to formulate Civil Code, finished 1804... Volta produces electricity from a cell... Letter post appears in Berlin... Danish law regulates Copenhagen's guilds, all guilds regulated in 1823... In Treaty of Ildefonso, Spain cedes Louisiana

Territory to France... Parliament's Arbitration Act is to resolve disputes in weaving industry... Baron Paul Thiebault pens book on theory, techniques of staff system... Some 20 million live in Holy Roman Empire, some 17 million in countryside.

Business Events

English East India Co. uses recruitment examinations to select new employees, adopted by British Civil Service in 1855... Some 200,000 workers are employed in cotton industry near Shanghai, follows tea plantations with hundreds of workers and porcelain factories with thousands in 1700s (other major industries in China are paper, sugar, iron and steel, silk, lacquer-ware)... Illegal opium trade evolves with China when foreign merchants need exchange to buy exports of tea, silk, porcelain... Marcus Samuel opens Shell Shop in London as a curio business (evolves as Shell Transport & Trading Co. for international commerce, is Royal Dutch Shell in 1900s)... Horse-drawn coal railway operates in Ruhr Valley... Atkinson textile mill, Manchester, employs some 1,500 workers under one roof... Regular cycles for charging iron furnaces are developed at Coalbrookdale, England (evolves by 1820s as factory with work norms, rational organizational structure, job descriptions for foremen)... Charles, Earl Stanhope uses iron to make printing presses... Some 800,000 workers are employed in British cotton mills, nation's leading industry... Berlin's Royal Porcelain factory uses first steam power in Germany... James White opens first British advertising agency in London (still extant under different name)... 52 private banks operate in London, 410 in provinces... By 1830 some 17 covered arcades with shops appear in Paris, copied throughout Europe and U.S... After issuing shares to raise needed capital, private company builds London's West India Docks (-1802 with Commercial Docks in 1802-07, London Docks in 1805, East India Docks in 1806, St. Katherine's Docks in 1828).

1801

General Events

Danes occupy Hamburg and Lubeck, exclude British ships from Elbe... First census of Britain shows 8 towns with over 50,000 people (notes 600,000 domestic servants)... England's Grand Union Canal opens for traffic... Horse-drawn trucks are used on iron railway in Surrey to haul coal, farm produce... Gerhard von Scharnhorst starts war college in Berlin for Prussian officers... Humphry Davy discusses possibility of electricity at Royal Institution... Bank of France is founded... Joseph Marie Jacquard gets lifetime income plus royalties on all looms sold, builds loom to weave figured-silk fabrics for textile manufacturers of Lyons (uses perforated paper to determine weaving patterns, idea from weavers of Lyons in 1720s, puts each pattern on different card, idea from mechanic of Lyons in 1740s, and automates process with rotating cylinder, idea of Vaucanson in 1741, to introduce digital technology, acceptance of innovation delayed until 1840s due to resistance of textile workers).

Business Events

Chivas Royal Scotch whisky is blended... London Stock Exchange forms, genesis 1773.

1802

General Events

J.W. Ritter devises first accumulator... Peshwa cedes independence to English East India Co... Humphry Davy devises incandescent light, not practical until Edison, Swan discover long-lasting filament in 1878-1879... Regular mail service begins between England, India... Portuguese explorers cross Africa from Angola to Mozambique (-1811)... Napoleon suggests idea for English Channel tunnel to Charles James Fox, formation of English Channel Company in 1881... Descroisilles, Rouen pharmacist, invents first coffee pot, two containers and filter (leads to first paper filters, invented by Melitta Benz, in 1918)... Col. von Massenbach, member of Quartermaster-General's staff, submits reports on need to create permanent Prussian general staff for strategic intelligence, to draft regulations and to make contingency plans for current operations, approved in 1803 for reorganization of Quartermaster-General's staff and used in 1806 for mobilization and offensive against French forces of Napoleon - a fiasco (is reorganized in 1807 as General Staff with four sections: strategy and tactics, internal administration, reinforcements, and artillery and munitions, provides operational plans in 1813 for deployment of Prussian-Russian armies)... Steam tug, <u>Charlotte Dunas,</u> is tested on English canal (although mechanically successful is banned for fear of destroying canal's banks)... British Royal Military College opens at Sandhurst... Tsar Alexander I forms secret committee to bring social reforms to Russia... Parliament passes Health and Morals Act of Robert Peale to protect pauper children hired as apprentices, England's first child labor law and world's first factory legislation (requires employers to conform to certain rules for hygiene, education and working hours - maximum of 12/day with no night work, leads to some employment regulations for all children in 1819, 10-hour work day with inspection in 1833 - limit of 48 hours/week for ages 9-13 and 68 hours/week for ages 14-18, 10-hour work day for all children and women in textile mills in 1847).

Business Events

G. Egestorff, German industrialist, tile, brick, coal, timber, sugar refining, water transport, steam locomotives, and pumps, and philanthropist (opens kitchens to feed impoverished working class), is born (-1868)... Chinese entrepreneur starts Hawaii's first commercial sugar mill, imports Chinese field workers in 1852... After inheriting wax business from uncle, started during French Revolution, Madame Marie Toussaud tours England with 35 wax figures (opens London exhibit hall in 1835 to become major tourist attraction).

1803

General Events

Fulton tests steamboat on Seine... Britain creates civil-service job for man to stand on Cliffs of Dover to sound the alarm if Napoleon attempts to land forces, abolished 1945... William Symmington demonstrates practical steamboat on Scotland's Clyde... Steam carriage is driven 4 miles in London... Jean Baptiste Say: <u>A Treatise on Political Economy</u> (views management as factor of production)... H.F. Fourdrinier, England, devises in this time process to mass produce paper, first U.S. production by Thomas Gilpin c. 1817 with secret device... M. Schonleutner is director of model farm in Bavaria (leads to school to train farmers)... Prague's Technical College is founded... An agreement is made by workers, owners of paper mill near St. Petersburg to let employees manage the mill (provides for election of foremen, allocation of pay by elected deputies, and determination of free firewood, profit-sharing, and hours by general assembly, is modified by government in 1818: foremen appointed by owner, work day at least 12 hours, children over 12 to work).

Business Events

First Australian newspaper appears.

1804

General Events

Napoleon Bonaparte is Emperor of France (-1814, 1815)... Trevithick builds first steam locomotive to haul weight, 70 men and 10 tons of iron ore (builds railway at Coalbrookdale in 1806, sails to Peru in 1816 to make, lose fortune in silver mines)... France adopts Code Napoleon... Royal Horticultural Society holds England's first flower show... Stein is (October 27) Prussian Minister of Trade.

Business Events

Sweden sees its first steam engine... Forces of English East India Co. defeat army of Indore... Russian-American Fur Co. founds New Archangel, Alaska (becomes known as Sitka - largest settlement on West Coast until San Francisco in 1850s, leads to 25 forts and posts to Ft. Ross, north of San Francisco, on Pacific Coast by 1812)... Daehnseldt seed business is started in Denmark, one of world's largest in 1980s with sales of some $80 million... German-born Winsor forms London's New Light & Heat Co. to light Lyceum Theater with coal gas... Hamburg merchant family of Schroders open banking firm in London (still extant)... First oil lamp, glass chimney and braided wick, of Swiss inventor Aime Argand is made in England.

1805

General Events

Morphine is isolated as a drug... Prussia abolishes internal customs duties... Holy Roman Empire dissolves when Francis I, Emperor of Austria, refuses Imperial Crown... Jean-Eugene Robert-Houdin, French magician (pioneers modern magic), is born (-1871).

Business Events

Truefitt & Hill, London's oldest barber shop in 1980s, opens for fashionable gentlemen... After starting Manchester textile business in 1798, Nathan Meyer Rothschild opens merchant bank in London, 150 accounts in 1835 and 41 by 1900 to focus on opportunities in Germany, overtakes old Jewish private banks of Warburgs, Bleichroders, Behrens and Mendelsohns, and Low Countries (with prior knowledge, private communications network faster than that of British government, of results at 1815 Battle of Waterloo, wins financial coup by first selling to confuse traders and then buying at low prices before rivals learn of victory, loses on Confederate bonds during U.S. Civil War, after conservative years of 1836-79 invests in South Africa mining, finances Trans-Caucasian Railway in 1883 and De Beers diamond monopoly in 1888, grows by 1900s with connections to 3 financial agencies in St. Petersburg, 3 Latin American banks, and NYC's M. Guggenheim & Sons)... Switzerland's Jura region's annual output of 100,000 watch movements forces Geneva watch makers to leave mass market and join Britain in quality market... After husband dies, Nicole-Barbe Cliquot-Ponsardin, age 27, runs small wine business (develops sparkling champagne as universal wine).

1806

General Events

England blockades (April) French coasts... Napoleon closes (November 21) continental ports to English imports, joined by Prussia and Russia in 1807, Austria in 1809 and Sweden in 1810 (leads to Britain's 1807 ban on all commercial shipping in waters of France, allies)... Bramah invents numerical printing machine for bank notes... Davy discovers electrolytic method to make potassium, soda... East India College is founded, England, to train personnel for India service (offers Oriental studies, mostly languages, and European studies, languages, mathematics, law, political economy and general history)... Paris Industrial Exposition encourages French business to develop machines for regaining industrial supremacy (features 1,422 exhibits, rewards inventors, mostly in textiles, chemicals and watchmaking, for devices that add speed, precision and simplicity in manufacturing process)... R. Wedgwood gets English patent for carbon paper... British forces take Dutch Cape Colony in South Africa... Albrecht Thaer pioneers crop rotation, founds Germany's first science institute to study agriculture.

Business Events

Britain's cotton industry employs some 90,000 factory workers, 184,000 handloom weavers... John Sutton starts London business as corn factory and agricultural seed merchant (gets Royal Warrant in 1858 as Britain's leading seed house)... Perfume business of Roger & Gallet appears in France (still extant)... Frederick Winsor forms National Light and Heat Co., renamed Gas Light and Coke Co. in 1812 and copied by 12 more utility firms by 1840s, to provide London with street lighting (supplies gas-lighting for Pall Mall area in 1807, most city streets gas-lit by 1842 and major European cities by 1818).

1807

General Events

French law gives 45 stockholders a trading monopoly on Paris Bourse, monopoly ends with 1987 law allowing buyouts... John Buddle uses crude wooden air pump to ventilate Wallsend Colliery, steam-powered pumps appear in 1840... Maudslay designs compact power unit, the 'table engine'... Prussia starts teacher training colleges, 17 by 1826... France's Code de Commerce regulates commercial partnerships and corporations, model for other European countries (exempts sleeping partners from any liability for firm's debts, basis for ownership shares later)... After defeat by Napoleon at Jena, Graf Gerhard von Scharnhorst gets authority to reform Prussian Army (-1814, requires officers to have liberal education, starts division schools to train officers in military arts, forms General Staff in 1809, basically unchanged until 1921 reforms)... Plowden gets English patent to preserve meat... Britain bans slave trade, continues to flourish for some 50 years until replaced by profitable palm oil shipments by West Africa for candles, lubricants, soap... Institute for Metal Workers appears in Denmark.

Business Events

73 private banks operate in England, some 100 in 1820s... London Coal Exchange forms to regulate industry... North West Co.builds Kootenae House, first trading post on Canada's upper Columbia River (builds 2nd post in Spokane area in 1810)... Odessa Exchange is formed in Russia, becomes major money and credit market for Black Sea ports... Debt of the English East India Co. is over 26 million pounds (continues to pay statutory maximum dividends of 10.5%/year despite loss of sales from domestic competition by 1808 and losses of almost 4 million pounds/year by 1812).

1808

General Events

After installing stationary steam engine in 1803 for rolling mill and operating a locomotive, too heavy for cast-iron tracks, in 1804, Trevithick gives rides for public amusement on steam-powered train in London... Davy demonstrates arc lighting, commercially successful in 1870s with generator of Gramme... Karl von Clausewitz writes historical study of generalship (notes comparison of Caesar, Prince Eugene of Savoy and Napoleon as difficult due to differing social, technological and political realities)... British and Foreign Schools Society forms to improve educational system, a national society in 1811... Engraving shows street carrier selling water in London... Napoleon abolishes Inquisition in Spain, Italy... Prussia's Royal Proclamation requires all military officers to be appointed, promoted on demonstrated ability... By 1827 Prussia uses 50 steam engines... Charles Fourier, French social reformer, develops plan for cooperative communities, "phalansteries", of 1,620 to operate agrarian-handicraft economics.

Business Events

Times of London sends Henry Crabb Robinson, first war correspondent, to Spain to report on Peninsula War... 150,475 merchants are members of guilds in European Russia, 40,993 in 1847... First Banco de Brazil is formed, liquidated 1829 and re-established 1851 (merges with Banco Commercial de Rio de Janeiro in 1853 to create nation's first substantial credit institution)... Jacques Mivart, French chef, opens deluxe hotel, London.

1809

General Events

Sweden creates world's first ombudsman office, genesis in 1792, to investigate complaints against administrative officials, adopted by Denmark in 1955 and in 1962 by Norway, New Zealand... Alex Soyer, French-born chef in London (creates patent sauces to be sold by 1706 business of Crosse & Blackwell), is born (-1858)... Berlin University gets Royal Charter for advanced study in science, first to stress research over education... German physiologist invents water voltameter telegraph... William Bundy, English mathematical instrument maker, invents "Patent Pin Machine" (after successful machine in 1824 by U.S. engineer Lemuel W. Wright leads to first commercial production of pins in 1833)... Heathcote invents bobbin net machine.

Business Events

Friendly Society of Ironfounders appears in England... Showman William Bullock opens Liverpool Museum in London with collected natural, artificial curiosities for paying customers.

1810

General Events

'Seehandlung' becomes Bank of Prussia, patterned after those of France, England and U.S... Branches of Italian Scientific Institute appear in Venice, Padua, Verona, Milan... King Ludwig I of Bavaria marries Therese of Saxony, celebrated by first annual Oktoberfest in Munich, seven million visitors in 1985... Frederick Koenig invents steam-powered press, used by The Times in 1814 (leads to high-speed press, invented 1846, by Richard Hoe in 1857)... French-born London merchant, Pierre Durand, patents the tin can... Napoleon issues decree to seize any U.S. vessel in French ports... John Leslie, Scottish professor, makes artificial ice... France makes sale of tobacco a monopoly... The Art of Making Money Plenty is published in this time... France builds first canal tunnels, boatmen refuse to enter long dark passages... Denmark holds first livestock show... Bank of France opens branch in Lille (-1814, opens branch in 1846 at Valenciennes)... Kriegsakademie is founded, Berlin to train Prussian officers in science of war (requires candidates to have graduated from gymnasia or pass six-day general examination on mental capacity instead of factual knowledge)... Though field obligations remain in force, Prussia grants peasants personal freedom (allows nobility to practice middle- class occupations)... Operative Cotton Spinner's Assn. strikes mills in Manchester.

Business Events

Birmingham firm builds arms-making plant for Russia at Tula (uses labor-saving machines, interchangeable parts)... England's first public rooms for billiards open in London for customers.

1811

General Events

Russia attempts to create special estate of factory workers to help manufacturers in recruiting free employees... French Press Agency is formed... Venezuela is first South American country to declare its independence from Spain, realized 1817... London's population is some one million, reached by Paris in 1840s and Berlin in 1880s... For second time Russia is unable to open Japan to foreign trade... Prussian Junkers grant peasants freehold on their holdings in payment for a percentage of land... Followers of "General" Lud destroy machines in English textile mills (-1815)... Civil Code of Austria is established... Japanese Government establishes translation bureau to study Dutch books on science... Charles Lamb: "The Good Clerk, A Character: with Some Account of 'The Complete English Tradesman'"... F.L. Jaun starts first Turner Society in Berlin (urges universal education and gymnastics)... Workers at six Russian woolen-cloth mills complain about non-payment of wages, various complaints on disorders elsewhere in Russia during 1796-1820s... Prussia's Trade Regulation Act restricts power of guilds, abolishes price-fixing authority of police.

Business Events

After acquiring rights for Appert's food preservation process, Durand sells rights to Bryan Donkin, John Hall and John Gamble (present canned food to Royal Society and Royal family in 1813 for approval, provide canned food to Arctic Expedition in 1814 - Royal Navy orders some 24,000 cans, appear in shops in 1830s, leads to production stamping process for cans in 1844)... Steam power is used at Leeds to haul coal on railway... London commercial sales room opens for commodity trading on Mincing Lane, used for trading since 900s by brokers handling Mediterranean wines and spices (is replaced by London Commodity Exchange in 1954).

1812

General Events

Prussia adopts Gymnasium educational plan... Planned development of London's residential Park Crescent estate is built (-1820)... Charles Babbage designs Difference Engine for automatic calculations, a special-purpose machine with fixed program to make complex calculations and print results... Royal Yacht Squadron appears in London... Philippe Girard invents machine to spin flax... Recently bankrupted commercial agent assassinates Prime Minister of Britain to protest war-time trading restrictions... Luddites petition Parliament to regulate wages, working hours... Paris provides regular water supply to wealthy districts, first in Europe... Prussia frees Jews.

Business Events

John Blenkinsop, Mathew Murray build railway engine for English colliery... A steam engine is built in Berlin, site later for 1,200 steam engines... Henry Bell operates steamship Comet, first successful steamboat in Europe, on the Clyde (leads to first steamer in Russia and Java in 1815, Germany in 1816, on Danube in 1818, India in 1819, and Switzerland in 1822)... Drury Lane Theater opens in London (still extant).

1813

General Events

Denmark declares bankruptcy... Work starts in London to build Regent Street as area for upper-class housing (-1827)... Humphry Davy: Elements of Agricultural Chemistry... Frederick S. Archer uses negatives to make photographic prints... Wilhelm von Gneisenau follows

Scharnhorst as Chief of Prussian General Staff (-1816, allows subordinate commanders to take independent action in handling changing circumstances, prepares strategic plans for campaigns of 1813, 1814)... Napoleon's personal staff is organized with secretariat of civilian secretaries, librarians and archivists, adjutant generals, officers d'Ordonnance as messengers, cabinet of intelligence as statistical bureau, and topographical bureau; Imperial Headquarters with Marshal Berthier's personal staff and general staff with adjutant-commandants for special assignments and positions for unassigned officers, engineering, military police, artillery and topography (commands Grande Armee of 11 divisions and 16-24 corps, each has semi-permanent general staff)... Parliament abolishes trade monopoly of English East India Co. with India (retains China monopoly to 1834, civil government of India until Sepoy Rebellion of 1858)... National Student Corp. appears in Germany (-1814)... Robert Owen: New View of Society (believes as men are the product of the social system, then society must be changed for the betterment of man)... Owen discusses psychological and social factors influencing work in address to manufacturing superintendents... French army requires two years of service for promotion of staff officers to rank of major.

Business Events

Two British ships seeking trade with Japan force Dutch trader out of Nagasaki... George Stephenson builds traveling steam engine for a colliery... Simon Fribourg starts family grain business in Belgium, evolves as worldwide Continental Grain Co. in 1921 with U.S. operation in 1928... John Jenkins: Art of Writing (discusses penmanship, evolves with use of steel nib pens in 1830s).

1814

General Events

Cape of Good Hope is a British Colony... Apprenticeship and Wages Act of 1563 is repealed... Napoleon is exiled to Elba (-1815)... Kingdom of the Netherlands forms, Belgium separates in 1830... England patents first successful spinning machine... John Lawes, agricultural scientist (turns estate into first agricultural research laboratory, tests artificial manures), is born (-1900).... England hires Gurkhas as mercenaries, still so employed (provides Nepal with foreign exchange).

Business Events

Dulwich picture gallery opens in London, first English public art gallery.... George Stephenson tests (July 25) first workable steam engine, Blucher, at Newcastle, first locomotive to operate faster than horse-drawn system... James Purdey starts gunmaking business in London to produce handcrafted sporting guns, so distinctive no two alike (evolves by 1980s to make only 70 custom guns/year, $13,000-$14,000, for list of buyers waiting up to 4 years)... After trying this and that, Josiah Mason learns father's trade of carpet weaving (becomes clerk in uncle's fancy imitation jewelry business in 1816, leaves in 1822 when firm is sold, with savings acquires business in 1824 making hoop rings and steel pens, makes just pens in 1829 - only some six others in Birmingham, runs partnership with brothers in 1842-56 in electro-plating copper with gold and silver, makes over 50 million pens/year by 1858 - 225 million/year by 1874, sells to Perry & Co. in 1875).

1815

General Events

John L. Macadam is Surveyor/General of British roads (uses crushed rock for surface of roads, evolves as macadamized roads)... Davy invents safety lamp for coal mines... German pharmacist F. Serturner is first to prepare morphine... 40 steam engines operate in Birmingham... Parliament's Apothecaries Act bans practice of unqualified doctors... David Ricardo: Essay on the Influence of a Low Price of Corn on the Profits of State... Technological College of Vienna is founded...

Congress of Vienna agrees to open international rivers to vessels of all countries, international commissions to regulate Rhine traffic in 1831 and Danube traffic in 1856... Robert Owen: Observations on the Effect of the Manufacturing System (urges legislation to counteract evils of new industrial practices on the character of people)... Congress of Vienna forms German Confederation of 39 independent states... Prussia acquires Ruegen Island, its first resort in 1818 (evolves by 1990s as most popular vacation spot in Baltic).

Business Events

In this time Benjamin Gott runs England's largest mechanized woolen mill, most weaving done by independent contractors - common practice of iron works, potteries, collieries, canal builders... Russian traders start post at Hawaii (-1816 when expelled on urging of U.S. traders)... With savings, John Doulton starts Doulton & Co. with John Watts, retired Watts replaced by son in 1835, to make utilitarian stoneware (is successful with drainpipes during sanitary revolution of 1840s, enters art pottery market in 1856, becomes Royal Doulton with warrant in 1901, makes bone china in 1902)... James Sanger, itinerant showman at Bristol fair, tours southern England with two caravans - during winters runs fruit and fish market stall at Newbury (after son George and brothers learn conjuring gives show at Stepney fair in 1848, gives winter show, London, in 1850 with performing animals, clowns, and pantomimers, tours with traveling tent show in 1854 - at Liverpool amphitheater during winter, during 1860s stages circuses at Manchester, Birmingham, Liverpool, Glasgow, Dundee, Aberdeen, Bath, Exeter, and Plymouth, leases Islington Hall for winter shows in 1870-71, buys London amphitheater in 1871, uses promotional techniques of P.T. Barnum in 1871 to compete with George Wombwell's Menagerie and Hengler's circus, stages Royal Thanksgiving Procession in 1872, stages "The Fall of Khartoum and Death of General Gordon", 300 guardsmen, 400 extras, 100 camels, 200 horses, fifes and drums of Grenadiers and pipers of Scots Guards, in 1886, drops lease in 1893 for traveling circus, 11 summer tours of Europe, theater shows and zoo)... After visiting vineyards in France, Madeira and Cape, John Macarthur starts producing Australia's first wine.

1816

General Events

Scottish clergyman Robert Stirling invents novel external combustion engine... Swiss-born John Pauly, Durs Egg design dolphin-shaped dirigible in England... Economic crisis in England spurs large-scale immigration of English to U.S., Canada... French chemist Joseph N. Niepce develops first photographic negative, development of photogram in this time by Thomas Wedgewood, Davy... Karl Wilhelm von Grolman is Prussia's new Chief of General Staff, distinct military unit in contrast to Napoleon's personal staff (-1819, forms unit into 3 "theaters of war" with each corps having chief of staff, 3 officers and each brigade with one officer - 87 in General Staff and 66 at corps level in 1873, adds military history section to provide professional training)... David Brewster, Scottish scientist and clergyman, invents kaleidoscope, device with mirrors to provide four images (-1817, becomes Victorian parlor amusement, evolves as objet d'art in 1980s)... Charles Dupin does efficiency studies of Royal Navy (-1820)... Parliament assumes responsibility to pay salaries of office holders... Germany's Baron Karl Drais von Sauerbromn devises bicycle, no pedals, with steering mechanism, propelled by striding rider, gets patent in 1818 (appears in England in 1818 as Hobby Horse or Dandy Horse)... John Trotter opens London's Soho Bazaar as charitable venture, provides stalls to relatives of those killed in recent wars (-1885, is emulated by Le Grand Bazar in Paris in 1825, Bazar de Brufflers in 1829, Bazar de Fer in 1830, and Galeries du Commerce et de L'Industrie in 1837).

Business Events

Canadians put steam-powered sternwheeler on Lake Ontario... Boston's Samuel Wells opens Paris banking house as correspondent for U.S. merchants (-1841)... U.S.-born French Huguenot Samuel

Courtauld III starts English silk business (tries to sell 1820-21, see business conditions improve 1823-25, forms Courtauld, Taylors & Courtauld partnership in 1828 silk business with handloom and power-loom weaving, dyeing and finishing of black silk for mourning - by 1850s England's biggest textile manufacturer, employs over 3,000 workers by 1880s with philosophy of benevolent despotism, acquires viscose rayon patents in 1904, makes investments during 1920s in France, Germany and Italy, signs agreement in 1928 with Imperial Chemical to divide world market).

1817

General Events

W. Cobbett: Paper Against Gold: The History and Mystery of the Bank of England... On advice of first French governors, Russia makes Odessa a free port on Black Sea to encourage trade... Parliament's Metropolitan Paving Act empowers Surveyors of Pavements to issue licenses for removing, regulating advertising signs... English workers in Derbyshire riot to protest low wages... David Ricardo: The Principles of Political Economy and Taxation (views capital as more significant in production than management)... Bank of Montreal is first chartered Canadian bank, opens London branch in 1818... R. Roberts, England, builds metal planer... Cayley proposes air screw to power a dirigible... Jean Baptiste Say: Catechism of Political Economy (stresses importance of planning)... Saint-Simon prepares four-volume study of industry (-1818)... Workers of Lille petition French Government for laws against new machinery.

Business Events

Joseph Baxendale, partner start English road haulage firm of Pickfords... Banque Rothschild opens in Paris (-1981 when nationalized by France's Socialist government, starts new house in NYC)... Bunge brothers start family trading firm for hides, spices in Amsterdam (moves to Belgium in 1850 and expands into grains, wool, cotton and coffee - later granted monopoly by King Leopold II to export ivory from Africa, leads to Argentine firm of Bunge & Born in 1876 by another brother to ship grain, products to Europe, later base for stock control of family empire, acquires NYC grain-exporting business after World War I, operational headquarters of billion-dollar trading business after World War II, evolves as 3rd or 4th largest U.S. grain trader, to run 117 firms in Brazil, 40 in Argentina and subsidiaries in Britain, Spain, Venezuela, Peru and Australia by 1990).

1818

General Events

Friedrich Harkort, student of British industrialization, starts workshop for engineers in Germany (devises puddling process for iron in 1829, starts foundry in 1832 to become industrialist)... First iron passenger ship appears on the Clyde... William Brown, Dundee flax-spinner manufacturer, begins essays to discuss management problems of his East Mill (-1823, uses observation and experimentation to study systematic management of textile operations, covers departmental organization, work flow, job tasks, record keeping, morale, giving orders, resolving conflicts, setting wages, and handling labor relations, as consultant advises other spinners)... Brunel patents underground tunneling shield, used to complete first tunnel between two London areas in 1843 before conversion to railway tunnel in 1860s... Institution of Civil Engineers forms, England, societies of mechanical engineers in 1847 and electrical engineers in 1871... Mary Woolstonecraft-Shelley: Frankenstein (attacks industrialization)... London's F.W. Cronhelm writes "first" book on accounting theory... Marshal Saint-Cyr founds school to train French staff officers... Argentine vessels capture Spanish garrison at Monterey in attempt to free Alta California from Spain... Britain offers prize to first person finding Northwest Passage (after some 27 attempts leads to discovery of North Magnetic Pole by 1831 Ross Expedition)... Clausewitz is director of the Prussian War College (-1830, stresses necessity for research, planning and preparing for military campaigns, observes practice of war modified by external factors).

Business Events

After getting secret liqueur recipe from master, Peter F. Heering, young grocery clerk, starts Copenhagen firm to make Cherry Heering (still extant)... Privately-owned, joint-stock bank appears in Copenhagen, genesis for National Bank of Denmark... Place to play chess opens in London, remodeled in 1848 by caterer John Simpson to become Simpson's Divan and Tavern and later Simpson's-in-the- Strand for dining by gentlemen, ladies only allowed in separate room... Smirnoff family starts Vodka business, Russia (passes secret recipe to family friend Rudolph Kunett after 1917 Revolution, starts vodka factory in U.S. in 1934, sells business to Heublein firm in 1939)... J. Henry Schroder & Co. opens in Britain as London house of Hamburg merchant bank, City's leading merchant bank 1849-1909 (specializes in 1853 in financing overseas railway construction and Latin-American governments, forms syndicate with Barings, Rothschilds in 1921, opens NYC branch in 1923).

1819

General Events

Travelers' Club forms in London for gentlemen having gone 500 miles from Britain... Switzerland's Francois-Cailer makes "first" known chocolate bar... England establishes 12-hour work day for juveniles, children under 9 banned from working in cotton mills... Steam-powered road vehicle operates in Paddington, England... Owen forms committee to establish experimental Village of Cooperation for 800-1,200 individuals... First horse-drawn omnibus appears in Paris, NYC in 1827 and London in 1829... Hawaii's King Kamehameha II abolishes Kapu, all-encompassing system of political, religious and social customs (orders temples destroyed and images burned)... By accident Danish scientist, Hans C. Oersted, discovers electromagnetism (leads to first electromagnet by France's Francois Arago in 1820, improved by U.S.' Joseph Henry in 1831, and theory of Ampere in 1827)... Prussia sets uniform tariff for all territories (by 1844 leads to Zollverein, economic market of 23 million people, of most German states to eliminate 38 tariffs, customs barriers).

Business Events

Modern Maypole dairy business appears in Birmingham (operates over 1,000 stores in 1914, is acquired in 1924 by Home and Colonial retailing chain)... Burlington Arcade with enclosed small shops opens in London's Piccadilly... Hudson's Bay Co. sends land expeditions to explore northern coast of Canada... German businessmen form organization to develop customs union of German states (is promoted by Friedrich List, admirer of Alexander Hamilton).

1820

General Events

Charles Wheatstone coins term "telephone" in 1820s to describe device for transmitting sound through wooden rods for short distances... Thomas Hancock patents process to use rubber in waterproofing (starts London public omnibus service in 1831-36)... Parliament declares future commercial policy should be guided by principle of free trade, by 1850 all major restrictions dropped... By this time, St. John's Wood near London is England's first suburban neighborhood... Use of guano as natural fertilizer appears in Europe... Alsatian inventor Charles Xavier Thomas devises "first" successful adding machine... Kamehameha II greets New England missionaries, erect mission house with pre-fabricated parts from Boston... Davy invents the magnet... Assn. for the Promotion of Technical Knowledge forms in Prussia... Ithiel Town patents truss bridge... Platinum is found in the Urals... Thomas de Colmar builds "first" workable calculating machine... London commercial men petition Parliament for free trade... Parliament lifts bans on exports of machinery to U.S...Pierre J. Pelletier isolates quinine, antimalarial drug, from tropical tree, followed by discoveries of strychnine, caffeine and digitalis by other French scientists... Frederick Accum: A Treatise on Adulterations of Food, and Culinary Poisons (attacks retailers for scandalous fakery, flees England after public outcry).

Business Events

Cosmorama, revised peepshow, opens in London as fashionable meeting place, lets 14 paying viewers see amazing scenes... Two silk merchants found Ecole Speciale de Commerce d'Industrie, oldest in France (becomes Ecole Superieure de Commerce in 1852, sponsored by Paris Chamber of Commerce in 1868)... E. Dehillerin cookware store opens in Paris (still extant)... London Magazine appears... Titus Salt starts apprenticeship with woolstapler (joins W. Rouse & Son, one of trade's biggest, in 1822, joins father's firm in 1824, starts wool business in 1834, innovates with cotton warp for women's fashion, runs 5-6 mills, hundreds of handcombers, in Bradford, center of international worsted trade, in 1840s, sponsors trips for workers, reorganizes firm 1850-72, builds Saltaire as model industrial village of 4,500 in 1853-72 with shops, dispensary, hospital, almshouses, community center, two churches, worker cottages, executive houses)... After touring England, F.A.S. Egells starts iron foundry, engineering works near Berlin (builds hydraulic press in 1824, steam engine in 1825).

1821

General Events

Friedrich Karl Freiherr von Muffling heads Prussian Great General Staff (-1829, organizes unit advising war minister into three sections of personnel matters, organization and training, maneuvers, deployment and mobilization plans, and technical and artillery matters, operates with 18 officers at Berlin, 27 at army corps and 20 at divisions, uses war games in military training)... Tsar attempts to close Pacific Coast north of San Francisco to any but Russian vessels (leads to diplomatic controversy, Monroe Doctrine of 1823)... Wheatstone demonstrates sound reproduction... Gewerbe Institute appears in Berlin to promote industrialization throughout Germany... First iron steamship is built in Birmingham... Julius Griffiths, England, builds 4-wheeled, steam-powered road vehicle... James Mill: Elements of Political Economy (gives first description to analyze and synthesize hand motions, sees planning as most important management activity, indicates control a necessity to prevent employee theft)... London Co-Operative Society is formed, some 500 such groups with 20,000 members in 1830s... Trade school opens in Berlin... T.J. Seebeck discovers thermoelectricity... Henri Saint-Simon: Du Systeme Industriel... Bank of England returns to gold standard, suspended 1797, Germany in 1870-73, Scandinavia in 1872, Holland in 1875-77, Austria-Hungary in 1879.

Business Events

Manchester Guardian appears as weekly, daily in 1855 (still extant)... First regular steamboat packet service begins between Dover, Calais... First public railroad is planned to operate 12 miles from Stockton on North Sea to coal town of Darlington, Stephenson is project engineer (operates in 1825)... Hudson's Bay Co., North America's oldest corporation, takes over over-extended North West Co. for fur monopoly in Northwest, Canada (runs chain of 173 trading posts).

1822

General Events

Babbage starts building model of Difference Engine to perform more complex mathematical functions than machines of Pascal or Leibniz, abandons project to design general-purpose computer in 1832... Niepce produces first photograph... King William I of Netherlands founds Societe Generale de Belgique, earliest known mutual investment company as developed by Scots in mid-1800s, with grant of lands, forests (enters private banking when Belgium is created in 1830, prints own paper currency until 1850, starts Congo venture in 1886 to acquire control over 75% of land's crops for export, evolves by 1960s as conglomerate with interests in banking, insurance, energy, steel, nonferrous metals, construction, real estate, electrical and mechanical equipment, chemical products and others in glass, paper, shipping and textiles - 1,261 firms including land's largest bank, and nearly 100,000 workers, by 1988 with assets of $66 billion, blocks takeover by De Benedetti in 1988)... John, David Ames improve 1817 process of Gilpin to make continuous strip of paper from wood pulp... Aaron Manby launches first iron steamer on Seine... Sweden College of Mines is founded... Lorenz Oken starts society in Germany to promote science.

Business Events

First mercantile establishment in California opens in Monterey... Anglo-U.S. merchants found Banco de Buenos Aires, dissolved 1836 (is followed by Banco de la Provincia de Buenos Aires in 1854)... Englishman tours Russian musket plant at Tula (sees use of specialized English machinery to make arms with interchangeable parts)... Stephenson builds first iron railroad bridge for Stockton-Darlington Railroad.

1823

General Events

Henri Saint-Simon: <u>Catechisme des Industriels</u>... England's Samuel Brown designs water-cooled engine, uses atmospheric-vacuum principle, to pump water from mines, leads to first operational water-cooled internal combustion engine of Lenoir in 1859-60 and Otto with four-stroke-cycle engine in 1876... W.W. Ellis develops form of football at England's Rugby School... Cologne holds first annual carnival... Michael Faraday liquifies chlorine... Mechanics Institute appears in London for education of workers, another institute in Glasgow... Royal Thames Yacht Club forms in London... E. Sabastien builds grand piano... Workers submit petition to Tsar Alexander I on "oppressions of the factory owner and low wages" (issues regulations for wage increases, reduces working hours from 14 to 13/day in summer and 12/day in winter, allows factories to send organizers of labor unrest to military)... England's budget for 1823-25 reduces duties on certain imports, first changes in mercantilism's protection policy... Charles Macintosh patents use of naphtha to waterproof fabric (joins Hancock in 1825 to make Macintosh raincoats, when unable to get sufficient supplies of rubber to meet demand, submits request in 1853 to Kew Botanical Gardens to develop rubber plantations in Far East with seedlings from Brazil)... First permanent school of watchmaking in Switzerland is started, follows previous attempts in 1776, 1781... With fares less than those of standard hackney coaches in public transportation, London's first horse-drawn cabriolet coach, originated in Paris, appears to carry two passengers under a hood, leads to use of Hansom cabs in 1834, 7,499 on streets in 1904, and four-wheeled coaches by 1865, 3,905 in use by 1904.

Business Events

Jacques M. Daguerre presents Dioramas in Paris for public amusement... William Greaves & Son is first in Sheffield with large-scale factory to handle production of steel, crafting of cutlery... Moscow Merchants' Assn. complains to Minister of Finance on increasing competition of small-scale peasant production, factory production soon replaced by cottage weaving.

1824

General Events

Prussian Army Lieutenant von Reisswitz designs complex wargame for military training, planning (despite resistance of military is approved by General von Muffling as training device, inspires first wargame club and magazine <u>Kriegspieler Verein</u>, becomes accepted by German army, gets credit for German victory in Franco-Prussian War)... In this time, first laboratory for chemistry is established by Justus von Liebig at University of Giessen, basis for Germany's role in chemistry... Britain captures lower part of Malay Peninsula from Dutch... Parliament's Vagrancy Act penalizes use of obscene advertisements... England abolishes its National Lottery... London's George S. Harris patents an advertising machine, four-wheeled kiosk with lanterns (is suppressed with London's Hackney Carriage Act of 1853)... Combinations Law of 1799-1800 is repealed (allows British workers to organize to raise wages, establishes penalties for violence, threats, intimidations)... British scholar and physician, Peter Roge publishes paper on persistence of vision to retain an image longer than it exists, leads to development of moving pictures... Edinburgh forms first British municipal fire force... Joseph Aspdin, Leeds bricklayer, patents Portland Cement, in general use after 1850 (appears in U.S. in 1872)... In guild reform Russia allows state peasants and private serfs same commercial and industrial rights as held by merchants... N. Sadi-Carnot pioneers study of thermodynamics with essay on heat, power.

Business Events

Pierre Parissot opens Belle Jardiniere, forerunner of modern department store, in Paris with one-price policy and cash only, followed in 1858 by London's Crystal Palace Bazaar... Syndicate of British financiers, politicians form Imperial Continental Gas to introduce Europe to commercial uses of gas (by 1900, operates 1,775 miles of gas mains in 10 major cities and 29 towns, shows features of modern multi-national organization by 1914)... John Lee Benham & Sons starts business in London as ironmongers, bathmakers and manufacturer of stoves and kitchen ranges with show rooms on ground floor and workshops above (gets first large stove contract in 1841, wins international prizes for stoves in 1851, 1855, 1862 and 1867, patents cooking apparatus for ships in 1862)... John Cadbury starts family's business as tea and coffee dealer (opens cocoa, chocolate drinking shop in Birmingham in 1831, makes 15 varieties of chocolates in 1841, gets Royal Warrant in 1853, employs 20 people in 1861 - over 200 in 1879, 1,500 in 1890 and 3,023 in 1900, makes Cocoa Essence with Dutch press, first pure cocoa in Britain without additives, in 1866, builds model plant in 1879 - first in City to work half- days on Saturdays, close on bank holidays and introduce piece-rate system, develops Bournville Village for workers in 1895, starts 2 cocoa estates in Trinidad in 1897, starts suggestion system in 1902, introduces UK's best-selling candy bar in 1905 to end Swiss dominance, forms works committee, year after Crossfields, in 1905, gives male employees pensions in 1906 - women 1911, exports 18% of volume in 1911 - plants in Australia in 1921, New Zealand 1930, Ireland 1933, and South Africa in 1937, sets minimum prices for chocolate, cocoa and candy in 1917 with rival J.S. Fry - joined by Rowntree in 1918, merges in 1919 with rival Fry to form Cocoa & Chocolate Co., forms Overseas Factory Committee in 1929, merges with Schweppes in 1969, acquires U.S.' Peter Paul candy in 1978, produces apple and drink mix products in 1982)... Two Calcutta merchants offer prize to first steamship sailing between England, Bengal under 70 days, won by <u>Enterprise</u> in 1825... By Act of 1823 Glenlivet is Scotland's oldest licensed distillery, bought by Seagrams in 1977... A share of Loughborough Canal is worth 2,200 pounds, mere 200 by 1872.

1825

General Events

Thomas Drummond invents limelight... Oersted discovers aluminum... Chemists M. Chevreul, J. Gay-Lussac patent method to make candles from fatty acids instead of tallow... Britain legalizes trade unions... By accident Jean Baptiste Jolly, French dyeworks owner, discovers kerosene removes dirt from fabrics (leads to first dry-cleaning service in 1866 by Pollars of Scotland after visit by Jolly's grandson and French patent for mechanized dry-cleaning machine in late 1860s)... Henri Saint-Simon: <u>The New Christianity</u> (notes inherent logic of industrial society, believes workers should receive just share of country's wealth, urges reorganization of society because new production methods assure greatest good for greatest number)... Parliament legalizes branch banking system... The Quarterly Review: "What can be more palpably absurd than the prospect held out of locomotives traveling twice as fast as stagecoaches?"... Michael Faraday isolates benzene... Hungarian Academy of Sciences is founded... Technological Institute appears in Stockholm... Norway's first steamboat is operated by postal service... First German polytechnical institute appears in Karlsruhe, Munich in 1827, Dresden in 1828, Stuttgart in 1829 and Hanover in 1831... London workers publish Trades Newspaper and Mechanics Weekly Journal... Britain lifts prohibition on machine exports... Brazil wins independence from Spain, 76 governments, 50% de facto military, by 1990... British doctor John Paris devises thaumatrope, rotating disk with two separate pictures, to show moving images (leads to blind Belgian scientist Joseph Plateau's phenkistiscope in 1833, to Austria's Simon Von Stampfer's stroboscope in 1833, to U.S.' kinematoscope, first with photographs, of Sellers in 1860, to France's Jules Janssen's chronophotography in 1874 and Emile Raynard's praxinoscope in 1876).

Business Events

New Zealand Colonization Co. is created in England, 2nd settlement company in 1839... Rug manufacturers Cyrus, James Clark start making shoes in England, major line in 1840s (is virtually insolvent by 1863 until revived by son William with strict financial controls, productivity measurements and cost accounting, promotes brand of quality shoes)... Hudson's Bay Co. starts trading post of Ft. Vancouver on Columbia River, Dr. John McLoughlin factor... World's first railroad line runs 12 miles from North Sea port of Stockton to coal mines of Darlington (allows use of private passenger coaches, lowers cost of coal over 50%), followed by U.S. in 1830, France in 1832, Ireland in 1834, Germany and Belgium in 1835, Canada in 1836, Russia and Cuba in 1837, Austria in 1838, Czechoslovakia, Holland and Italy in 1839, Switzerland in 1844, Denmark in 1847, Spain in 1848, Mexico in 1850, India in 1853, Norway, Australia and Egypt in 1854, Sweden in 1856, Union of South Africa in 1860, New Zealand in 1863, Bulgaria in 1866, Japan in 1872, China in 1883, and Burma in 1889.

1826

General Events

First German gasworks appears in Hanover... Benjamin Disraeli: Vivian Grey (uses word "millionaire" in novel, is used by New York Sun to identify 25 millionaires in City)... Swedish-born engineer John Ericsson builds model ship with unique screw propeller for Royal Navy (after approval builds screw-propeller tugboat, when rejected goes to U.S. in 1837 to build screw-propeller U.S.S. Princeton for U.S. Navy - explodes during trials in 1844, designs ironclad Monitor in 1861)... Parliament enacts incorporation legislation, other laws 1844-45 (is followed by Prussia in 1843, Hamburg and Berlin in 1860, and by France in 1867)... Experimental freight railroad is built in Germany... Unter den Linden in Berlin is lit by gas... Otto Unverdorben obtains aniline from indigo... Institute of Commerce appears in Gothenburg... Prussia, Mecklenburg sign commercial treaty, starts formation of German customs union... Parliament authorizes joint-stock banks, 70 by 1836... Large-scale riots destroy power looms in East Lancaster... University College of London is founded for nondenominational students excluded from other universities (opens in 1828 primarily for study of science, areas not emphasized at Oxford and Cambridge).

Business Events

Industry association forms in Brazil, renamed Confederacao Nacional da Industria in 1936... Bank of England opens branch in Manchester, Liverpool in 1827... Pilkington glassmaking business starts in Lancashire, sole British producer of plate glass in 1900s (sends salesman to U.S. in 1879 - agencies in Montreal in 1890 and Australia in 1895, fights attempts of Belgians in 1904 to control continental market for plate glass with Convention Internationale des Glaceries, develops first continuous glass-making process with Henry Ford in 1921 - U.S. license to Pittsburgh Plate Glass in 1930, joins 1904 Convention in 1934 with Pittsburgh Plate and Libbey Owens Ford, starts Argentine facility in 1937 - South Africa in 1950 and New Zealand in 1953, after 10 years of research invents revolutionary float-glass process in 1952 - commercial in 1959, licenses U.S. rights for process to Pittsburgh Plate in 1962)... Alfred, age 14, on death of father assumes ownership of Krupp Steel Foundry and secret for casting steel (employs 11 workers in 1831, 62 in 1834, 122 in 1846, 683 in 1849 and some 1700 in 1850, tours Germany in 1833 to capture steel market - success with cast-iron railway wheels in 1834, starts sickness and burial fund for workers in 1836, visits Britain in 1838 to study steel mills, produces first steel musket barrel in 1843 - Prussian Army not interested, develops rifled-cannon barrel in 1846, starts selling railway supplies in 1847 - develops seamless railway wheel, exhibits breech-loading steel cannon at 1851 London Crystal Palace Exhibition - no orders, shows new light cast steel cannon at 1855 French World's Fair - no orders, starts pension fund for workers in 1855, provides employees with housing, stores, life and accident insurance, pension fund, schools, apprenticeship programs, savings and loan bank, convalescent home, clubhouses, hospitals, dining halls and library by 1900, employs some 6,000 in 1864 - 21,000 in 1887 and 43,000 in 1902, gets credit for cannon helping Prussia to win Sedan battle in 1870-71 Franco-Prussia War, expands business after war with coal mines, steel mills, iron mines and works, and shipping company, after Vienna stock market crash in 1873 is forced to seek funds from Kaiser to pay bank loans - required to hire Kaiser's Karl Meyer to restore firm to sound financial basis, supplies guns to both Turkey, Russia during their 1877 war, after arming 46 nations, except Britain with its Armstrong and France with its Schneider, dies in 1887, is succeeded by son, Fritz - success by marketing nickel-steel armor to withstand shells, then chrome shells to pierce nickel-steel armor and then high carbon armor plate to resist chrome shells, is elected to Prussia's assembly in 1893, builds iron and steel complex at Rheinhausen in 1897 - still largest in Europe, commits suicide in 1902 after scandal, is followed by sister, Bertha, as not sanctioned to operate business by Kaiser marries Baron Gustav von Bolen und Halbach in 1906, changes name to Krupp with approval of Kaiser, to continue family dynasty)...

German cruise line appears on Rhine (still extant)... School teacher Louis Hachette buys small Paris book publisher and book selling business (issues its first periodical, for teachers, in 1827, buys rights for primary school texts in 1831, gets huge order, 540,000 primers and books, from government in 1833 after passing law for free primary school education, in 1852, idea from 1851 visit to London, begins building virtual monopoly selling books in train stations, issues travel guides in 1853, issues its first women's magazine in 1891, acquires, c. 1900, France's leading newspaper distributors and printing, binding firms by 1920).

1827

General Events

First Baedeker's travel guide appears... John Herschel proposes contact lenses... Niepce makes first photograph on metal plate... England's John Walker devises sulfur friction match, phosphorous match in 1833 and safety match in 1844... Austrian engineer Joseph Ressel invents screw-propeller for ships, tested on speedboat in 1829... Friedrich Wohler obtains metallic aluminum from clay... First French railway line opens from Saint-Etienne to Loire River for horse-pulled carriages, first passengers in 1832... German architect Karl F. Schinkel prepares plan for department store... George Pocock tests kite-drawn carriage successfully.

Business Events

Scottish sea captain John Clunies-Ross settles Cocos Islands in Indian Ocean (starts coconut plantations with imported indentured servants from Malaysia and Indonesia, is ruled by heirs until control by Australia in 1978)... Abel Sterns, Massachusetts, starts business career in Mexico (gets Mexican citizenship, moves to Los Angeles, acquires wealth as merchant by buying furs from U.S. trappers, selling Yankee dry goods and trading liquor for hides, tallow of rancheros, marries daughter of rich Bandani family, owns 12 ranches with over 200,000 acres by 1860s)... Geneva's

Vacheron & Constantin uses standardized plant layout to make watch movements (tries to make interchangeable parts)... C. Brewer & Co. appears in Hawaii to operate a sugar plantation, first member of "Big Five," American Factors, Alexander & Baldwin, Castle & Cooke, and Theo. H. Davis, to control Hawaii until W.W. II).

1828

General Events

Peasants revolt in Russia, average 23/year to 1854... Dutch discover how to make chocolate candy from cocoa... Russia's Ministry of Finance forms manufacturing, commercial councils to represent interests of merchants, rendered ineffective by legislation... Central German customs association forms... Goldsworthy Gurney builds steam carriage to travel road from Bath to London, invents crankshaft for steam-engine... London's Samuel Jones patents "Promethean Match," glass bead with acid... Robert Stephenson's Rocket wins Rainhill trials for steam locomotives with speed of 29 mph... Germany's Friedrich Wohler synthesizes urea, start of organic chemistry... J. Doherty forms Society for the Protection of Children Employed in Cotton Factories... J.S. Neilson, Glasgow, develops use of hot-air blasts to make iron, piston-air pumps developed in 1761 to make coke fires hotter.

Business Events

Crockford's opens in London as private club and gambling house (still extant as oldest in City)... First production of iron in France with coke instead of charcoal is started at Decazeville (appoints plant manager in 1827, resolves conflict in authority between board of directors and plant manager in 1839 with manager in charge of operations, is land's 4th largest enterprise in 1840s, contracts work to master craftsmen on piece-rate basis - masters to employ own workers and pay them a percent of master's rate or daily wage, eliminates role of customers in dictating production, quality standards).

1829

General Events

Pianist Frederic Chopin debuts in Vienna, popular artist in Europe... Parliament forms London Metropolitan Police force.. First Oxford-Cambridge boat race is held... Perth appears in Australia... Weavers destroy looms, machines at Rochdale mills... Mexico abolishes slavery... Physicist Oersted founds Polytechnical Institute in Copenhagen... French painter Claude Genoux develops papier-mache... First electro-magnetic clock is made... J. Bigelow coins term "technology"... French pharmacist Henri Leroux extracts salicin, basis for modern aspirin, from bark of willow tree.

Business Events

J. Alfred Novello starts London music publishing business... British start coffee plantations in Ceylon, replaced by tea plantations after blight... Daguerre, Niepce form partnership to develop inventions in photography... Liverpool and Manchester Railroad is built to carry cotton.

1830s

General Events

London's Adelaide Gallery, known as National Gallery of Practical Science, Blending Instruction with Amusements, shows some 250 machines, mechanical devices (evolves as amusement hall in 1840s, Royal Marionette Theater in 1852)... Marseilles printer devises "machine cryptographique" to do mechanical writing... Coffee evolves as major crop of Brazilian economy... Some 600 stationary steam-engines operate in France, 4,853 by 1847... Dutch authorities start agricultural system, crop controls, set prices, and sales by government contracts, in Indonesia (is eased in 1870s)... Mysterious Captain Swing, rural workers in England destroy threshing machines, rural riots again in 1843-44... John Doherty forms National Assn. for the Protection of Labor as federation of some 150 English labor unions (-?)... Cholera from India, 1826, appears in Russia, Central Europe (reaches Scotland in 1832)... First London restaurants appear, serve mostly French food (takes some 40 years for acceptance of women patrons as public dining considered improper for ladies).

Business Events

Ernesto Tornquist Co. begins as Argentine branch of German trading business (reorganizes as limited partnership in 1899 and joint-stock company in 1906 with interests in import-export trade, real estate, meatpacking, sugar, oil, and fishing, helps form Sociedad General Belga Argentina to finance business ventures, most in sugarcane and cattle)... Robert Fortune smuggles tea plants from China to India, cultivated in Calcutta's botanical gardens to start tea industry in India, Ceylon.

1830

General Events

Charles Sauria, J.F. Kammerer devise matches with phosphorous, sulfur and potassium chlorate... Europe's relative share of world manufacturing output is 34.2%, Britain with 9.5%, Hapsburg Empire 3.2%, France 5.2%, German area 3.52%, Italy area 2.3%, Russia 5.6%, U.S. 2.4%, Japan 2.8%, China 29.8%, and India with 17.6%... Joseph Whitworth devises screw gauge (proposes standard thread in 1841)... French tailor Barthelemy Thimmier patents sewing machine, machines destroyed by Paris tailors in 1839... Russian governor Baron Wrangell limits hunting of Alaskan fur seals... Chile exports nitrates, 300 tons in first year and 1.5 million tons in 1900... 26 steam cars drive on London streets... Mexico's colonization law prohibits immigration of Americans to Texas, restricts use of slavery... Self-acting spinning mule is devised in England, seen in U.S. mills in 1840s... James Perry patents steel slit pen... France seizes Algiers (-1962, elects Islamic government in 1990)... Employers, Rio de Janeiro, form Federation of Industry of the Federal District (-1941)... Pope Pius VIII admits "Money-breeding might be condoned."... Royal Geographical Society is an offshoot of Travelers Club (gets Royal Charter in 1859 to sponsor expeditions to explore unknown lands)... Britain produces 80% of Europe's coal, 50% of its iron and nearly all of its steam engines... German scientist Karl von Reichenbach discovers paraffin, used in candles around 3,000 B.C. by wealthy Egyptians (is patented as industrial process in 1850 by U.S. chemist James Young)... With creation of Belgium, State builds railway network, modeled on plans of Stephenson... France's July Revolution enables bourgeoisie, policies of King Louis Philippe favor middle class, to become major political and economic force, catalyst for industrialization.

Business Events

Lowther Arcade with small shops opens in London... Liverpool, Manchester line is Europe's first public railroad... Walter Hancock runs first English motor bus to carry fare-paying passengers... Wealthy businessmen start Political Union in England to enfranchise propertied men... Samuel M. Peto, cousin Thomas Grissell take over Grissell & Peto business building large breweries, fire offices (branches into public buildings and railways in 1830s-1840s, transforms Lowestoff port into holiday resort in 1840s-1850s, builds Canada's Grand Trunk Railway in early 1850s, Royal Danish Railway in mid-1850s, and railways in Portugal, Australia and Algiers in late 1850s, collapses in 1866 financial failure).

1831

General Events

Leipzig merchants' guild starts business high school, sponsored by City's chamber of commerce in 1887... Edmund Ruffin: Essay On Calcareous Manures (spurs use of fertilizers to increase agricultural production)... Budding, Ferrabee of England devise lawnmower, first electric lawnmower in 1958... National Union of Working Classes forms in Britain... Sadler's Committee: Condition of England Question (studies employment of children in factories)... Spring bed is patented... Belgium, Netherlands are separate countries... French silk-weavers riot in Lyons to protest wretched living conditions of workers, again 1834... Charles Dupin: Discours Sur le Sort des Ouvriers (covers industry, worker welfare and organizational efficiency, while Professor of mathematics and economics at Paris Conservatory of Arts and Professions teaches course to prepare students for industry)... House of Commons Select Committee studies steam locomotives for use on roads... Babbage, scientists form British Assn. for the Advancement of Science to correct failures of government, Royal Society in responding to needs of science.

Business Events

Gurney starts road steamer service between Gloucester and Cheltenham, a regular London to Birmingham service in 1833... Jonathan Carr starts career as meal and flour dealer (opens retail bakery shop in 1834, makes biscuits in new factory in 1837 - 72 kinds by 1860s, gets Royal Warrant in 1841)... Walter Hancock starts first steam-powered motor bus service between Stratford, London (is replaced by gas-engine Benz buses in 1895, trolley-buses in 1911).

1832

General Events

Operative Builders' Union forms in Britain... Dr. Henry Stephens makes commercial ink... Parisian Hippolyte Pixii, Amphere's mechanic, builds first rotary generator to produce direct electrical current... Babbage designs Analytical Engine as calculating machine, world's first computer, with punched cards, idea from Jacquard loom, and program of instructions by Lady Lovelace (lacks financial resources to build workable model)... Mass demonstrations for liberal causes appear in Hamburg, Germany... First Reform Act enfranchises Britain's upper-middle class... Karl von Clausewitz: On War (discusses science, art of war as extension of diplomacy, views strategy as use of engagements for object of war and tactics as use of armed forces in an engagement, identifies strategic elements as intellectual and psychological factors, size of forces, operational factors, terrain and logistics, identifies tactical elements as surprise, terrain and envelopment of attack, advises planning for chance and uncertainty in climate of war, describes desired qualities of commander as boldness, perseverance, intellect, courage, cunning, determination, decisiveness, and presence of mind for unexpected, recognizes use of assumptions, systems analysis, and quantitative techniques in making decisions)... Charles Babbage: On the Economy of Machinery and Manufacturers (covers division of labor, time-motion study, data acquisition)... Word "socialism" appears in England, France... Silver lode is found in Chile, more silver and copper found in 1840s-50s... Frederick Smith: Workshop Management: A Manual for Masters and Men, 3rd ed... Schilling, Russia, suggests electro-magnetic telegraph, "tested" 1837... James Montgomery: The Carding and Spinning Masters' Assistant; or the Theory and Practice of Cotton Spinning (provides "management" advice on operating a textile mill)... Swiss-born French and Russian General Antoine Henri Jomini opens Nicholas Academy in Moscow to train staff officers, his Summary of the Art of War in 1862 notes basic principles of warfare... Owen opens first exchanges where goods can be bought or sold according to time taken to make them.

Business Events

Prince Metternich commissions special chocolate cake from Eduard Sacher (builds Hotel Sacher in Vienna in 1876 - bankruptcy in 1930, is revived with family turmoil on ownership of secret cake recipe)... Austria's Linz-Budweiss railway uses passenger cars... George Palmer is apprenticed to uncle, a miller and confectioner (joins partnership of Huntley biscuit firm, founded 1822, in 1841 to make quality, hand-made biscuits, takes over with younger brothers in 1857 on death of Huntley, distributes to 700 retailers in nearly 400 localities in 1847, wins gold medals in 1867, 1878 and 1900 at international expositions, claims to be world's largest biscuit firm in 1874-75)... Barnett Samuel & Sons forms, London, to make musical instruments (becomes private company in 1901 with factory, 5 shops and patent for portable gramophone - Decca Dulcephone, goes public in 1928 as Decca Gramophone)... Andre, Edouard Michelin start machine shop, France... Scottish traders William Jardine, James Matheson start partnership in Canton, only Chinese city open to foreigners (smuggles Indian opium into China when unable to sell imported manufactured goods to buy exports, persuades Britain to use gun boats to preserve free trade in starting Opium War of 1839-42, moves headquarters to Hong Kong in 1841 when Britain forces China to cede Island, develops Island's major trading business with China through compradors to acquire interests in textiles, real estate, brewery, wharves, airline and godowns, closes China operations in 1954 to write off some $20 million in assets, reorganizes in 1984 as Bermuda Holding Co., picks first U.S. boss in 1988 to oversee 76,000 employees in 22 countries).

1833

General Events

Canada's <u>Royal William</u> steams from London to Quebec in 25 days... Britain's first Factory Act, 2nd 1850, establishes (August 28) system for factory inspection, regulates employment for child labor... Economist Friedrich List urges development of railroad system for Germany... John Wade: <u>History of the Middle and Working Classes</u> (studies formations of workers between 1780- 1832)... Owen forms Grand National Moral Union of the Productive and Useful Classes (-1835, starts working-class movement)... Karl F. Gauss, Wilhelm E. Weber build electric telegraph... Finland launches first steamship... Charity bazaars are popular in England... William Henry Fox Talbot, English photographer, develops camera obscura, paper prints... Anticlerical Mexican Government orders California missions, Mission San Gabriel in 1829 with 70,000 cattle, 4,200 horses and 400 mules, to make 50% of land, cattle available for private claims (leads to Pico family with over 700,000 acres, de la Guerra family with 488,329 acres, Castro family with 280,000 acres, Yorba family with 218,000 acres and General Vallejo with 50,000 cattle, 24,000 sheep and 8,000 horses in Sonoma Valley)... Britain shuts down commercial activities of East India Co... India's Civil Service is opened to Indians... French Department of Highways and Bridges is given responsibility to design national rail network... Kryptogaphique, early typewriter, is invented in Marseilles... France's Benoit Fourneyron builds first effective water turbine, used at Niagara Falls' hydroelectric station in 1895... Paris university students start Society of St. Vincent de Paul to help needy, homeless or unemployed.

Business Events

Three Boston merchants start trading house in Honolulu (start first sugar plantation in 1835 with 1,000-acre lease to partner William Hooper)... London Fire Engine Establishment is formed by rival local fire brigades with 80 full-time professionals... John Scott Russell builds six steam buses to operate between Glasgow, Paisley.

1834

General Events

Parliament abolishes East India Company's monopoly with China... Bavarian civil servant, Franz Xavier, creates shorthand system... William Horner, Bath schoolmaster, devises Xoetrope to view moving images... E.M. Clarke produces commercial electro-magnetic generator... Six English farmworkers are charged in taking illegal oaths to establish local union of Friendly Society of Agricultural laborers in Dorset, condemned to 7 years in Australia (after storm of protests, are pardoned after two years)... City of York, Canada, incorporates as Toronto... Refrigerator compressor is invented in Britain... John Bennet Lawes starts agricultural research station at Rothamsted (starts superphosphate factory near London in 1843, first tried as fertilizer in 1817 by Irish physician James Murray)... Owen forms Grand National Consolidated Trades Union in England, fails in general strike of over 500,000 members to win 8-hour day... German chemist F.F. Runge discovers carbolic acid... N.H. von Jacobi builds first electric motor powered by battery... London Statistical Society forms... Parliament's Poor Law puts most destitutes in work houses if they do not accept work (classifies anyone quitting work without an employers' certificate as a vagabond).

Business Events

Banco Economico opens in Rio de Janeiro, Brazil's oldest private bank... London Society of Builders forms, early employers' association to exchange information among members... Lloyd's of London classifies ships to set insurance risks, rates... Stead & Simpson Co. starts leather tanning business (employs some 6,000 workers to make boots in 1864, opens branch shops in 1886, 100 by 1889).

1835

General Events

Gas is used for cooking... Parliament outlaws bearbaiting... Alexis de Tocqueville: "Memoir on Pauperism," presented at meeting of Royal Academic Society of Cherbourg (discusses plight of underclass in England, Europe's most advanced country)... Texas declares succession from Mexico, Republic in 1836 with Sam Houston as President... Melbourne appears in Australia... Efforts are made to power railroad vehicles with electric batteries, successful in 1879... Samuel P. Newman: Elements of Political Economy (cites characteristics of good manager: perseverance, constancy of purpose in planning and directing efforts of others, discretion, and character, notes activities of manager as planning, arranging and conducting production processes)... Andrew Ure: The Philosophy of Manufacturers (gives first concept for factory system)... Charles Chubb invents burglar-proof safe... Talbot makes earliest negative photograph... Dutch Boers undertake Great Trek to Orange River (-1837)... Britain's Municipal Corporations Act establishes uniform city governments... Russia passes first factory laws on owner-worker relations (states that workers are unable to quit until end of contract, owners can fire workers at anytime, written employment contracts are not required, and work regulations are to be posted, leads to child labor law in 1845 with punishments for strikes and first law to protect Russian workers in 1882).

Business Events

Banque de Belgigue appears in Belgium as prototype investment bank, earlier industrial bank sponsored by King... After opening Paris news translation service, Charles Havas adds correspondents (sends data by semaphore, pigeons) to start world's first news agency (splits into Havas advertising, Agence France Presse in 1944), Reuter Telegram Co. in 1851, Associated Press and United Press in 1892 and TASS in 1918... Hawaii's first successful sugar mill opens on Kauai... Work is started, Britain, to build Great Western Railway... Holland & Holland, world's leading custom gunmaker by 1980s, opens in London... Lord Ward takes over Dudley estates, some 25,500 acres in 5 counties (develops iron trade, collieries and ironstone pits with mineral resources, despite less acreage is 7th largest in income of all nobles in 1883, starts steel production in 1890, with coal field exhausted and pits closed diversifies in 1930s with sand, gravel, real estate development)... Some 450 Rouen cloth manufacturers employ 300 spinners, 60 dyers, 60-70 printers... Allendale Insurance appears to provide property coverage, world leader in 1980s.

1836

General Events

Parliament limits loans to corporations to 33% of authorized capital (forbids borrowing until 50% of share capital is paid)... Royal Agricultural Society forms in Britain in this time... First London train is operated... Russia passes first comprehensive law on joint-stock companies... People's Charter movement is started, Britain, by Workingmen's Assn. (-1848)... Edmund Davey discovers acetylene... Adelaide appears in Australia... Balloon flight, 380 miles, is made from England to Germany... Workingmen's Assn. submits petition for manhood suffrage, abolition of property standards to Parliament... Serf-workers petition Tsar Nicholas for freedom, "liberty" in 1849... After receiving no assistance from guild, Dublin painters form trade union... France's Sorel makes galvanized iron... English chemist John F. Daniell builds battery to produce strong and steady current, used 1837 by Charles Wheatstone, William Cooke to send messages by wire... Friedrich Harkort, manufacturer of steam engines, power-looms, ovens and hydraulic presses, builds Germany's first steamship... Spinning, weaving mills appear in Esslingen and Augsburg, start of industrialization in southern Germany.

Business Events

Banque de Lille appears in France (leads to private bank in 1837, industrial bank later at Valenciennes)... J. Tetley starts tea business in England (still extant)... After 54-day crossing from London to NYC in 1832, London-based U.S. merchant Junis Smith and shipbuilder form British & American Steam Navigation Co. (launch British Queen in 1839, averages 16 days westbound and 14 days for eastbound trips).

1837

General Events

Some 10,000 weavers in Leeds are unemployed for three months... Euston Station with two hotels opens as London's first railroad terminal... Runge discovers aniline dyes in coal-tar... Rowland Hill: Post Office Reform (proposes penny postage stamp system, adopted 1840)... Victoria is Queen of Great Britain (-1901)... Iron ships are built in Liverpool... England's Edwin Chadwick proposes sanitary commission to study health problems... Wheatstone, Cooke patent electric telegraph... Isaac Pitman: Stenographic Soundhand, follows systems of Bright in 1588 and Thomas Shelton in 1638, used by diarist Samuel Pepys (closes private school in 1843 to publish shorthand manuals - 80,000/year by 1873, forms Isaac Pittman & Sons in 1886)... French economist Adolphe Blanqui "coins" term "industrial revolution," used by Friedrich Engels in 1845... Texas is recognized as independent State by U.S... England's H. Crawford patents galvanizing process... Russia hires Frederic Le Play, French engineer, sociologist and social reformer, to survey coal resources of Donets Basin, basis for area's industrialization... English is official language of India... Training center for Protestant nurses opens in Kaiserswerth... First German goods railway runs between Leipzig and Dresden, land's first long-distance railroad.

Business Events

Works to make textile machinery is built in Finland, 2nd in 1842... Boston merchant-capitalist

George Peabody starts international banking house in London (takes J.S. Morgan as partner in 1854)... Industrialist August Borsig starts iron foundry and factory to build engines in Berlin (makes first locomotive in 1842, some 500 by 1851 and 3,000 by 1880)... Alfred Krupp develops 20 horse-powered steam-driven forging hammer (sells steel rollers to goldsmiths, silversmiths and watch makers to flatten precious metals - basis for tableware)... Alfred Bird opens retail chemist and druggist business (as sideline develops baking and custard powders as artificial foodstuffs, when son takes over in 1878 develops egg substitute in 1890 and jelly crystals in 1895, sells 100 products in 1905)... Thomas Holloway, merchant and foreign commercial agent, is asked by client, vendor of leeches for therapeutic purposes, for aid in promoting product in England (produces Holloway's Family Ointment in 1837 to enter new field - successful in China, Turkey, Armenia, Middle East and India by advertising to fears, hope and vanity, by using foreign agents, and by giving free samples to captains of visiting ships, blocks brother's attempt in 1850 to compete).

1838

General Events

Public demonstrations to support People's Charter for male voters are held by 100,000 in Glasgow, 200,00 in Birmingham and 300,000 in West Yorkshire... Industrial Society forms, Denmark, to encourage industrialization... Francis Pettit Smith invents screw-propeller, effectiveness demonstrated by steamship Archimedes... Daguerre-Niepce method of photography is shown to Academy of Sciences, Academy of Arts in Paris (is challenged for original invention by Talbot in 1839 presentation to Royal Society)... Parliament switches mail service from coaches to railroads.

Business Events

French firm of Redouly & Cie, founded 1826, organizes Mutual Aid Society, profit-sharing fund run by employees... Steamer Sirius wins transatlantic race from England to New York with Great Western in some 15 days, starts era of transatlantic steamships... Tokugawa Shogunate grants Kikkoman brand name to Noda soy sauce brewery (advertises product with professional sumo wrestlers, story tellers, paper lanterns, umbrellas, world fairs - international recognition at Amsterdam's fair in 1883, uses specialist, formerly operator of employment agency, to recruit contract workers in 1854)... Aristide Boucicart, partner (sells out 1863) open Bon Marche shop in Paris to compete with other stores employing up to 100 people: The Lame Devil, The Poor Devil, The Little Sailor, The Two Maggots, The Iron Mask, Beautiful Farmer's Wife (although Kramm store with several thousand people prior to Revolution, shows trappings of world's first department store in early 1850s after absorbing adjacent shops and houses, reaches volume of $1.4 million by 1862, opens new store 1869 to display all kinds of goods, novelties)... Emerson Bainbridge, former draper apprentice, starts drapery partnership in Newcastle, among first with fixed prices (ends partnership in 1841, divides business into wholesale and retail, one of first, in 1849-52, forms Bainbridge & Co. in 1855, buys first factory in 1883, operates with 45 business rooms, 21 work rooms, 8 offices, and 600 workers in 1892, is sold to John Lewis Partnership in 1952)... Halifax immigrant Samuel Cunard proposes to British government to carry mail from Nova Scotia to London by steamships, first voyage of Britannia, sails and paddle-wheels, in 1840.

1839

General Events

London's Metropolitan Police Act prohibits posting of handbills without consent of property owner to prevent nightly papering of walls (regulates sandwich-men and walk chalkers)... Prussia's first labor law forbids children to work at night and on Sundays, holidays (limits those under 16 to maximum of 10 hours of work/day)... Antoine Becquerel devises first solar electric cell (leads to solar-powered steam engine of Augustin Mouchot, Abel Pefre at 1878 Paris International Exhibition)... Boers form independent republic of Natal in South Africa, annexed by Britain in

1843... First Henley Regatta is held... France's A.A. Giroux makes first commercial camera... William G. Armstrong, England, devises a harrow... Daguerre shows process to make photographs... William R. Grove devises first fuel cell (converts chemical energy into electricity without heat)... Talbot invents photographic paper to make negatives... First Grand National Horse Race is held at Aintree, England... Gentleman-adventurer James Brooke aids Sultan of Borneo to quell rebellious Dyaks (is given area of Sarawak as reward, ceded by family to Britain after W.W. II)... Dutch physicist Vorsselmann de Heer reports use of electro-magnetism for propulsion, based on article by Benjamin Silliman in 1838 and little electro-magnetic vehicle built by Professor S. Stratingh in 1835... M.H. Jacobi, Russia, discovers process of electrotyping... Kirkpatrick MacMillan invents crude lever-pedal bicycle (leads to front-wheel pedal-and-gear mechanism of French blacksmith Pierre Michaux and son in 1855, high bicycle of James Stanley in 1870, 'safety bicycle' of Guilmet in 1869 and Harry Lawson in 1879 with wheels of equal size, pneumatic tires, Dunlop, in 1888, and vertical pedal bicycle in 1978 of Korea's Man Te Seal, U.S.' Marione Clark)... Imperial Commissioner seizes illegal opium of British traders in Canton (starts first Opium War of 1839-42, 2nd in 1856-60)... Prussia limits work day for miners to 10 hours... Britain adopts postage stamp system to replace penny post... France signs commercial treaty with Texas, first European country to recognize its independence... French political leader Louis Blanc: L'Organization du Travail (notes "To each according to his needs, from each according to his abilities").

Business Events

Samuel Cunard founds British and North American Royal Mail Steam Packet Co., still extant as Cunard line... Colonel Chaves drives some 75,000 sheep from New Mexico to Mexico (leads to Don Baca, governor of Spanish New Mexico, running some two million sheep on 1,280,000 acre land grant with 2,700 herders)... F.G. Wakefield, partners form New Zealand Co. to colonize land, first settlements in 1788... Ten tea companies appear in Assam... English textile firm is represented in Russia by German-born L. Knoop (starts 122 Russian spinning mills by persuading clients to use his machinery, arranging credit, employing managers, designing plants, purchasing raw materials)... German-born Swiss John Sutter gets land grant of 50,000 acres at junction of Sacramento, American Rivers, CA (develops village of New Helvetia, buys Russia's closed Ft. Ross in 1841 for its lumber, forms partnership with John Marshall in 1847 to start sawmill on American River - discovery of gold in 1848 but not recognized until public announcement by President Polk in 1849, sells remaining interests in 1850 for $40,000)... Carl J. Hambro, 3rd generation banker, opens Hambro's Bank in London as branch for C.J. Hambro & Son, Copenhagen merchants and bankers (is one of City's most respected by 1877, merges with British Bank of Northern Commerce, backed by Scandinavian bankers, in 1920)... Moric Fischer takes over nearly defunct porcelain business, founded 1826, with 54 workers (revives Herend works near Budapest, success with Queen Victoria's order for large table service at 1851 London's World Exhibition)... Thomas Healey, former clerk, and partner acquire soap business of John Greene & Sons (joins Northern Soapmakers' Assn. in 1880 to set prices, prevent underselling)... James Spicer & Sons is formed, London, to make paper (starts pioneering branch house system in 1888 after contract with London school board, enters overseas markets with extensive product line)... Scotsman Alexander Lang Elder arrives at Port Adelaide, Australia (starts trading firm to serve farmers, evolves as one of land's largest in commodities trading and farm services).

1840s

General Events

Skiing evolves as sport in Norway... Iron rollers are used in Hungary to mill flour, replace traditional millstones.

Business Events

Swiss immigrant Ingold, investors try to charter British Watch and Clockmakers' Co. to make timepieces with interchangeable parts by machines, denied when opposed by Worshipful Company of Clockmakers.

1840

General Events

Some 54 steamboats operate in Sweden, 203 by 1860... Organized carnival events are celebrated in Rio de Janeiro, follows Portuguese tradition of celebrating prior to Lent (leads to first large-scale samba parades during Mardi Gras celebrations of 1930s)... Manchester school of economists supports free trade and opposes interference by state in industry, commerce (-1860s when many European counties begin to intervene in economic activities)... Potato fungus hits Ireland, blight leads to Great Famine of 1845-49 and some one million deaths by 1851 (forces some 2.5 million Irish to emigrate to U.S.)... Great Britain, Texas sign commercial treaty... England stops exporting criminals to New South Wales... Alexander Blain, Scotland, builds first electric clock... England issues world's first postage stamp, "The penny black"... Duchess of Bedford introduces afternoon tea ceremony... Britain, 24% of world trade, operates 24.3% of world's steam tonnage... Rowland Hill, Britain, introduces envelopes for postal service... Justus Liebig: Chemistry in its Application to Agriculture and Physiology, pioneering study of artificial fertilizers... James Young, Scotland, discovers that oil from shale with distillation can be used for illumination, patent 1850... Etienne Cabet: Le Voyage en Icarie (proposes social order based on communist principles, used unsuccessfully to start Texas community in 1848)... Lager beer is brewed in Pilsen, Bohemia... Rouen artisans Ratier, Guibal devise modern suspenders.

Business Events

Charles Mudie opens London newspaper, stationery store (starts circulating library, Mudie's Select Library with best in non-fiction, in 1842 - successful with rates lower than competitors, by 1860s is Britain's largest with 960,000 volumes)... Cunard starts steam-packet operation between Liverpool and Boston, subsidized by Britain... First professional photography studio opens in Lyons... Fry confectionery business creates chocolate bar.

1841

General Events

Lambert A.J. Quetelet establishes central statistical bureau in Belgium, model for other countries... Chef Alexis Soyer uses coal gas for cooking at London's Reform Club... Pharmaceutical Society forms in London... France passes first law to protect workers... Britain's Brighton shows population under 66,000, over 123,000 by 1901 with popularity as seaside resort... France's Jonual patents hydraulic turbine... Friedrich List: The National System of Political Economy (views bourgeoisie 'locomotive of the modern, capitalist economy', discusses role of international commerce, proposes economic policy for different stages of growth from savage, pastoral, agriculture, manufacture, and to commerce, puts national welfare before individual gain)... New Zealand is a British Colony... Japan's Shogun rejects report recommending end of seclusion, adoption of Western technology... Charles Mackay: Extraordinary Popular Delusions and the Madness of Crowds (cites inevitable mass manias through the ages: Tulipmania, South Sea Bubble, etc.)... Miners' Assn. of Great Britain and Ireland forms, Amalgamated Society of Engineers in 1850 and Amalgamated Society of Carpenters and Joiners in 1862... Talbot patents photographic process for printing... U.S.' Cyrus Hamilin starts missionary school at Bedek, Constantinople (gives courses on gospel, business and agriculture, genesis for Robert College in 1863)... Packet Siddons makes record passage of 15 days from Liverpool to NYC... France incorporates 260 companies, 994 in Britain during 1844... James Nasmyth invents steam hammer, follows use of steam power hammer by F. Cave, one of founders of French machine tool industry, in 1836... Paris' Place de la Concorde is lit by electric arc lamps.

Business Events

T. Carling starts Canadian brewery in London (still extant)... Brenninkmeijer family starts clothing business in Holland, over 500 shops, as C&A Modes, in Europe, Hong Kong, Japan and U.S. in 1988 empire of $3.4 billion... Ex-missionary Thomas Cook makes travel arrangements for 570 to visit Liverpool temperance meeting (plans temperance excursions in 1842-44 to launch pioneering travel agency, plans trips to Liverpool, North Wales in 1845 and Scotland in 1846, is joined by son John in 1851 - excursion traffic superintendent for Midland Counties Railway in 1856 and leaves father in 1859, arranges with hotels in 1864 to accept coupons for board, lodging to pioneer package tours, opens London office in 1865 - Australia in 1879, India in 1880, and Cairo in 1873, plans first U.S. excursion in 1866 - Palestine and Egypt tours in 1868, supplies Paris during siege in 1870-71, opens Egypt's Luxor Hotel in 1875, turns business over to John in 1878, for $15 million transports 10,000 troops, 200,000 tons of stores to Khartoum for Gordon Relief Expedition)...

On death of father Frederick T. Mappin, age 20, takes over Sheffield cutlery firm of 1825, successful with sportsman's knives to become one of largest in area by 1840 (buys out competitor in 1845, opens Queen's Cutlery Works in 1851, opens London shop in 1845 - City's largest by 1860, is youngest Master Cutler in 1855 after building export trade, retires 1859 after partnership dispute, enters heavy steel industry in 1860 in buying Thomas Turton & Sons - pioneers mechanization in manufacturing cutlery, joins Institution of Mechanical Engineers in 1862 - Institution of Civil Engineers in 1865, introduces first grinding machine for file cutting, challenges role of handicraft union in 1865, sponsors Technical School in 1884 - later department of technology at University of Sheffield)... Henry H. Gibbs graduates from Oxford (is partner in family's agency business for Spain and Peru in 1843 - head 1875, in late 1850s secures worldwide trading monopoly for Peru's guano, loses 3 Peruvian offices in 1880, opens house in Chile in 1881 for nitrates of soda - guano substitute, handles government bonds for Mexico to change commission house into merchant bank)... France's Maquet starts commercial manufacture of envelopes, existed in 1615 (follows 1820 announcement of an envelope by Brighton's brewer)... Punch, British humor magazine, appears... Alphonse Granier buys carbonated water spring at Vergeze, France (opens health spa in 1863, after losses, auctions property to Louis Rouviere in 1888, is acquired in 1898 by Louis Perrier, medical doctor, who sells bottled water for medicinal value, after being sold to England's A.W. St. John Harmsworth sells some 20 million bottles/year by 1930s, is acquired by France's Gustave Leven in 1947 - control to Exor S.D. after 1990 scandal, enters U.S. market in 1975, in 1987 buys Beatrice's Arrowhead bottled water division to capitalize on trendy fad, suffers catastrophe in 1990 with recall of 160 million bottles of tainted water).

1842

General Events

Werner von Siemens invents electro-plating process... Staffordshire miners strike in Northern England to protest cuts in wages, spreads to other industries (leads to arrest of hundreds of strikers and transportation of ringleaders to Australia)... Britain imposes income tax, no corporate tax until 1947... J.B. Lawes develops superphosphate in England as fertilizer, imports of Peruvian guano in 1840s from virtually zero to over 200,000 tons... Treaty of Nanking ends Opium War between China, Great Britain (confirms British possession of Hong Kong in perpetuity - acquisition of New Territories in 1898 for 99 years, opens ports of Shanghai, Canton, Amoy, Ningpo and Foochow for foreign settlements, grants British citizens full extraterritorial privileges, including right to enforce English law, conduct commercial enterprise and organize own civic government and police force within boundaries of settlements - extended by 1900 to U.S. and 16 other nations in Shanghai, its French Concession, 13 square miles, hosts British P&O Line, Blue Funnel Line, Royal Mail Steam Packet Co., Canadian Pacific Line, and U.S. Dollar Line while Hong Kong and Shanghai Bank, Russo-Asiatic Bank and Yokohama Specie Bank line famous Bund)... Edwin Chadwick, lawyer and leader of "sanitarians": Sanitary Conditions of the Laboring Population of Great Britain... Sweden starts elementary school system... French law requires plan for railway network from Paris, system in place by 1870s... Britain annexes Afrikaaner republic of Natal, South Africa (forces Boers north to form Orange Free State in 1852)... After a fire, Hamburg adopts pioneering dual system of drainage for storm water, sewage... Henry Bessemer invents first mechanical typesetter... Railway Clearing House forms, Britain, to handle intercompany exchanges of through traffic in oligopolistic industry, 4 firms in 1850 with 41.7% of traffic and 46.3% in 1870... Belgium adopts primary education system... Some 60% of cotton mill workers and 36% of iron workers in Boulton, Britain, are idle... Mines Act protects coal miners against work hazards, bans women and children under 10 from underground mining and forms inspectorate to supervise working conditions of boys, Inspection Act follows in 1850... Rothamsted station for agricultural research is established, Britain (studies use of artificial fertilizers)... England drops bans on imports of meat, cattle... Former foreman John Anderson heads Woolwich Arsenal's Brass Foundry (converts operation into engineering workshop with ideas, machines from Europe, U.S.)... Steamship travel begins between Bremen, NYC... W. H. Phillips tests steam-powered model aircraft.

Business Events

Somervell family starts shoe manufacturing, Britain (adopts welfare provisions and consultive works committee in 1880s, in early 1900s fights competition with new 'K' product line, in-stock system and aggressive marketing, opens first retail shop in 1934 - 44 by 1949 and 149 by 1957, goes public in 1949)... The Illustrated London News appears... Clayton & Shettleworth Co. appears to do foundry work (makes steam engines in 1845 and steam threshing machines in 1849 to pioneer use of steam power for agriculture in 1850s, opens Vienna office in 1857 - Australia and South America in 1870s, by 1883 produces 19,000 steam engines and 17,000 threshing machines to make Lincoln center of agricultural engineering industry)... German-born Charles W. Siemens goes to England to market electroplating process of brother Werner (sells water meter product of brother in 1852 and brother Frederick's invention of steel-making process in 1856 - first license to France's Martin ironworks, produces open-hearth steel at Birmingham in 1867, forms Landore-Siemens Steel in 1869, pioneers electric-arc steelmaking in 1879-80, forms Siemens Bros. & Co. in 1880 - 1/3 of Britain's electrical and telegraph business by 1891)... Joseph Swan becomes apprentice to chemist and druggist (joins chemical business in 1846, improves development of film in 1856 - first of 70 inventions, experiments with filaments for electric lamp - shows carbon filament lamp in December, 1878, after Thomas Alva Edison's test in October, patents high-speed bromide paper for photography in 1879, patents process in 1880 for vacuum light bulb - U.S. patent to Edison in 1879, wins British patent infringement suit against Edison in 1882, starts Swan United Electric Light in 1882 - attacked in UK market by Edison's Electric Light of 1882, forms Edison & Swan Light, Edison with 40%, in 1883 to make light bulbs - 10,000/week in 1883)... U.S.' David Haviland starts porcelain factory at Limoges, France (integrates French workmanship with U.S. marketing)... Adrien Philippe, French immigrant, and Comte de Patek, Polish emigre and Geneva watch manufacturer, devise stem-winding watch... French Huguenot Gustave Faberge starts jewelry business in St. Petersburg (develops workshop with over 500 artisans and branches in Moscow, Odessa, Kiev and London, joined by son Peter Carl in 1846-1920)... Peninsular & Oriental Line begins monthly service between England, Orient via Cape of Good Hope... F. Steinbeis heads Strumm ironworks (begins use of coal-fired blast furnaces in Germany).

1843

General Events

Joseph Fowle invents first tunnel drill powered by compressed air... First workmen's Co-Operative

Society appears in England... Flore Tristan: Union Ouvriere (proposes international union of workers)... Hancock devises vulcanizing process, pioneers British rubber industry... Bain seeks patent on "method for transmitting copies over a distance, by means of electricity" (abandons facsimile transmission project although theoretically workable, reality in 1925 when AT&T successfully introduces commercial process for sending news photographs and RCA transmits images internationally by radio)... In lecture at Popular Institute, Dr. Thomas E. Bowkett urges creation of building societies to improve living conditions of poor, 7 in 1849, 50 in 1865, 130 in 1868, 300 in 1879, 700 in 1887, and 1,000 in 1891 (starts business advising societies in 1857, joins Richard B. Starr, in business since 1857, in 1882 to form Starr Bowkett Ins. Co. to provide property insurance and fidelity guarantees)... England builds its first telegraph line... Britain's William S. Henson designs Aerial Steam Carriage with fixed wings and air-screw propeller, model tested unsuccessfully in 1847... Britain, France recognize independence of Hawaii... Britain's Nemesis sinks only Chinese warship (renews struggle over opium trade with Canton in favor, Peking in opposition)... Liebig publishes theory of fermentation... Cayley designs first biplane... Poet Bettina von Arnim prepares report on plight of proletariat for Frederick William IV.

Business Events

Houqua, most important of Canton's hong merchants (first dealings with U.S. traders in 1780s), dies, perhaps world's richest man... Tivoli pleasure garden, amusement park opens in Copenhagen (runs miniature railway)... The Economist, London financial paper, is published... Le Bal des Anglais opens in Paris, world's first nightclub... London's Aerial Transit Co. is first air transportation business, fails.

1844

General Events

William Siemens devises mechanical copying method... Friedrich Engels, partner in Manchester cotton plant: The Condition of the Working Class in England in 1844 (leads to meeting Karl Marx in Paris, joining Socialist League of Just in 1847, later the Communist League)... First Liverpool public bath, wash house opens... Germany's F.G. Keller invents wood-pulp paper to replace rags... Sweden's Gustaf Pasch proposes safe matches with combustion material on striking surface... Britain's George William starts Young Men's Christian Association, YWCA appears in 1855... Silesia handloom weavers revolt to oppose machinery, steam power... Denmark's Bishop Grundtvig starts first institute for adult education... Friedrich Harkort (founder of "mechanical workshops" in Ruhr, developer of German railroads): On the Obstacles in the Civilization and Emancipation of the Lower Classes... Parliament's Bank Charter Act eliminates all bank notes except those of the Bank of England, regulates money supply in relation to gold... Lin Tse-hsu: Illustrated Treatise on Overseas Countries (urges use of foreign techniques to industrialize China, is translated into Japanese in 1854-56, perhaps catalyst for Meiji reforms)... John S. Woolrich, Birmingham, builds steam-powered electro-magnetic machine... Britain's Factory Act establishes 12-hour day and no night work for women (provides safety regulations for textile industry)... Gustav Froment builds direct-current motors, powered by simple batteries, to operate calculating machines... France's La Maire devises first machine to manufacture cigarettes... In view of complex partnerships, i.e., Banking Company of Aberdeen with 446 partners, Britain's Companies Act initiates government policy over corporations (requires directors to make "full and fair balance sheet" as approved by auditors).

Business Events

Danish Society for the Promotion of Shipping forms... Cuban cigar factory, Fabrica de Tabacos de H. Upmann, starts in Havana, acquired in 1959 by Cuban government with takeover of Fidel Castro... Former manager of shoe factory in 1835, Moses P. Manfield, cordwainer's son, starts business with savings to make shoes for wholesale trade, large government contractor in 1858 (builds model factory in 1858, opens 3 retail shops in London in 1878-83 - 16 by 1889, 21 by 1895, Paris store in 1898, 16 on continent by 1916, and 30 by 1900, sells branded shoes at uniform prices in 1882, supervises 900 employees, plus 500 outside, in 1888, builds U.S.-style factory in 1892 to become England's largest maker of footwear)... Rochdale Society of Equitable Pioneers starts cooperative retail business, corporation legalized in 1852 to formalize movement... Great Britain, all iron with six masts and sails, is launched at Bristol, first propeller ship to cross Atlantic... Ville de Paris retail business employs some 150 employees, sales of some $2 million... First mechanical textile machines in France are used in Mulhouse mills... Finland's first industrial steam engine is installed, steam-powered sawmills in general use in 1870s.

1845

General Events

Britain outlaws Chinese Triads in Hong Kong, evolve as secret criminal societies... By accident during experiment in wife's kitchen without her approval, German-Swiss chemist Christian F. Schobein discovers smokeless powder, called "guncotton" later (is discovered independently by Germany's Rudoplph C. Bottger in 1846, development halted after 1847 explosion of English guncotton plant)... London's first public bath for working class opens... Britain abolishes duties on 450 items for more free trade... Copper is found in Central Australia... Because of poor harvests by 1855, some 550,000 Germans move to U.S... Russia passes first law to cover work of children (bans night work for those under age of 12)... London County Council starts to develop City drainage system... First railway in Empire outside Britain opens in Jamaica between Montego Bay, Kingston... German chemist Adolf Kolbe synthesizes acetic acid... British engineer M'Naught builds compound steam engine... Britain's Companies Act requires annual audits (grants limited liability to stockholders after 1855)... Prussia permits non-compulsory guilds, strikes banned... A. von Hoffman, German chemist specializing in coal tars, is professor at London's Royal College of Chemistry (launches study of chemistry in Britain)... Royal Agricultural College is founded, Britain... Entry for Northwest Passage is discovered by expedition of John Franklin (-1848 with no survivors, inspires dozens of subsequent expeditions to rescue him)... Robert Thomson, Scotland, invents crude pneumatic tire, "aerial wheels" (is re-invented by Dunlop for bicycles in 1888, perfected 1895-1905 for automobiles)... Parliament stops business of shipping orphans, children of poor families to work in U.S... After working for John Sutter at New Helvetia, John Bidwell acquires Mexican land grant of 22,000 acres to start Rancho Chico (starts first important farm, nursery in California, cultivates almonds, casaba melons, olive trees for oil, Chinese sugarcane, Egyptian corn, grapevines for wine)... William Armstrong patents hydraulic crane... First submarine cable across English Channel is laid... France's Joshua Heilman patents machine to combine cotton, wool... Friedrich Engels is "first" to use word "industrialization," John Stuart Mill in 1848 and Karl Marx in 1867... Railway links Berlin, Hamburg.

Business Events

Royal Stafford Co. appears in Britain to make fine bone china... Syndicate of merchant bankers, headed by Rothschilds, finances Nord Railway Co. in France... George Hudson, "The Railway King of England," gains control of 1/3 of Britain's railway system by combining small lines (uses dividends of existing lines to develop new roads, flees in 1848 when railroad mania collapses)... Grand Trunk Railroad appears in Canada (-1862 when refinanced)... Three years after Britain adopted an income tax, William Deloitte opens London accounting office (opens first U.K. office in NYC in 1890, offices in Cincinnati, 1905, Chicago and Montreal, 1912, Boston, 1930, and Los Angeles, 1952, forms alliance with U.S.' Haskins & Sells, 34 offices, in 1952, fails to merge with Price Waterhouse in 1984, joins Touche Ross, formed in 1947, in 1989, sets up DRT International, number 3 of Big 6 accounting firms, as umbrella organization in 1990 and cuts partners by 5% with economic downturn)... Edward Ind's Essex brewery, genesis in 1799 to brew beer for his new inn, merges with Coope Brewery, market leader in southern England (buys Ansell Brewery, popular in Midlands, in 1881, merges with Tetley brewing business, started 1822 in Leeds and acquired

Walker Cain brewery in 1960, in 1961 to form Allied Breweries in 1963, in 1968 acquires wine and spirits firm, a 1961 combine of firms of 1903, 1905 and 1953, buys, 1978, J. Lyons & Co. for food line, adopts, 1981, name of Allied-Lyons, one of world's largest in 1991 in food business, after failing to take over Elders IXL beats Reichmann family in 1985 to get Hiram Walker, distillery, oil and gas, for its liquor business, forms, 1988, venture with Suntory, in 1989 gets Dunkin' Donuts and in 1990 Whitbread's spirits unit and Mister Donut, buys 24% of champagne concern in 1991 and reveals foreign exchange loss of some $285 million, finance director resigns).

1846

General Events

Britain grants new government contract to Cunard to carry mail direct to NYC... Parliament abolishes Corn Laws of 1815, opens British agriculture to foreign competition... John C. Horsely makes first painted Christmas card... Electric arc lighting is used at Paris Opera... Catholic Church forms Assn. of Handicraft Apprentices, Germany... Paris, Rouen are connected by first French telegraph line... Parliamentary acts provide poor with public bathhouses... Sweden abolishes guild system, Finland in 1868... Sailors' Home is built as Liverpool hostel to improve living conditions for British seamen... Parisian chemist J. Dubonnet creates aperitif wine, starts company in 1908... Chaplain Adolf Kolping, Wilhelm von Ketteler form first Catholic journeyman's union.

Business Events

After Canadian-U.S. boundary is established, Hudson's Bay Co. moves northwestern headquarters from Ft. Vancouver to Ft. Victoria... As planned offspring from academic research laboratories of University of Jena, Carl Zeiss starts workshop to make optical instruments (forms partnership in 1866 with Ernest Abbe, professor of physics and mathematics, forms Carl Zeiss Foundation in 1888 to continue business, still extant)... First commercial bank in Denmark opens... John Dewar, son of crofter, starts wine and spirit business in Perth, Scotland (starts worldwide distribution of Scotch whisky in 1891-93)... William H. Wills joins family tobacco business, founded 1786 (introduces Woodbine machine-made cigarettes in 1888, joins 12 other manufacturers in 1901 to form Imperial Tobacco to fight market invasion of American Tobacco)... John D. Allcraft acquires family glove and leather manufacturing business, three employees, in Worcester (centralizes operations in 1853 - 200 employees in 1853 and 1,000 in 1878, goes international in 1884 with quality workmanship)... William D. Armstrong, son of corn merchant, starts Armstrong & Co. to make hydraulic cranes (builds 60 cranes/year in 1852 with 352 workers, creates mechanics institute c. 1852 - later free libraries and school for children of workers in 1866, tests breech-loading gun in 1857 - all muzzle-loading and smooth-bore artillery obsolete, is made Government's Engineer for Rifled Ordinance and Superintendent of Royal Gun Factory in 1859, restructures business in 1863 to become England's leading firm in armaments and Europe's largest private gunmaker, builds first warship in 1868 - 20 by 1882 and 127 by W.W. I, gets license for Gatling gun in 1870, accepts demands of workers after strike of 7,700 in 1871, starts Italian factory in 1885)... Loewe family fine leather business appears in Spain, by 1980s employs over 1,200 people with stores in London, Brussels, Tokyo, Hong Kong, New York and in Japan... Excursion trains appear in Birmingham, site of pleasure gardens in 1853, to provide leisure-time activities for public... Enclosed shopping mall appears in Brussels, "first" on Continent.

1847

General Events

Italy's Ascanio Solaro discovers nitroglycerin (leads to chance discovery of dynamite by Alfred Nobel in 1866)... On recommendation of British Railway Clearing House, Parliament requires all railways to adopt Greenwich time... Parliament's Ten Hours Bill limits work day for women, children 13-18 in textile industry, extended to all factories in 1867... Liebig prepares meat extract... George Boole: <u>Mathematical Analysis of Logic</u> (pioneers symbolic logic)... Richard Roberts uses paper with holes to guide riveting machines in building iron bridge in Wales... Prussian railway network covers some 3,000 kilometers of track, about 16,000 by 1875... German League Of Communists forms in London... Craftsmen's Educational Society forms, Denmark, to consider social, political reforms (evolves as union)... Europe is ravaged by typhus, cholera epidemics... Collapse of Europe's railway boom leads to mass unemployment... Montreal, Toronto are linked by telegraph line, linked with London in 1866... Liverpool is first English city with medical health officer, London in 1848 and required by law in 1854... William Hansen, London, patents safety razor with essential features of King Gillette's razor first sold 1904... French clockmaker Antoine Redier devises first mechanical alarm clock, first electric c. 1890... Foreign merchants handle some 90% of Russia's imports, 97% of exports... Britain, Brunei sign trade treaty (becomes British protectorate in 1888, starts oil production in 1929 - offshore in 1963, builds world's largest liquified gas plant in 1972, gets independence in 1894 - Sultan world's richest in 1988)... Britain's W.E. Staite devises first practical arc lamp... Fed up with arrogance of London-based Institution of Civil Engineers, George Stephenson, others form Birmingham's Institution of Mechanical Engineers.

Business Events

Gouin & Co. is formed, Paris, to build locomotives (evolves to build factory machinery, some 2,000 workers by 1855, before doing construction, engineering projects worldwide)... Fisons Group starts in East Anglia (evolves by 1980s as international pharmaceutical, chemical business of 63 firms with over 10,000 employees)... Cartier jewelry business opens in Paris, crown jeweler at one time or another for 21 royal families (diversifies in 1970s with licensed products in effort to become world's first billion-dollar luxury good business, global sales of some $400 million by 1985)... London's Savile Row, originally laid out in 1730s for fashionable residences, evolves with tailoring shops for gentlemen... Thomas Tilling starts public transportation business in London, 150 buses by 1912 (acquires Folkestone District Road Co. in 1914, East Kent Road Co. with British Electric Traction in 1916)... With backing of three U.S. rubber manufacturers, Stephen Moulton gets British patent for vulcanization (opens plant in 1848 to make clothing, sheeting, air cushions and waterbeds, when railroads become dissatisfied with rubber products of Manchester's Charles Macintosh & Co., industry's No. 1, supplies railways with rubber components for buffers, springs, and bearings in 1858)... Germany's Hamburg-American line appears to provide transatlantic steamship service... After running small brewery in 1826, J.C. Jacobsen starts Carlsberg Brewery, Copenhagen (assigns ownership of business to Carlsberg Foundation, formed 1876 to fund scientific research laboratory, in 1902 to distribute revenues for public needs)... Philip Morris opens shop on London's Bond Street (sells tobacco products by 1885, makes first U.S. cigarette, Marlboro, in 1924)... Ontario farmer Daniel Massey starts making farm machinery, (introduces first self-propelled combine in 1939, merges in 1953 with Ferguson tractor business, faces bankruptcy in 1956 from poor dealer network and excess inventories, is revived by acquisition of Argus Corp. to focus on sales of agricultural machinery outside of North American market - top seller in Britain, France and Scandinavia, evolves through acquisitions to operate 26 factories in 9 countries with strategy to provide emerging nations with one-stop agricultural centers)...

Werner von Siemens, former military officer (invents dynamo machine in 1866 and electric locomotive, loom in 1879), and J.G. Halske (leaves 1867) start business to make cables, telegraph equipment, signals, measuring devices and mechanical instruments in Berlin, Germany's 3rd largest public company in 1990 after Daimler-Benz, Volkswagen (builds Europe's first long-distance telegraph, Berlin to Frankfort, in 1848, opens branches in early 1850s in St. Petersburg and London with brothers of Siemens, formulates shop rules in 1855 with rights and duties of workers, seen in German factories as early as 1830s, employs 127 workers in 1857, 192 in 1867, 581 in 1872, 1,000 in 1882, 5,545 in 1890 and 81,795 in 1913 as 2nd largest in electrical market after AEG, lays telegraph line, 6,600 miles, from London to Calcutta and first transatlantic cable in 1874, builds world's first electric power transmission system, 1976, first electrified railway, 1879, and one of first electric elevators in 1880)... After arriving in London, Canada, in 1833 to farm,

John Labatt gains reputation for malt barley, teams up with master brewer to produce beer, Canada's 2nd largest after Molson by 1990s (survives U.S.' Prohibition, bankrupts all but 15 of Ontario's 65 breweries, by producing alcohol for export, buys Toronto brewery in 1946, makes deal with U.S.' Anheuser-Busch in 1980 to brew Budweiser in Canada, in 1980s acquires interests in other breweries, broadcast and entertainment field and food concerns)... Thomas Beecham opens apothecary (after hawking his patent medicines door-to-door, uses, following example of Thomas Holloway in 1855, mass advertising to sell Beecham's pills, a laxative, in 1859 to become leader in field, introduces "Pretty Girl" ads in 1890s, makes over 1 million pills/day by early 1900s).

1848

General Events

In face of rising unemployment and demanding statutory right to work, French students and workers force (February) abdication of king and formation of republic (leads to provisional government of poet Alphonse de Lamartine to guarantee right to employment, to set up national workshops, and to set minimum wage, is overturned, June, by military force as peasants, petite bourgeoisie and upper-middle classes gain victory over proletarian revolution)...England's John Stringfellow builds steam-powered monoplane, fails to sustain flight... London Institute of Actuaries forms... Uprisings are seen in Paris, Vienna, Venice, Berlin, Milan, Rome and Warsaw... Safety match is invented in Germany... Revolutionaries in Baden-Baden use railroad to escape Prussian Army, first military use of railroads (are used again in 1851 for Austrian mobilization against Prussia)... James Clarke, Physician in Ordinary to Queen, seeks injunction to stop patent medicine maker in selling "Sir James Clarke's Consumption Pills," unsuccessful... Austria abolishes serfdom... Public Health Act is England's first sanitary measure, follows with health board, medical officers and inspections in 1872 act... Switzerland reorganizes as federal union... Karl Marx, Friedrich Engels: "Communist Manifesto" (calls for "Workers of the world, unite!")... Some 22,500 water mills, 17,300 mill grain, are used in France for power (runs some 5,200 steam engines)... Fraternity of Labor forms in Berlin, starts German labor movement... James Young, Scottish chemist, uses oil spring at Derbyshire for lubrication... John Stuart Mill is first to use word "bureaucracy" in English... France abolishes slavery in colonies... France forms system of national workshops for work relief... Commission of the Luxembourg discusses common interests of employers, employees... Frederic Bastiat: Economic Harmonies (notes order beneath disorder)... Faced with lack of staple foods, rising prices, unemployment and bankruptcy of small, medium-sized firms, delegates to pre-parliamentary assembly agree on Basic Rights of German people (grants freedom in economic affairs and free choice of profession).

Business Events

John Aird starts contracting business, England (grows by laying gas and water mains)... Cunard line launches four steamers... Schaaffhausensche Bankverein forms in Germany, other joint-stock banks in 1851, 1853, 1856, 1870, and 1872... Alphonse Rothschild visits U.S., recommendation for U.S. branch rejected by French family... Surrey Music Hall is first in England so named, although Edward Winder, "Father of the Music Hall," presented music shows in Mogul Saloon during 1847.

1849

General Events

England repeals Navigation Laws of 1651, 1661, 1662 and 1823... Prussia allows tradesmen to join guilds... Britain bans cockfighting... Joseph F. Monier develops reinforced concrete in France, used in U.S. in 1875... Patent application is made, England, to improve keeping of ledger accounts with organized card index... France's Bourdan perfects pressure gauge for steam engines... Giuseppi Mazzini proclaims Rome a republic... Cayley tests glider with 10-year-old boy, uncontrolled flight in 1853 with adult passenger... Floris Nollet, Belgium, proposes to generate hydrogen, oxygen by electrolysis... August von Hoffman, director of Royal College of Chemistry, proposes to develop synthetic drug for quinine from coal tar (leads to discovery of coal tar dyes by aide Perkin in 1856)... Denmark abolishes guilds... Marcus Thrane starts labor movement in Norway to protest low wages, suppressed by government in 1851... Industrial Commission of the German Constitutional Assembly prepares industrial-representation plan for employee participation in business, use of employee consultation by Prussian mines in 1905... Some 650 stationary steam engines are used in Rhineland and Westphalia, about 12,000 by 1875... Working day in Germany reaches 15-17 or more hours/day... Italian-born Antonio Meucci invents acoustic telephone, telettrofono... Prussian law requires employers to pay employees in cash... Prussia's national assembly establishes savings and loan associations, consumers' cooperatives... Portugal makes Macao, possession since 1557, a free port for trade (returns land to China in 1976 after civil unrest, is allowed to administer territory).

Business Events

Ranchers Miguel Otero, Antonio Luna drive some 25,000 sheep from Santa Fe to Southern California, Sacramento... With approval of king, German Captain Henry Hackfield starts retail business in Hawaii, genesis of Liberty House retail stores... Wholesale tea merchant Henry Charles Harrod buys small grocers' shop in Knightsbridge, London (evolves as famous department store by 1900 with claim "Harrods Serves the World," is sold in 1959 to House of Fraser)... Schultz-Delitzsch forms first credit-association for workers... F.W. Raiffeisen creates co-operative savings bank to pioneer movement in Germany... After working for French news agency of Charles Havas, German-born Paul J. Reuter opens small telegraph office in Aachen as financial news service, provides carrier service Aachen to Brussels in 1850 (opens London office in 1851 to provide Stock Exchange with latest news from Continent exchanges - expanded to brokers and merchants, exchanges stockmarket quotations in 1856 with Havas and Wolff services, provides London dailies, not The Times, with news telegrams in 1858, incorporates 1865, opens Berlin office in 1866 - then Belgium and Holland, in dividing world market with Havas and Wolff in 1870 gets British Empire and Far East)... Prudential Mutual Insurance Investment & Loan Assn. forms, England (sells life insurance in 1854, acquires British Industry Life Assurance of Liverpool in 1859, is first insurance firm in 1872 to hire women clerks, handles 7 million policies as industry's largest, still is, in 1887)... Berlin's Bernhard Wolff opens first telegraph bureau for European papers (provides services to public with Continental Telegraph in 1865)... Robinson family, New York, opens San Francisco shop to sell produce, curios, shells (as sailors swap exotic birds, animals of trips for food, evolves as pet business, still extant, c. 1904)... Frederick Whinney joins Harding & Pullein, U.K. accounting firm, becomes Whinney, Smith & Whinney in 1894 (unites in 1979 with Cleveland's Ernst & Ernst, founded 1903, to form Ernst & Whinney, merges with Chicago's Arthur Young accounting, started 1894, to form Ernst & Young, in 1989, world's 4th largest).

1850s

General Events

Finland uses its first puddling process to make iron (builds railways by 1860, uses open-hearth process for making steel by 1880)... Nearly 94% of deaths in Europe are from infectious diseases.

Business Events

British capitalists form Amazon Steam Navigation Co... German firms in metal production, chemical production, chemicals, and electrical engineering use research laboratories.

1850

General Events

France's A. Mannheim devises modern slide rule... Austria paves first concrete road... D.D. Parmelle patents key-driven adding machine... England, France are linked by first underwater cable (-1851, Atlantic cable in 1867)... A variation in game of whist, first cited 1743, appears in Istanbul, called bridge in 1880s... Austria adopts Sunday as day of rest... Denmark sells Gold Coast properties to Britain... English textile workers get 60-hour week, lowered in 1874 to 10 hours/weekdays and 6.5 hours on Saturdays... Francis Galton invents teletype printer... London's population is some 2.3 million, Britain with 9 cities over 100,000 and 18 over 50,000... France introduces old-age insurance... School of Mines is founded in London, renamed College of Technology later... Joseph Paxton builds Crystal Palace in London, site of 1851 Great Exhibition... Britain launches its first clipper, Stornaway, 18 by 1860... Britain's Factory Act limits work week for women, children to 10.5 hours/day in all industries... Australia's James Harrison designs ice-making machine... Germany's R.W. Bunsen invents gas burner... University of Sydney appears in Australia... Charles Dickens: David Copperfield (is rags-to-riches tale of virtuous boy)... Austria, Hungary form customs union... Twelve different Swiss currencies are reduced to one as national medium of exchange... England's Amalgamated Society of Engineers forms as one of first large unions (provides social and economic benefits, advocates direct action and collective bargaining)... In this time Robert Mushet, Titanic Steel Co., develops harder steel alloy in England, predominant until Taylor's high-speed steel in 1888-90... W.E. Ketteler is Bishop of Maintz (-1877, urges better conditions for working class)... Herbert Spencer: Social Statistics (begins study of sociology).

Business Events

Existing since early days of City, over 250 street singers are cited performing in London along with itinerant street musicians, such as hurdy-gurdies, bagpipes, and violins (are regulated by 1864 ordinance)... Hill, partner use machines to make envelopes in this time, handmade cited in 1839... Edward V. Neale opens co-operative store, London (becomes Central Co-Operative Agency in 1851 - closes 1857, funds Co-Operative Society as educational center, fails in supporting strike of Amalgamated Society of Engineers and in forming a co-op productive association in 1852, forms Co-operative Wholesale Society in 1863 - membership of some 250,000 by 1870)... Chile's first woolen mill appears in Santiago... Switzerland's Lindt & Sprungli, formed 1845 to make quality chocolate, creates candy bar.

1851

General Events

Prussia operates 26 technical schools, Britain's first so-called in 1889... 18% of British people earn living from farms, 11% in 1871... Britain makes first grant for evening classes... England repeals (July 24) window tax (1696-)... Prussia, Hanover sign commercial treaty... Frederick Scott Archer, Britain, invents first practical glazed glass plate negative process for photography... First double-decker bus appears in London... Gold is discovered in New South Wales (spurs immigration)... Prussia adopts income tax, 2nd in 1891... Charles Babbage: Laws of Mechanical Notation (covers methods to study machine movements)... British census shows for first time that majority of people live in towns of 2,000 or more... Utopian socialists form Society of Equals in Chile, part of unsuccessful uprising against the government... By 1857, some 115 joint-stock companies appear in Paris... Paris builds Halles Centrales to centralize City's public markets... Queen Victoria, Prince Albert sponsor Great Exhibition in Crystal Palace, London's Hyde Park, to display world's technology (shows exhibits of England, raw materials and machinery, of Germany, Dresden china, Bavarian porcelain, sculpture, armor, and steel cannon, of France, turbine, photography, crystal, porcelain, silver, jewels, silks, tapestries, and perfumes, of U.S., soap, Colt revolver, dental powder, Indian maize, artificial teeth, bank books, Goodyear india rubber products, rifles, Borden meat biscuits - gold medal, and reapers, of Belgium, raw materials, chemicals, machinery, textiles, lace and imitation sable, of Holland, diamonds, of Austria, crafts and toys, of Spain, lace and swords, of India, ivory furniture, Koh-i-noor diamond, cashmere shawls, and howdah, of Canada, furs, fire engine, hides, sleighs, maple sugar, Indian regalia, and birch-bark canoe, and of Australia, hats made from cabbage leaves by convicts)... German constitution divides people into three-class suffrage by tax-paying capacity.

Business Events

French Compagnie des Messageries Maritime is started... Cook's travel agency offers British a grand tour of Europe... Royal Charter is granted to Falkland Islands Co. to start economic development of colony (-1982)... Castle & Cooke partnership starts in Hawaii, develops pineapple and sugar plantations... Aquascutum, London's Regent Street, shows new patented showerproof fabric for rainwear at Great Exposition... After dissolving partnership as wholesale and retail drapery, John Maple opens London furniture store (still extant)... Public laundries appear in Europe, U.S... George Barham joins law office as junior clerk (while apprentice in building trades in 1853 uses spare time to transport milk from areas of surplus to areas with shortages, buys London retail dairy in 1858, forms Express County Milk in 1864 - first branch in 1880, forms Dairy Supply Co. for wholesaling and manufacturing in 1866, founds Metropolitan Dairymen's Assn. in 1873 and Metropolitan Dairymen's Benevolent Institution in 1874, gets British rights for Laval cream separator in 1885)... "Octuple", "Sextuple" pooling agreements are signed by British railroads to protect their interests in Anglo-Scottish traffic... Steinweg family, piano-makers in Braunschweig since 1825, immigrate to U.S. when revolutions ruin business (leads to Grotrian-Steinweg piano works to continue in Germany, makes some 300 grand and 1500 upright pianos/year by 1990).

1852

General Events

Britain's Industrial & Provident Society Act establishes cooperative societies... Manchester funds free library... King's College, London, offers commercial courses, followed by Mercantile and Maritime College in 1850s and business courses at Belgian university, University of Zurich by 1900... French engineer Henri Giffard designs, builds and tests steam-powered dirigible, world's first sustained flight of 17 miles... First contract workers from China are employed on Hawaiian Islands... First Congress of Co-operative Societies is held, London... Lord Kelvin proposes "open-cycle" refrigeration process... First aeronautical society forms in France... Count Camillo de Cavour is Prime Minister of Sardinia-Piedmont, full unification of Italy in 1870 with joining of Rome... Foucault invents gyroscope.

Business Events

Pereire brothers, France, form Credit Mobilier as joint-stock enterprise to finance French railways and reconstruction of Rue de Rivoli, organizational model in 1867 for Union Pacific Railroad... Leopold Louis-Dreyfus starts small grain business in Basel, Switzerland (evolves as grain empire during 1900s in U.S., Russia, Argentina, Canada and Europe)... Charles Morton, 'Father of the Halls,' opens Canterbury musical hall, first in England for just musical programs (pioneers conversion of tavern concert rooms into musical halls - 28 in London and 300 in rest of country by 1868, is used in 1876 for variety shows, flourishes to 1912 when variety shows are slowly replaced by French-created revues)... Samuel Beeton publishes The Englishwoman's Domestic Magazine (advises social-climbing wives of business, professional men)... James C. Eno acquires chemist, druggist shop (launches three new products: tooth enamel, hair restorer and linseed poultice, leaves retail business in 1876 to make popular Fruit Salt with sodium bicarbonate)... Charles Shippam starts business as pork butcher in Chichester, famous for sausages throughout

Southern England with guaranteed overnight deliveries by railroad (adds potted meat in 1895 - soon principle product, changes family enterprise into limited company in 1913 with personnel philosophy "people matter before anything else," with increasing competition plans marketing strategy in 1934, is sold to U.S.' Underwood in 1964).

1853

General Events

Business institute appears in Antwerp... Blackheath FC is Britain's first rugby club ... Britain patents first process to make paper by pulping wood fiber... Prussia bans child labor under 12... Typographical Union, Argentina's first labor organization, forms in Buenos Aires... England drops duty on advertisements... By 1874 William Fairbairn, owner of Lancashire engineering works, devises "self-acting machines"... India builds telegraph system... Sweden takes over construction, operation of major railroads... Austrian artillery instructor Franz von Uchatius devises device to crank series of pictures around a limelight for moving images, idea used by Viennese magician Ludwig Dobler to present "dissolving pictures" throughout Europe... Eight stock companies form in Russia, start land's incorporation... First International Statistical Congress meets in Brussels... Britain re-adopts income tax, tried briefly during French Revolution and Napoleonic Wars... Frenchman makes double-lens camera to take pictures for stereoscopic viewer... By this time, Canada has granted 56 railroad charters, most in Ontario... Cayley tests model helicopters, styled on Chinese toys.

Business Events

Darmstadt Bank for Commerce and Industry, Germany's first large bank for business, forms as joint-stock company, Berlin Handelsgesellschaft in 1856, Deutsche Bank in 1870, Commerzbank in 1870, and Dresdner Bank in 1872... English East India Co. holds open competition, includes Indians, to select qualified applicants for India service in London, England's civil service personnel still chosen by patronage... First Cuban factory to make cigarettes appears in Havana... Baron Nathanial Rothschild, English branch, buys Brane-Mouton vineyard, a pioneer of Cabernet Sauvignon (leads to French cousins buying Lafite vineyard in 1868 to produce Bordeaux wine).

1854

General Events

Baron Haussman builds broad boulevards in Paris so troops can easily control revolutionaries... Electric telegraph links Paris, London... First reinforced concrete beam appears in Britain... Japan signs first commercial treaty with U.S... Working Men's College opens, London... Britain, U.S. sign Reciprocity Treaty to remove certain tariffs... Charles Dickens: <u>Hard Times</u> (views unionism as terrorism)... Parliament's Select Committee on Small Arms studies U.S. manufacturing operations, particularly Springfield Armory (reports factories of 500-700 workers in different industries mass producing metal goods by fabricating, assembling interchangeable parts, notes superiority of Chauncy Jerome's manufacture of clocks with specialized operations, warns Britain that U.S. manufacturers would become exporters to England in late 1800s)... After seeing Colt demonstration at 1851 Great Exhibition, Britain's Enfield Arsenal employs Cyrus Buckland of U.S. Springfield Armory to design, build gunstocking machinery (starts rifle production with interchangeable parts in 1857)... Dr. Abraham Gesner, Nova Scotia, patents process to distill pitchlike mineral to make kerosene... First kiosks appear in Berlin... Britain launches <u>Great Eastern</u>, largest ship of its time with paddlewheels, screw-propeller, five smokestacks and six masts for sails (is built to carry 4,000 passengers or troops, is used to lay Atlantic cable in 1865, loses $5 million in 8 years)... Great Britain starts civil service system, based on administration used in India (leads to U.S.' in 1871, 1883)... German watchmaker Heinrich Goebel invents first form of electric lightbulb... By accident Bessemer invents oxidizing process, converter to make steel (loses

U.S. patent battle to William Kelly in 1856, starts firm in 1859, licenses process to two steelmakers in 1861, sells firm in 1877)... Accounting Society of Scotland forms, first regional association.

Business Events

Sweden's Victor Theodor Engwall, obsessed to make world's best coffee, perfects Gevalia Kaffe (is named Coffee Purveyor to court by King Gustav V, 1907-1950)... After buying U.S. patents of Thomas J. Sloane to make screws with automatic machinery in 1846, John S. Nettlefold, owner of 1823 brass foundry and ironmongery, forms partnership to make woodscrews (takes over in 1874 when partners sell, lets son, Joseph, take over in 1878, acquires four competitors in 1880, installs Siemens furnaces in 1881, buys Bristol Screw Co. in 1898 for virtual U.K. monopoly, after 1900, 1902 mergers is Britain's largest integrated producer of iron, steel and coal in 1905 as Guest, Keen & Nettlefolds)... Louis Vuitton starts leather luggage firm in France for discerning customers (grows with 48 new stores worldwide after new president in 1977, achieves sales of $100 million in 1983, expands with leased departments and chain stores, goes public in 1984)... Argentine stock exchange, Bolsa, is created (functions basically as center for trading in gold, government securities, and bank stocks, trades corporate stocks after 1887)... I.M. Singer & Co. licenses French manufacturers to make sewing machines, followed by McCormick for reapers... Le Figaro is published, Paris... First industrial life insurance appears in Britain, introduced to U.S. in 1875 by Prudential Friendly Society.

1855

General Events

Henri-Etienne Denville devises new method to produce aluminum... London map of cholera epidemic helps solve public health crisis by pinpointing contaminated wells (evolves as science with formation of U.S.' ESRI in 1969 to design geographic information systems with satellite mapping for variety of business, governmental purposes)... France grants concession to build Suez Canal to Ferdinand de Lesseps (forms company in 1858, builds canal in 1859-69)... Paris holds World Exhibition... Edinburgh University creates professorship of technology... Chinese armament factory is started in Kiangsi, three more factories and naval shipyards in three provinces by 1860... David Hughes invents printing telegraph... Federal Polytechnic School appears in Zurich... First ice-hockey game is played by two teams from Royal Canadian Rifles... Science Reference Library opens, London... After four years as Orange Free State, Transvaalers found South African Republic, annexed by British in 1877 when it is unable to pay creditors... Dutch unions are granted legal rights to organize... Alexander II is Tsar of Russia (-1881, establishes State Bank in 1859, "emancipates" serfs in 1861)... Prussia launches its first screw-propeller steamship... Britain ends newspaper stamp tax, promotes growth of papers and advertising... Australia limits immigration of Chinese... By this time Melbourne workers in building trades win eight-hour day... Medoc region, next to Bordeaux, sets detailed regulations for wine producers.

Business Events

After 7-year draper apprenticeship William Whiteley goes to London to work for wholesalers, retailers (with savings opens first shop in Bayswater in 1863 - 18 employees in 1864, 622 in 1872, 2,000 in 1876 and some 6,000 in 1906 at store, farms and factories, after acquiring nearby shops is complex of 15 stores by 1876 as 'Universal Provider' to sell 'Everything from a pin to an elephant on short notice,' provides athletic club for employees in 1870, issues catalog in 1885, goes public in 1899, is sold to Selfridge's department store in 1927, closes 1981 as district can't support business)... Cunard steamship crosses Atlantic in 9.5 days... Inspired by success of Bon Marche, Les Grands Magasins du Louvre opens in Paris for carriage trade... French, German capital open Vienna's first investment bank, Creditanstalt, first Czech bank in 1863... Grand Hotel des Louvre, 700 rooms, opens in Paris, first in Europe to emulate scale, facilities of U.S. hotels... After buying small hotel earlier, William Claridge, former butler, buys neighboring Mivart's Hotel, is cited by

1860 Baedeker travel guide as "first hotel in London" (still extant)... Edward S. Gibbons is junior clerk in Plymouth's Naval Bank (joins father's pharmacy business and trades in stamps, with father's death drops pharmacy in 1862 to focus on stamp business, prints first monthly price list in 1865 - Gibbons Catalogue in 1880, issues first stamp album in 1870, after selling to Charles J. Phillips retires in 1890 with respectable fortune).

1856

General Events

Britain, Morocco sign commercial treaty... U.S. adventurer William Walker and 58 gringos, financed by Cornelius K. Garrison and Charles Morgan take over Nicaragua (-1858 when ousted by forces of Cornelius Vanderbilt)... Louis Pasteur is professor of chemistry at University of Paris (studies fermentation process for brewing industry, issues 1861 report on role of organisms in fermentation)... James Ramsden, working on local railway since 1846, develops plan for City of Barrow to build new port (grows with ironworks in 1859 and steel firm in 1866, is first mayor in 1867 with incorporation, sponsors flax firm in 1870 for employment of women, adds shipbuilding firm and steamship line in 1871, builds ocean dock in 1878)... William Perkin, experimenting with coal tar to make artificial quinine, accidentally discovers first synthetic dye, aniline purple, at Royal College of Chemistry (leads to discovery by German chemist Euden Lucius, a founder of Hoechst firm, of green dye in 1863, fashion success with wear by Empress Eugenie, and German chemical industry with all colors in 1870s - by 1914 Britain imports 75% of dyes from Germany)... William Marcroft helps form Oldham Building & Management Co. as co-operative society, workers share profits with customers (starts textile business - Sun Mill in 1866, reports only 4 of nearly 1,000 shareholders in 1867 as workers, pays dividend of nearly 30% in 1870)... Declaration of Paris establishes "Freedom of the Seas"... Machines in Joseph Whitworth's workshop operate to one-millionth of an inch... Japan starts Edo school to study foreign banks... First Japanese shipyard to build Western-style ships appears, others in 1861, 1864 and 1876... Agricultural high school opens near Copenhagen... Britain forms Department of Education... Jean-Marie Le Bris, France, tests two full-sized gliders in this time (-1868)... Britain's Joint-Stock Companies Act permits owners and managers, identified as separate groups, to form limited liability firms, granted to banks in 1858 and insurance firms in 1862 (expands role of accounting, leads to limited liability by France in 1867, Germany in 1870)... British, French ships bombard Canton (-1858, force China to open 11 more ports, accept missions, establish maritime customs service under British control, and legalize imports of opium).

Business Events

Switzerland's Credit Suisse is founded (still extant as worldwide financial enterprise)... London General Omnibus Co. is formed to provide public transportation... Seven railroads form pool to divide all receipts on traffic between London and Edinburgh, Glasgow and North of Scotland (-1870)... Swedish-born Victor Kullberg, former watchmaker apprentice in Denmark and Sweden, starts chronometer business in London, industry's major supplier 1860 onward with Thomas Mercer (-1943)... After joining small Yorkshire building firm in 1844, Samuel Pearson begins family construction business (gets railway, water supply contracts in late 1850s, enters London market in 1882, builds Spanish railway in 1888 and Hudson River Tunnel in 1889 to become one of large Imperial contractors with John Aird and John Jackson, with support of President Porfirio Diaz, builds Mexico City's Grand Canal in 1889 and Vera Cruz harbor works in 1895-1905 - one of nation's largest builders of docks by 1896, builds Mexican railway in 1898-1906 and Salina Cruz Harbor in 1899-1907, in addition to railway contracts in England handles 33 contracts in U.S., Brazil, England and Chile in 1900-1914 - each managed as separate venture)... After serving apprenticeship with firm of tailors and outfitters with several branches, David Lewis opens small Liverpool shop with men's and youth's clothing (sells women's clothes in 1864, opens Liverpool Bon Marche store in 1867 - 100,000 shoppers/week in 1877, makes clothes and sells toiletries, patent medicines, stationery and tobacco in 1870, opens Manchester store in 1877 - 2nd in 1884-86 and 3rd in 1885, adds tea items and 'Penny Readings' in 1882, watches in 1884, and food department in 1885)... Thomas Burberry starts London drapery business, success with water-resistant 'gabardine' fabric clothing (opens first U.S. store in NYC in 1978)... After studying U.S. banks, Wallenberg family, starts financial dynasty, opens Enskilda Bank, Sweden... Karl Bechstein starts Vienna piano factory (still extant)... German-Belgian group is granted right to build four major railroads in Russia (-1861, form Main Company of Russian Railways).

1857

General Events

Flex Du Temple successfully tests steam-powered model airplane, first successful flight of powered airplane... German scientist Hermann von Helmholte uses electromagnet to produce sound... National Assn. for the Promotion of Social Sciences appears in Britain... Economic crisis appears in Europe after speculation in U.S. railroad stocks... Oil is discovered in Romania and Russia's Caspian Sea area... Britain's Frederick Holmes proposes generator for incandescent light, based on idea of Floris Nollet (is installed in lighthouse in 1871)... Despite opposition of 44 Copenhagen guilds, freedom of occupation is granted to all Danish workers, by Norway in 1839 and Sweden in 1823 and 1846... Special train with dining, sleeping and observation cars is built for Napoleon III... Lyons is first European City with electrical street lighting, uses arc lamps... Denmark abolishes Sound dues for passing ships... Austria, German Zollverein countries adopt silver standard... France, Russia sign commercial treaty... Helmuth von Moltke is provisional Chief of Prussian General Staff, confirmed 1858 (-1888, supervises staff of 64 officers - 135 in 1871 and 239 in 1888, plans first rail-transport exercises in 1862, prepares plans for military victories in 1866, 1870)... India's Companies Act legalizes limited liability companies... Concrete mixer is invented in France... Pitlochry, Scotland, holds its first Highland Games.

Business Events

Moscow entrepreneurs form first joint venture to publish <u>The Messenger of Industry</u>, journal promotes industrialization (lobby to weaken French grip on Russia's railroads)... Tobacco manufacturing business starts in Londonderry, successful with pipe tobacco (moves to Belfast in 1863, opens London facilities in 1888 to make Park Drive machine-made cigarettes for Britain, U.S., Empire and Scandinavia, refuses to join formation of Imperial Tobacco in 1901 to fight American Tobacco, blocks takeover of American Tobacco in 1932)... In Scotland James and Marion Robertson devise special orange marmalade recipe (evolves as international food business by 1980s)... Beleek pottery appears in Ireland... North German Lloyd is transatlantic steamship company... Scottish engineer A. Wilson starts Vauxhall iron works in Britain, produces first car in 1903... Germany's Krupp sells first cannon to Egypt, Prussia in 1859 and Austria in 1866... Belgium's Neuhaus family enters confectionery field in prescribing chocolate at their pharmacy, grandson, Jean, invents filled bonbon in 1912.

1858

General Events

Manufacturer Baron W. Ohligs opens business institute, Vienna... France begins conquest of Cochin-China (-1864)... Japan, Britain sign commercial treaty... British Crown takes over powers, lands of English East India Co... First European oil well is drilled at Weitze, Hanover... Bessemer steel process appears in France... South Foreland lighthouse's arc light is powered by electricity... Peasant girl, Bernadette Soubirous, "sees" vision of Blessed Virgin Mary at Lourdes, major tourist attraction in 1900s... Lionel de Rothschild is first Jewish member of Parliament... France's Ferdinand Carre reveals mechanical system to make ice, close friend in audience at Gorrie's U.S. demonstration in 1850... Hawaiian king charters first bank, 2nd oldest West of the Rockies... British Army starts college to train staff officers... Local unions form Sheffield Trades Council,

Edinburgh in 1859, London in 1860, Glasgow in 1861, Dublin in 1863, and Birmingham in 1866... Keio University appears in Japan, Tokyo University in 1877 and Waseda University in 1882.

Business Events

John Fowler starts commercial production of steam plows in Britain, wins award from Royal Agricultural Society... Peugeot, started 1810 out of family textile mill, adopts lion trademark for metal products... P.T. Barnum presents "The Science of Money-making and the Philosophy of Humbug" on British lecture tour... British-born Charles Frederick Worth opens Maison Worth in Paris, later London, to launch French fashion industry with backing of Swedish financier Otto Bobergh (-1895, becomes dressmaker, fashion arbiter to French, Austrian courts to replace traditional seamstresses, uses first models to show designs, styles forerunner of tailor-made suit)... Sun Mill is limited liability company in Oldham, England, forerunner of area's 32 limited spinning firms in 1873-75... Bombay's Oriental Spinning & Weaving forms as limited liability company, forerunner of area's limited spinning firms in 1872-74... John J. Sainsbury, age 14, works in grocer's shop (starts family grocery business, Britain's largest in 1988 with 387 stores and assets of some $6 billion, with London dairy shop in 1869 - 2nd in 1876, starts wholesale depot in 1876, goes suburban in 1882 with experimental plush, spacious grocery store in well-to-do Croyden, adds bacon to product line, opens warehouse in 1891 for 14 branches - 115 in 1914, starts co-operative bulk buying in 1900 with other merchants - agree not to invade markets of others, buys farm in 1902, after W.W. I pioneers training centers for returning veterans, emphasizes store label in packaging bulk goods in 1920s, extends product line in 1930s to groceries, bacon and hams, cooked meats, fresh meats, dairy products, poultry, game and rabbits, adopts employee pension plan in 1934, acquires 30 Thoroughgood shops in 1936 for entry to London, operates 244 stores in 1938 and 240, half supermarkets, in late 1960s, opens first self-service grocery in 1950, drops deliveries to customers, credit, catering and wholesaling in 1950s, with some 30,000 employees sells some 1,000 products with family label in 1960s)...

Dutch-born Van den Bergh family moves to Oss, center of butter exports to England (after trouble with commission agents opens London office in 1868 for direct link to large buyers, expands buying organization to Germany, Switzerland, and Northern Italy, joins neighboring Jurgens family, its first experiments with margarine in 1871, in 1870s-80s to develop 'Butterine', opens margarine factory in 1872, forms British and Dutch firms in 1885, adds German factory in 1888, forms English holding company, Van den Berghs Margarine, in 1895 to raise capital for growth, acquires retail chain of Pearks, Gunston & Tee in 1896 - by 1906 with 3,120 retail customers, unable to merge pools profits with Jurgens, gets 40%, in 1908, merges with Jurgens in 1927 to form Margarine Unie NV in Holland and Margarine Union in England, linked by profit pool, before joining Lever empire)... Etienne Poulenc, pharmacist, buys Paris apothecary (expands by 1900 after making pharmaceuticals).

1859

General Events

England's Registrar's office uses difference engine to calculate actuarial tables, first use of computer technology by government... Britain legalizes peaceful picketing... Belgian-born French engineer, Etienne Lenoir, builds first workable, but inefficient, internal combustion engine, uses coal-gas and air... David Chadwick, professional accountant in 1843: <u>On The Rates of Wages in Two Hundred Trades</u>... Birmingham's Benjamin Baugh patents enamel metal, spurs widespread use of enamel advertising signs... Samuel Smiles: <u>Self Help</u> (notes "The spirit of self-help as root of all genuine growth in the individual")... Leon Scott demonstrates "Phonautograph" to British Association, shows for first time that sound is form of energy... R.L.G. Plante invents first practical storage battery... France's Louis Lemoine invents steam roller... Hung Ten-Kai: <u>New Writings to Help the Government</u> (urges modernization of technology to overcome traditional Chinese devotion to state, titles, official positions, moral credit from reputation and relationships, scholarship, arts and self-effacement)... British law allows hawkers, buy bread for resale, to keep 13th loaf/dozen as margin of profit, genesis for "bakers' dozen"... France captures trading settlement of Saigon, becomes key port for rubber-rich land... Exclusive St. James Club opens in London, by 1990 branches in Paris, Antigua and Los Angeles... Herbert Spencer: "The Morals of Trade" (lambastes business).

Business Events

John Barrans, Leeds, pioneers factory production of men's clothing with 30 Singer sewing machines... Westminster Palace Hotel is London's first with lift (provides 14 bathrooms for 300 bedrooms)... Irish-born Albert Grant forms Mercantile Discount Co., London, to launch new firms, fails 1860-61 (starts Credit Foncier, successful with feverish credit boom of 1862-66, and Credit Mobilier, named to suggest link with prestigious French investment bank, in 1864, merges two to finance 11 new firms 1864-66, is charged with corrupt bribery in 1874).

1860s

General Events

Open-hearth process for making steel is independently developed in France by Emile and Pierre Martin, Charles and Frederick Siemens in England... Rubber industry of Brazil is developed in Amazon Valley, continues expansion to 1910... Norwegian Svend Foyn invents harpoon gun and explosive harpoon head, leads to Norwegian inventions of floating factory ship in 1903 and ship's stern ramp in 1925... Topographers in several Dutch cities form mutual-aid societies... Skiing evolves as competitive sport... First worker strikes appear in Argentina... Siegfried Markus, Viennese inventor, experiments to make, operate motor carriages (fails until 1880s)... Alexis-Marie Lavigne, France, develops forerunner of store mannequin.

Business Events

Kit Burn's Sportsman Hall is popular British arena for sporting contests, i.e., dogs killing rats... Former chef to Napoleon III opens Kettner's Restaurant in London, claims to be first foreign eatery in Soho... Swiss G.F. Raskpt makes first reliable cheap watch... First Canadian stock exchanges appear in Montreal and Toronto, Winnipeg in 1903, Vancouver in 1907 and Calgary in 1913.

1860

General Events

Europe's relative share of world manufacturing output is 53.2%, Britain with 19.9%, Hapsburg empire 4.2%, France 7.9%, German area 4.9%, Italy area 2.5%, Russia 7.0%, U.S. 7.2%, Japan 2.6%, China 19.7%, India 8.6%... Siam establishes Royal Mint to issue coins, first paper currency in 1853... English chemist Greville Williams makes first synthetic rubber... First workers are imported from India to work sugar plantations of Natal, South Africa... First railway in Cape Colony opens, reaches Kimberley in 1885... Royal and Ancient Golf Club of St. Andrews, Scotland, sponsors first British Open golf tournament... Vladivostok is founded, Russia's only port on Pacific... Parliament passes Food and Drugs Act, strengthened 1872... Over 50 steam engines, first in 1797, are used in Cuba to process sugarcane, world's largest exporter... Carre demonstrates mechanical refrigerator at London exposition... National association of gymnastic clubs forms-in Germany... Copenhagen Workingmen's Assn. forms as self-help society to obtain better working conditions... Norway uses steam power, starts development of wood pulp industry... Italy's A. Pacinotti invents dynamo, first commercial generator by Gramme in 1869-70... British county magistrate reports on employment of children (notes children in Nottingham lace trade working from 2-4 a.m. to 10-12 p.m)... Lenoir, after discovering mixture of coal gas and air explodes, gets French patent for first practical 2-cycle internal-combustion engine, demonstrated 1863 (is improved in 1876 by Otto)... British Navy adopts ironclad warships... Anglo-French commercial treaty abolishes England's protective duties, in period to 1865 European powers lower tariffs in seven major treaties.

Business Events

James Spratt, inventor of special 'dog-cake,' and Charles Croft open pet shop in Holborn, England (start pet food factory in 1897)... Peek Frean & Co. forms to make biscuits (pioneers hiring women clerical workers in 1885, goes public in 1901, starts new products, pioneers assortments, in 1902)... Only 2 of 30 cloth mills in Russia's Simbirsk Province are owned by merchants (evolves by 1870 with 10 by merchants and 8 by gentry, 10 others of gentry closed and 2 leased to merchants)... Some 5,200 entrepreneurs do business in Paris, employ about 71,000 workers ... First successful private commercial banks in Russia appear, two prior were state banks... Machine works of Charles Baird, Scotland, is one of largest in Russia (employs 1,200-1,500 workers, operates country's first steam engines and steam-driven machines)... In this time Clavel enters synthetic dye field, evolves as Ciba to become largest Swiss chemical maker c. 1900 (merges with Basel rival, Geigy, in 1970, is attacked for using boys, Egypt, for chemical tests in 1976, sees diarrhea drug linked, 1978, to deaths of over 1,000 in Japan, forms venture, 1986, with Chiron to make genetically engineered vaccines).

1861

General Events

Henry Mayhew: <u>London Labour and London Poor</u>... French engineer, Germain Sommelier, develops jackhammer for excavating Mont Cenis tunnel... Britain drops last stamp tax on newspapers... German Commercial Law Code is enacted... Prussia, China sign commercial treaty... Britain opens Post Office Savings Bank... Belgian industrialist chemist Ernest Solvay devises new process to make soda, eliminates noxious wastes of Leblanc process... France, Britain and Spain send troops to Mexico to enforce payment of debt... Gold is found in New Zealand... Germany's J.P. Reis devises crude telephone device... First horse-drawn trams appear in London (-1953)... Germany imports Scottish workers from Dundee to train laborers in techniques of jute manufacture (hires U.S. workers in 1869 to train staff in use of U.S. machine tools)... Some 29% of France's population live in towns of 2,000 or more... Uruguay builds "first" industrial meat-packing plant... Some two million Russian serfs on estates of nobles are granted their freedom, allotted land by village communes... Saxony restores freedom of association for workers, spreads across North German Confederation by 1867 (leads to formation of labor unions, political parties).

Business Events

T.S. Mort builds world's first commercial plant for meat refrigeration in Sydney... Edwin Waterhouse is apprenticed to firm of accountants (is accountant and auditor for London & North Western Railway in 1861, opens office in 1864 - no accounting exam required until 1880, forms Price, Holyland & Waterhouse in 1865 - Price Waterhouse & Co. in 1874, opens NYC office in 1890 to gather data for English investors and Australia agency in 1896, hires first women member in 1924)... On death of partner, William H. Lascelles, age 29, takes over carpentry firm, improves efficiency in workshops by 1871 (patents 'Office Table' in 1870, devises new system of house construction with pre-cast concrete in 1875)... Assn. of German Chambers of Commerce and of Industry and Trade forms (follows chambers of medieval merchant corporations in Baltic, chambers in Rhineland, French models during Napoleonic years and chambers developed in Cologne during 1840s)... William Morris, English poet and craftsman, starts pioneer interior decorating firm with partner (designs Morris chair)... Frederick Englehorn, jeweler, starts BASF chemical business, Germany (develops successful indigo dye in 1897, joins I.G. Farben cartel in 1925, regains independence in 1952 after being dismantled by Allies after 1945, forms foreign joint ventures,

U.S.' Dow in 1958, in 1950s, after buying U.S.' Wyandotte Chemical, 1969, adds three more by 1985, in 1991 buys magnetic media business of Agfa-Gevaert to become world's 3rd largest in field)... New Zealand's Challenge business enterprise begins, Dunedin, as livestock partnership (opens London office in 1906, grows with fertilizers, 1920, breeding stock, 1922, motor cars, 1927, electrical appliances, 1937, land development, 1945, and bicycles, lawn mowers in 1962, in 1972 merges with another livestock broker, started 1864, to form Challenge Corp., acquires 28% of Tasman Pulp & Paper Co., formed 1952, in 1979 when New Zealand sells its stake, Fletcher gets 56%, combines with Fletcher, Dunedin construction firm of 1909, in 1981 as Fletcher Challenge with sales of $2 billion, buys U.S.' Crown Zellerback in 1983, majority share of British Columbia Forest Products in 1987 and New Zealand's Petrocorp, gas and oil, in 1988 and acquires government's Rural Bank)... Hong Kong and Whampoa Dock is first registered firm in Hong Kong (builds docks by 1865 and expands with shipyards, is fully acquired in 1977 by Hutchison trading in forming Hutchison Whampoa).

1862

General Events

Prussia, France sign commercial treaty, based on free-trade principles... F. Lassalle: <u>Working Class Programme</u> (urges State Socialism)... First subway section of London's Metropolitan Line shuttles passengers between above-ground railway terminals, under Thames in 1890 and electrified 1905... Britain's Limited Liability Act encourages accumulation of capital by issuing shares... Argentina enacts commercial and civil codes to establish modern legal framework for business (classifies business enterprises as simple ownership, partnership, limited partnership, and joint-stock limited liability, follows with 1869 law to create two classes of loans: secured by property and unsecured available for only short periods at high interest rates)... Iron Workers' Assn. forms in Britain... After work in 1850s Alexander Parkes shows plastic items, called celluloid later, in London... French government in Indochina puts 10% tax on all India opium imports (takes control of sales and forms opium monopoly, by 1918 licenses 1,512 dealers and 2,098 official shops)... German chemist isolates cocaine from cocoa leaf, used as opiate by South Americans from at least 1500 B.C... Western school of languages, sciences opens in Peking, Shanghai in 1863 and Canton in 1864... China starts naval shipyard, 2nd in Foochow in 1866, and arsenal, others in Nanking 1865 and Tientsin in 1867, in Shanghai, one of world's largest by 1870... Donation Fund of Peabody finances low-cost housing for London poor... Swiss Jean Henri Dunant proposes international relief organization, genesis for Red Cross in 1863... German Julius Sachs shows starch can be produced by photosynthesis... Denmark abolishes guild system... French engineer Beau de Rochas tries to patent four-cycle engine... Cooperative rural bank appears in Germany to provide credit for members, 49 in Switzerland by 1905, 11 in Britain by 1906 and 1,767 in France by 1907... Burma, Britain sign commercial treaty... Ferdinand Redtenbacher: <u>Machine Construction</u> (-1865)... Monaco opens Monte Carlo Casino.

Business Events

A. Opel starts sewing machine business in Germany, later makes bicycles, refrigerators and cars, first in 1898 (is acquired by GM in 1929)... Ireland's Guinness Brewery adopts harp brand.. Immigrant stone mason Thomas Cooper starts brewery (uses brewing methods of 1340 Queen's College Brewery of Oxford), Australia's only privately-owned brewery in 1980... Don F. Bacardi starts small rum distillery in Cuba, (moves to Puerto Rico with Castro's takeover in 1959, sells brand via complicated network of independent companies in 175 countries by 1980s, is divided by feud of 250-member family over control in 1986-90)... Aerated Bread Co. starts London business (after entering catering field runs some 100 tea-shops by 1900)... British merchants open London Buenos Aires and River Platt Bank, London Brazilian Bank (leads to other British banks and those of Germany, France and Italy to serve local immigrants)... Gilberts starts first factory in Uruguay to make Liebig's extract of meat... Henry P. Rowntree buys cocoa, chocolate business of William Tuke & Sons, York grocer (is limited company in 1897, buys cocoa estates in Dominica and

Jamaica - factories in South Africa in 1925 and Australia in 1933, considers merger with rival Cadbury in 1918)... William Pickle Hartley, age 16, runs mother's grocery store (when local grocer fails to supply preserves, starts making quality jams and marmalades - factories at Liverpool in 1874 and London in 1901, builds model village for workers in 1888, in addition to paying women 20%-40% more than competitors and free medical service provides profit-sharing plan in 1889, produces 600 tons of preserves/week by death in 1922)... After draper apprenticeship, John Player opens office in Nottingham as agent for lace thread and artificial manure, adds tobacco items later (buys 1823 tobacco plant of William Wright in 1877 to compete with city's 19 others, sells first brand, Gold Leaf, in 1877, uses sailor trademark in 1883 - success with advertising, opens new plant in 1884, incorporates in 1895, when threatened by American Tobacco and retail chains joins 12 other firms to form Imperial Tobacco in 1901).

1863

General Events

F. Lassalle, merchant son, forms General Assn. of German Workers, genesis of Social Democratic movement... First International Postal Conference meets in Paris... British Football Assn. forms to play soccer (codifies rules for sport, evolves by 1910 with 6,000 professionals)... France, Italy sign commercial treaty... Wilbrand manufacturers TNT... Australia's Victoria declares tokens of merchants, minted as English coins were too bulky for change, as illegal, NSW in 1868... William Smith: Advertise How? When? Where?... France's first Grand Prix de Paris is run at Longchamps... Henry C. Sorby discovers microstructure of steel, starts science of metallurgy... Poland drills first oil well... China employs Robert Hart, Scotland, to reorganize Maritime Custom Service (develops postal service in 1896)... When Mexico's bank fails to repay loans to French bankers, French forces seize Mexico City, make Maxmillian Emperor in 1864-67... Cambodia is French protectorate... French law permits joint-stock companies if their capital is not over specified amount, drops restriction in 1867.

Business Events

Barnard's Express and Stage Line begins as pony express service in British Columbia... Two chemists and two salesmen start Hoechst German pharmaceutical business (still extant)... Yorkshire Steel & Ironworks is Britain's first to depend on large-scale manufacture of Bessemer steel... Thomas E. Vickers takes over Naylor Vickers, one of three largest steel works in Sheffield (after series of patents incorporates 1867, produces marine shafts in 1868, screw-propellers in 1872, armor plate in 1888, and first artillery piece in 1890, acquires Maxim Gun Co. in 1897, acquires interests in submarine, aircraft and motor car operations - leading arsenal with W.G. Armstrong, buys 50% of Glasgow warship yard, retires 1909 as leader in world steelmaking - only Bochum and Krupp larger, evolves by 1918 as U.K.'s 3rd largest business after Coats, Lever Bros.)... Friedrich Bayer starts chemical business, one of pioneers of land's industry (introduces first synthetic pesticide in 1892, aspirin in 1899, and synthetic rubber in 1915, loses U.S. subsidiary and trademark rights in 1917, sold by U.S. to Sterling Drug in 1918, joins I.G. Farben Trust in 1925, develops first sulfa drug in 1935, after breakup of I.G. Farben, ordered 1945 Potsdam Agreement, emerges as independent firm in 1951, forms U.S. venture with Monsanto in 1954)... Henri Germain, son of Lyons lawyer, silk merchant, stockbroker and mine manager, forms, aided by local businessmen and Swiss bankers, Credit Lyonnaise as deposit bank, France's 3rd largest, 1991, after Credit Agricole and Banque Nationale de Paris.

1864

General Events

Societe Generale forms in France... Germany's J.F.E. Shultz invents smokeless powder... Clerks in General Post Office start Civil Service Stores in London to buy, sell tea (-1982, with success leads to Post Office Supply Assn. in 1865 with membership open to all civil servants, evolves as department store in 1927)... Fred Walton, England, invents linoleum floor covering... Co-operative Wholesale Society is federation of cooperatives (evolves with wholesalers, factories and farms, operates with 199 retail members in 1874, 1,035 in 1895)... Marx founds First International Workingmen's Assn. with representatives from English, French, Polish and Italian workers (-1876)... Pope Pius IX: "Syllabus Errorum" (condemns liberalism, socialism, rationalism)... Count Ferdinand d'Esterns contends in article that wind can power aircraft... Romania gives serfs their freedom... France permits strikes (although still illegal leads to union growth after 1868 act)... Octavia Hill starts movement in London to reform housing in slum areas... Training of social workers begins in London.

Business Events

Master Brewer George Killian makes first Irish Red lager (exports to U.S. in mid-1980s via Adolph Coors Co. of Colorado)... Germany's G. Junghans starts clock, watch manufacturing business (uses U.S. principle of interchangeable parts to become country's largest clockmaker)... Winter sports appear in Alps when Johannes Badrutt, owner of St. Moritz Palace Hotel, bets English visitors would prefer mountain activities to foggy London... Otto, partner start German factory to make gas engines, devise atmospheric gas-engine in 1867... Australian sugar plantations import Kanaka workers from Solomons, other Pacific islands... George Peabody & Co. reorganizes as J.S. Morgan & Co. (grants $50 million loan in 1870 to Prussia to become Europe's leading financial institution)... Grand Langham Hotel opens, London... John Lewis opens small haberdasher shop in London (leases nearby buildings for more space in 1875 - retail on first two floors and wholesaling on 3rd with restaurant, rebuilds as department store in 1895, acquires Peter Jones, Chelsea retailer, in 1906, adopts profit-sharing in 1920, sells stock in formation of John Lewis Partnership in 1929 - 2,460 participants in 1962, acquires T.S. Harries & Co. in 1929, expands in 1935 to operate 5 branch stores)... Martini and Rossi start making vermouth, popular drink in 1700s, in Turin (still extant)...

Heineken family acquires 270-year old De Hooiberg brewery, Amsterdam (opens 2nd brewery in Rotterdam in 10 years, after repeal of U.S.' Prohibition is first foreign beer to re-enter market, buys Amstel Brewery, founded 1870, in 1968 and Irish producer of stout, James J. Murphy, in 1970, after entering soft drink and wine industries buys Bokma distillery in 1971, expands during 1980s to buy breweries in France, Greece, Ireland, Italy and Spain, acquires U.S. importing firm and Hungarian brewery in 1991)... Merchants Banks opens in Halifax, incorporated 1869 (after adding branches in eastern Canada opens Bermuda bank in 1882 and Cuba in 1899, is renamed Royal Bank of Canada in 1901, land's largest and one of 10 largest in North America, adds six banks, including one in British Honduras, by 1926, sells island assets to Banco Nacional de Cuba in 1960, goes overseas in Britain, 1979, West Germany, 1980, Puerto Rico, 1980, and Bahamas, 1980, gets approval of U.S. Federal Reserve in 1991 to underwrite stocks).

1865

General Events

Britain paves first concrete roads... First International Telegraph Congress meets in Paris... Britain, German Zollverein sign (May 30) commercial treaty... Wolverhampton building trades are first in Britain to accept voluntary arbitration... Prussia, Italy sign (December 31) commercial treaty... Britain's Red Flag Act limits speed of all mechanical road vehicles to 4 mph in country, 2 mph in town (requires each self-propelled vehicle must be preceded by man with red flag, repealed 1896)... Jonas G.W. Zander, early physiotherapist, opens first medical-mechanical institute in Stockholm, by 1917 sells 73 items of exercise apparatus to institutes and spas from Baden-Baden to U.S.' Homestead Hotel... France, Belgium, Italy and Switzerland form Latin Monetary Union, joined by Greece, Spain, Romania, Finland, and several South, Central American countries after 1868...

First German association of women forms in Leipzig, leads to German Women's Assn. in 1894... First Socialist unions in Germany appear, 30 by 1894-95, as first Christian unions form by 1894-95... Pasteur treats silkworm disease, saves French silk industry... Nottingham pawnbroker William Booth starts Christian Revival Assn. in London, renamed The Salvation Army in 1878 (evolves by 1986 with 16,800 active officers, 1.5 million supporters worldwide)... London Metropolitan Fire Service forms to eliminate rival companies, NYC abolishes 125 volunteer engine houses with 1865 Metropolitan Fire Dept... Thaddeaus Lowe invents machine to make artificial ice... North German unified commercial code is accepted by all German states.

Business Events

Raffles Hotel opens in Singapore... First Finnish wood pulp mill appears, 9 in 1868-74 and 15 more by 1880... Britain's Whitwood Collieries adopts profit-sharing plan (-1875, influences U.S. use)... Printemps department store opens in Paris... W.H. Hughes starts Victoria Wine Co., Britain's oldest liquor retailer by 1980s with over 900 outlets (runs 63 stores by 1879 and 98 by death in 1886, is sold in 1929 to Taylor & Walker brewing firm, adds tobacco products in 1934, popularizes wine in 1960s during marketing war)... Joseph Hepworth acquires 1850s wholesale clothing business in Leeds, 500 employees in 1881 and 143 shops in 1905... Finland's Nokia Corp., 1988 multi-national conglomerate in high-tech electronics and communications with revenues of $5.25 billion, begins as wood-products enterprise (evolves in electric power, rubber products)... British merchants form Hongkong & Shanghai Bank in Colony, by 1988 one of world's 20 largest with $110 billion in assets and 2,000 offices in 57 countries (opens offices in Shanghai and London in 1865 - Japan in 1866, San Francisco in 1875, New York in 1879, Bangkok, Siam's first commercial bank, in 1888, and France and Germany by 1900, acquires Mercantile Bank in 1959, British Bank of Middle East in 1960, Hang Seng Bank in 1965 and Marine Midland Bank, U.S.' 15th largest, in 1980, opens own merchant bank, Wardley, in 1972 - largest in Asia servicing U.S., Cyprus, Gulf states, Singapore, Australia and New Zealand, after developing in-house computer system in mid-1960s uses automated teller machines in 1980, acquires NYC brokerage house in 1986)...

At age 14, Thomas J. Lipton, son of Scottish provision merchant, travels to U.S. by steerage class to wander country, worked as clerk for Virginia tobacco plantation, fireman in Charleston and clerk in NYC grocery store (returns to Scotland in 1869 with savings of $500, opens shop in Glasgow - success with Irish bacon and coupons known as "Lipton's Pounds," opens 2nd store in 1874 - 4 by 1878, opens first in England at Leeds in 1881 - London in 1882 with 72 by 1899, after selling tea from Ceylon plantations via shops in 1889 enters grocery trade to run over 100 stores by 1891, enters U.S. market at 1893 Chicago's World's Fair, adds sugar, jam, cakes, biscuits, confectionery and coffee to product line in 1890s, runs 242 shops in 1898 with factories and warehouses - is Knighted, enters Shamrock yacht in 1899 America's Cup Challenge - loses, sells to Van den Berghs margarine business in 1927, after losing in 1901, 1903, 1920 and 1930 yacht races is given trophy by U.S. public in 1930 for sportsmanship, dies in 1931 to leave most of estate to Glasgow poor).

1866

General Events

England closes last main turnpike... France's Francois Carlier invents first chemical fire extinguisher... Sweden controls sales of spirits... After previous failures by Britain's Royal Geographic Society, Dutch diplomat disappears after trying to smuggle rubber seeds from Manaus, Brazil's rubber Capitol (leads to 2nd failure in 1871 by Irishman for British capitalists)... Venezuela grants first oil concession (starts first drilling in 1883, allows exploration by Royal Dutch Shell in 1913 - production in 1919, discovers Lake Maracaibo field in 1926 - virtual control by Shell, Jersey Standard by 1937)... Method for training personnel for a specific task is developed in Finland... Society for the Cultivation of Heaths forms, Denmark, to improve agricultural methods... Master cabinet maker Henry Lemoine starts Patronage, funded by Paris, to revive craftsmanship being destroyed by industrial production (starts school of design in 1873 for apprentices with funds from individuals, business organizations)... Aeronautical Society of Great Britain forms, follows lectures on experiments with aerial locomotion by F.H. Wenham in 1850s... Union of Diamond Cutters appears in Holland... England starts manual training courses... Some two million Russian serfs on Crown estates are freed... W. Siemens develops dynamo to generate electricity, announced 1868... British patent for rigid steel dirigible goes to R.B. Boyman, follows idea for iron airship by France's Prosper Miller in 1851... Chinese population of Singapore is some 54,000, 224,000 in 1911 and 861,000 in 1958... Diamonds are found in southern Africa.

Business Events

Britain's first commercial dry-cleaning service opens... Great Tea Race from China's Foochow to London is sailed by 16 clippers (is won by Taeping, Ariel in virtual tie for first after logging 99 days over some 15,000 miles, Fiery Cross and Taitsing two days later)... Nobel invents dynamite, produces 12 tons in 1867 and 66,500 in 1897 for mining... Americans Charles, George Page form Anglo-Swiss condensed Milk Co. in Switzerland (begin production in 1867, introduce new product in 1878, end competitive battle in 1905 by merging with rival Nestle)... After dabbling in Australian gold fields, sheep farming and Melbourne merchant house, John S. Swire and brother, sons of Liverpool trader with business of 1816 evolving as importer of U.S. cotton, form Butterfield & Swire in Shanghai, partner leaves 1868, as agent for 1865 Ocean Steamship Co. (expands with White Star and Scottish Oriental lines to run branches in Yokohama, 1868, Hong Kong, 1870, Foochow, Swatow, Tientsin, Hankon, Kobe, Amoy, Chefor, and NYC, 1868, starts China Navigation in 1872 for shipping on Lower Yangtze, forms pool with rivals to reduce fights, runs Coast Boats for Manchuria and South shipping in 1874, merges with China Navigation in 1883, expands to Japan, Manila in 1880s-90s as a leading taipan of Shanghai, acquires Hong Kong sugar refinery in 1881, in 1898 builds Hong Kong dockyards, merges with Hongkong & Whampoa dockyards in 1972).

1867

General Events

Britain passes Factory Inspection Act... First Socialist is elected to North German Reichstag... England, U.S. issue patents to Tilghman for acid process, required to make paper of wood pulp instead of rags... Royal Commission reports few organized combinations of employers exist in Britain... Britain declares trade unions to be illegal... Otto and Eugene Langen, assisted by Gottlieb Daimler and Wilhelm Maybach (leave 1882), win gold medal at Paris Exposition for gas engine (open factory near Cologne in 1869)... Some 200 companies in Italy are corporations... Some 35% of Germany's population live in towns of 2,000 or more... First gold in Zimbabwe is discovered, Tati concession acquired by London and Limpopo Mining in 1870... German General Staff is divided into two parts: preparing and training, scientific assignments (are merged in 1898)... France's Companies Act minimizes government restraints on creation of business firms (encourages development of small, family-sized enterprises)... Metropolitan Streets Act regulates distribution of handbills, use of sandwich-men in London (requires approval of advertisements by Commissioner of Police)... Pall Mall Gazette prints articles attacking "foul advertisements" for patent medicines... Paris Exposition is held (presents 356 displays by U.S. manufacturers, introduces Japanese art to Europe)... Diamonds are discovered along Orange River, South Africa... Paris builds pneumatic postal system to deliver mail by underground tubes (-1984)... Prussia acquires mail monopoly of Thurn and Taxis family... Joseph F. Monier patents reinforced concrete process... Karl Marx: Das Kapital, Vol. I... Britain forms Dominion of Canada... British scientist William Thomson invents syphon recorder... North German Confederation forms (approves army budgets for four-year terms)... Johann Strauss the Younger, composer and musical director (oversees organization of some 200 with musicians, business staff): "Blue Danube".

Business Events

Cobb & Co. provides daily stagecoach service between Auckland, Hamilton in New Zealand (runs chain of 20 restaurants by 1881)... Germany's Agfa starts making dyes, produces photography supplies later... Factory to make Longines watches appears in Switzerland... Galleria Vittorio Emmanuele opens in Milan, Italy (is built with English capital as early modern urban center to enclose shopping arcade of stores, shops on two major thoroughfares)... Elegant Plaza-Athenee hotel opens in Paris, Ritz Hotel in 1898... France's Pierre Michaus starts making bicycles... Paperback series of books is published in Leipzig... Public meat market, slaughter house opens in Paris (-1974, becomes 10-acre site, Paris' largest park, for center of sciences and technology)... Alexander Macmillan starts London publishing business (opens U.S. branch in 1896 and Canada in 1905 - by W.W. I in India, Far East and Australia, urges in 1890 that publishers should not supply books to discount retailers - Net Book Agreement in 1900, helps form Booksellers' Assn. of Great Britain and Ireland in 1895 and Publishers' Assn. in 1896, fights takeover in 1988)... Owen Owen, son of tenant farmer, joins uncle's Liverpool drapery business (opens shop in 1868 - success with low profit margins, high turnover, clear labels, and financial controls, employs 120 in 1873, joins brother in London department store opposite William Whiteley's retail business, buys Burlington Carriage Co. in 1907 to import French cars)... W. & S. Butcher is Sheffield's first with steelworks in U.S., 5 more by 1917...

Canadian Bank of Commerce is opened, first charter of 1858 is purchased in 1866 by Toronto financier William McMaster (by 1874 expands with 24 branches in Ontario and offices in Montreal and NYC, opens Winnipeg branch in 1893 and branches to serve Yukon Gold Rush in 1898, acquires three banks in 1901, 1903, and 1906 from British Columbia to Prince Edward Island, merges in 1961 with Imperial Bank of Canada, founded 1875, to form Canadian Imperial Bank of Commerce, adds investment bank in 1988 and Merrill Lynch Canada in 1990, gets right to underwrite U.S. stocks in 1991)... Henri Nestle, Switzerland, introduces new condensed milk product (sells business operating in 16 countries to three local businessmen in 1875, makes first chocolate in 1904, takes over Anglo-Swiss in 1905, acquires Cailler, first to mass-produce bars, in 1929, evolves by 1960s with 180 factories in 34 countries, 75,000 employees and sales of $1.5 billion from variety of food products).

1868

General Events

Trades Union Congress forms, Manchester, as central confederation to coordinate efforts of unions to secure legal status, granted by 1877 Trades Union Act... Two students of Adolf Baeyer, Munich, patent alizarin synthetic dye, impractical (becomes practical in 1869 when Perkin devises new process, joins Germany's BASF to manufacture product in England, to make 453 tons in 1873)... Game of badminton appears in Britain... First known bicycle race is run in Paris... George Leclanche devises zinc-carbon battery, forerunner of modern "flashlight battery"... Shogunate is abolished in Japan with restoration of Meiji Dynasty (moves Capitol from Kyoto to Edo - renamed Tokyo, adopts to Meiji Constitution in 1889)... Aberdeen's Thermopylae sails record voyage from China to London in 91 days (-1907)... First Japanese workers are brought to Hawaii to work sugarcane fields... First Chinese-built steamship is launched... First aeronautical exhibition is held at London's Crystal Palace... Mushet develops tungsten steel, leads to chromium steel by France in 1877, manganese steel by Britain in 1882, nickel steel by France in 1888, stainless steel by Britain in 1911-20... Britain's John Stringfellow tests model triplane, unsuccessful... Japan runs first steam-powered train... French scientist H. Mege-Mouries devises suet-and-milk mixture as cheap butter substitute, oleo, for military use, wins prize from Napoleon III (leads to commercial production in 1873 and substitution of vegetable oil in 1907, exports to U.S. limited by 1886 Act to 1950).

Business Events

Heinrich Caro, after working at Manchester Dyeworks 1859-66, joins Munich's BASF (synthesizes numerous dyes and devises industrial processes for their manufacture)... German Trades Assn. forms... England's Robert T. Humber makes bicycles, produces first light car in 1900... Charles Schneider, French capitalist (transforms Schneider et Cie into international munitions power with 182 works in France and 230 foreign operations, including Czechoslovakia's Skoda), is born (-1942)... Artist Edouard Manet does first advertising poster, pioneered in 1867 by Jules Cheret (leads to Henri Toulouse-Lautrec's Moulin Rouge poster in 1891)... Lesage family clothing business opens in Paris, specializes in elaborate French needlework favored by top designers (uses 90 seamstresses by 1980s to turn out 400 different designs, 18,000 hours of labor, for sales over $8 million/year)... Enrique C. Creel manages store in Chihuahua for Kentucky-born father (on death of father in 1871 starts own business with loan of 300 pesos, leading merchant in area by 1879, marries daughter of Chihuahua's political boss, 10 million acres of land and 500,000 cattle, in 1880, starts Banco Minero de Chihuahua in 1882 with four partners - Mexico's 4th largest by 1910 with offices over Northern Mexico, with two partners starts Banco Mercantil in 1899, stockholders of elite, to finance industrial development of Monterrey, c. 1900 tries to build trust in flour milling and meatpacking, is governor in 1904-10 to reform state government, is Ambassador to U.S. in 1906, is embroiled in politics after 1911 maderista revolution to protect interests, power)...

Edward C. Guinness takes over Dublin family brewery on death of father, produces 350,000 barrels in 1868, 725,000 in 1875 and 1.2 million in 1886 (by 1870 cuts product line to three for specific markets: porter for Ireland, Extra Stout for Britain and Foreign Extra Stout for rest of world, registers harp in 1875 with Trademark Registration Act, incorporates in 1886 as world's largest brewery)... Haub family, worth some $2.6 billion by 1990, starts retail business (buys 50% of stock of U.S.' Great Atlantic & Pacific Tea Co. in 1979-80, by 1989 evolves as Tengelmann Group, West Germany's largest private retailer and Europe's largest supermarket chain, with some 4,000 Tengelmann, Kaiser's and Plus stores)... Jamsetji Tata, Bombay Parsee, starts textile trading firm (after manufacturing textiles, begins mission to industrialize India).

1869

General Events

J.F. Tretz, Europe's first, uses chain drive with unit for bicycles... Germany's Social Democratic Party forms... Britain takes over inland telegraph firm, first use of term "nationalization"... Jonathan Gable, Far East missionary, invents jinrikisha, small two-wheel-hooded vehicle with long shaft pulled by one or more men... William S. Jovan devises logic machine, first quicker than individual to solve complicated problems... France's Fareo develops principle of hydrofoil... Mexico drills its first oil well, first major field in 1904 near Tampico (leads to new discoveries in 1910, managed by Royal Dutch Shell with Jersey Standard to produce over 50% of nation's output, and major find in 1932 by British firm)... Typographical Assn. forms in Denmark as social, benevolent society... Fraser's Magazine: "The Great Force" (castigates British advertising for impacts on commercial standards, interests of public)... French Empress Eugenie opens Suez Canal, costs some $80 million for 100 miles from Port Said to Suez... Britain abolishes debtors' prisons... Clipper Cutty Sark is launched (-1922, after undistinguished sailing record in tea trade, sails from Sydney to London in 73 days to beat rival Thermopylae in 1885 wool race by 7 days)... First postcards appear, Austria... Assn. of German Unions forms for mutual support... Britain's National Line launches Holland with compound-expansion engine, first appearance of triple-expansion marine engine in 1873 by Britain and France... France's Guilmet devises chain drive for bicycles, not used... North German Confederation adopts freedom of occupation, free movement of labor... Douglas, visited by some 25,000 tourists 1830-40 from Ireland and Britain (reaches high of 634,512 in 1913), is new capitol of Isle of Man... Wilhelm Liebnicht, August Bebel form Social

Democratic Workers' Party (urges Marxist class war)... Paul Schutzenberger, Sorbonne chemist, prepares cellulose acetate, patent for industrial process to England's Charles F. Cross, Edward J. Bevan in 1884 to make artificial fiber.

Business Events

Folies-Bergere delights Paris... Two of first mechanized mills in Japan to process raw silk are built by two Fukushima sake breweries... First German employers' association forms in printing industry, central federation of associations in 1919... Skoda Works is started at Pilsen, Bohemia, as engineering firm, evolves to make military equipment... After visiting U.S. to recover from broken love affair (enjoyed riding on Pullman luxury railroad car), Belgian Georges Nagelmackers starts similar railroad service in Europe... Group of entrepreneurs forms Moscow Merchants' Society of Mutual Credit... United Co-operative Baking Society of Clydeside is Britain's first wholesale baker... With license from Otto and Langen, Crossley Bros. of Manchester starts making gas engines, 40,000 by 1900s... Joseph Rowntree joins brother's cocoa and chocolate business, sole owner 1883 (sells first gum and pastilles, a French monopoly, in 1881, employs work force of 200 in 1883 - 800 in 1894 and 4,000 in 1906, introduces new brand of Elect cocoa in 1887, builds new factory in 1891-98 to process chocolate).

1870s

General Events

Felix Du Temple tries to fly powered, man-carrying plane (gets lift-off from inclined ramp but fails to sustain flight)... 276 incorporated companies do business in Prussia... Some 500 foreigners, most British, are employed by Japanese Ministry of Industry as engineers, technical instructors (-1885).

Business Events

Sweden's R. Nobel builds Russia's first modern petroleum refinery to process Caucasian oil... Four paper mills appear in Japan... Chile's sodium nitrate resources are developed for fertilizer... In late 1800s, Hirose Saihei, 1824-1914, develops Sumitomo merchant house of some 200 years by modernizing copper mining (evolves with interests in lumber, machine manufacture, foreign trade and banking to become Sogo Shosha in 1985 with revenues of $53 billion from machinery, 30%, metals, 29%, chemicals, 24%, food, 6%, and 3% in textiles).

1870

General Events

Britain handles 42.3% of world's merchant shipping, volume of trade greater than that of France, Germany and Italy combined and three times more than U.S... Diamonds are discovered at Kimberley, South Africa... Institute of Chartered Accountants of England and Wales forms... Chartered banks hold 73% of all assets of Canadian financial institutions... World produces .5 million tons of steel, 29 million in 1900 by U.S. as largest producer... Japan establishes Ministry of Industry... Argentina formulates federal constitution, national government in 1880 after years of conflict between Buenos Aires, provinces... Li Hongzhang, High Commissioner for the Northern Ocean, is responsible for China's foreign affairs (-1895, as leader of Self-Strengthening movement, evolved in 1860s, urges arsenals and factories to overcome superiority of foreign military technology)... Using ideas of Floris Nollet and Dan Soren Hjorth, Zenobe T. Gramme builds first high-voltage electrical generator (produces first continuous current for arc light, invents alternator in 1878)... Charles Robert: La Suppression des Greves (proposes labor share in profits)... Improving on toy helicopters of Launoy and Bienvenue, France's Alfonse Penaud devises basic "motor," twisted rubber band, for model helicopters (lacks only lightweight power supply for full-sized craft)... Britain requires competitive examinations for certain civil service positions...

Britain starts national telegraph service... National Union of Elementary Teachers forms in Britain, first permanent union of teachers... Japan starts overseas study program for students, enrolls 380 by 1872... German law requires corporations to have two boards, supervisory board to represent stockholders and executive board to make operating decisions... Britain grants property rights to women... Parliament helps farmers with fair rents and tenure, freedom to sell leases... France's Lentheric invents hair net in this time (leads to Marcel salon, Paris, in 1882)... With defeat of French forces, world military study Prussian military methods, particularly wargaming (is generally accepted by W.W. I, credited for Japanese victory over Russia in 1904-05 and used by Germans in 1939 in planning Ardennes breakthrough to turn Maginot Line)... Trade unions of construction workers in Victoria, Australia, win legal recognition (leads to trades and labor councils by 1880, first union congress in 1879).

Business Events

Austro-Hungarian Chamber of Commerce is first to go abroad with office in Constantinople... Congress of commercial and industrial interests forms in St. Petersburg, followed by Moscow in 1882 and Nizhnyi Novgorod in 1896... Vaudeville theater opens, London... Merchant bank of Lazard Bros. & Co. opens in London... Gerardo di Nola business appears near Naples (evolves by 1980s as one of Italy's largest producers of premium pasta)... Salesman and department manager, John Barker, leaves William Whiteley's emporium to open small London drapery shop with wealthy merchant James Whitehead (sells draperies, groceries, furnishings, and hardware by 1880, pioneers Saturday half-days, operates with 60 departments and 1,400 employees by 1893, acquires fashion store in 1907)...

Former provincial samurai Yataro Iwasaki, head of family trading office in Nagasaki, acquires small Japanese coastal shipping firm of Tosa clan, names business Mitsubishi, Three Diamonds, in 1873 (with acquisition of government ships expands coastal, overseas service to build trading house, with government subsidy, leaders want to reduce Japan's dependence on foreign lines, enters international market with Shanghai trade, is rewarded for loyalty by government leasing 32 of his 40 ships to suppress Satsuma Rebellion in 1877, is forced by government to end shipping war by merging with 1882 Hokkaido line, KUK, in 1885 to form NYK, becomes Zaibatsu, joins Mitsui, Sumitomo and Yasuda, in 1886 with non-shipping ventures, acquires valuable Tokyo real estate in 1890s when Japan needs funds for military build-up, continues to grow under Baron Koyata Iwasaki with interests in industrial machinery, electrical equipment - license from Westinghouse in 1923, chemicals and aircraft production - Zero plane during W.W. II, enters oil business in 1956 with Royal Dutch Shell, produces first cars in 1959, evolves by 1985 with interests in fuels, 31% of sales, metals, 21%, machinery, 19%, foods, 14%, and chemicals, 8%, 226 offices worldwide, 13,865 employees and sales of $68.6 billion, 2nd largest to Mitsui of nine Sogo Sosha, general trading houses, producing almost 25% of Japan's GNP, buys 51% of NYC's Rockefeller Center in 1989 for $846 million)...

With German unification Georg von Siemens starts Deutsche Bank in Berlin, world's 18th largest by assets in 1987 with interests in autos, Daimler-Benz, department stores, Karstadt and Horton, construction, metals and engineering, shipping and tourism, Hapag-Lloyd, chemicals, porcelain, machine tools and plastics (goes overseas, 1873, with London branch, with foreign business survives economic crisis of 1873-75 and buys other banks, evolves with secretariat by 1900)... Cecil John Rhodes, British adventurer and empire-builder, visits brother in South Africa to make fortune as diamond prospector (goes to Britain in 1873 to study at Oxford, returns to South Africa to become assembly member in 1881 - largely responsible for annexation of Bechuanaland in 1884, monopolizes diamond production of Kimberley with creation of DeBeers Consolidated Mines in 1888, gets Royal Charter in 1889 for British South Africa Co. - forms Rhodesia in 1895, is South Africa's prime minister in 1890 - censored in 1896 for plot to overthrow Transvaal Republic)... Amstel Brewery appears in Amsterdam... Britain's W.N. Sharpe Holdings starts greeting card business, acquired by U.S.' Hallmark in 1984... Former minister, J.C. Van Marken, starts Royal Netherlands Yeast and Spirits Factory, Delft, in belief that well-treated workers will be productive, viewed by some Dutch employers as a Communist... Grand resort Eden Roc appears in Cannes, French Riviera.

1871

General Events

Britain ends practice of purchasing military commissions... Germany adopts gold standard... Britain annexes Kimberley diamond fields, South Africa (produces nearly one million carats in 1872 and two million in 1880, regulates ownership and exploitation of claims in 1873 by registering titles - limit of 10 until dropped in 1880 to allow consolidations, leads to first mining board at DeBeers in 1874, a company in 1880, and Board for Protection of Mining Interests in 1881, directors from four mines form detective department to stop smuggling by workers)... Britain's Criminal Law Amendment Act makes picketing illegal... General Miribel forms French Army General Staff, modeled on Prussian organization... Protestant, non-denominational unions form in Holland... William I, King of Prussia, is Emperor of Germany (makes Prince Otto von Bismarck Chancellor to 1890)... Paris is ruled by Commune for two months (decrees all industrial enterprises be worker cooperatives)... England, Wales start bank holidays (follows custom of banks closing one day to exchange checks)... Germany's population is some 41 million, France with 36 million, Japan with 33, Britain with 26 and Italy with 26.8... W.S. Jevons: The Theory of Political Economy (covers labor and fatigue, cooperation of labor and management in industrial partnerships, work-study, profit-sharing)... F. Wenham, developed device in 1870, and Browning conduct first wind-tunnel experiments... Japan begins to dissolve fiefs, remove daimyos from governance, and disband private armies of daimyos... Spanish Socialist Party forms, Italian party in 1890s... British telegraph engineers form professional society, is Institution of Electrical Engineers in 1889... First daily paper, universal education and postal service appear in Japan... Cigarmakers' Union and International Workmens' Assn., a branch of Socialist International, form in Denmark... Henry Fawcett: Pauperism, Its Causes and Remedies (urges profit-sharing as solution for inefficiencies)... Technical school appears in Japan, becomes engineering department of Imperial University... Leaders of Meiji government tour Europe, U.S. to study possible applications of business practices for Japan... Some 50% of Germany's labor force is in forestry and agriculture, under 35% in 1900.

Business Events

Regional association of German textile, iron enterprises forms to lobby for free trade, a national body in 1873... Britain's Albion Lamp Co. starts pioneering oil stove business... Cunard White Star line launches S.S. Oceanic, first of large modern luxury liners... German industrialist August Thyssen, specializes in operating small enterprises and mines, starts Thyssen A.G. as puddling and rolling mill on Ruhr (builds business as Europe's largest)... Liamin is first merchant mayor of Moscow... Maggs family starts milk processing plant, Britain (after absorbing competitors becomes United Dairies in 1915)... After working as grain merchant, insurance broker and silk maker, German-born Christian A.H. Allhusen starts Newcastle Chemical Works to make alkaline with new Solvay process... German-born Alfred Beit goes to Amsterdam to learn diamond trade (becomes clerk at Kimberley branch of Hamburg merchant house, forms diamond partnership with Paris' Jules Porges et Cie in 1880, buys claims in 1886 after discovery of gold in Transvaal's Witwatersrand, joins Wernher in 1889 - largest mining group in South Africa in 1890s, supports Rhodes' British South Africa Co. with funds in 1889, joins Rhodes and Leander Jameson to overthrow Boer Republic in 1895)... After working for diamond merchant Porges, German-born Julius C. Wernher goes to South Africa to trade in rough stones, aids Porges in 1876 to form Griqualand Diamond Mining to buy claims - first in area to go public in 1880, returns to Paris in 1880 - replaced by Beit, when Porges retires reforms business in London in 1889 as Wernher, Beit & Co. to develop group system of mining in Transvaal, with German and French investors forms African Ventures Syndicate in 1903, floats Central Mining & Investment Corp. in 1905).

1872

General Events

Some 32,000 friendly societies, some 4 million members, exist in England... England, France sign commercial treaty... Japan National Railroad forms (is forced into bankruptcy by political pork-barreling and union featherbedding in 1980s, privatized 1987)... National Union of Agricultural Workers forms, England... England's Adulteration Act makes manufacturers list ingredients of products... Persia grants concession for economic development to Britain's Reuter (cancels grant, awards new concession to Imperial Bank of Persia with right to exploit mineral resources in 1889)... Lodygin devises crude incandescent lamp in Russia, developed in 1880 by England's Joseph Swan... Robert Angus notes coal burning in Britain causes acid precipitation (leads to report in early 1900s by English scientist C. Crowther, H.G. Rustin that "acid rain" kills or reduces yields of farms)... Copenhagen bricklayers strike for shorter working hours... Yap islanders use stone money, introduced by U.S. adventurer David O'Keefe... French physiologist Etienne Marey devises chromatographe to produce succession of images on band of film... Dutch Catholics form first union... England, Scotland play first international soccer match... Japan's Banking Act establishes national banks, modeled on U.S. system... German engineer Paul Haelein tests internal-combustion engine to power dirigibles (fails as engine is too heavy, feeble for practical use)... Parliament requires mine managers to be certified for competency.

Business Events

Contractors form London Master Builders' Assn... Armstrong forms Iron Trades Employers' Assn. to fight unionism (fails to form permanent group with absence of marine firms)... Shiseido, Japan's No. 1 cosmetic maker by 1980s with 25,000-store distribution network, forms (in 1985 diversifies into paper diapers, liquid detergents, pricey boutiques, restaurants, trendy cafes to swank salons, health foods, health clubs and personal care products, 1986 sales of $2.4 billion)... England's National Federation of Associated Employers forms (opposes unionism of woolcombers, spinners and weavers)... London Stock Exchange installs ticker-tape machine (lists over 2,000 brokers in 1878 - 5,567 in 1905, bans advertising of members in 1885, prohibits members acting as both jobbers and brokers in 1908, sets minimum commission for brokers in 1912, admits first women members in 1973)... Banks form first Japanese joint-stock companies, 10 large-scale joint-stock enterprises by 1884... First Japanese railroad opens between Tokyo, Yokohama, nationalized in 1906... I.M. Singer sewing machine business opens sales office in France, "first" U.S. direct investment in country... Japan's first private mechanical cotton-spinning mill is started, first agricultural school is founded and first fair to promote exports is held in Kyoto...

William H. Lever joins father's wholesale grocery business (leaves in 1885 to start works to make Sunlight Soap - packaged, branded, and promoted, forms Lever Bros. as limited company in 1890, goes public in 1894 - England's largest holding company by 1920, starts horizontal integration in 1899, starts plantations in Solomon Islands in 1902 and Belgian Congo in 1911, fails combine soap makers in 1906, starts Nigerian merchant business in 1910, enters margarine market in 1914, courts disaster in 1920 in trying to buy Niger Co., greatest rival in West Africa, is transformed from ill-organized collection of firms to modern industrial organization by former accountant Francis D'Arcy Cooper in 1925, joins rival Margarine Union, combine of Jurgens and Van den Burgh, in 1927 to form Unilever, plans new organizational structure for 49 manufacturing firms and 48 separate sales organizations in 1931)... Giovanni Pirelli, after noting use of French rubber in 1860s, starts Milan business to make rubber products (makes insulated cables for growing telegraph industry in 1879, bicycle tires in 1890 and automobile tires in 1899, starts Spanish tire plant in 1902, forms cable partnership with Britain's GE in 1914, forms international corporation in Switzerland in 1937 to consolidate all non-Italian operations, starts production in Turkey, Greece in 1962, joins British tiremaker, Dunlop, through stock swap in 1971 - part 1981 after bickering on accounting methods, buys U.S.' Armstrong Tire in 1988 after losing Firestone to Bridgestone).

1873

General Events

Economic crisis sweeps Europe with fall in wheat prices (leads to gradual abandonment of free trade)... Cambridge offers university extension courses... France's Amedee Bollee builds steam car... With flood of cheap agricultural imports from Continent, "Great Depression" evolves in Britain (-1896, slows technological innovation)... Britain smuggles some 2,000 rubber seeds out of Brazil for $25, planting fails (smuggles 70,000 seeds in 1876, success in Malaya)... Vienna's international trade exposition gives first demonstration in use of electricity to drive machinery (features Russian Mountain roller-coaster, based on ice slides used in Russia during 1500s)... Zanzibar abolishes slave markets... Germany adopts mark as monetary unit, replaces 9 different currencies... Britain's Maj. W.C. Wingfield develops modern game of lawn tennis... Canada's Royal Montreal Golf Club is first in North America, U.S.' "first" at Foxburg, PA, in 1887... South Russian Union of Workers forms in Odessa (follows earlier educational associations, friendly societies of skilled workers in 1860s-1870s)... First Australian Factory Act protects children, women... Color photographs are first developed... Economic depression appears in Germany (-1874), triggered by collapse of Vienna stock exchange... French pharmacist Limousin devises the tablet, first prepared in England in 1843, although most medications appear in powders, pastes or lozenges... Herbert Spencer: The Study of Sociology (applies Social Darwinism to natural selection of entrepreneurs).

Business Events

National Federation of Employers forms, Britain... J. & W. Horlick forms, Britain (patents powdered food for infants, dyspeptics and invalids in 1874, patents malted milk in 1883, incorporates in Wisconsin in 1885, is acquired by Beecham Group in 1969)... With English rights to Belgium's Solvay process to make soda, John Brunner and Ludwig Mond start chemical business... Family fruit orchard business of Chivers & Sons prepares first jam (adopts employee profit- sharing in 1891, diversifies with jellies, custard powders and canned food in 1900 - 1,000 employees in 1902, uses research and development in 1902-29 to find new products)... Tuborg Breweries forms in Copenhagen (acquires King's Brewhouse, Denmark's first in 1400s, in 1890s to form United Breweries, provides workers with health insurance, old age fund, retirement programs, interest-free loans, vacations, travel grants, day nursery, kindergarten, social activities, Christmas gifts, funeral aid, and awards for seniority, forms Tuborg Foundation in 1931 to fund public projects)... As first non-military modern enterprise in China, China Merchants' Steam Navigation Co. is formed, first steamship company owned, operated by Chinese (is funded by compradors, merchant-middlemen from 1842 as go-betweens for foreigners and China, who also invest in China's first modern large-scale mining enterprise, Kaiping Mines, in 1878, railway in 1879, Tientsin telegraph in 1880, machinery manufacturing firm in 1883, and Shanghai Cotton Cloth Mill in 1890)... Villa d'Este, historic palace on Lake Como, is regal hotel... Dai-Ichi Kokuritsu (First National) Bank, founder Eiichi Shibusawa issues stock to avoid family-controlled zaibatsu, is first formed under Japan's National Bank Act of 1872 (issues currency until Bank of Japan takes over in 1883, after acquisitions from 1912-1964 merges with Nippon Kangyo Bank, founded by Japan in 1897 to finance farmers and industry and become commercial bank in 1950, in 1971 to create Japan's largest bank, Dai-Ichi Kangyo)... Rio Tinto forms as Spanish mining concern (sells, 1954, most of Spanish holdings for properties in Australia, southern Africa and Canada)

1874

General Events

Britain, Europe are linked by telegraph... Britain's Factory Act sets 56.5 hours for work week... France institutes factory inspection (bans women working underground, child labor)... First trade unionist is elected to Parliament... England's Edward Butler gets motorcycle patent, followed in 1885 by Maybach and Daimler, in 1889 by Felix Millet of France, and in 1894 by first mass-produced cycles of Germany's Hilderbrand, Wolfmuller... Institute of Journalists, Britain's oldest professional journalistic society, forms in London... Forced lubrication for machines appears in Britain... Denmark suppresses International Workingmens' Assn., replaced by Central Trade Union (dissolves 1879)... Women's Protective and Provident League forms, Britain... Germany's Wilhem Wundt starts world's first psychology laboratory in this time... Holland regulates child labor... International Postal Congress meets in Switzerland, one of land's first international meetings... Japan's Ministry of Finance creates 4-year school in finance, bookkeeping... Count von Zeppelin designs dirigible as big as ocean liner, lacks only suitable power plant... Eiichu Shibusawa, government administrator (Ministry of Finance), entrepreneur (helps start several hundred new firms) and organizer (Tokyo Chamber of Commerce, Bankers' Ass'n.), co-founds Japan's first business school.

Business Events

One of first newspapers owned by Chinese appears in Shanghai... Lewis Tomalin opens Jaeger clothing store, London (is successful with "Dr. Jaeger's Sanitary Woolen System")... Jesse Boot turns father's small herbalist shop, Nottingham, into proprietary medicine business (advertises patent medicines at cut rates in 1877 - starts branches, starts first factory in 1877, operates 126 shops in 1897 - 251 in 1901 and 560 in 1914, in 1901 buys Day's 65 shops and two warehouses in London and starts national advertising for Boots Cash Chemists, opens prestigious department store in Nottingham in 1903, losing faith in business sells to U.S.' Rexall Drug Store chain in 1920)... After working at uncle's butcher shop John L. Johnston wins contract to supply French forts with food (invents 'Johnston's Fluid Beef' as blended meat extract, Bovril brand name in 1887, sells Bovril to Spiers & Pont, restaurant owners, hoteliers and caterers, in 1887, sells out to venture capitalist E.T. Houley in 1896, enters health food market in 1899 with malt tonic, starts branches in Argentina in 1908 and Australia in 1909, buys 'Marmite' yeast extract and 'Ambrosia' baby food in 1920, introduces creamed rice in 1936)... Barnato Bros. forms in South Africa to deal in diamonds (opens London office in 1880).

1875

General Events

Britain's Trades Union Act grants unions legal status, right to strike, and protection of union funds, revised 1906... Universal Postal Union forms (July 1)... Turkey declares bankruptcy... Deutsche Reichsbank opens in Berlin to control circulation of bank-notes (replaces provincial coins as legal standard with mark in 1878)... Bedford Park is London's first garden suburb (-1881)... International Metric Convention meets... In this time Swiss are first to perfect process to make milk chocolate for candy... Japan's Ministry of Education opens U.S.-type business school (sponsors commercial college by 1883)... London finishes building main sewer system... Parliament passes Public Health Act... Britain buys some 176,000 shares, 42%, of Suez Canal stock from Khedive of Egypt to start role in area, nationalized by Egypt in 1956... Vienna's Siegfried Narcus "develops" benzyne-powered vehicle... J.L. Stoddard gives series of travel lectures, first travel lectures by Burton Holmes in 1892... Parliament's Conspiracy and Protection of Property Act allows peaceful picketing.

Business Events

British carriers in Calcutta form trade association to pool interests... First roller-skating rink opens in London... France's Minier chocolate factory is lit by electricity... After apprenticeship with draper and working in Farmer & Rogers' Great Shawl & Cloak Emporium's Oriental department, Arthur L. Liberty, when denied partnership, opens East India House to sell Oriental silks (adds space in 1883 for Arab tea room, decorating studio, furniture and cabinet factory, and Oriental antiques, opens costume department in 1884, opens Maison Liberty with couture salons and workrooms in 1889, goes public in 1894, evolves as Liberty chain-store business)... Rank family business starts in renting Hull windmill to process flour (builds roller mill in 1885 to increase capacity, incorporates in 1889 to build new mills, opens London headquarters and mill in 1904 - next mill in 1913, in 1930 buys Ireland's Goodbody mills to become Britain's leading wheat dealer and produce 30% of nation's flour, combines seven firms as London Flour Millers in 1932, goes public in 1933)... Grand Hotel Le Richemonde opens in Geneva... So-called Edison of Japan, land's first telegraph manufacturer, is formed (begins making electrical equipment and hydro-electric generators in 1890s, joins Japan's 1st incandescent lamp maker, founded 1890 and renamed Tokyo Electric in 1899 to make land's first radios in 1924, to create Toshiba in 1939, makes Japan's first fluorescent lamps in 1940, first radar in 1942, first broadcasting equipment in 1952 and first digital computer in 1954, makes black-and-white TV sets in 1949, is rejuvenated with new president in 1980, is world's first to make powerful 1-megabyte DRAM chip, starts joint ventures with Seimens, 1985, and Motorola, 1986, introduces popular laptop computer in 1986 before 1987 scandal with U.S. on selling secret submarine technology to U.S.S.R. - chairman, president resign in shame).

1876

General Events

British law sets Plimsoll Line, maximum loading limit for ships... Japan's Technical Art School opens with Western craftsmen as teachers... Cayley designs helicopter, never built (leads to Italian Enrico Forlanini's helicopter in 1877, built and tested, and French mechanic Paul Cornu's machine in 1907)... British build China's first railroad near Shanghai, first all-Chinese line in 1909... Britain passes Industrial and Provident Societies Act... Germany forms Bundespost as state monopoly, Europe's largest in telecommunications in 1987 with sales of $30 billion and bureaucracy of 550,000 (plans deregulation in 1988)... Germany's Karl von Linde devises first ammonia compressor for refrigeration, first patent, 1872, to U.S.' David Boyle... Richard Wagner begins Bayreuth Festival in Bavaria to showcase German music, followed by yearly Salzburg summer concerts of Vienna Philharmonic in 1877-1910 and Salzburg Festival in 1920... First French national conference of labor unions meets... Local government starts brewery in Sapporo, Japan, to provide market for area's barley (follows Japan's first brewery in 1870)... Korea becomes independent nation... Col. von Verdy de Vernis designs new war game with umpire... German engineer Dr. Nikolaus Otto designs first practical four-stroke-cycle gasoline engine, stationary (follows previous engines of Lenoir and Alphonse Beau de Rochas, is followed in 1880s by lightweight, high-speed engine of Daimler)... Alphonse Penaud patents design for full-size airplane... Belgium's King Leopold II forms International Assn. for the Exploration and Civilization of Africa (-1908 when ousted from Congo, acquires some 900,000 square miles by 1880s).

Business Events

After returning from Philadelphia Centennial Exposition, E. Faure-Perret reports to Swiss manufacturers that U.S. plants are getting higher productivity, lower prices with large-scale production using interchangeable parts, demonstrated by Waltham at 1878 Paris exposition... International Railway of Ontario & Maritime Provinces forms... Central Assn. of German Industrialists is first stable organization to represent big business (-1919, joins large landowners to demand state protection, high tariffs to block cheap British imports and grain from U.S., India), follows first group in 1820s and temporary confederation in 1850s... After working in small chemical works, Germany's Fritz Henkel starts family business, worth $2.7 billion by 1990, making bleaching powder with three workers, some 80 by 1900s (introduces Persil washing soap in 1907 - successful with extensive advertising, diversifies in 1920s, acquires business with pioneering synthetic detergent in 1935, retains lead in German market after 1950s battle with Unilever, Procter & Gamble and Colgate-Palmolive, starts foreign operations in 1970 with buy of French detergent maker, evolves by 1970s as world's 4th-largest in washing, cleaning products...

Royal Aquarium opens, London, for public entertainment... Nagelmackers forms Cie Internationale des Wagon-Lits to provide European railway transportation for passengers (starts Orient Express from London to Istanbul via Paris in 1887 - closed 1977, acquires Thomas Cook & Son travel agency in 1927-28 and 1882 British Pullman for transportation from London to Cairo)... John Jackson, age 25, starts business as engineering contractor, one of Britain's largest by late 1890s... Edwin Foden, shoemaker's son, acquires control of Platt & Hancock agricultural engineering firm to build traction engines, mechanical threshers (builds new engine in 1887 with low fuel consumption, introduces 6-ton steam-powered truck, introduces motor-lorry in 1931, drops steam vehicles for diesel trucks in 1935 - builds 1,750 in 1940-44)...

George Singer starts making bicycles in Midland, adds cars 1904-05 (introduces Singer Ten light car in 1912 - makes 1,350/year in 1913, acquires two Coventry car works in 1920 and 1922, adds Sparkbrook Mfg. in 1925 and factory in 1926 to make 9,000/year, acquires Aster Engineering Works in 1928, builds 28,000 cars, 15% of nation's output, in 1929 with 8,000 employees, industry's 3rd largest, reorganizes in 1937, joins Rootes Group in 1955)... Samuel Vestey, Yorkshire provisions merchant, sends son to U.S. to buy exports for Liverpool, successful with corned beef from waste not wanted by Chicago packers (opens first cold store for meats in Liverpool in 1890 - Union Cold Storage evolves as one of world's largest, expands by trading with Russia, China and establishing refrigeration facilities for perishable foods, buys two tramp steamers to start Blue Star Line in 1909 - 5 more ships by 1912 to become one of world's largest refrigerated fleets by 1925, adds Argentine operation in 1915, operates 2,365 retail butcher shops in 1925, evolves as world's largest meat retailer by 1987 with 250 companies in 25 countries, family worth some $2.3 billion by 1990)... Sanderson Bros is first Sheffield steelmaker to invest in U.S. manufacturing, others in 1896, 1901, 1910 and 1919)... Bass, Britain's leading brewer in 1990s, is first firm, founded by family in 1777, to gain trademark protection under 1875 trademark law.

1877

General Events

Queen Victoria is Empress of India, independence in 1947... <u>S.S. Paraguay</u> carries first Argentinean frozen meat to France, successful in 1878... Belgium adopts compulsory education for children aged 6-9... Switzerland adopts factory inspections... With rubber seeds smuggled from Brazil, Kew Gardens supplies seedlings for planting in Ceylon... Bell & Coalman get British patent for refrigeration, success with 1880 Melbourne-London shipment to establish British monopoly of marine meat refrigeration for 14 years... The All England Croquet Club, formed 1868, holds first Wimbledon tennis championship (pays professionals first legal prizes in 1968, signs first merchandizing contract in 1978 to give Japanese textile firm right to use "Flying W" trademark, $12 million in profits by 1987)... Joseph Monier patents reinforced concrete beams... Britain annexes South African Republic... Germany passes Patent Protection Law... Swiss Louis Rochet founds Blue Cross to fight alcoholism... Raynauld devises "Praxinoscope" to view moving images... Imperial University of Tokyo is founded... British Board of Trade approves use of steel to build bridges... France's Charles Cros proposes theory to record sound vibrations, fails to raise money for model machine called phonograph... Moscow's first permanent circus opens... Swedish engineer Gustav de Laval invents mechanized cream separator that greatly lowers production costs, basis for rise of Danish butter industry (starts firm in 1883).

Business Events

With winnings from Newmarket races printer James Smith opens Bon Marche, London's first designed department store... New Glenfiddich distillery produces Scotch whisky... Edward Wood heads Freeman, Hardy & Willis, maker of shoes and boots (operates 40 retail outlets in 1881 - 132 in 1891, 310 in 1900, 450 in 1910, 482 in 1916 and 820 in 1926)... Mitsui Trading Co. contracts to provision Japanese Army in defeating Satsuma Rebellion of samurai (after becoming bank for new Meiji government, grows with ventures in paper, textiles and machinery, evolves by 1985 as empire of $70.1 billion, Japan's largest Soga Shosha, with interests in energy, 25%, machinery, 16%, foods, 15%, iron/steel, 14%, chemicals, 11%, and non-ferrous metals, 10%)... George Andre opens shop in Nyon, France, to sell flour, dried vegetables, Italian pasta (evolves by 1990 as $1.0 billion Swiss business in food processing, commodity trading, aviation, shipping, cattle ranches, hardware worldwide)... James S. Tata, founder of India's largest enterprise, starts pension system (adopts college scholarship program in 1892).

1878

General Events

Economist W.S. Jevons presents paper to British Assn. for the Advancement of Science, postulates ups and downs in economy are caused by sunspot cycles... Air compressor is invented, Britain... Germany outlaws (October 18) socialists... Germany adopts factory inspection... D. Hughes invents repeating rifle... Britain's Factory and Workshop Act regulates hours, conditions of employment... German engineer Karl Benz builds motorized tricycle, tested at 7 mph... Electric street lighting appears in London... David Hughes invents microphone... Mannlicher makes repeating rifle... The Great Twelve and Seventy-Two Minor Livery Companies, societies of trade guilds from 1200s, form Corporation of The City of London... National Union of Russian Workers forms in St. Petersburg... German scientists, Emil and Otto Fischer, determine chemical composition of aniline dyes, leads to development of nation's chemical industry... Prussia nationalizes all railways, all other German states by 1900s... Social Democratic Assn. forms, Denmark, to promote socialism... Marey studies work and fatigue, Mosso in 1888... Swiss professor of economics Victor Boehmert studies participation of workers in profit-sharing plans, shows 81 firms using such schemes... Sweden's Baron Nils Nordenskjold makes first complete voyage of 6,400 miles of Northeast Passage (-1879)... Adolf Stoecker forms Christian-Social Workers' Party, Germany... Actor Henry Irving manages London's Lyceum Theatre.

Business Events

Allen and Hamburg start pioneering British pharmaceutical business... Arthur W. Gamage, former drapers' apprentice, and partner open London shop to sell hosiery (grows by buying in quantities to undercut prices of rivals as 'Peoples' Popular Emporium' with departments of haberdashery, furniture, gardening, sports and camping equipment, clothing, toys and motoring needs, acquires sports club in 1907 to promote sports and camping gear, prints 900-page mail-order catalog in 1911, employs over 2,000 employees 1930, closes 1972)... First National Bank is Japan's first to go abroad with office in Korea... John K. Starley, after working in uncle's business, starts firm to make bicycles, financed by owner of Coventry haberdashery (produces Rover, first practical safety bicycle, in 1885, makes electric car in 1888, goes public in 1896, shows self-propelled bath-chair at 1899 Royal Automobile Show, with collapse of bicycle market in late 1890s enters car market in 1904, drops bicycle line in 1912)...

Julius C. Drew, after working in tea importing business, opens Liverpool tea shop (forms Home and Colonial Trading Assn. with John Musker, opens 1st London store in 1885, runs 4 stores and 9 tea shops in 1888 - 107 outlets in 1890 and over 500 by 1906, is sold in 1919 to Jurgen's margarine business)... George A. Touche joins accounting firm of Alexander C. Niven as apprentice (is secretary of newly-formed Industrial & General Trust in 1899 - director 1898 and chairman 1908, forms London accounting firm in 1899, after Birmingham office opens offices in Toronto in 1909, Montreal and Vancouver in 1911, Winnipeg and Chicago in 1913, Cleveland in 1919, and Paris in 1929 to evolve as Touche Ross International)... After working for London publisher since 1876 reading manuscripts and handling advertising, Alexander T. Watt starts informal literary agency, formal 1885 (is only reputable literary agent until late 1880s, sees J.B. Pinker as first major competitor in 1896)... Marcus Samuel, son of trader in Oriental shells, and brother form Marcus Samuel & Co. in London and Samuel Samuel & Co. in Japan (after first syndicate in 1885, join French Rothschilds in 1890-92 venture to export Russian oil in bulk, Standard uses cans, with oil tankers, fleet ready 1892, via Suez Canal, after striking oil in Borneo form Shell Transport & Trading Co. in 1897 for Asian markets)... After being forced to give funds to government in 1860s to quell rebellion, Sumitomo is allowed to continue by new Meiji state of 1868 (mortgages assets to revive Besshi mine with French technology, starts bank in 1897 with subsidiaries in copper wire, electricity and metals, chemicals in 1913 and life insurance in 1925, manages NEC in 1932 until dissolution by Occupation in 1946, reforms as Sumitomo Group in 1950)... Tokyo Stock Exchange forms, patterned on those of U.S. (reforms 1949, is 2nd largest market by 1980s)... Canada starts fur farming... Missionary, commercial interests form African Lakes Trading Co. at Lake Nyasa... London Trading Bank opens to handle funds of building societies.

<h1 style="text-align:center">1879</h1>

General Events

Chile, world's No. 1 copper producer, fights nitrate war with Bolivia, Peru (-1882, acquires lands of Bolivia, Peru to supply 73% of world market in 1894)... German businessman Gustav von Meuissen forms foundation to finance school of business administration (opens Cologne Handelschochscule in 1901)... Germany passes protectionist laws... First tanker to transport petroleum appears on Caspian Sea... First collegiate hockey game is played by two teams, most students at Montreal's McGill University (leads to formation of Amateur Hockey Assn. of Canada in 1887, first professional International Hockey League in Northern Michigan in 1904)... Oslo, Norway, holds first large skiing contest... British churchman W.L. Blackley proposes plan for old-age pensions... Fahlberg, Remser discover saccharin... London's first telephone exchange is built... French Workers' Party forms... Scottish professor James Clerk Maxwell proves existence of radio waves... Francis Galton's paper covers psychology of individual differences, pioneers psychological tests... Finland's Trades Act makes striking workers pay for damages (fines workers who stop working contrary to law, contracts)... Linde starts research on industrial refrigeration, requested by Germany's Brewers' Union... German tariff protects farmers against U.S. imports... Australia legislation protects workers, shortens hours, provides insurance... First Australian trade-union congress meets... E. Richter is first to use word cartel (describes business combination in opposing agreement by German iron producers to maintain high prices, follows growth of such groups in 1870s from economic slump, protective tariffs)... Gilchrist Thomas, police-court clerk, devises new method to make steel with low-grade iron ore (shows value of metallurgical theory to resolve industrial problem).

Business Events

Siemens and Halske demonstrates first locomotive powered by electricity at Berlin trade fair (is tested by Edison in 1880, is used by electric tramway in 1884)... Ferdinand de Lesseps forms French Panama Canal Co. (-1889 when ruined by corruption and mismanagement, is acquired by U.S. 1894-04)... British Chamber of Commerce opens office in Paris... London Institute of Bankers forms... British United Africa Co. forms to trade with West Africa... Hermes opens fine saddle shop, Paris (adds other fancy leather products to compete in automotive age, evolves to operate over 200 elegant stores worldwide by 1980s)... Hong Kong trading business of Jardin, Matheson & Co. challenges John Swire's dominance of steamer trade on Yangtze River (retaliates by slashing rates and starting sugar refinery on Hong Kong to attack Jardin's sugar business)... Hungarian-born David Gestetner, after selling copying process in U.S. and London, patents improved process (licenses patents to Fairholme & Co. in 1881, forms Automatic Cyclostyle business in 1893 to make duplicating machines - first rotary in 1902 and electric in 1908, opens NYC office in 1893 - legal problems, starts sales branches in 1919)... Tokio Marine and Fire, Japan's largest non-life insurance firm in 1991, is formed to insure cargo, offices in London, Paris and NYC in 1880 (underwrites first fire insurance in 1914).

1880s

General Events

Game of bingo, based on Italian game of tumvula, appears... Rubber production grows in Brazil's Amazon Basin, declines after 1910 with competition from East Indies... Ministry of Finance promotes development of Russia (starts with railroads, mostly developed by Jews and naturalized Germans, and heavy industry operated by steam, electric power)... Immigrants from China, Japan, Korea and Portugal go to Hawaii to work in new sugar industry... Some 90% of Japan's foreign trade is controlled by British, U.S. interests (drops to 80% by 1890, 60% by 1900)... Berlin hosts 56 breweries, 300 machine shops and iron foundries with 20,000 workers, garment industry employs some 60,000.

Business Events

Harold Bowden develops Nottingham's small Woodhed Angois & Ellis as leading maker of bicycles (employs 2,000 by 1918 as Raleigh Cycle Co.).

1880

General Events

Britain adopts one uniform time to replace local times... France's G. Bouchardat makes first synthetic rubber, follows 1860 research of England's Greville Williams (is used in patents for industrial production by Britain, Germany in 1910)... Society for the Regulation of Street Music and Street Musicians forms in London... British inventor devises a thermostat... Institute of Chartered Accountants in England and Wales gets Royal Charter, insolvency primary business of accountants... Swiss suggest international legislation to protect workers... England's first Employers' Liability Act grants workers compensation for injuries not their fault... Parliament sends committee to U.S. to determine why range-fed cattle threaten English market (spurs investments of English, Scottish investors in U.S. cattle ranching corporations)... Japan sells governmental enterprises to certain wealthy families, spurs development of Zaibatsu organizations... Europe's relative share of world's manufacturing output is 6.13%, Britain with 22.9%, Hapsburg Empire with 4.4%, France with 7.8%, Germany with 8.5%, Italy 2.5%, Russia 7.6%, U.S. 14.7%, Japan 2.4%, China 12.5%, and India with 2.8%... Herman Miller invents tin can, made for 50% the labor cost of those made in U.S... Britain introduces parcel post service... Some 100,000 men work 25,000 barges on 4,800 miles of British canals, navigable rivers (after slipping into pastoral obscurity are revived by pleasure boating in 1960s)... Canada forms Bell Canada, land's largest phone system in 1991 (starts acquiring small telephone firms in 1954, buys Northern Electrical, small equipment maker, in 1957 from AT&T's Western Electric, invests in satellite joint venture, Telesat, in 1970, Northern Research for R&D in 1971 and directory publishing in 1971, forms international unit in 1976, creates Bell Canada Enterprises, Montreal, as umbrella to separate unregulated, natural gas in 1983, and real estate in 1985, and regulated activities, buys UK's STC, world's 12th largest in telecommunications equipment, in 1990).

Business Events

Birmingham Small Arms, BSA, makes rifles, bicycles and motorcycles (-1914)... Rhodes, Beit form De Beers Mining Co., South Africa (acquires control by 1890 of some 95% of world's diamond production)... Paralyzed Margarete Steiff uses pieces of felt left over from her dressmaking to make small stuffed elephant pincushions in Giengen, Germany (becomes success with annual output of 5,000 stuffed animals, sells stuffed bears to U.S. buyer at 1903 Leipzig trade fair - one decorates White House room in 1906, sells some one million "teddy bears" in 1907)... First oil gusher of Baku field near Caspian Sea is drilled, developed by Sweden's Nobel Bros. Petroleum Co. in 1883 and Caspian & Black Sea Co. of Baron Alphonse de Rothschild in 1884...

Barney Barnato starts Baranato Diamond Mining Co., South Africa (merges with De Beers in 1888)... Yasuda, Japan's 5th largest issuer of life insurance in 1989, appears... Iraq's Kadoorie family moves to Hong Kong (begins business by developing land, evolves as $1.5 billion empire by 1987 with 25% of China Light & Power, 30% of Hongkong & Shanghai Hotels and share of Schroeder Wagg Bank)... Mechanic Henry Curry manages Leicester Tricycle Co. (starts business to make, sell bicycles in 1888, opens first retail store in 1904 - 7 by 1910 and 221 by 1939 to sell mainly bicycles and radios)...

Yokohama Specie Bank incorporates to finance trade, handle foreign exchange and provide financial information (becomes Japan's major foreign exchange bank with NYC office, site of 14 Japanese trading companies, in 1880, Bombay in 1894, Hawaii in 1899 and Los Angeles in 1913)... Oswald Stohl, age 14, helps mother run Liverpool's Parthenon Music Hall (after managing theatrical agency acquires Cardiff Music Hall in 1890 with mother - chain of 8 in 1890s, forms 'Moss' Empires in 1899 with other music hall operators to handle 13 theaters - employs 2,200 in 1904, builds variety theater, London Coliseum, in 1902-04 as club with restaurant, reading room, and lounges, gets double licenses from City to offer variety and drama - drops variety shows for regular productions in 1931, takes over Alhambra Theater and London Opera House, becomes Stohl Picture Theater, in 1916, forms Stohl Film Co. in 1918 to distribute films - one of two top distributors, starts Stohl Picture Productions, largest producer in 1920s, in 1920 - last production 1929 with financial troubles, forms Stohl Theaters Corp. in 1939)... After working for McKesson & Robbins, U.S.' largest drug house, Henry S. Wellcome forms Burroughs, Wellcome & Co., England, with exclusive rights for McKesson preparations outside U.S. (opens house in Australia in 1886, starts research activity in 1894 - others in 1896 and 1903, takes over business in 1895 - facilities in Capetown and Milan in 1905, Montreal and NYC 1906, Shanghai 1908, Buenos Aires 1910 and Bombay in 1912, consolidates nine firms, research laboratories and museum as The Wellcome Foundation in 1924)... By 1889 mechanical system, suspended from ceiling to carry cash from clerks to central cashier, appears in British stores... Evans, most famous of England's song and supper rooms, closes due to popularity of music halls... Sixteen Canadian oil refiners form Imperial Oil Co., Canada's largest in 1991 is 69.7% owned by Exxon (grows coast-to-coast by mid-1890s, sells controlling interest in 1898 to Standard Oil to pay for expansion, discovers, 1920, oil in Northwest Territory and gas near Edmonton in 1924, gets Alberta gusher in 1947, builds longest crude oil pipeline in non-Communist world from Alberta to Wisconsin, finds crude on land near Bearfort Sea in 1970, buys Texaco Canada in 1989)... John Hutchison starts Hong Kong trading firm (in mid-1960s buys part, all in 1977, of Whampoa to become Hutchison Whampoa and buys control of A.S. Watson's drugstores, supermarkets and soft drinks to near bankruptcy in 1975, sells 103 firms in 1976 to recover from complex acquisitions, buys share of Hongkong Electric, 1985, Canada's Husky Oil, and U.K.'s Cluff Resources, gold and minerals, in 1987, and Australian paging firm and U.K. mobile phone service in 1989, sells trading unit in 1990, buys U.K.'s largest container port and U.K.'s Millicom, cellular phone system, in 1991).

1881

General Events

Berlin introduces first electric streetcar... Britain's Army, Navy abolish flogging... First permanent labor organization in Denmark, follows central labor union in 1874-79, is formed by skilled workers... Electrical power station is built in Milan, Italy... New Zealand passes Chinese Immigrants Act... Paris hosts International Exposition of Electricity, features Thomas A. Edison's electric light system.

Business Events

Richard D'Oyly Carte, producer of Gilbert and Sullivan works, builds Savoy Theater, lit by electricity, in London... Rudolphe Salis opens first cabaret, Chat Noir, in Paris... Canadian Pacific Railway, first proposed 1840s and chartered 1878, begins construction, reaches Pacific Coast in

1886... Some 90 manufacturing plants do business in Tokyo (shows some 537 workers in governmental machine shop, viewed as large-scale operation)... After acquiring land in 1873 when assuming 1865 concession of American Trading Co., British North Borneo Co. is formed to govern island, Royal Charter 1882... W. Siemens powers first electric generator with steam engine... Kinraro Hattori, son of secondhand-goods dealer, starts shop to sell, repair foreign-made timepieces in Tokyo, genesis for 1984 business of Seiko in timepieces, clocks and camera shutters, printers and computers, electronics, men's watches and semiconductors, computers and liquid crystal displays for sales of some $3 billion... Paris Chamber of Commerce sponsors Ecole des Hautes Etudes Commerciales... John E. Beale opens Bournemouth gift shop, Fancy Fair, for well-to-do tourists at seaside resort (by 1900 adds stationery, toys, books and leather goods)... After selling crude steam-powered submarine to Greece, Basil Zaharoff, agent for Anglo-Swedish Nordenfeldt, sells two to Turkey to counter Greek threat (becomes known as "Merchant of Death" for arms deals)...

After designing wallpaper and fabric, Rene Lalique designs jewelry in Paris (realizes success with Art Nouveau designs and elegant glasswork)... Dudley, Frank Docker start small business to make paint, varnish (build factory in 1887, merge five of Midland's leading carriage and wagon firms in 1902 to form Metropolitan Amalgamated Railway Carriage & Wagon - Frank, on board of BSA in 1906, masterminds acquisition of Daimler Motors in 1910)... Oki Electric, Japan's 10th largest by 1991 in electronics, is formed as Meikosha Co. to make, sell phones (add software line in 1970 and PCs in 1981, starts U.S. unit in 1984)... Two western frontier bankers join U.S.' James J. Hill to form Canadian Pacific Railway, 7th largest in North America in 1991 (with 25-million-acre land grant builds railroad, 1882-1885, to Pacific nearly 6 years ahead of schedule, charters ships in 1886 to carry tea, silk to West Coast - foundation for steamship line, hotel chain and telegraph services, faces competition in 1917 when Canada combines several railroads to form Canadian National System)... After talks with Thomas A. Edison, Siemens gets license to make incandescent bulbs (forms centralized organization in 1882, becomes joint-stock company, funds from Deutsche Bank, in 1897).

1882

General Events

International society for chefs de cuisine forms, Paris, to advance cooking (starts publication and professional schools, sponsors competitions)... Diamond Trading Act establishes regulations for South Africa market... Professor Jaigoro Kano develops sport of Judo from martial art of jujitsu... U.S.-born Hiram S. Maxim invents recoil-operated machine gun... London Chamber of Commerce forms... Berlin Philharmonic Orchestra is formed by musicians as cooperative venture... Hague Convention establishes 3-mile limit for territorial waters... First Russian Factory Act sets hours of work (-1886)... Oriental Socialists Party is first Japanese group to seek improvements in working conditions (focuses efforts on industries of textiles, munitions)... Europe's first school to train foremen opens in Germany... First dairy-farm cooperative in Denmark forms... Typographers form Norway's first national union, follows local unions and bargaining activities in 1870s... First attempt to build tunnel under English Channel is stopped for political reasons... Society of Musicians forms, London, to promote music and profession, incorporates 1892... Jules Marcy pioneers motion pictures with chronophotography.

Business Events

Bank of Japan is founded... After leaving Otto's Cologne factory, engineer Daimler (patents petrol-engine in 1889), designer Maybach (devises carburetor in 1893) start Stuttgart factory to build cars... Jewish trader Herman Tietz starts Hertie Waren-und Kaufhaus in Berlin (after surviving bank takeover in 1930s and near elimination during W.W. II, evolves as West Germany's 3rd largest department store business)... Shanghai Electricity Co. is founded... U.S. interests form British Pullman Palace Car Co., acquired 1906-07 by Davison A. Dalziel... When Japan subsidizes shipping firms to compete with Mitsubishi, Hokkaido Un'yo Kaisha forms (after ruinous competition, signs agreement on Government urging with Mitsubishi in 1885 to limit competition, becomes National Company, NYK, in 1885 with some government ownership)... Thomas P. Hewitt, after apprenticeship with father, starts watchmaking business (after visiting U.S. in 1888 returns with machine tools to reorganize production, employs some 1,000 workers in 1893 - still use traditional methods, after producing 60,000 watches/year by 1893 and 50,000 1893-1910, fails in 1910 because of inefficiencies, obsolete designs and 50 models)... Osaka Spinning, uses steam power, is formed in Japan as limited company, forerunner of area's 19 limited spinning firms 1887-89... John James Fenwick, after draper apprenticeship, working for silk mercers, and selling insurance part-time, opens shop to provide Parisian elegance in London's prestigious area as mantle maker, furrier (visits customers in homes, after one failure opens 2nd store in 1890 - basis for department store, opens London fashion store in 1891, follows Continental custom with Christmas promotion in 1902)... Moreau family confection business begins in Switzerland (still extant)... Samuel J. Moore, after meeting John R. Carter selling his innovative sales forms, forms firm to make patented business records, New York factory in 1883 and new British firm in 1886 - bought by Lamson Store Service in 1889 (buys printing firm in 1899, starts firm in 1909 to make boxes and forms, sells forms with enclosed carbon paper in 1925, consolidates as Moore Corp. in 1929, acquires Lamson in 1964-1977, starts joint venture with Japanese printer in 1964, supplies UPS in 1991 with portable terminals to track packages, replace forms).

1883

General Events

Britain's Francis Galton develops the questionnaire... English metallurgist Robert A. Hadfield patents manganese steel, first of special super hard alloy steels... Germany passes first health insurance law, financed by employers, employees, and state, unemployment insurance law in 1884 and old-age and invalidity insurance law in 1889 - France with social insurance in 1905 and Britain in 1908... Swan creates synthetic fiber... Central Committee of Trades Unions forms in Oslo... After trying to pay workers for loss of jobs from dissolution of the corporation, English judge rules against West Cork Railway: "Charity has no business sitting at the board of directors"... French aeronauts Gaston, Albert Tissandier test electrically-powered airship twice, fail for lack of power... Development of synthetic organic drugs begins with creation of antipyrine, followed by phenacetin in 1887 and aspirin in 1899... Daimler builds first high-speed internal combustion engine, first used in motorboat (builds automobile in 1886, starts Daimler Motor Co. in 1890)... Sydney-Melbourne railway opens.

Business Events

Swedish General Electric Co. forms (evolves by 1980 as international manufacturer of electrical equipment and household appliances, decentralized into 40 profit centers)... Bremen merchant Adolph Luderitz buys land, turned over to Germany in 1884, in Southwest Africa from native chief to start trading post... Paul Gauguin, prosperous French banker and market analyst for 11 years, quits business to paint... Magnus Volk starts electric tramway, Britain's first, at Brighton resort (is followed by London line in 1887-90)... Emil Rathenau, with rights for Edison's patents, forms Edison Corp. of Germany to compete with Siemens & Halske (becomes Allgemeine Elektrizitats-Gesellschaft, AEG, in 1887, evolves as land's largest electrical business)... Edwin Guthrie is first British accounting firm to open U.S. office... Shipping magnate George Nipper opens Grand Hotel, renamed Windsor later, in Melbourne (is acquired by Grand Coffee Palace Co. in 1886, is classified as historical landmark in 1973, is acquired by Federal Hotels in 1976 and Oberoi International Hotels, backed by Saudi Arabian financing, in 1979, after $5-7 million re-opens with elegance restored to outlast Australia's other grand hotels: Sidney's Metropole, Brisbane's Bellevue, and Perth's Esplanade)... ASEA, Sweden, is founded to make electric dynamos (after merger in 1890 buys rival in 1933 to become land's electrical equipment maker, controlled by Wallenberg family, enters U.S. market in 1947, buys 20% of Electrolux, electrical appliance maker, in 1962, forms joint venture with Owens-Corning Fiberglass in 1962, begins nuclear power venture with Sweden - full control 1982)... Tokyo Electric Lighting, land's first electric utility, is formed, first power plant 1887 (is nationalized in 1938, helps to form public system of 9 regional firms, each a service monopoly, in 1951 and listed on Tokyo exchange, is regulated by MITI in 1965, forms Energy Conservation Center in 1977, joins Toshiba, Texaco, GE and others to build coal gasification plant on Mojave Desert, CA, in 1982 to reduce dependence on foreign oil, builds coal-burning generator, first since oil crisis, in 1984, forms telecommunications network for industrial, public services in 1986 and cable TV in 1989)... CP blacksmith finds copper, nickel in Canada's Sudbury Basin (is developed with 1890 patent by Orford Nickel & Copper to process ore)... Sheep station boundary rider, Charles Rasp, discovers massive lode of silver, lead, zinc in Broken Hill area, New South Wales (leads to Broken Hill Proprietary Co. to mine ore - closed 1939, finds iron ore deposits in southern Australia in 1887).

1884

General Events

W.H. Walker invents roll film... After apprenticeship and learning production engineering at Armstrong's Elswick Works, Charles Parsons gets key patents for first practical steam turbine to generate electrical power, 300 produced by 1889 (starts manufacturing business in 1889 - Cunard's *Carmania* is first steamship with steam turbine for main propulsion in 1905, sells U.S. rights to George Westinghouse in 1896)... British elite form Jockey Club in Hong Kong (evolves with monopoly on colony's horse racing and gambling, picks first Chinese chairman in 1986)... Berlin Conference establishes rules for European powers to colonize Africa... Japanese citizens are allowed to migrate to Hawaii... Germany's production of dyes is four times that of Britain, exports 80%... Socialists League is formed, Britain... Russia abolishes poll tax, last of serfdom... Germany's Paul Nipkow patents scanning disc, used by John Baird in 1920s for photo-mechanical transmissions... Sidney and Beatrice Webb, George Bernard Shaw form Fabian Society, London (rejects Marxism and violent class struggle for social change with gradual, democratic means)... International Prime Meridian Conference selects Greenwich, England, as Prime Meridian for world (is superseded by Coordinated Universal Time in 1972 to maintain international time in Paris with 150 atomic clocks worldwide)... German colonizes mineral-rich Southwest Africa (-1915)... Gold is discovered in Transvaal (starts development of Johannesburg)... First deep underground railroad, London's "Tube," is built... Emile de Laveleye: <u>The Elements of Political Economy</u> (states employer's duty is to train employees, good business is government's responsibility, piecework is answer for low productivity)...

Charles Renard and Arthur Krebs, Army engineering officers, fly balloon, La France, in 5-mile flight with lightweight battery for power, first practical airship... French law legalizes professional societies, labor unions and trade associations (allows strikes)... Russian railway links iron ore of Krivoi Rog with coal in Donets Basin, only two iron mills in Southern Russia by 1887... First streetcars to use overhead trolley lines appear in Germany.

Business Events

Tranmontin & Sons, one of 15 left by 1900 and last of Venice's gondola makers in 1988, is founded (evolves by 1980s to make 25 boats/year, 440 boats left in Venice from some 5,000 in 1700s)... Augustus D. Klaber is U.S. agent for Gestetner's duplicating process (opens NYC office in 1893 to sell Gestetner equipment and supplies, acquires rights to sell rotary Neostyle copiers in 1899, starts London business to sell Roneo machines, markets only dry copier in 1900 - agencies later in Canada, Russia, India, U.S. and Japan, buys 40% of maker in steel office furniture)... Russian-born Michael Marks, travelling peddler, opens stall, self-service and self-selection, at Leeds Knicknach open market, Tuesdays and Thursdays, to sell all goods for a pence (runs 'Penny Bazaar' at Warrington in 1887, stalls at Birkenhead, 1890, Wigan, 1891, Bolton, 1892, and Manchester, 1894, with business too much for one forms equal partnership with Thomas Spencer, cashier, dies 1905, for a distributor in 1894, runs over 40 Penny Bazaars, most in covered market halls, by 1903, runs over 60 outlets, 30% in market halls and arcades, in 1907 with open displays, runs 140 branches, under 10% in market halls and arcades, in 1914)... German banker Adolf von Hansemann, others form New Guinea Co. to oversee islands in western Pacific.

1885

General Events

Karl Marx (post.): <u>Das Kapital</u>, Vol. II... Seamless steel tube is invented, Germany... Lenoir, inventor of electric ignition system in 1883, devises automobile spark plug... Russia creates Peasant Land Bank to buy land of gentry for resale to peasants... English fashion designer Redfern creates first lady's suit... England opens first public labor bureau... Gold is found in Transvaal, South Africa... Charles S. Tainter invents dictaphone... Karl Auer von Welsvach invents incandescent gas mantle... First Leipzig Fair is held, Germany... Czar Alexander III commissions St. Petersburg jeweler Carl Faberge to make Easter egg for Empress (continues custom for 31 years)... Germany annexes Tanganyika, Zanzibar... South Africa's Kimberley is linked to Capetown by railroad... Some 18.4% of Germany's population live in cities of 20,000 or more, 34.5% by 1910... Siam opens for British trade... Australia forms wage boards to set wages for industry... Unions of shoemakers, textile workers and joiners form in Denmark... Labor Party of Belgium is formed... Sovereignty for German New Guinea is transferred to New Guinea Co. (-1898)... Hamburg conference makes first international agreement on transatlantic shipping rates... St. Moritz Tobogganing Club forms in Switzerland, starts first organized winter sport in Alps for tourists (builds first sole bobsled run in 1903)... Hindu middle-class professionals form Indian National Congress (demand more employment of Indians in civil service).

Business Events

After forming Benz & Co. in 1883, Benz builds first operable automobile with internal combustion engine (patents auto in 1886, is world's No. 1 automaker in 1899, merges with Daimler, 1890, in 1926 to compete with Ford)... German East Africa Co. forms to carry out nation's treaties with tribes near Bagamoyo (cedes all rights to Germany in 1889)... U.S.' Parke-Davis pharmaceutical business appoints London agent, spurs development of British drug industry... German-born Siegfried Bettman starts Triumph Cycle Co., England, to make bicycles (makes first car in 1923, receivership 1939 and Triumph Motor 1945)... U.S.' George Eastman starts Eastman Co. in London, Eastman Photographic Materials in 1889 (starts factory in 1890 to make and develop film, incorporates as Kodak in 1898 to dominate British market - 1,400 employees in 1918 and 4,400 in 1938)... William Evans, after managing grocery store, opens own (starts baking bread in 1890 - three shops by 1895 to pioneer chain of small groceries in South Wales, with idea from U.S. quack doctor introduces 'Welsh Hill's' mineral water in 1903 - eight factories by end of W.W. I and 57 by 1934 in England, Wales)...

Candy maker George Cadbury builds Bournville Garden City near Birmingham for employees... Singer plant is built in Scotland, first significant U.S. investment overseas (produces 8,000 machines/week)... Assn. of Manufacturers forms as Denmark's first permanent association of employers... Daimler uses Otto gasoline engine to power a bicycle (operates 4-wheel petrol-powered wagonette in 1887, within 10 years sells engines to French automobile firm of Panhard & Levasseur - piano-maker, William Steinway, unsuccessful in selling engines in U.S.)... <u>Great Eastern</u> ocean liner, after bankrupting number of firms, ends career as floating Liverpool carnival with music hall, souvenir stalls... Yamaha, watchmaker and medical equipment repairman, tinkers with his first reed organ, completes building one in 1887 to launch Yamaha as world's No. 1 maker of musical instruments in 1954 (starts business in 1889 to make reed organs, builds upright pianos in 1900 and grand pianos in 1902, diversifies with wooden airplane propellers in 1920, makes pipe organs, 1932, guitars, 1946, motorcycles in 1954 - spun off 1955, motorboats and outboard motors, 1960, yachts, 1965, car engines, 1966, snowmobiles, 1968, golf carts, 1975, and all-terrain vehicles in 1979, introduces first electronic organ in 1959, adds wind instruments, 1965, stereos, 1968, and revolutionary portable keyboard synthesizer in 1983, expands with microchips in 1971 and mass production of integrated circuits in 1990s).

1886

General Events

Japan's first labor strike occurs at Kofu Amamiya paper mill... First true oil tanker is launched... France's P. Heroult, U.S.' Charles M. Hall independently discover practical method to make aluminum... Gold is discovered in Southern Transvaal, South Africa (is financed, organized by Consolidated Goldfield of Rhodes and associates, controls most of output by 1890 via some 450 companies)... English Lawn Tennis Assn. forms... French chemist Henri Moissan produces fluorine... Britain sees first Amateur Golf Championship... Tientsin School of Military Engineering is founded, China... Jules Verne: The Clipper of the Clouds (describes air vessel with air screws instead of sails)... Russia's labor law defines procedures and conditions for employment, abrogation of labor contract by owners, workers for non-payment of wages, beatings, severe insults, violations of working conditions, unsafe work... Scandinavian Labor Congress is formed by members from Sweden, Denmark and Norway... Railroad workers in Argentina form La Fraternidad.

Business Events

New cotton mills appear in Japan, 33 by 1894... Britain charters Royal Niger Co... Charles W. Wallace forms Shaw Wallace & Co. from moribund Calcutta Trading Co. (becomes India agent in 1891 for Burmah Oil, exporter of kerosene from Rangoon refineries, is board member of Burmah in 1902, with D'Arcy prospects for oil in Persia in 1905 - discovered 1908, forms Anglo-Persian Oil in 1909 - Burmah major owner)... Alfred C.W. Harmsworth, after leaving school for journalism career, is editor of Coventry paper (fails publishing booklets in 1887, issues Answers to Correspondents in 1888 with items from other publications, issues Comic Cuts for young readers in 1890 and Home Sweet Home in 1891, acquires first newspaper, London's ailing Evening News, in 1894, launches Daily Mail, first for mass market, in 1896, revives ailing Weekly Dispatch and launches Daily Mirror paper for women in 1903, acquires Sunday Observer in 1905 and Times in 1908, builds publishing empire by 1917 with world's largest circulation)... William Knox D'Arcy forms Mount Morgan Gold Mining (negotiates concession in 1901 with Persia to explore for petroleum, forms Concession Oil Syndicate in 1905 with Burmah Oil)... William Price buys small London retail dairy store (evolves as Great Western & Metropolitan Dairies, joins wholesalers in 1915 to form United Dairies, quasi monopoly over London wholesale, retail market by 1917)...

Hugo Hirst, Gustav Byng start electrical equipment wholesale firm, London (is General Electric, independent of U.S.' GE, in 1889, makes light bulbs in 1893 and electric motors in 1896, goes public in 1900, forms firm, 1910, to install telephone exchanges, begins TV work in 1935, buys profitable radio and TV business in 1963, acquires rival Associated Electrical Industries, 1967, in hostile takeover, merges with English Electric, owner of pioneering Marconi Co. in radio and electronics, in 1968, buys U.S.' A.B. Dick Co., office equipment, in 1979 and RCA's medical diagnostic equipment maker in 1981, fails in 1985 to acquire Britain's Plessey, defense and telecommunications, forms joint ventures with Plessey and Siemans in 1988 and GE, appliances and electrical products, in 1989, divides Plessey with Siemens in 1989, forms joint venture with France's Alcatel Alsthom, once CGE, in 1989 to combine their power generation, rail transportation and electrical distribution businesses, buys defense business of British electronics firm, Ferranti International, in 1990)... Sandoz Ltd. begins pharmaceutical, chemical business in Basel making synthetic dyes (to compete in world market with Germans, forms Swiss cartel, Basel AG, in 1918 with Ciba and Geigy, dissolves Basel AG in 1951, acquires dietetic products firm in 1967, buys U.S., Dutch firms in seeds in 1976, adds Sweden's WASA Group in 1982 and construction chemicals of Martin Marietta in 1985, contaminates Rhine to North Sea in 1986 after warehouse fire spills tons of chemicals into river)... Barbier family asks Andre Michelin to run its 1863 rubber business, renamed Michelin 1889 (devises detachable bicycle tire in 1891, creates Michelin Man trademark in 1898, opens London sales office in 1905, starts Italian plant in 1906, New Jersey in 1908, and invents spare tires, develops tubeless tires, 1930, and tire treads, 1934).

<h2 style="text-align:center">1887</h2>

General Events

Independent Labor Party forms in Britain... Arts & Crafts Exhibition Society begins British arts and crafts movement... France's G. Zede designs world's first practical seagoing submersible... Some 79 of Germany's largest firms do business as joint-stock companies, 77 in 1907, with 6 corporations, 16 by 1907... Germany's Heinrich Hertz demonstrates reflection property of radio waves (leads to Britain's Edward Appleton studying atmospheric ionization in 1924, genesis of radar)... Rene Panhard, Emile Levasseur get French patents for road carriages... When London's Trafalgar Square is closed to open meetings, troops are used to quell riot by workers, members of Democratic Federation... Japan's Private Railway Regulation Act sets standards for industry... Labor Party forms in Norway... British law requires all goods exported from Germany be labeled "Made in Germany", soon sign of high quality.

Business Events

London Electricity Supply Corp. forms (uses idea of electrical engineer Sebastian de Ferranti to build network of large power stations, leads to 3,000 in U.S. and 250 in Britain by 1900)... AEG, Germany's counterpart to U.S.' General Electric, is formed with aid of Thomas A. Edison (introduces Olympia typewriters in 1908, is acquired in 1980s by Daimler-Benz group, one of Germany's largest conglomerates)... Herbert Austin is manager of small engineering firm (sells patent rights for sheep shearing machinery in 1893 to Frederick Wolseley for shares, buys works in 1895 to make equipment instead of assembling parts, adds machine tools and bicycle parts to product line, looking for new products builds first car c. 1895 - 2nd 1896, makes Wolseley Autocar in 1898, wins 1,000-mile trial in 1900, starts firm in 1905 to build cars - 1,500/year in 1914, enters receivership in 1921 after post-war financial crisis, reorganizes 1921-22 - one of big three in 1920s-1930s, employs 8,000 workers in 1922 - 20,000 by 1939, makes 45,562 vehicles, success with small car, in 1929 and 76,492, omitting commercial vehicles, in 1939)... Montague Gluckstein, after working in family's 1841 tobacco business, gets catering rights for New Castle Jubilee Exhibition, later other contracts for Glasgow, Paris and London (joins relative Joseph Lyons, operator of refreshment stand at Liverpool Exhibition, in 1894 to open first Lyons tea shop, copies Gatti family's chain of inexpensive restaurants and cafes, in London, adds others to build chain of restaurants and tea shops, acquires Trocadero Music Hall and Trocadero Restaurant, serves haute cuisine at popular prices, in 1896, opens first Cornerhouse Restaurant in London in 1909, in addition to teashops, restaurants, catering, four London hotels and bakeries, enters wholesale tea trade in 1904, acquires 10,000 acres of tea plantations in Nyasaland)...

Japanese soy sauce cartel, Noda Shoyu Associates, forms to stabilize prices, market shares (-1917, contributes to patriotic, civic and charity activities in 1894, opens bank in 1900 to finance members, starts joint research laboratory in 1904 - activity of some individual brewers in 1800s, forms Noda Charitable Society in 1905 to provide poor relief, education for impoverished students)... John M. Fells, Emile Garcke: Factory Accounts, leading English work on cost accounting to W.W. I... Daimler builds four-wheeled vehicle powered by internal-combustion engine... British East Africa Co. (-1895) gets 50-year lease of land by Sultan of Zanzibar, governed as protectorate in 1889... Wilhelm Diethelm starts Bangkok trading business, $1.2 billion worldwide enterprise by 1990.

1888

General Events

London match girls strike for higher pay, better factory health and safety, prelude to growth of trade unionism... John Gregg: Script Phonography (moves to U.S. in 1893 to give shorthand classes at Industrial Institute)... France floats Russian loan... China's first railway opens, November 24... World's first beauty contest is held at Spa, Belgium... Aeronautical Exhibition is held in Vienna... Hawaii grants railroad franchise to Dillingham (evolves as 1982 diversified business of $1 billion)... Oil is found in Borneo... Gestetner devises first typewriter stencil... Brazil emancipates slaves... Miner's Federation of Great Britain forms... France's Felix Millet patents "self-propelling bicycle" with engine, few built... Claude Monet starts series paintings, a commercial success... Social Democrat party forms in Sweden (supports evolutionary change c. 1900, private ownership in 1930s, and generous welfare state in 1950s, plans tax overhaul, world's highest in 1987 at 56% of GNP, and market orientation in late 1980s to manage limited government resources).

Business Events

Canadian Pacific builds, world's largest, Banff Springs Hotel, "finest hotel on North American continent", near Calgary... Financial Times is published, London... King of Matabele grants mining concessions to Rhodes in return for protection... Rhodes combines Barnato Diamond Mining, De Beers to form practical monopoly for Kimberley... Ernst Abbe takes control of Zeiss works (innovates with work analysis, continuous training to improve skills, productivity)... Lever builds Fort Sunlight as model community for workers... German company is granted authority to build first link of Baghdad railway from Constantinople to Ankara (-1892)... Anglo-American Oil is formed to market U.S. oil products overseas (puts British interests under Standard Oil's control)... Moulin Rouge club opens in Paris with famed Can-Can dancers... After acquiring control of family tea importing business of 1700s in 1850s, Edward W. Fyffe visits Canary Islands for wife's health (starts shipping bananas, follows some exports of bananas and tomatoes to Liverpool, to London, dominates city market to 1892)... Vickers is Britain's leading armaments manufacturer (is Britain's 6th largest firm by capitalization in 1905 - 4th in 1919 and 9th in 1948, acquires Wolseley Tool & Motor Car in 1901-06 - Westinghouse Electrical in 1918-38 and Metropolitan-Cammell Carriage and Finance in 1929-69, is Britain's 4th largest business in 1907 with 22,500 workers - 44,162 in 1935, runs branches in Buenos Aires, U.S., Italy, Canada, France, Rio de Janeiro, Hungary and Shanghai in 1914 - joint ventures in Spain, Italy, Japan, Russia and Turkey, absorbs Armstrong, almost insolvent, in 1927 to form English Steel, adds operations in Switzerland, Romania and Poland by 1930)...

John B. Dunlop, Irish veterinarian, devises pneumatic tire for bicycle (patents tire in 1889, invalidated 1892 for prior invention in 1845, forms Pneumatic Tyre & Booth's Cycle Agency Co. with syndicate of du Cros, acquires patents to attach tires to rims in 1890, buys French factory in 1892, control 1909, and German factory, control in 1910 - sold 1915, opens U.S. plant in 1893 - sold 1898 to Canadian interests, goes public in 1896 as Dunlop Pneumatic Co., signs licensing agreement in 1898 with U.S. Rubber, acquires General Rubber Goods business in 1900 and rubber mills in 1901, starts wheel plant in 1906, opens Japanese plant in 1909 to make tires for rickshaws - 40% to local interests in 1931 and sells in 1941, signs licensing agreement with Russia in 1910 and produces first airplane tires and golf balls, is holding company in 1912, buys Macintosh waterproof products in 1926, starts Canadian operation with independent Dunlop Co. of 1898 in 1927 -Australia in 1928, South Africa and Eire in 1935, and India in 1936, patents latex foam in 1929 - commercial products in 1933)... International Woodscrew Union forms, cartel lasts to W.W. I... Brothers W.M., R.R. Foster begin modern Carlton and United Breweries near Melbourne (export beer in 1901 to serve Aussies in Boer War, combines with six other breweries by 1907, by 1986 sells Foster lager in 80 countries).

1889

General Events

Germany sets minimum retirement age at 70, 65 in 1916... London dockworkers Bill Tillett and John Burns, pioneer industrial unionism, lead strike of 13 weeks for higher pay and minimum work of 4 hours, shows increasing use of strikes by workers... Brassiere is invented, Paris... England's Mogul v. McGregor upholds cartel rebate, followed by 1894 Maxim v. Nordenfelt to uphold cartel agreement... Woodcutters form Norway's second national union, followed by Iron and Metal Workers, Iron and Metal Laborers in 1890s... Germany's first general strike is held by workers demanding legislation on worker security, employment of women and children, factory safety, protection of wage levels... Belgium passes factory inspection law... Artificial silk of French chemist Count Hilaire de Chardonnet, invented 1884, is shown at Paris Exhibition... Charles Booth: Life and Labour of the People in London... Workers hold first May Day celebration in Paris... Eiffel Tower, 1,056 feet in height with hydraulic elevator, is built for Paris' World Exhibition, viewed at first as a monstrosity... Sweden passes first factory act... Swedish industrial workers back Social Democratic Party... Second International Workingmen's Assn. forms.

Business Events

Brunner-Mond creates Salt Union as combine of 64 firms... Barnum & Bailey Circus appears in London... Benjamin Seebohm Rowntree joins family's cocoa works to improve employee relations (-1936, hires women welfare workers in 1891, installs suggestion system in late 1890s)... Delhi Cloth & General Mills Co. forms in India to produce textiles, diversifies in 1912 by starting and/or acquiring manufacturing and retailing enterprises... D'Oyly Carte opens London's Hotel Savoy (hires Cesar Ritz as manager and Auguste Escoffier as chef - uses card index for tastes of rich and famous, is target, along with exclusive Connaught and Claridge's chain, for takeover in 1988 by Trusthouse Forte)... Dublin-born William Harvey du Cros forms Belfast syndicate to acquire John Boyd Dunlop's pneumatic tire patent, Pneumatic Tyre & Booth's Cycle Agency (survives invalidation of master patent in 1892, with small subsidiaries in France, Germany and U.S. starts main assembly plant at Coventry in 1893, acquires rubber estates in Ceylon, Malaya - 60,000 acres by 1917, is 14th largest British manufacturing company in 1918)... Raffaelo Esposito, owner of celebrated Naples pizzeria, creates modern pizza to honor Queen... Yamauchi family starts Marufuku Co., renamed Nintendo Playing Card Co. in 1951, to make, sell traditional Japanese playing cards (in 1980 devises hand-held liquid crystal video game and forms U.S. branch for coin-operated video games, introduces home video hames to Japan in 1983, as Nintendo hits U.S. in 1986, devises new super video game system in 1991 with improved graphics, sound).

German-born Frederick R. Simms meets auto pioneer Daimler at Bremen Exhibition (forms Simms & Co., consulting engineers, in 1890 to sell Daimler engines in England, forms Daimler Motor Syndicate in 1893 - sold to Henry Lawson in 1895, starts Motor Carriage Supply Co. in 1898 - lasts to 1900, forms Simms Mfg. Co. in 1900 to make cars and commercial vehicles, with rights from Germany's Robert Bosch starts Simms Magneto in 1907 - lasts to 1913, starts Simms Motor Units in 1913 and subsidiary of Standard Insulator in 1915, forms new Simms Motor Units in 1920 - lasts to 1926)... British Bank of the Middle East, known as Imperial Bank of Persia, opens in Teheran, is acquired in 1960 by Hongkong and Shanghai Banking Corp., later operations in Iraq and India... Harrods retail store, London, is limited liability company (appoints Richard Burbidge, former manager of Whiteley's emporium, as general manager in 1891 - managing director in 1894, opens theater ticket agency, restaurant, hairdressing salon and catalog business, adds athletic club in 1905 and pension plan for managers in 1906, opens Harrods Buenos Aires in 1913 and drops co-operative image to become exclusive store for wealthy with Royal Warrant, is sold to House of Fraser in 1959).

1890s

General Events

Fewer than 3,000 factories, some 200 use steam power, operate in Japan, over 30,000 by 1908... Workers in Chile form "resistance societies" to seek better working conditions... H.G. Wells: Little Wars (gives instructions for war game).

Business Events

After entering banking field in 1885, Mitsubishi invests in Japanese railroads, property.

1890

General Events

Graf von Leo Caprivi is Chancellor of Germany (-1894, resigns after displeasing agrarians by emphasizing industry over agriculture)... Some 50,000 Australian workers in shipping, mining and shearing strike for union recognition, defeated when public backs employers (leads to formation of Australia's Labor Party)... Financial crisis hits Argentina, heavy urban unemployment despite growth of beef and corn industries (is aided by Baring Bros., London financial agent for Europe, helps Argentina to stabilize currency, adopt gold standard for more credit from London, Europe)... Europe's relative share of world manufacturing output is 62.0%, Britain with 18.5%, Hapsburg Empire 4.7%, France 6.8%, Germany 13.2%, Italy 2.5%, Russia 8.8%, U.S. 23.6%, Japan 2.4%, China 6.2%, India 1.7%... Britain's first electrical power station is operated at Deptford... Emile von Behring discovers antitoxins... Japan holds first general election... Switzerland adopts social insurance... Alfred Marshall: Principles of Economics (synthesizes previous theories to formulate system of equilibrium)... Clement Adler's Eole is first full-sized aircraft to leave ground with own power (fails to sustain flight)... French professor Etienne Jules Marey shows filmed series of photographs... Eugene von Bohm-Bawerk: Capital and Interest (presents model for investment decision analysis)... Germany forms industrial courts to settle disputes on wages, employment of women and children... Ratchet train runs at Zermatt to take skiers up mountain at Alpine ski resort... James Dewar gives details of vacuum flask to Royal Institution, marketed by 1902 with name of Thermos by German Rheinhold Berger... All-steel railway bridge is built over Scotland's Firth of Fourth... Friese-Green prints first motion picture on celluloid film... First international congress to protect workers meets in Berlin... Britain's Working Classes Act finances slum clearance for low-income housing... London, Paris are linked by telephone line... World's first electric subway opens in London... Edward Guinness, head of Ireland brewery, forms The Guinness Trust to provide poor with housing... Swiss shipbuilder Escher Wyss builds first aluminum steamboat as a yacht... Britain produces 8 million tons of iron/steel and 5.0 in 1900, U.S. at 9.3 and 10.3, Germany at 4.1 and 6.3, France at 1.9 and 1.5, Austria at .94 and 1.1, Russia at .95 and 2.2, Japan at .02 and Italy at .01 and .11... Socialist unions, first appeared in 1860, unite to form General Commission of Free German Trade Unions, largest on continent... Economic depression hits Australia (-1893, causes over 40 land companies to fail, Federal Bank, later 12 others, closes in 1893).

Business Events

Peruvian Corp., society of bondholders headed by W.R. Grace, assumes national debt of Peru (gets concessions for silver mines, guano deposits and 5 million acres of land)... Small Indonesian company is chartered to drill for oil in Dutch East Indies (hires Henri Detering in 1896, CEO in 1900, to form sales arm, joins Royal Dutch Petroleum with Shell Transport and Trading Company and France's Rothschilds to form Asiatic Petroleum in 1903, marketing organization for Royal Dutch Shell in 1907)... British banking house of Baring Bros. declares bankruptcy (leads to U.S. panic of 1893)... Louis Rothman, age 21, opens tobacco shop on London's Pall Mall, family operated Ukraine tobacco factory (with success of handmade, exotically blended cigarettes opens show room in 1900, gets Royal Warrants from Edward VII in 1905 and Spain's King Alfonso XIII in 1910)... Banca di Roma fails, causes financial panic in London and Paris... After patenting cigarette machine in 1872 (is managing director of NYC's National Cigarette Tobacco in 1890-95), Bernhard Baron enters England's growing market with Baron Cigarette Machine Co... After working in father's 1879 shop selling objets d'art, Joseph Duveen and brother start business to sell art to wealthy U.S. industrialists (open London's Bond street store in 1893, acquire art collections of Oscar Hainauer in 1906 and Rodolphe Kann in 1907, open galleries in Paris in 1908 and NYC in 1912, contract with Bernard Berenson, leading expert in Italian art, for advice 1911-37)... Tamesaburo Furukawa, Japanese entrepreneur (is worth $1.8 billion by 1990 from Nippon Herald Films and some 50 entertainment-related companies), is born... Brewery is started in Manila, named San Miguel (outsells imported brands by 5 to 1 by 1900, forms corporation in 1913, diversifies with soft drinks in 1922, ice cream, 1925, and first non-U.S. Coca-Cola franchise in 1927, loses independence to Marcos crony in 1984 - out 1986, forms joint venture with Japanese glass container business in 1991)... Munich-based Allianz insurance is formed by Carl Thieme (joins in a consortium of German, Austrian, Swiss and Russian firms to insure world commerce in 1890, open offices in UK, 1893, Switzerland, 1897, and Holland, 1898).

1891

General Events

Law for Protection of Workers regulates hours for German workers... Beatrice Webb: The Cooperative Movement in Great Britain... Count Alfred von Schlieffen is Chief of German General Staff (-1905, prepares, 1892-1905, detailed strategic plan for two-front war with France, Russia)... Paul Goehre, theological student: Drei Monate Fabrikarbeiter und Handwerksburche (covers research while working at Saxony machine-making factory)... New Zealand forms system of public employment agencies, followed by Germany in 1890s... Argentine government forms Banco de la Nacion, land's largest commercial bank by 1983... Social Democratic Workers' Clubs appear, Germany, for physical, political education of working class... Spencer Wilkinson: The Brain of an Army (notes significance of Germany's general staff)... R.W. Cooke-Taylor: The Modern Factory System (discusses use of technology)... Catholic labor movement appears in Italy, named Italian Confederation of Workers in 1918 with some 1.5 million members by 1921... French engineer, entrepreneur Levasseur designs prototype of modern automobile, not motor on bicycle frame... Polytechnical Society forms in Moscow, Society of Technologists in St. Petersburg in 1894... London's Institute of Chartered Secretaries and Administrators is formed by company executives, Royal Charter in 1897... Pope Leo XIII: "Rerum Novarum" (upholds right to private property, insists material goods meet needs of humanity, supports right of workers to have living wage)... Russia starts building Trans-Siberian Railroad (-1904)... Denmark passes Old-Age Pension Act, health insurance law in 1892 and industrial injury act in 1898... Otto Lilienthal begins over 2,000 glider flights, popular sport in Germany, in 1890s to study airplane design (-1896, says "Sacrifices must be made" before death after crash)... General strike is held in Belgium for manhood suffrage... Textile workers in Northern France organize May Day demonstration for 8-hour day, suppressed, 10 killed, by police... Paris Anarchists lead workers' demonstration, attacked by mounted police... German workers get rights to form bargaining units, to negotiate with employers... Canada opposes free trade with U.S., endorsed 1988... Charles F. Cross, England, files for first patent for industrial process to make viscose rayon (leads to Viscose Syndicate in 1893, license of British rights to Courtaulds in 1904 for production in 1907).

Business Events

After building his first car in 1889, Armand Peugeot, previously maker of tools and steel stays for hoopskirts, makes world's first commercial car sale (makes first diesel-powered car in 1922)... Charter of British South Africa Co. is extended north of Zambezi River... A. & F. Pears is public company with Thomas J. Barratt as CEO (after spending only 500 pounds/year in 80 years for advertising, ups amount to 126,000/year - nearly 1 million by 1903 to pioneer mass consumer advertising in Britain, uses endorsements and illustrations of contemporary artists in ads)... Charles V. Pugh, brother start Whitworth Cycle to sell bicycles (take over ailing Rudge Cycle in 1894, make first bicycles in 1898 to fight U.S. imports, provide easy payment plan, after receivership in 1904 is named Lanchester Motor)... With savings, John Mackintosh opens pastry shop, wife tends business while he works in textile mill (with success from toffee specialty quits mill job and rents small warehouse in 1894, forms Steam Confectionery Works in 1895 - 1,000 employees by W.W. I, advertises in 1896 as Toffee King with wide range of flavors, gives away free samples by caravans touring villages and towns, becomes limited liability company in 1899 to finance expansion, distributes to Northern Europe in 1902, introduces toffee de luxe in 1914, runs quality control lab in 1925, acquires Unilever's chocolate business of A.J. Caley in 1932)... Portugal charters Mozambique Co., financed by British interests...

Philips Incandescent Light Works is started in Eindhoven, Holland, by Frederick and eldest son, inventor of improved filament in 1890 for mass production of lightbulbs (hires son Anton in 1893, tries to sell unprofitable business in 1893 as Holland a poor market with few power stations, is revived by Anton with exports to Germany, shows first profits in 1895 in producing 500 lamps/day, when depression occurs in 1900-02 exports lamps to France, Spain and Italy, after price war forms cartel sales organization with AEG, Siemens & Halske and 13 small factories - 10.5% market to Philips, signs pact in 1906 with GE and Siemens-Halske to exchange patents, forms joint patent organization in 1911 with AEG, Siemens & Halske and other large factories - employment at 2,500 and 10,000 by 1927, incorporates in 1912)... Switzerland's BBC Brown Boveri is formed to make electrical generation equipment (builds Europe's first steam turbines in 1900 after opening branches in Germany, France and Italy, forms joint venture with U.S.' Gould to make electrical equipment in 1979 and one in transportation with Thyssen in 1990, merges with ASEA in 1991 to form enterprise, 2nd largest in Switzerland after Nestle, with 1,300 firms worldwide to compete with Siemens, GE).

1892

General Events

Holland adopts income tax... Portugal declares bankruptcy... Austria-Hungary adopts gold standard... Gold is found in Western Australia... By this time 30% of French miners, engineers and foundrymen are unionized... Two Englishmen patent first electric radiator... Nitro-cellulose process to make rayon appears in France... Germany's Statistical Office forms labor department... Germany signs commercial treaties with Austria, Italy, Switzerland, Spain, Romania, Belgium, Russia to reduce agricultural duties... Emile Raynaud shows animated drawings at Paris' Theatre Optique... South Africa finishes building Cape-Johannesburg Railroad... Keir Hardie is first socialist member elected to Parliament... Sergei Wilte is Russia's Minister of Finance (-1903, makes industrialization No. 1 priority)... Alfred Marshall: Elements of Economics in Industry... Rudolph Diesel, student of Karl von Linde, gets German patent for oil engine, first built successfully in 1897 (is used by first ocean vessel in 1913)... Japan builds first locomotive.

Business Events

Hotel Chateau Frontenac opens in Quebec City, Canada... James A. Watson, working for firm of wholesalers, gets exclusive rights to sell Norwegian fish in U.K. (forms Newcastle business in 1903 to handle exports of Norwegian canners, promotes popular Skipper brand with advertising, markets product abroad in 1906 - sued by French canners, increases work force of 100 to 1,000 by 1913, one of first to use scientists for product quality and nutritional content, sells to Lever Bros. in 1923)... Emil Kirdorf is General Director of Germany's Gelsen-Kirchen Mining Co. (starts Rhenish Westphalian Coal Syndicate in 1893, largest German mining cartel by 1906)... U.S.' A.L. Teele is first advertising consultant in England... Holland's Protestant employers form association... Campari appears in marketplace... U.S.' M. Guggenheim & Sons, formed 1875 (buys part of

Colorado silver mine in 1879, builds world's largest smelter in 1888), opens small smelter in Monterrey, by 1910 largest private enterprise in Mexico (forms Chilean copper business in 1908 - by 1924 2nd largest in land, buys Chilean mountain of copper ore - sold to Anaconda Copper in 1923, starts Chilean nitrate venture with J.P. Morgan & Co. in 1916, with new processing technology buys 35-square-mile tract of Chilean nitrate land, buys Lautaro Nitrate Co., Chile's most important, in 1929, merges interests in 1931 with Chile to form industry monopoly).

1893

General Events

Belgian troops quell riots during general strike... France, Russia sign commercial treaty... Germany signs commercial treaties with Romania, Serbia, Spain... France, Switzerland start customs war (-1895)... Amsterdam shows factory safety devices... Polo players at swank Hurlingham Club, Buenos Aires, wear knitted-cotton, soft-collar shirts, sold in City's sports shops by polo star Lewis Lacey (leads to polo shirt, designed by Lacoste, in 1926)... Greece opens Corinth Canal... Keir Hardie, others form Independent Labour Party in Britain, becomes Labor Party in 1906 (holds minority roles in government in 1924, 1929-31 and governs 1945-51)... Emile Durkheim: The Division of Labor in Society... France holds trial on corruption of Panama Canal Co... Rosa Luxembourg starts Social-Democratic Party in area of Poland... British miners are killed by troops during Featherstone Massacre, followed by Tonypandy violence of workers in 1911... German agrarian interests form league to lobby for lower taxes on agriculture.

Business Events

First British factory to make storage batteries starts operations... Samuel H. Benson opens British advertising agency, pioneers role of advertising in marketing process (fails to form association of advertising agents)... To replace willow bark for relief, Felix Hoffman, Bayer chemist, re-discovers aspirin for rheumatic father, follows work of France's Charles Gerhardt in 1853 (loses brand name in 1919 Treaty of Versailles)... Benz builds four-wheeled car, first with engine specifically intended for automobile... Meng Lo-shuan transforms old Chinese family business in cotton cloth in this time into business empire with 24 branches in Peking, Shanghai and other Chinese cities... Hugo Stinnes starts German coal-trading firm with some $12,500 (forms Rhenish-Westphalian Electric in 1898, forms Coal Board syndicate in 1903, starts coal shipping firm in 1905, organizes 3 companies in 1916 to exploit Belgium's industry, transportation and agriculture, starts overseas trading firm in 1917, expands interests in 1920s to create Konzern by 1924 with 24 coal mines, 21 iron mines, 7 oil fields and refineries, 16 earth, stone and ceramic works, 29 smelters, 20 metal and machinery works, 3 telegraph companies, 4 shipyards, 80 electrical plants, 8 paper and chemical plants, 4 shoe factories, 47 electrical and gas utilities, 10 railways, 9 shipping companies, 9 holdings in forests and sawmills, 3 cotton and coconut plantations, and 10 banks and holding companies with philosophy of "Do anything with your capital except hold it in reserve," leaves business to sons in 1924, insolvent 1925)... German cartel in heavy industry forms, produces more steel in first year than all of Britain... Compagnie Francaise Thomson-Houston forms with patent rights from U.S.' firm of same name (creates Alsthom in 1928 to manufacture electrical equipment).

1894

General Events

Italian engineer Guglielmo Marconi builds first radio equipment... Blackpool, England's largest resort city by 1980s, builds replica of Eiffel Tower to attract tourists to Irish Sea area... Gold field is found in Transvaal... Russia, Germany sign commercial treaty... First railway over Andes is finished... Agricultural workers riot in Sicily... Dutch Labor Party forms... B.F.S. Baden-Powell is first European with successful man-flying kite... Karl Marx (post.): Das Kapital, Vol. III... Bath

Club opens in London (-1981, provides City's only swimming facilities)... Motor cars make trial run from Paris to Rouen... Maxim tests steam-powered flying machine in this time in Scotland... New Zealand passes world's first minimum wage law, 8-hour day law in 1897... French Trade-Union Congress approves use of general strike... New Zealand creates industrial conciliation, arbitration boards... South Australia starts compulsory arbitration of industrial disputes... Typographers forms first trade union in Finland... Britain adopts inheritance tax... Sidney, Beatrice Webb: History of Trade Unionism... Various trades form unions in France... New Zealand is first country to grant suffrage to women over age of 21... Modern school opens in China (provides courses in foreign languages, mathematics, natural sciences, commerce)... Australia's Warren Hardgrave invents box kite (uses 4 box kites in 1894 to lift himself some 16 feet into air)... Hawaiian government is overthrown by U.S. Ambassador John L. Stevens, no authorization from Washington, and planters led by Sanford P. Dole (is annexed by U.S. 1898, gets Statehood in 1959)... Socialist leaders, unions organize general strike in Belgium for equal manhood suffrage... Christian unions appear in Germany (-1895)... Britain's Building Societies Act regulates promoters... Prince Hohenlohe is chancellor of Germany (-1900, repeals restrictive combination laws preventing unions joining forces)... Quebec holds first winter carnival.

Business Events

Parisian bistro opens in Paris, named Maxim's later when waiter Maxim Gaillard takes over business... T. Bata starts shoe business in Czechoslovakia (operates in 28 countries by 1932, is nationalized late 1940s)... Watch business, known later as Omega, appears in Switzerland... Industrial confederation for employers forms in Germany as defense against labor organizations... U.S.' GE forms subsidiary Thompson Electric in Britain... With British rights for German process to extract alumina from bauxite ore, British Aluminum pioneers new industry... S. Simpson business to manufacture men's clothing is started (patents DAKS self-supporting trousers in 1934, goes public in 1935, opens Piccadilly store in 1936, employs 3,300 workers in 1939, introduces DAKS skirts in 1952, forms DAKS USA to sell in North American market)... Fritz Hoffmann-La Roche, son of wealthy silk merchant, and German pharmacist buy chemical wholesale house in Basel, Switzerland (is dissolved and reorganized in 1896 with father as partner to make pharmaceutical products, re-finances business in 1898 to achieve first success with orange- flavored cough syrup - by W.W. I operates on 4 continents, is public corporation in 1919 - success by W.W. II with vitamins and painkillers, fearing Nazi invasion, forms Canadian subsidy in 1930s, by 1946 operates worldwide with 18 subsidiaries and some 6,000 employees - some 29,000 employees, 60 affiliates in 32 countries by 1970s in selling Librum, Valium and Larodopa, enters bioelectronics field in 1966, shows sales of $5.3 billion, profits of $384 million, in 1988, after failure to acquire U.S.' Sterling Drug, restructures in 1989 with $4 billion for global market)...

After starting nitroglycerin business with Stockholm merchant in 1864, Alfred Nobel, inventor of blasting cap to control detonation of nitro in 1863, blasting gelatine in 1875, and smokeless gunpowder in 1887, buys A.B. Bofors-Gullspang munitions works, fame in 1930s for rapid-fire anti-aircraft gun (loses control of nitro business to Wallenbergs in 1978, is re-acquired in 1984 with formation of Nobel Industries, adds defense electronics firm, Pharos, in 1986, after being accused of illegal smuggling of weapons to Iran, Iraq in mid-1980 is charged, dropped 1988, for alleged kickbacks of $60 million to Indian middleman on sale of $1.3 billion in 1986, acquires #1 laser business, CA, in 1990).

1895

General Events

China, Japan sign treaty (for first time lets foreigners manufacture in Chinese treaty ports, 136 operations, 49 Japanese, by 1913)... Russian Alexander Popov invents antennae for radio transmissions... Le Cordon Bleu cooking school opens in Paris... German Assn. for Mercantile Education forms, sponsors all of nation's schools of business by 1920... Brothers Otto, Gustav

Williamthal fly first glider above height of takeoff... Russian physicist K. Tsiolkovsky proposes liquid-fuel rockets for space travel... First Venice Biennale art exhibition is held, tourist attraction in 1900s... France's Auguste, Louis Lumiere patent Cinematographe, first system for filming, printing and projecting moving pictures on screen (give first public showing of two-minute newsreel at Paris' Hotel Scribe)... Fabian Society founds London School of Economics and Political Science to train young men in progressive thought, enlightened ideas... French trade unions form Confederation Generale du Travail... Automobile race runs from Paris to Bordeaux, winner finishes with average of 15 mph... Marconi invents radiotelegraphy (sends long-wave signals over a mile, receives first transatlantic wireless signals in 1901)... After three years of trials and error, Hiram Percy Maxim, son of U.S.-born inventor, designs crude gas-powered tricycle (is hired by Pope Mfg., largest U.S. maker of bicycles, as chief engineer to make motor vehicles)... Skaladenowsky brothers show moving pictures in Germany, followed by Edison's exhibit in 1896... Ernest Rutherford sends radio message nearly a mile... China grants territorial concessions to Germany, given to Russia and France in 1896, Germany and Japan in 1897, Britain and Japan in 1898, France and Japan in 1899, Russia in 1900, Japan in 1901, and Belgium, Italy, Austria in 1902... In searching for process to make cheap diamonds, France's Henri Moissan discovers acetylene gas (when demand drops for calcium carbide used to produce the gas, is used by BASF dye-makers to make fertilizer with nitrogen in 1913)... Trade-Union Congress at Limoges plans program to destroy capitalists regime of France with general strike... Kiel Canal links North Sea with Baltic... Electric locomotive is introduced, followed by diesel-electric around 1924... Scotland's A. Shields patents first practical milking machine... Lord Kelvin, president of Royal Society: "Heavier than air flying machines are impossible"... Henry Irving is first actor knighted.

Business Events

German manufacturers in consumer goods form confederation (merge with industrialists in 1919 to form National Federation of German Industry)... Rival Carlsberg, Tuborg breweries sign agreement, lasts to year 2000, to consult each other on common interests, to share profits and losses, to participate in modernization, and to regulate competitive factors, revised 1903 (join as one enterprise in 1970)... Peugeot puts pneumatic tires on cars... Daniel Swarovski starts Swiss factory to make crystal (by 1980s employs over 7,000 people in 15 production centers and 42 sales subsidiaries as world leader in machine-cut crystal)... Russia-Chinese Bank opens in China, followed by Sino-American Bank in 1910 and Banque Industrielle de Chine in 1911... World's oldest athletic-shoe business, J.W. Foster & Sons, appears in Britain (develops Reebok shoe, is discovered at 1979 trade show by U.S.' Paul Fireman, former distributor of fishing and camping equipment, to acquire U.S. rights, with market success acquires Reebok from Foster family in 1984 for $700,000, sales of $900 million by 1986)... Michelin makes first pneumatic tires for cars (opens U.S. plant in 1907)...

Spinning-factory, designed by Francois Hennebique after developing reinforced concrete in 1880s, is built at Tourcoing, France, with concrete frame, glass panels... John C. Dennis, brother open London bicycle plant, use parts from supplier to assemble bicycles (experiment with motorized tricycles in late 1890s - first car-tricycle in 1899, incorporate in 1901 - public in 1913, build first commercial truck in 1904 for Harrods - 4 models of lorries by 1907, after winning Dewar Trophy in 1907 get order from Post Office for fleet of delivery vans, build fire trucks in 1908 - 250 by 1937, go international in 1919)... Ernest Petler, twin brother Percival build, aided by father's foreman in ironmongery, first oil engine for car (form Yeovil Motor Car & Cycle Co. in 1896 to build paraffin oil engine in contest for best self-propelled road vehicle, form new engine business in 1901 - new company in 1911 with fresh capital, build 1,500 engines in 1911 - seaplanes during W.W. I, form venture with Vickers in 1920 to make semi-diesel engines - full control in 1926, work with autogiros in 1933-35)... Monague S. Napier buys family's business, precision machinery for arsenals, banks and mints, from father's estate (contracts in 1899-24 to make cars for S.F. Edge's Motor Vehicle Co., introduces first commercial 6-cylinder engine in 1904, employs work force of 1,000 in 1906, make 8,582 large, powerful hand-built cars, Napier, by 1924 to compete with Rolls-Royce, develops Lion airplane engine in 1914, ends car production in 1924, is bought by English Electric in 1942)... London Press Exchange is founded, top British ad agency in 1930s (develops international network in 1948, after losing lead to U.S.' J. Walter Thompson and S.H. Benson in 1950s-60s is acquired by U.S.' Leo Burnett agency)... Galeries Lafayette opens Paris flagship department store, 1989 sales of $3.1 billion with provincial stores, 118 Monoprix and Inna discount supermarkets (plans posh NYC store in 1990 for Trump Tower).

1896

General Events

Lumiere brothers show movies in NYC... France builds first electric submarine... Parliament passes Conciliation Act to resolve labor disputes... Poland's Karol Adamiecki designs harmonogram as graph with critical path to resolve complex production problems, presented to Society of Russian Engineers in 1903 (precedes U.S.' Program Evaluation and Review Techniques, PERT, c. 1957)... Athens hosts first modern Olympic games, organized by French Baron Pierre de Courbetin... Britain erects first all-steel building... Danish Federation of Trade Unions forms... J. Slater Lewis: The Commercial Organization of Factories... Some 435,000 workers, about 261,000 women - most peasant girls under 16, are employed by private plants in Japan with 100 employees or more... Construction is started in East Africa to build 879-mile railway from Kenya to Uganda (-1901, imports Asians for work)... Sweden's C. Johansson develops gauge blocks for precision measurements, mass produced in 1918 by Major W.A. Hoke... Spanish, Italian, German and French immigrants in Argentina form Social Party... Germany passes law against unfair competition... Imperial Chinese Railway College, Southwest Jiaotong University in 1972 with studies in science, engineering, management, and liberal arts, appears at Emei, Sichuan (is instrumental in developing country's first electric and diesel locomotives)... Danish Employers' Confederation forms... German Protestants form National Social League to promote trade unionism... First London-to-Brighton, most fashionable resort in land, car run is held.

Business Events

First Alpine ski school opens at Liliefeld, Austria... Britain's Daimler Motor Co. is started with German firm's patents... World's first automobile show, International Horseless Carriage Exhibition, opens in London... Holland's Vereniging family fortune of $2.5 billion, mostly in consumer goods and chemicals, in 1987, begins with formation of coal cartel... Pioneering Trafford Park Industrial Estate near Manchester is registered as public company (provides land, facilities in early 1900s for factories of Rolls-Royce, Ford, British Westinghouse, others)... Proprietary Articles Trade Assn. forms in Britain to withhold goods of members from price-cutting retailers... Charles E.H. Friswell, one of Britain's first successful car agencies, opens to sell Peugeot cars in London (sells Standard cars in 1905)... Engineering Employers' Federation forms in Glasgow (absorbs National Employers' Federation in 1918, sponsors new national body, National Confederation of Employers' Organization to cover 45 industries, to act with trade union congress, orders general lock- out, covers 250,000 workers, in 1922 to uphold employers' right to manage and impose wage reductions, wins after 4 months)...

Wilts United Dairies is formed as wholesale business (enters London wholesale market in 1901, joins City's other wholesalers, Dairy Supply, Great Western & Metropolitan Dairy Supply and F.W. Gilbert Dairy, in 1915 to form United Dairies to dominate market)... Palace Hotel opens at St. Moritz, spa during Middle Ages, to provide elegance for those at Swiss winter resort... Ashanti Goldfields Corp. signs mining lease with Ghana, taken over in 1968 by London and Rhodesian Mining and Land Co... Barclay & Co., genesis in 1736 when James Barclay joins goldsmithing and banking firm using sign of black spread eagle, occurs when 20 banks combine to avoid takeovers (acquires 17 private banks in 20 years, as largest in London links branches with computer in 1959, issued Barclaycard in 1966, enters U.S. consumer finance market in 1980 in buying American Credit and 138 financial offices of Beneficial, for 1986 deregulation merges its merchant bank with two other financial firms, sells California banks to Wells Fargo in 1988, sells U.S.

consumer finance units to Primerica's Commercial Credit in 1989, as UK's largest bank in assets buys German, French banks in 1990)... Siemens completes, continent's first, subway for Budapest.

1897

General Events

Japan adopts (March 1) gold standard... Beatrice, Sidney Webb: Industrial Democracy (pioneer use of cards to compile research data)... Adolph Spiltler discovers casein plastics... Charles A. Parson's Turbina is first steamship to use steam turbines... London licenses first motor bus, 3,000 motor omnibuses on London streets by 1913 (replace horse-drawn carriages by 1916)... McCreary patents air-washer to purify air in buildings... South American-born Pedro P. Poulet builds first liquid fuel rocket engine in Paris... Henry Tate, sugar refiner, opens Tate Gallery in London with funds, art work... First electric cabs are seen in London, withdrawn by 1898 for unreliability... Croatian timber merchant David Schwarz tests aluminum airship in Berlin (crashes after several miles with leaking gas)... Steel Labor Union is first labor organization formed in Japan... Royal Automobile Club forms... Parliament's Workmen's Compensation Act makes (August 5) employers liable for work injuries... Denmark takes first reliable census of manufacturing... Commercial school opens in Shanghai... Government of China is petitioned to abolish traditional social discrimination against business, to protect native commerce and industry, and to fund industries (leads to Imperial Edict to let all government officials to invest in industry)... Some 499 foreign businesses operate in China, 6,800, including major banks, in 1923... Australia issues postage stamp to raise money to support home for consumptives, world's first stamp for charity... Germany writes commercial code to standardize regulations for businesses, trading companies... Germany's highest court confirms legality of cartels in Pulp Cartel case (rules cartels are in public interest, 4 in 1875, 106 in 1890, 205 in 1896, 350 in 1905, 1,500 in 1925, 2,100 in 1930)... France's Alder fails to fly Avion III... Labor Union Promotion Society forms, Japan, to advocate factory legislation... Workers' Volunteer Society, Assn. for Study of Socialism are started in China to promote trade unionism, leads to temporary unions in steel, railways, shipbuilding and printing.

Business Events

Standard Bank is founded in Salisbury, Rhodesia... Samurai-born Nakamigawa Hikojiro, former teacher and newspaper editor, is hired by House of Mitsui's failing bank, founded 1876 (revives operation with modernization, purchases two silk mills, acquires paper mill, modernizes iron works, starts cotton mill, employs college graduates to change traditional attitudes)... Teak exporter H.N. Andersen starts East Asiatic Co., Denmark (evolves by 1980s as largest Scandinavian trading enterprise with 38 cargo ships and some 40,000 employees worldwide)... Bovril drops plan for illuminated sign in Edinburgh after public furor, similar reaction of Dover citizens in 1901 to planned advertising sign of Quaker Oats on White Cliffs... Grand Guignol Theater opens in Paris to present gory melodramas (-1962)... Marconi gets British patent for wireless telegraph (forms Wireless Telegraph Co. in 1900, sends signal over Channel in 1899 and Atlantic in 1901)... B. Seebohm Rowntree is first Director of Labour Department for family candy business (starts House Magazine in 1902, hires works doctor in 1904, forms trust for adult education in 1904, adopts 8-hour day and pension plan in 1906, in 1919 hires 'social helpers' for women workers, adopts 5-day week, and forms Central Works Council, used during W.W. I, begins Oxford Conference for Works Managers in 1919 to train foremen, forms Psychological Dept in 1922, rules in 1923 that appointments of foremen must be approved by workers, forms Management Research Groups in mid-1920s, 8 in country by 1935, with Urwick, C.F. Merriam to improve efficiency by exchanging views, research with other managers)...

Engineering Employers' Federation, Britain's first permanent association of employers, is victorious over unions with lockout... William Stephenson is apprenticed to general merchandising firm (meets F.W. Woolworth in 1904 while on business trip to England, joins British F.W. Woolworth in 1909 - director in 1920 and president in 1932 to build chain from 529 stores to 768 by W.W. II)...

S. Pearson & Son incorporates as world's largest contractor, grandson Weetman in charge 1897 (reconstructs business as holding company in 1919 to invest in newspapers, Lazard Bros., and oil exploration in 1920s, passes business to heirs in 1927, helps form British Airways in 1935).

1898

General Events

Workers, peasants riot in Italy... France, Italy sign commercial treaty... Russia adopts gold standard... Following 1874 formula of English research chemist, Bayer sells Heroin, trademark name, as family remedy for aches, pains, coughs and diarrhea (-1925 when outlawed by Geneva Convention)... Boxers, Righteous and Harmonious Fists Society, appear in China, encouraged by Empress, as antiforeign, anti-western movement (-1901)... New Zealand adopts old-age pensions... Industrial workers start Russia's Social Democratic Party... Confederation of Swedish Trade Unions forms, local and national unions seen in 1880s (holds direct negotiations with Swedish Confederation of Employers in 1936)... China grants concessions to Britain (inland waterways, railroads - virtual monopoly until international consortium in 1910), Germany (mines), Russia (land), and France (land)... Peter Elfelt makes first Danish motion picture, produces feature film in 1903... Aero Club of France forms in Paris... Japan formulates Civil Code, traditional familial system as key legal institution...

Brazilian Alberto Santos-Dumont makes power flight in dirigible in France (wins Deutsche Prize in 1901 for 7-mile flight in Paris)... China starts reform program to speed building of Peking-Hankow Railway (-1905), to buy Western arms, to start naval training, to start schools (Peking University), to develop budget system, to abolish sinecures of mandarins (is revoked after Empress Dowager imprisons Emperor)... With small grant from Vienna aviation association, Wilhelm Kress, Austrian piano maker and inventor who tinkered in aviation for some 34 years, starts building full-scale, manned flying boat (fails in 1901 test when plane capsizes, may have been over-powered as Daimler works mistakenly sent larger gasoline engine than ordered)... Baseball appears in Puerto Rico with U.S. troops in Cuban war... Germany's Kaiser threatens to imprison anyone encouraging strikes or impeding strike-breakers.

Business Events

Escoffier, master French chef, heads kitchen at London's Carlton Hotel (-1921, organizes kitchen into interdependent specializations for efficient food preparation)... Johannesburg Stock Exchange is founded, South Africa... Zeppelin forms Joint Stock Co. for the Promotion of Airship Travel in Stuttgart, Germany (makes first flight of 18 minutes in 1900)... Cesar Ritz, son of Swiss peasant, transforms Paris mansion of Francois Mansard into elegant hotel... Louis Renault builds his first car with own transmission (after forming business with two brothers, makes world's first sedan, develops best-selling taxis by 1914, expands with trucks, tractors and aircraft engines in 1920s-1930s)... Pierre Azaria combines his electrical generating firm with three others to form Compagnie Generale d'Electricite, becomes Paris-based Alcatel, founded 1879, Asthom in 1991 (after France nationalizes, 1946, electric utilities, diversifies into appliances, electronics and telecommunications, swaps, 1969, its data processing and appliance business to Thomson for its heavy equipment maker, Asthom, in 1976 gets French shipbuilding giant, Chantiers de l'Atlantique, after being nationalized in 1982, trades its defense and consumer electronics to Thomson for its communications business, goes public in 1987, tops AT&T in 1989 as world's No. 1 maker of telecommunications equipment, systems, and cables, in 1990 takes over, pending EC approval, Fiat's telecommunications unit, enters U.S. market, 1991, with buy of Rockwell International's transmission equipment division)... With British rights for Emile Berliner's gramophone, William B. Owen forms Gramophone Co. to compete with Seamen's National Gramophone (acquires French phonograph business in 1899, exchanges record pressings with U.S.' Victor Talking Machine in 1902 - informally divide world market, buys Zonophone Co. in 1903, opens first British factory in 1906, by 1914 operates in Austria, France, Germany, India, Russia, and Spain, is acquired

1920-21 by U.S.' Victor, merges in 1931 to form British-dominated Electrical and Musical Instruments, EMI)... Ariel Cycle Co. produces first motor tricycle (makes cars in 1900 and motorcycles in 1905)... Edwin White, brothers start Wolverhampton ginger beer manufacturing and retailing business (enter milk market in 1913, by 1923 build Midland Counties Dairy as land's largest private dairy company).

1899

General Events

British Navy launches first its turbine ship... Contract for building Baghdad Railroad is granted to German interests... Britain buys Niger Co... German Social Democrats abandon strict Marxism... New university at Birmingham forms Faculty of Commerce, offers 3-year course... Norwegian Federation of Labor forms... South African war between Boers, British begins (-1902)... Inspired by work of Lilienthal, Scottish Percy F. Pilcher tests gasoline-powered Hawk (dies during experiment)... First full-scale school of social work opens in Amsterdam... Basic agreement for collective bargaining is formulated in Denmark by central union, confederation of employers after major strike (provides employees with right to bargain, establishes national mechanism to resolve labor disputes, copied by Norway in 1935, Sweden in 1938, and Finland in 1948).

Business Events

Bayer's Carl Duisberg forms five-man directorate to manage internal operations and external affairs... U.S.' J. Walter Thompson Advertising Agency opens British office, first such U.S. branch overseas... British Westinghouse is created... A.D. Klaber, inventor of first British rotary duplicating machine, forms Neostyle Mfg. Co. (becomes Roneo, is acquired in 1966 by Vickers to prevent U.S. takeover)... Assn. of Netherlands Employers is formed... Nippon Electric Co., NEC, started by two Japanese businessmen with Western Electric holding 54% (sells its interest, letting NEC have access to patents, in 1925 to ITT, is resold in 1959-77 to Japanese investors) to make communications equipment (evolves as primary supplier to Nippon Telegraph & Telephone, by 1960s operates with 40 subsidiaries, minority interests in some 40 others, and some 30,000 employees, starts U.S. venture in 1978 to make telephone equipment, is world's largest semi-conductor business in 1980s, plans to take on IBM, AT&T in 1990 global markets)... Mobil starts subsidiary in South Africa (after pressure by U.S. antiapartheid groups and U.S. tax policies, leaves in 1989, largest U.S. firm in country, for net loss of $140 million)... Walter Rathenau joins board of AEG... Kenneth C. Irving, New Brunswick, Canada, entrepreneur (runs some 300 companies in oil, shipbuilding, forestry, etc., worth some $5.6 billion, by 1990), is born... Shinjiro Torii peddles Spanish wine to Osaka pubs, by 1990 Suntory with sales of $5.4 billion.

1900s

General Events

Britain's first practical vacuum cleaner appears... Sochi evolves on Russia's Black Sea as resort for elite, hosts over 250 sanitariums by 1988.

Business Events

Royal Mail Shipping Group forms in Britain (as complex of 120 interlocking subsidiaries, collapses 1930 after paying spurious dividends, most subsidiaries revived by trustees)... United Fruit starts Tropical Radio Telegraph to communicate with plantations in Panama, Honduras (evolves by 1980s as profitable international telecommunications subsidiary, TRT, for United Brands)... J. & P. Coates, Paisley sewing-thread business, is Britain's largest manufacturer with some 5,000 employees, first in 1919, 5th in 1930 and 8th in 1948... J.C. Van Marken: Industrial Social

Organization (describes management practices of 1870 Nederlands Yeast & Spirits Fabrik: savings bank in 1871, joint employer-employee committee in 1878, social department and sickness fund in 1880, employee housing in 1880s, plant paper in 1882 - oldest in continuous publication, profit-sharing plan in 1885, widow fund in 1886, employee clubhouse in 1890, nursery school in 1893, disabled fund in 1895, and family care program in 1930, cites hierarchy of needs)... Pedro Ferrer, wife start Freixenet in Spain to make sparkling wine (becomes world's leading producer with operations in U.S., Mexico, France, China).

1900

General Events

Labor Representation Committee, forerunner of Labor Party in 1906, forms (February 27) in Britain... France establishes 10-hour working day... London's underground is electrified... Society of Righteous and Harmonious Fists starts (May 31) Boxer Rebellion to rid China of all "foreign devils" (-1901 when suppressed by British, U.S., French and Japanese forces, force China to pay $333 million indemnity)... Fessenden is first to transmit human speech by radio waves... Paris subway opens (July 2)... New German Chancellor Bernhard von Bulow names Count Arthur von Posadowsky-Wehner Secretary of State for Internal Affairs (improves sickness and accident insurance plans, makes industrial courts mandatory for communities over 20,000, extends child labor laws to cover cottage industries, encourages construction of working-class housing)... Zeppelin flies (July 2) his first dirigible for 18 minutes (proves reality of dirigibles, last Zeppelin dismantled in 1940)... British mine act outlaws (July 30) child labor... Strikes appear in Belgium, Germany, Austria, Western Bohemia... Britain passes act for railway safety, workmen's compensation act for sickness... Germany abolishes private postal services... After experimenting with asbestos waste since 1893, Ludwig Hatschele, Austrian textile manufacturer, makes first asbestos-cement sheets... First glass-fiber is developed, Germany... Norway's Johann Waaler gets German patent for paper clip...

Long-distance buses appear (August 27) in England... Paris holds world's fair (exhibits tools equipped with Taylor's high-speed steel - hailed by European engineers and industrialists, escalator of U.S.' Otis and Scandinavian design in textiles, porcelains and furniture)... Finland's first nationwide agreement is obtained by typographers, founded 1890... Japan's Peace Policy Law prohibits unions and strikes, repealed 1925... World's tanker fleet, ships over 2,000 dwt, is composed of 109 vessels, 2,991 above 10,000 dwt by 1969... Edmund Fouche devises oxyacetylene torch... Deutschland liner beats (September 9) Kaiser Wilhem der Grosse in race from Hamburg to NYC in 5 days, 11 hours, 45 minutes... Germany passes (October 1) workman's compensation act... Belgium adopts (October 26) old age pensions... German engineer patents (November 30) front-wheel drive for cars... Nicaragua sells (December 1) canal rights to U.S. for $5 million... Germany's population is some 50 millon, 54% in industrial cities... Hamburg-American Line, world's largest shipper, makes Hamburg world's 3rd busiest port after NYC, Antwerp... After starting land's first telephone service in 1889 Japan's Ministry of Communications gets monopoly for system.

Business Events

London Daily Express is published... William Muldoon is world's first professional wrestling champion... Swedish textile mill, founded 1853, with some 2,000 workers is largest industrial operation in Scandinavia... After leaving New Mexico mining in 1892 to develop Los Angeles oil field, Edward L. Doheny starts Mexican Petroleum (starts drilling in 1901, successful by 1910)... France's Henri Fayol presents views on industrial administration to engineering, mining conferences (-1908)... Norwegian Employers' Confederation forms... Societe Parisienne d'Electricite forms, provides financial services to three large electrical-utility firms... Chinese Chamber of Commerce appears in Hong Kong, Shanghai chamber in 1904... Over 30% of all cotton goods produced by Moscow industrialists are sold at Nizhnyi fair, traditional market of

Russian merchants... Edward Moss opens London Hippodrome as music, circus hall (-1982, presents revues and variety shows in 1912, after dance bands and musical comedies, is Talk of the Town cabaret, restaurant in 1958)... Selwyn Edge forms British Motor Traction Co. to control automobile patents (fails to form monopoly)... John Benn, after working for father's trade journal, acquires Hardware Trade Journal, business of 25 papers by 1925 (publishes books in 1920)... Gerard N.C. Mann forms partnership to build car bodies and sell, service cars of various makes, 80 in 1907-08 and 36 in 1936, for gentry of Norwich, East Anglia (by 1919 runs 10 showrooms, garages with over 1,000 employees)... Alfred Mond forms Mond Nickel (creates Imperial Chemical Industries in 1926 with Brunner, Mond & Co., Mond Nickel, Nobel Industries, United Alkali and British Dyestuffs)... After working at U.S.' Wanamaker's, Austin L. Reed persuades father to open new branch of Reed & Sons, men's outfitter, in London (forms National Assn. of Outfitters in 1902, opens 2nd branch in 1905, forms Austin Reed of 1980s in 1906 with larger London store - 31 shops by 1939, gets rights to retail men's wear on Cunard's transatlantic liners, grants exclusive agencies for shirts, collars to leading retailers of Europe and Empire, founds Regent Street Assn. in 1925)... Michelin tire business publishes Guide Michelin for French motorists (lists first restaurants in 1926, uses stars for quality in 1929)... First modern department store, The Sincere Co., in Hong Kong, Wing On store in 1907, is started by 12 partners, Chinese merchants from Hong Kong, Australia and U.S., and 25 employees (forms corporation and starts Bible study group in 1907, evening school for English, Chinese and commercial mathematics in 1911, opens Canton branch with hotel, factories in 1912 and Shanghai branch in 1914, forms insurance and investment firm in 1915, social clubs and funds for sick and needy workers in 1922, and life insurance firm in 1923, operates in 1925 with some 3,000 shareholders, 4,000 store and factory employees, innovates with glass display windows, fixed prices, individual receipts for sales, employment of women clerks)... First Fiat automobiles are made in Turin, Italy, founded in 1899 by nine industrial amateurs - Giovanni Agnelli I in charge by 1907 (promotes business by racing against cars of Panhard, Peugeot and Mercedes, returns to authority after workers seize plant after W.W. I but can't operate it, survives early 1920s with bank loan from Morgan bank, introduces "Topolino" in 1936 as people's car, is succeeded in 1945 by Vittorio Valletta, signs contract with U.S.S.R. in 1966 to build billion-dollar plant before retirement)...

Philips electrical factory provides medical care to employees (starts employee welfare program in 1905, provides free medical assistance in 1909, starts Sick Benefit Fund in 1909 - dropped with Health Insurance Act of 1931, starts employee housing program in 1910 - some 7,000 units by 1951, forms band in 1911 - orchestra in 1930 and choir in 1937, forms entertainment society in 1912 and sports association in 1913, sponsors employee relief fund in 1916, provides gardens for growing vegetables in 1917, and creates Philips Cooperative Society in 1918)... Manon makes handcrafted chocolates in Brussels (still extant)... Austro-Hungarian Emil Jellinek, financier and diplomat, buys 36 racing cars, named after daughter, from Daimler Engine (after seeing first win in 1901, leads to Daimler registering Mercedes mark in 1902)... Aluminum Co. of America, Alcoa, begins its Canadian operation (in 1929, after U.S. antitrust order, becomes separate firm, in 1950, after U.S. courts order Mellon and Davis interests to end their joint ownership, is an independent entity, opens giant power complex in British Columbia in 1954 to run smelters, is renamed Alcan in 1962, changes supply plans when Guyana nationalizes its raw resources in 1971 and Jamaica takes over 70% of its assets on the island in 1977, builds world's largest aluminum can recycling plant, Kentucky, in 1989, in 1990s works with Jaguar to make an energy-saving aluminum car).

1901

General Events

Blickensderfer Electric makes first electric typewriter... Motor-driven bicycles appear in Europe... Peter C. Hewitt invents mercury vapor arc lamp... International Federation of Trade Unions forms... Labor riots appear in Spain... Asphalt trust concedes (February 13) to Venezuelan expropriation demands... Madrid enacts (February 14) martial law to quell tax protests... Britain enacts Miners' Eight-Hour Bill... Britain grants unions legal status, right to strike, protection of union funds and use of peaceful picketing... French miners end (May 6) 3-month strike... Work is finished on Mombasa-Lake Victoria Railway in Africa (1896-)... France's L. Gaumont invents method to synchronize film projector with gramophone... Great Britain grants Australia commonwealth status, New Zealand in 1907... Holland's Christian Eijkman identifies rice germ, leads to development of vitamins... Britain's Taff Vale Judgment limits right of workers to strike (holds unions liable for damages caused by its officials, allows suits by employers for damages)... Argentina's first national central labor organization is formed, some 160,000 members by 1919... Paris opens (July 1) new electric railway... Thomas H. Holding forms The Assn. of Cycle Campers, world's first camping club... Mexico places under federal control those mineral deposits found on "national lands" to prevent U.S. interests in controlling its oil industry... Deutschland sets (July 17) east-west transatlantic record of 5 days, 11 hours, 5 minutes... France requires car registration for those driving over 18 mph... Confederation of Mexican Workers forms... Chinese Imperial Edict forbids (October 10) buying of positions in public service... Marconi sends (December 13) first transatlantic telegraphic radio message from Cornwall to Newfoundland... Britain makes boxing a legal sport... Although a blast furnace had operated, used Dutch manual, in 1851, Japanese government forms Yawata Works to make steel (produces bulk of land's steel by 1920, during 1930s is combined with other steelmakers as Japan Iron & Steel, dissolved in 1950 to spawn Yawata Iron & Steel and Fuji Iron and Steel, buys two steelmakers in 1967 and 1968, merges with Fuji to form Nippon Steel in 1970 - 3rd largest in 1991 after Italy's IRI and Germany's Thyssen, diversifies with electronics in 1986, forms joint ventures with IBM Japan and Hitachi, invests $200 million in Oracle software in 1991).

Business Events

Cabaret Uberbretti opens in Berlin... A. Milne, flour mill owner, forms South American Petroleum Syndicate to prospect for oil in Peru (reorganizes in 1903 with Peruvian Corp. and London merchant house of Balfour Williamson, finds major discovery in 1905)... AB Lux begins to make mantles for paraffin lamps in Sweden (reorganizes in 1919 as AB Electrolux to make electrical appliances)... Three U.S. businessmen start American Electrical Novelty & Manufacturing Co. in London, called Ever Ready Electrical in 1906... D'Arcy, adventurer with fortune from Australian mining, and Burmah Oil Co. get exclusive rights for 60 years, canceled 1932, by Persia to develop oil, gas reserves... Barnum & Bailey Circus tours Germany (surprises military by loading circus cars at one end of train, used for mobilization in W.W. I)... Doulton pottery works gets Royal Warrant (produces Toby mugs in 1930s)... Imperial Tobacco is formed by Wills, Players and other manufacturers to compete with American Tobacco... George Beale, after working for Maypole Dairy in 1884, forms Meadow Dairy with support of Dutch margarine merchant family of Van der Berghs, formal control in 1912 (operates 16 food shops in 1906 - 90 in 1909 and 800 by 1926, acquires Home & Colonial Stores in 1927 before creation of Unilever in 1929)...

After managing Rover Cycles racing team in 1895 and working for Dunlop Rubber in 1900, John D. Siddeley buys car agency to sell Peugeots, later Siddeley Autocars (asks Wolseley Motors, Vickers subsidiary, in 1905 to make engines of his design, is Wolseley's general manager in 1905-09, starts Siddeley-Deasy Motor in 1909, after acquisition in 1919 by Armstrong forms Armstrong Siddeley, joins Armstrong aircraft subsidiary in 1920, forms Hawker-Siddeley in 1934 as major aircraft manufacturer)... After developing toy kits to teach children mechanics, Frank Hornly patents 'Meecano,' registered 1907 to become 'The World's Most Famous Toy' (starts German wind-up toy train business in 1920, makes electric trains and accessories in 1925, makes Dinky toys in 1933)... Former reporter, William E. Berry, starts Advertising World (starts small publishing business with brother in 1905 - severed 1937, acquires 1822 Sunday Times in 1905, after selling to Hulton publishing group acquires Amalgamated Press, paper mills in 1926 to build Allied Newspapers as empire with 58 weeklies, 21 monthly periodicals and 4 publishing subsidiaries)... After hearing of 1901 Spindletop oil gusher, Weetman Pearson starts buying, 600,000 acres, and leasing, 300,000 acres, land to look for oil south of Tampico (gets Mexico's biggest oil concession from Diaz regime in 1906, completes refinery pipeline by 1908 - 72 distribution agencies, forms

Compania Mexicana de Petroleo, El Aguila, by 1909, as one of three firms controlling Mexico's oil industry, fights "great oil war" with U.S. interests, forms Anglo-Mexican Petroleum Co. to distribute Mexico's oil in Britain, Continent, sells Mexican Eagle Oil in 1919 to Royal Dutch Shell)... Sweden's Scandia forms to make cars at bicycle factory, trucks in 1902 (merges with rival in 1911 and makes buses, leaves car market in 1920s, makes military vehicles during W.W. II, imports Volkswagens in 1948)... War correspondent Hishiro Mitsunaga starts Telegraphic Service for faster communications with news and Japan Advertising, allows clients to pay bills with ad space (merges two, evolves as Dentsu, in 1907, gets Japanese rights in 1908 for United Press wire).

1902

General Events

F.A. McKenzie: The American Invaders (decries U.S. takeover of British industry)... Diesel engine is used on French canal boat (after try by Cunard Line is used on Russian tanker in 1904 and Danish Selandia, first large vessel, in 1912)... Germany receives (January 16) rights to build Konia-Baghdad railway... Transatlantic carriers combine (January 30) to raise rates 100%... France's Lebaudy brothers launch first practical airship... Portugal declares bankruptcy... Germany passes protectionist tariff... Anglo-German fleet seize Venezuela's Navy to recover debts... France passes Public Health Act to improve living conditions for working class... Trieste uses (February 14) martial law to quell rioting strikers seeking reduced hours... Berlin subway opens (February 15)... Louis Renault invents drum brake... Great Britain, Persia agree (March 22) to link Europe, India by telegraph... Preussen, largest and most sophisticated sailing vessel ever built, is launched in Hamburg as ideal windjammer... Commercial affairs school opens in Wuchang, China... W. Nurman discovers hydrogenation process... German unions confederate (April 9)... Belgian trade unionists call general strike for universal suffrage... French artillery captain tests gasoline-powered gliders suspended from tower (uses Wright brothers' data to make gliders)... 10 days of rioting ends (April 18) when Belgium refuses to grant Socialists right to strike... International Miners Congress demands (May 22) nationalization of mines... For first time German government representatives attend (June 21) union congress... France sets (June 27) 10.5 hours as minimum working day...

Worker's Party, Belgium, breaks up (September 15) when radical Socialists try to dominate new party... Some 60% of French miners strike (October 9)... Britain's Education Act establishes secondary education... Werner Sombert: Der Moderne Kapitalismus (gives "first" discussion of capitalism, socialism as opposite systems)... After general strike, Austria grants general manhood suffrage, effective 1907...Danish labor unions and cooperatives, union bank and bakery, start Stjernen Brewery to share in industry profits, to show unions can operate profitable business and to provide work for union members (-late 1960s)... Vilfredo Pareto: Les Systemes Socialistes... Japanese government sponsors Industrial Bank of Japan to provide long-term financing for businesses (receives U.S. permission after W.W. II to continue after severing governmental ties, helps form Nippon Steel in 1970, is allowed to start foreign branches in 1971, acquires New York merchant bank in 1985 and primary dealer in U.S. Treasury securities in 1986).

Business Events

Industrial Bank of Japan, modeled on Credit Mobilier, appears, seen in 1990 as Japan's most reliable bank... Helene Rubinstein opens her first beauty salon in Melbourne, Australia (opens London salon in 1908, Paris in 1912, and New York in 1915 - by 1917 with operations in Philadelphia, New Orleans and San Francisco)... Eastman Kodak opens retail outlets in London, Lyons... Swedish Employers' Confederation forms (negotiates with Swedish Central Confederation of Unions in 1936, first nationwide collective agreement with union confederation c. 1940)... Maudslay Motor Co. appears in Coventry, Standard Motor Co. in 1903 (produces 750 cars/year in 1913 - 53,000 in 1939 as Britain's 6th largest with 13% of market)... U.K.'s Imperial Tobacco and U.S.' American Tobacco end their market war by dividing the world markets (after giving

American the U.S. and Imperial the U.K., form British-American Tobacco, American with 66% share until forced to sell by Supreme Court in 1911, as a cartel for the rest of the world, wins, BAT, success in 1907 after massive billboard campaign in China, gives Chinese millions of free samples in 1909 to get sales of 25 billion cigarettes/year by 1920, buys U.S. ciagrette firm, Brown & Williamson, in 1927, acquires, 1933, Boots drug chain from U.S.' Liggett)... U.S.' Citicorp bank opens first Asian branches, 83 by 1990 for income of $362 million... With aid of J.P. Morgan, Orford and Canadian Copper, plus five smaller firms in industry, form New Jersey-based International Nickel (forms Canadian subsidiary in 1916 - parent after restructuring in 1928, acquires Mond Nickel in 1929 to control world's output - 85% of non-Communist production in 1950s, acquires ESB Ray-O-Vac, world's No. 1 maker of batteries in 1975 - sold early 1980s, is renamed Inco Ltd. in 1976)

1903

General Events

Argentina bars (January 10) importation of U.S. beef for sanitary reasons... W.H. Stearn, F. Topham develop method to produce artificial silk, viscose rayon... W. Siemens develops electric locomotive... K. Tsiolkovsky proposes liquid oxygen as fuel for space travel... Workers' Education Assn. forms in Britain to improve adult education, follows Cambridge extension lectures in 1873... German banking syndicate, headed by Georg von Siemens, gets (March 5) concession to build Turkey-Baghdad railroad, Baghdad Railway Co. with first concession 1888... Emmeline Pankhurst forms Women's Social & Political Union to get voting rights for women... Dutch railway workers strike (April 6-11)... Panama, abetted by French and U.S. interests for construction of Panama Canal, declares independence from Columbia... Britain sets 20-mile-per-hour speed limit for automobiles... First motor taxis, use taximeters, appear in London, 8,397 by W.W. I... Holland adopts (April 11) law punishing railway, civil service strikers... Octave Mirbeau opens (April 23) play "Business is Business"... Russian Social Democratic Labor Party, formed 1898, meets in London, splits into Mensheviks, Bolsheviks led by Lenin, Trotsky... Social Democratic Party forms in Finland... Chinese Government establishes regulations, rewards to encourage growth of business... Dutch trade unionists strike to protest anti-strike legislation... Paris, Rome are linked (May 23) by telephone... Norway's Roald Amundsen is first to complete east-to-west voyage of Northwest Passage (-1905, first west-to-east passage in 1942)... Berlin International Monetary Conference sets (July 16) rate for trading gold-based with silver-based currencies... British Trade Unions Congress opposes (September 8) proposed customs reform with preferential tariffs for colonial goods... Britain passes (December 17) Employment of Children Act... Germany sets quality standards to prevent adulteration of wine, France in 1905.

Business Events

Trusthouse Forte hotel business is started in Britain to restore quality of old coaching inns... The Institute of Directors, world's largest group of business leaders, forms in London, Royal Charter in 1906... Annual Tour de France bicycle race is started as pioneering commercial venture in sports by two Paris newspapers (evolves by 1980s with annual budget of some $7 million)... Duisberg visits U.S., sees trusts as blueprint for future (proposes in 1904 paper that large size and administrative coordination are required to reduce costs in production, sales and administration, leads to consolidation in Germany's chemical industry)... To counter AEG's merger with Union, Siemens & Halske forms Siemens-Schuckert-Werke to combine its high-voltage production and research with Schuckert's manufacturing plants and sales organization (distinguishes in corporate structure between high and low-voltage technology, forms "common departments" after W.W. I to clarify lines of authority, forms Siemens Cable Cooperative in 1921 and Siemens Relay Cooperative in late-1920s to resolve conflicts of interest in parent firms)... Mexico gives Mexican Telephone & Telegraph, backed by U.S. interests including AT&T, permission to operate in Mexico City, similar concession to Swedish consortium, including Ericsson, in 1905 (is nationalized in 1915 while Ericsson thrives, is run in 1925 by ITT to expand system nationwide, acquires Ericsson in 1932 - called Telmex after W.W. II, goes public in 1953 - nationalization in 1972, is sold in 1990 to Southwestern Bell, France Telecom, Grupo Carso)... After starting in 1894 as newsprint manufacturer, Albert E. Reed & Co., now Reed International, goes public, by 1991 U.K.'s largest publishing and information group and Europe's 3rd largest after Bertelsmann and Hachette (for next 60 years grows by acquiring U.K. pulp and paper mills, begins making packaging materials in 1930s, goes into building products in 1954, enters Canada and Australia in 1960 and Norway in 1962, buys International Publishing and 29% of Cahners Publishing, other 71% in 1977, in 1970, sells Mirror Group Newspapers to Maxwell in 1984 to ease debt load and improve coordination, sells building and decoration products in 1986 and paint and do-it-yourself firms in 1987, buys Octopus Publishing, U.K.'s 2nd largest in books, in 1987, sells paper and packaging units for acquisition fund - over five by 1991).

1904

General Events

W. Rubel invents offset printing... China signs (January 13) treaty of commerce with U.S. (opens Manchu ports and Mukden to international trade)... Japan stops (January 15) all steamship service to U.S... British chemist F.S. Kipping develops first practical formula for silicone, not utilized until W.W. II... French scientist, Leon Guillet, discovers stainless steel, fails to develop discovery... Germany signs commercial treaties with Belgium, Russia, Switzerland, Serbia, Austria- Hungary... Australia's Workers Party forms (April 26)... Britain acquires part ownership of Cunard steamship line (acquires telephone system in 1912, Marconi Radio Telegraph in 1913 and Anglo-Persian Oil in 1914, amalgamates railways in 1921, partially nationalizes electrical utilities in 1926, forms iron, steel monopoly in 1932, national coal cartel in 1936 and government airline in 1939)... After 13 years, Trans-Siberian Railroad is finished (July 31), takes 21 days from Paris to Vladivostok... First telegraphic transmission of photographs is made between Munich, Nuremberg... Paris conference discusses white slave trade... Strike starts in Milan, soon spreads throughout Italy... Following formation of labor groups in 1880s-90s and political activities in 1890s,Labor Party is elected to govern Australia, re-elected 1908-09, 1914-17, 1929-31 and 1941-49... Max Weber: The Protestant Ethic and the Spirit of Capitalism (argues teachings of Calvin stimulated entrepreneurship)... France adopts 10-hour work day... Oil workers, Austria-Hungary, win (August 8) shorter hours and sanitary improvements after uprising... International Congress of Miners demands (August 9) minimum wage, 8-hour day... First radio transmission of music is aired at Graz, Austria... Thorstein Veblen: The Theory of Business Enterprise... Swiss Dr. George Wander develops Ovaltine as nutritious food concentrate for ailing patients... London Symphony Orchestra opens first season, organized as cooperative society with structure of joint stock company... Federation Internationale de Football Assn. forms to govern sport of soccer... World's first omnibus, built by Heinrich Buessing to carry 20 people, is tested in Braunschweig, Germany.

Business Events

Carl Linstrom Co. is started in Berlin to make phonographs, records... General Funerals, French cartel, is granted rights for most of nation's funeral business (is challenged in 1984 by franchise operation of Michel Leclerc)... Aristocratic auto buff, Charles S. Rolls, opened ad agency in 1902 to sell gasoline cars by installment plan, becomes selling agent for elegant cars made by engineer F. Henry Royce, resigns 1910 when board rejects manufacture of Wright Aeroplanes (breaks Monte Carlo-London speed record in 1906, merges interests with Royce in 1906, introduces first Silver Ghost car in 1907 to challenge Napier cars in exclusive market - sells 2,813 in 1907-16, 3,360 in 1919-25, and total of 100,000 by 1985 with 65,000 still running, starts driving school for chauffeurs in 1908, by 1912 forms experimental department for developing auto and airplane engines - Merlin liquid-cooled in 1937 and jets in 1942, starts making airplane engines in 1914 - world's largest manufacturer in 1918, makes airplane engines for first transatlantic flight in 1919, introduces luxury Phantom series in 1920s - one Silver Spirit made every three months in 1980s, buys ailing car business of W.O. Bentley in 1931, produces 65% of Free World's gas turbine engines for commercial use in 1957)... Lithuanian-born Montague M. Burton opens retail clothing business in Chesterfield, 5 shops by 1910, 51, 8 in Ireland, by 1918, 364 in 1928 and 600 by 1939 with over 200,000 employees (to employ fellow Jews working in deplorable workshops starts factory in 1906, as Europe's largest clothing business builds world's largest clothing factory, 100 acres with housing for 8,000 employees, in 1921, employs over 100,000 in 1950, declines in 1950-70 with competition of jeans, casual wear)... Renault designs France's first vehicle for public transport... John J. McLaughlin, Toronto chemist and soda fountain supplier, creates Canada Dry ginger ale... Plush Ritz Hotel, named after Swiss hotelier, is built, London's first steel-framed building (opens 1906 for wealthy patrons)... Courtauld family silk business gets rights for viscose syndicate's process, patented 1891 by Charles F. Cross (starts U.S. subsidiary in 1911, by 1918 produces 40% of world's rayon, forms Foreign Relations Committee in 1928 to oversee foreign operations - Denmark and Spain in 1926 and Italy, France and Germany in 1927, agrees with ICI in 1928 to stay out of each other's markets)... Following Duisberg's proposal, Hoechst and Cassella & Co. form organization to acquire interests in dyestuff industry (expands with Kalle & Co. in 1907, leads to creation of IG Farben in 1925)... After quitting job as doorman for London's Savoy Hotel, Guccio Gucci opens small saddlery in Florence (evolves with separate Italian, U.S. branches in 1980s overseeing 150 emblem stores, 200 franchised shops and 2,500 outlets worldwide peddling some 14,000 different products with red and green band, with some 50 lawsuits in 1980s as grandson and nephew, Maurizio, fight patriarch Aldo for control, leads to Aldo going to jail, evidence from son, in 1986 after pleading guilty to $7 million in tax fraud, Maurizio fleeing to Switzerland in 1987 to avoid charges of fraud and illegal currency trade - cleared 1989 to take charge, and Investcorp buying 50% stake in 1988 from minority shareholders for $200-300 million to back Maurizio as CEO)... First Rolex timepieces are made, Switzerland (sells watches in 1950s for $600, $11,000 and up by 1990 as status symbols).

1905

General Events

Some 140,000 workers, peasants march (January 21) on Winter Palace, St. Petersburg... Larderello, Italy, uses geothermal power to generate electricity... Moscow is hit (January 23) by general strike... Finnish workers call general strike to protest Czar's infringements of constitutional rights... Danish Postal Service proposes centralized personnel function (starts job analysis program in 1916, forms personnel department in 1927)... First Simon-Benet tests of metal ability appear, France... Czar orders (February 12) study of living conditions for workers... First efficient tungsten filament lamp is devised, Germany... Riga Polytechnical Institute is only commercial institution of higher learning in Russia... Britain sets (March 22) maximum of 8-hour day for child miners... French Socialist Party forms... General Bronsart von Schellendorff: The Duties of the General Staff... Safety glass is invented... Germany signs commercial treaties with Bulgaria, Abyssinia... Father Gapon presents petition of grievances, identifies abuses by businessmen and industrial autocrats, to Czar... Sun Yat-sen forms union of secret societies in China to oust ruling Manchus... First motor buses appear in London... Netherlands Federation of Trade Unions forms... Chinese boycott U.S. goods to protest exclusion of Chinese immigrants... First harvest of Malay rubber is produced for under 9 cents/pound, Brazil's Manaus rubber runs $3/pound... Telephone links (April 1) Paris, Berlin... Russian Workers' Soviet Congress demands (April 7) democratic constitution... Striking workers at Ivanovo-Voznesensk textile center form (April 15) first soviet, win demands... Shanghai boycotts (August 5-25) U.S.goods... Belgian law limits (August 15) work week to 6 days... Budget Meakin: Model Factories and Villages: Ideal Conditions for Labor and Housing (describes desired social relations, health plans, communications, incentives and rewards, suggestion system, workmen's counsels)... British trade unions, some 1.5 million members, support (September 8) free trade, 8-hour day... Leon Trotsky, leader of St. Petersburg Soviet of Workers' Deputies, urges worker soviets to prepare for revolution... Over one million workers demanding political reforms hold (October 28-30) general strike in Russia... Czar Nicholas II grants (October 30) subjects constitutional rights... Factory councils form in Russia after unsuccessful revolution, prototype for soldiers' and workers' councils in 1917.

Business Events

General Electric acquires control of Tokyo Electric, pioneers U.S. investments in Japan... Rene Coty starts perfume plant near Paris... Russian businessmen try to start political party... London Automobile Assn. forms... Controlling interest of Zeiss Optical Works, Germany, is transferred to Ernst Abbe Foundation (distributes all profits to employees)... International Harvester opens plant in Sweden to compete with European firms (starts French, German plants in 1909)... In Germany, BASF, Agfa and Bayer consolidate interests for 50 years... Austin Motor Co. is started in Britain (makes its first small car in 1922, gets 37.3% of 1929 market and 24.3% in 1939)... George Kenning, age 24, takes over family business selling paraffin, pots, matches, and soap in local markets and distributing petroleum products door-to-door (opens first agency in 1910 to sell BSA Royal Enfield motorcycles - Ford car agency in 1916, by 1922 operates some 100 agencies in 28 countries to sell cars of 6 makers, sells first tires in 1936 - UniRoyal distributor in 1955)... Gabriel Voisin, Ernest Archdeacon and Louis Bleriot build France's first airplane factory near Paris... Walter Edge of Atlantic City, NJ, opens first U.S. ad agency, Dorland, in London (opens offices in Paris, Berlin and Brussels before W.W. I, followed after war by J. Walter Thompson, Erwin Wasey, Lord & Thomas, and McCann-Erickson)... Oppenheimers, German family with major share of Premier Diamond Mining of South Africa, buy small Consolidated Mines Selection (by 1917 acquires some of richest gold-bearing land in country, forms Anglo American in 1917 with financing by J.P. Morgan and U.S. banking interests, acquires diamond fields in German Southwest Africa, now Namibia, in 1920 to break 1888 monopoly of De Beers, takes over De Beers in 1929, by 1957 grows with uranium, chemicals, real estate, banking, manufacturing and insurance, is land's largest gold producer in 1958, dismisses 60,000 workers after strike in 1987, seven die in violence, sells share of Consolidated Gold Fields in 1989 and buys U.S. gold mining firm, faces difficulties, 1990-91, with sluggish demand for diamonds, counters with advertising program, and gold)...

Consolidated Zinc forms to mine Australia's mineral-rich Broken Hill area (after combining with New Broken Hill and Imperial Smelting finds world's largest bauxite deposit in 1955, merges with 1873 Rio Tinto in 1962 to form RTZ Corp., in 1968 acquires U.S. Borax, gets Papua New Guinea copper mine in 1969, sells consumer products of Borax in 1988 to Greyhound, now Dial, buys BP Minerals, includes U.S.' Kennecott formed 1915 by Guggenheims, J.P. Morgan for mining, shipping Alaskan copper which buys Chilean copper mine in 1925 and Utah Copper in 1936 and then sold to BP in 1981, from British Petroleum in 1989)... Sweden's Ericsson is hired to run a Mexican phone system, started by Lars Ericsson in 1876 to repair telegraph equipment and make telephones, 1878, and combined receiver-speaker handset in 1885 (is hired, 1908, to modernize Bangkok's phone system, starts Paris factory in 1911, sees Russian holdings nationalized in 1918 and merges with Stockholm phone company - named L.M. Ericsson in 1926, sees Ivan Kreuger, Match King, gain control in 1930, after his suicide, sees ITT, Kreuger creditor, take over in 1932 and sell out to Wallenbergs in 1960, introduces computer-controlled exchange in 1975, develops "office of the future" in 1980s, sheds computer business in 1988, tops AT&T, Siemens to get CGCT, French phone equipment business, in 1987)... Norsk Hydro is started by two Norwegian entrepreneurs to use electricity generated by waterfalls to extract nitrogen from air for fertilizer (as largest chemical firm in Scandinavia wins concession with partners for offshore drilling - North Sea strike in 1969 leads to Norway upping its share of firm to 51%, diversifies with aluminum in 1967 and fish-farming in 1969, buys fertilizer firms in Holland, 1979, Sweden, 1981, U.K., 1982, Germany, 1985, and France, 1986, acquires two British firms in petrochemicals in 1981, begins producing at Oseberg field, major find, in 1988, buys 300 Danish gasoline stations in 1990).

1906

General Events

Trades Dispute Act exempts British unions from damages caused by strikes, lifted in 1980s by Thatcher Government... Holland begins to drain Zuider Zee... France holds first Grand Prix motor car race... International conference bans night-shift work for women... Werner Sombart: "Why is there no socialism in the United States?"... Britain's A.J. Penty starts guild socialism movement to promote industrial self-government... General Confederation of Labor forms as Italy's first national union, some two million members by 1920 as nation's largest... England's Workman's Compensation Act adopts principle of employers' liability, first developed in 1880... Austria, Serbia begin customs war... Some 6,000 workers are fired (May 1) after May Day strike, Germany... Norway adopts unemployment insurance... Alarmed by amount of foreign ownership, Norway limits foreign investments in natural resources... Arsene d'Arsonval, F. Bordas of Paris devise freeze dry process, discovered independently in 1909 by U.S.' Shackwell (is used for coffee in 1934 and for other foods in 1946-47 by U.S.' E.W. Flosdorff)... France's Eugene Lauste is (August 11) first to patent talking film... Russian agrarian reforms of Stolypin lead to rise of Kulaks, word first used for greedy moneylenders and merchants, in acquiring relatively large farms and labor, eliminated by collectivization in 1929-34... Sweden establishes machinery for voluntary conciliation of industrial disputes...

France suppresses strike of Nord miners (quells strikes by Nantes doctors in 1907, Midi vineyard workers in 1907, construction workers in 1908)... China forms Patent Bureau, previously inventor would register patent claim with Maritime Customs Service... Paris hosts first Gordon Bennett International Balloon Race (-1938)... After disappointments with power flights in dirigibles, Brazilian-born Alberto Santos-Dumont makes Europe's first sustained plane flight... China, Britain agree to reduce opium production... French engineer Robert Esnault-Pelterie designs air-cooled, fan-shaped engine for planes (is built, used later in enclosed fuselage of steel tubing)... Peasants burn (September 10) 142 Russian estates, crushed by Cossacks... Switzerland hosts (September 17) international conference for worker protection... Strike of French Confederation General Du Travail for 8-hour day is unsuccessful... Zeppelin's dirigible, funded by lottery and gift from Kaiser, makes successful flight of some two hours at speed of 24.5 mph (carries 5,000 pounds of ballast, 11 people)... German Social Democratic Party opens (October 15) school for political education of workers... Germany's Arthur Korne telegraphs (October 17) pictures... Aero Club holds first official balloon race in Britain... Metal workers' union signs Italy's first collective agreement with ITALA auto firm... After studying U.S. schools of business in 1904, Ignaz Jastrow founds Berlin's Handelshockschule to train students for business careers (offers courses in business administration, economics, law, economic geography, economic history, science, technology, languages and those for training business teachers).

Business Events

British operation of Columbia record business, founded by Edison, is started (merges in 1931 with 1907 Gramophone Co.)... Dalziel forms General Motor Cab, joined by United Motor Cab in 1907... William Maxwell Aiken starts Royal Securities Corp., first bond-selling company in Eastern Canada (moves to England in 1910, after buying and selling firms invests in first paper in 1911, buys controlling interest of Daily Express in 1916 to build newspaper empire as Lord Beaverbrook)...

After becoming retail general manager of Chicago's Marshall Field department store, quit in 1904 when denied senior partnership and rejected in opening branches in London and Paris, Harry G. Selfridge moves to London to start retail store with backing of Sam Waring, London's major furniture retailer (after withdrawal of Waring in opposition to grand plans in 1907 forms Selfridge & Co. in 1908, opens elegant store, 130 departments and staff of 1,800, in 1909 in 'London's Greatest Gala Shopping Week,' acquires 3 satellite businesses in 1913, publishes The Romance of Commerce in 1918, is forced to retire in 1939 for debts from lavish spending)... M. MacKinnon starts first commercial production of Drambuie liquor, family's secret for helping "Bonnie Prince Charley" to escape in 1746... French engineer A. Darracq starts Milan business to make taxi cabs, produces first Alfa Romeo car in 1914... By this time, Britain's Vickers and Armstrong have market-sharing agreements for global distribution of armaments with Germany's Krupp, France's Schneider... With marriage to Bertha Krupp, Gustav Krupp assumes management of family enterprises (produces armaments during W.W. I, revives business with French withdrawal in 1920, produces steel bridges and rails for railroads during Germany's recovery, advises President Hindenberg in 1933 against appointment of Hitler as Chancellor - later enthusiastic supporter of Hitler and his armament program, is succeeded as head of enterprise by son, Alfred, in 1943)... Rihachi Mizundo, kimono shop worker, opens Tokyo baseball equipment store (by 1934 produces bats, balls, uniforms, golf clubs and skis at Osaka factory, builds gliders during W.W. II and furniture, frying pans after War before returning to sporting goods, by late 1980s runs 60 golf schools and produces over 30,000 products with 3,700 employees for sales of $1.2 billion)... German industrialists begin making fertilizer from lime, reduces dependence on Chile's nitrates... Electrical engineer and inventor, alternator in 1987, spark plug in 1902, starter in 1912, and regulator in 1913, Robert Bosch, started workshop in 1886, shortens workday for employees to 8 hours (starts U.S. business in 1909 - confiscated W.W.I, introduces power tools in 1928, adds appliances and car radios in 1933, dies in 1942 - 90% of firm goes to charity, after rebuilding with end of W.W. II introduces world's first electronic fuel injection system in 1967 and forms joint venture with Siemens to make appliances, returns to U.S. in 1974 with South Carolina plant, and develops first electronic fuel injection system in 1967 and forms joint venture with Siemens to make appliances, returns to U.S. in 1974 with South Carolina plant and develops first electronic ignition system, introduces first antilock braking in 1978, in late 1980s develops system to use one wire to replace many with semiconductor controllers)... Shojiro Ishibashi, elder brother take over father's, a former samurai, small Kyushu clothing business (focus on traditional footwear, start, 1923, making rubber soles, form Bridgestone in 1931 to make tires).

1907

General Events

Architect William Willett urges British lawmakers to adopt daylight-savings time to conserve fuel, provide more daylight hours to train soldiers (despite opposition of farmers, is adopted in 1916 after Germany)... France's Tourand designs first gasoline-powered tractor system for pulling equipment, followed by International Harvester in 1918 and Harry Ferguson in 1939 with hydraulic power... Imperial College of Science and Technology is created in London from 1845 Royal College of Chemistry, 1851 Royal School of Mines and 1884 The City and Guilds of London Institute... Tethered helicopter, designed by Louis and Jacques Brequet, is tested in flight, followed by attempt of Igor Sikorsky, Russia, in 1910 - successful in U.S. in 1939... Hamburg dockworkers strike March 2) to end night shifts, broken by 2,000 British strikebreakers... Claude G. Johnson, Lord Montague of Beaulieu: <u>Roads Made Easy by Picture in Pen</u>, one of first road maps in Europe... France builds first reinforced concrete bridge... France, Japan guarantee (May 6) free trade, change spheres of influence in Far East... Londoners see first airplane over City... British legislation provides contributory old-age pensions... Peking-Paris auto race, 8,000 miles, begins (June 10), won (August 10) by Italy's Prince Borghese... Britain's union membership rises by 60% by 1914... Lumiere brothers develop (June 10) three-color photography, follows 1867 work of James Maxwell... France passes (June 22) law to control fraud in wine industry... Paint spray gun is invented... Portugal declares (August 3) Sunday a day of rest... Britain launches <u>Lusitania</u>, world's largest steamship (sets new east-to-west record of 5 days, 54 minutes)... Carl Hagenbeck opens modern zoo in Berlin... Finnish unions form Federation of Labor, sawmill society largest with 4,300 members, woodworking with 4,200 and paper with 3,500 (organizes as Confederation of Finnish Trade Unions in 1930)...

Britain's Advertisements Regulation Act grants local authorities power to regulate unsightly signs, result of pressure from 1893 National Society for Controlling the Abuses of Public Advertising... <u>Journal of Applied Psychology</u> appears in Germany... Some 58% of all German mining workers are employed by firms with 1,000 employees or more, 46% in 1895 and 33% in 1882, and some 5% of all German manufacturing workers are employed in firms of 1,000 employees or more, 3% in 1895 and 2% in 1882... Argentina drills first oil wells, discovery of first major field in 1931 (is developed by state oil firm in 1910, is organized as state-owned corporation in 1923, first vertically integrated state petroleum firm outside of Russia to evolve as Argentina's largest enterprise)... French bicycle dealer, Paul Cornu makes (November 3) first helicopter flight, breaks up on landing after 20-second flight... Railway workers strike (November 10) in India...British are reported (December 11) to fear Japanese competition in trade.

Business Events

Premier Electric Heaters, Birmingham, pioneers electric heaters in Britain... Austria's Post Hotel hires Hannes Schneider to teach skiing... Paris jeweler, Louis Cartier, devises wristwatch for aviator Alberto Santos-Dumont... William G. Baker starts Ealing Studios, London, to produce movies... Coty perfume business commissions Rene Lalique to design vials, later does bottles and flasks... Siemens & Halske electrical business forms management secretariat to coordinate activities with Siemens-Schuckert... Lancashire Steam Motor reorganizes as Leyland Motors to make gasoline-driven dust carts, vans and fire engines (makes 3-ton lorry in 1914 - 6,000 in 1914-18, enters Rolls-Royce market in 1922 and refurbishes 3,000 lorries for civilian use, makes buses in 1925, discontinues steamers in 1926, sells vehicles in 54 countries in 1932, exports 20% of 1939 output, merges in 1951 with Glasgow's Albion Motors for wider range of commercial vehicles - only producer in late 1950s in medium and heavy lorry market, purchases Coventry's financially-troubled Standard Triumph in 1961 to become only British firm to make full line of trucks, buses and cars, after missing opportunity in 1958 buys rival Associated Commercial in 1962 to block acquisition by rival British Motor, acquires Rover Co. in 1966 for Land-Rover market, forms British Motor Holdings in 1967-68 to save Rootes Group from Chrysler takeover and then, with government urging in 1968, forms British Leyland with other ailing automobile firms to run 77 U.K. factories, 66 overseas plants with staff of 185,000)...

After visiting U.S. to do odd jobs, Ivar Kreuger, Swedish entrepreneur and international swindler, returns to start Stockholm building business (extends operations with partner in 1910 to Finland, Russia and Germany, starts match business in 1913, forms Swedish Match in 1917 to revive Sweden's role in international match market, forms International Match in 1923 as holding company, 250 match factories with absolute monopolies in 15 countries, de facto monopolies in 9 countries and market dominance in 10 countries, acquires interests in 1926-27 in newspapers, mining and L.M. Ericsson Telephone - full control in 1930, lends Germany some $125 million in 1929 - other loans to France for $75 million and $184 million to 13 countries, is investigated in 1930 by Swedish Investigating Commission for financial irregularities - report reveals records as fraudulent, defaults on $250 million to U.S. investors in 1931 - bonds marketed by Boston's renowned Lee, Higginson & Co. and signed by Ernst & Ernst accounting firm, is exposed as one of history's largest stock swindlers after suicide in 1932)... Britain's first picture palace is London's Balham Empire... Industrialists form Finnish General Employers' Federation to bargain with central union organization (accepts commercial, agricultural members after W.W.I)... Parisian chemist, Eugene Schueller, devises land's 1st synthetic hair dye in kitchen sink (after peddling products to local salons forms L'Oreal, 12% of world's cosmetic market in 1991, after expanding into shampoos, soaps is 1st in industry with radio advertising, 1920s, dies in 1957 with successor selling soap business in 1961, adds popular hairspray in 1962, goes public in 1963, buys upscale Lancome cosmetics in 1965, enters pharmaceutical field with acquisition, buys 49% of publisher, Marie-Claire, in 1977, after acquiring cosmetics firms gets cosmetics business, including Ralph Lauren and Gloria Vanderbilt lines, of Warner Communications in 1984, acquires France's No. 1 toothpaste producer and Helena Rubenstein beauty products in 1988, after getting maker of skin care products in 1989 buys 47.5% of Lanvin perfumes in 1990)... Yokohama brewery, Japan's first is opened 1864 by U.S.' William Copeland as Spring Valley Brewery (closes 1884, reopens as Japan Brewery in 1885 with Japanese investors), adopts Kirin name, label brand in 1888 (becomes land's leading brewer in 1950s after U.S. splits major rival, Dai Nippon, into Asahi and Sapporo after W.W. II, adds soft drinks in 1970s, in 1972 forms joint venture with Seagrams to enter liquor field, forms Kirin Australia in 1976, in 1980s buys Coca-Cola bottlers in New England and Japan, in 1988 adds wine line, licenses Molson to produce its beer for North America and forms information system subsidiary, in 1989 gets Napa Valley vineyard and adds four new beers, two more in 1991)... Tata Iron and Steel is financed entirely by Indians (leads to Tata Chemicals in 1939, Tata Engineering and Locomotive in 1954, collaboration with Daimler-Benz to make trucks in 1954, Voltas manufacturing conglomerate in 1954, Tata Tea in 1962, loses "managing agency" system to control subsidiaries with 1970 antitrust law)... Detering forms international Royal Dutch Shell by combining U.K.'s Shell Transport & Trading with Royal Dutch Petroleum (is structured, British with 40%, with dual headquarters in London and the Hague, joins, 1928, joins oil "As Is" cartel to fix world prices, in 1983 is world's 12th largest industrial group).

1908

General Events

Britain, Australia sponsor old-age pensions bill... France's Henri Farman is (January 13) first to complete heavier-than-air flight over circular course of at least 8 kilometers... Germany's Ludwig Roselius patents basic process to make decaffeinated coffee... Georges Sorel: <u>Reflections on Violence</u> (advocates overthrow of government by general strike of workers)... Wilbur Wright successfully demonstrates Wright plane in Paris (promotes growth of licensed companies in Europe)... NYC-Paris auto race of 20,000 miles begins (February 12-July 26)... London conference doubles (February 10) transatlantic fares... German Army tests experimental armored cars with machine guns in maneuvers, not used as no one knows how to use them (is followed by 1911 plan of Austrian officer for armored vehicle with machine guns and treads - rejected as not practical, leads to British tanks in 1916, tests by German military in 1917 - operational units in 1918)... Thomas H. Holding: <u>Britain Campers Handbook</u> (launches recreational camping)... Swiss-born chemist Jacques Brandenberger, France, invents transparent wrapping to give shiny appearance to fabrics (gets Swiss trademark in 1912, forms Societe de Cellophane in 1915, sells U.S. rights to Dupont, with world rights builds major industrial enterprise)... Henri Farman is (March 1) first to carry passenger in plane... Union of South Africa is created... Port of London Authority is formed... Britain's Coal Mines Regulation Act provides miners with 8-hour work day... <u>Lancet Medical Journal</u> declares (July 2) men wearing colored shirts as slovens... Paris tribunal extends (July 7) copyright law to cover moving pictures... After destruction of his dirigible by static electricity, German public views Zeppelin as national hero instead of a crazy inventor, continues to provide him with donations... Japanese patent for world's first cultured pearl, discovered first around 1900 by teenage carpenter and government marine biologist, is granted to Kokichi Mikimoto, son of noodle vendor (builds business to produce some 75% of world's pearls)... After scandals on King Leopold's use of forced labor in Congo Free State to exploit its resources, Belgium annexes (August 19) land, pays King Leopold 120 million francs for territory (forms Belgian Congo)... Canada forms (September 12) Civil Service Commission... Finnish bakers establish a maximum of 48 hours/week... Attempt of Eastman Kodak to form international cartel is blocked by French law... G.A. Smith, Charles Urban invent Kinemacolor, two-colored film process, in England... Seven European nations compete (October 1) in first international soccer match... France hosts (October 12) first international conference on roads... England, U.S. postage is (November 1) 2 cents... Liege workers demonstrate (November 23) for 8-hour day... Dutch physicist, H.K. Onnes liquifies helium, Nobel Prize in 1913 (spurs superconductivity race with development of oxide compounds in 1980s, barium in 1986)... Germany labor law permits (December 9) no work for those under 13... Shippers of various nations hold North Atlantic Shipping Conference to regulate prices, rebates.

Business Events

AEG builds Berlin turbine factory, world's first steel and glass building... Japanese trading house of Mitsui ships Manchurian surplus of 2,800 tons of soybeans, later becomes oil substitute, to Britain in trade for scarce cottonseed, linseed oils... Braun-Menendez family start Sociedad Anonima Importadura y Exportadora de la Patagonia, evolves by 1960s as Argentina's most influential dynasty with ships, piers and shipyard, airline, 22 stores, 600,000 sheep on ranches, and interest in banking, insurance and chemical enterprises (is started in 1873 with visit to Patagonia by Buenos Aires bookkeeper Jose Menendez to observe commercial possibilities of region with vessels rounding Cape Horn, opens trading post at Punta Arenas)... Nineteen of largest German manufacturing firms are involved in 10 or more diversified activities, only 3 so diversified in U.S... After inventing, suffered from acute indigestion, and operating shredded wheat business in Canada, U.S. lawyer Henry Perky starts British food company... First true fashion show is held in London to present Lady Duff-Gordon's collection, emulated by Paris fashion houses of Paquin, Poiret... Flick family industrial empire, steel, chemical and paper interests, is started in Germany... Victoria's Empress Hotel, Canadian landmark, opens... 1873 Anglo-New Zealand mercantile and trading firm of Joseph Nathan markets Glaxo dried milk for infants, invalids (enters pharmaceutical field in 1924 with vitamins, introduces Ostermilk, vitamin-fortified, in 1930s, and adds chemical products, forms Glaxo Laboratories in 1935 as subsidiary, goes public in 1947, blocks hostile takeover by Beecham in 1970s, in 1980s sheds non-drug firms, opens North Carolina research facility in 1988, faces challenge to patent for Zantac in 1991 by Tabatznik, generic pharmaceuticals group)... Robert Blackburn builds first airplane (advertises aircraft business in 1910, builds Mercury, first British plane with steel-tube fuselage, in 1911, enters commercial air operations in 1919 with North Sea Aerial Navigation Co. - soon fails, continues as Blackburn Aircraft with orders from Air Ministry, reorganizes in 1938 with insolvency, amalgamates with General Aircraft in 1948)... Engineer Geoffrey De Havilland builds first airplane, sells first in 1910 (is chief engineer for Aircraft Mfg. Co. in 1914 until closing in 1920, forms De Havilland Aircraft in 1920 - first commercial success with Moth airplane, 7,278 by 1932, in 1925, operates in 1937 with 5,191 employees, 38,311 in 1944, to build 200 airplanes, 2,327 in 1941)... France's Pathe Freres, industry pioneer, produces first movie newsreel... Louis Vuitton, Paris, sells trunk for some $83, same model $8,000 in 1989...

India's Bank of Baroda opens to take over state treasury functions as joint private and state enterprise, nationalized in 1969 (incorporates with new company law in 1936, engages in mostly short-term lending to finance regional agriculture and manufacturing industries before India's independence in 1947, starts East Africa branch in 1953-58)... Germany's Melitta-Werke Bentz & Sohn forms to sell coffee, coffee paraphernalia (enters U.S. market in 1985, shows worldwide sales of $1.5 billion in 1989)... Camillo Olivetti starts firm to make typewriters, Italy's first (presents first machine in 1911, expands with office furniture, 1930, teleprinters, 1938, and adding machines in 1940s, builds first mainframe computer in 1959, business sold to GE in 1964, and buys 1896 Underwood typewriters, is acquired by Pirelli-Fiat syndicate in 1964, introduces 1st electronic typewriter in 1978, buys Swiss maker of typewriters, Hermes Precisa, in 1981, acquires 80% of UK's Acorn Computer in 1985, Volkswagen's ailing office products maker in 1986 and buys firm in bank automation in 1986).

1909

General Events

Trade Boards Act, first proposed by Samuel Whitebread in 1808, enables government to form trade boards, four in industries with weak unions by 1917, to set legal minimum wage rates... Sweden adopts universal suffrage... French communications industry is paralyzed (March 17) by strikes... Osborne Judgment mandates funds of British unions are not to be used for political purposes... France cuts (April 4) tariffs on U.S. goods for preferential rates to France... First electric toaster appears... Enrico Forlanini develops hydrofoil independently of Alexander Graham Bell... Britain enacts old-age pension... German universities admit first women... Paris mail, telegraph workers unionize (May 6)... France denies civil servants' right to strike... Zeppelin II flies (April 9) 400 miles in 22 hours... Rheims, France, hosts first international air meet... French high court rules (June 1) postal union illegal... Vatican denounces (July 8) feminine fashions as immodest... French aviator, Louis Bleriot, is (July 25) first to fly over English Channel... National Christian Federation of Trade Unions forms in Holland, Catholic workers form central organization later... Anarchist unions form Brazil's first central labor organization... Nationwide strikes begin (August 4) in Sweden... Aviation society forms in Moscow... Wrights start flying school in France near Spanish border... Barcelona is paralyzed by general strike... Paris reports (September 18) over 1,000 women wanting flying instruction... First all-Chinese railroad is built (October 2) between Peking, Kalgan... France offers (November 28) working women eight weeks vacation after childbirth.

Business Events

Finnish Cooperative Wholesale Society forms, starts country's cooperative movement... When German Army refuses to buy latest airship, Zeppelin forms German Airship Transport Co., world's first commercial "airline" (starts service with Deutschland in 1910, adds deluxe passenger flights in 1911, by 1914 carries some 10,000 passengers on 1,588 flights)... Alfred Hugenberg, ardent supporter of National Socialism during 1920s-30s, is chairman of Krupp industries... Syndicate of wholesalers pressures eight French metal-fabricating, light machinery companies, including Peugeot, to agree not to sell their products direct to retailers, consumers... William L. Stephenson opens first British F.W. Woolworth variety store in Liverpool, 20 by 1912, 44 by 1914, London store in 1924, 494 in 1931, 529 in 1933, 768 by W.W. II and 988 throughout Britain and 96 in London by 1982... After importing Ford cars in 1903, Percival L. Dewhurst starts British plant to assemble Ford cars (sells 1,023 Model-Ts by 1911, after producing 3,000 vehicles in 1912, installs moving assembly line for mass production in 1913-14 to make 6,000 vehicles in 1913)... Russian-born ballet impresario Sergi Diaghilev forms Ballets Russe in Paris, revolutionizes art form (-1929)...

After working in brewing industry since 1901, James F. Taylor goes to Canada to represent London financiers on Lake Superior Corp. (supervises complete financial reorganization and modernization of Algoma subsidiary in 1913-17 to produce one million tons of coal, iron ore/year, is chairman of Lake Superior in 1917 - resigns 1918, after advising and managing other firms, opens independent consulting office in Montreal to rescue over-extended companies, after working with Armstrong's Newfoundland Power & Paper 1925-27 supervises dis-memberment of Armstrong's industrial empire in 1929)... Israel M. Sieff joins family business in cloth, scrap and waste (joins family friend, Simon Marks, in 1919 as director of Marks and Spencer retailing business, creates personnel department in 1926, adds welfare department in 1933, staff canteens in 1930s, medical aid services in 1934, textile laboratory in 1935, pension scheme in 1936, and Merchandise Development Department in 1936 to provide technical advice to suppliers, is chairman in 1964 with death of Simon)... Rinj Shino, billionaire Japanese entrepreneur in 1980s, is born, credited for combining family firms into leisure business empire in Western Japan... After starting Cologne firm in 1899 to make cars (loses support of backers), Dr. August Horch starts new firm to make Audi cars (joins other makers, 1932, to form Auto Union, is acquired, 1971, by Volkswagen)... Michio Suzuki starts loom works (develops inexpensive cars in 1947, makes engine for motorized bicycles in 1952, is named Suzuki Motors in 1954 and makes 1st motorcycles, makes minicars, 1955, delivery vans, 1959, and small trucks, 1961, opens first overseas plant, 1967, in Thailand, with domestic market going upscale, begins auto exports in 1974, makes motorcycles in Taiwan, Thailand and Indonesia in 1975, distributes Peugeot cars in Japan in 1988, sells 5.2% share to GM in 1981, in 1986 enters joint venture with GM to make cars in Canada and forms U.S. subsidiary).

1910

General Events

Militant British miners strike (January 3) for 8-hour day... Swiss railways are nationalized... France adopts Old-Age pensions... Germany warns (January 18) U.S. it is ready for trade war... Union of South Africa becomes dominion, independent republic in 1961... Germany produces 13.6 million tons of iron/steel and 17.6 in 1913, U.S. with 26.5 and 31.8, Britain 6.5 and 7.7, France with 3.4 and 4.6, Austria with 2.1 and 2.6, Russia with 3.5 and 4.8, Japan with .16 and .25 and Italy with .73 and .93... German firms produce rayon hose for women... Charles P. Steinmetz: Future of Electricity (warns of air pollution from burning coal and water pollution from sewage)...

New Zealand Labor Party forms, re-forms 1916 after competition with militants (wins office 1935-49, 1957-60, 1972-75, 1984-)... First Jewish kibbutz, collective settlement, appears in Israel, some 300 in 1980s face reforms with government bailout of $3.6 billion in 1989... Romanian Social Democratic Party forms (February 13)... Japanese army builds first air base... French inventor Georges Claude starts development of neon lighting with invention of long-life electrode, first used in U.S. by Los Angeles Packard dealer in 1923... Painter Filippo Marinetti, fellow artists launch movement to portray age's dangers and machines (flourishes through 1920s)... France's Baroness de Laroche is (March 8) first woman to get pilot's license, first U.S. woman in 1911... London County Council starts Westminster Hotel School, 7 more in City and 18 elsewhere by 1914... Germany's Futtinger is first to devise automatic transmission for cars, electronic controlled transmission by France's Renault in 1965... Hendon is London's first airport (-1959, starts airmail service in 1911, Heathrow airport in 1928)...

Australia adopts first penny postage and issues its first Commonwealth bank note... Professor Karl Harries, Berlin, perfects (April 2) artificial rubber process... Some 200,000 German workers are locked out (April 16) as negotiators fail to agree on wage increases... Paris hosts (May 18) first conference on air traffic... China abolishes slavery... Britain's first labor exchanges appear... Hamburg employers replace (August 5) 2,400 of 10,000 striking dockworkers with British workers... Free Trade Congress meets (August 9) in Antwerp... Rudolph Hilferding: The Finance Capital (describes imperialism as last stage of capitalism)... French plane is first to fly from Paris to London... Some 50,000 British dockworkers, supported by 10,000 mine workers in Wales, are fired (September 3) during strike... Paris international conference debates (September 19) value of unemployment insurance... Japan annexes Korea, renamed Chosen (-1945)... Some 150,000 workers are laid off (October 2) as 700 Lancashire mills close... France is paralyzed (October 12) by nationwide strike in transportation industry, leaders arrested for fomenting national unrest... First dirigible flies (October 18) over English Channel... Militant coal miners strike in Wales wins (November 7) wage hike.

Business Events

Alfred Dunhill opens London factory to make briar pipes... Walter Haefner, Swiss billionaire in 1988 as owner of nation's largest car importer, Amaq, and Uccel computer company, is born to missionary in Tibet... French hairdresser Marcel Grateau devises permanent wave for hair... Dutch-born Anthony Fokker starts small aircraft factory, flying school near Berlin (designs first practical synchronized machine gun and fighter plane during W.W. I, returns to Holland in 1918-19 with smuggled planes, equipment to start Netherlands Aircraft Factory in Amsterdam, produces F-7, most successful airliner of its time, in 1924, moves to U.S. and operates 3 factories during 1920s to make popular Fokker Trimotor - reputation for reliability ruined with 1931 crash killing Knute Rockne)... U.S.' Oscar Hammerstein opens London Opera House, converted to City's grandest movie theater after failure... Teams in Eastern Canada form National Hockey Association, replaced by National Hockey League in 1917 with Boston first U.S. team in 1924... Goring Hotel opens in London, claims to be world's first with central heating and bathrooms in every bedroom... London's Palladium Music Hall opens (becomes mecca for vaudeville, stages spectacular revues in 1922-28, cinema and variety shows in 1928)... 30 banks operate in Canada with 2,367 branches... Marconi Wireless applies for licenses to operate 18 radio stations in Asia, Africa, Australia and West Indies (wins judgments for patent infringements in 1911 against British Radio Telegraph & Telephone and Clyde Steamship and United Wireless in 1912, signs 1912 pact with Germany's Telefunken to exchange patents)...

Thomas B. Russell forms Incorporated Society of Advertisement Consultants (is first British advertising consultant hired by political party, Liberals, in 1910, gives first advertising course at London School of Economics in 1919)... Business League forms in Midlands as lobby group... BSA acquires Daimler Motors, Ariel motorcycle in 1944 and Triumph motorcycle in 1951 ... With money from U.S. flying prizes, Thomas O.M. Sopwith opens flying school, Sopwith Aviation Co. to build airplanes (produces 5,497 Camels, 5,466 Strutters, and 1,847 Pups by 1920 with some

3,000 workers, is one of 200 firms making airplanes in 1914 - 771 in 1917, 1,529 in 1918, and 18 in 1925, liquidates business in 1920 after strike and market collapse to join H.G. Hawker Engineering as director for motorcars and motorcycles, as CEO shifts to all-metal aircraft in 1925-28 - by 1933 one of Britain's largest aircraft firms, Hawker Aircraft, making 7 models in two factories for government, acquires Gloster in 1934 and Armstrong Siddeley Development in 1935 - CEO of Hawker Siddeley Aircraft in 1936, builds 40,089 aircraft during W.W. II - first English jet plane in 1941 and vertical takeoff fighter in 1960s)... By this time Nomura, started in 1872 as Osaka currency exchange, shifts focus of business to stock market by forming its first underwriting syndicate (starts bank in 1918, bond department goes independent as Nomura Securities in 1925)... Tata business, India, grants leaves with pay, 8-hour day in 1912 (sponsors Indian Institute of Science, modeled on Johns Hopkins University, in 1911)... Swedish salesman, Axel Wenner-Gren, sees opportunity for selling vacuum cleaners door-to-door, learned in U.S., after noting model in Viennese store (works for two Swedish vacuum cleaner makers, 1912, to improve design of models, when two firms merge as Electrolux in 1919 handles distribution of cleaners when idea for mass production is rejected, scores publicity coup in 1920s when Pope Pius XI approves their use in Vatican, sells most of sales agency to Electrolux by 1930)... Namihei Odaira builds electric motors, genesis for modern Hitachi, to prove Japan need not depend on foreign technology (becomes independent of electric utilities in 1920, in 1930s-40s makes vacuum tubes, light bulbs, radar and sonar, closes 19 plants for W.W. II, in 1950s is designated supplier to NTT, spins off metals and cable units in 1956, chemicals in 1963, with help of MITI builds first computer in 1965, makes color TVs and builds plants in Southeast Asia in 1960s, puts out an IBM-compatible computer in 1974, sold in U.S. via Intel to 1979 when National Semiconductor takes over distribution, after FBI agents catch employees buying IBM software secrets, settles civil suit in 1982 for $300-500 million plus $2-3 million/month for eight years for use of technology, buys 80% of National Semiconductor in 1989 for direct control over U.S. distribution).

1911

General Events

Germany, Russia finalize (January 6) pact to build railway from Baghdad to Berlin (-1940)... Strikes of railwaymen, metal workers force (January 11) Britain's Interior Minister to resign... Joseph Schumpter: The Theory of Economic Development (notes critical role of "creative entrepreneurship")... German Government, industry form Kaiser Wilhelm Institute for research... Hamburg pharmacist, Beiersdorf, creates cold cream preparation, Nivea, for 1882 business... Japan passes first factory law to restrict employment for those over age 13 (sets maximum of 12 hours/day for work, grants two days/month for holidays)... Britain's first escalators are at London subway station... Italy establishes (April 6) state life insurance... Britain is paralyzed by railway, mining and coal strikes (-1912, leads to 1912 minimum wage law)... French law forbids use of English words in business when French equivalents exist, used to convict some 40 firms 1977-87... Japan signs commercial treaties with Britain, France, Germany... Buenos Aires-Valparaiso railroad opens... Germany's Walter Gropius designs Fagus factory as modern glass, concrete structure... Italy uses (August 3) plane for reconnaissance over Tripoli, first military use of planes... Sun Yat-sen, supporters overthrow Manchu Dynasty ruling China... British start (September 9) airmail service between Windsor, London...

Joseph J.C. Joffre, Marshal of France, devises Plan XVII to attack Alsace-Lorraine in event of war with Germany... General strike hits (September 18) Valencia, uses martial law to suppress strike... Switzerland's Dreyfus brothers patent cellulose acetate fabric... Imperial Decree requires (December 7) Chinese to cut braids... Germany adopts special state-supported old-age pension plan for white-collar employees... State of Northern Rhodesia is formed, administered by South Africa Co... Britain forms Army Air Battalion, Royal Flying Corps in 1912... Mexico hires aerial circus of John Moisant barnstorming Southwestern U.S. to scout for rebels along Rio Grande... Italy uses first aerial bombing to fight Turks in Libya... After several unofficial flights in 1910, Britain begins first airmail service in India, flown by France, Italy, U.S., Japan and Germany in 1912... When license for National Telephone, private firm, expires, British Post Office, telegraph monopoly since 1879, takes over monopoly (introduces public red phone booths in 1936).

Business Events

Henri Le Chatelier: <u>Principes d'organization scientifique</u> (translates Taylor's work)... After searching 13 years for gold around the world with no success, Harry Oakes discovers lode in Northern Ontario (dies in 1943 leaving estate of some $200 million)... White Star Line, absorbed by Cunard Line in 1934, launches unsinkable <u>Titanic</u>, world's largest and fastest luxury liner, to capture North Atlantic traffic of wealthy (-1912 when sunk by iceberg)... Ford builds factory in England... Although denounced Gieves & Hawkes is first posh Savile Row tailor to sell ready-to-wear suits (operates 35 shops in Japan by 1988)... Bertone business, Italy's oldest coach builder for Ferrari, Lamborghini, Alfa Romeo, and Lancia cars, is started... Self-taught mechanic Henry G. Ferguson, opens Belfast motorcar, farm implement business (starts business with partners in 1925 to make plows for Ford tractors, Fordson dropped 1928, at Evansville, IN, after developing tractor unit system forms Ferguson-Brown in 1937 to make tractors and agricultural equipment, by verbal agreement lets Ford produce tractors with his design in 1938, 306,221 produced until cancellation by Ford in 1947 to make its own tractors, sues Ford in 1952 for patent infringement - in largest award gets $15-20 million, creates Ferguson Research in 1950 to build 4-wheel drive vehicles - no production before death in 1960, merges British, U.S. interests with Canada's Massey-Harris in 1953 - firm's largest stockholder)... Harry Pickering opens Harry's New York Bar in Paris (adds 2nd in Venice in 1931, Florence 1952, Los Angeles 1972, San Francisco 1986)... Mario Danieli, brother start steel business in Northeastern Italy (operates with crude furnace, 40 workers in 1955, grows in 1960 with son, Luigi, from steel production to engineering, construction of steel plants)... U.S. trained Hashimoto Masujiro starts Tokyo's Kwaishinha Motor Car Works to repair, import and make cars (using Dat, "fast rabbit" in Japanese, as logo, makes Japan's first car in 1913, renames business Dat Motors in 1925, merges with ailing Jitsuyo Motors in 1926, introduces son of Dat car in 1931, is acquired in 1933 by Tobata Casting, is spun off in 1933 as Nissan Motors, is Japan's first mass-producer of cars in 1936).

1912

General Events

Russia adopts workmen's insurance... Switzerland builds first diesel locomotive... Thailand sends officers to France to learn flying (return to build airport and start mail service, evolves in 1967 as Thai International to serve 41 cities in 30 countries by 1986)... Chinese Imperial Government recognizes (February 13) new Republic... International Lawn Tennis Federation forms... Some one million British miners strike (March 1), urged to return to work by miner's union (gets minimum wage from Parliament)... Italians are (March 5) first to use dirigibles for military purpose... French army creates (March 5) autonomous aeronautics unit... Troeltsch: <u>Protestantism and Progress</u>... France's Henri Seinet is (March 7) first to fly nonstop London to Paris... Ruhr miners strike (March 10)... J. Ellenhammer tests rotary-winged flying machine, Copenhagen (leads to 1918 test near Budapest, 1921 model of George de Bothez for U.S. Army - contract canceled as impractical, 1923 test, France, by E. Oemichen, first successful flight in 1937 by Germany)... Russian army breaks (April 18) gold miner's strike in Siberia...

After 144-day strike, Paris taxi drivers return (April 19) to work... After contacts by Webbs and Samuel Gompers, Friendly Society forms in Tokyo, starts Japanese labor movement (leads to General Federation of Labor in 1919, Farmers' Union in 1920 and Communist Party in 1922)... Hungary monopolizes (May 2) world's most important natural gas reserves, Transylvania... Some 100,000 British dockworkers strike (May 29) for minimum wage... Left-wing dissidents from 1906 General Confederation of Labor form Italian Syndical Union, some 500,000 members in 1919...

A. Bogdanov: Tektology: The Universal Organization Science, Vol. I (-1927, proposes theory of systems in dealing with organizing and disorganizing processes of nature and society, attacked by Lenin)... Some 200,000 British transport workers hold (June 11) nationwide strike... Ramsay MacDonald submits bill to Parliament to legalize informal agreements of organized employers, unions... Belgian workers strike (June 30) for universal suffrage... U.S. cowboy Guy Weadick starts Canada's annual Calgary Stampede... British National Health Insurance Act takes (July 15) effect... Lisbon is paralyzed by general strike... J. Vedrines is (September 9) first to fly over 100 mph... Australia starts (September 14) building 1,000-mile railroad to link Port Augusta, Kalgoorlie (-1917)... In experimenting with acetylene and hydrogen chloride, German chemist, Fritz Klatte, accidentally discovers milky mixture which solidifies on exposure to sunlight (forms Greiheim Electron to exploit product - patent elapses in 1925 before finding commercial use for plastic)... First all-metal plane is flown (November 3) in France... African National Conference forms.

Business Events

Research chemist Harry Brearley, Firth-Brown Research Laboratory in Sheffield, makes technical breakthrough for development of stainless steel in 1914... Australia's last stagecoach line closes in Queensland... French firm of Bourjois creates first rouge makeup... After building bicycles and motorcycles, William Morris starts business making cars, 51% of Britain's market in 1929 and 26.9% in 1939... After working as assistant manager in aunt's celebrated London music hall, Lilian Baylis uses temperance hall to produce Shakespeare plays, operas and ballets for working-class audience (re-opens in 1931 as Sadler Wells Theater to become old Vic)... India's 1889 Delhi Cloth & General Mills Co. hires Shri Ram (-1963, as CEO transforms textile business into diversified empire with interests in sugar, edible fats, alcohol, ceramics, plastics, rayon tire cord, heavy chemicals and some 400 retail stores - some 30,000 employees and sales over $70.5 million in 1965)...

Anglo-Persian Oil, Royal Dutch Shell, German interests and negotiator Armenian Calouste S. Gulbenkian form Turkish Petroleum Co. to search for oil in Mesopotamia, forced by U.S. to accept Jersey Standard, others in 1922... Kuhara Copper Mining business appears in Japan (is acquired in 1926 by Y. Ayukawa in forming holding company to operate over 80 enterprises in 1930s)... Edward Cadbury: Experiments in Industrial Organization (cites practices of candy business in employee selection, education, remuneration, discipline, health and safety)... After visiting U.S. Louis Renault, Andre Citroen urge use of time and motion studies and assembly-line production, used to make munitions in 1915 and cars in 1919... Aalsmeer, Holland, holds its first flower auction (forces bidders to bid against clock's deadline)... A.J. Renner starts Brazilian textile business in Porto Alegre (evolves as S.A. Matarazzo Reunidas, Sao Paulo, as combination of meat and food companies)... Subsidiaries of General Electric, Westinghouse and Germany's Siemens produce some 66% of output of Britain's electrical industry...

Dutch electrical business of 1891 is incorporated as N.V. Philips' Gloeilampenfabrieken, changes to holding company in 1920 (starts pension fund for office, technical employees in 1913 - all personnel in 1929, starts research laboratory in 1914 - physical laboratory for radio research in 1926 and laboratory for movie sound equipment in 1929, starts glassworks in 1915 to ensure supply, provides fund in 1916 to help children of employees get higher education, forms Social Economic Department in 1917 to assist employees in surviving wartime shortages, starts first foreign subsidiary in Belgium in 1919 - others in Spain in 1920, Switzerland 1921, Poland 1922, Norway and Italy 1923, Brazil 1924 and Australia in 1926, forms alliance in 1919 with GE as electric lamp cartels appear in Britain and Germany, adopts midwife service in 1920 - advisory service for infant care in 1921 and household school in 1924, forms Labor Department in 1921 - Personnel Council in 1920s, starts training program for foremen in 1921, joins International Incandescent Lamp Price Assn. to regulate prices, signs patent agreement in 1924 with European makers of incandescent filament lamps to regulate quotas, prices and quality - ended 1939, forms trade school for young workers in 1928 - recreational center and monthly publication in 1929, employs some 20,000 Dutch workers in 1929 - 10,000 in 1927, 8,100 in 1925, 3,100 in 1915 and

400 in 1900, starts small U.S. factory to make X-ray equipment in 1934 - basis for North American Philips in 1941, prepares plans in 1938 for possible war - trustees for British Empire and North, South America with headquarters in Dutch West Indies, puts personnel officers in all major divisions in 1945, creates Department of Social Affairs in 1946 to centralize, coordinate all personnel activities and to develop employees as human beings, forms Social Psychological Service and starts "Training Within Industry" program in 1946)... Hamburg-American's Imperator is world's largest luxury liner at 50,000 tons, uses crew of 1,100 for 4,100 passengers... Imperial Tobacco Co. of Canada forms, aided by B.A.T. (absorbs rivals in 1921, General Cigar in 1930, 1949 and Brown & Williamson in 1950, acquires two winemakers in 1964 and 1966, closed-circuit equipment maker in 1967, S&W Fine Foods and Pasquale foods in 1969, forms Imasco as holding company in 1970, after buying, selling several food chains in 1970s acquires Shoppers Drug Mart chain in 1979, adds Hardee's Food Systems, 1981, Burger Chef from General Foods, 1982, Mid Atlantic Peoples Drug Stores, sold 1990, and Rea and Derick in 1984, gets Genstar, founded 1951 to win Canada's largest trust company, in 1986, buys Roy Rogers restaurants in 1990 and goes for Rochester S&L)...

Tokuji Hayakawa starts Tokyo metal shop to make belt buckles, his design (introduces Ever-Sharp, first mechanical pencil, in 1915, after Tokyo earthquake and moving to Osaka, introduces Japan's first crystal radio sets in 1925 - vacuum tube radios in 1929, incorporates as Sharp in 1938, mass produces TV in 1953 - color TV in 1960, mass produces microwave ovens in 1962, opens first U.S. office, and solar cells in 1963, develops first desktop all-transistor-diode calculators, builds factory, 1970, to make microchips, develops first electronic calculator with liquid display in 1973, first solar-powered calculator in 1976 and first credit card-sized calculator in 1979, introduces color copiers and FAX machines, No. 1 in U.S. by 1989, in 1984, develops desktop color FAX machines in 1990)... Union Bank of Switzerland, largest in land ahead of Swiss Bank and Credit Suisse and world's 33rd largest in 1991, is formed by merger of two banks, founded 1862 and 1863 (opens NYC office in 1946, runs 81 branches in 1962, in 1967 buys Interhandel, cash-rich Swiss financial concern, and opens its first full-fledged foreign unit in London, gets four savings banks in 1968, in 1970s forms foreign subsidiaries to underwrite securities, acquires London brokerage in 1986 for deregulation - heavy financial losses by 1989, acquires German bank, 1986, and forms Australian subsidiary, 1987)... Karl Rapp starts Munich shop to design aircraft, named BMW in 1917 (makes first motorcycle in 1923 - speed records 1929-37, after acquiring defunct automobile maker with license from Austin, starts building cars in 1928 - sports cars in 1933, builds aircraft engines in 1930s, after being dismantled after W.W. II, makes one-cylinder motorcycle in 1948, is bailed out of financial mess, cars too large and expensive, by Herbert Quandt in 1959, introduces sports sedans for upscale niche in 1961 - sales soar in 1970s-80s, introduces luxury line in 1986, sales decline with rise in value of DM and Japanese competition)... Arthur Andersen, after working for Price Waterhouse, 1907, and teaching accounting at Northwestern, 1908, starts public accounting firm with partners (by 1920 runs six offices and goes overseas after W.W. II, in early 1970s develops Center for Professional Education, Illinois, as world's largest consulting firm, 40% of revenues, in 1988, operates in 54 countries, 66 in 1990, in 1989, U.S. 59% of revenues and 55% in 1990, is world's 4th largest in accounting in 1991).

1913

General Events

Telephone line links (January 13) Berlin, NYC... Russian Duma rejects (February 6) proposal to open legal profession to women... Holland, Switzerland adopt Old Age and Sickness Insurance...Sweden develops diesel-electric rail-car, leads to GM's diesel locomotive in 1935... Britain's share of world trade is 14.15%, 10.75% in 1929 and 9.8% in 1937... Trade Union Act lets British unions use funds for political purposes... Britain forms Airship Department to build transatlantic airships, Vickers builds R-100 and Royal Airship Works builds R-101 in 1924... Belgian workers hold (April 14) general strike for universal suffrage, Government promises (April 24) reforms... Russian engineer Igor Sikorsky flies (May 13) world's first 4-engine plane...

Fredrich Bergius determines process for converting coal dust into oil... Institute of Labor Management forms in Britain, incorporated in 1924 as Institute of Personnel Management by specialists in business, government... Rene Lorin proposes basic idea for jet propulsion... China opens (June 5) bank, NYC... Krupp executives get (August 5) light jail terms for bribes to secure defense contracts... Werner Sombart: The Jews and Modern Capitalism (notes role of Judaism in stressing self-control, hard work, moderation, sobriety, thrift)... German plane carries (September 7) passengers on Paris-to-Berlin flight... Germany launches (September 8) Zeppelin LZ, largest at 520 feet (goes down during hurricane)... First airplane race for Schneider trophy is held, 61 mph by fastest "hydro airplane" (leads to 340 mph in 1931 race and nearly 450 mph in 1934)... French aviator Roland Garros flies (September 23) 558 miles across Mediterranean.

Business Events

Taylor's The Principles of Scientific Management is translated into German...Lord Northcliff's Daily News announces prize for first flight across Atlantic, won in 1919... Process for synthetic production of ammonia is developed by Carl Bosch of BASF, based on research of Fritz Haber in 1908-09 (is used by Germany to make gunpowder during W.W. I when blocked in acquiring Chilean nitrates)... Ten largest German firms are Krupp, AEG, Gelsenkirchener Bergwerks AG, Siemens-Schuckert-Werke, Deutsch-Luxemburg Gewerkschaft Deutscher Kaiser, Phoenix, Siemens & Halske, Harpener Bergwerks AG, and Hohenlohe with chemical giants Bayer, 13th, BASF, 14th, and Hoechst, 18th... German steelmakers agree to invade Britain, U.S. markets in Far East... Siemens-Schuckert plants are managed with central administration (coordinates communications, marketing and purchasing, supervises accounting activities and devises operating procedures), traffic, marketing and finance functions... Prada, elegant leather goods, opens Milan store (still extant)... Reuters news agency forms a bank, sold 1917 (uses radio technology in 1923 and teleprinters in 1927, faces ruin, 1941, until Winston Churchill persuades British newspapers to buy Reuters, joined in 1947 by Australian and New Zealand papers).

1914

General Events

Some 25% of British workers are union members, about 7% in U.S... Bank of England is authorized to issue paper money over legal limit... Russian flyer carries (February 26) 17 passengers in twin-engine plane... Belgium adopts Old-Age, Sickness and Disablement Insurance... Switzerland extends regulations against female, child labor... Some 3 million workers are union members in Britain and Germany, France with one million and U.S.' AFL with two million... In this time, Britain's F.W. Lanchester devises equations to construct models for military operations (-1915, pioneers development of Operations Research)... British Government acquires (May 20) controlling interest in cash-short Anglo-Persian oil company, basis for British Petroleum in 1954 (makes finds in Iraq, 1927, and Kuwait, 1938, joins secret cartel, "As Is", in 1928 to fix world production and prices for 20 years, after Iran assets are seized in 1951 coup resumes operations in 1953, 40% of consortium, with return of Shah, makes find in Alaska's Prudhoe Bay, 1969, and North Sea, 1970, swaps Alaskan reserves in 1970 for share, all in 1987, of U.S.' SOHIO, sells Britain 20.15% more in 1975, public offerings in 1977, 1979 and 1987, buys Kennecott Copper in 1981, sold 1988, buys Purina Mills in 1986, acquires Britoil, North Sea gas and oil, in 1988 and sells most of mineral business to RT2, in 1989 sells $1.3 billion of oil properties to Oryx while UK forces Kuwait to reduce its 21.6% in BP to 9.9%, buys Petromed, Spain's 3rd largest oil refiner, in 1991)... Manchester, Britain, builds first modern plant to treat sewage with bacteria... Brassiere is patented...

Edward Kleinschmidt invents teletypewriter... Emile Pouget: L'Organisation du surmenage (notes significance of Taylorism)... British mine and railway unions join (June 4) construction strike, two million workers out... Bismarck is (June 20) world's largest luxury liner... Some 160,000 strike (July 22) in St. Petersburg... W.W. I begins when Austrian Archduke Ferdinand is assassinated

(July 28) in Sarajevo (-1919)... Britain's Nautical Almanac Office uses multi-unit calculator to compile astronomical tables, used in 1931 at Woolwich Arsenal to compute ballistics.

Business Events

William Crawford starts British advertising agency to serve retail accounts, gets reputation for political campaigns... After opening shop in 1901, Russian-born Elcon, Sidney Myer open department store, San Francisco's Emporium as model, in Melbourne (open first factory in 1915 and buying office in 1916, capitalize in 1917 for $1 million - $30 million in 1956, open Store for Men in 1920, give grants in 1931 to provide work for unemployed, open holiday house for staff in 1946, use punch-card accounting in 1947 - computer center 1970, form charitable trust and open Brisbane store in 1955, open first regional shopping center in 1959, merge with Farmer's Western Stores in 1960, is first Australian retail store with sales over $200 million in 1962, plan network of Target discount stores and supermarkets in 1964 - 25 centers by 1969 and 71 by 1978, run 48 department stores in 1978, form Meyers Overseas in 1979 for trading activities, form holding company in 1981 to oversee 43 Country Road/Dynamite stores, 59 Red Rooster fast foods, 68 liquor stores, 38 department stores, add 62 Grace Bros. stores, 69 Target stores, 152 apparel discount stores, and 27 limited department stores by 1984)... After arriving in Australia for Swedish Match Trust, mechanical engineer, Carl Friden, devises a calculator (after shipboard contact in 1916, is hired by Marchant Calculating Machine, CA, starts Friden Calculating Machine business in 1933 to make rotary calculators)... Some 17 multinational manufacturing firms operate in Continental Europe, 9 German - Siemens with plants in Russia, France, U.S., Britain, Spain and Austria, 4 Swiss, 1 each in France, Holland, Sweden, and Belgium, Solvay with branches in Russia, France, Germany, U.S., Britain, Spain, Austria and Italy after going international in 1864, while 9 U.S. firms have European branches... Brothers Hernand, Sosthenes Behn acquire Puerto Rico Telephone (form International Telephone & Telegraph in 1920)... 1847 Siemens & Halske, 1883 AEG control Germany's electrical industry... In London Swiss-born Charles Nessler, barber cum surgeon, invents machine to heat and wave hair, invents false eyelashes later (opens salon in NYC after W.W. I to serve rich women, sells permanent wave business to Cleveland firm in 1928)... Germany's Krupp is first to develop successful method to weld stainless steel... Accounting and Tabulating Co. of Great Britain is formed as U.S. subsidiary of 1909 Powers Accounting Machine Co. (goes independent in 1919 as Powers Accounting Machines, merges with French distributor in 1929 to form Powers-Samas Accounting Machine, is acquired in 1945 by merchant banker Morgan-Grenfell and Vickers - subsidiary of Vickers in 1955, merges with British Tabulating in 1959 to create ICT)...

With funds from lover, Gabrielle "Coco" Chanel opens milliner's shop (with flare for clothes goes to Paris in 1917 to open fashion house with backing by Wertheimer - popular in 1920s with simple, elegant jersey dress, twin sweater set, and understated knitted suit to liberate women from whalebones and feathers, launches fads of bobbed hair in 1920s and deep tan, slacks in 1930s)... Rolex is first wrist watch to out-perform pocket timepieces (devises world's first practical water-and-shockproof watch in 1926)... Antonio Puig starts Barcelona perfume business (challenges international perfumers in 1950s, innovates with creative packaging in 1963, launches men's fragrance in 1981)... After moving to England, French-born Carter starts pioneering business to make potato crisps, followed in 1920 with commercial production by Frank Smith to dominate snack food market in 1920s-1930s... Yoshihiro Inayama starts Japanese steel business (helps create military force before losing all in W.W. II, forges Nippon Steel as world's largest after War, is chairman of Japan Federation of Economic Organizations, land's most powerful business lobby, in 1980)... Some 16 firms operate in Britain with over 200 branches each, butchery firms of Eastmans, James Nelson & Sons with each over 1,000 outlets and Maypole Dairy, Boots, Liptons and Home and Colonial all over 500... Gaumont movie studio is built at Sheppards Bush, followed by Paramount in 1924, British National Studios in 1926 and British International in 1927... Cole family, Australia, opens their first variety store in Hollywood, Victoria, a larger store in 1919, two more in 1922, Melbourne store in 1924, 17 stores by 1929, 27 in 1932, 31 in 1934, 64 in 1938 with staff of 3,300, 82 in 1940, 85 in 1946, 93 in 1948 with staff of 5,160, 200 in 1955 including department stores, 240 in 1956 after acquiring chain, 300 in 1959 with purchase of grocery chain - 2nd in 1960 to operate 265 stores, first supermarket in 1962 - 100 by 1968, 553 in 1964, first discount store in 1968 with U.S.' S.S. Kresge - first K mart in 1969 with 100 by 1986, for total of 1,518 outlets of all types as Cole Meyer, Ltd. in 1986 (forms central buying in 1923, goes public with 8 stores in 1927, issues staff journal in 1928, starts savings plan in 1934, diversifies with two small grocery chains in 1949, tries experimental discount stores in 1967, adopts discount policy for supermarkets, converts variety stores to self-service in 1974, runs 195 variety stores, 271 supermarkets, 69 grocery stores, 6 country stores and 33 K marts with staff of 47,000 in 1977, acquires liquor and footwear chains in 1981, opens first Super K mart stores to combine food and variety items in 1982 - 19 by 1986, merges with D. Myer Emporium, Australia's 3rd largest retailer in 1985, appoints first woman general manager in 1985, buys fast food chain, 36 places, in 1986)... Sixteen of 30 largest British firms have at least one foreign plant.

1915

General Events

German Army uses psychological testing center to select motor-transport drivers... Norway's Labor Disputes Act establishes labor court... Werner Sombart: The Quintessence of Capitalism (cites pirates on high seas as early form of business organization)... Threatening new aggression Japan presents (May 9) some 21 economic demands, including extensive mining and fishing rights, to China... Britain, trade unions negotiate Treasury Agreement (bans strikes, guarantees collective bargaining)... Sport of handball appears in Germany... Britain opens its first automatic telephone exchange... Parliament passes Rent Restriction Act, Excess Profits Duty... First radio-telephone communication links (July 27) Japan, U.S... Britain forms Ministry of Munitions to oversee industry with 700,000 workers... Hawaii's Duke Kahanamoku introduces sport of surf riding to Australia, U.S. in 1916.

Business Events

Ghia design studio for cars opens in Turin, Italy... Raffles Hotel barman concocts Singapore Sling drink... London milk wholesalers, Wilts United Dairies in Northern England form United Dairies (by 1917 acquires some of largest retail chains - 13 by 1920, operates 32 subsidiaries with 700 shops and over 50 creameries, 60 shops and 40 creameries in London and suburbs in 1950, acquires Cow & Gates processed milk products in 1959 to become one of world's largest food businesses)... Chandris Cruise Line appears in Greece (enters new upscale market in 1989 with Caribbean Fantasy Cruises)... After helping build a plane in 1909, Charles Richard Fairey starts Fairey Aviation with order for 12 planes from previous employer (tries making car bodies in 1919, declares liquidation in 1921 to reform, designs over 50% of British military aircraft in 1925, makes 5 models by 1929, designs Swordfish in 1935)... After mining and smelting ores Broken Hill Proprietary begins producing steel, soon land's largest (after opening coal, iron mines buys Australian Iron and Steel in 1935 and other steel firms for virtual monopoly of steel industry, starts shipbuilding in 1940, in partnership with Esso Standard finds offshore gas in 1965 - oil in 1967, exports iron ore, manganese, coal in 1960s-70s, buys Utah International's overseas assets from GE for $700 million to expand in U.S., South Africa, Canada, Chile and Brazil, expands with vertical integration, petroleum and steel, in 1980s)... Citroen is founded, Europe's first to mass-produce cars.

1916

General Events

China grants commercial rights for Inner Mongolia, Southern Manchuria to Japan (-1931 when invaded by Japanese forces to create puppet state of Manchukuo)... David Lloyd George is Britain's Prime Minister (-1922, begins reforms in 1919-20 by expanding programs in health and education, pensions, unemployment insurance and subsidized housing, builds over 200,000 units)... Germany puts (February 3) textile industry under government control... Germans protest (February 8) food shortages in Berlin... Britain recruits (February 13) 400,000 for farm work... National Bank of Philippines is chartered... Germany's Auxiliary Service Law establishes work councils as grievance committees... Britain creates Department of Scientific and Industrial Research... Britain starts National Savings Movement, adopts "summertime"... France's Paul Languein develops sonar... Germany issues (March 20) rationing cards for food... In searching for new methods, Lenin starts compiling series of notebooks on workings of capitalist finance and production (although favoring Taylorism, condemns Scientific Management, after Russian Revolution advocates Taylor system for industry, government)... France's gunpowder production is reorganized according to Taylor system (sends engineers to U.S. to learn secrets of production)... Britain's Ministry of Munitions creates Industrial Welfare Department... Emerging middle-class, led by Hipolito Iriyan, overthrow Argentina's ruling class of large landholders, beef barons and export merchants allied with foreign interests, mostly British (-1930 when overthrown by military coup, over 36 more military takeovers by 1982).

Business Events

Henri Fayol: <u>General and Industrial Management</u> (notes functions of planning, organizing, command, coordination and control, U.S. publication in 1949)... DKW appears in Germany to make steam-powered engines (produces first motor car in 1927, joins Audi, Horch and Wanderer to form Auto-Union in 1932, symbolized by four linked rings)... Joseph Wickham Roe: <u>English and American Tool Builders</u> (views manufacturing system with interchangeable parts as of U.S. origin)... Britain charters Aircraft Transport and Travel (starts first regularly scheduled flights for public in 1919 between London and Paris, adds mail service in 1919, is acquired by Daimler Airway in 1920, uses cabin boys in 1922 to serve passengers, U.S.' United with nurses as attendants in 1930)... Federation of British Industries forms to promote overseas trade (advocates tariff protection)... British Celluloid is registered (markets cellulose acetate as Celanese in 1921, changes name to British Celanese in 1923, is acquired by Courtaulds in 1957)... British Commonwealth Union forms to foster trade in empire and represent business in Parliament... John M. Carras, Greek billionaire in 1989, is born (builds father's shipping business as international operation after moving headquarters to New York and then to London).

1917

General Events

Britain issues Bread-cards... German Independent Labor Party forms... Britain creates Ministry of Labor... Britain puts wool, cotton and food under state control... Petrograd Soviet issues (March 16) Order One to abolish authority of army officers... Russian Czar Nicholas II abdicates (March 16)... British mail service sells postmark space to raise revenues... Vladimir Lenin: <u>The State and Revolution</u> (views State's essential functions as accounting, control)... Trans-Australian Railway opens for traffic, each state with different gauge track (runs tea and sugar train to supply workers on line, evolves by 1980s as railway store for small localities)... Whitley Commission on Relations Between Employees and Employers recommends British industry form councils of employers and workers to consider trade, wages, working conditions, education and training (leads to 73 such groups by 1921, abandoned in 1930s)... Austria holds first Salzburg music festival... Russia's Kerensky government establishes (April 17) 8-hour day (ends capital punishment)... Walther Rathenau, managing director of Germany's AEG: <u>The Days to Come</u> (discusses plans for rationalization, standardization in collective economy)... Mexico adopts New Constitution (requires natural resources belong to Mexico, establishes minimum wage and 8-hour day, arbitration of labor disputes, and agrarian reform, leads to 1918 decree to make oil a national resource and change foreign titles into concessions)... Germany's Imperial Parliament approves limited partnerships of employees, employers (begins co-determination movement)... Pan-Russian Peasant's Congress of All Councils of Workmen's and Soldiers' Delegates favors (April 28) democratic federal republic for Russia... A.K. Erland, Danish mathematician studying technical problems of telephone company, anticipates waiting-line mathematical model... France adopts income tax... Russia assigns (June 19) women volunteers to war service... Berlin halts (August 23) private bathing to save water, coal... German Navy Zeppelin flies to German East Africa, covers some 4,200 miles in 95 hours... Kerensky Government proclaims (September 15) Russian Republic... Finland declares independence from Russia (establishes 8-hour day)... Britain places (October 17) embargo on Sweden, Norway, Denmark, Holland to stop supplies to Germany... Bolsheviks seize (November 7) power in Russia, Kerensky flees (November 15) as Lenin takes over (-1924, formulates prescriptions for nation's political, economic, and social conduct - thought challenged in 1989, proposes scientific system to resolve problems and plan for future, claims Russia's state result of iron laws of history)... First Soviet Government is formed (November 8) with creation of Council of People's Commissars, headed by Lenin (issues 'peace decree', 'land decree' nationalizes all private land - legalized for homes in 1990)... Izvestia, Soviet Government newspaper, appears (prints first ad, Pechiney French aluminum packaging company, in 1989)... Bolshevik Government adopts forcible requisitioning, nationalizes banks, confiscates all church property, repudiates national debt and gives control of factories to workers (instructs workers to join Government-controlled unions in 1918, requires peasants to turn over food surpluses to Government in 1920)... Britain's licensing law allows brewers to acquire pubs, by 1989 Bass, largest brewer with over 7,000 plus of total 82,000, and Allied-Lyons, Whitbread with over 6,000 each (leads to consideration in 1989 to end 239-year old "tied house" monopoly system)... Canada nationalizes 1896 Canadian Northern Railroad.

Business Events

Ernest Oppenheimer forms Anglo-American mining business in South Africa, evolves as world's largest gold producer... Nikon camera business appears in Japan... Assn. of British Advertising Agencies forms, rejected for Royal Charter as members are from limited companies and scope of activity too restricted (is Institute of Incorporated Practitioners in Advertising in 1927)... Business interests start Copenhagen School of Economics and Business Administration... After apprenticeship with Singer Motors and military service, William E. Rootes takes over family's business distributing cars of Singer, Austin, Humber, Clyno, and others - largest in 10 years and biggest exporter (acquires coach builder in 1925, opens London headquarters in 1926, buys three manufacturers in 1934-37 to make cars, forms Rootes Group in 1932 with reorganized Humber to mass-produce cars - nearly 43,000 vehicles in 1938 as one of Britain's 'Big Six' with 10% of total market, starts Australian plant in 1946 - Venezuela in 1963, evolves as world's 12th largest in volume in 1960, gets capital from Chrysler in 1964)... By 1932, British advertising agency Dorland opens 32 offices in Europe, South America and Commonwealth... Mitsubishi makes first car... Marks family regains control of retail store business (after eliminating wholesalers for direct links with suppliers, goes public in 1926, operates 126 stores in 1927, 234 in 1939 as Europe's largest retailer, 228 in 1947, 237 in 1958 and 252 in 1977, adopts self-service after W.W. II).

1918

General Events

Britain starts national food kitchens, rationing to cope with food shortages... Worldwide influenza epidemic appears (-1920 after some 20 million deaths)... Germany establishes 8-hour work day... U.S.S.R. Constitution places all power with Soviets of deputies representing workers, peasants and soldiers... Moscow Central Labor Institute trains skilled workers in simulated factory conditions... Soviets move (March 5) Capitol from Petrograd, formerly St. Petersburg, to Moscow... Bolsheviks change (March 7) name to All-Russian Communist Party (adopts Socialism in 1989-90)... Ferdinand Leger: "Engine Rooms" (glorifies modern machinery in painting)... Kingdom of the Serbs, Croats and Slovenes is formed in Balkans... Professor Junkers, engineering staff develop F-13, most widely used transport plane of its time (is ousted from firm in early 1930s by government takeover)... Soviets create (June 11) Peasants Committee to distribute land... First

Constitution of Russian Soviet Federated Socialists Republic is promulgated (July 10) to proclaim dictatorship of proletariat in restructuring the society... U.S.S.R. forms first collective farms with pooled resources to replace previous cooperative agricultural societies, some 4,700 in 1914... Oswald Spengler: <u>Decline of the West</u> (-1922, gives cyclical view of history with-eclipse of Western Civilization as inevitable)... Britain grants voting privileges to women over 30... Central Cooperative Union forms, Germany, to advance joint interests of employers and employees... Soviets complete (June 28) nationalization of industry... Airmail route is developed from France to South America (reaches Dakar by 1925, Buenos Aires by 1928, Santiago by 1929, ends operation in 1932)...

Catholic unions form Italian Confederation of Workers, follows movement started in 1891 (shows some 1.5 million members in 1921, Italy's 2nd largest federation)... Lenin approves U.S.S.R. League for Scientific Organization of Work (establishes laboratories to simulate factory conditions to study psychophysical variables of work)... Moscow University, first formed in 1755, re-opens... Czechoslovakia, Poland and Hungary are proclaimed republics... Alexander Moss invents turbo-supercharger for airplanes, standard equipment by 1938... Britain creates independent Air Ministry for RAF to function with War Office, Admiralty... British Labor Party adopts nationalization of major industries as major goal... Lenin: "Immediate Tasks of the Soviet Government" (in speech recommends use, modification of Taylorism... "The task that the Soviet Government must set in all its scope is - to learn to work... We must organize in Russia the study and teaching of the Taylor System and systematically try it out and adapt it over to our purposes"... plans to recruit U.S. engineers to help install system despite opposition of Soviet Labor Union and some party members, is used by Leon Trotsky to improve army's efficiency)... Industrial Welfare Society forms in Britain... Oil is discovered in this time in Maracaibo, Venezuela... Mexico's Confederation of Labor forms, AFL as model... Right-wing nationalists form Italian Labor Union... U.S.S.R. creates League of Time to educate workers on value of time-and-motion study... Red Army establishes system of military Commissars, perhaps to counteract influence of former Imperial Army officers... Germany signs (November 11) armistice... Britain provides free elementary education (creates ladder of opportunity from elementary school to higher levels)... After armistice, German ex-soldiers form unions... Radio links England, Australia.. France cancels (December 4) trade treaties to prepare for post-war economic battles... During Soviet Union Civil War (-1922) Bolsheviks are unsuccessful in turning over industry to trade unions, committees of workers.

Business Events

German industrialists Hugo Stinnes, Albert Vogler propose consolidating iron and steel industry as horizontal combination to share resources in marketing, purchasing, capital allocation, and research... Portuguese immigrant Antonio P. Ignacio founds Industrias Votorantim, Brazil's largest non-government industrial group in 1989 with interests in textiles, cement, paper, steel, chemicals and mining, in buying textile factory at auction of failed banks' assets... Central organizations of German employers, unions agree on mutual recognition and collaboration... Noda Soy Sauce Co. is incorporated by members of 1887 cartel (-1964 when renamed Kikkoman Soy Sauce Co., forms committees for sales, research, organization and production in 1918, sees unionization of workers in 1921, forms central personnel function in 1922 to administer programs in education, medicine, housing, burial, retirement and savings, forms work teams in 1923, forms Zaibatsu in 1926-36 with six manufacturing firms and four enterprises in transportation and finance, sees largest pre-war Japanese strike in 1927-28 by some 3,500 workers for 218 days)... Manolete, Spanish bullfighter, is born (-1947 when killed by Miura bull, leaves estate of some $4 million)... After toiling in bicycle shop as apprentice since 1905, working for Osaka Electric Light Co., and hearing about discoveries of Edison, Konosuke Matsushita, born 1894, starts small business to make reliable electrical sockets with wife and brother-in-law, 28 employees by 1920, 600 by 1931 and some 10,000 by W.W. II (makes electric heaters in 1927, foot warmers in 1930, and radios in 1931, views production in 1932 as means to eliminate poverty and create prosperity, after developing clanlike organization to embrace employees and families, decentralizes, central control with accounting and "bank" for funding capital investments, business with product divisions, each a profit center, in 1933 - centralizes 1945-52 to cope with post-war confusion and recession, decentralizes 1953-55, re-centralizes in 1955-60, and decentralizes again in 1960-73 to eliminate headquarters staff, acquires post-war technology by joint venture with Philips - ties with RCA, introduces Panasonic brand in 1955, forms U.S. subsidiary in 1959 - sales over $150 million by 1969, is accused of "dumping" color TV sets in U.S. in 1970, is forced to change pricing in Japan by 5 associations of housewives, as largest Japanese maker of consumer electronic products, some 5,000 with 120 plants and 19 centers abroad, forms Overseas Training Institute in 1972, forms U.S. firm in 1981 to sell U.S.-made goods to Japan and help U.S. firms enter Japan's market, starts Semiconductor Research Center in 1985 - R & D at $1.8 billion and $2.4 billion in 1988 with 55,000, 12,000 overseas, patents, creates Human Electronics in 1987 to study consumer trends to make "more human" products, with sales of $27 billion, about $40 billion by 1990, from 110 factories, 69 abroad, with 170,000 employees endows foundation in 1988 with $26.9 million to finance studies for better understanding of Japan and other countries, donates 0.1% of U.S. sales, about $5.1 million, in 1989 to U.S. charities and cultural activities, dies 1989, viewed by Japan as "god of management" for building world's No. 1 consumer electronics firm, over 14,000 products with brands of Panasonic, Technics, Quasar, National)...

Madeleine Vionnet opens fashion salon in Paris (-1940, devises innovative diagonal "bias cut" in 20s to change modern fashions, employs some 1,200 workers by closure)... Britain's first industrial cooperative research assn. forms, 24 more by 1923 but only one lasts after cut of Government funds... Some French firms provide family allowances, adopted by New Zealand as governmental program... France's Latecoere airline forms (-1933 when part of Air France after reorganizations in 1921, 1927)... U.S. interests control 87% of Chile's copper output... Increase in price of rice causes rioting in Japan... Krupp, consortium of banks form UFA to produce movies, one of two major studios, Bioscope the other, in Germany.

1919

General Events

Radicals Karl Liebknecht, Rosa Luxemburg and Karl Radek form (January 1) German Communist Party (leads to short-lived soviet republics in Munich, Brunswick and Bremen)... Britain adopts 48-hour work week... National Socialist Party forms (January 5) in Germany... Communist Party appears in Hungary (reforms itself as Hungarian Socialist Party in 1989)... British Post Office denies license for radio transmission as it would be "interfering with important communications" (grants first license in 1921 to BBC)... First Japanese radical labor union appears... German troops crush (January 12) revolution of Spartacists in Berlin, leaders of German Communist Party killed... Britain's Electricity Supply Act abets coordination of private and public power systems for new industrial revolution, Germany in 1919 and U.S.S.R.in 1920... With threat of nationwide coal strike, Prime Minister Lloyd George calls on Parliament to create special commission to make recommendations on future of British coal industry... Some 200,000 in Britain, Ireland strike (January 28)... Germany's Weimar Republic requires each mining, iron and steel firm with over 1,000 employees to have equal representation of management, employees on supervisory council... Walter Gropius, others found Bauhaus, Germany, to develop modern painting, sculpture, architecture, industrial arts (is closed by Nazis in 1933, is chairman of Harvard's architecture department in 1937)... J.W. Alcock, A.W. Brown of RAF make first non-stop transatlantic flight from Ireland to Newfoundland in 16 hours, 27 minutes... 1870 General Commission of German Trade Unions re-organizes as General German Federation of Labor, joins General Assn. of Christian Trade Unions (leads to 1920 Federation of Unions of German Workers)... Benito Mussolini, followers start (February 23) Fascist political movement in Italy... Riots of trade unionists throughout Buenos Aires are caused by police, soldiers firing on pickets at Vansena Iron Works in "Tragic Week"... Parliament's Industrial Courts Act establishes system for handling labor disputes... International Labor Organization forms in Geneva, endorses 8-hour work day... U.S.S.R. airs first radio broadcast, regular programming in 1922... First civil air route is opened between Berlin, Weimar... R-34 Zeppelin, given to Britain after W.W. I, completes first round-trip transatlantic crossing, 108 hours westward and 75 hours back... German mark is 8.9/dollar, 3.9 in 1920 and 88 in 1921... Third International forms (March 4) in Moscow to foster world revolution, first 1864-1876 to coordinate working-class movement... Italy starts (April 4) public air service, Rome-Naples, by dirigible... France adopts (April 17) 8-hour day... Ministry of Reconstruction issues first important British work on scientific management (views business welfare as necessity)... British Government investigates trusts... Finland's Act on Associations says labor organizations are legal... Moscow Narodny Bank opens first branch in London (pioneers Soviet ventures in international business)... Estonia is recognized as democratic republic, Latvia in 1921 and Lithuania in 1922... Holland adopts (July 11) 8-hour day... Moscow creates Central Aerodynamics and Hydrodynamics Research Institute, approved by Lenin as demonstration of modern power... Britain restricts (July 17) luxury imports to protect balance of trade... Madrid subway opens (October 18)... Labor Union Confederation forms in Paris, evolves as 2nd largest after Confederation Generale du Travail... Germany stops (November 1) railways for 10 days to save coal... Communist factory councils, Berlin, call strike (November 4), not supported by many workers... Ross Smith, crew in converted bomber win air race over some 7,000 miles between London and Darwin, Australia, in 27 days, 20 hours... Northern Italy is paralyzed by strike (December 3)... Britain plans air service from Egypt to South Africa (builds 21 landing fields for use of Imperial Airways, first continuous flight of Cobham in 1925-26)... Germany nationalizes (December 18) electricity.

Business Events

Canadian forester Ellwood Wilson starts world's first bush-flying activity in Quebec, Alaska's first in 1922, to survey trees for Laurentide Co. (evolves as Ontario Provincial Air Service during 1924-40s)... Polish-born fishmonger Abraham Belzberg, founder of family dynasty, starts new home in Calgary, Canada (-1976, develops used-furniture store as profitable operation, starts City Savings & Trust in 1962 to finance family's real estate ventures - consolidated later as Western Realty, sells Western Realty for $43 million in 1973 - attacked by minority stockholders for being cheated, after failures by sons to acquire eight major U.S. firms, purchase Scovill in 1985 for $523 million)... U.S.' Sylvia Beach opens Shakespeare and Co., Paris, as book store (-1941, becomes Left Bank center for writers, musicians of Lost Generation)... First Citroen car is made in France, first in Europe by mass-production... Lord Leverhulme acquires herring firm Bix and 300 shops for economic development of two Scottish isles (renames business MacFisheries, sells personal venture to Lever Bros. in 1922)... Rowntree cocoa works creates Workers' Council to improve industrial relations... Dutch businessmen form Royal Dutch Airline, KLM, 38.2% owned by Holland in 1991 (serves London, 1920, Copenhagen, 1920, Brussels, 1922, Paris, 1923, and Indonesia in 1927).

Paul Schlumberger forms partnership with sons, Conrad with science background and Marcel with engineering expertise (pioneers discovery of oil, gas deposits by electrical charting of rock formations, finds oil in 1927 - Soviet Union first client in 1929 as French firms refuse to reveal secrets to outsiders and non-French firms doubt claims, opens Houston office in 1946 - headquarters in 1956 and later Netherlands Antilles, hires investment banker and socialist Jean Riboud to be in charge of finance in 1950 - CEO of family enterprise in 1965, starts diversification from drilling equipment into oil-drilling in 1952, acquires French maker of electric meters and instruments in 1969, approves firing of grandson of founder Marcel as president in 1975, acquires Fairchild Camera & Instruments in 1979 for $425 million - sold 1987 for $122 million, becomes world's No. 1 oil exploration firm in 1980s - highest profit margin of world's 1,000 leading industrial companies with only AT&T and IBM having higher stock value/share, when Riboud retires in 1985 with cancer, names Michel Vailaud successor in 1986 after bitter family fight - replaced by U.S.' D.E. Baird as first non-French CEO)... B. Seebohm Rowntree gives lecture series for supervisors, executives of Britain's Ministry of Munitions (becomes Oxford Management Conferences)... Alsatian hair stylist Charles Jundt opens beauty salon in London's famed Ritz-Carlton Hotel (grosses some $500,000/year with cosmetics in 1936 as Charles of the Ritz when sold to Coty cosmetics business)... Confindustria is formed in Italy by employers, 103 associations and 75,000 firms with 2.5 million employees, to bargain with labor unions (joins other central employer organizations of Confagricotura, represents some 500,000 landowners with 1.8 million workers, and Confcummercio, represents some 50,000 firms with .3 million employees)... Farman Airline appears in France (evolves with others of 1923,1925 and 1929 as Air France in 1933)... Tropical Oil Co. gets contract to develop oil fields of Colombia... British Employers' Confederation forms as central organization for employers to bargain with trade unions... Canada's Grand Trunk Pacific Railroad declares bankruptcy... English Electric is formed by number of firms making appliances... Robert R. Hyde forms Industrial Welfare Society to disseminate information about good practices in managing men... Hydrogen Syndicate Corp. is formed in Berlin to market hydrogen, nitrates for fertilizers, industrial uses...

Siemens & Halske, AEG and Auer merge incandescent lamp operations as Osram for overseas competition, becomes Europe's largest supplier of light bulbs... John E. Colon, after flying in W.W. I, starts wholesale and importing business for street corner stalls, mostly wholesaling by 1929 (opens first Tesco food fair store in 1931 - 100 in London in 1939, opens Britain's first modern food warehouse in 1934, innovates with company branches in 1930s, opens first self-service outlet in 1947 - 20 by 1950 and over 140 of total of 185 in 1959, adopts lost-leader promotions in 1959, takes over 212 traditional grocery stores of John Irwin, Sons & Co. in 1960, adopts Green Shield trading stamps in 1963 after Fine Fair, others adopt Sperry & Hutchinson trading stamps in competitive war to 1967, runs 834 self- service stores, 4th behind Co-op, Fine Fair and Allied Suppliers, in 1968, by 1977 runs one hypermarket, 53 superstores, 393 supermarkets, 195 self-service food stores, 63 Home 'N Wear Stores, 19 furniture stores)... Bank of China, now People's Republic International Bank, opens branch in Hong Kong... Reginald C. Rootes joins brother in selling motorcars (founds Rootes Argentina SA, one of first English car distributors in Latin America, in 1931, is CEO of Rootes Group with reorganized Humber, subsidiaries of Hillman and Commoner, in 1932 to mass-produce cars)... British branch of Hoover vacuum cleaner business is started... W.O. Bentley starts making fine cars in England (-1931)... Junkers F-13 is first all-metal civilian airliner... Brazil builds first automotive assembly plant... Dance Hall Palais de Danse opens in London (popularizes jazz music in 1921 with Dixieland Jazz Band)...

Some 109,000 drivers, around two million by 1939, operate cars on English roads... For first time world price of gold is determined by five gold bullion dealers meeting twice-a-day at N. M. Rothschild & Son in London... Daimler Air Hire appears in England, part of Imperial Airways in 1924... International Chamber of Commerce forms to "promote private enterprise and increase trade" (arbitrates disputes in 1923 to settle problems between firms in different countries, issues first commercial reference for disputes in 1936, evolves with of some 7,566 members by 1964)... Frick & Co. airline flies in Switzerland (-1920 when replaced by Ad Astra line)... Handley Page Transport airline appears (-1924 with creation of Imperial Airways)... Frederick Bull, Norwegian engineer, devises punch-card machine (sells patents to Georges Vieillard, French bank employee, in 1931, incorporates 1933, unveils tabulator in 1935 to compete with IBM, builds its first computer in 1952, after defaulting on loan payment in 1964 sells 50%, later 66%, to GE, becomes Honeywell Bull in 1970 when GE sells computer business, in 1975 merges with French company, formed 1966 by government to ensure survival of land's computer industry - Honeywell out in 1982, merges with three French computer firms in 1983 to form Groupe Bull, after annual subsidies since 1963 sees losses in 1981-84, forms venture with Honeywell, NEC in 1987, buys Zenith's computer business in 1989, is 3rd largest Europe-based computer maker in 1991 after Siemens-Nixdorf, Olivetti)... After producing dyes in 1895, Rhone chemical business, Lyons, starts Brazilian branch to make perfumes for carnivals, soon Brazil's largest (in 1922 merges to form Rhone-Poulenc, by 1970 is 3rd largest chemical business in Europe, after losses is nationalized in 1982, in 1980s sells 20 firms and adds 30, in 1990 gets 35%, Hoechst owns 65%, of France's 3rd largest drug maker).

1920s

General Events

Marconi is instrumental in forming Italian National Research Council to promote development of all sciences, governed in 1988 by 163 scholars elected by 63,000 scientists (launches $800 million program in 1988 to reorganize over 150 research institutes into 5 large research centers)... Soviet planners hire German Ernst May, used factory techniques to build modern housing settlements in Frankfurt, to plan workers' city of Magnitogorsk... Tavistock Clinic appears in London as out-patient facility to provide families, organizations with psychotherapy (evolves as Tavistock Institute of Human Relations to pioneer use of behavioral science research, group dynamics and action research for business in 1940s, sponsors experiments of Eric Trist at British coal mines in late 1940s to develop use of autonomous groups/teams in new design of work organization)... Harmonization Society, financed by private funds and government subsidies, forms in Japan to promote labor-management cooperation... U.S.S.R.'s Central Labor Institute is fountainhead for use of Taylorism, time-and-motion studies.

Business Events

Women's Commercial & Savings Bank, world's first so managed, appears in Shanghai... Canton merchants' guild forms Merchants' Volunteer Corps with Russian advisors as private army to destroy roving bands of mercenaries (goes underground after 1924 attack by Nationalists murder leaders)... Adopted father of Shoji Uehara, 1987 wealth of $1.4 billion from non-prescription drug maker, launches Taisho Pharmaceutical Co.

1920

General Events

Britain, Austria adopt unemployment insurance... Australian high court gives Conciliation and Arbitration Court authority to regulate working conditions for state employees... All-India Trade Union Congress forms (sponsors series of strikes in 1928)... Germany's J.B. Rieffert heads army's psychology unit (-1931, pioneers use of group interview technique to select new officers)... Milan sets aside 99 acres for industrial fair, "La Fiera Campionaria" (becomes business showcase after W.W. II)... German Worker's Party becomes (April 1) Nationalist Socialist German Worker's Party... Chinese Labor Corps of some 180,000 coolies in France, recruited in North China by Allies during W.W. I for construction and supply projects, disbands... Lenin forms Commission for Elaborating the Plan for the Governmental Electrification of Russia (leads to 1920-21 campaign to push for country's revival with national plan for electrification of Soviet Union and construction, 1927-32, of massive V.I. Lenin power station, world's largest hydroelectric plant, with assistance of U.S. engineer Hugh Cooper, first foreigner to win order of Red Star, on Dnieper River with complex of canals and dam to provide, dream of Catherine the Great, unbroken navigation from Northern Russia to Black Sea)... Spanish Communist Party forms (June 1)... First Danish airline appears, Sweden in 1924 and Norway in 1928 (evolve as SAS in 1946)...

In mass meeting at Munich beer hall, Adolf Hitler calls for immediate socialization of great department stores, mostly Jewish-owned, for leasing at low rates to small middle-class merchants... Soviet Union nationalizes all factories... British Communist Party forms (August 1)... International Court is formed, The Hague... Britain produces 9.2 million tons of iron and steel, 7.4 in 1930 and 10.5 in 1938, U.S. with 42.3, 41.3 and 28.8, Germany with 7.6, 11.3 and 23.2, France with 2.7, 9.4 and 6.1, U.S.S.R. with .16, 5.7 and 18.0, Japan with .84, 2.3 and 7.0, and Italy with .73, 1.7 and 2.3... Defeat of Count Peter Wrangel's troops ends (November 16) organized resistance to Bolshevik regime... Britain, France sign pact to aid their oil companies to acquire Middle East concessions in preventing growth of possible competition in area... Spain's Juan de la Cierva tests autogiro (is successful in 1925, gives practical demonstration in 1927, flies over English Channel in 1928)... France hosts conference to promote Scientific Management... Histadrut labor federation forms, Palestine, to build modern economy and socialist-welfare society for Jews (evolves by 1980s to represent 80% of Israeli workers, provides comprehensive health care and other welfare benefits, operates enterprises, 66% of total agricultural output, as land's 2nd largest employer)... Britain's Amalgamated Engineer Union forms, follows industrial unions in 1910-14 (leads to Transport and General Workers' Union, National Union of General and Municipal Workers in 1921)... Germany's Workers' Council Act gives employees a voice in management, follows first representative worker groups in 1881 (is abolished by National Socialists in 1933, is re-established by Workers' Constitution Acts of 1952, 1972)... League of Labor Unions forms in Japan... France forms Credit Agricole to grant government-subsidized loans to farmers (goes international in 1984 as farmer-owned cooperative with assets of some $90 million)... Chile holds presidential election (shows shift in power from traditional rural landlords to cities)... Norway's Trade Union Opposition supports industrial unionism, idea from U.S.' International Workers of the World (is adopted by Norwegian Federation of Labor)... League of Nations creates (December 14) credit system to revive Europe... First Belgian airline appears (-1923 with formation of Sabena national line).

Business Events

Charles J. Bartlett joins London branch of GM as accounting clerk, CEO in 1926 (buys 1903 Vauxhall Motors in 1925, introduces profit-sharing in 1935, forms Management Advisory Committee in 1941 to handle grievances, sees unionism in 1950s, retires 1954 after making 130,000 vehicles/year with work force of 14,500)... After serving in Royal Flying Corps, giving flying instruction in 1918, and forming Cobham & Holmes Aviation to give air shows and joy rides, fails for lack of capital, Alan J. Cobham joins in forming De Haviland Aircraft to make planes (starts Alan Cobham Aviation in 1927 to survey airline routes - Africa 1927-31, starts Cobham-Blackburn Airlines in 1927 to serve Africa with cooperation of Imperial Airways, forms Air Speed to design planes, forms Flight Refueling in 1934 with Imperial, with Shell buys Imperial in 1937, sells back in 1948 and wins USAF contract in 1948)... Steamship business of S. Instone & Co. starts Instone Airline (-1924 when absorbed by Imperial Airways)... Oscar Deutsch, partners start Victory Motion Pictures as film distributor, develop improved sound system in 1920s (achieve success in 1927 when Film Quota Act requires exhibitors to show so many British films, operates 26 theaters by 1933 - 142 by 1936 as Odeon Theaters to compete with Gaumont British and Associated British Picture Corp., merges with United Artists' theaters, 68, in 1937 to become 3rd largest circuit before taking over houses of Paramount-Astoria)...

Frederick J. Marquis takes over London's David Lewis retail business with several branches (forms central publicity unit in 1922 and buying office in 1923, opens Glasgow department store in 1929 - Leeds in 1932, Hanley in 1934 and Leicester in 1939, acquires London's Selfridges in 1951)... Germany's AEG signs cooperative agreement with U.S.' GE... After breeding horses, operating Mills Horse Show Wagon, and serving in military, Bertram W. Mills presents circus at London's 1886 Olympia Exhibition Hall (becomes 'The Great International Circus' with European performers, tours in 1930 - 47 towns in 1937)... Marconi opens world's first public broadcasting station in Britain... Master shoemaker Adi Dassler starts Adidas, Germany (evolves by death in 1978 as $1.9 billion/year business worldwide in sports shoes, clothes, equipment)... After financial panic nearly wipes him out, Tamesaburo Furukawa switches from jewelry to movie field with Nippon Herald Films (as world's oldest billionaire in 1987, manages theater chain to distribute foreign films and Herald Group of 50 entertainment-related firms, includes golf courses, ski schools and restaurants)... After serving as infantry captain and staff positions focusing on organization, Lyndall F. Urwick leaves family firm after dispute to join Rowntree candy business as assistant to Oliver Sheldon in organization office (resigns 1928 to serve as director of Geneva's International Management Institute, forms Urwick, Orr & Partners in 1934 for management consulting)... Karl Aldrecht, 1989 billionaire with brother running 1,853 ALDI discount stores in Germany, Belgium, Spain, Austria and Denmark with interests in Iowa and Idaho, is born... Charles Higham's ad agency signs agreement with Chicago ad agency of William H. Rankin to handle Rankin's clients in Britain and vice versa... Germany's Hugo Stinnes starts building colossal trust with Austrian, Swiss and German interests in shipping, mining, utilities, manufacturing, finance and trading (-1924)... Firm is started in Hiroshima to produce cork, Toyo Kogyo in 1927 (makes machine tools in 1929, impressed by Ford trucks used in 1923 earthquake relief effort makes motorcycle/truck hybrid in 1931, after making rifles makes prototype passenger car in 1940, by 1949 turns out 800 trucks/month, after demand for its 3-wheel trucks during Korean War produces 4-wheel truck in 1958 and minicar in 1960, licenses Wankel engine technology from Audi in 1961 - first rotary engine in 1967, is Japan's No. 3 automaker in 1964 - named Mazda in 1988, gains diesel technology by license in 1965, exports to U.S. in 1970 - plant 1985, sells 25% to Ford in 1929, imports Fords in 1988)... When defeated Germany cedes its interests in Romanian oil, Belgium interests, Societe Generale as main participant, form firm, Petrofina, to acquire the properties (after losing assets during W.W. II expands overseas in 1950s, forms U.S. subsidiary in 1956, gets 30% of a North Sea field in 1971, with North Sea profits buys UK's Charterhouse Petroleum and U.S. oil properties, is subject of battle in 1982 for control by Groupe Bruxelles Lambert, land's 2nd largest holding company, and Societe Generale, land's largest holding company, resolves conflict with 1990 agreement to share authority, signs agreement in 1991 with Russia for oil exploration).

1921

General Events

Colombia's SCADTA airline forms, oldest continuous in Americas (evolves with 1933 SACO to form Avianca)... Britain's Safeguarding of Industries Act abandons free trade... Karl Capek: "R.U.R." (coins term "robot" in play, they destroy mankind)... Britain reports (January 14) 927,000 jobless, 3.5 million in U.S... Australia adopts tariff to protect industries launched during war... Joseph Stalin is General Secretary of U.S.S.R. Communist Party... Austria is hit (January 20) by general strike... Switzerland bars (January 24) imports of foreign labor... Airmail service evolves between Cairo, Baghdad (-1926)... German architect Mies van der Rohe designs all-glass tower... Japanese Labor Federation forms, membership of 300 unions with one million members by 1923 (is revived in 1946)... British Broadcasting Co., BBC, is created (starts radio broadcasts in 1922)... To inject some vitality in U.S.S.R.'s economy, Lenin proposes (March 12) New Economic Policy (allows small farms, firms to operate with state-controlled foreign trade, industry and agriculture, promoted by Nikolai I. Bukharin, dismissed from Politboro in 1929, purged by Stalin in 1937-38, and rehabilitated in 1988)... Aircraft designer and builder Edmond Rumpler shows aerodynamic car at Berlin motor show, followed by streamlined Chrysler Airflow in 1934, conceived in 1929, and Lincoln Zephyr in 1936... Reparation Recovery Act imposes (March 24) 50% duties on German goods, reduced (May 20) to 26%...

First Anglo-Soviet trade agreement is signed... Britain's Railway Act combines all railroads except four... Britain declares (March 31) state of emergency with thousands of coal miners on strike, settled after three months... U.S.S.R. counts population of 136 million people, Japan with 78 million, Germany with 60 million and Britain at 42.5 million... British Musicians' Union forms... Lenin bans all opposition groups, factions in U.S.S.R. to establish one-party dictatorship (-1989)... Persian Cossack officer Reza Khan overthrows Persian Government (founds Pahlavi "dynasty" as Shah in 1925, names land Iran in 1935, is succeeded in 1942 by son, Shah Reza Pahlavi)... H.G. Wells: Washington and the Riddle of Peace (predicts coming financial catastrophe)... Carl Kottgen, electrical engineer for Siemens, and others form National Board for Efficiency in Germany to urge rationalization movement based on Scientific Management... German scientist Friedrich Bergius liquifies (June 25) coal for oil... Paul Jaray, chief of design and development at Zeppelin works, tests model cars in wind tunnel (designs 1934 Czech car Tatra)... U.S.S.R. creates classification system to determine relative rates of remuneration for plant personnel... Hitler heads (July 29) Nationalist Socialist German Workers Party... Mao Tse-Tung, young librarian, forms Chinese Communist Party with small group of intellectuals (starts peasant unions and rural soviets in 1927, wins 1946-49 Civil War to form People's Republic in 1949)... German mark drops (August 15) to 88/dollar, 225/dollar on November 4... I. Hamilton: The Soul and Body of an Army (views ideal span of control as 3 to 6, follows Napoleon's maximum of 5 in early 1800s, Clausewitz's 10 in 1830 and Fayol's 6 in 1916, leads to H.L. Dennison's 6 to 12 in 1931, V.A. Graicunas' 6 in 1933 and T. Hainmann's, W.G. Scott's no definite limit for ideal span in 1970)... U.S.S.R. is threatened by severe famine, saved by U.S. relief efforts of Herbert Hoover (leads to decision by Lenin to slow collectivization of farms, to encourage peasants to sell food surpluses on open market)... Germany declares (August 29) state of emergency to combat economic crisis... All-Russian Scientific Management Conference meets in Moscow to formulate program for rationalizing production, 2nd assembly in 1924... National Institute for Industrial Psychology forms, London, to advise business on management research... Rome is hit (November 9) by general strike as railway workers clash with Fascists... U.S.S.R. defines union as "school of administration, a school of economic management, and a school of Communism" (purges independently-minded union officials in 1929)... Mussolini forms (November 7) National Fascist Party, begun in 1919 as reaction to post-war revolutionary movements... Some 300,000 in Vienna protest (December 1) high cost of living.

Business Events

First Aston Martin car is made in Britain... Germany's Braun AG begins to make kitchen blenders, home food preparation equipment... Air operation appears in Australia to serve Outback, evolves as Queensland and Northern Territory Aerial Services, Qantas, in 1922... B. Seebohm Rowntree, labor director for 1889-1936, is CEO of father's candy business (-1941, installs profit-sharing plan, full-time psychologist, employee testing and time-studies, union approved, by 1923, builds confectionery as world's 3rd largest, employment goes from some 7,000 in 1924 to 10,000 by 1939)... John Lee: Management: A Study of Industrial Organization (urges Britain to modify Scientific Management with industrial psychology)... Thomas N.R. Morson starts pharmaceutical business, Britain, with 6 products, over 50 by 1925 as importer, manufacturer, wholesaler, and retailer...

Billy Butlin opens hoop-la stall at Bedminster fair, sells at small margin for high volume (opens stall outside circus in 1922, after opposition to forming Stallholders Assn. to resist higher rents, opens four stalls at Skegness for holiday makers - successful with U.S. Dodgem cars, gains concession in 1930 for all stalls at provincial amusement park, opens first holiday park, field started in 1920s, in 1936 with dining and recreation halls, club rooms, gymnasium, chalets, tennis courts, bowling and putting greens, swimming pool and lake - 2,000 first summer and 5,000 in 1939, opens 2nd holiday camp, largest of nearly 100 in 1939, in 1938 - 3rd in 1945, runs two luxury hotels in Bermuda and luxury holiday village in Grand Bahama 80 miles from Miami, sold 1953 after failure, in 1946, after opening camps in 1959 and 1962 sells leisure business in 1972 to Rank Organization)... B. Seebohm Rowntree: The Human Factor in Business: Experiments in Industrial Democracy... Polish-born Isadore Ostrer, former stockbrokers' clerk and director of Lothbury Investment banking and underwriting house in 1919, forms Ostrer Bros. Merchant Bank (buys French interests in Gaumont Co., film distributor for films of Leon Gaumont, in 1922, is director of large textile concern in 1923, after 1927 Film Quota Act forms syndicate of Gaumont and two film distribution agencies, after acquiring 116 theaters of Lord Beaverbrook in 1928 runs chain of some 2,000 cinemas in 1928- 29, adds Gainsborough Studios to produce movies, after 5-year battle sells Gaumont-British to J. Arthur Rank in 1941)... Deruluft airline is a joint venture of German interests, Soviet Union (-1941).

1922

General Events

German mark hits (January 2) 7,260/dollar... B. Seebohm Rowntree: Industrial Unrest (notes true function of industry as form of social service, sees need to improve industrial relations by cooperation, for trained managers, for more democratic conditions)... France accepts (March 15) raw materials instead of currency for German reparations... Eng, Massole and Vogt develop sound system for films in Britain, fail to continue work... Unemployed Glasgow workers go on hunger march to London... Geneva hosts (April 10) international economics conference... U.S.S.R.'s Council of Commissars restores (April 12) private ownership of cars... London radio station airs first broadcasts... Egypt is (May 9) sole legal trader in opium, cocaine, hashish, morphine... Mexico expropriates (May 14) 1.9 million acres for land reform... Communist revolt in Bulgaria forces (April 21) King Boris to flee (-1989 with overthrow of Communist rule)... Lucerne says (May 27) cheese industry is hurt by U.S.-made Swiss cheese... Peng Pay starts Peasants' Union in China (joins Communists in 1923 to found Peasant Movement Training Institute)... Socialists, Budapest, win (June 4) parliamentary seats... Greece grants (July 24) Macedonian oil rights to Anglo-Persian Oil Co.... British possessions implement "Stevenson Plan" to restrict production of crude rubber on plantations (leads to drastic rise in world prices, causes Ford, Firestone to start Liberia rubber plantation in 1924)... Soviet oil trust hires U.S. oil firm to modernize petroleum facilities in Caucasian field... Collapse of mark imperils (October 23) Germany... Finland's Labor Agreement Act allows employers to prevent workers joining unions... Italian Fascists march on (October 30) Rome, full power (November 25).

Business Events

Thomas Lipton: "There's no fun like work"... Aero Lloyd Warschau appears in Poland, joins 2nd of 1925 to form Polskie Linje Lotnicze, LOT, in 1929... Edward A. Deeds joins in forming General Sugar Co. to combine over 100 Cuban firms, president to 1947... Britain's Cunard line sponsors first world cruise for tourists... Champion Hannes Schneider starts famous Austrian ski school .. Baron Phillippe de Rothschild takes over father's declining Bordeaux vineyards (builds Chateau Mouton Rothschild as maker of top-ranked wine)... Coco Chanel couture house, Paris, creates provocative perfume, named No. 5 after her lucky number (leads to perfumes of fashion designers Norell, Lauren, Halston, Calvin Klein and Oscar de la Renta in late 1960s-70s)... Charles, George Hurst start Kenya brewery to make Tusker beer, wins 8 gold medals in international tastings by 1980s (exports to U.S. in 1986)... William Lyons, age 21, partner open shop to make Swallow motorcycle side-cars (becomes Swallow Side-Car & Coach Building in 1926, makes first Austin-Swallow cars in 1927 and first Jaguar cars, so named in 1935, in 1931, goes public in 1935, instead of making Jaguar cars services bombers 1940-45, becomes Jaguar Cars in 1945, acquires Daimler cars in 1960, Guy Motors in 1961 and Coventry Climax Engines in 1963, merges with British Motor in 1966)... Britain's Daimler Airway is formed by merger of Daimler Air Hire, Aircraft Transport & Travel... Suliman Abdul-Aziz Al Rajhi, 1989 billionaire after making fortune with money exchange business (invests deposits as devout Muslims accept no interest), is born in Saudi Arabia.

1923

General Events

Union of Soviet Socialists Republics is created (January 1)... Le Corbusier: Toward A New Architecture... French Army occupies (January 25) industrial Ruhr for reparations... Sidney, Beatrice Webb: The Decay of Capitalist Civilization... German mark trades (February 1) at 47,500/dollar, 136,000 (June 22), hits 12 billion (October 21), 40 billion (October 23), and 4 trillion (November 15)... Some 2,000 private factories, at least 15 workers each, operate in U.S.S.R. (are closed by central planning in 1929)... Communist-organized and allowed by local warlord, Peking-Hankow Railway Workers' General Union, China's largest, stops railroad with strike, supported by Provincial Council of Trade Unions in Hankow until brutally suppressed with deaths of labor leaders... Communist Party appears in India... Norwegian inventor develops artificial wood... Alfred Marshall: Money, Credit and Commerce... Health forces (March 9) Lenin to retire, troika of General Secretary Joseph Stalin, Comintern leader Grigori Zinoviev, and Lev Kamenev, head of Moscow Communist group, takes over... International Criminal Police

Organization, Interpol, forms in Vienna as clearing house for police information (resumes operation in 1946)... Despite objections of rickshaw men, Beijing starts building China's first electric streetcar line... British housewives boycott (May 2) over-priced sugar, tea... Bread prices rise (May 15) in Paris, highest mark since 1870... Germany forms Cartel Court with authority to adjudicate abuses... City of Copenhagen uses psychological test to select new employees... Paris restaurants draw (July 1) color line to please U.S. tourists... Mussolini bans (July 16) gambling in Italy... U.S.S.R. forms Central Council of Scientific Organization of Labor to direct, coordinate 60 local, regional institutes in study of work, training and motion-and-time studies... Most bread in Berlin costs (November 6) 140 billion marks... German work week is set (December 14) at 54 hours, 59 for heavy industry... Hjalmar Schacht is Germany's Commissioner of Currency (stabilizes mark with new monetary issue backed by gold and mortgages on property of commerce, industry and banks, ends inflation with rigorous monetary policy which idles some 300,000 civil servants, office employees, workers)... After abolition of Sultanate in 1922, Turkish Republic is created at Capitol of Ankara with Mustapha Kemal as president (-1938, abolishes customs of polygamy and wearing of fez in 1925, introduces divorce in 1925, introduces new civil, criminal and commercial law in 1926 - based on Swiss, Italian and German legal systems, changes name of Constantinople to Istanbul in 1930, grants women voting rights in 1934, introduces use of family names in 1935)... German civil servants receive (December 17) only 50% of salary... American Country Club opens in Bucharest, first in Balkans... Canadian National Railroad appears (-1933).

Business Events

Willy Messerschmitt starts aircraft factory, Germany... Oliver Sheldon, assistant to B. Seebohm Rowntree: The Philosophy of Management (cites management functions as finance, administration, preparation, production, facilities and distribution, pioneers reconciliation of Scientific Management with social ethic as management needs to consider the 'personal' side, such as employee welfare, and 'impersonal' side, as well as operations)... Farman brothers, plane makers, design racing automobile with aerodynamic lines... First Japanese airline appears (is absorbed with 1925 J.A.L. by 1928 N.K.K.K. in 1929, is dissolved 1945)... After operating office supply business, John Moores and two mates, soon bought out, start Littlewoods betting business, Britain's largest private company in 1987, with football pools in spare time (quits job in 1926 to work full-time on business, starts Littlewoods Mail-Order Stores, renamed John Moores Home Shopping Service in 1959, with club membership in 1932, starts Littlewoods Chain Stores in 1936 - Blackpool first in 1937 and 24 by 1939, 52 by 1954, over 70 by mid-1960s, 108 by 1984 and 175 by 1987, runs 14 factories during W.W. II to make war supplies, starts credit mail business in 1952, Brian Mills mail-order in 1959, 6 mail-order firms by 1968, and Littlewoods Warehouses in 1960, evolves with wealth of some $2.8 billion in 1987)... Isao Nakauchi, 1988 billionaire with 14.9% of Daiei, Japan's largest supermarket/discount chain (expands family drug store business to become Japan's largest retailer), is born... Air Union appears in France (-1933 when part of Air France)... Suntory blends Japan's first domestic whisky... Siemens, Furukawa Electric form Fuji Electric to make electrical equipment (spins off Fujitsu, communication unit making phone equipment, in 1935)... Krupp fires any workers refusing to work 10 hours/day... With Spain in shambles after military coup, ITT, financed by Citicorp, buys three private phone companies, combined as Telefonica de Espana (wins service concession in 1924, sees assets frozen in 1939 to please German backers of Franco, is nationalized in 1945, starts long-distance direct dialing in 1960 - international 1971, enters satellite communications in 1967, buys minority share in Chile's phone system in 1990 from Alan Bond and wins bid with consortium to manage Argentinean network, joins AT&T in 1991 to develop private international network to link U.S., Mexico, Caribbean, Spain, Italy with fiber optics cable).

1924

General Events

Lenin dies (January 21) after denouncing Joseph Stalin... Mussolini abolishes (January 24) all non-Fascist trade unions... Ramsay MacDonald forms (January 23) Britain's first Labor government (-November 6)... Chamonix, France, hosts (January 31) first Winter Olympics... Dobrolet is U.S.S.R.'s first airline, merges with 1925 Ukvuzduchput to form Aeroflot in 1932 - world's largest in 1980s with 2,500 planes (forms joint ventures with Western firms and buys Western planes in 1989, seeks U.S. business travelers in 1990)... Norway launches first open-ocean factory ship for whaling (leads to International Whaling Commission in 1946 to regulate hunting, not effective until 1980s)... Insecticides are used for first time... Moscow creates central office for developing rockets.. Scottish inventor John L. Baird transmits first pictorial television image... Mussolini polls (April 7) 64% of popular vote to control Italy's parliament... Hugo Eckener, airship pioneer, flies ZR-3 from Germany to U.S... First Chilean labor code regulates labor commissions, hours, wages, vacations, social security, unions and disputes... Joseph Stalin: "The combination of the Russian revolutionary sweep with American efficiency is the essence of Leninism"... Britain, U.S.S.R. sign (August 8) trade agreement... Some 1,000 die as Canton tradesmen rise (October 16) against Sun Yat-sen... Spiral-bound notebooks appear... British seize (November 4) customs at Alexandria, force Zaghlul Pasha to resign... Following work of C.T.R. Wilson, Cambridge researcher Edward Appleton finds radio emissions bounce from ionized layer of atmosphere (is refined by Robert Watson Watt, chief meteorologist at British Royal Aircraft Establishment, to locate storms, gets patent in 1935 for radar)... Le Corbusier designs "rational" worker housing for Pessac, France.

Business Events

Swedish Confederation of Employers starts apprentice-training committee (starts supervisory training in 1950)... International Congress on Scientific Management meets in Brussels to reconcile approaches of Frederick W. Taylor, Henri Fayol... Swiss association forms to protect interests of makers, sellers of finished watches (is followed by producers trust in 1926, collective agreements on outputs, prices and exports in 1928, holding company for watchmakers in 1931, and cartel by federal law in 1934)... Finnish Society for Scientific Management in Agriculture forms... Siemens & Halske sign cooperative agreement with U.S.' Westinghouse, 20 years after pact of AEG with General Electric... First Czech airline appears, 2nd 1927... With government subsidy, Imperial Airways is formed by merger of 1922 Daimler Airway, 1919 Handley Page Transport, 1920 Instone Air Line, and 1923 British Air Marine (serves India, 1929, Cape Town, 1932, Singapore, 1933, and Australia, 1935)...

On death of father Willard G. Weston, age 27, takes over 1882 chain of Ontario bakeries, biscuit factories (after quintupling annual profits to over $129,000 by 1928, raises money on North American stock exchanges to finance expansion in U.S., Europe - buys biscuit and confectionery firm of William Patterson, invades Britain in 1934 with purchase of Aberdeen's Mitchell & Muir's biscuit division and enters bread baking with takeover of London's Chibnalls - 4 others later in Scotland, Wales, North West, and Midlands to develop market for Canadian wheat with financing by U.S. bear speculator Bernard Smith, forms Allied Bakeries in 1935 - one of wealthiest men in British food business in 1938 with 22 bakeries, 189 retail shops, 620 bread routes, and 4,187 employees, enters Parliament in 1936, while buying U.S., Canadian bakeries during W.W. II diversifies in wholesaling and paper-making, starts to acquire Canada's Loblaw grocery chain, 400 stores in 1988, in 1947 - control in 1953 to become Canada's largest maker of bread and Empire's largest biscuit maker with operations in Australia, South Africa, and India, buys London's Fortnum & Mason, purveyors of fine food, in 1951 despite public outcry over foreign control, after fighting Spillers and Rank buys 16 plants, 900 shops in 1953, operates 34 North American enterprises, including U.S.' National Tea Co., in 1954, with approval of West Germany's Economic Minister Ludwig Erhard buys interest in Deutscher Supermarket, chain of 100 stores, in 1958 despite opposition of local grocers, acquires two Canadian food wholesalers of franchised independent grocers in 1959 - Weston business Canada's largest retailer and wholesaler, forms Glenhuron Properties in 1963 to invest surplus cash at favorable long-term rates, acquires Britain's Fine Fair chain of 750 supermarkets, started in 1950s, in 1963, evolves as billion-dollar empire with some 100 North American subsidiaries and over 100 subsidiaries of Associated British Foods in 1988)... Solel Boneh construction is formed, British Palestine, by Histadrut (spins off Koor manufacturing in 1944 to provide employment for relocating Jews)... After buying Montreal's Bonaventure Liquor Co. in 1916 (sells liquor by mail, legal during Canada's Prohibition), Sam Bronfman, son of Manitoba frontier hotel owner, starts small Quebec distillery as Distillers Corp., Seagram in 1975 (in 1928 buys Joseph E. Seagram & Sons distillery business to become world's largest, when U.S. Prohibition ends, 1933, holds world's largest supply of rye and sour mash whiskeys and purchases three U.S. distilleries)... Land developer, Philip Hills, buys Beecham estate and pill business, Beecham's Pills in 1928 (adds consumer products, i.e., Macleans toothpaste, 1938, Eno Fruit Salt laxatives, 1938, Brylcreem hair care, 1939, to line, develops, 1959, world's first partly synthetic penicillin, and popular antibiotic Amoxil in 1961, acquires Massengill drugs, 1971, Calgon bath products, 1977, Jovan fragrances, 1979, Bovril foods, sold 1990, in 1980, J.B. William with Aqua Velvet, Sominex and Geritol in 1982, Germain Monteil cosmetics and Yardley soap in 1984, and cosmetics Norcliff Thayer, Tums and medications, in 1985, sells non-drug firms in 1987-1990).

1925

General Events

Emile Houdry devises catalytic cracking process to refine petroleum, commercial use in 1937... Japanese Ministry of Commerce and Industry is created (plans land's industrial policy after 1927, becomes Ministry of International Trade and Industry, MITI, in 1949 to direct post-war economic revival of Japan)... Mussolini's Fascist regime governs Italy (-1945, ends parliamentary government in 1928, introduces Fascist Confederation of Workers' Syndicate to replace unions... Communist KPD, Berlin, forms (February 1) to organize workers against Fascism... Germany's F. Fischer, H. Tropsch develop process to make synthetic oil... Sabena Airline links (February 12) Belgium, Belgian Congo... Hitler reorganizes (February 27) banned National Socialist Workers Party... German chemist Bosch invents industrial process to produce hydrogen... Shah of Iran begins industrialization with construction of railroad from Persian Gulf to Caspian Coast... Austria issues (March 2) shilling as new currency... J. Arthur Rank, inherited father's fortune from flour mills, starts Religious Film Society to produce movies for Methodists (starts building cinema empire of some 600 theaters, 24 movie companies)... Belgian Labor Party gains (April 5) first legislative majority... Germany's Central Federation of Labor adopts principle of industrial unionization... After being impressed by strength and lightness of recently purchased bicycle, Marcel Breuer designs tubular-steel chair, follows with Isokon recliner in 1936... Britain restores (April 28) gold standard (leads to nationwide general strike in 1926)... General strike in Shanghai briefly paralyzes (May 30) international settlement, French Concession... Paris exhibition features machine-age art in exuberant geometric patterns, spawns Art Deco movement to 1939... Belgium signs (June 1) commercial treaty with Japan... Adolph Hitler: <u>Mein Kampf</u>, Vol. 1 (advocates economic self-sufficiency, elimination of trade unions)... Berlin's Herr Schaetzle demonstrates (June 20) wireless phone for cars... Britain averts (June 21) nationwide strike with bonuses to miners... First practical British bread-wrapping machine is devised, first wrapped sliced-bread in 1928... By 1939 total number of coal mines in Germany drops from 2,940 to 1,540... Britain passes (July 31) Unemployment Insurance Act... In developing its First Five-Year Plan, Soviets use principles of Taylorism for factory organization... France, Germany sign (August 14) customs treaty... U.S.S.R. drops (October 4) 11-year-old partial prohibition laws... Hong Kong is paralyzed by general strike, again in 1989 to protest suppression of compatriots in Beijing and fear of takeover in 1997... Berlin bans (November 2) skyscrapers as health hazard... Germany's Paul Vierkotter devises camera flashbulb... With no enforcement of 1917 Constitution on ownership of resources, Mexico passes law to limit concessions of foreign firms.

Business Events

English firm of Spear's advertises sausages free of all preservatives... London shopkeepers form Regent Street Assn. to handle mutual problems... German major steel producers, Rheinelbe, Thyssen, Krupp, Hoesch, Rheinische, Stalwerke and Phoenix, plan to form Steel Alliance (after two drop out and three show no interest, form commission to combine administrative interests while retaining legal autonomy, leads to union of 12 firms, oldest facility of 1562, in 1926 to become world's 2nd largest iron and steel enterprise after U.S. Steel, operates with central administrative staff for finance with cost department, sales, and general administration, advisory departments of legal, tax and real estate, social and political economy, patent and purchasing, and four operating groups: mining, raw materials, smelting and refining and sales, adds Mitteldeutsche Stahlwerke in 1926 for plate and sheet metal products)... Tsai Wan-Lin, Taiwan billionaire by 1989 from Cathay Life Insurance and Cathay Construction after starting fruit and vegetable stand, is born to poor rice farmer...

Pierre, Jacques Guerlain create Shalimar perfume... Compagnie Internationale De Navigation Aerienne appears, part of Air France in 1933... Ford Motor Co. starts subsidiary in Germany... Austria's Oskar Barnack devises Leica, first successful 35-millimeter, hand-held camera (-1981 with bankruptcy)... Second International Management Congress at Brussels finally reconciles approaches of F.W. Taylor, H. Fayol... Conciliation Society forms, Japan, to promote management familism, welfare benefits and workers' councils... Ford Motor Co. begins to assemble U.S.-made cars in Japan, joined by GM in 1926... Shipping company consolidates several small airlines in Berlin to form Deutsche Aero Lloyd... With three key firms of BASF, Bayer, AG Farbwerke Hoechst and four smaller firms, Duisberg creates IG Farben to make dye-stuffs, controls over 90% of Germany's tar-dye production and over 50% of world's tar-dye market (dissolves 1945)... In formation of IG Farben, Agfa is created by combining photography interests of member firms (merges with Belgium's Gevaert in 1964 with Bayer holding 60%, 100% in 1981).

1926

General Events

After allowing some Fascist strikes to pressure industry to accept state control, Mussolini creates special ministry of corporations to fix wages, working conditions as way to control whole economy... Rhine, Ruhr steel industries form (January 14) combine of $150 million... Britain forms General Electricity Board... J.M. Keynes: The End of Laissez-Faire... Mexico nationalizes (February 11) church property... Germany adopts unemployment insurance... By this time, U.S.S.R. receives most of ordered 24,600 Fordson tractors... For first time, Shanghai Municipal Council seats (April 14) Chinese members... Germany grants (April 16) jobless unemployment benefits for 39 weeks... Mexico nationalizes minerals, oil... Some 78% of Soviet population works in agricultural sector, 71% in 1928 and 51% in 1940... Picture is transmitted (April 30) by radio between London, NYC... R.H. Tawney: Religion and the Rise of Capitalism... When government fails to renew subsidy to mining industry, British unions call (May 3) for general strike of 4 million workers to support coal miners (-April 12)...

Norway's Erik Rotheim invents aerosol spray, followed by disposable spray can of New York's Julian F. Kahn in 1939 (is used commercially in 1941 for insecticides)... In Rome, Fascists add (June 29) hour to work day for economic efficiency... Two Argentina railroad unions form socialist central labor organization, followed by Communist central union in 1929... French test (July 7) neutralizer of auto exhaust to purify city air... Collapse of franc leads (July 23) to new government... Mexican Catholics start (July 28) trade boycott to protest religious restrictions... French law penalizes excessive company profits... Soviet landowners are required (August 1) to pay taxes in securities instead of in kind... French tennis professional, Suzanne Lenglen gets (August 2) $200,000 to tour U.S... Ralph B. Perry: General Theory of Value... European Steel Cartel is formed (September 30) by Norway, 36.5%, Germany, 25.4%, Sweden, 20.5%, Yugoslavia's 14.1% indirectly owned by Germany's IG Farben, and Switzerland with 3.5%... Republic of Lebanon is created (evolves as banking center of Middle East after W.W. II until Civil War in 1975)... Alfred Mond: Industry and Politics (gives English model of business rationalization)... Italy bars (October 23) women from civic offices... Belgium adopts (October 26) new currency to stabilize economy... Jan Christian Smuts: Holism and Evolution (pioneers evolution of systems theory)... British coal strike ends (November 19) with no settlement.

Business Events

French tennis player Rene Lacoste starts sport clothing business with simple short-sleeved sport shirt, first marketed as Izod with crocodile emblem in 1933 (enters U.S. market in 1951 - fad in 1960s-70s, is acquired by General Mills in 1969)... Following example of Manufacturers' Assn. in Boston, Rowntree forms first British Management Research Group, members from some 25 non-competing large manufacturing firms, to promote efficient management... After meeting American with photos of greyhounds chasing mechanical hare in Oklahoma City, Alfred C. Critchley starts greyhound racing in England (forms Greyhound Racing Assn. in 1927)... Vehbi Koc starts small construction materials firm in Istanbul, Turkey (starts Ford dealership in 1928, forms joint venture with General Electric in 1946, evolves by 1988 as Koc Group with over 116 firms, including interests in automobiles, household appliances, food, banking, insurance, construction and tourism, with family wealth of some $1 billion)... Balair starts flying, joins 1920 Ad Astra in 1931 to form Swissair... Benz automobile firm joins Daimler Motor Co. to form Daimler-Benz to make Mercedes-Benz vehicles, worldwide conglomerate by 1980s... Major British manufacturers of explosives, dyestuffs and alkalis form Imperial Chemical Industries, ICI (operates with central headquarters coordinating functional departments, signs marketing agreements to give IG Farben rights for Europe, DuPont rights for U.S., and Solvay & Cie rights for Belgium, ICI with exclusive rights for Britain and Empire...

Sakichi Toyoda starts Automatic Loom Works, technology from British firm in 1929 (opens automobile department, copies U.S. designs, in 1933, shows first car, a flop, in 1935, after sending engineer to study U.S. Packard plant, spins off car unit in 1936, goes public in 1937 as Toyota, name selected by numerologist as more favorable, Motor Co., makes trucks in 1939 when forbidden to make passenger cars)... Deutsch Luft Hansa is formed by Deutscher Aero Lloyd, 1919, and Junkers, formed by airplane manufacturer in 1921 (starts Eurasia Aviation, seized 1941, with China in 1930, runs Europe's most comprehensive air route system, serves U.S.S.R. via Deruluft, in 1931, starts world's first regular transatlantic airmail service, Berlin to Buenos Aires, in 1934, is allowed by Allies, now named Deutsche Lufthansa, to fly to London in 1954, Paris in 1955 and South America in 1956, sees first profits in 1963, buys 49% of Euro-Berlin France, regional airline of Air France, in 1988).

1927

General Events

Italy's Labor Charter designates Fascist unions as sole representatives of workers (makes strikes, lock-outs illegal)... For first time, planes are used in Canada to dust crops with insecticides... Mexico grants unlimited concessions to foreigners for lands developed prior to 1917 (revokes 1918 decree to open oil concessions for negotiations, leads to oil lands reverting to U.S. firms when Mexico's Supreme Court finds Petroleum Law unconstitutional)... University of Manchester takes over Manchester College of Technology's Department of Industrial Administration, formed after W.W. I... After 1926 general strike, Parliament passes Trade Disputes Act, makes general strikes illegal, and Trade Union Act, curbs union powers... Chou En Lai leads (March 21) general unions of workers to take over Shanghai, overthrown (April 12) by Shanghai Chamber of Commerce, Green gang of gangsters and foreign community after killing thousands - Chou escapes... Britain puts 33.5% import duties on tires, spurs local plants by Goodyear, Firestone, Goodrich and Italy's Pirelli... Socialists riots appear in Vienna... Stalin assumes control of Soviet Union (-1953, purges 6,500 supporters of Leon Trotsky by 1930)... Austria ski instructor Hannes Schneider hosts first Arlberg-Kandahar ski race (attracts racers throughout Europe to competition)... Berlin, Buenos Aires are linked (August 3) by wireless... Leo Theremin invents earliest known electronic musical instrument... Moscow hosts first exhibition of space flight... Industrial Health and Safety Center appears in London... Norway elects (October 27) first Labor Government... Germany passes Unemployment Insurance Act... China uses lottery to raise funds for famine victims... World's first large air lift is flown by Western Canada Airways, carries drilling machinery to Hudson Bay...

R.H. Tawney: <u>The Acquisitive Society</u> (discusses accumulation of wealth)... British Broadcasting Corporation, BBC, gets government charter (is financed by licenses on radio sets, two million in 1927)... Chiang Kai-shek forms China's Nationalist government in Nanking (eliminates working men's organization first formed in 1919-21, begins civil war with Communists)... U.S.S.R. prepares first Five-Year Plan (uses services of foreign specialists in Scientific Management to prepare Gantt charts for implementation in 1929-33, uses some 45 U.S. firms by 1930 to carry out plan)... France adds elegant <u>Ile de France</u> to fleet of three luxury ocean liners... Colombia nationalizes (November 18) oil industry... Chiberta Golf Club opens near Spanish border, France's oldest golf area.

Business Events

VARIG airline of Brazil is started by state of Rio Grande do Sul, private investors (reorganizes in 1945 as foundation - employees with 50% of stock, starts first international flight in 1955 between Rio de Janeiro and New York, becomes largest privately owned airline outside U.S.)... Vickers-Armstrong combination forms in London with interests in machinery, shipbuilding and armaments... International Management Institute, Lt. Col. Lyndall Urwick as director, is formed at Geneva by Edward Filene, others as clearing house for management information (-1933)... Thomas Cook & Son arranges first air-tour for tourists for trip from NYC to Chicago (is absorbed by Belgium's Wagonslits in 1930s, reorganizes in 1942 as British business)... Mille Miglia, most dangerous and glorious of great Continental road races, is first held on 1,000-mile loop in Northern Italy... Siemens & Halske oversees plants with central administration for finance, plants and traffic... German airline, Kondor Syndikat, forms for traffic to South America (-1941)... British International Pictures appears from assets of British National and its Elstree Studios (forms Associated British Cinemas, 80 houses in 1929 and 160 in 1931, in 1928, produces 200 films, most of any British production company, in 1929-39, becomes Associated British Picture in 1933 with Wardour Films to compete with Gaumont-British Pictures)...

With 4 million trees from Philippines, Henry Ford starts rubber plantations in Brazil's Upper Amazon River to break monopoly of producers in Malaya, Ceylon (builds Ft. Landia, community of some 3,000 with schools, churches, hospitals, stores and recreational facilities, abandons project after investing some $20 million to work two million acres with 2,000 people, is sold in 1946 for some $250,000)... Japan's Nomura securities firm opens NYC office (sponsors company song in 1929, is first Japanese securities house to return to NYC in 1953, spurs personal investment in 1958-62 by distributing savings chests to Japanese households, between 1980-87 doubles work force abroad to 2,000, is first Japanese security house in China in 1982, opens London office in 1982, buys seat on London Stock Exchange in 1986 and is one of two Japanese firms to be named primary dealer in U.S. Government Bonds, operates as world's largest securities firm in 1988 with assets of $372 billion, U.S.' Citicorp, $204 billion, and Merrill Lynch, $55 billion, and 12,000 employees, 38 offices in 21 countries, 131 branches in Japan, to serve 5 million customers and handle 17% of all stock traded in Japan, Daiwa Securities with 12%)... Y. F. Chang, Taiwan billionaire in 1988 as world's largest container shipper Evergreen Group, is born... Edward Bronfman, Toronto-based billionaire 1988 with interests in energy, financial services, and consumer products after being forced out of family Seagram business by Montreal cousins in late 1940s to build Edper Enterprises with brother, is born... British ad agency W.S. Crawford opens offices in Berlin, Paris by 1932.

1928

General Events

Countries agree to build inter-American Highway (finishes 62% of Central America, 87% of South American sections of Pan-American Highway by 1940)... John Baird sends TV images of London to NYC... Congres Internationaux d'Architecture Moderne forms in Geneva... Soviet peasants protest (March 22) food shortages... U.S. accepts (March 27) new Mexican oil-land laws...

Business Research Institute, Stockholm School of Economics, issues first report... Sweden's Collective Agreements Act limits actions of unions, management during contract period, creates Labor Market Court to resolve employer-employee disputes... De Freyssinet develops pre-stressed concrete for construction... Turkey drops (April 9) Islam as state religion, drops Arabic letters for Latin alphabet... Iran establishes Banque Melli Iran as first government bank... French Aeropostate starts service to South America... Alexander Fleming accidentally discovers penicillin in contaminated culture dish (is tested for practical applications in 1938-40 by Dr. Howard Florey, is developed for commercial use in 1943)... Charles Kingsford-Smith, crew in Fokker Trimotor, Southern Cross, make (May 31-June 8) first flight of some 7,800 miles from California to Australia, first non-stop flight in 1931 by Major Clyde Pangborn, Hugh Herndon... Soviet Union invites German-born Albert Kahn with 25 engineers, architects from his Detroit engineering firm to design Stalingrad Tractor Plant (in full charge of heavy industry sector in first Five-Year plan builds 521 factories in two years and trains some 4,000 engineers and apprentices, helps design 2nd Five-Year plan)... Nationalist flag flies (June 8) over Beijing with Chiang Kai-shek as (October 6) chairman of Nationalist Government... Argentina nationalizes oil sector... First Mexican airline appears... France devalues (June 24) franc to 25.5 francs/dollar...Brazil's economy collapses with over-production of coffee... U.S.S.R. lists 47,000 engineers, 289,900 by 1941...

First Italian airline is formed... U.S.S.R. increases coal output from 35.4 million tons to 128 million by 1937, steel from 4 million tons to 17.7 million... Junkers F13, first built 1919 and workhorse of Lufthansa 1926-32 by carrying 4 passengers in closed, heated cabin, makes first East-West crossing of Atlantic before crashing in Labrador after 37 hours... Soviet Union's Amtorg Trading Corp., Moscow Automobile Trust visit 4 plants in Detroit... Airship Graf Zeppelin, 775 ft. in length and 100 ft. in diameter, returns (November 1) to Germany after flying 4,400 miles in 69 hours (starts first transoceanic airline service to Brazil in 1931, retires in 1937 after 590 flights).

Business Events

Lyndall F. Urwick: "Principles of Direction and Control," <u>Dictionary of Industrial Administration</u> (gives first principles for control activity of management)... Aluminium of Canada is founded... Van Doorne brothers start Dutch car-repair business (start building DAF trucks and buses in 1930, cars in 1959)... Elegant Peninsula Hotel opens in Hong Kong near new railroad station, terminus for completed Paris, Moscow, Beijing and Hong Kong rail line... Fritz Thyssen heads family steel, iron ore trust (-1951, supports Hitler in 1930s)... International Corp. for Chemical Enterprises forms in Basel, Switzerland (provides funds to finance German chemical activities in Norway, Switzerland, Spain, U.S. and Italy)... Leading Hotels is formed by 38 Europeans with properties in Europe, Egypt (coordinates promotions for 210 independently-owned luxury hotels worldwide in 1988)... After closing Dearborn tractor plant Henry Ford shifts production to Cork, world's largest tractor facility (makes modified Ford cars in 1931 to capture 54% of British market in 1934, signs first labor contract in 1944)...

Financier Pierre Bermond's Hotel Royale Monceau in Paris provides visitors with elegance, prestige... Frank Samuel takes over ailing United Africa Co. (merges with Niger Co., Lever Bros. subsidiary, and African & Eastern Trade Corp., revives business in 1930s with trade in vegetable oils and other commodities, diversifies into ships, Palm Line, motor vehicles and refrigerated foods, acquires maker of heavy construction equipment in 1937, opens Kingway Store, modeled on those of U.S., in 1947, opens plywood factory in 1948, brewery in Nigeria in 1949, furniture factory in 1953 and concrete plant in 1954)... Benjamin Benetau is first fisherman on France's West Coast to put motor on fishing boat (evolves by 1987 as world's top maker of sailing yachts, opens $3.5 million U.S. assembly plant in 1987 to challenge some 300 small manufacturers)... Airwork is formed to service private planes, under 1,000 centers by 1935 (trains pilots, navigators and services aircraft in 1939-45, is most successful of independent airlines in 1945-56, merges with seven independent competitors to form British United Airways in 1960, adds two more lines in 1962, with withdrawal of BOAC gets right to South America market in 1965, operates in 1964 with 130 planes, 59 helicopters and 7,000 employees to handle over 1.5 million passengers and 84,000 tons of freight, adds 10 major subsidiaries in 1965, merges with Caledonian Airways in 1970-71 to form British Caledonian Airways)... Frank Murphy leaves advertising to start Murphy Radio (produces first sets in 1930 - 80,000/year in 1935 as market standard, resigns 1937 to start furniture manufacturing business with marketing approach, "New Conception of Business," that shopkeepers should be consumer's advisor rather than a manufacturer's agent, provides workers with employment security, reasonable working conditions and above-average wages, uses market research, liquidates with W.W. II)... Barnett Samuel & Sons forms Decca Record Co. after exporting 22% of Britain's gramophones in 1927 (buys firm making records in 1929 and moribund U.S. record company, Brunswick with Bing Crosby, in 1932, forms American Decca in 1934, Crosby leading artist, to become leader in popular music, in late 1930s expands into radar business, in 1979 sells record business to German-Dutch Poly-Gram and military electronics, communications to General Electric)... Kazuo Tashima, helped by a German trader and an optical engineer - both leave 1931, forms Osaka firm to make quality optical equipment (makes first camera in 1920 - Minolta brand in 1933, introduce popular Vest camera in 1934, makes optical equipment during W.W. II, rebuilds destroyed facilities, 1945, with U.S. recovery loans, in 1950s-60s expands to Southeast Asia and diversifies in office equipment, overtakes Nikon in 1973 as U.S. market leader, introduces best-selling copier in 1974, exports some 80% of sales in 1975, introduces fully automated camera in 1985 to compete with Canon's AE-1, forms venture with Mazda, Sumitomo in 1990 to make car engines, body parts in Indonesia, sells Polaroid instant cameras with Minolta name in 1990)...

Jules Thorn starts Electrical Lamp Service Co. in London to sell imported lamps (after acquiring radio and lamp firms, restructures in 1936 as Thorn Electrical, is Britain's largest maker of radio, TV sets in 1960s, buys Robinson Radio Rental to become world's largest TV rental firm in late 1960s, after buying host of small firms, gets struggling Electrical & Musical Industries, formed 1931, in 1979, reforms in 1985 to focus on music, technology, rental and retail, buys U.S.' Rent-A-Center in 1987 for $594 million, gets 50% of Chrysalis Records in 1989 and adds music publisher, Filmtrak, in 1990, in 1991 sells European light bulb business to GE, gets approval in 1991 to buy control of Thames Television).

1929

General Events

Turkey adopts (January 11) metric system... Britain's share of world's manufacturing output is 9.4%, U.S. with 43.3%, U.S.S.R. 5.0%, Germany 11.1%, France 6.6%, Japan 2.5% and Italy with 3.3%... Oil is discovered in Brunei (generates revenues of some $3 billion/year by 1980s)... After purge trials of engineers in 1928, U.S.S.R.'s Communist Youth League is given task to prepare engineers for industry... In this time, some 1,500 U.S. experts from RCA, DuPont, G.E., etc., work in Russia on technical contracts... Germany reports (February 15) 3.2 million unemployed... Soviet Union prepares unified accounting system to monitor performance of Five-Year Plan, tested 1931... Air Orient is formed, part of Air France in 1933... Soviet Union, Ford sign contract for construction of plants to make 100,000 vehicles/year... Unemployed Glasgow workers hold hunger march to London... German engineer Felix Wankel patents rotary engine, not practical until 1951... International Conference on working women meets (June 11) in Berlin... As plant operations had been coordinated by management, Soviet Central Committee now defines committee of workers and Communist Party plant committee as basic units of industrial management of an enterprise in network of state financial and production planning (lets each factory to make plans, records, evaluations of performance)... Australian Labor Party wins government national elections... After 21 days, 7 hours and 26 minutes, Graf Zeppelin ends (August 2) flight around the world, three stops... Tootal's devises first crease-resisting cotton fabric, Britain... Mexico adopts labor code... U.S.S.R. calls (September 24) for 5-day week... Alves Reis, Portuguese international swindler, is convicted in conspiring to defraud Bank of Portugal, jailed to 1945... During Chile's depression (-1933), government forms Corporacion de Fomento de la Production to finance industrial growth... Yugoslavia is formed as Serbo-Croat-Slovene Kingdom with Alexander I as King... First rocket plane, invented by automaker Fritz von Apel, covers (September 30) nearly two miles in 75 seconds... Institutional Revolutionary Party forms in Mexico, controls government to present time... Henri De Man: <u>Joy in Work</u> (studies work motivation, results similar to those of Herzberg in 1960)... Bank for International Settlements picks (November 8) Switzerland as site of world bank... Soviet Union creates Intourist... International pact is signed to protect fledgling overseas airlines (limits liability on suits from crashes... Britain grants (December 19) 7.5-hour day to coal miners.

Business Events

After resigning as manager of Atlantic City Woolworth variety store, James Marshall, partners start retail business in Rio de Janeiro, revolutionizes retail business of Brazil... Latin American Panagra airline is a joint venture of Pan-American, W.R. Grace & Co. (is acquired by Braniff in 1966 for $30 million, is acquired by Eastern in 1982 for $30 million)... General Motors, Ford assemble some 98% of 26,000 cars made in Japan, forced to leave country later after protectionist laws... Enzo Ferrari starts exotic-car factory in Modena, Italy, joins plants of Lamborghini, De Tomaso, Maserati... After working at race courses, William Hill starts London bookmaking business (opens credit office in 1934, launches football wagers, Scotland, in 1937 with postal betting, goes public 1954)... Metal Box is Britain's first can-making business, technology not known until 1927... GM buys Opel Motor Works, Germany's largest, (evolves as Europe's largest manufacturing plant on 500 acres to make at peak some 5,000 vehicles/ month with 24,000 employees)... Franz Burda inherits 3-man printing shop (evolves by 1980s as one of Europe's largest press empires with 12 magazines, including popular TV-radio guide and slick-picture weekly)... Unilever is created as one unified holding company by Margarine Union of Britain, holding company started in 1885 by William Lever to make Sunlight Soap, and Margarine Unie, holding company jointly owned and operated by Van den Berghs of Holland and Jurgens of Germany since 1908 (establishes special committee reporting to joint Anglo-Dutch board for administering operations and overseeing Continental Committee, Overseas Committee for Britain and sub-committees for soaps, margarine and oils and fats, is $33 billion conglomerate in 1989 with some 500 decentralized subsidiaries in about 75 countries)...

George S. Livanos, London-based (joins secretive Goulandris shipping family of Andros) billionaire in 1988 after inheriting largest Greek fleet in 1950s, is born (weds sisters to shipping tycoons Aristotle Onassis, Stavros Niarchos)... Dunlop Rubber Co. produces first foam rubber... After visiting U.S. in 1911 to work as necktie peddler and operate women's underwear factory, Abdul Majeed Shoman returns to Palestine with $75,000 to start first Palestinian Arab Bank, 350 branches in 45 countries by 1980s... In opposition to Carl Bosch's proposed Super Board of Control to oversee most of Europe's chemical industry, ICI rejects exchange of technical information with IG Farben... Eastern Telegraph, formed 1872 to own one of every three miles of world's cable by 1896, joins other firms, including Marconi Wireless, to form Cable and Wireless to fight ITT (is nationalized by Britain in 1947 - privatized 1981-1985, forms Mercury Communications, government mandated rival to British Telecom, with BP and Barclays in 1982, buys control of Hong Kong internal phone system in 1984 - 20% is sold to China in 1990, joins C. Itoh, Pacific Telesis in 1990 to form International Digital Communications, picked to compete against Japan's former overseas communications monopoly, joins Motorola, Spain's Telefonica to develop cellular phone system for UK for use in 1992).

1930

General Events

To eliminate 10-13 million landed farmers, kulaks, Stalin starts (January 5) forming giant agricultural cooperatives, to operate like State-owned factories, by collectivizing all agricultural land, livestock and equipment of farmers (grants farmers free use of state property, divides income from farms among farmers on quality and quantity of work... In 1989 collective peasants can own house and garden, stable and cow, sell surplus for private income, lease land for 50 years or more and pass tenancy to heirs)... Mahatma Ghandi heads non-violent protest, India, against Britain's salt tax to prevent manufacturing of salt... During decade, Chile shifts mining from traditional nitrates to copper... France passes National Workman's Insurance Law... All central unions in Argentina join together into one organization (dissolves with military dictatorship in 1943)... Danish labor unions form Workers' Educational Assn. to operate training programs for members during decade... After successful revolution, first since 1889, Geutlio Vargas is President of Brazil (-1945, eliminates democratic constitution in 1937 to proclaim Estado Novo, places all trade unions and employers' organizations under control of Ministry of Labor, bans all strikes as subversive)... Tape recorder is developed in Germany... France passes (February 8) social security bill... After Soviet government purges, Stalin creates State nomenklatura in 1930s to execute his orders (evolves as distinct social caste to dominate governmental bureaucracy)... Picture telegraphy begins between Britain, Germany... Amy Johnson makes solo flight from London to Australia in 19.5 days... Thousands of Russians flee (March 1) collectivization to Poland... In 1930s France's Couplex and Givelet invent "first" electronic organ, follows electromechanical organ of U.S.' Thaddeau Cahill in 1895... After unsuccessful attempts by U.S., British, Danish, Italian and German flyers, Germany's Wolfgang von Gronau is first to fly Arctic Great Circle route from Europe to North America, followed by Lindbergh's from NYC to Tokyo in 1931 and Russian plane from Moscow to U.S.' Vancouver in 1937... Japan acknowledges (May 6) China's customs autonomy... French airmail links (May 13) Paris, Brazil... Holland's Post, Telephone and Telegraph Service uses psychologist to select new employees, used during 1950s to study effects of organizational changes...

During 1930s Wo Lee Wo Triad appears in Hong Kong as secret fraternal association (evolves in gambling, narcotics, prostitution, loan-sharking, etc.)... German General Staff forms special section for rocket development... All-India Radio Network is created, used first radio transmitters in 1926... Iran takes over banks, railways, telephone and telegraph system (establishes government monopolies in tobacco, opium, sugar, cement and wheat)... Charles Kingsford-Smith flies in record time, 9 days and 22 hours, from London to Australia ... British Coal Mines Act allows cartel of coal industry (signs agreement with Poland, German syndicate declines to join, in 1934 for exports to Scandinavia)... Uruguay wins first World Cup of soccer, global sport by 1990s with TV viewers in millions... U.S.S.R.'s Nizhni Novgorod plant, designed by Cleveland's engineering, consulting firm of Austin Co., with model city, named Gorky in 1932, for workers, starts producing Ford vehicles... General strike, riots paralyze (November 15) Madrid... Holland, Scandinavia sign economic pact... Britain abandons airships with crash of R101... Soviet-built plant, designed by U.S.'s Albert Kahn and supervised by International Harvester, begins making tractors at Stalingrad (opens with 2nd plant in 1933 to produce crawler tractors)... Frank Whittle submits plan for jet engine to British Patent Office, no interest by private industry for next two years (loses patent in 1935 when unable to pay renewal fee, builds first engine in 1937 - 2nd explodes in 1938, achieves reliable performance in 1940, is flight-tested in 1941, is recognized in 1948 with award of $400,000, knighthood)... Geneva hosts (November 28) economic conference to discuss spreading depression... General strike, Spain, supports (December 16) revolution... U.S.S.R. takes (December 22) control of all food supplies... Germany's Hermann Julius Oberth, space age pioneer, develops model jet motor... Britain forms secret Industrial Intelligence Center, becomes Ministry of Economic Warfare, in this time to identify targets in enemy's war production... Over 25% of Japan's upper house and 12% of lower house members have commercial ties with zaibatsu.

Business Events

Mainbocher fashion salon opens in Paris, famous for elegant design (opens New York house in 1940)... Two industrial groups in France form marketing firm (shows land's trend in vertical integration)... After working as apprentice in uncle's leather and fur shop in Florence since 1925, Adele Casagrande, brother start small leather shop in Rome, renamed Fendi after marriage (present first collection in 1954, evolves by 1980s as Italy's leading fashion house with sales of $40 million, some 380 employees and 200 stores worldwide)... Independent Radio Normandy of International

Broadcasting Co. airs commercial radio programs to Britain...Vauxhall Motors makes Cadet cars, its first mass-produced model... Battista Farina starts Pininfarina, Italy's premier design firm for cars (after creating Ferraris, Peugeots and Alfa Romeos, styles Allante for Cadillac in 1987)... British, Dutch teagrowers in Far East agree to cut production of cheaper varieties of tea... Cepsa builds Spain's first refinery in Tenerife, second in 1964 at Cadiz, to pioneer Nation's petroleum industry (opens research center in 1975, evolves by 1980s as diversified group of 37 firms producing everything from crude oil to bottles, 1987 sales of $2.4 billion)... Jacques Maus, Swiss billionaire in 1988 with Maus Freres, Switzerland's largest retail chain with 78 department stores, 70 boutiques, 22 hardware stores, supermarkets and restaurants plus controlling share of Le Printemps and other department store chains in France, is born... Lee Seng Wee, Singapore billionaire with interests in banking, plantations, rubber, pineapple and palm oil, real estate, publishing and insurance in 1980s, is born... Aristide Merloni opens small machine shop in Italy's Fabriano to make weighing machines (makes appliances in 1957, buys out major Italian rival in 1988 to become one of fastest-growing in European market by making customized products with mass-production)... In early 1930s Alsatian skier Charles Diebold revives nearly deserted Val d'Isere as French ski resort... Citizen Watch Co. starts making timepieces, Japan (diversifies in 1970 with watchmaking equipment, adds office and electronic equipment by 1990 as market for watches declines, plans computers for 1990s to chase rival Seiko Epson)... Hudson's Bay forms oil and gas subsidiary (acquires Henry Morgan department store chain in 1960, in 1970 moves headquarters from London to Winnipeg then Toronto, sells gas, oil properties and fur houses in 1980s to run 490 stores by 1992).

1931

General Events

Germany's unemployment in January reaches 4.9 million, 6 million by 1932... Oswald Spencer: Mankind and Technology... Work ends in building first trans-African railroad to link Benguella, Katanga... British Labor Party ousts (March 10) Oswald Mosley for Fascist program... Tariff Truce convention fails (March 17)... Germany, Austria propose (March 21) customs union, canceled September 3... France's Henri de France transmits TV from Toulouse to Le Havre, first regular TV by Post Telecommunications Authority... Germany uncovers (April 11) alleged Communist industrial spy network... Winkler is first European to launch liquid-propelled rocket... U.S.S.R. experiments with television (airs regular programs in 1939 at Moscow, Leningrad)... London sends (May 8) first overseas TV broadcast... Farmers Party comes (May 8) to power in Norway... Pope Pius XI: "Quadragesimo Anno" (rejects unfettered competition, dictatorial reorganization of economy)... Austria's national bank controlled by Rothschilds, Vienna's Credit Anstalt, folds (May 11), partly due to withdrawal of French credit in reprisal for Austrian-German customs union (begins Europe's economic collapse)...

France's Aristide Briand proposes (May 14) European Custom Union... J.V. Stalin: "New Methods of Work, New Methods of Management"... Soviet Union contracts (June 1) with U.S. to build 90 steel plants... Germany's Konrad Zuse starts building Z1 calculator, forerunner of modern computer (-1938, followed by Britain's Colossus, designed by Alan Turing's team, in 1941-43 to break German codes, first all-electronic calculating device, never fully operational, of U.S' John V. Atanasoff, Clifford Berry in 1942 as prototype computer, U.S.' Mark I in 1944, U.S.' BINAC and ENIAC in 1946, Britain's EDSAC and IBM's SSEC in 1948, U.S.' UNIVAC I in 1951 - first transistorized in 1959)... Britain's Supermarine is first plane to top 400 mph, designed by Reginald Mitchell (uses aerodynamics to design Supermarine Spitfire, basic fighter plane for RAF during W.W. II)... German Danatbank declares (July 13) bankruptcy, closes some 3,000 German banks... Rene Clair: "Give Us Our Freedom" (is first film to show social effects of mass-production)... Britain gets (August 1) loan from France, U.S. to help cover estimated deficit... European nations adopt protective tariffs in retaliation to U.S.' Smoot-Hawley Tariff... Germany's Dornier Do-X, world's largest passenger plane carrying 100 passengers at some 140 mph, makes (August 27) first transatlantic flight... Soviet Union's First Conference of Industrial Executives supports use of Gantt charting... London sees (September 10) riots as Parliament raises taxes, cuts wages of public employees to cover deficits... British sailors of Atlantic fleet strike (September 15) to protest pay cut... British publisher John Benn starts Friends of Economy to persuade politicians to use private initiative instead of government intervention... British abandons (September 21) gold standard... Sweden, Norway, Egypt drop (September 27) gold standard... Brazil destroys millions of pounds of coffee to maintain prices... Unemployed riot (September 30) in London to protest cuts in benefits... Cuba, Java and 6 other countries limit sugar production, exports... Hitler gains (September 30) commercial support from publisher Alfred Hugenberg... Swissair forms as merger of 1919-20 AD ASTRA and 1926 Balair (after profits for 38 consecutive years prepares for de-regulation in 1988 with Galileo electronic reservation system with 9 airlines, interest in Austrian Airlines, and joint operations with SAS, KLM, and France's UTA)... Labor Government is defeated (November 25) in Australia, possible reaction against socialism... Spain seizes (November 29) estates for land distribution... Japan drops (December 11) gold standard.

Business Events

Kinetic Chemical produces first Freon gas, discovered later to destroy Earth's ozone layer... German industrialists, Hugenberg, Kirdorf, Thyssen and Schroder, finance 800,000-strong Nazi party... Sestriere, run by Fiat auto, is Italy's oldest resort in Alps... Gramophone, Columbia Graphophone and Parlophone Co. form Electric & Musical Industries, EMI (buys Capitol Records in 1951, develops new scanning X-ray in 1972 to become market leader, sees financial problems in late 1970s)... IG Farben, over 550 production sites in 5 plant groups, forms central committee to coordinate groups, to make strategic plans (by 1938 evolves with working committee and central staff offices of finance, economic, purchasing, press, tax, public relations, insurance, transportation)... Industrialist George M. Booth, horrified by crash of pyramided investment trusts, starts immutable investment portfolio First British Fixed Trust, adds flexible unit trust in 1934... British Works Management Assn. forms, evolves as Institution of Industrial Managers... Germany's Krupp develops tungsten carbide alloy stronger and harder than steel (revolutionizes mass-production by providing tools to machine precision parts, leads to need for industrial diamonds, previously discarded as of little value, to sharpen alloy tools, diamond grinding wheel in 1934 and industrial-grade diamonds outselling gem-grade diamonds by 1937)... Canadian barber Kenneth Thomson buys first radio station and newspaper (pioneers leveraged buyouts in 1940s by borrowing on future profits to build newspaper monopoly, evolves as $6.9 billion empire in 1988 with newspapers and 74% of Hudson's Bay Co.)...

Aristotle Onassis, after making fortune in Argentina as tobacco importer, acquires 6 old freighters, 54 by death in 1975 for fleet larger than some oil companies (builds world's largest tanker of 15,000 tons in 1938, at urging of Greek Government takes over National airline in 1957, after losing some $30 million in 1974, sells back Olympic Airways, orders 10 dry-cargo ships in 1960s for stable cash flow during unstable oil market, orders 10 very large crude carriers, 215,000 tons, for service on long-term charters to oil companies after Suez Canal is closed during Six-Day war in 1967 - mistake with rise in inflation, buys Swiss bank in 1968 - no growth after 6 years, prepares plan in 1968 for $360 million industrial development in Greece - no action, takes financial loss by failing to take over Belfast shipyard in 1970, prepares plan in 1973 for $600 million refinery for New Hampshire - no action, expands fleets in 1973 with ultra-large crude carriers, $80 million each, to operate in 1975-77 spot market - financial loss with oil embargo and mild depression, cancels three vessels to lose some $17 million)... Clinique La Prairie opens in Montreux, Switzerland (by 1990 serves some 70,000 well-heeled clients seeking rejuvenation)... Ishibashi family, worth some $1 billion by mid-1980s, starts Bridgestone Tire, Japan's largest in 1982, to make automobile and airplane tires and golf balls (provides employees with lifetime employment, low-cost housing, company stores, vacation lodges, cafeterias, wedding halls and bachelor dormitories, in 1946, after losing overseas plants in W.W. II, resumes to make bicycles, Japanese plants escaped damage, in 1951, signs assistance pact with Goodyear to gain technology).

1932

General Events

Japan takes (January 2) Manchuria... BBC takes over Baird Co.'s work in television... Holland finishes Zuider Zee drainage project.. Oslo convention establishes (February 7) economic cooperation between Belgium, Holland, Scandinavia... Aldous Huxley: Brave New World (describes life in world of A.F. 632 with ethos of mass-production)... Japanese slash prices to undercut competitors in world markets... De Beers closes (February 18) diamond mines... Unemployed hold Great Hunger March to London... Soviet Union opens massive large production plant, counterpart to Detroit's River Rouge facility, on Volga to produce Ford cars... Graf Zeppelin starts (March 2) regular airline trips to South America... Britain's Imperial Airways serves 22 countries, carries some 34,000 passengers over 1.7 million miles... U.S.S.R. prepares 2nd Five Year Plan... League of Nations Economic Committee holds (April 1) debt, tariffs bar world recovery... During British study of motivation, women workers are allowed to leave work after finishing day's quota...

Swiss engineer Gerhard Muller invents first rope-tow for skiers... Britain's share of world manufacturing output is 10.9%, U.S. with 31.8%, U.S.S.R. 11.5%, Germany 10.6%, France 6.9%, Japan 3.5% and Italy 3.1%... Some 30 million are unemployed worldwide... Britain raises (April 21) tariffs to 20%, 33.3% on steel... Fritz Mietzsch, Joseph Klarer discover first sulfonamide drug... Gustav Cassel: The Crisis of the World's Money System... Some 6 million die in U.S.S.R. during famine (-1933), blamed on Stalin's policies... Britain's R.S. Willows de Glossop claims (August 9) invention of wrinkle-proof fabric... British military uses Operations Research, used during W.W. II to resolve problems in radar systems, anti-aircraft gunnery, anti-submarine warfare, civilian defense, convoy size and bombing raids on Germany... U.S.S.R. opens (October 9) world's largest hydroelectric plant on Dnieper River... Institute of International Economics and Management is formed, Copenhagen... Persia cancels (November 28) concession of Anglo-Persian Oil... Chile's Santa Maria Technical University is founded to develop engineers... England's Whipsnade Park opens, prototype modern zoo with open-range exhibits... South Africa quits (December 27) gold standard... Ibn Saud creates Kingdom of Saudi Arabia... U.S.S.R. bars (December 29) food handouts to housewives under 36... First operational Telex works in Britain... Chaco War erupts between Bolivia, Paraguay after discovery of oil on border (-1935)... Venice holds first film festival... Moscow changes Tverskaya Street, built in 1400s to become home of fashionable shops, to Gorky Street, re-named Tverskaya in 1990.

Business Events

U.S.' Forrest E. Mars starts candy business in Britain (acquires small pet food business of Chappel Brothers in 1934 to dominate market in 1957 as Petfood Ltd.)... With declining sales of his wooden stepladders, milk stools, etc., Ole Christiansen starts making quality wooden toys in Denmark (devises Lego toys in 1934, produces plastic toys in 1947, develops toy building bricks by 1950, employs some 3,500 workers in family enterprise by 1982 - sales of $230-350 million and $650 million in 1986-87, introduces first educational toys, TC for "Technic Control", to combine computer software with programmable toys, for U.S. schools in 1987)... Federation of Swedish Industries opens Institute for Supervisory Training... France's Jean Mantelet devises practical hand-powered rotary vegetable mill (develops Moulinex as France's leading maker of small appliances, sales of $435 million in 1982)... Bogner ski-clothes business is started in Munich (invents body-hugging pants in 1952, introduces ski clothes with dazzling fashion designs in 1985)... H.P. Gibson & Sons devises Tri-Tactics as war game... After flying for Mexico Corporacion Aeronautica de Transportes, operated 1929-32 by U.S. adventurer T.T. Hull until acquired by Pan Am,- New Zealand pilot Lowell Yerex starts Transportes Aereas Certo-Americanos in Honduras, extended with American Export's airline (sells controlling interest to U.S. investors, including Howard Hughes, to build railroad for Peron in Argentina)... After operating an advertising agency, Robert Ricci helps mother, Nina, open Paris fashion house (grows from 40 employees to 450 in 1939 with fame in dressing mature and elegant women, opens first boutique for ready-to-wear in 1979 - by mid-1980s with shops in Geneva, Tokyo, Hong Kong, Buenos Aires and Los Angeles)... Hungarian-born Alexander Korda, in movie business since 1917 in Hungary, Austria, Germany, Hollywood and France, forms London Film Productions to revive British film industry (opens Denham Studios in 1936 to rival Hollywood facilities, is ousted in 1938 when financially over-extended, goes to Hollywood, is first film-maker knighted in 1942, sells holdings in United Artists in 1944 to refloat London Film, ousted 1951)... Germany's Siemens & Halske operates worldwide with some 200 companies, 109 in Europe, 13 in Africa, 27 in Latin America, 33 in Asia, 10 in Australia and New Zealand, and 3 in U.S...

As a result of Japanese religious movement Matsushita adopts new philosophy: "A business should quickly stand on its own based on the service it provides the society... Profits should not be a reflection of corporate greed but a vote of confidence from society that what is offered by the firm is valued... When a business fails to make profits, it should die - it is a waste of resources to society"... Salvatore Ligresti, Italian billionaire in 1988 with interests in construction, insurance, bathroom fixtures, real estate, etc., is born... With collapse of Swedish Match empire, Wallenberg family uses extensive financial resources to build $50 billion empire, by 1987 operates 20 companies, Stora Kopparberg as Europe's largest forest products company, Saab-Scandia automaker, Swedish Match, Electrolux, and Hasselblad cameras, to account for 33% of Sweden's GNP and 44% of firms on Stockholm Stock Exchange... Standard Oil of California discovers oil in Bahrain...

Matsushita announces 250-year plan for electrical enterprise... Nozomu Matsumoto founds, Osaka, Gospel Electric Works to develop land's first hi-fi speaker, introduced 1937 under Pioneer brand (moves to Tokyo in 1938, makes turntables and amplifiers in 1955 and hi-fi receivers in 1958, incorporates as Pioneer Electric in 1961, land's #1 audio equipment maker in 1960s, builds world's first car stereo in 1963, opens branches in U.S., Europe in 1966, develops Laser disc video player in 1970, forms joint venture with MCA in 1977 and sells first LD player to GM in 1979, sells LD players in U.S., Japan 1981, in 1980, sluggish sales as public buys VCRs, builds world's first car compact disc system in 1984 and branches into office automation with LD technology, builds optical memory disk in 1985, buys IBM-MCA venture, over 1,400 patents for laser-optical technology, and opens manufacture of LD players to others, joins U.S.' Trimble in 1989 to develop computerized car navigation system)... Yung-ching Wang borrows $200 from father, Taiwanese tea merchant, to buy rice mill, destroyed by Allied bombs in 1944 (starts Formosa Plastics, takes on resin project when rejected by other business groups, in 1954, buys technology from Japan, starts resin processor in 1958 and chemical firm in 1965 to make rayon from discarded wood in logging yards, in 1980-88 buys 14 U.S. related firms, builds Texas plant in 1981, in mid-1980s, with plastic market near saturation, builds plants to make chemicals for semiconductors, invests in Texas-based oil, gas properties with 218 producing wells and starts gas processing plant, buys Alcoa pipeline plant in 1988, is blocked, 1990 and 1991, by China in building projects, is Taiwan's largest conglomerate in 1991 with estimated personal wealth over $1.2 billion).

1933

General Events

Argentina launches program of national economic recovery with contracts for large shipments of beef, wheat to Britain... London Economic Conference fails to achieve international cooperation in fighting depression... Hitler is (January 30) German Chancellor, sole leader in 1934 with death of Hindenburg... Romanians destroy (February 1) Standard Oil office... Spain's Associations Law forbids members of religious orders to engage in trade, industry (abolishes church schools, nationalizes church property)... After payment in gold, Saudi Arabia grants oil concession to Standard Oil of California (forms California Arabian Standard Oil to develop concession, discovers first oil in 1934 and first major field of 47 in 1938, is restructured in 1946 as Aramco with

California Standard, Jersey Standard, Texaco, Socony-Vacuum)... Reichstag gives (March 23) Hitler power to rule by decree... Nazis ban (March 28) Jews in business, professions, schools... Germany adopts Four-Year Plan to abolish unemployment (uses public works to drop unemployment from 6 million to under one million in 1937)... Air France is formed as national airline by merging 5 lines... Labor Party wins Norwegian election... High-intensity mercury vapor lamps appear... Canada drops (April 25) gold standard... Germany's Inherited Estates Act maintains size of farms... Government buys wheat crop of Argentina, dumped on international market for best price...

London Passenger Transport Board takes over all private, pirate bus operations... Hitler breaks up (May 2) all trade unions, replaced by Labor Front in 1934 to ban strikes, lockouts... Twenty-one nations sign (August 25) wheat agreement to combat worldwide glut... After research since 1926 by Hans Busch, Germany's Ernst Ruska devises first operational electron microscope... National Socialist Government of Germany forms National "Estate" of Germany Industry to promote cooperation between business, party... German Post Office starts (October 1) telex communications between Hamburg, Berlin... Holland sets production limits for pork, beef and dairy products... Denmark slaughters inferior cattle... Nazis take over (November 1) Germany's largest press, Ullstein... German financier Hjalmar Schacht devises financial system of Mefo-bills to provide credit for rearmament, job creation, large-scale public works, imported raw materials... Mussolini's Instituto per la Ricostruzione Industriale, IRI, is government trust to rescue banks and sell their unwanted assets (soon holds Alfa Romeo, three regional phone companies and three major banks, Banca Commercial Italia, Credito Italiano, and Banco di Roma, by 1937 consolidates firms in shipping and steel, builds Naples aircraft engine plant in 1939)... U.S. recognizes (November 17) U.S.S.R... U.S.S.R. sees starvation as national disaster.

Business Events

Ceylon, India growers limit tea exports... Dutch, British, French and Siamese rubber growers adopt production quotas... P.F. Florence: The Logic of Industrial Organisation (cites need for more efficient organization of British industry, better managers)... Danfoss, perhaps Europe's largest maker of refrigeration parts in 1980s, is started on Danish farm by Clausen brothers... Lyndall Urwick: Management of Tomorrow (discusses organization theory)... Innocenti business appears in Milan (produces Lambretta motor scooter in 1947)... Jersey Standard, Socony-Vacuum form Standac to distribute petroleum products in China, Japan... First Dinky toys, miniature models of actual cars first made in U.S., France c. 1915, are made by Liverpool factory (closes British plant in 1959, continues manufacture in Hong Kong)...

Germany's Siemens & Halske reorganizes for changing market, internal growth (increases autonomy of operating units grouped in 4 divisions, divides central headquarters into administrative and technical branches)... German engineer Ferdinand Porsche, after showing first electric car at 1900 Paris World Exhibition and working for Daimler Benz 1923-29, builds small, rear-engine car (is backed by Hitler in 1935 to mass produce "Volk auto" for workers)... Hang Seng Ngan Ho, means Evergrowing Native Bank, opens in Hong Kong, evolves as Hang Seng Bank to handle remittances between Hong Kong, Chinese cities and trade in gold, commodity markets (offers first savings, checking accounts in 1952, is acquired in 1965 by Hongkong and Shanghai Bank, designs worldwide index for Hong Kong stock market in 1967, is City's 2nd largest bank in mid-1980s with over 100 branches)... At age of 31, S.G. Warburg, descendant of Pisa's Italian-Jew money-changer Andrea del Banco in 1500s, flees family Warburg Bank in Hamburg to London (builds S.G. Warburg & Co. as City's leading financial house, engineers one of earliest hostile takeovers of post-war period in 1958, pioneers development of Euromarkets in 1960s, acquires Britain's 2nd-oldest trading house, Akroyd & Smithers, and No. 2 broker, Rowe & Pitman, in 1986 before banking deregulations to capture 20% of British equity market and 10% of government bond market, with capital base of $1.1 billion to compete in world markets fends off raid by U.S. investor Saul P. Steinberg in 1987)... Sakip Sabanci, Turkish billionaire in 1988 with interests in rubber and textiles inherited from peasant-born father, is born... Britain's ICI is first to discover polytene... Frederik H.F. van Vlissingen, Dutch multi-billionaire in 1988 from consumer goods, financial services and chemicals, is born... After skiing in early 1900s, Gray Rocks, in Laurentians north of Montreal, installs first ski lift (offers ski packages in 1951 to become popular resort.

1934

General Events

League of Nations reports (January 5) U.S. leading world in recovery... Gordonstoun School opens in Scotland (provides physical development with education, basis for future management development programs)... Turkey issues (January 9) first Five-Year Industrial Plan, aided by U.S. experts... General strike occurs in France... Britain introduces driving test to license drivers... Stalin fears (January 27) capitalists will choose war to overcome depression... French luxury liner, Normandie, is launched, largest afloat until Queen Elizabeth in 1938 (crosses Atlantic in 107 hours, 33 minutes in 1935)... After close ally, Leningrad Party leader Serge Kirov, is assassinated, Stalin begins purge of managers, engineers, scientists and military personnel to rid Communist Party, Soviet Union of undesirables (-1938 after sending some ten million to Siberian prison camps)... Austria, Hungary, Italy pledge (March 1) economic cooperation... Wernher von Braun tests liquid-fuel rocket, reaches height of 1.5 miles... Young journalist Francois de Saulieu develops truckers' guide for France, some 2,000 entries by W.W. II...

Longest air race from England to Australia is contested by 20 planes, 9 finish, from 7 countries, winning time is under 71 hours... German law allows surveillance over business associations... Dr. Rudolph Kuehnald tests (March 20) radar for German navy... Switzerland's Banking Act reinforces bank secrecy, follows trust-secrecy established by Liechtenstein (obligates banks not to divulge information about any account, protects wealth of Germans from Nazi inspection)... U.S.S.R. completes economic sovereignty of Communist Party over industrial management (permits plant managers to issue orders with party committees to report on short-comings)... U.S. joins International Labor Organization... Some 1,000 are arrested (April 20) in Paris riot of 6,000 for jobs... Berlin police ban (April 23) fortune telling, horoscopes... In this time, U.S.S.R. changes focus from building plants to production... Hitler ennobles (May 1) labor...

Airmail service begins between Australia, England... German Labor Front is special Nazi agency to 'oversee preservation of labor peace'... Hitler stops (June 6) paying all foreign debts... German university student Hans von Ohain, 23 years, begins work on jet propulsion (joins Heinkel Aircraft in 1936, keeps work secret to avoid meddling by Air Ministry bureaucrats, unveils engine in 1939 - Hitler opposed, makes flight test in 1939 - Luftwaffe refuses to see world's first jet, leads to Air Ministry funding Messerschmitt, arch rival of Heinkel, to build plane in 1942 - ready for mass-production in 1943 but Hitler wants fighter remade as bomber)... U.S. missionary introduces football to Japan (survives war as only naval cadets allowed to play game, evolves with play by some 200 colleges in 1980s)... Italy establishes state corporations... Some 40,000 factory, farm workers attend first Soviet fashion show of clothes to change monotony of garments issued by Dress and Lingerie Trust... Britain's Workmen's Compensation covers industrial diseases... Germany plans 900-mile autobahn system of 4-lane highways to reduce unemployment... China taxes (October 14) silver to stop exports to U.S... Dutch government gets emergency powers to regulate trade, industry... Canada's Companies Act gives regulations to establish security for investors, shareholders, creditors.

Business Events

Morris Motors operates Britain's first moving assembly line for cars... Following lead of some local banks in late-1920s, Magasin Du Nord, Copenhagen department store, appoints personnel inspector to oversee employee activities... U.S. baseball is adopted in Japan with formation of Tokyo Giants, joined by 6 other teams to start pro league (follows first introduction in 1873 by

Horace Wilson, U.S. professor at Tokyo University)... Management consulting business of Urwick, Orr and Partners forms in England... Sanko steamship business appears in Japan (evolves in 1970s as world's largest operator of tankers, continues to expand after 1973 Arab oil embargo, files for bankruptcy in 1985 with debts of $2-4 billion, Japan's largest since W.W. II)... U.S.' Eli Lilly pharmaceutical starts foreign subsidiary in London... British Iron and Steel Federation forms... European Aeronautical Society opens world's first airline office in London to sell tickets for London-Paris dirigible trip (files for bankruptcy after prototype dirigible explodes, 2nd is seized by sheriff)...

Cunard Line launches luxury liner Queen Mary (-1967, crosses Atlantic in 3 days, 23 hours and 57 minutes in 1936)... Hamburg bank of M.M. Warburg & Co. opens New Trading Co. in London to finance small, medium-sized firms... Taro Iketani, family wealth over $1 billion in 1988, starts Tokyo Steel, world's largest electric furnace-steel maker in 1980s... London, Midland & Scottish Railway starts air service to London, Belfast and Glasgow to compete with small airlines of 1933... J. Arthur Rank co-founds British National Films to make religious movies (-1969, forms General Film Finance in 1936 as holding company to acquire 25% of U.S.' Universal Pictures and controlling interest in General Film Distributors, after buying West End cinema starts Pinewood Studios in 1936, acquires Gaumont British Pictures in 1941, acquires 600 Odeon Theaters and four studios in 1942 to dominate UK film industry)... After developing popular refrigerator in 1930s, Electrolux buys rival, Volta, for retail distribution (prospers until 1960s when victim to management infighting, declining profits)...

Mokichi Morita, CEO of Japan's leading celluloid maker of 1919, forms Fuji Photo with government grant, no domestic supplier, as independent firm to make film, Japan's No. 1 by 1991 and 2nd in world (with aid of German specialist to correct product deficiencies produces black-and-white film in 1936, color in 1948, runs four plants and research lab in 1945, starts first overseas venture, Brazil, in 1955, U.S. in 1958 and Europe 1964, adds magnetic tape in 1960, forms Fuji Xerox in 1962 with Rank Xerox to sell copiers in UK, after providing private-labels for others, sells film in U.S. under own brand, with new CEO expands with videotypes, floppy disks and medical equipment, introduces world's first 35 mm disposable camera in 1987, forms venture with BASF's U.S. unit in 1989, buys U.S. firm making photographic chemicals and joins DuPont to buy UK imaging concern, starts unit to produce image processing semiconductors in 1990).

1935

General Events

Oil pipelines open between Iraq, Haifa and Tripoli... U.S., Brazil sign (February 2) trade accord... Persia's name becomes Iran... Sidney, Beatrice Webb: Soviet Communism: A New Civilization?... Germany establishes (February 17) 8-hour work day... Canada passes labor legislation covering wages, hours, employment and social insurance... U.S.S.R. sells (March 22) Chinese Eastern Railway to Japan... New Zealand Labor Party wins its first general election (-1938, introduces social reforms)... Belgium devalues (March 29) franc... University of Uppsala devises first Swedish qualification test for Royal Navy (prepares selection test later for Swedish State Railway, leads to use of aptitude test in 1944 by Central Conscription Bureau)... Moscow opens (April 23) first section of subway (1933-)... Kurt Lewin: A Dynamic Theory of Personality (pioneers development of field theory)... Britain's Department of Scientific and Industrial Research devises process to remove salt from sea water to recover metals... Nazis plan (September 23) to buy all Jewish firms... Green-belt scheme around London is adopted... India establishes Reserve Bank system... League of Nations votes (October 19) to boycott Italian exports for its invasion of Ethiopia... German inventor Konrad Zuse revolutionizes computer field by adopting binary system for programming... British mathematician Alan Turing develops hypothetical machine to test mathematical propositions... Hungary adopts (October 28) 8-hour work day... Soviet Union brands one million former officials, merchants and noblemen as "class strangers", deported from Leningrad, Moscow and other cities... Soviet Union adopts Stakhanovism to increase work output (uses some features of Trotsky's "shock worker" system in 1920s to operate model factories with high-output workers).

Business Events

Societa Industria Farmaceutica Italiana, Sicily, enters drug industry... Yunosuke Aoki starts restaurant chain in Japan (is brought to U.S. in 1964 as Benihana of Tokyo by son Hiroaki, 15 operations by 1970s)... Allen Lane's Penguin Books, small London publishing house, introduces first modern, low-priced paperback books (opens U.S. branch in 1939, leads to U.S.' Pocket Books in 1937, Bantam books in 1945)... Germany's AEG makes first tape-recorder using plastic tape... Bank of Canada is formed... Three private airlines, Hillman Airways, Spartan Air and United Airways, join to form British Airways (merges in 1939 with Imperial to form state-owned British Overseas Airways Corp.).

1936

General Events

BBC starts regular television service... Fluorescent lighting appears... Mussolini nationalizes (March 23) key industries... France proposes (April 8) international commission to govern Europe... German troops occupy demilitarized Rhineland... Germany launches diesel-electric vessel, Wupperthal... Some 50,000 Mexican railworkers strike (May 18)... Germany launches dirigible Hindenburg, 803 feet in length, for passenger service to U.S. (explodes on landing in Lakehurst, NJ, in 1937, ends era of airships)... Spain takes over (July 28) industry... Joseph A. Schumpeter: The Theory of Economic Development... Civil War breaks out (July 31) in Spain (-1939)... Swedish law confirms rights of electrical workers, foremen to organize and bargain with employers... Britain's Factory Act, revised 1948, sets minimum standards for health, safety, welfare and hours for women and children... German scientists develop magnetic levitation to operate high-speed trains, tested in 1970s by U.S., Japanese, West German firms...

France, Switzerland, Holland drop (September 27) gold standard... Helicopter, designed by Heinrich Focke, is tested in Germany (sets flight record in 1937, forms helicopter company in 1937, leads to first practical helicopter of A. Flettner for German Navy in 1940)... British Labor Party rejects (October 6) alliance with Communists... Hermann Goering heads (October 19) Reich's four-year economic plan... France's Popular Front Government passes several laws on industrial relations (establishes workers' delegates in businesses, first appeared in 1885 and required in 1890 law for all coal mines)... John Maynard Keynes: The General Theory of Employment, Interests and Money (advises governments to increase money supply to overcome depression).

Business Events

Nestle registers Unilac as Panamanian holding company in case Nazis invade Switzerland... Italy's Fiat introduces "Topolino" as people's car... All-Japan Industries Assn. forms... Neal Spencer, brother start London factory to make dry-cleaning equipment... Dentsu, news and advertising, is seized by Japan in forming Domei as propaganda bureau (in 1943 all ad agencies are consolidated as 12 entities, Dentsu controls four, after dismantling of Domei in 1947, grows by financing TV broadcasting in 1950s, is world's largest ad agency in 1973, gets 1% of revenues from foreign advertisers in 1980, forms venture, 1981, with Young & Rubicam as U.S.' largest and 2nd in world, joined by French agency in 1987, after foreign billings reach 7% of revenues in 1986 loses No. 1 position in 1987)... Japanese-educated Lee Byung-Chull runs rice mill in Korea, genesis for Samsung, South Korea's leading chaebol in 1990 with sales of $35.6 billion, as a group of 29 public, private firms, ranging from sugar, textiles, paper, electronics, aerospace, watches, petrochemicals, heavy industry, insurance, department stores, hotels and hospitals as one of land's oldest industrials, in 1991 (trades dried fish in 1938 and incorporates as "Three Stars", with end of W.W. II invests in transportation and real estate, with almost all destroyed by Korean War rebuilds with surviving brewery and importing for UN personnel, starts profitable sugar business, only one at time, in 1953, starts textile firm in 1954 and enters banking and insurance in 1954, in 1960s diversifies in paper, department stores, newspapers and electronics, starts ventures in shipbuilding, 1974, petrochemicals, 1977, aircraft engines, 1977, and broadcasting in 1979, loses these facilities with takeover of new regime).

1937

General Events

Britain's share of world manufacturing output is 9.4%, U.S. with 35.1%, U.S.S.R. 14.1%, Germany 11.4%, France 4.5%, Japan 3.5%, and Italy 2.7%... B. Seebohm Rowntree: The Human Needs of Labor... Italy adjusts (March 3) pay for family size to promote births... Japanese forces invade China... France nationalizes Schneider-Creuzot armament factories... Bolivia seizes (March 16) Standard Oil properties... Stalin gives (June 13) leaders 10 days to reorganize tractor, auto industry or face trial... British mathematician Alan Turing presents proof, "On Computable Numbers," that a computer, like the brain, could process any kind of information... Japan occupies (August 8) Beijing... Italy withdraws from International Labor Office... In October, Japan labels some goods "Made in USA" to make U.S. products appear cheap, shoddy... German pilot Hanna Reitsch makes first successful helicopter flight in Focke FW-61... Britain starts building chain of 20 radar stations... Germany's Walter R. Dornberger starts developing V-2 rocket... Mexico takes over (November 4) Standard Oil's 350,000 acres of oil lands... Mexico grants (November 12) concessions to Shell Oil... French scientist Daniele Bovet discovers first antihistamine... U.S. asks (December 26) Mexico to slow industrialization... Oil is discovered in Alberta, Canada.

Business Events

Physician Takeshi Mitarai starts Japan's Canon photography business (introduces revolutionary camera, AE-1, in 1976 with built-in micro-processor, unveils laser copier in 1987, employs 35,000 in 130 countries in 1988)... Michelin develops first radial-ply tires, patent in 1946... Spanish-born Balenciaga opens Paris fashion house (-1968)... Although tried as early as 1867 in U.S., Switzerland's Nestle develops first instant coffee, suggestion from Brazilian coffer growers in 1930, after 8 years of research, patent in 1938... Swedish industry, University of Uppsala start joint research program to design special psychological tests to select employees, used by some 20 firms in 1955 (follows use of first selection tests by Swedish manufacturers in 1928)... Penniless Suliman Saleh Olayan is hired as dispatcher by Aramco in building trans-Arabian pipeline, later a subcontractor (by 1987 is worth over $1 billion with interests in 25 firms in real estate, food importing, transportation, insurance and construction)...

After attending Hamamatsu Technical High School, Soichiro Honda starts business to make piston rings for Toyota (after rejections for poor quality sells rings to small firms unable to buy better rings, builds plant in 1939 to make quality rings with financing from Toyota, supplies Japanese Navy with parts in 1941, with $3,300 starts Honda Motor Co. in 1948 to make motorized bicycles)... Unilever buys Thomas J. Lipton business (adds dehydrated soups, 1940, and Pepsodent, 1944, but loses U.S. soap market in 1946 after P&G introduces first synthetic detergent, Tide, acquires Birds Eye Foods of UK, 1957, Good Humor ice cream, 1961, National Starch, 1978, Lawry's Foods, 1979, and Ragu sauces, 1986)... Firms controlled by Electrolux form Saab to make military aircraft for Sweden, Marcus Wallenberg board member 1939 (makes first plane, 1940, and car, 1947, acquires truck maker Scania in 1969 and two arms makers, drops proposed merger with Volvo in 1977, in late 1970s is success with upscale cars for U.S. market, sells, 1989, 50% of car business to GM, after Swedish property developer gets 22% of voting stock in 1990 sees, 1991, Wallenberg family buying stock back at a premium to launch a takeover to defend empire)...

After collaborating as pioneers making cars and trucks for 21 years, two Japanese firms, one formed in 1918 to build trucks and other in 1922 to make cars with license from UK's Wolseley, form Tokyo Motors, adopts Isuzu brand in 1938 (sells trucks for military in 1943, is renamed, Isuzu for "50 bells", in 1949, during Korean War gets orders to become top maker in diesel engines and trucks, builds cars for Rootes Group in 1953, makes diesel-powered cars in 1961, soon discontinued for noise, sells GM 34.2% in 1971 for stable partner, starts own U.S. dealer network in 1981, by 1990 loses U.S. market share with rise in value of yen)... Malayan Airways forms (starts first scheduled flights in 1947 when resumed by Mansfield & Co., shipping line, to link Singapore with other Malayan cities, serves Vietnam, Sumatra and Java in 1951 and Borneo, Brunei, Thailand and Burma by 1958, sells 10% to BOAC, 20% more in 1959, in 1948 and 30% to Qantas in 1959, is Malaysian Airways in 1962 with formation of Malaysia, when Singapore secedes in 1965 buys control from BOAC, Qantas in 1966 to form Singapore Airlines in 1967, world's 5th largest in 1991, serves Melbourne, Bombay, Rome and London by 1971 and Osaka, Athens, Zurich and Frankfort by 1972, is dissolved by Singapore, Malaysia in 1972 to form two lines, Singapore international and Malaysian domestic, serves 25 cities in 20 countries in 1974, flies to San Francisco in 1978, forms Abacus reservation system in 1988 with Cathay Pacific and Thai International, forms alliance in 1989 with Delta, Swissair to cover 288 cities, 82 countries).

1938

General Events

Britain's share of world manufacturing output is some 9.2%, U.S. with 28.7%, U.S.S.R. 17.6%, Germany 13.2%, France 4.5%, Japan 3.8%, and Italy 2.9%... Some 30,000 Italian farm workers go to (January 8) Germany to aid labor shortage... P.M.S. Blackett, others develop management technique of Operations Research in Britain (forms "Blackett's Circus" with three physiologists, two mathematical physicists, one astrophysicist, one army officer, one surveyor, one general physicist, and two mathematicians to solve complex problems in war, defense efforts)... Otto Hahn, Fritz Strassman achieve fission of uranium at Berlin's Kaiser Wilhelm Institute... Mexico raises (January 19) tariffs on U.S. goods 100-200%... Chiang Kai-shek's government in China creates industrial cooperatives, each a self-operated social unit, as economic defense against Japanese invasion, occupation...

Austrian physicists, Lise Meitner, former colleague of Otto Hahn, and Otto Frisch deem atomic fission process feasible in Sweden... Sweden's central organizations of employers, unions sign basic labor agreement... Hungarian journalist H. Biro patents ball-point pen (goes to Argentina in 1940 to perfect invention - patent 1948, sells first in 1945 in Buenos Aires, starts international distribution in 1948)... German troops take over (March 12) Austria... France cancels Labor Code... H.M.S. Rodney is first vessel equipped with radar... When firms are unable to pay $40 million in higher wages, Mexico seizes (March 18) properties of 17 U.S., British oil companies (declares itself "rector" of national economy to run businesses for social welfare and profit)... New nickel-chrome alloy, required for engines, is discovered...

During strike, British auto workers occupy (April 13) 213 factories... Britain recognizes paid vacations... BBC broadcasts (May 31) first TV game show... Helmut Schreyer, Germany, devises system of vacuum tubes for computers... Germany adopts (June 22) mandatory national service to ease labor shortage... Mexican unions seize (July 11) five U.S. mines... German troops take over (October 3) Sudetenland, Czechoslovakia's border area... Prince Franz Josef II rules Liechtenstein (-1989, transforms principality from rural community into one of Europe's richest enclaves with postage stamps, bank secrecy and low taxes - base for some 25,000 foreign corporations)... National airlines of Denmark, Norway and Sweden discuss joint service to NYC... During bitter labor dispute Mexico expropriates foreign oil holdings, first action by non-Communist state (results in state formation of PEMEX, world's 14th largest producer in 1991, to run petroleum properties (by 1970 becomes a net importer of oil, is revived with major discovery in 1972, contributes 50% of government revenues 1982-85, when prices collapse in 1985 lowers investments in facilities, sees exports drop from 2/3 to 1/3 by 1990, forms exporting arm in 1989, borrows, first time in eight years, to finance oil exploration in 1990 and plans to invest $4 billion through 1996 to upgrade refineries and products, after government pressure closes 58-year old Mexico City refinery in 1991 to reduce thick air pollution)... When Venezuela threatens nationalization, foreign oil firms agree to increase their royalties.

Business Events

Cunard line launches luxury liner Queen Elizabeth (-1967)... IG Farben, DuPont divide world market in synthetic fibers... Hotel Kuckkockuhr, Switzerland, offers guests opportunity to participate in weekend mystery theater, similar entertainment at 1869 Mohonk Mountain House, NY, in 1985... Born to wealthy Sao Paulo family in hard times, Sebastiao Ferraz De Camargo Penteado, partner form business to build roads (builds billion-dollar construction firm, largest in Brazil, by 1989 with interests in banking, cement, ranching and mining)... Belgium's Solvay, Britain's ICI and Germany's IG Farben sign secret cartel agreement to regulate chlorine exports to prevent rise of rivals in other countries...

Chinese-born Liem Sioe Liong goes to Java to work for uncle in small trading business (during Indonesia's struggle for independence, 1945-49, supplies rebels with food, medicine and arms, after friendship with Suharto, President of Indonesia, gets monopolies on clothes, cement, etc., evolves as multi-billionaire in 1988 with interests in Indonesia's largest private bank, largest cement company and Hong Kong finance and trading conglomerate)... Siemens & Halske demonstrates first modern electron microscope in Berlin, followed by first U.S. model of RCA in 1940 - portables in 1942 by RCA and GE...

Work is started in Germany to build Wolfsburg, company town with some 85,000 people in 1960s, as community to produce Volkswagens (makes 1,785 Beetles by 1945 - 2,350,000 in 1971 as largest industrial company in Germany and world's 4th largest auto maker with over 9,000 dealers in 140 countries, ships first Beetles to U.S. in 1949 - 600 in 1950, introduces Karmann Ghia model in 1955, denationalizes business with private sale of stock - retains 20% for Lower Saxony and 16% for Bonn, acquires Auto Union in 1965 to make Audi cars, acquires NSU Motorenwerke AG in 1969 to get Felix Wankel's patents on rotary-piston motor, introduces super-Beetle - flops, discontinues German production, after making some 21 million Beetle sedans, in 1977 and Beetle convertibles in 1979, still produced at plants in Brazil, Mexico and Nigeria)... Kiichiro Toyoda builds first Toyota plant in Central Japan, develops Toyota City of some 290,000 by 1980s (employs some 52,000 workers in 8 plants by 1980s, provides such services as housing, schooling, free hospitals, sports center, cooperatives for food and clothing, mountain resort)... U.S.' Texaco acquires Canada's McColl-Frontenac in hostile takeover, sells to Imperial Oil in 1989.

1939

General Events

Switzerland's Paul Muller synthesizes DDT, follows work of Othmar Zeidler in 1874... Mexico seizes (February 13) U.S.' United Sugar Co... To prevent smuggling of art objects, Italy declares grave robbing as illegal (forms world's first special police unit in 1969 to recover stolen art works)... 1937 Trans-Canada Air becomes Air Canada... Germany takes over (March 15) Czechoslovakia... K.V. Kantorovich: "Mathematical Methods in the Organization and Planning of Production" (pioneers linear programming at Leningrad State University, English translation in 1960)... France's Joliot-Curie demonstrates possibility of splitting the atom... Joseph Schumpeter: Business Cycles... Chilean Development Corp. is created to encourage domestic industrialization... Institute of Automation and Control is formed in Moscow (works on mathematical methods for organization, production planning)... German troops invade (September 9) Poland to launch W.W. II (-1945)... Iran creates loan bank to provide capital for building houses... Wehrmacht infantry division requires some 40 Military Occupational Specialties, some 900 in West Germany Bundeswehr division of 1980s... Chile allows workers to join unions... Germany adopts 10-hour day to ease labor shortages... Enigma machine, Germany's secret complex coding device, is smuggled from Poland to Britain (quickly leads to Oriental Goddess, Ultra electronic computers to decode Enigma messages).

Business Events

Siemens & Halske with affiliated companies is world's 4th largest private-sector employer with 185,000 employees after Vereinigte Stahlwerke, IG Farben and U.S. Steel... Imperial Chemical Industries, Courtalds form British Nylon Spinners... Germany's Heinkel makes first jet-powered flight, first rocket-powered flight by Messerschmitt in 1941 and first supersonic flight by U.S. plane in 1947)... To compete with Venice for tourists, first annual Cannes film festival is planned, revived 1946... Iran grants concession to develop mineral resources to Holland's Algemeen Exploratie Mattaschappig... Wilfred Brown is managing director of Glacier Metal Co., medium-sized British metal working business (-1965, transforms traditional corporate structure into industrial democracy with Works Council)... Swiss Bank Corp. opens first U.S. branch, 300 branches and subsidiaries by 1989... Havana's famed Tropicana night club opens... Abdul-Aziz Al Sulaiman, Saudi Arabian billionaire in 1988 (builds business empire from father's, first Saudi Finance Minister, cement franchise and real estate), is born... Bank of Basel opens NYC branch to protect European funds... Pan Am begins regular flights to Europe... Two electrical equipment firms, one started, 1875, as Japan's first to make telegraph equipment and transformers, electric motors and hydroelectric generators in 1890s, and other, Tokyo Electric in 1899, formed in 1890 as land's first maker of incandescent light bulbs and first radios in 1924, merge as Toshiba (is first in land to make fluorescent lamps in 1940, makes radar, 1942, black-and-white TVs, 1949, and broadcasting equipment in 1952, makes land's first digital computer in 1954, in 1980s invests in telecommunications, semiconductor and computer units, as world's first in 1985 to make 1-megabit DRAM chip, forms ventures with Siemens, 1985, and Motorola, 1986, puts out popular laptop computer in 1986).

1940

General Events

Britain rations (January 8) sugar, butter, meat... Canada looks for oil near Prince Edward Island in Gulf of St. Lawrence... Britain forms Operations Research team to determine optimum use of new radar defense system... Germany occupies (April 9) Denmark... Britain adopts National Government under leadership of Winston Churchill (-1945)... Stalin closes Central Labor Institute, fountainhead in 1920s for Soviet Taylorism, time-and-motion studies... German women save (May 7) hair to make felt... Germany takes (May 28) Holland, Belgium... Norway surrenders (June 10) to Germany... Nazis occupy (June 14) Paris... Britain forms Scientific Advisory Committee... Soviets annex (July 21) Lithuania, Estonia, Latvia (after civil disturbances are given some rights in 1989 to control own trade, industry and resources and to run market economies, seek full independence in 1990)... Vichy France dissolves (November 9) all labor unions.

Business Events

Finnish employers, unions sign January Agreement, Basic Agreement to set regulations for negotiations, shop stewards, dismissal of workers, social welfare units and use of time-and-motion studies... Alex Szekely opens Rancho la Puerta in Tecate, Mexico, for wealthy desiring healthful living, first in North America (opens Golden Door health resort in Escondido, CA, in 1959 to pamper health faddists, $3,500/week in 1980s)... In 1940s Ahmed Juffali, Saudi Arabia, gets concession from British electronics firm to provide Taif with electricity (evolves by 1988 as billion-dollar E.A. Juffali & Bros., largest private business in peninsula as trading company with contracting and industrial subsidiaries, with franchises for Daimler Benz, Michelin, Siemens, IBM, etc.)... Basque gunsmith Avelino Arrieta starts making handmade shotguns in Elgoibar for discerning users at fraction of cost, time of London makers.

1941

General Events

Brazil adopts first system of minimum wages... Britain starts clothes rationing (urges use of "utility" clothing)... Central Psychological Laboratory, German Army: German Psychological Warfare (cites personnel practices used in indoctrination, preparation of soldiers for service)... Italy tests workable jet plane at Milan... German troops invade (June 21) U.S.S.R... Spain forms Instituto Nacional de Industria as state holding company to encourage industrial growth, Spain's largest industrial enterprise, staff of some 170,000, by 1980s with over 60 companies producing coal, electricity, aluminum, aircraft, ships, and wood pulp (owns main steel centers and two regular airlines, holds interests in fertilizers, uranium, electronics and handicrafts, is in top 20 of European enterprises)... Britain flies its first jet aircraft... With Harvard doctoral dissertation, Norway's Trygve Haavelmo pioneers field of econometrics to use statistical probability for economic testing and forecasting, published 1944 (wins Nobel Prize for Economics in 1989)... Servico Nacional de Aprendizagem Industrial is formed in Brazil to provide technical training for industrial workers... After father's abdication, Reza Pahlavi is new Shah of Iran (-1979 when overthrown by revolution led by Ayatollah Khomeini, tries to modernize country by breaking up large estates, granting women right to vote, educating people, industrializing with oil revenues, and reducing power of religious leaders)... Outward Bound program is started in Wales to develop one's confidence to survive in wilderness, used later in management development programs... France's "Charter of Labor" establishes enterprise committees in business firms... Japan attacks (December 7) Pearl Harbor, Hawaii.

Business Events

Britain's Calico Printers Assn. patents first polyester fiber, developed by John R. Whinfield and J.P. Dickson (is marketed in 1950 by ICI and in 1951 as Dacron by DuPont).

1942

General Events

W.H. Beveridge: Report on Social Insurance and Allied Services (proposes freedom from want, disease, ignorance, squalor and idleness for all in England, designs comprehensive scheme of social security, financed by central taxation, is basis for post-war 'cradle to grave' program of Labor Government)... Magnetic recording tape is invented... Japanese use war game to plan for Battle of Midway... Germany deports (March 7) Belgians to Germany to ease labor shortages... Uthwatt report proposes new approach to town planning in Britain (recommends green belts around major cities, new land use controls)... Joseph Schumpter: Capitalism, Socialism and Democracy (notes process of "creative destruction" that "incessantly revolutionizes the economic structure from within, incessantly destroying the old one, incessantly creating a new one")...

Vatican forms Institute for Religious Works as banking enterprise (makes dubious investments in mid-1960s)... Vichy France tells (October 20) French workers where they must serve in Germany... Brazil's Consolidacao das Leis do Trabalho codifies all labor regulations (assigns Ministry of Labor, Commerce and Industry authority to grant status to unions, to assist in presenting grievances to labor courts and providing welfare activities, and to review union finances, establishes trade-union tax to provide funds for union administration and social welfare activities, establishes working hours of 8/day for 6 days and regulations for working women and children, and sets tenure rule whereby employees with 10 years of service cannot be dismissed except for "grave misbehavior")... CP unites ten local airlines to form Canadian Pacific Air (pioneers polar route in 1955, is sold in 1987 to Pacific Western line).

Business Events

After apprenticeship in German wholesale linen and woolen firm, Grete Schickedanz marries boss (after W.W. II, starts anew to build Quelle as Europe's largest mail-order catalog business by 1980s, with estimated family wealth of $2.2 billion retires 1987)... Martin Hilti makes industrial fasteners in Liechtenstein, billion-dollar business by 1988... When father dies, Li Ka-Shing, 14 years, supports mother and younger brother in Hong Kong as junior salesman for toy manufacturer (starts plastics firm, Cheung Kong, at age of 22, is first Chinese taipan, traditionally British, in Hong Kong in acquiring Hutchison Whampoa's great trading house in 1979, is multi-billionaire, richest in Hong Kong, in 1988 with interests in Canada's Husky Oil and Imperial Bank of Commerce, Hong Kong container terminal handling 45% of world's biggest container port, and real estate in Canada, Hong Kong)... Seagram forms partnership to buy Paul Masson wines, sold 1987 (buys distilleries in West Indies, 1942, and adds Mumm and Perrier-Jovet champagne and Chivas Bros. Scotch after W.W. II, in later 1950s, with ready cash, acquires host of unrelated firms from Israeli supermarkets to Texas gas fields)... Tadao Kashio starts Tokyo machine shop, genesis for Casio Computer in 1990s (starts to develop a computer, joined by two brothers, in 1950s after reading about abacus besting an electric computer in 1946, incorporates, 1957, and unveils innovative electric calculator, Japan's first, makes 1st desktop electronic calculator with memory in 1965, exports to U.S. in 1970, in 1970s survives fierce calculator war along with Sharp, unveils digital watch in 1974 to dominate market, introduces electronic music synthesizers, 1980, pocket TVs, 1982, and thin card-sized calculators in 1983, with price competition in mid-1980s starts plants overseas and invests in R&D for sophisticated new products, puts out electronic diary 6 months after Sharp in 1988, opens plants, San Diego and Tijuana, in 1990 and forms unit to exploit its technology by selling components).

1943

General Events

Maurice Allais, Nobel Laureate in Economics in 1988: In Search of An Economic Discipline (argues state-run monopolies are most efficient when setting prices, allocating resources according to market forces)... German forces surrender (January 31) at Stalingrad... J.M. Keynes proposes international currency union... German engineer S. Junghans develops continuous casting of steel... Military junta overthrows Argentina's government (makes Col. Juan Peron Director for Department of Labor, responsible for developing nation's trade union movement)... In fighting for survival in Afghanistan's Little Pamir Mountains, Kirghiz tribe adopts amanat system of agriculture whereby wealthy herdsmen lend livestock to those less fortunate for use of byproducts (leads to larger herds, doubled in 5 years, trade with neighboring tribes and visits by wandering tinkers, tradesmen)... France's Jacques-Yves Cousteau, Gagnan devise aqualung... Italy declares (October 13) war on Germany.

Business Events

Canadian-born Jack Kent Cooke, after buying and selling encyclopedias door-to-door, managing Ontario radio station and buying U.S. radio station, claims to be millionaire (reaches billionaire status in 1980s with Cooke Cablevision, Los Angeles Daily News, Washington Redskins pro football team, and New York's art deco Chrysler building)... Inguar Kamprad, age 17, starts business career in Sweden selling ball-point pens (evolves as IKEA, retailer of unassembled furniture and other household goods with 85 stores worldwide, 3 in U.S. in 1985-89, with worth some $1.7 billion in 1987)... Marcus Wallenberg's private airline replaces Sweden's international carrier (opens Stockholm - NYC route in 1945).

1944

General Events

Greenwich Royal Observatory installs quartz-crystal clock... Germany introduces rocket-powered airplane, ME163B-1 Komet... Over 100 nations create International Civil Aviation organization in Montreal... Soviet troops cross (January 4) Polish border... Sweden's Central Organization of Salaried Employees is formed by merger of 1931 union of employees in private business, 1937 union of employees in public service (grows to represent 42 affiliates by 1955 with total membership of some 337,500)... International Air Transport Agreement establishes freedom to fly over other countries... Welsh miners strike (March 8), threaten to paralyze British war industry... Britain, U.S.S.R. and U.S. propose formation of United Nations... Britain's Butler Education Act provides comprehensive secondary educational system of modern grammar and technical schools... Soviet forces reach (March 17) Romania... Britain establishes Ministry of National Insurance... William Beveridge: Full Employment in a Free Society... Allied forces invade (June 6) Continent... British astronautical societies plan space exploration... Germany launches first V-1 jet-propelled flying bombs, developed by Hermann Oberth, to strike London, V-2 rockets later in year... Spain tests Talgo streamlined, lightweight train at 105 mph... Free French troops retake (August 25) Paris... Holland forms Foundation of Labor, existed clandestinely during war, to improve management, union relations... Allied Control Commission ships Italian goods to U.S., allocated to NYC importers on prewar quota basis... Bulgaria announces that all cooks who spoil food will be classified as saboteurs and shot... While "Battle of the Bulge" is being contested with U.S. forces, German headquarters tests tactics in war game... U.S. troops invade (October 25) Philippines.

Business Events

Swedish confederations of employers, unions sponsor joint program of vocational training... Pilkington subsidiary is first to make fiberglass... Hubert Beuve-Mery starts France's Le Monde... Lars-Erik Londberg starts construction empire, billion-dollar group with construction, real estate, industrial, and banking interests in 1988, building residential housing in Sweden... Tokio Marine and Fire merges with Mitsubishi Marine Insurance and Meiji Fire Insurance (resumes foreign business in 1956 with affiliation with Mitsubishi, buys U.S.' Houston General Insurance in 1980, forms Tokio Reinsurance, Switzerland, in 1982, opens offices in Madrid, 1989, Istanbul, Milan and Santiago in 1990, gets 10% share of Philadelphia-based investment counseling firm in 1990 and starts program to adapt policies for individuals).

1945

General Events

Germany leaves (January 4) Belgium... On taking office as head of state General Charles De Gaulle nationalizes (January 16) Renault car business to punish founder-owner Louis Renault for allegedly collaborating with Nazi occupation, one of nation's most dynamic enterprises in 1980s with freedom to operate as private business (follows with nationalization of three largest banks, Air France, major factories, and gas, electric utilities)... New Zealand Airline is nationalized (is sold in 1989 to consortium, Qantas, American, Japan Air lines and New Zealand investment group, for $413 million)... Soviet troops invade (January 21) Germany... International Bank for Reconstruction and Development, "World Bank," is formed... Government of Argentina is overthrown by coup led by Col. Juan Peron... France promises (March 24) Indochina financial autonomy in empire... Robert Rossellini: Open City" (starts postwar Italian movie industry)... Britain's Wages Council Act sets minimum wages for industry... Red Army enters (April 23) Berlin... Germany surrenders (May 7)... Clement Attlee's Labor Party wins (July 5) British elections (-1951)... Japan surrenders (August 15)... Britain, U.S. sign (September 24) oil pact... Arabs threaten (October 24) oil embargo if U.S. aids Zionists... Workers' Ski Cooperative is formed, Yugoslavia, by 10 former partisans (adopts name of Elan in 1952, provides equipment for Swedish ski team in 1972 Olympics - continues sponsorship with champion Ingemar Stenmark, evolves to employ some 1,100 workers in 1983 for sales of some $45 million)... "Black markets" in food, clothing and cigarettes, medium of exchange with candy in some areas, appear throughout Europe... Britain adopts family allowances... Britain nationalizes (November 3) civil aviation... Federal People's Republic of Yugoslavia, Tito Chief of State, is formed (November 29)... Atomic Research Center is established in England (starts first atomic pile in 1947)... Let Us Face the Future proposes governmental welfare program in post-war manifesto of British labor movement... Faced with completely disrupted economy Holland issues Extraordinary Labor Degree (forms Board of Government Conciliators to formulate and implement nation's wage policies, sets minimum wages for unskilled adult workers based on costs required by family of four, 10% more for semi-skilled workers and 20% more for skilled workers, sets maximum wages with differentials for skills, sex, age, marital status, and cost-of-living)...

U.S. occupation of Japan begins with General Douglas MacArthur as commissioner (-1952, dissolves terrorist Black Dragon Society, approves first trade union law in 1945, Wagner Act as model, and Anti-Monopoly Law of 1947)... Britain, U.S. and Soviet Union sign Potsdam Agreement (dismantles major combines in Germany's coal and steel industries, by 1949 Germany operates 668 factories, 30% in iron and steel, 25% in chemicals, 13% in mechanical engineering and 10% in aeronautical sector)... British science-fiction writer, Arthur C. Clarke, proposes communications satellites (predicts use in year 2000, reality in 1962 with Telstar I)... On demise of Fascist regime Italian General Confederation of Labor is created to represent Christian Democrats, lose control to Communists in 1947... Bank of New Zealand is nationalized... U.S.S.R. produces 12.3 million tons of steel, 65.3 in 1960 and 148 in 1980 as world's largest producer... Britain's Distribution of Industry Act seeks to reverse economic decline of such stagnant areas as Northeast England and South Wales, visualized by 1940 Barlow report... Britain approves free labor union and political parties for its sector of Germany... Communists establish Polish People's Republic, sponsored by U.S.S.R. (is transformed with first democratic elections in 1989, is governed by non-Communist majority in 1990)... Basketball appears in Yugoslavia when Belgrade rival clubs, Partizan and Red Star, begin sports rivalry (evolves as growth sport with indoor arenas in 1960s, land's first world championship in 1970, NBA players in 1989).

Business Events

Standard-Triumph car business is formed, Britain... Thomas Schmidheiny, 4th-generation heir to Switzerland's most successful industrial dynasty with 1988 wealth of some $2.6 billion from Holderbank, world's largest cement firm, and Anova Holding in construction, electronics, packaging, real estate, banking and watches, is born... After W.W. II, Korean-born Nakajima, Japan's richest in 1988 with fortune of some $3.4 billion, starts pachinko machine business (becomes world's largest maker)... After war, Swiss Max Schachenmann takes over family's calcium carbonate business, billionaire by 1988 to control 60% of European, 25% of North American markets... Rudolph A. Oetker, West Germany, takes over family baking powder business (rebuilds and diversifies to build billion-dollar empire by 1988 with West Germany's largest food firm and interests in some 70 businesses, such as beverages, banks, luxury hotels, insurance, and brewing)... Y.Z. Hsu operates Shanghai textile factory (flees to Taiwan in late 1940s to develop business of $4.2 billion in cement, synthetic fibers and department stores)...

Brazilian employers are required to provide social service programs to employees for social peace... After apprenticeships at Molyneux and Lelong houses, Balmain opens Paris fashion house (after losing nearly $6 million, drops haute couture in 1980s to focus on ready-to-wear, perfume licensing)... Chateau Mouton-Rothschild uses great artists to design wine labels... During occupation period, Noda Soy Sauce Co. is revived for post-war business (forms consensus decision-making labor council in 1950 as substitute for management-labor negotiations, is investigated in 1951-54, 1956 by government for anti-trust violations, starts automated continuous process technology in 1950s, opens international office in 1957 at San Francisco, starts new subsidiary in 1961 to pack, distribute fruit, vegetable brands in Japan for such firms as Del Monte, is U.S.' best selling soy sauce in 1976)... Pan Am reopens NYC-London service... Albrecht brothers take over family grocery business in Ruhr (build billion-dollar chain of discount stores by mid-1980s)... Italy's Costas family replaces small cargo fleet with U.S. surplus Liberty ships, evolves as Mediterranean cruise line, six ships with four more by 1993, by 1990 with sales of $260 million... In two months after Japan's surrender, Masaru Ibuka, engineer, and Akio Morita, scientist, start small business to convert standard radios for shortwave broadcasts and repair phonographs, Tokyo Telecommunication Engineering in 1946 and Sony in 1958 (get contract in 1949 to make equipment for radio stations, see first success in developing Japan's first tape recorders in 1950, for $25,000 get non-exclusive rights from AT&T in 1953 for its 1948 transistor technology to launch the consumer electronics revolution, make one of first transistor radios in 1955, enter U.S. market in 1956, make pocket-sized radios in 1957, show first home video recorder in 1964 and integrated circuit-based radio, introduce Trinitron color TV tube in 1968 and Betamax VCRs in 1976)... After confiscation of properties, Alfried Krupp, succeeded father in 1943, is convicted by Occupation for use of slave labor during war (is released in 1951, due to Cold War, to continue family enterprise, regains control, pledges to sell holdings in iron, steel and coal, in 1953, builds, India, steel plant in 1953, opens, Greece, nickel mines in 1955 and starts producing titanium, first European manufacturer, after recession of 1966-67 is forced to sell shares to public, passes control, 1967, to private foundation with death, sells 25% of firm to Shah of Iran in 1975, after strike by steelworkers in 1987 blocks takeover by Thyssen in 1988 and forms trading division)... Hachette, French publisher, launches Elle (starts line of paperbacks in 1953, becomes land's largest publisher by 1990s as media empire on five continents with 75 magazines, papers).

1946

General Events

London Airport opens... U.N. holds (January 30) first General Assembly... Albania, Hungary, Transjordan and Bulgaria become independent... Italy's Gaggia invents coffee espresso machine... Britain's Labor Government repeals (February 13) 1926 law banning strikes... Britain nationalizes (February 14) Bank of England, then British European Airways operated by railroads and coal industry... International Labor Organization declares rights of all to equal pay for equal work... Brazil's labor court system to resolve grievances of workers in Ministry of Labor is made an independent activity... France recognizes (March 6) Ho Chi Minh's Vietnam state... Britain's Gold Coast is (March 29) first British colony with African parliamentary majority... Col. Juan Peron is President of Argentina (-1955, 1973-74, sponsors first Five-Year Plan to encourage industrial growth with revenues from agricultural exports, establishes government monopoly for purchasing and exporting grain production, later meat)... Milovan Djilas: The New Class (exposes development of Communist Party oligarchies)... Japan's Labor Relations Adjustment Law establishes procedures to settle labor disputes...

Iran reveals (April 7) giving U.S.S.R. 51% control of oil for 25 years... Argentina nationalizes telecommunications industries (sells 40% to Spain's telephone company in 1988, Chile sells part of telephone system to Australia's Alan Bond)... France nationalizes (May 17) all independent coal mines... By 1960, some 80% of British investment is in Commonwealth lands, by 1981 over 30% in North America and 23% on Continent... France adopts (May 22) social security... Tapio Wirkkala, Finnish designer of elegant functional, wins recognition for Scandinavian style with show... West Germany's industrial production reaches only 33% of 1936 level... Britain adopts (June 17) bread rationing... France launches Monet plan for economic recovery... Nuremberg war trials reject defense of responsibility to follow orders... France bars (August 8) economic reunification of Germany... By 1947, 45% of East Germany's factories are 'property of the people' (takes over all natural resources in 1947, banks in 1948)... Yugoslavia adopts new constitution (copies economic apparatus of U.S.S.R. - local managers report to some 215 agencies in Belgrade, signs economic agreements with Poland, Czechoslovakia, Hungary, Albania and Bulgaria in 1946-47, announces first Five-Year Plan for economic development in 1947, is expelled from

Cominform and denounced by U.S.S.R. in 1948, passes first decentralization law in 1951 to turn over all enterprises to workers' councils - tried unsuccessfully by Poland in 1956 and Czechoslovakia in 1958, starts program to let unemployed contract for work in western countries, establishes governance of enterprises by 1969 constitutional amendment - workers' councils to make policy, select managing director, and appoint executive committee to advise on short-term technical matters and commission to advise on long-range technical issues)... Evita Peron begins purge to rid Argentina's unions of traditional leaders (-1951)... Kuwait, one of poorest nations, pumps first oil (holds foreign assets of nearly $100 billion by 1990)...

France forms agency to hold majority interest in enterprise formed just before W.W. II to develop natural gas discovery in southwest France and publicly-traded firm formed by Vichy to find oil (discovers large gas field in 1951, finds oil and gas in Algeria, nationalized in 1971, Gabon, 1956, and Congo in 1957, consolidates petroleum activities in 1966, Elf trade name in 1967 and Societe Nationale Elf Aquitaine name in 1976 with France holding 70%, launches Sanofi in 1973 to oversee pharmaceuticals, cosmetic activities, buys U.S.' M&T Chemicals in 1977, and Texasgulf, mining and chemicals, in 1981, adds Atochem, created by France to nationalize its chemical industry, in 1983 and Pennwalt chemicals in 1989, acquires perfumes from Avon, Continental Flavors & Fragrances in 1988 and 1989, in 1991, as world's 8th largest in petroleum industry with 53.9% owned by France, pays $1.35 billion for Occidental's North Sea holdings and takes large part of CEPSA, Spain's refining enterprise)... Scandinavia Airlines System, SAS, is formed as a public-government consortium by Denmark, Norway, Sweden (flies to Buenos Aires, 1946, Bangkok, 1949, and Johannesburg, 1953, buys, 1957, 50% of Sweden's domestic carrier, sold 1990, starts Scanair for charter service in 1961 and Danair in 1971 for domestic flights, with U.S. 1978 deregulation sees first loss in 18 years in 1980, targets businessmen, most stable passengers of market, to regain profits in 1982, in 1989 coordinates routes with All Nippon, Lan Chile, Canadian Airlines International).

Business Events

Congress of Unione Siciliana meets in Havana, U.S. exile Lucky Luciano in charge, to discuss U.S. crime business... International Management Institute appears in Geneva... Piaggio of Genoa introduces popular Vespa motor scooter, one of Italy's first industrial successes after war (-1987 after selling some 10 million)... Sweden's central confederation of employers, unions sign Basic Agreement to create joint enterprise councils in firms, tested in 1942 by firm using British model... Former civil engineer before joining mother's Paris hosiery business, Louis Reard designs daring bikini, first called 'atome', bathing suit, modeled by striptease dancer as professional models refused to wear scanty attire (catches on in 1950s with Brigitte Bardot - 20% of U.S. swimsuit sales by 1984, leads to Rudi Gernreich's topless bathing suit in 1964 and his thong suit in 1974)... Washington SyCip opens one-man accounting office in Manila (evolves by 1980s as largest consulting, accounting firm in area and leading legitimate fixer in Pacific Rim)... Canada's Butchart Gardens, started 1904 in Victoria, are opened to public, by 1990 handles over 500,000 tourists/year with staff of 300... Paris closes city-sanctioned brothels (considers reopening houses, based on government-monitored Eros Centers in West Germany, in 1990 to slow spread of AIDS)... Bertelsman AG, started printing hymnals in 1835 to evolve as world's largest media enterprise in 1991, returns to publishing, plant blown up by Nazis in 1940 (starts Germany's first book club in 1950 and record club in late 1950s, in 1964 buys UFA, TV and film production, and 25%, controlling interest in 1973, of publisher of Stern and Der Spiegel, acquires 51% of Bantam Books, rest 1981, in 1977, gets Arista Records in 1979, starts America Circle books, records club in 1980, folds 1984 after losses)... Mitsubishi zaibatsu is split into 139 separate entities by U.S. Occupation.

1947

General Events

Britain nationalizes (January 5) coal mines... Irish coffee is created by accident at Ireland's

Shannon airport, refueling stop for transatlantic flights, when catering chef Sheridan adds whipped cream for final touch... British troops replace (January 13) striking truck drivers... Truman Doctrine provides U.S. funds for recovery of Greece, Turkey (starts Cold War)... India grants commercial banks, largely short-term lending to finance agriculture and manufacturing industries with working capital, independence to handle long-term loans and investments... Actor Laurence Olivier is knighted, first of craft raised to life peerage in 1970... World Bank opens (May 9), gives France $250 million reconstruction loan... Britain's Kenneth Wood devises crude Robert Kenwood Chef food processor, followed by Pierre Verdun's Robot-Coupe in 1963 and his automatic Magimix, sold in U.S. as Cuisinart, in 1971... Hungarian-born physicist, Dennis Gabor invents holography while at Britain's Thomson-Houston Co., new industry after advent of laser in 1960... Ludwig Erhard, chairman of West Germany's Economic Council, advocates socially responsible market economy to combine state social policies with free enterprise... Finland tries (May 25) collectivized agriculture... Soviets nationalize (May 30) mines in occupation zones... Economist Jean Monet is France's commissioner-general to restore economy with centralized planning... Britain's Minister of Labor pleads (June 1) for British women to work... Japan's labor law establishes minimum standards of work for all workers... U.S. Occupation Authority provides series of training programs for Japanese supervisors, adds management programs later... U.S. grants Philippines its independence...

Soviet occupation forces in Austria take over (August 4) U.S.' Vacuum Oil, Britain's Shell refinery as German assets... Britain grants (August 15) independence to India, Pakistan... Finland's Collective Agreement Act establishes official labor court... National Congress of Industrial Unions forms in Japan, controlled by Communists... Argentina law requires employers to recognize labor unions (requires unions to acquire government recognition)... Britain puts (August 27) curbs on food, motoring, travel... Australia creates coal board to govern industry... Romanian peasants strike (October 17) over currency reforms, Kent cigarettes underground medium of exchange... Japan forms Fair Trade Commission to administer anti-monopoly act... Belgium, Holland and Luxembourg form (October 29) Benelux customs union... Britain orders boards of German coal, steel companies of Ruhr to have equal numbers of representatives from stockholders, employees (is adopted by 1951 Co-Determination Act, similar laws by Holland, Sweden and Norway)... General Agreement on Tariffs and Trade, GATT, is formed with headquarters in Geneva, sponsored by U.S... Peruvian International Airways is first to use radar... Australia nationalizes (November 27) banks... Japan's new constitution creates Ministry of Labor... U.S. presents Marshall Plan for post-war recovery of Europe (requires involved nations to prepare comprehensive modernization plan to integrate economies)... U.S.' Jack Kramer helps form international pro circuit for tennis players... Australia nationalizes Qantas, its international carrier (in 1958, Pan Am earlier in 1957 but blocked by U.S. in crossing states, offers world's first complete round-the-world flights, buys, 1958, Fiji Airways, renamed Air Pacific in 1971 and nationalized 1978, gets 29% of Malayan Airways in 1979).

Business Events

Emilio Pucci starts fashion business in Italy... First Swedish chair in business administration is sponsored by industrial funds... First store of Sears, Roebuck de Mexico opens in Mexico City, 6 more by 1953... Italy's "Shoeshine" is first foreign-language film to win an Oscar, spurs land's post-war movie industry... British Institute of Management is formed... British ad agency, Colman, Prentis & Varley, opens 11 overseas offices by 1960... Cathay Pacific Airways is started in Hong Kong by American, Australian... Servico Nacional de Apprendizagem Commercial forms in Brazil to provide training for employees in commercial trade...

Some 70 Japanese executives form Doyukai to develop post-war managerial ideology... France's Georges Salomon abandons teaching career to join small business of parents making band-saw blades, metal ski edges (convinces parents to produce ski bindings - leading supplier by 1960, starts selling ski boots in 1979 - No. 2 by 1980s, acquires Chicago maker of high-priced golf clubs in 1985)... Japan's only private gambling concession (requires most of profits, eventually $2 billion/year, be distributed to towns, prefectures hosting events and Japan Shipbuilding Industry Foundation) is given in motorboat racing to Ryoichi Sasakawa, former 1931 leader of Fascists political party with private army of 15,000 (expands to operate bicycle, horse and motorcycle racing, contributes some $1.35 billion to various charities in 1971-80s, establishes $45 million grant in 1980-83 to create U.S.-Japan Foundation for research, a $19 million grant in 1984-85 for Scandinavia-Japan Sasakawa Foundation for research and education and $15 million in 1984 for Great Britain-Sasakawa Foundation for maritime research)... Former auto racer Enzo Ferrari, Italy's greatest car designer, starts building racing machines as elegant cars near Modena with 400 workers, builds 55,000 by 1989 but most too valuable for collectors to drive... First airport duty-free store opens at Ireland's Shannon airport to promote Irish whisky and woolens, $5.5 billion industry in 1984 with Duty-Free Shoppers, San Francisco firm of 160 stores around Pacific Rim, top retailer in 1988 with sales of some $2 billion...

With backing from textile magnate Marcel Boussac, Christian Dior opens fashion house, 3 work rooms and 85 employees, in Paris (introduces New Look fashion in 1948 as antithesis of rigid, masculine style of war years, introduces perfume line and visits U.S. to sign licenses - 320 by 1987 to pioneer trend, runs House of Dior in 1953 with 28 work rooms, over 1,000 employees in 8 firms and licensed businesses on 5 continents, is succeeded by Yves Saint Laurent in 1957, Marc Bohan in 1962 and Italian designer of ready-to-wear Gianfranco Ferre in 1989 to pioneer trend of internationalism in European fashion)... U.S.' Max Masius, William Ferguson acquire British operation of Albert Lasker's Lord & Thomas to start Britain's Masius ad agency (goes global in 1960s)... Rank Organization increases output of movies when Britain puts stiff tariffs on imports, rescinded 1948, of foreign films (loses UK market after 1948 with flood of U.S. films, reverses fortunes, 1956, in deal, rejected by IBM and Gestetner, with Haloid, now Xerox, to provide financing for 1/3 of profits in forming Rank Xerox, after 20 years of dubious investments in host of unrelated areas for sluggish performance sees revival by new CEO in 1983 to trim overhead, dumps firms at rate 1½/day, joins MCA in 1988 to build Universal Studios theme park, in 1990 absorbs Mecca Leisure Group, bingo parlors, casinos, hotels and clubs)... Windjammer cruises for vacationers begin in West Indies, fleet of five sailing ships by 1992...

Koo In-Hwoi starts Lucky Chemical in Korea to make facial creams, later detergents, shampoo, toothpaste to become land's only plastics maker (starts trading company, basis for Lucky-Goldstar Group as 3rd largest in South Korea after Samsung, Hyundai, in 1953, forms Goldstar in 1958 to make electric appliances, first to make radios, 1959, refrigerators 1965, TVs, 1966, elevators and escalators, 1968, and washing machines and air conditioners, 1969, builds first privately-owned refinery in 1967 with Caltex, starts petrochemical production in 1977, runs, in 1980s, 24 diversified companies from copper mines, oil refineries, plastics, agriculture, to brokerage house, starts 1982, TV factory in Alabama to head off protectionism, forms 1984, biotech venture with U.S.' Chiron, in 1986 builds world's largest single-unit petrochemical plant in Saudi Arabia, with heavy debt reorganizes in 1989)... Nestle acquires Alimenta dehydrated soups, Crosse & Blackwell foods in 1960, Findus, Swedish frozen foods, in 1962, Beringer wine in 1971, Libby, McNeil & Libby canned foods in 1976, and Beech-Nut baby food in 1978, sold 1989 to Ralston Purina (introduces Taster's Choice coffee in 1966)... Chung Ju-Yung, after repairing trucks for U.S. military, starts Hyundai Engineering & Construction, first Korean contractor to win overseas contracts (starts Hyundai Motor, 1967, to assemble Fords, in 1970s gets $1 billion contract to build port in Jubai, saves money by importing Korean parts and risks ruin by not insuring cargos to achieve success, despite no experience builds, 1973, world's largest shipyard, in 1975, with aid of Mitsubishi Motor, builds land's first car, Pony, opens institute in 1977 to train engineers, forms Hyundai Electric in 1983, ships Pony cars to Canada, sells 5 times target of 5,000, in 1984 for sales of $4 million in 1985, ships subcompacts, Excel, to U.S. in 1986, makes first Korean-designed car engine in 1991 and selects three core areas, motor vehicles, electronics and petrochemicals, as required by government of all industrial groups).

1948

General Events

Twenty-three nations sign (January 1) General Agreement on Trade and Tariffs to reduce international trade barriers... Britain nationalizes (January 1) inland transport... Tikon Khrennikov is chancellor of U.S.S.R.'s Composers Union... Manchester University's Mark I is prototype electronic computer, first to use U.S.' J. von Neumann's binary code and stored program... Czech Communists threaten (February 2) strike if economic demands not met... Britain ends bread rationing... Britain's Liverpool operates first port radar system... British Electrical Authority is created to govern nationalized utilities... Communists take over Czechoslovakia (-1989 when ousted by people)... When U.S.S.R. seals off Allied access to Berlin, airlift is started (-49 with 277,264 flights in 15 months delivering over 1.8 million tons of food, coal and vital supplies, including candy for children, for city of 2 million)... Venezuela requires foreign oil companies to split their profits 50-50 with government, adopted later by other petroleum countries... Under terms of Marshall Plan, European Organization for Economic Cooperation is formed (April 16)... New Italian Constitution recognizes rights of workers to organize (allows management-worker committees)... Israel forms (May) independent state... Administrative Staff College is formed in Britain to train senior, middle-level managers... Western Allies carry out currency reform in West Germany by replacing worthless Reichsmark with Deutsche Mark, eliminates 90% of cash holdings... After noticing cockleburs sticking to socks and dog on hikes in 1941, Swiss engineer George de Mestral invents Velcro fastener to replace buttons and zippers, patented 1955... Sweden's Industrial Council for Social and Economic Studies is formed...

Free Italian General Confederation of Workers is formed by Christian Democratic unions after leaving Communist- dominated Italian General Confederation of Labor... Britain establishes (July 5) National Health Services (evolves by 1980s as Western Europe's largest employer with 800,000 people, falls into disarray in mid-1980s with budget of some $34 billion, 6% of GNP with Sweden at 9.6% and West Germany at 8.1%, surgery delays with 700,000 waiting, closure of hospital beds and demoralized staff)... Verghese Kurien begins work at Indian experimental dairy in Anand (starts small cooperative, Kaira Dairy Milk Producers Union, is extended by government nationwide in 1964, evolves by 1989 as world's largest agricultural development program with 6 million dairy producers in 50,000 cooperatives in 500 cities, towns throughout India to stabilize milk prices, prevent exploitation of small farmers)... Afrikaaners' National Party wins South Africa election, establishes Apartheid (eases some regulations in 1985 by suspending forced resettlement, abolishing laws prohibiting interracial marriages and sexual relations, increasing leasehold and freehold rights to blacks in urban areas and granting blacks some political power, starts reforms in 1990)... Britain, U.S., France and Benelux create International Ruhr Authority, joined by West Germany later... Siegfried Giedion: Mechanization Takes Command (studies problems arising from modern technology)... Operations Research Society of the United Kingdom forms... AIESEC, International Association of Students in Economics and Business Management, is formed as international internship exchange program by students from seven lands (evolves by 1980s to cover some 30,000 students at 400 universities in 61 countries)... U.S. abandons (December 9) plans to deconcentrate Japanese industry.

Business Events

Axel Stringer, son of small Hamburg publisher, starts Hamburger Abendblatt, Germany's first post-war paper (starts tabloid Bild Zeitung in 1952, Europe's largest paper with circulation over 5 million, acquires Die Welt in 1953, expands with acquisition of Berlin's Ullstein publishing house to create Europe's largest news publishing enterprise)... Federation of Swedish Industries starts management development program, land's first, at Yxtaholm... First Land-Rover is made in Britain... Ferdinand, son Ferry build first cars to bear Porsche family name in West Germany, win first racing victory at Innsbruck in 1948... British, French Rothschilds invest in U.S. New Court Securities (acquire full control in 1981 to start investment bank)... Hanson family trucking interests are nationalized by Britain's Labor Government (after running group of truck dealerships, sell business in 1964 to Wiles Group)... Japanese Federation of Employers' Assn. forms to participate in formulation and administration of public labor policy... Swedish confederations of employers, unions start joint program to use time-and-motion studies, follows first Swedish use of job analysis in early 1940s by glass factory... Nejat F. Eczacibasi gets loan from newly-established industrial development bank for long-term loans to start Turkey's first modern pharmaceutical business (by 1980s evolves as group of four pharmaceutical firms with 22 licenses from international firms, four building companies and two paper products companies)... Portsea Inland Mutual Co-operative Society opens Britain's first self-service shop... Swiss-born Ernest Bader starts British chemical business (pioneers industrial democracy in settling disputes with Chemical Workers' Union with joint ownership, 40% of profits goes to staff for merit, charities in Third World and 60% for taxation, reserves)... After quarreling with brother, founder of Adidas sports shoe business, Rudolf Dassler starts rival Puma athletic shoe business in Bavaria...

After supplying navy with parts during W.W. II, Soichiro Honda starts Honda Motor Co. with 20 employees to build motorized bicycles with surplus army engines, world's largest manufacturer of motorcycles in 1960 (produces engines for farming in 1952, forms American Honda Motor Co. in 1959, wins all motorcycle classes at Britain's Mile of Man races in 1961 - recognized for dependability and quality, opens first foreign plant in Belgium in 1962 - 49 in 30 countries by 1980, despite opposition of government builds his first automobile, sports car, in 1963 - wins Mexico Grand Prix in 1965, is first to win all five Solo World Championships in motorcycle Grand Prix races in 1966, introduces first passenger car in 1967 and withdraws from racing, shows Civic car in 1972 - Accord in 1976, exports cars to U.S. in 1973 - displaces Toyota, market leader of foreign-built cars since 1975, in 1986, opens first U.S. plant in 1982 - Nissan in 1988 and Toyota planned for 1988, introduces Acura cars for upscale buyers, pioneers market for Japanese, in 1985 to compete with elegant European models, after reentering racing, reputed to spend over $100 million/year on Grand Prix events, wins 15 of 16 Formula One races in 1988)... Karl Heinz Kipp buys Swiss textile firm, Alfred Massa (switches from textile wholesaling to retailing in 1960s, sells chain, 26 variety stores in Germany, in 1986 to become multi-billionaire and buy 4 Swiss hotels)... Son of wealthy orange grower, Jaweed Al-Ghussein flees Gaza to Egypt (after graduating, meets Arafat, from Cairo's American University and working as civil servant for Kuwait, persuades Palestinian contractors to let him borrow their firm's name to bid for $400,000 contract, launches engineering firm with profits of $40,000 in mid-1960s, moves business to Abu Dhabi, builds multi-million-dollar construction business at thriving Capitol of United Arab Emirates and becomes Minister of Finance for PLO by 1980s)... London Press Exchange ad agency goes global by 1966... Spain's Jumberca begins to make textile machinery near Barcelona, world leader by 1988 with exports to 70 countries and over 300 patents...

After working in real estate and military service, Maxwell Joseph starts buying small London hotels (takes over chain of Grand Hotels in 1957, buys Europe's largest block of 1,200 flats in 1958, forms Grand Metropolitan Hotels, world's largest in profits by 1965, in 1962, to consolidate operations acquires Home & Continental Investment Trust in 1965 to get two merchant banking firms, buys drink wholesaler, Levy & Franks with Chef & Brewer pubs, in 1966, buys three of best hotels in Paris in 1967 - largest hotel group in France with five, buys NYC's Royal Manhattan Hotel in 1969 and acquires Express Dairies, in 1970 buys Mecca Group, betting shops, dance halls and bingo houses, and Berni Inns, 130 steak houses and 15 hotels, to run 2,000 eateries in Britain, mostly pubs, in 1989, in 1971 drops bid for Cunard Line and buys brewery Truman Hanberry Buxton, 1,200 pubs, to top Watney Manns - buys it 6 months later to get 8 breweries, 7,000 pubs in England and over 3,000 in Belgium, in 1975 operates 13 hotels in Europe, including Carlton at Cannes, and 55 in Britain, introduces Bailey's Irish Cream in 1979 - world's No. 1 liqueur in 1989, starts Huckleberry hamburger chain in 1980 - sells 18 units in 1983, buys U.S.' Liggett Group, tobacco, drinks, pet food and sports goods, in 1980, acquires Inter-Continental Hotels, 83 in 46 countries, in 1981 from Pan American World Airways for $500 million, sells 100 hotels, last of original business, to Seibu Saison Group for $2.3 billion in 1988, buys U.S.' Pearle Vision Centers, 1,200 eye-care places, in 1985 for $385 million, after interval is succeeded by Allen

Shepherd as CEO in 1986 to sell operations worth over $4 billion by 1989)... U.S. firm, transported thousands of workers from China, Caribbean to build Panama Canal 1903-1914, creates Colon Free Zone, evolves by 1980s as a commercial center with 1,600 firms and 12,000 workers to move some $4 billion in goods/year... IBM forms World Trade unit, sales over $100 million in 1954 and $350 million in 1960... Budapest Stock Exchange closes (reopens, first in post-Communist Middle Europe, in 1990)... Michael Sumichrast flees Czechoslovakia after communists take over (after making millions in Ohio real estate returns in 1990, starts firms to invest in projects, 600 possible but frustrated by maze of red tape)... Shanghai's Butterfield and Swire buys Hong Kong's new Cathay Pacific Airways, goes public in 1986 with China buying 12.5% in 1987 (with assets nationalized by People's Republic in 1949 moves business to Hong Kong, goes public in 1959 as Swire Pacific, global sales by 1990 of some $3.3 billion/year, gets, 1965, Coca-Cola franchise for Hong Kong, in 1990 buys 35% of Dragonair, 38% owned by China, to operate with interests in U.S., Japan, U.K. and Australia).

1949

General Events

Cambridge University's EDSAC is first computer with full-scale electronic- stored program... Confederation of German Trade Unions forms... Hungary forms (February 1) People's Republic, goes democratic with free elections in 1989... Romania, U.S.S.R., Albania, East Germany, Bulgaria, Hungary and Czechoslovakia form Council for Mutual Economic Assistance, Comecon chartered 1959 (brokers bulk of East bloc's bartered trade, encourages members to specialize in making certain goods, and sets production goals to meet joint needs, starts to dissolve in 1989 as Poland, Hungary seek commercial ties with West)... Britain ends clothes rationing... Britain nationalizes (May 1) gas industry... Council of Europe is created in Strasbourg... George Orwell: Nineteen Eighty-Four (warns technology an instrument of tyranny, used by Chinese in 1989 to resist, attack government oppression)... Japan's Army takes over (May 8) civilian jobs... Ireland drops membership in British Commonwealth... 12 nations form North Atlantic Treaty Organization (supports unification of West, East Germany in 1990)... Bolivia declares (May 30) state of siege with labor unrest... Ludwig Erhard, West Germany's first economic minister, advocates Social Market Economy... Japan revises Occupation's Anti-monopoly Act (permits cartels in 1953 revision)... With advice of U.S. technicians, Iran prepares Seven-Year plan for economic development... Finns mobilize (August 18) army to fight Communist-led strikes against Socialist Government... After withdrawing from Communist-dominated World Federation of Trade Unions, International Confederation of Free Trade Unions is formed by U.S.' CIO, unions of other countries... Simone de Beauvoir: The Second Sex (inspires Feminist Movement)...

Britain devalues (September 18) pound 30% to fight dollar deficit... France, Canada and 17 other nations devalue (September 19) currency... U.S. cancels reparation removals to assist Japan with its economic recovery... Argentina's new constitution establishes land reform, nationalization of industries and regulation of foreign trade... After 4-year civil war, China forms (October 1) People's Republic (spurs exodus of entrepreneurs to Hong Kong while Nationalists flee to Formosa)... Geoffrey de Havilland designs Comet, world's first jet airliner (is adopted in 1952 for service to South Africa)... After 8 years, Labor Party loses (December 10) elections in Australia... After almost 350 years of Dutch rule, Indonesia gets (December 28) independence... Hungary nationalizes (December 29) all foreign and privately-owned industry... Czechoslovakia closes all private shops (allows private shops, restaurants in 1990)... Italian Labor Federation is formed by Republicans, Social Democrats (merges with Free Italian General Confederation of Workers in 1950 to form Italian Confederation of Workers' Union, dissidents form Italian Workers' Union)... By 1990 value of shares on Tokyo Stock Exchange zooms 25,000%, nearly three times pace of NYSE... COCOM, Coordinating Committee for Multilateral Export Controls, is formed to keep Western technology from communist lands (liberalizes rules in 1990).

Business Events

Caledonian Market in North London, started as cattle market in 1855, moves to Bermondsey Square (becomes center for dealers in everything from antiques to knickknacks, opens at 7 a.m., according to old law of commerce, "market ouvert," that "anyone who buys stolen goods in hours between sunrise and sunset cannot be prosecuted for doing so")... Konrad Henkel joins family business, chemical colossus built by Fritz Henkel on success of Persil wash powder before W.W. I, as a chemist (as head 1965-80 builds $5.1 billion operation by 1987 - family's wealth of $2.9 billion)... To raise money for taxes, Lord Thynne family's Longleat House is first stately home opened to paying public (adds Safari Park in 1966, 13 attractions by 1988)... After moving from Baghdad to Shanghai in late 1800s, Jewish Kadoorie family goes to Hong Kong (evolves as billion-dollar empire in 1988 with interests in Hongkong & Shanghai Hotels, China Light & Power, banking, carpet business)... Germany's Volkswagen ships first Beetles to U.S., sells some 9.5 million by 1989... German inventor Han Liebherr devises tower crane to erect tall buildings (invents hydraulic ditchdigger in early 1950s, achieves sales of some $1.1 billion by 1980)... Michelin introduces first steel-belted radial tire, original idea for tire in 1913 by two Englishmen who lacked technology to make it (sells to U.S. in 1966 via Sears and to Ford for Lincoln Continental cars in 1976, opens first U.S. plant in 1975)... First annual Caribbean Baseball Series is played.

1950

General Events

Japanese law permits number of pre-war U.S. investors, such as IBM, B.F. Goodrich, and National Cash Register, to resume operations... British "productivity team" studies intensive mechanization on U.S. farms... Japan's labor movement is united with formation of General Council of Trade Unions... Holland's Industrial Organization Act creates Social Economic Council, members from management, labor and government, to coordinate product and industry boards for advice on social, economic issues and problems... West Germany's co-determination law requires firms in iron, steel and coal industries to put employees on boards... Syria, Lebanon form (March 13) customs union, later dissolved... Japan's Commercial Code dilutes role of stockholders while increasing power of managers, directors... Some 12.46% of West Germany's labor force, 28.2% in France, works in agriculture, forestry or fishing, 7.5% in 1973 and 12.2% in France... Avro, first turbojet transport plane, flies (April 18) Toronto - NYC in one hour... Austria ends wartime rationing... In 1950s East Germany builds Iron Works City as model workers' community, in decay by 1990 unification with West Germany... European Payments Union forms (June 1)... Italy designs 10-year economic plan... After attempts since 1919 France enacts basic law for collective bargaining (specifies contracts to cover union rights and workers' freedom of opinion, wages, conditions of hiring and firing, plant committees, welfare services and programs for vocational training, apprenticeships)...

Korean War begins (June 25) with invasion of North Korean troops... China puts villagers into five categories: landed proprietors, rich, fairly rich, poor peasants, agricultural workers (uses public meetings to expose injustices of landowners, moneylenders)... Japan's Foreign Investment Act requires governmental approval of all transactions involving payments in foreign currency (establishes control of technology and imports with MITI, which issues list of 33 desired technologies, mostly in heavy industry with electronics, jet aircraft, automation in 1959)... China bans traditional buying, selling of wives as arranged by families and/or matchmakers (use birth signs to determine marriage date) and grants wives equal rights... Dr. W. Edward Deming, professor of statistics at New York University's business school, gives proselytizing speech on quality control to Japanese Union of Scientists and Engineers (leads to society's annual Deming Prize in 1951 for excellence in quality control).

Business Events

Arabian-American Oil opens world's longest pipeline of 1,066 miles from Persian Gulf to Sidon (opens 753-mile pipeline from Saudi Arabia to Sidon later in year)... Swedish confederation of employers opens nation's first residential school for management development... Copenhagen's Magasin du Nord reports use of assessment center to meeting of International Assn. of Department Stores (describes process: group discussion of case problem, written proposal for job description, interviews, instruction of subordinates, written self-description, chairing a meeting)... Britain's Bernard Matthews, student auctioneer, buys 20 turkey eggs on sudden impulse (evolves to become Europe's largest producer of turkeys by 1960, innovates with light-controls for off-season breeding, growing small and large turkeys, processing and promoting consumption of turkey parts)... Danish Employers' Confederation establishes training program for managers in 1950s... Italian Baseball Federation forms, teams in 12 cities by 1986... U.S.' M.M. Zimmerman founds International Assn. of Food Distribution, Paris... Sanyo electrical business appears, Japan, to make bicycle lamps (evolves by 1980s as land's 2nd largest consumer electronics producer behind Matsushita with yearly sales of some $9.5 billion)...

Belgian-born diamond cutter Gerard Blitz, Gilbert Trigano start Club Mediterranee vacation business in France (opens first "village", emphasizes singles, on Majorca with 200 surplus U.S. Army tents to handle some 2,300 vacationers first season - 45,000 in 1960, 293,000 in 1970, 770,000 in 1980 and over 1 million in 1990 at 110 resorts in 33 countries with sales over $1 billion, appoints managing director and opens first hut village in 1954, opens Club Med ski resort in Switzerland in 1956, is sold to Baron Edmond de Rothschild in 1961, opens first bungalow village in 1965 and U.S. Club Med in 1968, acquires 45% of Italian resort business with villages in Italy, Greece and Tunisia in 1976, acquires Club Hotel, leader for 12 years in seasonal time-sharing resort business, in 1977, runs 90 villages in 40 countries on 5 continents in 1981 - world's 11th largest hotel chain, promotes vacations for U.S. families in 1984, forms subsidiary to operate villages in North America and Asia, fastest growing areas in worldwide network, plans resorts with China in 1984, after conflicts opens resort in 1986 with Chinese management, in 1987 plans $100 million, 610-foot, 5-masted schooner for sailing vacations in 1990, in 1989 buys 34% of French vacation-flight marketer with no-frills villages to fight low-cost, packaged tours of rival Club Aquarius with Go Voyages, opens first upscale resort, $60 million village, in 1989 and plans 1990 deal with U.S.S.R. for summer villas)... Seat, Spanish Government major stockholder until Volkswagen buys 75% in 1986, starts building cars, world's 6th largest by 1988 with small, medium cars...

Werner Otto starts mail-order house, Otto-Versand, in Hamburg, sales of $5.5 billion by 1986 (acquires U.S.' Spiegel mail-order in 1982, forms joint-venture with Japan's Sumitomo trading house in 1985, world's largest by 1990 with firms in France, Belgium, Spain and Britain)... Britain's Debenham owns 110 of 140 department stores owned by groups with 5 each... Tsukamoto prepares 50-year strategic plan for Japan's Wacoal Corp. (opens boutiques, employees trained and paid by cosmetics manufacturers, in lingerie departments of prestigious department stores, enters U.S. market in 1977 - 50 by 1985)... After surviving Nazi labor camps, George Herscu opens small dairy bar in Australia, basis for real estate empire (pleads guilty to making illegal payments to building union in 1983, after spending $1.5 billion to acquire 4 U.S. department store chains, Bonwit Teller, B. Altman of NYC, Sakowitz of Houston and Parisian of Birmingham, and real-estate businesses of Merrill Lynch and others, launches Forest Fair, first of 7 suburban shopping malls with theme-park rides, miniature golf courses, hypermarkets and microbreweries, in 1989, faces bankruptcy in 1990 with $1.2 billion takeover debt)... As sideline, Japan's Genshiro Kawamoto builds home for resale in early 1950s, multi-billionaire by 1989, with properties in Japan, 3,000 apartments and several office buildings, Hawaii, $173 million spree leads to law to ban ownership by non-resident aliens, and California, aims to invest $500 million for new tracts of rental homes... Safra family, founded Beirut's Banque du Credit Nationale, moves to Brazil while son Edmond runs Beirut bank (gets Brazil's Ponte Frio $230 million appliance group by marriage and runs Banco Safra)... After moving headquarters from Berlin to Bavaria after W.W.II,

Siemens begins computer research and development project, basis for area's growth as "Silicon Bavaria" in 1980s after U. S. electronics firms arrive in late 1970s... In this time Marbella Club, area's first grand-luxe resort, appears on Spain's Costa del Sol... Saturday Evening Post runs article on neglected Grand Cayman Island (starts tourist industry)... After W.W. II victors seize Allianz's foreign holdings, allowed to keep a share in Spanish firm, Allianz repurchases, 1950s, lost holdings in Italian, Austrian insurance firms and dominates German market (forms UK subsidiary in 1973, buys Brazilian firm in 1974, forms Los Angeles subsidiary in 1977, adds, 1979, insurance firms in Dallas and Minneapolis, loses 1981 hostile takeover of UK's Eagle Star insurance to BAT in 1983, acquires Italy's 2nd largest insurance firm in 1984, buys, on 3rd try, a British insurance firm in 1986, acquires insurance holdings of French firm in 1989 as white knight and buys Hungarian insurance firm, in 1990 wins control of former East German insurance firm, wins U.S.' Fireman's Fund Insurance for $1.1 billion, as Germany's largest in insurance gets 23% share of Dresdner Bank, Germany's 2nd largest)... After five years of financial problems, Toyota restructures, is saved by Korean War by orders for trucks (makes popular 4-wheel drive Land Cruiser in 1951, Crown car, used mostly as a taxi, in 1955, and Corona car in 1957, fails, 1957, in U.S. market with Crown cars, opens driving schools in 1961 to broaden Japanese market, re-enters U.S. with popular Corona, inexpensive but luxurious, in 1965, puts out best-selling Corolla subcompacts in 1968, is world's 4th largest car maker in 1970, tops Volkswagen in 1975 as No. 1 exporter of cars to U.S., opens first U.S. plant in 1984, shows upscale Lexus line in 1989, is accused of dumping Previa minivans in 1991 by U.S. auto makers)... After Mitsui zaibatsu is split into over 180 separate entities in 1946, 27 leaders of former Mitsui companies form new Mitsui group (after growth in petrochemicals and metals evolves by 1991 as world's 2nd largest trader after rival C. Itoh).

1951

General Events

Arabian-American Oil shares (January 2) profits with Saudi Arabia... After serving in post-war industrial posts, Velimir Marton, trusted Communist with little business background, is made manager of small Zagreb meat-packing plant (develops business by 1964 as Yugoslavia's largest company, some 3,500 workers, with sales of $37 million from 4 farms, 4 large factories, 60 food shops, 8 restaurants, one hotel and fleet of 150 trucks)... Elliot Jacques: The Changing Culture of a Factory... Some 300,000 strike (March 12) in Barcelona to protest high cost of living... West Germany's Investment Aid Act provides assistance to coal, iron and steel industries... After sharing 30% of oil revenues since 1946 with Iran, Anglo-Iranian Co. is nationalized (March 15)... France, West Germany, Italy, Belgium, Holland and Luxembourg form (March 19) European Coal and Steel Community... Greece adopts civil service code, Egypt 1952, Israel 1955 and Iraq in 1956... Some 46% of Britain's population work in commerce and industry, West Germany 41%, U.S. 30%, Italy 29%, Japan 20%, and India 10%... Israel uses regular examinations to select applicants for government positions... India prepares first Five-Year plan to industrialize... Egypt ejects (October 8) British from Suez...

People's Republic of China classifies corruption, waste, bureaucracy, bribery, tax invasion, theft of state property, cheating on government contracts, and stealing economic information as Eight Evil Winds (-1952)... Engineer Emerik Blum, deputy minister of electricity in Belgrade since 1947, starts Elektroprojekt in Sarajevo to design electric power systems, transmission lines (expands with Elektrorement, business repairing electrical equipment, after approval of both workers' councils renames growing united concern as Energoinvest in 1958, despite Belgrade's charges of capitalism, hires U.S.' McKenzie & Co. in 1968 to improve organization structure, accepts Obod, consumer appliance business, in 1970 as new activity - part by mutual consent in 1971, evolves by 1972 with some 22,000 people and sales of $160 million, 50% in exports, from 35 factories, 6 mines and 6 divisions of automation, aluminum, electrical equipment, processing equipment, consumer products and metals and minerals, spends $5-6 million/year on research, development and scholarship)... Festival of Britain commemorates century since 1851 Great Exhibition... Ferranti Mark I computer, first commercially manufactured computer, is installed at Britain's Manchester University... Britain develops (November 17) world's first nuclear-powered heating system.

Business Events

Kanebo and Toyobo, two cotton textile firms, are largest corporations in Japan, 4 of 10 largest in textiles... Britain's J. Lyons and Co. uses LEO, world's first business computer, to calculate payrolls and optimum mixes for tea blending... Kurosawa produces "Rashomon," Oscar award wins recognition for Japan's film industry... After watching wife make sausages, Sweden's Ruben Rausing devises machine for septic packaging of liquids (introduces sterile vacuum packages in 1961 to keep liquids fresh without refrigeration, evolves as world's biggest liquid-food container business, Tetra Pak with sales $2.2 billion by 1989)... With borrowed funds from relatives, Robert Maxwell, eldest son of Czechoslovakian laborer fleeing to Britain at start of W.W. II, buys controlling interest of publisher, renamed Pergamon Press, of scientific and technical journals (gets exclusive rights to back, current issues of German scientific publisher, is labor member of House of Commons in 1964, is found guilty of misrepresenting firm's financial position in 1971 - loses Pergamon and House seat, regains Pergamon in 1974 after settling suit, acquires struggling British printing and communications business in 1981 for $22 million - Maxwell Communications global in 1987 with sales of some $5 billion, debt of $2 billion, while rival Murdoch has sales of $13 billion and debt of $6 billion, buys Mirror Group with Britain's 2nd largest paper in 1984 for $191 million)... Wild-animal trainer Gunther Gebel-Williams, cited as world's greatest showman, begins career with Germany's Circus Williams (with its purchase by Ringling Bros. and Barnum & Bailey in 1969 becomes international star for feats)...

At age of 13 Alan Bond moves from Britain to Australia (quits school in 1952 to work as Freemantle sign painter, after borrowing some $700 from relatives to invest in land, gets first $1 million in 1957, forms Progress Development in 1959 to buy shares in 14 firms, incorporates in 1969, Bond Corp. Holding in 1974, after going into debt to finance deals in 1960s faces ruin in mid-1970s with collapse of Australia's property market, adopts policy to acquire and build cash-generating firms for stability, when asked to block takeover of Swan Brewery buys business in 1982, wins, 1983, America's Cup in sailing, in hostile takeover gets Castlemaine Tooheys, Brisbane brewer, in 1985 for 42% of market, sells $350 million assets to make the deal, after buying Pittsburgh's Iron City beer in 1986 buys U.S.' 1853 G. Heileman, 4th largest with 10% of market, 2.7% by 1991 after market war between Anheuser Busch and Miller, with 13 regional breweries acquired 1959-80, in 1987 for $1.75 billion, pays $700 million for broadcasting interests of Australian TV pioneer, Kerry Packer, in 1987, after trying to land Allied-Lyons, $7.4 billion in beer, liquor and food, and Lonrho, $5.6 billion in mining, hotels and agribusinesses, gets, 1988, Australia's Bell Group, NYC's St. Moritz hotel, $180 million in cash, and share of British Satellite Broadcasting as debt balloons to some $10 billion, with soaring interest rates, sagging property values, and skidding profits, loses $762 million in 1988-89, faces bankruptcy in 1990, in 1991 puts G. Heileman in bankruptcy, sheds Australian holdings to avoid financial collapse and steps down as CEO to face personal bankruptcy)...

Koor Industries, Israel's largest industrial in 1991, makes first diversification, Telrad, in telecommunications, follows with 1952 Finnish venture to make artillery, steel in 1954, rubber in 1955, defense electronics in 1962, chemical firm in 1963, food processor in 1970 and 1983 jet engine venture with United Technologies (shows first loss in 20 years in 1986, after losses in 1987, 1988 shows $303 million deficit in 1989, suspends payments to creditors in 1990, gets $100 million in loan guarantees from government in 1991)... With end of occupation, group of Japanese bankers start airline, lease pilots and equipment from Northwest Airlines (reorganizes in 1953 as Japan Air Line with government, public owning equal shares, flies to San Francisco, 1954, Hong Kong, 1955, Bangkok, 1956, Singapore, 1958, Europe, 1961, and Moscow in 1967, suspends flights to Taipei in 1954, subsidiary for Taipei in 1975, in favor of service to Beijing and Shanghai, after crash in 1985 kills 520 sees most of top executives resign for tragedy, loses monopoly for international routes in 1987).

1952

General Events

West Germany joins World Bank... British Overseas Airways launches (May 2) first commercial jet service with De Havilland Comet planes (takes 23.5 hours, 40 hours usual, for flight to Johannesburg)... General Batista, President 1940-44, overthrows Cuban Government (-1959 when ousted by Castro)... Britain, France and U.S. end occupation of West Germany... Egyptian King Farouk is overthrown (July 23) by military coup led by Major General Mohammed Naguib Bey (-1954, forms civil service commission, sets salary grades for government employees)... Austria devises oxygen process to make steel, adopted by Japan in 1957 - all Japanese firms use process by 1961... Saudi Arabian Monetary Agency forms... China reports (September 7) 40% of farm workers in cooperatives... Bolivia nationalizes (October 31) mining operations, Cuba in 1959-60, Chile in 1971, Guyana in 1971, Peru in 1973 and Nicaragua in 1979... Holland, Luxembourg start Multi-National European School System for multilingual, intercultural graduates, joined later by other Common Market countries... West Germany's Works Constitution Act establishes 2-tier system of directorships for large corporations with supervisory board, two-thirds of members from stockholders and rest from employees, and managerial board to make daily operating decisions (requires all firms with at least five employees to have work councils with co-determination rights on social-welfare issues, allotment of work, and vacation time, provides regulations for working hours, leaves, training, welfare services, disciplinary cases, job and piece rates, and grievance procedures, restores collective bargaining outlawed by Third Reich, adjusts pensions to reflect negotiated wages)...

SAS opens (November 19) commercial service between Canada, Europe... General strike occurs (December 6) in Tunisia to protest murder of labor leader... Japan joins World Bank (gets first loan in 1956, last in 1966 for total of $862.9 million for 31 projects - repaid by 1990, contributes to bank in 1970, 2nd largest after U.S. by 1990)... Japan's telephone monopoly is reorganized as Nippon Telegraph & Telephone, NTT, land's largest employer in 1991 (holds 10% of separate agency formed for international service in 1953, seeks aid of Hitachi, Fujitsu and NEC in 1968 to design, build computers, after years of stalling opens procurement, previously used suppliers mostly staffed by NTT retirees, to U.S. firms in 1981, develops public FAX network in 1981 and videotex service in 1984, loses monopoly in 1984, starts international unit in 1985 to enter global market, sells shares, 23.75%, to public in 1985 and 1987, selects AT&T, Motorola, Ericcson in 1990 to devise mobile telephone system)... IRI, after emerging from W.W. II with Corniglano steel plant to expand industry, gets national broadcaster (in 1950s buys large bankrupt textile works, rest of regional phone companies and Alitalia airlines, raises funds, 1955, to build, operate Autostrada when government is unable to finance road construction, as ordered starts to develop economy of southern Italy in 1957).

Business Events

Swedish Employers' Federation form Council for Personnel Administration (funds land's first university chair for personnel administration in 1956)... Engineer Heinz Nixdorf starts Nixdorf Computer, a success in minicomputers, software and private telecommunications, with advance payment from customer to pioneer West Germany's computer industry (buys first U.S. firm in 1977, expands in 1984 to provide tailored services to clients, after losing $251 million in 1989 needs quick recovery or alliance to survive Europe's shakeout in computer industry)... After training with Fath, Piguet, Lelong and Schiaparelli, Hubert de Givenchy opens Paris fashion house... To protect its home market Schweppes licenses Pepsi Cola to produce its soft drinks in U.S... Chow Yei Ching flees Communist China to study engineering in Taiwan (starts Hong Kong elevator sales business in 1970, after riding colony's construction boom of 1970s diversifies into office equipment - sales of $77 million by Chevalier Holdings in 1988 from fax machines, telephone switches, portable computers)... Said Khoury, two partners form Consolidated Contractors in Aden with $30,000 loan, sales of $500 million in early 1980s with oil boom, to work as subcontractor for Bechtel's in building Aden's first oil refinery... Australian-born Rupert Murdoch inherits two ailing newspapers in Adelaide, by 1988 builds News Corp. as leader in worldwide communications with television in 22 countries, films, magazines, books, 10 publishers, newspapers, 60% of Australian market and 36% of Britain's, and interests in printing plants, sheep farms, airlines, real estate, etc. (starts to acquire British papers in 1969 - U.S. in 1973 to run 80 in Australia, Britain and U.S. in 1980s, acquires Twentieth Century Fox in 1985, gets U.S. citizenship in 1985, acquires Metromedia, 7 stations, in 1986 to build 4th U.S. TV network, pays $1.5 billion for Australia's largest media company, Herald & Weekly Times Group, in 1987)... Astin Motor, Morris Motor form British Motor Corp., world's 4th largest making 200,000 vehicles/year before being topped as Europe's largest by Volkswagen in late 1950s and Fiat in 1960 (acquires car body supplier, appliance manufacturer in 1963, makes nearly 700,000 cars/year in 1963 - 63% of Britain's output, acquires last independent body supplier in 1965 for economy of scale - 14th largest corporation outside U.S., evolves in 1966 as British Motor Holding with Jaguar, Daimler Motor, Guy Motors and Coventry Climax, merges in 1968 with Leyland Motor to form British Leyland)...

After flying peninsula's first mail route in 1949, Luis Coppola, backed by father-in-law, makes "ridiculously low offer" for run-down Los Arcos Hotel in La Paz, opens luxury hotel Finisterra in 1971 (pioneers growth of lower Baja California for tourists)... Nissan returns to car business after building only trucks, airplane engines during W.W. II (enters U.S. market with Datsun cars in 1958, is Japan's 4th largest auto maker by 1980, introduces upscale Infiniti line in 1989, "takes over" Fuji Heavy Industries in 1990 to rescue failing Subaru)... J. Arthur Rank returns to family milling business (turns over control of film interests to British investors, acquires Hovis-McDougall milling in 1962 to dominate UK's flour industry, buys Corebus, packaged grocery products with overseas plants, in 1968)... Japan Helicopter and Aeroplane Transport begins service as domestic carrier (evolves as All Nippon Airways to start international flights in 1987 with privatization of JAL)...ICI, DuPont alliance loses U.S. antitrust suit... Matsushita forms electronics venture with Philips, 2nd in 1991 for digital compact cassettes (makes TVs, refrigerators and washing machines in 1953, buys, 1954, major share of Victor Co. of Japan, forms New York subsidiary in 1959, by 1960 makes vacuum cleaners, tape recorders, stereos, color TVs, National, Panasonic and Technics brands, to become land's largest maker of home appliances, in 1974 buys Motorola's U.S. TV plants and its Quasar brand).

1953

General Events

Last London tram car, first used in 1861, is ceremonially burned... First Asian Socialist Conference, Rangoon, proposes (January 15) land reform for peasants... After storm tide breaches dikes in vulnerable River Delta region of Holland, kills some 1,800 people, work on Delta project of dams, dikes and channels is started to seal Oosterschelde estuary during dangerous storms (-1986, costs some $5 billion)... Guatemala expropriates (February 13) 234,000 acres of United Fruit for land reforms (leads to government overthrow in 1954 by United Fruit with CIA help)... India opens (February 20) $140 million power system, based on TVA...

Major Soviet journal denounces cybernetics as pseudo-science, an Institute of Cybernetics in 1963... Comet jet airliner crashes (May 2), third for plane (is withdrawn 1954 after metal fatigue accidents, is recommissioned in 1958 for first transatlantic service by BOAC to beat Boeing's 707, Douglas' DC-8)... By agreement of central federations of unions, employers in Holland, all firms over 40 workers must form internal commissions to handle employee grievances... Queen Elizabeth II rules (June 2) Great Britain... Soviet tanks quell (June 17) general strike of thousands of workers rioting against East German Government after increasing production quotas for construction workers... Eurovision appears (June 25), first U.S.-Europe TV transmission by Telstar satellite in 1962... Some 8.38 million Chinese work in small business, some 160,000 after Mao's "socialist transformation" as State closes small enterprises, over one million in 1965 before Cultural

Revolution, some 140,000 by 1978 and over 7.5 million in 1983 after change in leadership (declines in 1989 with crack-down on democratic movement)... Korean armistice is signed (July 25) by United Nations, North Korea... Britain drops sugar rationing (opens door for Canada Dry, 7-Up, Coca-Cola, Pepsi-Cola)... Soviet premier Georgi Malenkov (-1955) presents (August 5) changes to Supreme Soviet: workers on collective farms to get more land for personal use and fair compensation, more investments in consumer-goods sector... New Zealand's Edmund Hillary, Sherpa guide Tenzing Norgay are first to scale Mount Everest, some 150 others by 1980s to develop Nepal's climbing industry (leads to 10,000 tourists in 1960, nearly 250,000 in 1988, and devastation of resources)... Two million protest (August 8) in Paris over expected cutbacks in civil service, leads to (August 13) general strike... After overthrow of Mossadegh, Shah returns (August 22) to power in Iran (allows consortium, BP, five U. S. oil companies, and French petroleum firm, and some independents to operate)... Britain's share of world manufacturing production is 8.6%, 4.0% in 1980... Jacques-Yves Cousteau, James Dugan: The Silent World, sells 5 million copies (leads to Cousteau Society for environmental education, Foundation Cousteau for marine preservation).

Business Events

Onassis, owner of 91 ships, acquires control of Monte Carlo Casino, several hotels in Monaco... Brazil's Federacao das Industrias do Distrito Federal opens productivity center in Rio (starts training program 1956)... Maurice Girodias starts Olympia Press, Paris, to publish conventional works along with erotica... Fiat, Olivetti open Italy's first school of business in Turin, a Palermo school in 1956... First Japanese commercial-television broadcast airs... With support of local merchants, Tyrone Guthrie starts Canada's annual Stratford Shakespearean Festival (draws some 450,000 viewers, about 45% from U.S., in 1988 to net $820,000)... With earnings from chain of Japanese movie theaters, started after W.W. II with father's small-town playhouse, Hisao Tsubouchi acquires bankrupt Kurushima Dockyard (as autocratic boss, breaks unions, fires employees and instills fear in workers, creates business empire of 180 firms with sales of some $3.3 billion in 1980s)...

After joining brother in Paris pharmaceutical business, James Goldsmith, age 20, descended from Frankfurt merchant banking family going to London in 1895, elopes with disinherited daughter of Bolivian tin millionaire Don Patino (after almost losing French business, gains control of Bovril British food company in 1957, lacking money to pay hospital for birth of son in 1959, wins stake playing backgammon, assembles huge British food conglomerate, Cavenham, in 1960s by buying ailing firms and selling weak operations, acquires U.S.' Grand Union grocery chain in 1973 for $62 million, buys Diamond International, one of first leveraged buyouts, in 1982 - after dismemberment gets $500 million and 1.6 million acres to go after St. Regis and Crown Zellerbach, is blocked in takeover of Goodyear Tire in 1986 by public outcry - profits by $93 million, sells most of U.S. assets prior to October 1987 market crash, after liquidating British, French interests, shows 1988 net worth of $1.2 billion with holdings in Grand Union, Paris publishing house, Guatemala oil wells, some 2.5 million acres of U.S. timberland and $800 million in cash to run three menages, after getting 30% of food giant Ranks Hovis McDougall with Jacob Rothschild, Kerry Packer launches 1989 hostile takeover with partners of BAT, $21.2 billion deal financed by junk bonds with plans to pay debt by selling parts, forces European firms to revise survival strategies, joins others in 1989 to acquire Mexico's largest airline for $140 million, drops BAT takeover in 1990 when stymied by U.S. regulatory delays)...

London's Gore Hotel opens Elizabethan room for visitors to experience dining, amusements of 1558-1603... Laura Ashley begins Britain's leading fashion house by making scarves on kitchen table (opens shop in 1967 - success with elegant dresses and Victorian-style prints, opens San Francisco store in 1974, opens first English country hotel in 1990, plans 15-20 "country house" hotels for U.S.)... Air Congo is joint venture of Belgian investors, Congo Belge investors including Sabena... England calls up two Kray brothers for National Service (after court-martials evolve in 1960s as land's most successful criminals by intimidation, media darlings and night club operators)... Vargas government forms Brazil's petroleum monopoly, Petrobras (after team, led by U.S. geologist Walter Link, outrages public with 1953 report that prospects are slim for discovery of oil, finds oil land in 1957, by 1973 produces only 10% of needs, sets price of gasohol at 65% of gasoline in 1979, in mid-1980s cost of alcohol twice that for gasoline, finds Iraq field in 1980, explores Amazon jungle, first drilling in 1917, in 1986 to develop wells by 1990, drills in Angola, Gulf of Mexico, agreement with Texaco, in 1987, finds two new fields in 1988 to triple land's oil reserves, still imports 40% oil in 1991, with annual inflation of 1,765% in 1989 suspends dividends for first time, in 1990 spins off subsidiaries, fertilizer, and liquidates trading and mining units to focus on oil, gas, plans in 1990 to raise crude oil output to 71% of demand by 1995)... After being carved up by Allies after W.W. II, Thyssen steel business begins anew with its Bruckhausen complex, its only asset (with reviving West Germany economy prospers sufficiently to acquire, 1973, manufacturing giant, Rheinstahl AG, with everything from shipyards to locomotives, buys, 1978, U.S.' Budd, car parts, in first overseas venture, spun off in 1985 as Transit America, with demand for steel declining, develops its trading activity in 1980s as largest contributor to sales).

1954

General Events

Ad hoc Paris Club is created by officials from 16 industrial countries to review debt of Third World nations... Soviet Union finds diamonds in Northern Siberia, produces one million carats in 1965 and two million in 1971... Giulio Matta, 1938 director of Milan Institute of Industrial Chemistry, develops high-strength polypropylene plastic, wins Nobel Prize in 1963... Tito rules out (January 31) Soviet centralized government, economy for Yugoslavia... Gordon Richard is first professional jockey knighted... West Germany joins NATO, Western European Union... London gold market opens (March 22), closed 1939... France devises Value-Added tax... Britain starts (March 24) trade with Hungary... Toronto opens (March 30) Canada's first subway... Sultanate of Oman, home of Sinbad the Sailor and source of frankincense for Queen of Sheba, discovers first oil... Switzerland's Federal Institute of Technology, St. Gall Graduate School of Economics and Swiss Foundation for Applied Psychology offer integrated management program, leads to 1962 graduate program by St. Gall Graduate School of Economics, Business and Public Administration... Britain tests first controlled flight of vertical take-off plane... Eight major U.S., European oil companies combine (May 10) to resume oil production in Iran... West Germany, France sign cultural and economic agreement...

Norway, Sweden, Denmark and Finland form common labor market... 100 chemical elements are known, nine c. birth of Christ, 12 c. 1500 and 84 c. 1900... Argentina's secret law establishes employer groups, requires agreements with labor unions... Pope opens (June 2) 8-station TV network Eurovision... Britain ends (July 3) wartime food controls in dropping meat rationing... University of Naples offers management training course... Britain licenses Independent Television Authority as commercial network to compete with state-owned BBC... First production cooperatives in China appear, used to develop heavy industry in 1955-57... Britain ends (July 27) 72-year presence in Egypt... Sweden approves (October 30) national healthcare system... Friendship Farm appears in Northeastern Province of China as state enterprise (evolves with 465,000 acres, population of 110,000, 137 schools, 134 hospitals, 62 ships, over 1,000 tractors, 444 combines, 60,000 pieces of farm equipment and 300 heavy trucks, is decentralized in 1984 from 287 "production teams" to contract farm units of single families, two or more related families and/or at least five households under elected manager)... Bulgaria's Todor Zhivkov is Communist Party's first secretary, head of state and party chief in 1971 (resigns in 1989 after democratic upheaval)... Twelve European countries form Centre Europeen pour la Recherche Nucleaire... Japan adopts 1st foreign aid budget, 2nd largest donor in 1988 after U.S. and No. 1 in 1989 with outlay of $9.13 billion.

Business Events

Vidal Sassoon, once shampoo boy in East End and high school dropout, opens London hairdressing salon, line of hair-care products generates annual sales of $120 million by 1990... With some 660,000 workers, India's cotton textile industry is largest, followed by railroads, jute textiles, electrical manufacturing and metal products... Business associations, industries sponsor West Germany's first seminar for executive development... Liddell Hart: Strategy: The Indirect Approach... Booz, Allen & Hamilton opens first office of U.S. consulting firm in Europe, over 50 others by 1966... After working 35 years as houseboy for wealthy Kaaki family and running money-changing business with partner, Salem Ahmed Bin Mahfouz founds first Saudi-owned bank (is billionaire in 1988 with 52% of Jiddah's National Commercial Bank, largest in Saudi Arabia, and interests in Luxembourg holding company, U.S. bank)... SAS pioneers first commercial polar route, Copenhagen to Los Angeles... Italy's Isveimer is founded as special investment bank to aid South's growth... Mariucci Mandelli opens two-room fashion atelier, Krizia, in Milan, financed by $200 loan on motorcycle (does $200 million in sales by 1988 with practical clothes for working women as one of Italy's leading designers)... Toshimine Kobayashi builds Japan's first superstore, combined supermarket and discount store, in Kyoto (by 1989 runs 300 in Japan while moving to boutiques, large shopping malls)...

After making antiaircraft guns during W.W. II and becoming one of four major suppliers to NTT in 1950s, Fujitsu is encouraged by MITI to build Japan's first computer (with support of MITI, works on mainframe computers and expands into semiconductor production in 1960s, spins off its FANUC unit, maker of industrial robots, in 1972, begins acquiring U.S.' Amdahl in 1972 for its computer technology, makes IBM compatible computers in 1974, forms venture with Siemens in 1978, ICL in 1981, unveils, two-year market lead, HEMT computer technology in 1980, makes it first super computer in 1982, is sued, 1985, by IBM for illegally copying its software, gets limited rights, 1988, from arbitrator to inspect, duplicate IBM's mainframe system and pays $833 million for past use of software and annual fee, opens research facility, one focus is on neuro computer technology to transfer human skills to a machine, in 1988, evolves by 1990 with plants in Spain, Ireland, Australia, Singapore, Malaysia, U.S., South Korea and R&D centers in U.K., U.S. and Spain, buys 80% of ICL, U.K.'s maker of mainframe computers, in 1990, is sued, 1991, by Texas Instrument for patent infringements)... KLM forms aerial photography and survey unit, first in 1921 (lists stock in NYSE in 1957, starts helicopter service for North Sea oil wells in 1965 and commuter service line for Holland in 1966)... Mitsubishi Trading, Mitsubishi Corp. in 1971, is reorganized by merger of three of old trading firms to become lead firm of Mitsubishi constellation of companies (forms Mitsubishi International in NYC in 1954 as exporting arm).

1955

General Events

U.S. tuna boats are seized by Ecuador, Chile and Peru for violating offshore 200-mile limit... Italy, West Germany, France form European Union... Rail line opens (February 28) between Hanoi, Beijing, Moscow, Berlin... Italian unemployment insurance covers lost wages for any under-40-hour work weeks... Britain plans to build 12 nuclear power stations... Scandinavian states form Nordic Council... London's Narinder Kapary develops first optical fibers... Austria regains (July 7) sovereignty... Britain's share of world trade is 19.8%, 8.7% in 1976... Deutsche Lufthansa resumes airline service... British aeronautical engineer, Christopher Cockerell, patents first practical hovercraft, independently developed by France's Bertin firm (after demonstration in 1959 across English Channel, is used commercially in 1963)... Military junta exiles (September 22) Peron from Argentina, returns to rule 1973-74... Israel discovers (September 23) oil... Japan's Liberty Democratic Party appears (governs until losing Parliamentary seats to Japanese Socialist Party, headed by woman, in 1989 from Recruit bribery scandal, farm policies and 3% consumption tax to increase savings)... Universal copyright convention goes into effect... Marshal N.A. Bulganin is new leader of U.S.S.R. (-1958, orders decentralization for agricultural planning)... Government, business create Japanese Productivity Center... Canada, U.S.S.R. sign (October 11) trade accord, grant most-favored status to each other... Annual planning for U.S.S.R. is assigned to State Economic Council, leaves long-range planning to Gosplan... Sweden adopts National Health Insurance... Soviet Union grants managers more authority to make decisions on production mix, amount of output, specifications for manpower needs, classification of manpower... Tank-supported marines seize (November 16) Buenos Aires labor headquarters... Chile requires profit sharing for all workers in copper industry... South African Coal, Oil and Gas Corp. is created to produce crude oil by coal gasification... Eight East-European Communist nations form Warsaw Pact... Jack Heginbotham, British railroad engine driver, is put in Coventry, condemned to ostracism and silence by his fellow mates, by union for violating its solidarity (commits suicide in 1956 from ordeal).

Business Events

Commercial television programs appear in Britain... Fashion designer Mary Quant, others start Bizarre boutique in London's Chelsea district... Mitsubishi Petrochemical is formed by Mitsubishi Group of Japan, Shell Petroleum... Unable to compete with big trading houses and banks, Hong Kong trader Y.K. Pao visits London to buy first ship (builds fleet of some 200 vessels by 1980 - world's largest privately-owned navy, acquires Hong Kong and Kowloon Wharf and Godown Co. in 1980, acquires 1925 British trading business of Wheelock Marden in 1985, is billionaire in 1988 with interests in real estate, hotels, banking and airline, Dragon-air only rival to Colony's line)... Vickers scraps plans, 80% finished, for advanced jet airliner when RAF, BOAC cannot fund development costs (cedes market to DC-8 on drawing board, Boeing's 707 in prototype)... Brazil's Minas Gerais industrial federation starts training program for industry, based on U.S. model... Dr. Inaba leads team of 500 engineers with Fujitsu's entry into factory automation, new venture called Fujitsu Fanuc in 1972 (licenses control, motors to Bulgaria in 1974 - later plant in Sofia, forms GMF Robotics with GM in 1981 to control 50% of world market by 1982, forms GE joint venture in 1987 to develop numerical controls)... Rolls-Royce is first British industrial firm to install a computer... Daimler-Benz starts U.S. plants to make trucks, buses... Guinness brewery issues popular Book of Records (in 1970s acquires hodgepodge of over 200 firms, after new CEO in 1981, sells 140 in two years, acquires U.K. newsstand chain, health spas, 7-11s, and Bell scotch in 1984, in 1991 buys Curzcompo, Spanish brewer, for $900 million to get 22% of beer market, seeks to buy Union Cervecera from Carlsberg for 28% of the market).

1956

General Events

Extensive mineral deposits are found in Siberia... First Pan-American Management Conference in Chile meets in Santiago (provides first management seminars, taught by U.S. instructors, for middle and top-level executives)... After abolishing alcohol rationing in 1955, Swedish report shows alcoholism, worker absenteeism up nearly 200%... USDA exhibit opens in Rome, spurs rise of supermarkets in country... Pope Pius XII: "The State ought not to try to take the place of private industry"... Britain ends (June 13) 74-year control of Suez Canal... To deter tax dodgers, Italian law requires all stock transactions be reported... U.S.-built kitchen gadgets are latest craze in Paris, sell for twice U.S. prices... European Productivity Agency sends researchers to U.S. universities to study business, economics, psychology, etc...U.S.S.R.-Yugoslav paper recognizes (June 20) different routes to Socialism... Poland's Poznan strike, crushed by military, leads to rise of workers' councils... When Hungary seeks to withdraw from Warsaw Pact, Soviet tanks crush revolution (becomes democratic republic in 1989)... John McCarthy designs Lisp computer language for artificial intelligence... John Osborne: "Look Back in Anger" (champions struggling working class in play)... At 20th Soviet Communist Party Conference, Secretary Nikita Khrushchev denounces Stalin... Japan joins UN... Britain raises bank interest rate to 5.5%, highest since 1932... Pollock, Weber: Revolution of the Robots... Richard Wooley, Britain's Astronomer Royal, views prospects of space travel as "utter bilge"... Transatlantic cable telephone service begins...

Belgian Industry-University Foundation is created as cooperative venture by industry, management centers at Universities of Brussels, Ghent, Liege, Louvain... Egypt nationalizes (July 26) Suez Canal Co. after U.S., Britain refuse aid to build Aswan Dam... Japanese law promotes domestic machine-tool industry while MITI encourages firms to set prices, allocate products and form cartels (exempts industry from 1947 Anti-Monopoly Law, restricts industry in 1960 to few firms, those with less than 5% of market to stop production in 1968, allows firms left in industry to form joint operations in 1971 and cartel in 1978 for U.S., Canadian markets - 3.7% of U.S. market in 1976 to 50.1% in 1981)... When Egypt nationalizes the Suez Canal, Israel, backed by Britain and France, invades (October 29) the Sinai (blocks, November, Suez Canal to stop oil deliveries to France and Britain, leads to demand for supertankers to by-pass canal)... Kenji Mizoguchi's film, "Street of Shame", leads to Japanese ban on prostitution... West Germany unions lobby to win shopping hours of 8 a.m. to 6:30 p.m. Monday-Friday, 7 a.m. to 2 p.m. Saturday.

Business Events

Holland's N.V. Philips forms Ergomics Group to adapt machines, equipment to workers (follows "human engineering" used by U.S. military)... After working with Dior, Paquin and Schiaparelli, Pierre Cardin, later designer of fashions and consumer products, opens Paris shop to sell men's clothing accessories (designs first gowns for women in 1957, after acquiring Maxim's of Paris opens 8th branch in NYC in 1985)... International Tin Council is formed as cartel by producers, buyers to control, stabilize world market (collapses in 1985 when non-council producers, i.e., Brazil, increase exports, drops rescue scheme in 1986 with inability of members to reach agreement on what to do and increasing use of substitutes)...

France's Lip Co. produces first commercial watch powered by battery... Fagor, cooperative firm in Spain's Basque area, starts making electrical domestic appliances (with 6,700 workers, 30% of total of area's 110 cooperatives, exports technology to 20 countries by 1988)... Yoshihisa Tabuchi, after graduating from Waseda University, joins Nomura Securities as salesman, CEO in 1985 after big break in 1980 as his new investment fund goes from $970 million to nearly $4.5 billion in two years (makes Nomura Japan's top brokerage house with 129 offices and 10,000 full-time employees, 2,500 part-time saleswomen sell financial products door-to-door, replaces Toyota as Japan's most profitable firm in 1987, enters global financial market in 1987 with Daiwa, Nikko and Yamaichi, funds from Japan's huge trade surpluses)...

After escaping Nazis, Ralph Reichmann reaches Canada to start tile-importing business, Olympia Floor & Tile, joined by parents and brothers, Albert and Paul, in stages (enter real estate market in 1960 to build warehouse - by 1963 Albert and Paul Toronto's biggest industrial developers, buy $20 million lot from bankrupt real estate magnate William Zeckendorf in 1965 - site for Canada's largest suburban office complex, form, Albert and Paul, York Developments and incorporate, family, as Olympia & York Developments, launch Canada's largest office-construction project, First Canadian Place, in 1974, enter U.S. market in 1977 with buy of 8 Manhattan office buildings for $320 million, enter stock market in 1979 to build $1.2 billion portfolio with interests in some of Canada's biggest firms, win development contract in 1980 to build NYC's Battery Park City and World Financial Center, buy Gulf Canada for $3 billion in 1985, fail to get Hiram Walker liquor business in 1986 to offset failing oil prices, play white knight in 1987 with quiet restructuring of Santa Fe oil, rail and real estate giant, take over London's huge Canary Wharf 71-acre development in 1988 to bet it will be Europe's new business center, run $8.4 billion empire, Olympia & York as largest owner of NYC commercial real estate, with over 60, 14 in NYC, U.S. office buildings and extensive holdings in Canada, in 1989, plan $210 million, 60-story office tower, city's tallest, for Moscow, lend Campeau $250 million in 1990 to rescue failing retailing empire, with $700 million stake, 38%, in Campeau Corp. lead bankruptcy recovery efforts in 1990)... Rockefeller interests form Fundo Crescinco, Brazil's first mutual fund, 1,400 investors in 1957 and 44,800 in 1963... "First" British launderette opens, Falmouth, for yachtsmen, crews of merchant ships needing fast service, some 10,000 in 1980s... Masatoshi Ito takes over family's Tokyo department store, begun in 1913 as clothing shop, to build Ito-Yokado as land's 2nd largest supermarket chain (is invited to U.S. in 1961 by NCR, seeks to replace traditional abacus with the cash register, and attend seminar on self-service retailing, by 1965 runs six superstores, low-priced food, clothing and household products, in high traffic areas of Tokyo, 140 by 1991, starts Famil, family-style restaurants with U.S., Chinese and Japanese food, chain, 323 by 1982, and follows with Denny's restaurants, 353 by 1991, starts York Mart supermarkets for areas unable to support superstore in 1975, 42 by 1991, gets rights in 1984 for Robinson's department stores, 2 by 1991, and in 1985 for Oshman's sporting goods stores, 2 by 1991, buys 58 7-Elevens in Hawaii in 1989)... Marks and Spencer starts "Operation Simplification" to reduce its paperwork (in 1970s acquires three Canadian chains, Peoples, general merchandise, D'Allairds, women's clothing, and Walter, clothing, in 1980s runs 281 stores in U.K., innovates using Technical Services unit to set rigid quality standards for suppliers, by eliminating timeclocks, customer receipts, refunds on returns, and stock-order forms, by using sales force for market research and by requiring executives to work on sales floor a certain number of hours/month, issues its charge card in 1985, enters U.S. in 1988 to buy New Jersey's King Super Markets).

1957

General Events

Regular air service begins between London, Moscow... 71 cities in world have over one million inhabitants each, 16 in 1914... Egypt nationalizes (January 15) French, British banks... U.S.S.R. launches first earth satellites in space... International Atomic Energy Agency forms... France, West Germany, Italy, Luxembourg, Belgium, and Holland form (March 25) European Common Market, Britain, Ireland and Denmark join 1972-73, Greece 1979-81, and Spain, Portugal in 1985-86 (plans world's largest integrated market in 1992)... China launches "anti-rightist" campaign to purge society of resistance to reforms... Nikita Khrushchev, first secretary of Communist Party's Central Committee, plans sweeping reorganization of industrial production (divides industry into 92 regions to decentralize, 3 in 1932 and 30 in 1956)... Cairo University forms institute of business administration... C. Northcote Parkinson: Parkinson's Law and Other Studies in Administration... Malaya is independent republic with Singapore as self-governing state in 1959, nation in 1965... Ghana, former British colony, is first of 48 states in Africa to win its independence... Britain encourages aircraft industry to reorganize in specialized groups... Europe adopts Common Agricultural Policy.

Business Events

One of first U.S.-style supermarkets in Eastern Europe opens in Zagreb, Yugoslavia... Fiat enters U.S. auto market (leaves 1983)... By 1967 U.S. ad firms acquire 32 British agencies... Nestle Alimentana creates international Management Development Institute, IMEDE, in Switzerland to provide programs for middle, top-level managers (affiliates with local universities in Geneva)... Britain's Ralph Coverdale starts training program with planned experiences and teamwork building, used by organizations for management development... Isao Nakauchi starts Daiei retailing business (evolves by 1980s as Japan's largest retailer with 174 self-service super stores)... With death of Christian Dior, Algerian-born Yves Saint Laurent is designer for fashion house (shows first collection in 1958, after being drafted for military service and replaced by Marc Bohan opens own fashion house in 1962, shows pants for women in 1967 collection, operates over $100-million business in 1973 - couture a loss of $1 million, ready-to-wear earns $15 million, three fragrances over $10 million and men's clothes at $20 million, grants 100 licenses, Dior with 130 and Cardin with 285)... After exporting to local firm in 1919, Coca-Cola forms Japanese subsidiary (introduces Georgia canned coffee in 1975 - later adds Aquarius sports drink and Mone, honey and lemon drink, with over 700,000 vending machines wins 92% of cola market by 1990)... Pearson business buys Financial Times paper and 50% of Economist magazine (gets 54% of Chateau Latour wine in 1963 - sold 1988, buys 56% of Longman publishing - rest 1982, acquires Penguin Books and Royal Doulton china in 1971, then Madame Toussaud's museum in 1978, fights off, 1986, takeover scare of Hutchison Whampoa, in 1988-89 sells oil production business and buys French financial paper and 22.2% of Elsevier publishing, buys, 1990, U.S.' Cuisenaire, teaching materials, to operate in six areas: periodicals, book publishers, entertainment, investment banking, oil services, fine china)... After being split into 10 distinct West German institutions, forced to close its East German branches and stripped of its overseas operations by Allies in 1945, Deutsche–Bank is reassembled from its West German parts (by 1970 grows from 345 to 1,100 branches, in 1969 launches Eurochecks, good anywhere in Western Europe, to combat U.S. credit cards)... Accounting firms of Coopers, formed in U.K. in 1854 to open offices in Brussels, 1925, NYC 1926, and Paris, 1930, and merge with three others after W.W. II, and Lybrand, started 1898 to gain reputation for auditing and add offices in Berlin, 1924-1938, Paris, 1926, and London, 1929, merge, named Coopers & Lybrand in 1973 (agrees in 1990 to accept, admits no guilt, penalties for 1986 audit of failed Denver-based Silverado Banking, is world's 5th largest in 1991).

1958

General Events

Holland nationalizes (January 3) banking... International Institute for Strategic Studies forms in Brighton... Canada adopts hospital care for all... London installs first parking meters... Benelux countries abolish (February 3) 97% of internal trade curbs... Mao Tse-Tung launches "Great Leap Forward" to industrialize China with People's Communes in countryside (increases collectivization to eliminate mutual aid teams and co-operatives of 1950s land reform, fails to stimulate industrial growth)... Egypt, Syria form United Arab Republic (-1961)... Pope John XXIII heads Catholic Church (-1963)... France is crippled (April 1) by 24-hour strike of public workers... Oil-rich Venezuela establishes stable democracy (after squandering wealth from 1970s oil bonanza, is rent in 1989 by mobs opposing Government's 89% rise in gas prices, hikes in bus fares)... Poland declares (April 14) strikes illegal, unions put under Party rule... A.K. Rice, Tavistock Institute of Human Relations: <u>Productivity and Social Organization: The Ahmedabad Experiment</u> (reports research started during W.W. II on sociotechnical systems)... Brussels hosts World Exhibition... U.S.S.R. allows (June 24) ILO to study Soviet labor practices... Instituto De Estudios Superiores De La Empresa business school opens in Barcelona, one of Europe's largest by 1988... Japan launches (December 6) world's largest oil tanker, one million barrels, at Kure... British fashion designer Mary Quant lifts skirts above knees, mini hemline by Andre Courreges in 1964.

Business Events

BOAC begins first transatlantic jet passenger service from London to New York, Pan American later in year with daily service for NYC-Paris... After starting only successful British ad office in U.S. in 1948, Britain's S.H. Benson ad agency opens first subsidiary in Kenya to serve clients, by 1960 adds offices in India, Malaya, Australia and Canada (acquires agencies in Spain, France and Germany in 1967, is sold in 1972-73 to U.S.' Ogilvy & Mather)... Chicken ramen, world's first instant noodles, appears, 130 million packages sold by 1989 (leads to first "cup of noodles" in 1971, 378 kinds with self-heating Hot Line foods in 1988, Super Boil noodles in 1989)... After working as police reporter, Maurico de Sovsa starts comic strip, one of Brazil's hottest in comic-publishing with staff of some 200 artists by 1988 and licensed products... Vatican sells 40% of Ares Serono Holding to financier Michele Sindona (is controlled, after owner and Sindona sell out, by Fabio Bertarelli, son of former CEO, to become billionaire by 1988 as Italy's leading producer of natural drugs)...

After first job as porter in 1936 with Sotheby's, London art-auction house, Peter C. Wilson is CEO (-1980, sells seven French Impressionist paintings in 1958, over twice what anyone expected, to start dominance of major auction houses over dealers in selling art, opens offices in Europe, Asia and Latin America, buys NYC's Parke Bernet Galleries, U.S.'s largest art auctioneers, in 1964 to become world's largest, uses television satellite in 1965 in first auction to link NYC and London, goes public in 1977)... After hawking used furniture, sporting goods at family's British Columbia store, Dave Ritchie holds first auction to raise cash to repay bank loan, by 1990 auctions $450 million of equipment/year... Three years after landing in U.S. from Naples, Sbarro family opens Brooklyn deli, 136 shops in 1985 and 306, plus first European unit, by 1990 for sales of $149 million.

1959

General Events

Fidel Castro seizes (January 1) power in Cuba... U.S.S.R. uses installment plan to purchase certain goods... Buenos Aires transport workers start (January 19) general strike... Canada opens two offices in U.S. to promote immigration... First section of London-Birmingham M-1 Motorway opens for traffic... Soviets agree (February 7) to help with China's industrialization... Castro demands (April 3) U.S. restore Cuba's sugar quota... A. Dannevig, Norwegian fisheries inspector, attributes decline of fish to rise of water acidity (is independently reported by E. Gordon, Canadian ecologist, that acid precipitation could affect bedrock, soil and lakes)... Left-wing Gaullists form (April 14) Democratic Work Union... Arab nations hold (April 16) first oil conference... Yasir Arafat forms Al Fatah organization (heads PLO in 1969, is seen by Arab leaders in 1974 as sole speaker for Palestinians)... St. Lawrence Seaway, $500 million project, opens (April 25) to allow ocean vessels in Great Lakes... U.S. exhibitors demonstrate model all-electric kitchen in Moscow show... Italian law makes Government responsible for minimum economic standards, to incorporate national collective agreements as law... Jan Tinbergen: "The Theory of the Optimum Regime" (notes convergence of industrial societies)...

Cuba takes over (May 18) U.S. sugar mills... Large natural gas field is found in North Sea off coast of Holland, first major oil strike in 1969... Soviet Union shifts emphasis of enterprise incentives for managers from gross output to costs... Cuba nationalizes (May 23) seven airlines... Oil is discovered in Kingdom of Libya... Seven States of French West Africa form customs union... Soviet Union reduces work week for engineers from 45 to 42 hours... Cuba seizes (June 25) 2.35 million acres for land reform... Brazil, Argentina, Bolivia, Chile, Paraguay, Peru and Uruguay form free trade zone... 68 World Bank nations approve (October 1) new International Development Assn... West Germany opens (October 27) Volkswagen to private ownership... France drops (November 5) 200 import curbs... Japan's MITI raises trade barriers to protect land's new computer industry.

Business Events

Les Halles, Paris' central wholesale market for over 800 years, moves to new location... Basque priest advises Spanish workers in Mondragon area to form co-op (evolves by 1980s as enterprise of 80 commercial, industrial ventures with nearly 20,000 employees)... Metra International appears in Paris as management and research consulting business... European Conference on Personnel Administration meets... Matsushita electrical concern forms three-member Executive Council to make all major decisions, one responsible for short-term tactics and domestic business, one responsible for finance, accounting and international operations, and K. Matsushita to formulate long-term strategy... Britain's Allied Suppliers is formed by Home and Colonial Stores, Liptons, Meadow Dairy Co., Perarks Dairies, and Maypole Dairy... Small group of Europeans and Americans, including actor William Holden, start exclusive resort of Mt. Kenya Safari Club (is acquired 1967 by Khoshoggi as birthday gift for son, is sold 1986 to Rowland to raise money for financial difficulties)...

Pepsi-Cola licenses U.S.S.R. to sell its soft drinks in Soviet Union, 25 Soviet-owned bottling plants by 1989 (swaps syrup in 1972 to sell Soviet vodka in U.S. - handles obsolete Soviet submarines in 1989, negotiates in 1986 for Pizza Hut joint venture in U.S.S.R., inks $3 billion pact in 1990 to expand plants to 50, swaps syrup for vodka and merchant ships as ruble not easily convertible)... Swissair provides meal service with 36 specialties to first, deluxe class passengers... De Beers makes synthetic diamonds... Norway's Jacob Stolt-Nielsen, grandfather bought first ship in 1891, launches Parcel Tankers to carry 58 different liquids at once, 60 ships, 25% of world's fleet, by 1988... With $2 million from Arab Bank, Munib Al-Masri starts Engineering & Development Group, one of first in Middle East to explore for water with geological mapping (gets sales of $150 million in late 1970s, gives over $1 million/year to Palestine causes)... Geoffrey Crowther is CEO of Trust House hotel chain, Britain's largest hotel group (-1971, starts chain of motor-hotels in provinces and London, by 1970, as largest caterer, runs 203 hotels in U.K., Ireland, and 21 abroad as well as restaurants, motorway service cafes, amusement arcades and cigarette kiosks as Trusthouse Forte, battles to take over London's exclusive Savoy hotel chain, with Connaught and Claridge's, in 1988)...

After working as "washy-washy boy" for U.S. artillery unit during Korean war, age 12, working as Seoul factory janitor, age 14, to manage two stores and factory, Baik Sung-Hak, age 19, starts business making hats, by 1990 is one of richest in South Korea with 3,800 people at 19 plants in 5 countries, including U.S., to gross $85 million from plastics, corrugated boxes and baseball caps... Paris Chamber of Commerce, assisted by Harvard and sponsored by European Productivity Agency and International Chamber of Commerce, founds premier business school, Institut Europeen D'Administration Des Affaires, INSEAD, in Fontainebleau... After argument over treatment of employees with research director of Shofu Industries, maker of ceramic insulators, Kazuo Inamori, 27-year old chemical engineer, starts Kyoto Ceramics, Kyocera with 1989 sales of $2.5 billion as dominant producer, 64% of global market with focus on quality and service, in high-tech ceramics, with seven friends, $40,000 (opens first U.S. plant in 1969 - later Mexico and Brazil, buys ailing Yashica for optical, metal- machining technologies in 1983, is named by Nikkei Business in 1983 as Japan's most effective manager - well-disciplined army with workers formed in "amoebas" as flexible, relatively autonomous teams to form, dissolve for needs of projects, forms $100 million foundation in 1984 to award innovators missed by Nobel prizes, adds 8 plants in Western Europe in 1989, is most admired by 1989 poll of Japanese executives for entrepreneurship and technological progress - 90% of products from own R&D of $100 million/year).

1960

General Events

France devalues (January 1) franc... Guatemala, El Salvador, Honduras, Costa Rica and Nicaragua form Central American Common Market... Belgium, Japan, Norway, South Africa, U.S. and Britain declare Antarctica a "scientific preserve"... In 1960s Christel Kuemmerer, West Germany, proposes flextime to recruit housewives, mothers into labor market... Cuba puts (February 21) all industry under government control... With oil priced at $1.80/barrel, Saudi Arabia, Iran, Iraq, Kuwait, and Venezuela form Organization of Petroleum Exporting Countries, OPEC, as oil cartel (negotiates with oil firms in 1964 for greater share of profits, starts oil boycott in 1967 after Six Day war, sets oil price/barrel at $2.18, stops shipping oil to U.S. in 1973 after Yom Kippur War, puts price of oil/barrel in 1974 at $10.95, $14.59 in 1979, $35 in 1981)... Cuba seizes (June 29) Texaco's oil refinery... Belgium grants (June 30) Congo independence... By 1962 Singapore increases its manufacturing base to 605 factories with 28,642 employees, over 2,400 plants employing some 280,000 workers in 1977)...

With funds from Rockefeller and Ford Foundations, Rice Institute, "first" international center for agriculture research, is started at Los Banos, Philippines (develops new strain in 1968 to increase rice productivity of Third World lands)... France grants some 40,000 patents during year, only 16,000 to French citizens... Cuba nationalizes (August 7) all U.S. property, follows U.S.' cut in sugar imports by 95%... After working in North China since 1920s and Philippines after W.W. II to improve lot of peasants with educational, cooperative work, health and political programs, Jimmy Yen, viewed by scholars and scientists as one of 10 "modern revolutionaries," forms Institute of Rural Reconstruction to train teams from Third World countries to better the life of their communities... Mexico nationalizes (September 27) all utilities... UN admits (September 30)

15 new African nations... With $100, missionary Bruce Olson, age 19, joins Stone Age Indian tribe with epidemic diseases in Colombian jungle (by 1988 creates 10 health centers, 16 agricultural programs, 8 cooperative trading posts and 12 bilingual schools, all staffed by Motilones)... Col. Joseph Mobotu seizes power of Congo, Zaire in 1971 (is president in 1970, with drop in world copper prices in mid-1970s causing economic problems heads government system of Kleptocracy with graft top to bottom)... Britain, Sweden, Norway, Denmark, Switzerland, Austria and Portugal form European Free Trade Assn. (drops almost all customs duties by 1966)... Peter Sellers stars in film "I'm All Right, Jack" (satires idleness of British welfare state)... Cuba nationalizes (October 14) banks, major companies... Belgian Socialists lead (December 29) strike against government prosperity plan.

Business Events

W. Brown: Explorations in Management... N.V. Philips starts job enrichment program for assembly workers, followed in 1966 by Texas Instruments and 1967 by Oslo's Norsk Hydro... Mitsui Polychemical is formed by Mitsui Group with DuPont technology... British Aircraft Corp. is formed by merger of Bristol Aircraft, English Electric, Hunting Aircraft (maintains profitable operation until nationalized with Hawker-Siddeley in 1977 to form British Aerospace)... Marisa Bellisario, first woman to head major Italian company, is hired by Olivetti as program analyst (heads Olivetti Corp. of America in 1979, is CEO of Italtel Telecommunications in 1981, transforms deficit-ridden giant into profitable operation by slashing costs and changing traditional manufacturing activities to electronics)... Italian employers form Intersind to represent their interests in collective bargaining, joins bargaining groups of Central Confederation of Italian Industry, General Confederation of Italian Agriculture, and Italian General Confederation of Commerce... Department store chain of Marui Co. issues first Japanese credit cards...

Olivetti & Co., world leader in stylish office machines, rescues financially-troubled U.S. Underwood Corp. (after losing some $50 million on Underwood and ailing computer business, is saved in 1964 by syndicate of Fiat, Pirelli, several financial institutions)... While visiting U.S. in 1960s, Otto Beisheim, Swiss-based multi-billionaire by 1989 with department store chain in 14 countries and interests in office equipment, etc., discovers "cash and carry" (is first to introduce system to Europe, an instant hit)... Funded by industry, Foundation for Management begins projects at Bristol, Cambridge, Leeds Universities (recommends business schools for London, Manchester in 1963, leads to Council of Industry for Management Education in 1967)... After apprenticeship at two Paris fashion houses, Valentino achieves success with first show in Rome, becomes Italy's leading designer... S.S. France is launched, converted to Norwegian cruise ship later... ICI adopts organizational development to manage change (-1983)... U.S.' Charles F. Feeney, Robert W. Miller start Duty-Free Shoppers in Hong Kong for Japanese tourists, billionaires by 1989... Two wealthy Texans open exclusive Tiger Tops game lodge in Nepal in 1960s, visited by some 8,000/year in 1980s... Italy's leading high-tech Selenia firm forms joint venture with Raytheon to make air control equipment, with nearly 25% of market runs 9 firms, 13,000 employees, to show annual sales of some $1.2 billion by 1988... By 1990 Sicilian Mafia, "the Octopus", evolves to control global $160 billion heroin market...

Over 12 U.S. firms and many in Europe claim rights to 278 polypropylene-related patents... Lawyer Mark McCormack opens office, International Management Group global in 1990 with 1,000 people in 43 offices in 20 countries, to represent golfer Arnold Palmer (builds him a financial empire by 1991 with two aviation agencies, golf design business - 40 courses under construction, six car dealerships, and golf management firm, 300 employees, for 15 resorts and golf courses worldwide), soon gets Jack Nicklaus, leaves 1970, and Gary Player as clients to handle golf's Big Three (opens London office in 1960 - 10 European countries, Budapest in 1988, by 1990, shows sales of $25 million in 1975 - over $700 million in 1990 with client management 29%, television and films 28%, corporate marketing, i.e., Nobel Foundation, Mayo Clinic and Ringling Bros., 23%, and event management, i.e., Pope's 1982 tour of British Isles, 20%, in 1987 buys Nick Bolletieri's Tennis Academy for some $8 million in vertical integration and firm of baseball agents later in horizontal growth out of golf and racquet sports)... Jorge Martinez builds Grupo Sidek in Guadalajara, Mexico, with steel mill, $300 million conglomerate by 1990 (-1969, plans $1.1 billion development, 1,250 acres, for Puerto Vallarta in 1986).

1961

General Events

Britain drops (January 1) farthing as legal tender... U.S.S.R. trade fair opens in London... Moscow approves (January 18) Khrushchev's plan for agricultural decentralization... Organization for Economic Cooperation and Development forms to encourage world trade, aid underdeveloped countries (supersedes Organization for European Economic Cooperation formed under Marshall Plan in 1948)... Argentina, Bolivia, Brazil, Chile, Colombia, Ecuador, Mexico, Paraguay, Peru, Uruguay and Venezuela form (February 18) Latin American Free Trade Assn., followed by Caribbean Common Market in 1973...Albania breaks with Soviet Union, allies with China (adopts rigid isolationist foreign policy in 1978, opens in 1989-90)... Roald Sagdeyed helps form Science City as informal think tank in Siberia (heads floundering space program in 1973 and Superconducting Institute in mid-1980s)... South Africa quits (March 15) British Commonwealth... Pope John XXIII: Mater et Magistra (discusses social injustice, opposes materialism, urges more participation by workers in industry decisions)...

United Nations General Assembly condemns Apartheid... Cuba joins (May 1) Communist bloc... France designs first supersonic jet with cruising speed of 1,450 mph... West Germany revalues mark to stimulate trade (causes shift of short-term funds from London, New York to West Germany)... China reverses policy to stress pragmatism in economy... 125 nations ratify treaty to ban production, possession of cocaine (allows Peru's National Cocoa Enterprise to distribute pharmaceutical cocaine)... Britain drops (June 19) protectorate over oil-rich Kuwait... India outlaws traditional dowry custom, continues as some parents of brides incur lifetime debt (leads to sex-selection clinics as big business)... German drug Thalidomide starts scandal by causing birth defects, perhaps 20,000 in 20 countries throughout Europe... East Germany puts up (August 8) Berlin Wall to stem flow of refugees to West, some 144,000 in 1959 and 199,000 in 1960 for total of 3 million from 1949 (reopens in 1989 with democratic reforms)... Burma is (August 8) world's first Buddhist Republic... New British "Red Brick" universities are established at Sussex and Essex, 14 more by 1966...

Tanganyika Conference meets to preserve African wildlife... Britain's Ministry of Education starts management studies program via Technical Colleges of Advanced Technologies at six universities, postgraduate management programs by seven universities in 1963... Khrushchev assures world that U.S.S.R.'s economy will overtake U.S.' by 1970... Tanganyika gets independence (forms United Republic of Tanzania with Zanzibar in 1964, uses extended family system as basis for some 8,000 cooperative villages in 1967 with all crops bought, distributed by government and all major industries operated by state-owned companies)... EEC admits (December 7) 18 African nations as associates...Sofreto, French Society for the Study and Realization of Urban Transport, forms in Paris to sell technology developed by City's Metro system (evolves to design, build subways worldwide)... Portugal's Goa, acquired 1510, is retaken by India... Soviet Union's Yuri Gagarin is first man in space, followed by U.S.' Alan Shepherd.

Business Events

Famous Isle of Man Tourist Trophy event for motorcycles is won for first time by Honda, provides prototype for new machines (causes demise of Britain's BSA in 1973, Norton in 1976, Triumph in 1983)... Hitachi starts advanced management program, uses GE's program as model (starts program in 1964 for middle-managers)... Joan Woodward, pioneer of contingency management in 1950s: Industrial Organization... In this time 21 branches of U.S. banks operate in European centers, over 100 by 1971 (leads to expansion of English, French banks overseas, mostly in colonial markets)... Katanga hires Col. Michael, "Mad Mike," Hoare as mercenary during Congo conflict, pioneers use of mercenaries in Africa (gets death sentence in 1982 by South Africa for unsuccessful attempt to overthrow Communist government of Seychelles)... Tom Burns, G.M. Stalker: The Management of Innovation (studies mechanistic, organic organizational structures)... After discovering group in Liverpool club, record store manager starts promoting Beatles (-1970 as world's best-selling recording group after U.S. debut in 1964)... Some 25 farm families from San Joaquin Valley, CA, begin move to Australia's Outback near Queensland border to launch land's cotton industry, world's 10th largest producer in mid-1980s with 1.1 million bales... Damri Darakananda, 55, starts joint venture in Thailand with Japan's YKK to make zippers (after expanding into thread, buttons and plastic items, buys out YKK as Saha-Union, diversifies from textiles to Nike shoes, IBM computers, and Computerland franchise)... After serving as Rhodesia agent for British mining company and investing in farms, car dealerships, and mines, Rowland "Tiny" Rowland rescues London & Rhodesian Mining Co., Lonrho (by 1987 builds $4.7 billion conglomerate with variety of 800 companies in Britain, France, Ghana, Kenya, North America, Pacific Basin, South Africa, Zambia, and Zimbabwe, despite public opinion acquires South Africa's Western Platinum for $75 million)...

New Zealand raider Ronald A. Brierly folds financial tip sheet to raise $40,000 from subscribers to launch investment business, spans four continents with assets of $7 billion by 1986 via three Hong Kong holding companies (gets Higbee Co., Cleveland-based department store chain, for $70 million in 1984 as first major U.S. acquisition, U.S. investments total some $600 million and 70 enterprises by 1987, blotches 1990 investment in Cummins Engine to face racketeering charges)... Japan Credit Bureau, owned by financial firms and big banks, starts credit-card business, controls 39% of Japan's market and does business in over 100 countries by 1990 (enters U.S. market in 1990)... Group Koike, formed as Japan's first industrial design firm in early 1950s, styles classic bottle for Kikkoman soy sauce (by 1990 is Japan's No. 1 with nearly 300 employees, sales of $30 million)... Bass brewing business, U.K.'s largest in 1990s, merges with regional brewer (merges with Charrington United, Carling Black Label lager and pubs, in 1967 to form nationwide network of breweries and pubs - 25% market share by 1970, starts Crest Hotel chain in 1969, acquires Coral Leisure, hotels and gambling, in 1980, adds Horizon Travel with packaged holidays in 1987, acquires all of North American Holiday Inns in 1987-1990 for $2.23 billion - spins off Holiday Inns' Harrah's casino business, acquired 1979, and Embassy Suites, so named 1984, as Promus Companies, in 1990 sells Alexis Lichine wines to begin $1 billion renovation of Holiday Inns and plans to dispose of over 3,000 pubs to placate government)... Caledonian Airways, Scotland, begins service (buys British United Airways, a merger of eight lines in 1960, in 1970 to form British Caledonian in 1971).

1962

General Events

Saskatchewan, Canada, starts first community medicare program in North America... China, Albania sign (January 13) accord for economic cooperation... Carl A. Petri: Communication with Automata (introduces new modeling technique as means for conceptualizing systems of dynamic logic, diagrammed by A.W. Holt as "Petrie Nets")... E. Liberman: "The Plan, Profits and Bonuses," Pravda (urges less bureaucratic planning and controls for U.S.S.R., advocates profit sharing for workers and managers, is adopted by some 243 enterprises, including tea and tobacco industries employing some one million workers, is opposed in 1964 by Soviet Finance Ministry as capitalistic)... African Nations form (June 17) Common Market... Pope John XXIII opens 2nd Vatican Council (-1965, ends ban on eating of meat on Fridays, lets nuns wear secular clothing, introduces power sharing by Pope and bishops, encourages orders to re-examine traditions)... Khrushchev advocates foreign experience in management research, training and practice be studied and applied where possible in report to Communist Party Plenum... After 132 years of French colonial rule, Algeria wins (July 3) independence... Britain, France start Concorde supersonic jet project, begin tests in 1965 and commercial service in 1976... After 307 years as British possession, Jamaica is (July 6) independent... Royal Canadian Air Force Exercise Plan for Physical Fitness pioneers aerobics... Khrushchev splits Communist Party into separate industrial and agricultural branches for more efficiency (after weakening authority of local party barons, loses power in 1964 when Party, army and secret police oust him)... Britain licenses betting shops... Ahmed Zaki Yamani is made Saudi Minister of Petroleum by King Faisal (after leading OPEC to broker oil prices in 1973, is fired 1986)... Joaquin Hernandez Galicia, "La Quina," is untouchable leader of Mexico's powerful oil workers' union, some 200,000 members (after extravagant living, is arrested, three underlings jailed for various crimes, in 1989 for arms smuggling, murder of federal agent in government crackdown on corruption)... U.S.S.R. plans (August 7) gradual end to one-family houses in urban areas... With reorganization of earlier post-war group, Italy creates EFIM, 3rd largest state-owned enterprise by 1988 with sales of $3.9 billion from transportation, aircraft, defense projects, aluminum, glass, plant engineering... Brazil seizes (October 16) its U.S. phone system... Cuba is barred from buying U.S. cars (leads to Havana selling antique cars to tourists in late 1980s for hard currency)... Japan builds commercial airliner, YS-11 a flop.

Business Events

Steve Shirley starts F. International computer consulting business (operates ad hoc organizational structure by 1985 with over 1,000 free lance consultants in Britain, Holland and Denmark)... Brenninkmeyer family, owners of Dutch retailing empire, acquires NYC apparel store Ohrbachs, followed in 1970s by acquisitions of U.S.' A&P, Grand Union, Gimbel Bros., and F.A.O. Schwarz by other European firms... Rolling Stones, English rock group featuring Mick Jagger and Keith Richards, forms (records 39 hit albums by 1989 as leader in business)... Mitsui & Co. joins U.S., Australian interests to start Australian coal venture, other joint projects in 1966, 1968 to mine iron ore in Australia... U.S.' Unimation produces world's first industrial robot... After flogging Caribbean records from car in British inner cities, Chris Blackwell launches Island Records business, first hit in 1964 with Reggae tune (sells $200 million music production and publishing empire, world's largest independent, to London's PolyGram, owned by Philips as world's No. 3 with sales of $1.7 billion, in fight for global market with Sony, No. 1, and Warner Communications, No. 2)... After fleeing Hong Kong in 1941 to island and acquiring interests in Hong Kong real estate and Macao trading firms in gold, toys and textiles, Stanley Ho wins Macao's gambling monopoly (develops gambling business by 1987 to account for 45% of Island's budget, 20% of GNP, and employment of 420,000).

1963

General Events

National referendum approves Shah's "White Revolution" in Iran to provide land reform, women's rights and secular education (after opposition banishes Islamic cleric Ayatollah Khomeini 16 months later)... France bars (January 14) Britain from Common Market, again 1968... Tsukuba Science City evolves some 37 miles from Tokyo (provides site for some 50 government, private research agencies with over 8,000 scientists)... Volunteers of U.S. Peace Corps visit Kuna Indian village on Panama's San Blas islands (-1971, revive traditional handicraft of poor women with Cooperative de Productos de Mola, successful cottage industry of 200 women making native garments for export, tourists)... Pope John XXIII: Pacem in Terris (insists on human rights to basic education, just wage, safe working conditions, social security and insurance, private property and "food, clothing, shelter, rest, medical care, and necessary social services")... A.K. Rice: The Enterprise and its Environment... Malaya, Singapore, Sarawak, North Borneo form (September 16) Malaysia... Organization of African Unity is formed by 32 nations... Norway's Labor Party Government of 28 years is replaced by coalition of non-socialist parties... Indonesia takes over (September 20) all British firms... Friction welding is invented... U.S.S.R.'s Ekonomicheskaya Gazeta sponsors informal management development programs for top enterprise executives (leads to creation of "Business Clubs")... Ludwig Erhard, father of West Germany's 'economic miracle' 1949-57, is chancellor (-1966)... Leningrad Public Institute for Social Research is formed to study socio-psychological problems resulting from technological innovations... Soviet delegation studies educational program of Harvard Business School... Argentina voids (November 11) all foreign oil contracts... African countries form development bank with $250 million... Soviet Union's industrial system reorganizes as 47 regional councils... Renault grants four-week paid vacations in labor contracts to some 65,000 workers, established normal pattern in 1953 with three-week paid vacations... Kenya gets (December 12) independence.

Business Events

Hilton Hotel opens on Park Lane, London's first high-rise building... Palestinian Izzedin Aryan opens pharmacy in Jordan to sell drugs, mostly from U.S., Europe (evolves by 1989 as head of Balsam Pharmaceutical, West Bank's largest drug manufacturer)... Philips demonstrates first audio cassette at Berlin's Radio TV Exhibition... Of those employed in German manufacturing 6.2% work in firms under 10 employees, 2.1% for Britain, 2.4% for U.S., 8.7% for Benelux, 10.8% for France, 18.5% for Italy... Building on research of Makoto Kikuehi (joins Sony in 1974 as head of R&D) at MIT, IBM discovers basic principle of microwave communications... After developing White Greeting Cards, James Hanson and Gordon White sell successful business (merge their Wiles Group with family interests to form Hanson Trust in 1964 to buy and sell firms, start independent Hanson Industries in U.S., White as CEO, in 1973 while Trust acquires variety of 24 firms, sales over $120 million, by 1979, by 1989 run $12.5 billion empire, U.K.'s 7th largest group with array of some 175 firms).

1964

General Events

Otto Wichterle produces first soft contact lenses, Czechoslovakia... Government, industrialists and public officials form Japan's Cooperative Consultation Committee of the Association of Petrochemical Industries to give guidance to MITI... Conservative Ian Smith is Prime Minister of Rhodesia (declares unilateral independence from Britain in 1965, forms republic in 1970, accepts biracial government in 1978)... Britain, France agree (February 6) to build channel tunnel... Soviet Union's Council for Complex Problems of Cybernetics forms section on Theoretical Questions of Organization (issues first book, Organization and Management, in 1968)... European Coal and Steel Community, Euratom join (February 25) EEC... Japan builds world's longest tunnel, 33.5 miles between islands of Honshu, Hokkaido (-1985 for some $2.8 billion, three times original estimate, projects losses of some $26 million/year)... Britain grants licenses to drill for oil, gas in North Sea... Peru passes Agrarian Reform Law, Chile in 1967... Leonid Brezhnev replaces (October 17) Khrushchev as first Secretary of U.S.S.R.'s Communist Party (-1982, leads to revelations of organized crime in 1988 trial)...

Jacques Ellul: The Technological Society (views technology as Frankenstein monster)... North Rhodesia becomes (October 24) Republic of Zambia, ends 73 years of British rule... Intelsat forms to manage, coordinate global satellite communications for 11-member nations, 114 countries and 13 satellites in 1987... First bullet train begins 4-hour service, 6.5 hours usual, between Tokyo and Osaka, some 2.7 billion passengers by 1989 with one fatal accident... Marshall McLuhan: Understanding Media (notes new technological age forming global village with new morals)... U.S. industrialist Edward Lamb visits U.S.S.R. (informs leadership on management science and education, leads, in 1965, to departments in 18 universities to develop organizers of industrial production and agreement with MIT to collaborate on management education programs)... Palestine Liberation Organization, PLO, forms at Arab League meeting in Cairo... Vatican drops (November 23) Latin as official language of Roman Catholic liturgy... Japan drops ban on ordinary citizens taking vacations abroad, some 5.5 million annually to spend $11 billion by 1989... Eleven nations offer (November 25) $3 billion to save British pound... East Germany starts mass-producing Trabant cars with Duraplast bodies, motorcycle-size two-stroke engines (joins with Volkswagen in 1990 for new model to replace lemons).

Business Events

Horst-Dieter Esch, 20-year-old son of welder, visits U.S. to study, work (after returning to West Germany starts construction business, by 1982 industry's 3rd largest with connections to GM, Saudi Arabia and English engineering group)... Hattori Seiko Co. is official timer for Tokyo Olympics (introduces Quartz watches in 1969, enters U.S. market in 1970, by 1980s is world's largest seller of timepieces)... Britain's Hardy Amies, France's Cardin are first to show men's clothing with designer label... London's Windmill Theater, site for non-stop vaudeville since 1930s, closes... Radio Caroline, first offshore pirate station, starts commercial radio broadcasting to compete with BBC (-1969)... German, Belgian firms form Agfa-Gevaert photography business as joint venture... Virginia-based ILM Corp. starts Jamaican subsidiary to do its data processing, followed in 1981 by Pacific Data Services, Dallas, to subcontract computer work to data centers in China and by Caribbean Data Services of American Airlines to process passenger information on Barbados... Chicago's Libby, McNeill & Libby opens Europe's largest cannery in Vauvert, France (is accepted after initial resistance by farmers, unions to invasion by "American giant")...

Japan Export Overseas Pearl Producers' Assn. forms legal cartel (handles almost all of world's South Sea pearls)... After wandering around Europe working as artist, cartoonist and actor, Brooklyn-born Bob Guccione starts Penthouse magazine with borrowed $150,000 and credit from printer and paper manufacturer, abetted by publicity of British postal officials (sells some 235,000 copies of first issue - success with sophisticated eroticism in showing pubic hair, couples to out-do Playboy, opens London Penthouse Club and invades U.S. market in 1969, launches Viva in 1973 as pornographic Cosmopolitan for women - losses of some $3 million by 1975, claims circulation of 3.7 million in 1975 - 4 million in 1982)... After raids in late-1950s by U.S. search firms pirating talent for U.S. multi-nationals, Egon Zehnder International, pioneering European headhunter, appears in Zurich (with 67 partners is No. 1 in Europe with revenues of $55 million by 1990, No. 3 in world, $80 million, after Korn/Ferry $103.3 million, and Russell Reynolds, $85 million, leads to Tamas Toth's Budapest subsidiary of Vienna's H. Neumann International in 1989 - 1990 joint venture with NYC headhunter)...

Despite opposition of MITI, Honda starts making cars (opens first U.S. plant in 1982, 4th largest car maker in Japan in 1980s)... Container ships appear in international trade... Japan's New Otani Hotel begins business, 18 worldwide, 2,000-room Tokyo Hotel largest, by 1989's opening of Beijing hotel... After running small furniture-making business, Terence Conran opens first Habitat home-furnishing store to sell trendy housewares in London, chain of 32 in Britain, France, and Belgium by 1977 (opens first U.S. store in 1977 - 15 by 1987, buys Mothercare group of some 400 stores worldwide in 1981, by 1987 runs 900-store empire, both sides of Atlantic, selling furniture, housewares and clothes, core of business is 250- member Design Group as modern Bauhaus)...

When buccaneering father dies, Yoshiaki Tsutsumi, illegitimate son, inherits most of family business, built after W.W. II by buying out impoverished aristocrats unable to pay inheritance taxes, of railroads and leisure operations (by 1989 is multi-billionaire with suburban Tokyo railroad, national chain of Prince Hotels, and ski resorts) while legitimate son, Seiji, gets retail business (runs Seibu Saison Group, includes Japan's largest department store chain, supermarkets and service firms, total sales of $28 billion in 1987)...Juan Carlos Schidlowski, fugitive king of penny stocks in 1989, leaves Chile to study in U.S., work for cosmetics firm (starts trading penny stocks for New Mexico broker in 1978, starts OTC Net brokerage in 1979, closed 1982, in Denver - Forbes Salesman of the Year in 1982, after 1986 conviction for tax fraud and conspiracy flees to Barcelona to sell penny stocks to gullible Europeans, after making millions returns to Chile in 1988 when Spain cracks down on boiler-room shops)... After fortuitous discovery, Reuters gets non-U.S. rights to Ultronic System's electronic stock price reporting system, computerized transmission eliminates traditional ticker-tape, handles all financial data from government securities to futures by 1990 (starts, 1971, financial news service for banks and, 1973, Monitor electronic system for foreign exchange trades, goes public in 1984, acquires, 1985, Rich trading room systems and, 1987, Instinet to operate 200,852 terminals in 128 countries as world's leading distributor of computerized data in 1991)... With losses from new refrigerator, Electrolux sells large share to ASEA, controlled by Wallenbergs (sells U.S. Electrolux to Consolidated Foods in 1968, goes private in 1987, after 1970, acquires over 300 firms, including U.S.' National Union Electric, its Eureka vacuums, in 1974, Tappan appliances, 1979, and Italy's Zanussi appliances, 1986, to become Europe's No. 1 in appliances, buys White Consolidated Industries, appliances, in 1986 to become U.S.' 3rd largest in appliances after Whirlpool and GE, acquires U.K.'s Thorn EMI in 1987, world's No. 1 in $45 billion white goods market with sales of $5.1 billion, buys Roper's garden tools in 1988 and Hungarian refrigerator maker in 1991, sells its commercial cleaning service in 1990).

1965

General Events

Soviet Union fails to stimulate economy with price reforms, profit incentives... Syria nationalizes (January 3) major industries... Mexico establishes special maquiladora manufacturing zone (lets U.S. firms ship parts duty-free to Mexican assembly plants, levies only value-added duties on shipments back to U.S.) along U.S. border (evolves to provide facilities to over 600 U.S. assembly plants, RCA largest with some 6,000 employees, to take advantage of low labor costs, when Mexico peso loses 82% of value against U.S. dollar in 1982 grows to 850 plants employing some 250,000 Mexicans by 1987, some 1,250 plants with 300,000 jobs and 800,000 supporting jobs, 10% of Mexico's labor force, by 1989)... London Business School opens, closest thing in Europe to U.S. business school... Japan's Productivity Institute forms management academy for middle-managers... Britain bans (February 8) TV cigarette ads... Switzerland extends ban on foreign investments in country... Indonesia seizes (February 26) U.S. rubber plants... Nikolai K. Baibakov heads U.S.S.R.'s Gosplan, central planning unit responsible for coordinating some three million enterprises and organizations with some 200,000 industrial plants, 93 million workers, making 20,000 different classes of products (lets some operations plan on basis of orders, adopts new bonus system based on profitability and sales to replace one with physical output based quotas negotiated by individual enterprises with Gosplan)...

Syria nationalizes (March 4) nine oil companies... In this time, French mathematics professor, Rene Thom develops catastrophe theory to explain discontinuous or abrupt changes in processes... Soviet Union joins International Union for Protection of Industrial Property... Indonesia nationalizes (March 21) Goodyear and four U.S. oil firms... World Bank forms court to settle disputes between businessmen, foreign governments... U.S.S.R. launches (April 23) its first communications satellite... Unions in 10 countries agree to close all ports in Americas to ships trading with Cuba... Britain adopts (May 24) metric system... Lee Kuan Yew is Prime Minister of newly independent Singapore (after surviving 1986 recession shows 11% growth in 1988 as leading economic tiger in area, 138 commercial and 67 merchant banks in 1989 to close on Hong Kong as financial center, invests in R&D to develop industries in biotechnology, telecommunications and artificial intelligence)... U.S.S.R. buys (August 11) Canadian wheat for $450 million... Over 68% of Japanese live in 561 cities...

Japan launches (September 27) world's largest tanker, 150,000 tons... Electrical power is lost in parts of Canada, Northeastern U.S. when simple relay switch malfunctions in Ontario (blackouts some 30 million people)... Business Week: "Eastern Europe Breaks Out of Its Bonds" (notes economic revival with some features of capitalism)... England's Terence Pamplin devises electronic player piano... Ester Boserup, Danish economist: The Conditions of Agricultural Growth (shows population pressures spur new technologies)... France launches (November 26) its first satellite... In this time Professor Funakubo, Japan's Medical Precision Engineering Institute, starts to develop artificial limb for thalidomide babies born without arms (devises electric arm, more precise than hydraulic ones, in eight years, key step in technology of "mechatronic" robots)... Common Market Commission, Coal and Steel Authority and Euratom merge (December 12)... Britain imposes (December 17) oil embargo on Rhodesia, U.S. on 28th... Japan's stock market sees massive sell-off, threatens Yamaichi Securities with bankruptcy... Non-profit International Executive Service Corps forms, U.S., to give managerial, technical aid to private firms in developing nations, over 12,000 projects in 90 countries by 1991.

Business Events

Royal Dutch Shell Group starts to plan complete system to produce, refine and distribute petroleum products worldwide... Luigi Danielli, CEO steel business started by father in 1911, hires daughter Cecilia as assistant (after taking over for father expands business by building some 50% of world's 250 mini-mills for 1985 revenues of some $139.2 million and over $300 million in 1989 as key in revival of Soviet's clumsy steel industry)... BP finds natural gas in North Sea, oil in 1970 after spending some $1 billion... Hisashi Hirano visits U.S. to study K Mart operations (changes family's 53-year-old electronics shop with high prices into Mr. Max mass-retailer, Japan's hottest-growing chain of discount retail stores, huge floor space, low prices and parking, for 1989 sales of $5.2 million)... After serving Balenciaga and Courreges, Ungaro opens Paris fashion house with $5,000, successful with seductive feminine styles (runs, unique among 24 French fashion houses, with no outside underwriting, a $130 million firm in 1978 with 2,000 employees, $450 million and 6,000 employees by 1987 after winning prestigious Golden Thimble, France's highest fashion honor, in 1981 and 1982)... After buying Toronto FM station in 1960, Edward S. Rogers wins cable franchise, one of first in Canada (by 1988 controls 23% of market and Canada's biggest cellular phone business, Cantel, sells U.S. cable interests in 1988 to acquire CNCP Telecommunications, telex firm owned by Canadian National Railway and Canadian Pacific, to battle Telecom Canada, owned by Bell Canada and nine local phone monopolies, for phone service)...

U.S.' Robert Pomeranz of Roberts Co. acquires Britain's 1812 Arundel textile machinery plant with obsolete equipment in Stockport, center of trade unions influenced by Communists (after taking over substitutes hot-drink machines for teakettles, after strike, gives in to workers but stipulates break time of only 10 minutes, when workers continue brewing tea traditional way smashes all kettles, installs modern soap dispensers - rejected by workers, puts in new manufacturing methods - rejected by workers, lays off workers in 1966 after work stoppages from new methods - strike by Amalgamated Engineering Union, fires strikers, closes business in 1968 to expand operations in Belgium, Italy and Spain)... Former U.S. State Department interpreter, Japanese-born Masumi Muramatsu returns to Tokyo to start Simul International, dominates city's interpreting industry by 1989 with sales of $22 million/year, 40 interpreters and school with 150 students... After building Remy Martin as international success after W.W. II, Andre Renaud leaves 51% of firm to oldest daughter, 49% to younger, after death (leads to irreparable family split in 1973 when sons-in-law openly battle for control of cognac dynasty)...

After selling her hand-knit sweaters to help out family, Giuliana Benetton, eldest brother Luciano start Benetton business to make, sell trendy casual clothes, over 5,483 franchised stores in 80 nations, including 700 plus in U.S. and first plant in 1987, by 1989 as billion-dollar business (after 3-year effort in financial services, sells units in 1990 to focus on sportswear and 1989 ski-equipment firm to enter skiwear field, forms joint venture with Seibu Saison in 1990 for Asian markets, plans to expand Middle Europe chain of 20 shops in Czechoslovakia, Hungary and Poland in 1990 and open 50 shops, two factories in U.S.S.R.)... After apprenticeship with Andre Meyer at family's Lazard Brothers' office in NYC, Michel David-Weil, descendant of three Lazard brothers starting New Orleans clothing store in 1847 (open banks in Paris, London, lose control in 1919 to S. Pearson & Son - regained 1984, and NYC), returns to Lazard Paris, CEO in 1975 when father dies (turns barely profitable New York branch, one of last family houses on Wall Street, around by focusing on selling financial advice and hiring four bankers from Lehman Bros. in 1978, six money managers from Oppenheimer & Co. in 1981 to run investment department, assets from $880 million to $9 billion by 1988, and trader in 1981 from Morgan Stanley, oversees 730 employees and over $100 million in capital, more profits/employee than rivals, in 1988)... Genshiro Kawamoto, son of provincial kimono maker, buys first building, 10 floors of bars, in

Tokyo for $1.7 million, worth some $62 million in 1990 to become billionaire with Ginza real estate... Fashion designer, Emilio Pucci, Italy, introduces bodysuits in vivid patterns, rage in 1990 with spandex tights, leggings and bodywear.

1966

General Events

Sweden starts plant to make fish-protein concentrates... Japan forms special council to crack down on alleged piracy of trademarks, designs by foreign manufacturers... EEC adopts common agricultural policy (resists U.S. demand in 1990 to end subsidies)... Iran opens (March 15) oil terminal at Kharg Island... Central African Customs Union forms... Montedison, Italy's 2nd largest enterprise, is created when state-dominated Edison acquires Montecatini... Britain nationalizes (July 27) steel industry... Cayman Islands passes new trust law (registers over 11,000 firms, charters some 300 new banks by 1981)... Chile creates National Copper Corp. to control production, sale of nation's copper (nationalizes U.S.' Anaconda in 1969)... Tunis bans (August 13) mini-skirts... Mao Tse-Tung launches (August) China's Cultural Revolution to revitalize Communism by attacking "reactionary bourgeois ideology," bureaucrats (unleashes several million Red Guards of student zealots to crush Four Olds of ideas, culture, customs and habits)... Austria adopts decimal currency... General Park Chung Hee seizes South Korea (with Western economists builds Korea as world trader, claims world's highest annual growth rate of 12% in 1988)... Arab League boycotts (November 20) Coca-Cola, Ford for supporting Israel... Britain forms Ministry of Science and Technology... British Prime Minister Harold Wilson urges (November 30) Europe to avoid U.S. economic domination... Ottawa pension fund, Caisse de Depot de Placement, drops government ties (with $29 billion in 1990, as does $38 billion confederation of credit unions, provides funds for economic development of Quebec seeking economic freedom from Canada).

Business Events

Supermarkets appear in Europe, Far East... Lebanese Intra Bank declares bankruptcy... For first time in history of Royal Dutch Shell Group, an American, Monroe E. Spaght, President of U.S. Shell Oil, is managing director, joins six other regional directors in consensus decision-making body to oversee some 500 operating companies... Staircase building, each level with progressively higher echelon of employees, is built in Dusseldorf, Germany, by insurance firm (gives visual image of organizational structure)... Birell, non-alcoholic beer, is first brewed in Switzerland, Japan birthplace of dry beer in 1987 when Tokyo's Asahi Breweries pioneers new fad... Business Horizons: "Group Management, European Style" (notes collegial management practice in Holland, West Germany - typical board of Ruhr iron and steel enterprise with four equal directors supported by Secretariat with legal, secretarial, public relations, statistical, organizational and economic activities)... Freddie Laker starts London's Laker Airways as charter carrier (starts innovative low-cost, no-frill Skytrain service between New York and London in 1977)...

Saint Laurent starts Rive Gauche chain of shops to sell ready-to-wear clothes (runs 172 by 1983)... Texas' King Ranch acquires land in Venezuela (builds cattle spread of 52,000 acres, operates land holdings of some 160,000 acres in other South American countries)... Cunard line lays keel for Queen Elizabeth II, last of grand luxury liners (is used for fancy cruises in 1980s)... Electro-Technical Center at Komatsu, Japanese maker of construction equipment, combines mechanical functions with electronics to develop specialized robots... Studebaker closes its last automobile plant in Canada, continues with diversified activities... Pittsburgh Steel starts industry's first joint venture overseas in Belgium with Armco Steel... For first time, The London Times no longer puts classified ads on front page... Japan's Fukuyama Steel is world's largest (with rise in value of yen cuts some 8,000 employees of some 10,000 in 1987)... After working in cotton fields near Adana, Turkey, and starting textile business, Omer Sabanci dies, business group of 51 firms with 31,000 employees, 166th of biggest outside U.S. in late 1980s, goes to five sons... Norwegian Caribbean Lines, six ships by 1988 including Norway to revolutionize market as largest liner with restaurants, bars, shops, cafes, theater, casino and recreational facilities, pioneers Caribbean cruise market of 33 lines with some 108 vessels by 1990... After working as a gofer in travel agency since age of 16, Harry Goodman, son of London sweatshop worker, opens travel agency, International Leisure Group sells 2.5 million vacations, 20% of British market as 2nd largest, in 1988 (operates charter airline, Air Europe, in 1979 to create network of low-fare small carriers on Continent by 1989, enters hotel field in 1985 - out in 1987 with profit of $60 million)... Giovanni Agnelli is CEO of family's Fiat business, owns 39.5% (tops Volkswagen in sales in 1967 as Europe's No. 1 carmaker - world's 4th in 1980 with financial troubles, invests $15 billion in 1982-87 in R & D to improve productivity - Europe's lowest-cost carmaker, in 1983 introduces Uno subcompact cars and leaves U.S. market - poor quality, bests Ford in 1986 to buy Alfa Romeo, in 1987 gets 54% of Italy's market, 61% in 1988, 7.2% of French, 4.6% of German and 3.7% of British market - 15.6% of Europe to Volkswagen's 14.6% in 1988 as world's 6th largest, in 1988 introduces Tipo car to compete with VW's Golf and Ford's Escort and gets sales of $34 billion, $2.1 billion in 1960, from cars, turbines, jet fighters, swaps railcar business for Italy's jet-engine operation, trucks, Iveco with 20% of Europe market, and diesel engines with interests in insurance, department stores, publishing, telecommunications - venture with Spanish enterprise, concrete, etc., as Italy's largest single private business, 22 plants and some 157,000 employees - 1.3% of all Italian workers, to represent over 25% of value of Milan Stock Exchange reveals, 1990, plans to swap stock with Alcatel Alsthom and merge their units in car batteries, Italian telecommunications activities)... France's Thomson, started 1893, merges with Hotchkiss-Brandt, appliances, defense electronics, cars and postal equipment, to form Thomson-Brandt (is Thomson-CSF in 1968 after 2nd merger, in 1969 transfers its Alsthom, started 1928, to CGE, now Alcatel Alsthom, for its appliances and data processing activities, after technical bankruptcy is nationalized in 1982, in 1983 swaps its civil telecommunications to CGE for its military and consumer electronics, acquires, 1986, assets of Moktek, semiconductors, and trades its medical unit plus $800 million for GE's GE, RCA consumer electronics, forms, 1988, joint venture in flight electronics, gets U.K. microprocessor maker in 1989, forms venture in 1990 with Philips to develop HDTV, gets, 1991, 50% of Pilkington Optronics as world's 4th largest in consumer electronics).

1967

General Events

Japan imports its first hydraulic robot (uses 118,800 robots, electronic and hydraulic, by 1987, U.S. with 25,000)... Belgian-born Raul de Thuih stops (January 5) forging rare stamps, gets funds from American Philatelic Society to retire... Computers use keyboards... Overseas direct dialing begins between London, Paris and NYC, regular service 1971... GATT puts South Korea on protective tariff list, removed 1990 after hefty trade surpluses from 1986... Supertanker Torrey Canyon goes aground (March 28) off Cornwall, spews 120,000 tons into water in world's first major oil spill... James Molloy III designs world's first electronic piano... Fikret Abdic is CEO of Bosnia-Herzegovina's industrial enterprise Agrokomerc (with imperial powers builds tiny milk-processing plant into $183 million food conglomerate, 13,500 employees in 1985)...

U.N. puts trade embargo on Rhodesia when white minority government unilaterally declares independence (-1980)... New Greek government bans (April 24) mini-skirts, bearded tourists in May... After years of negotiations, 53 nations make tariff cuts in Geneva to stimulate world trade (pledge food program to help developing countries)... Organization of Future Research Congress, sponsored by Britain's Mankind 2000, meets in Oslo... Pope Paul VI: Popularum Progressio (cites need for Third World economic development)... Egypt closes (June 6) Suez Canal as Israel seizes Gaza in Six Day War... British law makes it an offense to supply pirate radios on ships in international waters (shuts down most operations while Radio Caroline continues with supplies from Amsterdam)... Wimbledon holds first open tennis tournament for professionals, amateurs (leads to unionization of players in 1972, boycott of Wimbledon in 1973 to support suspended Yugoslavia's Nikki Pilic, Men's Tennis Council in 1974 as governing body of sport with players eventually holding 3 of 9 seats, and walkout in 1988 by players to form Assn. of Tennis Professionals to run their own grand tour in 1990 with 18 tournaments, $1 million or more, to challenge Grand Slam events, Davis Cup matches of International Tennis Federation)... Arabs hold (August 7) general strike in Jerusalem to resist Israel... Chile's Agrarian Reform Act allots land to needy peasants... First World Lacrosse Championship is held... Commission des Operations de Bourse is formed to monitor Paris Stock Exchange for irregularities... First stage in building underground shopping complex of some 1,000 stores in downtown Toronto, Canada, is finished (evolves with 3 miles of malls to protect users from weather and traffic, limits growth in 1980s to stimulate ground-level development)... Sweden's Svante Oden identifies acid precipitation as serious environmental hazard... French wheel-less aerotrain travels 215 mph on cushion of air... Mexico gives (October 29) 2.5 million acres to 9,600 peasant families... Nigerian Civil War begins when Ibo ethnic group, many in professional, managerial and technical work, tries to form Biafra (-1970 with surrender)... Montreal hosts Expo '67 World's Fair... Sweden changes from left-to-right-lane driving... Britain devalues (November 18) pound from $2.80 to $2.40... International Assn. of Bureaucrats appears to lampoon traditional inaction... Jean-Jacques Servan-Schrieber: The American Challenge (warns U.S. firms will dominate Europe).

Business Events

Ottobrunn research and development plant of German aerospace firm adopts first known use of flexible-working-hours system to reduce traffic problems to, from factory (is used by 10 West German firms by 1969, is used by 40 U.S. firms in 1970 - some 3,000 in 1973, appears in Japan in 1971)... Canada asks Quebec's Clouston Foods, major seafood business, to identify commercial potential of spider crabs, irritant in fouling nets and propellers of East Coast fishermen (develops new industry of Atlantic Snow Crab)... Antony Jay: Management and Machiavelli... After working four years as French distributor for U.S.- based key maker, France's Serge Crasnainski starts KIS as instant key machine business (with gung-ho sales force grows as worldwide empire, sales of $22 million in 1980 to $293 million in 1984, to provide retailers with compact machines to print business cards, cut keys, engrave bracelets, process film, repair shoes, sell croissants, etc., is attacked in 1986 for fraud by customers, former disgruntled employees and for dubious business practices by government)...

Mitsubishi, Zaibatsu before W.W. II and now a Soga Shosha, is composed of 25 enterprises, followed by Mitsui and Sumitomo groups, each with 17 enterprises, to top C. Itoh, Marubeni, Nissho Iwai, Toyo Menkakaisha, Nichimen and Kanematsu-Gosho... International Work Simplification Institute forms... IBM's World Trade Corp. forms European System Research Institute... Miss Dior boutiques appear with ready-to-wear clothes... After losses of $20 million in 1966, Cunard sells Queen Mary luxury liner to Long Beach, CA, as floating tourist attraction... France's Antoine Riboud uses $200 million container maker as base to build BSN, 3rd in world after Nestle and Unilever by 1989 (is $7 billion food conglomerate, brands of Evian mineral water and Dannon yogurt, after buying Belgium's Maes Group breweries and Britain's HP Products in 1988)...

Khun Sa starts "opium wars" to take over Burma's opium networks run by rogue elements of Chinese Kuomintang Army (as drug lord, called "The Money Tree," levies protection tax, some $200 million in 1988, on 10-20 drug factories processing poppies from some 250,000 acres)... Daniel Ludwig, U.S. shipping tycoon, starts project to clear 2.5 million acres in Amazon Basin to grow trees for wood pulp (tows mill from Japan)... James C. Abegglen starts first U.S. full-line management consulting business in Japan for Boston Consulting Group... Gillette Co. buys Braun, West Germany's maker of small appliances with lean, understated look... Gerard Pelisson, Paul Dubrule build their first hotel, 184 Novotels by 1979 as Europe's No. 1, near Lille, pioneers 3-star hotels in niche between quaint inns and luxury hotels (launch 2-star Ibis hotels in 1973, buy Mercure chain in 1975, open 1st U.S. hotel, 1979, in Minneapolis, form Accor in 1983 to combine Jacques Borel restaurants, started 1957 to become Europe's largest by 1975 when it takes over Belgium's Sofitel chain of luxury hotels, sold to Accor in 1980, in 1984 enters package vacation tours market with majority share of Africatours, largest in Africa, after visiting Disneyland,

McDonald's training schools opens Accor Academy in 1985, opens first budget hotel, Formula 1, 1985, goes Pacific with Ted Cook's Islands in the Sun, 1986, and Asiatours and Americatours in 1987, markets Pacquet cruises in 1986, in 1987 starts Hotelia with health care for senior citizens and Parthenon chain of residential hotels in Brazil, in 1988 opens theme part north of Paris and fails to buy Hilton International chain, fails to merge with Club Med in 1989, in 1990 buys U.S.' Motel 6, low-budget pioneer with 554 units, for $1.3 billion and 26.7% of Belgium's Wagon-Lits, some 300 hotels in Europe, Thailand and Indonesia, with Societe Generale to become world's largest hotel operator, 1,421 hotels and 3,112 restaurants in 62 countries, after Bass's Holiday Inns in 1991)... Kim Woo-Chong, To Dae Do start South Korean textile exporting firm, genesis for Daewoo Group, 4th largest chaebol, in 1991 (at request of President Park Chung-Hee takes over government-owned machinery plant, unprofitable for 37 years, in 1976, with turnaround in 9 months forms Daewoo Heavy Industries, by 1980s takes over two more state-owned enterprises, GM Korea becomes Daewoo Motor Co. as land's 3rd largest, and shipyard, still unprofitable and drag on group, in 1980s handles export deals, Pontiac, Caterpillar, Northern Telecom, Boeing Lockheed, General Dynamics, Daimler-Benz, United Technologies, to exchange low-cost goods for technology, in mid-1980s enter electronics industry with acquisitions).

1968

General Events

Daccra convention of Indian beggars passes resolution on minimum amount of alms... Tupolev TU-144 is first U.S.S.R. supersonic airliner... Big ranches of Peru's highlands are gradually replaced by large cooperative operations... Three largest French labor federations call (May 11) general strike to support students wanting more control of universities and overthrow of "capitalist establishment," by 20th, millions of workers seize factories and Government raises minimum wage by 35% on 26th... Latin American Catholic bishops meet in Colombia (condemn economic situation in Latin America, propose reorientation of Church to support poor instead of traditional oligarchies, launch movement of Liberation Theology)... U.S.S.R. starts (July 15) commercial flights to U.S... Hungary develops New Economic Mechanism, first in Eastern Bloc to move away from Soviet's central planning model (grants factory managers limited freedom from tyranny of rigid central planning, lets small-scale entrepreneurs and profit-oriented collectives operate)... Soviet forces suppress liberal reforms of Alexander Dubcek (returns to government in 1990 with overthrow of Communists in Czechoslovakia)... Student unrest appears in Rome, Copenhagen, Tokyo, Paris and West Germany... Britain's Race Relations Bill bans discrimination in employment, housing, etc., on basis of color, race or national origin... Nafta-B, joint Soviet-Belgian company, is formed to market U.S.S.R.'s crude oil in Europe (is Belgium's 2nd largest firm by 1977)... European currency crisis eases (November 25)... Auroville is founded, India, as center for organic farming, showplace by 1989 with 2,000 acres of formerly arid, eroded land.

Business Events

Seiko introduces first electronic watches, forced to withdraw first models for defects (-1969, is followed in U.S. by Hamilton's Pulsar in 1969)... After 280 years, Lloyd's of London plans to admit foreigners as members... Cardin's pendants for men shock fashion world... Merger of Japan's Yawata, Fuji results in world's 2nd largest steel enterprise after U.S. Steel... Fiat, 15% ownership (acquires control), and Michelin's Citroen form joint venture to coordinate investment, sales, manufacturing and research activities... Management Today reports 66% of top 120 British firms with no other hierarchy than chairman, managing director... Cunard scraps Queen Elizabeth (after being sold to Chinese investor, Hong Kong, for floating California campus, burns in 1972)... Alan Sugar, Britain's PC and consumer electronics king in 1988 with annual sales over $1 billion, starts Amstrad as wholesale distributor of cassette players, speakers and other electronic gear for cars (gets first success in 1978 with stereo unit for lorry drivers, goes public in 1980 for immediate net worth of $8 million, introduces first word processing computer in 1985 and Europe's first inexpensive IBM PC clone in 1986, success using established technology for low prices to make mass markets out of specialty markets)... Taiwan's Y.F. Chang, son of ship carpenter, buys old freighter (as multi-billionaire runs world's largest container shipping business by 1989)... Salvatore Torrisi founds Agriculture Industrial Development, Sicily, to devise new industrial technologies to protect and harvest crops, 200, 50 in 1981, scientists and technicians by 1989... Tennis pro Billie Jean King wins $1,800 in Wimbledon singles, $279,100 for No. 1 woman in 1989, while Rod Laver gets $4,800, $310,000 for top male in 1989... Former general Park Tae-jin is CEO of South Korea's POSCO, started in early 1960s (with technology, loans and aid from Japan evolves after 1984 as world's 2nd largest steelmaker, used as model by Third World nations)...

After arranging Nepal trip for U.S.' Sierra Club in 1967, Leo Le Bon forms Mountain Travel, first to specialize in adventure tours... Big Comic is published in Japan for men in their 20s, pioneers trend of firms, such as Mazda and Matsushita, using comic strips to explain technical subjects to workers, customers... After running textile business after high school, Yasumichi Morishita, son of storekeeper, founds Aichi Co., moneylender and stock speculator that becomes, despite being twice convicted, sentences suspended, for stock fraud and extortion, core of complex corporate web by 1990 (opens Gallery Aoyama in 1988, after spending over $1 billion on art is Japan's 2nd most profitable house in 1989, buys 6.3% of Christie's auction house in 1989 for $54 million, plans to spend $365 million yearly on art in 1990s).

1969

General Events

France sells (January 2) Maginot line, built in early 1930s for defense, for housing... Britain starts open university so anyone, anywhere can take courses regardless of educational background... Rome hosts conference of 39 nations on pollution of the seas... English, French are official government languages in Canada... R. Frisch of Norway, N. Tinbergen of Holland win first Nobel Prizes for Economic Science...Peru seizes (February 6) holdings of International Petroleum... First home yogurt maker appears... Maxim Gorky is built, used for cruises by Soviet Union in 1974 (runs fleet of 27 ships for Mediterranean, Black Sea, Baltic and Caribbean cruises in late 1980s)... London School of Economics and Political Science is closed by student disorders... Colombia, Venezuela, Peru, Ecuador, Bolivia and Chile form South American Common Market... Peru seizes (June 24) all major tracts of private land... Sindona is financial advisor to Vatican (invests Church funds, eventually loses up to $200 million, in personal financial enterprises, is convicted of fraud for largest U.S. bank failure in 1974, commits suicide in 1986 after being sentenced to life in prison by Milan court)... Libya's King Idris is overthrown by coup of Muammar al-Qaddafi, army officers (expels U.S. military personnel from Wheeler Air Base near Tripoli, forces oil companies to raise prices and accept higher taxes, tries to close private enterprise in 1973, tries to nationalize all private business in 1981 - shopkeepers close doors, opens Libya to exports in 1988, makes black market a "people's market" and allows private enterprise)... Denmark legalizes (June) pornography...

Sweden forms Svetab as state-owned venture capital enterprise, followed in 1975 by joint venture capital business of 29 German banks and London Unlisted Securities Market in 1980 for venture capital stocks... Brazil starts Embraer to build aircraft for air force (evolves to make, sell commuter planes for U.S. market, forms joint venture with British firm in 1984 to win RAF contract)... First transatlantic hijacking lands (October 31) in Rome... Sweden's 1890 state-controlled LKAB iron-ore company adopts project management system (operates as world's largest exporter of iron-ore with seven divisions, some 8,000 employees)... British creativity consultant Edward de Bona coins "lateral thinking" as process to solve problems with apparently illogical reasoning (forms Supranational Independent Thinking Organization to help governments develop creative thinking, introduces creative thinking courses in schools of Britain, Israel, Australia, New York and Venezuela)... Denmark holds (November 1) 6-day sex fair in Copenhagen Sports Palace... Britain finds oil reserves in North Sea (starts production in 1975, works nine fields by 1978, is petroleum self-sufficient by 1980)... U.S.' Senator Gaylord Nelson proposes Earth Day to honor the environment (launches global ecology movement)... France, West Germany build first Airbus plane to compete with U.S.' Boeing (form Airbus Industrie, joined by U.K. in 1979, in 1970, is adopted by Air France in 1974, gets first non-partner order from Eastern in 1978, wins 20% share of commercial jet market in 1988, flies A320 plane, electronic controls and five computers limit use of pilot to takeoffs and emergencies, in 1989, with 765 planes ordered faces, 1990, managerial problems with high costs and diffusion of responsibility, in 1991 floats its first international bond issue to finance new plane and gets $2 billion order from Kuwait Airways and $6 billion order from Federal Express).

Business Events

Volvo begins Quality of Work Life program to combat labor turnover, absenteeism and wildcat strikes (leads to job enrichment and job rotation programs, new factory and new organizational structure with work teams in 1973)... Giorgetto Giugiaro creates international Ital Design to fashion products with elegant appearance, practicality for consumers, manufacturers... St. Laurent introduces maxi-skirt in fashion collection... France's Vittel Mineral Water Co. invents plastic bottle... VFW-Fokker is formed by German, Dutch aircraft firms (-1980)... With help of father, Hong Kong's Gordon Wu gets $2.5 million loan to start property development business (after building $100 million hotel in Canton and $400 million power station in Southern China, year ahead of schedule, runs $190 million real estate business with properties of $440 million by 1989, plans $1 billion, 181-mile "super highway" in 1988 to link Hong Kong, Canton)... Hartmut Esslinger starts frog design in West Germany, evolves by 1988 as world leader in industrial design with Sony's Walkman and Apple computers to its credit...

After inheriting family shipping business, Ronald Li, Colony's 3rd richest man in 1988, helps form Far East Stock Exchange, merged with 3 others in 1986 to form Hong Kong Exchange (is arrested in 1988 for closing Exchange 4 days during worldwide financial crash of October, 1987)... After working as stage manager since 1965, Cameron MacKintosh, son of London timber merchant, produces first show, Cole Porter revival fails (puts on hit, "Side by Side By Sondheim", in 1976, with Shubert Organization stages "Little Shop of Horrors" and "Cats", first megahit with record advance of $6 million, in 1982, follows with "Phantom of the Opera", advance of $18 million, "Les Miserables", and "Miss Saigon", U.S. advance of $25 million, by 1991)... Michael Ashcroft is executive for British cleaning firm (starts building own Hawley Group as service conglomerate, industrial cleaning to car auctions with sales of $842 million in 1986, in late 1970s, buys 1969 employer in 1986 for $240 million, with 10% of U.S. market in Central-station alarms buys U.S.' ADT home-alarm firm in 1987 for $635 million to snag 40% of security market)... Japan's National Football Assn. is formed for corporation-sponsored teams, 54 teams in three divisions by 1989... High-school drop-out, Richard Branson, launches Virgin Records, successful with Mike Oldsfield as first artist, later Sex Pistols, Boy George and Genesis, in 1973 to spawn chain of record shops (takes up Laker's dream of cheap flights to U.S. with Virgin Atlantic Airline in 1984, by 1988 is Britain's 9th-richest with $480 million business, sells 25% to Japan's largest communications firm, Fujisankei, in 1989 for $150 million)... Mitsubishi is a Boeing subcontractor... First Avon ladies appear in Japan, 3% of Japan's competitive $9 billion cosmetics market by 1989 (sells 60% in 1990 to Japanese direct-mail firm for $408 million while Shaklee sells 78% to Yamanouchi Pharmaceutical for $350 million which then buys U.S. parent for $392 million)... Fiat acquires upscale Lancia, Ferrari car makers (merges its earthmoving equipment arm with that of Allis Chalmers in 1973).

1970

General Events

Britain's merchant fleet has over 1,600 cargo ships, 614 by 1986... Jean-Francois Revel: Without Marx or Jesus (rejects socialism as failure)... Romania raises some $11 billion in foreign loans in 1970s to spur industrial growth with huge petrochemical complexes and steel mills, fledgling electronics industry, and shipping canal (becomes economic disaster in 1980s with shortages everywhere by 1989 in effort to pay debt by exports)... Student riots, strikes of workers urge governmental reforms in Italy... East Bloc countries form (May 14) Comecon Investment Bank (consider abolishing Comecon in 1990)... Pioneering research survey agency appears in Georgia, U.S.S.R. (is upgraded to party research center in 1981, takes public opinion poll in 1985)... Due to language misunderstanding, Korean student ruins experiment with organic polymers at Tokyo Institute of Technology (leads to 1975 study of odd residue by researchers, two Americans and one Japanese, to discover plastics as conductors of electricity)... Libya is first Arab-oil exporting country to demand substantially higher prices for crude oil... London declares (July 16) emergency when 47,000 dockworkers strike for two weeks... MITI spends $36 million to develop remote-controlled undersea oil-drilling rig (fails as do five other projects for some $250 million by 1989, loses $2.5 billion trying to start aluminum smelting industry)... During 1970s U.S. pressures Mexico to spray marijuana fields with weed killer...

Floppy disk appears to store computer data... Dr. Kenneth Cooper's aerobic conditioning of Brazil's soccer team helps them win World Cup, Rio with over 2,000 aerobic centers in 1989 - Corpore with five and 8,300 members... China orbits its first satellite... China, Albania sign trade agreement... Brazil builds 2,000-mile Trans-Amazon Highway from Recife on Atlantic to Peru (-1980s, is opposed by environmentalists, protectors of Indian tribes)... European Common Market, Yugoslavia sign trade agreement... After riots in Polish cities by workers protesting food shortages and higher prices, Gomulka is replaced as government head by Edward Gierek... Marxist Salvador Allende is (November 3) President of Chile (-1973)... Inventor-scientist James Lovelock proposes Gaia theory, first noted by Scottish geologist James Hutton in 1785, in early 1970s that earth functions as giant organism, first major scientific conference by American Geophysical Union in 1988 with rising interest in worldwide industrial pollution... Saudi Arabia begins first development plan with borrowed money (with rising oil revenues and foreign workers, some three million in 1989, spends some $640 billion by 1990 to modernize society)... Britain grants (November 11) financially-troubled Rolls-Royce $100,000... Andrei Amalrik: Will the Soviet Union Survive Until 1984?... By 1990 Whistler, British Columbia, evolves as leading North American ski complex... British researcher A.R.E. Singer, University of Swansea, finds key way to make spray steel, perhaps biggest advance since the blast furnace.

Business Events

Fortune: "Europe's Love Affair with Bigness" (notes mergers to battle U.S. giants invading Europe)... Israeli businessman Abraham Levy designs cardboard sun shield to fit inside car's front window (is brought to Los Angeles by two immigrants, sales of $2 million from $4 auto shades)... After advising corporate clients on dealing with Saudi Arabia in 1960s, deal-maker Adnan Khoshoggi, son of personal physician to late Saudi king and nephew of Saudi defense official (starts deals with government contract in 1956 to supply trucks for Saudi Army), becomes exclusive agent for 80% of all Saudi arms purchases (charges fees, 5%-15% on huge orders, for arranging contracts, loses commissions on Defense Projects when stopped 1975, with estimated fortune of some $4 billion, mainly invested in U.S., by 1986 lives lavish, sybaritic life before disastrous investments bankrupt his Triad America Co. in 1987)...

Gold on free market is under official price of $35/ounce... Cartier jewelry starts major diversification program in 1970s by licensing products in endeavor to become world's first billion-dollar luxury goods company, sales of some $400 million in 1985... Kentucky Fried Chicken opens first U.S. fast-food business in Japan, 434 units by 1985 (leads to McDonald's, Wimpy's, Wendy's, Burger King, Baskin-Robbins, Dairy Queen, Pizza Hut, Mister Donut, Shakey's Pizza, and Dunkin' Donuts, an industry of some $85 billion in 1980s)... Japan's Komatsu starts robotic research (produces first model in 1973 for forging)... Coupon Clearing Service is started in Tijuana, Mexico, to handle market promotions of U.S. firms (processes over one million/day by 1986)... Nippon Steel is world's largest... Anthony R. Gurka, British expatriate, starts Commercial Trademark Services, Hong Kong, to track down counterfeit products... By this time, 54 of France's 100 largest firms use divisional organizational structures with centralized headquarters to oversee operations, 50 in West Germany, 57 in UK and 80 in U.S... After training as psychiatrist and opening nursing home, London's Michael J. Sinclair, son of hairdressers, builds nursing homes, private hospitals throughout Britain, Mideast during 1970s (opens first U.S. nursing home in 1983 - loses $400,000, switches business to supply medical personnel, after six acquisitions in 1986-89 builds Lifetime Corp. into major supplier of nurses to home health care industry, 1989 revenues of some $460 million)... In 1970s, Les Pompes Guinard, France's largest industrial-pump manufacturer, abandons large factories for small, geographically-dispersed shops with under a few hundred workers in each (replaces some shop foremen with local wise men that workers can see when in trouble)... Robert Holmes a Court begins career buying bankrupt woolen mills in Western Australia (makes $8 million in 1979 unsuccessful struggle with Murdoch for control of Ansett, one of Australia's two domestic airlines, buys British film maker Associated Communications for $85 million, starts takeover of Broken Hill Proprietary in 1983 - largest shareholder by 1986, makes $40 million on USX raid, acquires 2nd newspaper and stakes in Texaco, British Sears, and other firms by 1988)...

Former West Germany playboy, Johannes Thurn und Taxis, multi-billionaire in 1988 with private bank, real estate in West Germany, Brazil and Canada, supplier of rare metals, and family breweries, hires consultant Booz Allen for advice (divests six castles, non-productive assets to start new businesses in Germany, Brazil)... In mid-20s, Charles and Maurice Saatchi, sons of Iraqi Jew who arrived in Britain in 1947 to start successful textile business, open London advertising agency (after buying three British agencies go public in 1975 for growth capital - 500 employees in 1976 to 7,000, 12,000 in 1986, at 150 offices in 28 countries by 1980, acquire London's staid Compton Partners, U.K., in 1975 to become U.K.'s 5th largest and No. 1 by 1979, gain fame by promoting Conservative Party's winning campaign in 1978-79, is Europe's No. 1 by 1981 and world's No. 5 by 1985 with billings of $3 billion, invade U.S. in 1982 with acquisition of Compton Communications - 3 more later, in 1985 enter consulting field by buying Hay Group, 9,000 clients worldwide in 1990, for $125 million, sold 1990 for some $88 million to focus on advertising, and Howard Marlboro, sales promotion, for $414 million)... Heineken buys James S. Murphy, Irish stout... Carlsberg, Tuborg breweries form United Breweries, use Carlsberg name in 1988 (diversifies with Carlsberg Biotechnology in 1983 to use its R&D resources, signs licensing pact with Anheuser-Busch, 1985, and John Labatt in 1988)... Only two ocean liners, <u>S.S. France</u> and <u>Queen Elizabeth 2</u>, ply North Atlantic from NYC to Southampton.

1971

General Events

Ecuador, U.S. sign (January 30) accord to settle fishing dispute... West Germany's Works Constitution Act extends rights of work councils over social welfare, economic and personnel matters (requires firms to inform, consult with employees on company affairs)... U.S.S.R. expands (February 14) consumer production in new 9th Five-Year Plan... Twenty-three oil companies agree (February 14) to increase payments to six Persian Gulf states... Britain drops (February 15) pound for decimal system... Chilean peasants seize (February 17) farms... Algeria seizes (February 24) French oil assets... Chile buys (March 26) Bethlehem iron mines... Soviet Union tests unmanned prototype space station (after series of Salyut experiments, launches MIR in 1986 as 3rd-generation station)... Western oil firms sign (April 2) 5-year pact with Libya...

Canadians form Greenpeace to oppose slaughter of whales, seals (operates by 1985 with 1.5 million supporters in 15 countries to fight for number of environmental issues with budget of some $16 million)... EEC finance ministers meet (May 8) to discuss dollar crisis... Soviets contract (June 17) with U.S.' Mack Trucks to build a plant... After civil disorders of Catholics, Protestants in Northern Ireland since 1969, Britain invokes (August 25) emergency powers to arrest suspected leaders of Irish Republican Army (is financed, some $7 million annually by 1980s, by underground activities of IRA-controlled businesses, such as social clubs, pubs and West Belfast's fleet of 600 taxis)... Chile bars (September 28) payment for seized copper mine... Caribbean nations form Common Market... People's Republic of China joins (November 15) UN, Taiwan out... Turkish farmers get (November 20) $35 million from U.S. to stop growing opium poppies... Libya nationalizes (December 12) BP properties.

Business Events

U.S.' National Semiconductor opens two plants in Penang, by 1989 some $1 billion invested by U.S. electronics firms in Malaysia as world's largest exporter of microchips... U.S.' Peter Shayne starts shrimp farm business in Ecuador with $20,000 (evolves by 1981 as world's largest exporter of farmed shrimp with revenues of some $20 million)... Robert Calvi, advisor to banker Sindona, is general director of Italy's Banco Ambrosiano (collapses in 1982)... Japanese joint venture is started by McDonald's, Den Fujita (after working as interpreter for U.S. occupation forces, peddling appliances to GIs, and graduating from law school, starts trading company in 1950s to import women's accessories - accounts with 250 department stores and retail outlets by 1980s) and bakery, shares later acquired by Fujita (despite objections of U.S. firm, opens first restaurant in urban location on Tokyo's Ginza to set world's record for McDonald's with sales of $14,000 in one day, evolves as No. 1 fast-food business in Japan by 1986 with yearly sales of $770 million, McDonald's largest foreign operation, from 560 stores, 480 owned by Fujita)... After pressure by Labor Government in 1960s to build jet engines for Lockheed TriStar plane, Rolls-Royce declares bankruptcy after underestimating contract costs (leads to Britain taking over jet engine works, separate car enterprise is sold to public and merges with Vickers engineering firm in 1980)... Japanese textile industry puts self-imposed quota on textile exports to U.S... Japan launches world's largest ship, oil tanker Nisseki Maru at 372,400 tons... England's Dunlop, Italy's Pirelli merge tire interests (-1981)...

Moet champagne business merges with Hennessy Cognac empire... First Hard Rock Cafe, serves ribs, burgers, and U.S. pop music, opens across from Buckingham Palace, spawns places in Stockholm, NYC, Dallas and Tokyo for sales of $32.5 million in 1987... With lack of business, Singapore's new Hyatt Regency hires feng shui master to rid hotel of unhappy spirits, occupancy rate rises... By 1986 Japanese firms open 50 plants in Britain, 50 more 1987-89 in preparing for 1992 European integrated market... After gambling in property developments while practicing medicine, Kichinosuke Sasaki starts Togensha real estate business, multi-billionaire by 1989... John D. Elliott, after getting MBA degree from Melbourne University and working as consultant for McKenzie & Co., buys tiny jam maker, Elder's IXL with 1987 sales of $7.6 billion (gets old-line agribusiness in 1981, buys Carlton United Breweries in 1983, blocks takeover of Brierly to win Australia's largest brewery, Foster's, for $700 million in 1982, gets Carling O'Keefe Brewery, Canada's No. 3, for $297 million in 1986, after buying Courage, Britain's 6th largest brewery with cash of $160 million, in 1986 for $2.5 billion - largest overseas takeover by Australian business, sells its wine and spirits division for $80 million and floats pubs as public firm for $1.9 billion, after stock battle gets 19% of Broken Hill, Australia's largest corporation in steel, minerals and energy, in 1986 for $1 billion)...

Japan's Dai-Ichi and Nippon Kangyo banks merge, world's largest in 1989 with assets of $384 billion... Pehr Gyllenhammer is CEO of Volvo, 1988 sales of $16.1 billion (puts two union delegates on board in 1971 before required by Swedish law, as Sweden's highly educated, well-trained labor force doesn't like factories opens pioneering Kalmar plant in 1974 with work teams to assemble components for making cars, experiments building cars in 1987 without using assembly lines, opens new $220 million Uddevalla complex of six plants without assembly lines, each self-managing team of 7-10 workers puts together four cars/shift with fewer hours of labor and better quality than its other plants, in 1989, spurs use of self-managed teams in U.S., Europe by 1990, forms $45 billion alliance with Renault in 1990)... Thailand's Dumri Kontuntakiet takes over family's rice-exporting, whisky business (by 1988 starts new enterprises, about one/year, in shrimp farming, tin-plating and toy making in partnership with U.S.' Hasbro)... Australia's Rod Laver is first tennis millionaire.

1972

General Events

Britain, Iceland begin cod war over fishing limits (-1976)... Pakistan nationalizes (January 2) 10 industries... Civil war in Lebanon begins... Donnella H. Meadows, others: The Limit to Growth: A Report for the Club of Rome's Projects on the Predicaments of Mankind... EEC accepts (January 22) Britain, Ireland, Denmark and Norway as members... Idi Amin ousts some 60,000 native-born residents of Asian heritage, most shopkeepers and traders resented for wealth and racial insularity, from Uganda, forced to leave behind all possessions except for $100 in cash... Swedish law requires all firms over 500 employees to have two workers on corporate boards... U.S.S.R. agrees (March 4) to help develop Libyan oil fields... Australia adopts equal pay for comparable work for both public and private organizations (leads to higher employment of women, more women working part-time, fewer women entering labor force in five years)... Britain is devastated by national strike of coal miners, again 1974 and 1984... Milan's Bocconi University begins pioneering MBA program, emulated by Madrid's Instituto de Empresa during year... Bangladesh nationalizes (March 26) main industries... Philippines' President Ferdinand Marcos declares martial law when barred from 3rd term (-1981, issues 971 decrees and directives, some secret, to seize businesses, create monopolies, grant exclusive import licenses, and guarantee bank loans for relatives and cronies, rigs markets in bananas, coconuts, pharmaceuticals and sugar, awards favorites with development projects, is ousted by Corazon Aquino in 1986 after popular revolt)...

Canada adopts controls to regulate foreign investments in nation's resources... Chile's President Allende seeks (April 18) to nationalize ITT property... All major international airports adopt anti-hijack measures... Canada, U.S. sign agreement to rid Great Lakes of pollution... Iraq nationalizes (June 1) Western-owned Iraq Petroleum... France's hard-right party, National Front (opposes immigrant workers), forms, Italian Social Movement follows... By 1988 Soviet trade with West rises from $7 billion to $41 billion, U.S.' $2 billion from mostly grain... Massive strikes oppose (October 11) Chile's government...By 1988, Hungary forms 140 joint ventures with West... Costa Rica sets aside private reserve, 10,500 hectares, to preserve forests as tourist attraction... Britain allows commercial radio (considers deregulation in 1989 to create three new channels)... Britain freezes (November 6) wages, prices to fight inflation... West German act mandates boards of supervisors to give stockholders and employees equal membership (covers over 5 million employees of some 600 firms by 1972)... East Germany nationalizes last 12,000 industrial firms into state conglomerates, only 17,000 private retailers left by 1990... BOAC and BEA, formed as British European Airways after W.W. II for domestic market, combine as British Airways (is privatized in 1987, acquires British Caledonian, in 1987, in 1988 forms alliance with U.S.' United and buys 10% of its Apollo reservation system, joins, 1989, KLM to buy part of Sabena, resumes talks in 1991 when deal collapses).

Business Events

Mitsubishi gives Harvard $1 million for Japanese studies... Christian David, holds 10% of world's heroin market with partners, prefers 80 years in U.S. prison to extradition to France for 1966 death of police officer... Bobby Hull of Chicago Black Hawks, NHL pro team, signs contract for $2.7 million with new World Hockey Assn. to play for Winnipeg Jets... South Africa's luxurious $5 million Blue Train starts service on 1,000-mile run, 25 hours, between Pretoria, Cape Town... Steel firms in Holland, West Germany form Estel... S.S. France, world's longest and most elegant liner with crew of some 1,000, begins luxurious cruise to 29 ports worldwide (provides 1,200 passengers on 91-day voyage with accommodations from minimum of $5,065 to $99,440)... Kenzo, young Japanese designer, presents fashion show as spectacle, starts trend... Sony is first Japanese firm to make TVs in U.S... Fujisankei introduces televised home shopping to Japan, starts U.S. operation in 1987... Japanese firms stop importing Malaysian ore as too dirty for processing, leads to lawsuit by villagers against Mitsubishi for radioactive contamination... Running small tool-repairing collective in China's Jiangxi Province, Zhang Guoxi gets idea for Yujiang Carved

Wood Factory (sells house for $380 to start workshop making furniture, Buddhist shrines and intricate carving, by 1988 oversees some 3,000 people in 32 factories, six commercial firms, seven joint ventures, and offices in Japan, Hong Kong and West Germany, hires bodyguard in 1987 as viewed by some party members as a dangerous bourgeois class element)... U.S.' Tandy opens electronics plant in low-cost South Korea, rising wages and labor strikes appear in late 1980s... Fujitsu funds Japan-America Institute of Management Science, Hawaii, to foster cross-cultural programs... GM buys 360-acre plantation, Brazil, to test cars (by 1990 is one of GM's most profitable units growing coffee, nets $100,000/year, to subsidize facility)... Alec MacKenzie: The Time Trap (starts time-management boom with over 500,000 copies in 12 languages)... Self-Employed Women's Assn. is formed in Ahmedabad, India (helps women vendors win right to sell produce in market)... BAT tries to enter U.K. tobacco market, retreats by 1984 (enters retail field in 1970s to buy U.S. chains, i.e., Saks Fifth Avenue, 32 stores, in 1973, and Marshall Field, 22 stores, in 1982, along with U.K.'s Argo and Jewelers Guild Shops, expands as BAT Industries, renamed for public opposition to smoking, after 1982, tobacco 73% of earnings, to operate in retailing financial services, insurance and paper products, sold 1990, by 1984, tobacco 55%).

1973

General Events

West Germany's Labor Promotion Act (provides 3 months of wages to employees of bankrupt firms)... Australia establishes Prices Justification Tribunal (adjusts wage structure for inflation)... Banks in Japan, West Europe close (March 2) to handle monetary crisis from dollar devaluation... Gustavo Gutierrez, Peruvian priest: A Theology of Liberation (urges political activism to help poor in Third World countries, is investigated by Peru's episcopacy)... Norwegian law establishes "company assemblies" with one-third worker membership... Iran nationalizes all foreign-operated oil firms... East, West Germany establish diplomatic relations, unification in 1990... Siberia-to-Eastern Europe pipeline starts (April 21) pumping oil... Al-Quaddafi starts Popular Revolution to eradicate Libya's bourgeoisie, bureaucracy (eliminates all private enterprises and all rental properties, freezes bank accounts, forms People's Committees to supervise daily life, declares in 1978 that Libya is a state without a government with al-Quaddafi as leader of People's Revolution)... Canada forms Foreign Investment Review Agency to screen foreign takeovers, approve foreign investments in Canada... Libya nationalizes (June 11) U.S. oil firm, all foreign oil firms (September 1)... Yom Kippur War begins with Egypt's invasion of Israeli-held Sinai Peninsula (leads to embargo, Oct. 21, by Arab oil-producing nations to force U.S., Europe to pressure Israel to withdraw from occupied Arab territory - price of oil rises from $1.79/barrel in 1970 to over $13 in 1974, forces nations to conserve energy by developing carbon cloth, lighter than aluminum and stronger than steel, heat-resistant ceramics, new alloys of dissimilar metals and carbon-fiber plastics)...

Chile's Allende government is overthrown (September 9) by military coup, aided by CIA, ITT... E.F. Schumacher: Small Is Beautiful: Economics as if People Mattered (urges in pioneering work that human-scale and decentralized methods are required for economic growth by Third World countries, attacks use of economic bigness and centralization to develop such nations)... Cousteau Society forms to enhance public awareness of fragile environment, to explore world's resources... Arab League agrees (December 6) to "gradual withdrawal" of funds from Western banks to fund Arab development projects... After strike by coal miners and oil embargo, Britain cuts (December 13) work week to three days to save energy... Peru nationalizes (December 30) U.S.-owned mining firms... Haile Selassie is overthrown as ruler of Ethiopia (leads to Marxist-Leninist government, with famines and civil war adopts capitalist reforms in 1990, keeps state ownership of land but allows individual enterprise, free market economy)... Ophthalmologist Slava Fydorov at Moscow Eye Clinic devises new cornea eye operation in this time (by 1989 oversees main clinic, uses assembly line with conveyor belts, lazy-Susans and TV monitors, nine treatment centers across U.S.S.R., and two factories with some 5,000 employees to handle some 220,000 patients, 5,500 foreigners, in $75 million/year business, earns $35,000/year and enjoys telephone-equipped car, airplanes, roomy apartments, country dachas, 53 horses, foreign vacations and yachts, plans foreign clinics, floating hospital for sheikhs of Persian Gulf in late 1980s)... First OPEC oil shock forces Japan to reshape its economic base (phases out energy-intensive industries)... After overthrowing Allende, General Augusto Pinochet rules Chile with absolute authority (-1990, after rousing dormant economy with deregulation, 1975, and privatization realizes growth averaging 6%/year after 1985 with legacy of extensive pollution).

Business Events

Moet wine business acquires some 1,500 Napa Valley acres, considers Italian and South African vineyards in 1989 (despite jeers sees eight more French houses in California by 1989)... Tokuchichi Hasegewa purchases 14 paintings of actor Edward G. Robinson's collection for Japan's Nichido Gallery, started by father in 1928, to become significant dealer in international world of art... London Stock Exchange accepts first women members... London-based BAT Industries, formerly British American Tobacco Co., acquires U.S. retail department-store chain of Gimbel Bros. (after failing to upgrade its image and compete with "off-priced" and discount stores, seeks buyers in 1986 for 144- year-old retail business)... London-based Reuters news agency starts Monitor, 24-hour currency-information service for international traders... By 1988, Sanwa Bank, 275 branches in Japan in 1988, puts $385 million into U.S. acquisitions, including $233 million purchase of California network of Lloyds Bank, 113 branches, in 1986 to become State's 7th largest bank... After employer, Elf Aquitaine, accepts suggestions to diversify into drugs, France's Rene Sautier founds Sanofi with backing of Elf, a $3 billion enterprise in prescription drugs, biotechnology, and swank consumer brands, i.e., Van Cleef & Arpels perfumes, by 1988 (after 175 acquisitions bids for U.S.' A.H. Robins pharmaceutical)... After borrowing $8,000 from friends, Tsuneo Kusunoki opens English-language school in Japan, 90 throughout land by 1989 (starts international-exchange organization in 1985 to arrange home stays, starts travel agency in 1988 to handle language-study trips, forms joint venture with Portland, OR, college in 1988 so Japanese can study abroad, plans language schools for Japanese in NYC, London, Paris, Brisbane and Madrid in 1989)...

Egyptian-born Refaat El-Sayed returns to Sweden to start Micro-Chem Development as biotechnology business (after 24 patent applications, gets loan of $325,000 from Electrolux to buy penicillin factory and start Fermenta)... U.S.' Joseph Dunkle teams up with Seibu Saison, Japan's largest retailer, to start chain of ice cream stores, 35 units and 28 Aunt Stella cookie stores by 1989... Pakistani Agha Hassan Abedi starts Luxembourg's Bank of Credit & Commerce International, 400 branches in 73 countries in 1988 before charges by U.S. Customs of money-laundering for cocaine lords (pleads guilty in 1990)... Australian financial journalist Chris Skase, partners get $12,000 bank loan to buy small Melbourne hotel (when group splits in 1977, gets Qintex, acquired in 1975, to operate small TV station, after acquiring chain of jewelry stores, timber resources, radio stations and electronics firm, hits big time in 1987 with buy of Australia's 3rd-largest TV network for $640 million, fails on $1.5 billion bid for MGM/UA Communications in 1989 when unable to secure deal with $50 million letter of credit, runs $2 billion empire built by frenzied deals with interests in four resorts, TV stations and Hollywood's Hal Roach Studios, owing $500 million to Hong Kong, Chase Manhattan banks files for bankruptcy in 1989)... Ricoh Electronics pioneers Japanese manufacturing in U.S., four plants by 1989...

Colombian-born Carlos Lehder is caught smuggling marijuana into Florida (after serving jail sentence takes over Norman's Cay, Bahamas, in 1978 to develop drug distribution network for Medellin families with goal to unify traffickers in joint management council as The Cartel, buys Colombia newspaper in 1981 for propaganda, is indicted by Florida for smuggling, is arrested by Colombia and extradited to U.S. for trial in 1987, gets life imprisonment without parole in 1988)... Japan's Taiyo Bank and Kobe Bank merge, merger with 1876 Mitsui Bank in 1989 forms world's 2nd-largest bank, assets of $371 billion after Dai-Ichi Kangyo's $380 billion (is followed by Sumitomo, $370 billion, Fuji, $358 billion, and Mitsubishi, $347 billion in assets, face hard times in 1990 with sharp rising interest rates, 27% drop in value of yen since 1988 and collapse of three-year super-bull market on Tokyo Stock Exchange)... Japanese licensee, Ito-Yokado as Japan's second largest supermarket chain, gets rights, Southland, for 7-Eleven chain of convenience stores, 11,551 stores by 1991 (buys 75% of Southland, U.S. parent of 7-Eleven, for $400 million in 1990)... Italian industrialist Franco Mattioli bankrolls fashion designer Gianfranco Ferre, Italy's hottest stylist in 1987 with 82 boutiques and worldwide distribution by Marzotto textile group... Gordon White starts U.S. autonomous branch, Hanson Industries, of Hanson Trust (starts with buy, 1974, of animal feed firm, continues with Hygrade, 1976, Interstate United food service, 1978, sold 1985 for over 3 times original cost, McDonough tools and shoes, in 1981, and U.S. Industries conglomerate in 1984 to run amalgam of low-tech enterprises using bank debt to buy firms with poor management on unrealized market value).

1974

General Events

Some 269,000 British miners strike (February 9) for higher wages, get 35% raise (March 6)... Romanian dictator Nicolae Ceausescu launches national campaign to distract people from economic woes, U.S. Kent Cigarettes are medium of exchange as Lei loses value (starts export program in 1980 to retire foreign debt, begins to rebuild Bucharest in 1983 - displaces over 40,000 residents by 1989, in 1986 institutes 7-day work week and imposes pay cuts up to 30% on workers unable to meet production quotas, by 1988 reduces debt to $5 billion while generating shortages and repression, ignores democratic reforms sweeping East Bloc in 1989, is slain by popular uprising in 1989 - new government gets $1.7 billion foreign-exchange surplus, leads to democratic elections in 1990)... Arab nations end (March 13) oil embargo on U.S., keep high prices... Portuguese Government is overthrown by military coup (begins democratic reforms, grants independence to Portugal's colonies in Africa)... Air Gabon starts air service to Europe, throughout Africa... Libya nationalizes three U.S. oil companies... India arrests (May 2) 700 union leaders to avoid rail strike... Turkey resumes (July 1) sale of opium... Mexico starts herbicide program to spray drug-growing areas (causes share of U.S. heroin market to drop 80% to 30%)... International Maize and Wheat Improvement Center, Mexico, produces (September 2) new plant varieties... International Bauxite Assn. is formed by producing countries in seeking higher prices for resources...

Edward Heath's Conservative Government is toppled by strike of coal miners, fail to overturn Thatcher government with bitter strike in 1984-85... Panama, Columbia, Costa Rica, Venezuela ask OAS to lift (September 6) sanctions against Cuba... M. Mesarovic, E. Pestel: Mankind At The Turning Point (views prospects precarious in report for Club of Rome)... Greece abolishes (December 8) 142-year-old monarchy... I.R.A. explodes (December 21) bomb in Harrods... Benin with widespread poverty nationalizes key firms, banking and insurance services in Marxist revolution (evolves by 1989 as probably West Africa's leading conduit for illicit trade to neighboring countries, principally Nigeria, plans to sell off unprofitable state-owned enterprises in 1989 as nation faces economic crisis)... Mexico opens Cancun international resort, some one million tourists in 1987 and 137 finished hotels in 1989, on Yucatan Peninsula to provide employment for area and lure workers from Mexico City...

Carlos Andres Perez is President of Venezuela (-1979, after drop in oil prices and economy collapses in 1980s is President in 1989 to face public rioting, looting and killing after adopting economic austerity measures to get $4.32 billion in credit from IMF)... Some 1,600 square miles of Japan's Inland Sea are polluted (December 24) by oil spill... Khaled Abu Suud is financial adviser to Kuwait's Emir (uses oil revenues to invest in world markets, portfolio of some $200 billion in 1989, makes biggest coups in 1974 with $350 million stake in Daimler-Benz, worth $2.5 billion in 1989, and $700 million profit on privatized BP in 1987, targets BP, operator of its petroleum field with Gulf Oil before 1975 and world's largest, for acquisition in 1988)... Collapse of copper prices makes Zambia one of world's poorest lands (sees riots in 1990 after $.07 rise in cornmeal prices)... MITI funds project, $47 million by 1991, to raise performance of solar cells...

Number of European golfers increases 242% by 1990 to 2.5 million players, U.S. with 25 million for 13,738 courses, for 3,500 courses, Britain with 2,300.

Business Events

Chase Manhattan Bank reports 30 of world's largest oil companies show an average increase in profits of 93%... Regine's disco club opens in Paris, branches later in Manhattan, Rio... Namco imports video games to Japan (designs popular Pac Man video game in 1980)... Charly Records is started, Britain, with British, Dutch licensing rights to Sun Records catalog (pioneers reissue record business)... With $10,000 Italian fashion designer Giorgio Armani shows first collection of male clothes (features wrinkled linen jackets for understated elegance, unshaven models to start fad), over 2,000 stores worldwide sell merchandise by 1989 in addition to boutiques in Milan, Bologna, London, New York, Los Angeles and Paris... After father dies, Kerry Packer takes over father's business empire (evolves as multi-billionaire by 1989 as Australia's largest magazine publisher, 70% of market, with interests in textiles, chemicals, livestock, construction, properties and financial services)... Murdoch publishes Star supermarket tabloid (sells, circ. 3.6 million, to rival National Enquirer, circ. 4.1 million, in 1990 for $400,000)... In this time, Bolivian rancher Roberto Gomez uses his fleet of planes to ship cocoa leaves to Colombian buyers instead of transporting cattle.

1975

General Events

Scottish Daily News, first workers' cooperative national paper, appears... For first time since W.W. II, British unemployment tops one million... After 13 years of struggle, Angola gets (January 13) independence... Britain, West Germany, U.S., Japan, Canada, France and Italy hold first annual meeting to discuss joint economic problems... EEC opens (February 11) all nine nations to doctors from any member... After 10 years of study and 14 months of digging, work stops on English Channel project, first considered by Napoleon in 1802 (leads to Eurotunnel, British and French consortium, with monopoly franchise to build and operate crossing, gets financing up to $9 billion by global consortium of 200 banks for largest private venture ever taken, plans 1985-87, builds 1988-93)... Japan's percentage of working women in managerial jobs is .9%, 1% in 1987 with U.S. over 10%... European Space Agency is formed by 13 nations, 33 launches by 1989 with $2.1 billion worth of contracts... Kuwait nationalizes its petroleum industry... Egypt reopens (June 5) Suez Canal, closed in 1967 Arab-Israeli War... Britain's inflation rate hits (June 13) 25%... First International Woman's Year World Conference meets in Mexico City, adopts 10-year plan to improve status of women... In Italian elections, Christian Democrats win (June 16) 35.3% of vote, Communists, new name in 1990, 33.4%... Gerhard Mensch: Stalemate in Technology: Innovations Overcome the Depression...

First Japanese-language word processor appears (-1979)... International Whaling Commission bans (June 27) hunting of finback whales... Canada adopts metric system, modified in 1985 due to public resistance... Argentina's Isabel Peron grants (July 8) wage demands to stop general strike... In this time Colombia smuggler Fabio Ochoa, handles cars, liquor, electronic appliances, cattle, emeralds and coffee, is persuaded by drug entrepreneur Pablo Escobar Gaviria to run cocaine to U.S. (acquires control of domestic industry and U.S. wholesale market with personal army of over 2,000, amasses estimated fortune of $2 billion in mid-1980s)... Canada closes (July 23) Atlantic ports to Soviet fishing trawlers... Soviets swap (October 20) 10 million tons of oil to U.S. for 6 million tons of grain... World bank regulators, supervisors worldwide form Cooke Committee, Switzerland, to exchange quick, reliable information to resolve international banking problems... Professor Erno Rubik, Hungary, devises colored-cube puzzle to aid students to understand 3-dimensional objects, world's sales by 1986 of some $100 million (devises new puzzle, "Rubik's Magic", in 1986)... Britain opens (November 3) first underwater pipeline to North Sea oil field... After 470 years, Mozambique wins (November 11) independence from Portugal... Italian, French

Communist Parties disavow (November 17) violent revolution... India files tax case against U.S.' Time, Inc. to tax profits on stories about India... Full-scale civil war appears in Lebanon between conservative Christians, leftist Muslims, aided by PLO (causes only two of 92 banks to close by 1985)... Pro-Palestinian terrorists capture (December 23) 11 oil ministers, Vienna... By 1990 arms exports of Czechoslovakia yield $850 million/year, limited by democratic reforms in 1990... By 1990 East Germany earns some $600 million as landfill for western Europe.

Business Events

El Pollo Loco opens in Mexico to serve char-broiled chicken (evolves with 92 outlets, opens first Los Angeles eatery in 1980 - over 200 local imitators, sells 20 U.S. units to Denny's in 1983 - plans 500 by 1989)... While serving as pilot with Swissair, Moritz Suter starts small independent regional airline, named Crossair in 1978 (shows profits of $681,000 on sales of $23 million in 1983)... After working in insurance underwriting and merchant banking, David Shilling, 22, opens successful small shop for women's hats, London... Tunisia's Tarak Ben Ammar starts Cathago Films to provide on-site services to foreign movie makers (evolves to produce films)... Bell Canada severs ties with AT&T (forms new patent holding company in 1983 to manage diversified operations outside regulatory oversight, represents 13% of all shares on Toronto Stock Exchange by 1985)... Kentucky Fried Chicken opens place in Hong Kong, closes for lack of business... With death of husband, Amalie Lacroze de Fortabat, Argentina's richest woman in 1989 with net worth of $1 billion, takes over family's cement monopoly, chain of radio stations, oil companies and real estate, 17 ranches... Impa is started in Sicily to do steel work, by 1989 handles complex heavy engineering projects in energy, railroads, heavy machinery and construction for mostly governmental clients... Canon's AE-1 launches electronic era of photography, Minolta first with autofocusing system in 1985... Wolfgang Ley starts Escada fashion house in West Germany, 1988 sales of $193 million in U.S. and $300 million in world...

After graduating from Kansai University, Yasuyuki Nambu starts Temporary Center employment agency to lure Japanese housewives into work force, largest of some 350 rivals in 1987 as 31,000 wives look for work (runs 74 branches across land in 1989 with restaurants, venture capital firm, travel agency, and firm leasing sculptures, plans floating office ship for crowded Tokyo in 1989)... Privately-funded International Foundation for Art Research appears in NYC (coordinates efforts to end global market in art theft)... With $25,000 from friends, electronics entrepreneur Stan Shih, Taiwan, starts Acer to assemble U.S.-made computers, later develops own computers and acquires small U.S. firms (goes public in 1988, plans Malaysia plant in 1990 to cut costs and get sales of $1 billion)... Subaru popularizes 4-wheel-drive passenger car for suburbia... West Germany's fashion designer Jil Sander shows first collection, industry of $12 billion by 1988 with Mondi running 50 stores in U.S.... After working for Nomura Securities, Akio Mikuni starts bond-rating service, breaks with traditional Japanese practice to calculate merit of each company... South Korea's Kim Suk-Won inherits father's Ssangyong cement firm (builds chaebol group, sales of $6 billion in 1988, by diversifying in oil refining and using cement business to construct large hotels in Asia and U.S., buys local jeep manufacturer to enter automaking - later Britain's Panther sports car maker, plans Korean venture with Volvo in 1989)... AEG-Telefunken devises world's first commercial videodisc system... Sumitomo Bank rescues failing Mazda Motor, a success by 1990 (leads to Fuji Heavy Industries saving Subaru of America in 1990)... Prodded by Fiat, owns 74% by 1990, small Turin engineering firms form Comau to make robots, $817 million in sales in 1989... U.S.' Campbell's Soup buys Belgian confectioner Godiva... Briton Anne Willan opens La Varenne, Paris cooking school for English-speaking students.

1976

General Events

Italy launches commercial TV in Europe when Supreme Court allows private stations, followed by France in 1984... Generalized System of Preferences is created to give Third World nations duty-free status on some exports... Spain drafts (January 19) 70,000 railmen to halt strike... Scottish weavers reject proposal by Harris Tweed Assn., major unions and government to modernize wool production with power looms... Area around Seveso plant, Northern Italy, is contaminated by dioxin cloud after an explosion (leads to evacuation of residents for six years)... Britain slashes (February 19) welfare spending... Anglo-French supersonic Concorde makes first commercial flight, 1500 mph (makes first operating profits for British Airways in 1982 and Air France in 1983 with no hope to recover start-up costs of some $4.3 billion to build 14 planes, spends $36 million to plan second generation plane, 1875 mph, in 1990)... Rene Levesque, representing Parti Quebecois for secession from Canada, is elected Premier of Quebec in upset victory (-1985, loses on 1976 referendum to negotiate sovereignty status with Canada, sponsors law in 1977 to make French official language of province, loses 140 corporate headquarters by 1985)... Rail strike hits (April 20) Japan... MITI forms consortium of six firms to produce world's highest-capacity memory chip... Italian Government takes over ailing Maserati car business...

Canada cancels (May 18) contract with Lockheed after its bribery scandal... Canada's Alfred N. Dunlop devises solid paint... Elliott Jacques: A General Theory of Bureaucracy (shows organizations can be stratified by time spans required at different levels for work assignments)... Non-aligned nations call (August 20) for rearrangement of international economic relations... Prince Bernhard, Netherlands, resigns (August 26) from military, business posts after Lockheed bribery scandal (leads to indictments of Japanese officials taking $1.6 million from Lockheed)... Elf Aquitaine, French state-run oil conglomerate, is secretly approached by Aldo Bonassoli, Italian "inventor," and Alain de Villegas, glib Belgian Count (reveal "unique" device so an airplane can locate oil deposits and detect submerged enemy submarines by gravitational waves, are given $150 million by 1978, are exposed in 1983 scandal)... Death of Mao Tse-Tung ends (September 19) China's Cultural Revolution...

After Angola's independence in 1975, Marxist Popular Liberation Movement, supported by U.S.S.R. and Cuba, wins struggle for power (evolves with weak economy, black market flourishes with "beer standard," 24 cans of Heineken, as basic exchange value, tries free-market recovery plan in 1988 to end price controls on fruit and vegetables, invites foreign investment, plans to sell state enterprises in 1989)... Swedish Socialists lose (September 19) first general election in 44 years... Brussels opens (September 20) subway... Haranbee Savings & Credit Society of Kenya is saved from default by Government (is revived in one year by Technoserve, non-profit U.S. economic development consulting business)... Saudi Arabia selects U.S.' Bechtel Group as construction manager for project to build Jubail as new ultra-modern city, industrial complex (uses some 1,600 California engineers, 41,000 workers from 39 countries in 15-year effort)... Peter Hall, former chairman of Britain's Fabian Society, devises enterprise zones to revitalize urban areas (is introduced to U.S. in 1978 by Stuart Butler, economic historian from University of St. Andrews, and proposed as legislation by Congressman Jack Kemp in 1980)... Romania, U.S. sign (November 21) 10-year trade pact... Cayman Islands lures investors with passage of Confidential Relationships Law for banking practices... Britain is forced to seek financial assistance from IMF to avert economic crisis...

With economic chaos and guerilla insurgency, military overthrows Argentina's civilian government (-1983)... With foreign grants and private funds, Muhammad Yunus, former professor of economics, starts Bangladesh rural bank, Grameen Bank with branches in 15,000 villages to serve over 500,000 clients by 1990 (lends money, poverty only qualification, to poor in groups for self-employment, is non-government bank in 1986 - 60% of shares held by borrowers, after lending over $100 million by 1990, default rate of 2-3%, serves as model for 18 developing nations)... Engineer Guy Dejouany heads state-owned Compagnie Generale des Eaux, formed 1853 to pipe water of Seine to Paris apartments, with 33 million customers in Europe, world's biggest and wealthiest water utility (begins diversification in steam heating and related services to water business, in 1980s goes into hospitals, Europe's largest with British chain in 1980, toll roads, airports, cable TV, Canal-Plus world's No. 2, office buildings, and pollution controls to hold stakes in over 1,200 subsidiaries, run by headquarters staff of 15, by 1990 for revenues of $17.8

billion)... France persuades Peugeot, Citroen to merge.

Business Events

Short of cash Fiat accepts Libya's investment of some $400 million for 15% ownership (when rejected for Pentagon contract for ties with Libya, buys stock back in 1986)... Assn. of Surfing Professionals plans international tour circuit... London's posh Dorchester Hotel is acquired by Mideast investors... Carrefour, pioneered hypermarkets in 1963 to run 115 by 1989 in Europe, South America as France's largest grocery chain, introduces generic brands to Europe (following Bigg's, joint venture of U.S.' Super Valu, Euromarche and others, in Cincinnati in 1984, opens its first U.S. hypermarket in Philadelphia in 1988, followed by Wal-Mart in 1988-89 and Super Valu in 1989)... After transforming father's 50-person metal-hose factory into Italy's largest independent auto-component producer, listed as Gilardini, with 1,600 employees in 16 years, Carlo De Benedetti is new CEO of Fiat (resigns after three months when Agnelli rejects his bold plan to revive struggling auto firm, starts building new empire with Compagnie Industriali Riunite, failing canning company, as base to buy string of small manufacturing firms, forms three personal holding companies by 1988 to run collections of enterprises throughout Europe)... Pan Am begins Tokyo-NYC service... Volkswagen builds U.S. plant... Former gang bodyguard Rodriguez Gacha works for Pablo Escobar, head of Medellin Cartel (works way up to midlevel cocaine dealer, pioneers new distribution route through Mexico to U.S. to become drug lord, is slain by police in 1989 shoot-out)... Japanese sports promoter, Atsushi Fujita, puts on Tokyo's Coca-Cola Classic, pioneers overseas college bowls (fans' enthusiasm for U.S. football in Asia)... McDonald's of Canada meets Soviet delegation at Montreal Olympics for restaurant in U.S.S.R. (after bureaucratic maze signs joint venture, one of 1,400 by western firms by 1990, in 1988, opens $50 million fast-food eatery, largest in 11,300 chain, to handle 15,000 customers/day with 605 employees, some 27,000 applicants, on Moscow's Pushkin Square in 1990 to waiting lines)... Anita Roddick starts mixing first cosmetics with natural ingredients on kitchen table, Britain's Retailer of Year in 1990 with 464 Body Shops, 300 products, worldwide for sales of some $90 million.

1977

General Events

European Commission tries to outlaw "butterships," floating supermarkets, usually West German, selling duty-free goods at sea... Kenya bans big-game hunting... Rhodesia opens (February 23) industrial zones, shopping areas to blacks... Saudi Arabia allocates (March 7) $1 billion in aid to black Africa... Mexico discovers "sea of oil"... Until new law was passed, Japan was viewed as "process patent" country since local firms could legally patent any foreign-invented medicine if they had devised "unique process" to make it... Infant Formula Action Coalition, joined by International Nestle's Boycott Committee of 70 church, labor and other groups, starts worldwide boycott of Nestle products for failing to observe code of World Health Organization (forces them to comply by 1982)... 107 nations fail (April 2) to create fund to stabilize commodity prices... Spain legalizes (April 9) Communist Party...

First Russian mini-computers appear, U.S. in 1965... U.S. drops membership in ILO for Soviet influence and non-observance of principles, procedures (returns 1980)... Britain, Canada, West Germany, France, Italy, Japan and U.S. meet (May 7) to discuss global recession... With death of Steve Biko in police custody and suppression of black movement, U.N. Security Council votes mandatory embargo on sales of arms, strategic equipment to South Africa, leads to voluntary oil embargo (puts trade embargo on Iraq in 1990 for its invasion of Kuwait)... Some 30,000 Romanian coal miners hold violent strike on withdrawal of certain job benefits, rioting by some 5,000 Brasov workers in 1987 over pay cuts... Forced by U.S. tariff hike, Japan curbs (May 17) TV exports... U.S.S.R. Constitution states each citizen has a right to a job... Failure of Brazil's coffee crop leads to rise in coffee prices worldwide... Canada forms Via Rail to take over failing passenger services of Canadian Pacific, state-owned Canadian National Railway (cuts 405 trains/week to 191 in 1989 to reduce subsidies, budget deficit)... Oleg Vinogradov is artistic director of Kirov Ballet (modernizes traditional ballets, adds new works, employs London promoter in 1989 to license products)... Pravda denounces (June 23) Eurocommunism for seeking power by elections... Israel, U.S. create Tel Aviv's Binational Industrial Research & Development Foundation with $60 million (by 1989, provides seed money to finance nearly 250 commercial ventures from optical equipment to computer software, industry ships over $3 billion in electronics exports in 1988)... OPEC freezes (December 21) price of oil at $12.70/barrel... By 1982 Canadian firms buy some $10.9 billion of U.S. property (is No. 1 foreign real estate owner in U.S.).

Business Events

U.S. fashion designer Geoffrey Beene shows collection of clothes in Italy (gets some $1.3 million on investment of $135,000)... Isoda is President of Sumitomo Bank, keystone of Sumitomo Group of enterprises (replaces consensus rule with authoritarian leadership)... For first time in its history, Sotheby Parke Bernet Group sells stock to public... Iceberg Transport International is formed to provide Saudi Arabia with water from ice floes... Humanization of work is theme of VIII Congress of the European Assn. of Personnel Management in Spain... Michael Hatcher, partners form salvage company in Southeast Asia (by 1983 finds $12 million worth of rubber, tin and other scraps from sunken W.W. II ships in Asian waters, discovers Geldermalsen, Dutch East India merchant sunk during 1752 storm, to recover 127 gold ingots and nearly 170,000 pieces of Chinese export porcelain, worth some $15.3 million in 1986 auction, on investment of some $500,000)... After 94 years of operation, Orient Express ends famed London-Istanbul train service (after acquisition by London's Sea Container's Group of U.S. entrepreneur James Sherwood, refurbished for $20 million, begins London-Venice Orient Express in 1982 for nostalgic tourists, plans luxury railroad service in 1990 for Singapore-Thailand, leads to plush train service between Chicago, Washington in 1989 by sponsor of Europe's Nostalgie Istanbul Orient Express in 1988 for trip from Paris across Russia, China to Hong Kong)...

Perrier, world leader, exports mineral water to U.S. (sells fruit-flavored drinks in 1985, after string of acquisitions, nine brands including Maine's Poland Spring, California's Calistoga and Arrowhead, U.S.' largest processor of bottled water, and Texas' Oasis Water, gets 20% of U.S. market, No. 1, in late 1980s, loses fizz with worldwide recall of tainted bubbly in 1990)... Three former Harvard Business School graduates form MMG Patricof Group as venture capital business (pioneers leveraged buyouts in Europe, by 1988 offices in Paris, London, NYC and Palo Alto)... After civil strife in Lebanon's Bekaa Valley in 1976, Serge Hochar revives Chateau Masar as one of world's great wine houses... Llario Floresta takes over Sicily's ITEL Communications with 20 people, by late-1980s employs 750 in field of advanced communications technology... Japan's Harunori Takahashi begins building empire, $7 billion in 1989, with troubled computer-parts importer (uses EIE International to oversee interests in resorts/leisure activities, 25 hotels from London to Australia and two golf courses, six under construction, and electronics, holds stakes in 15 firms, transportation, shipping, two air cargo lines and aircraft leasing, real estate, office space in Tokyo, Osaka, Hong Kong and Los Angeles, Japanese banks, and Australian gold mine, in 1989 plans $300 million Regent Hotel for NYC, bids for Ramada chain, and invests in Pacific Airlines as debt nearly equals assets)...

When British industry rejects research to determine economic implications of design decisions for assembly lines, Geoffrey Boothroyd goes to U.S. (gets $400,000 research grant from National Science Foundation, gets industrial support in 1978 - later Digital Equipment, GE, Westinghouse, Xerox, IBM in 1983 and Ford in 1984, forms business in 1981 with Peter Dewhurst to commercialize concept, software sales of $414,000 in 1988 with GM as major customer)... Olympic gold-medal skier Jean-Claude Killy starts ski-wear manufacturing firm, Veleda S.A., in Paris, one of Europe's biggest with 1987 sales of $35 million... U.S.' Nike leads athletic-shoes firms to South Korean ventures... RCA asks Sony to make Beta VCRs for sale under RCA label, denied (asks Matsushita which devises VHS).

1978

General Events

Japan, U.S. ease (January 13) trade tensions... U.S. supertanker, Amoco Cadiz, goes aground off Brittany Coast, spews some 60 million gallons in Europe's worst oil spill (is ordered to pay some $155 million in 1990 for damages to French fisheries and tourist industry, followed by U.S.' worst oil spill, some 10 million gallons, of Exxon Valdez in 1989 to pollute some 1,000 miles of Alaskan shores)... Protesting Moscow workers form (January 26) unofficial labor union... France takes over Usinor and Sacilor, ailing steel firms (ends subsidies, total of $16 billion, in 1985, merges two in 1988 to make 97% of land's steel, pays $570 million in 1990 to buy J & L Specialty Products, U.S.' No. 2 stainless producer, to challenge world's No. 1, Nippon Steel)... Canada's Human Rights Act forces liberal new mandates on all employers (makes military put women in combat units)... Sweden is (January 29) first nation to curb aerosol sprays to stop destruction of ozone layer... International standards for private computer networks are formulated, adopted by Japan in 1988 but not U.S. with 70% of world market... China, Japan sign (February 16) $20 billion trade pact... Thousands of Chinese flee (May 1) as Vietnam abolishes some 30,000 private shops in South... City Club of Rome: Beyond the Age of Waste... After four days of rioting in Iran, Moslem leaders ask (May 11) halt to modernization, return of Mosque lands seized by land reforms... Italy elects (July 8) first Socialist president... Former Italian Prime Minister, Aldo Moro is kidnapped, murdered by Red Brigade... For first time in Europe, gold goes over (July 28) $200 at London market...

Japan's Depressed Industries Law provides financial assistance, certain exemptions from anti-monopoly law to firms in declining industries... General strike paralyzes (October 2) Guatemala... John Paul II is (October 23) first non-Italian Pope in 455 years... Thousands clash (October 30) with police in nationwide oil strike, Iran, to demand expulsion of all foreigners with oil jobs... During French elections, Communist candidates get 27% of votes, 15.5% in 1981, 11.3% in 1984, and 9.82% in 1986 election, lowest since 1932 when 8.4% votes for new party... U.S. dollar hits (November 1) post-War low of 175 on Tokyo exchange... Shah of Iran puts (November 6) country under military control... After anti-Shah strikes (December 4) cut oil production by 30%, millions march in Tehran against Shah, Shah flees (January 16, 1979)... After power struggle in China Deng Xiaoping is new leader ("retires" 1989)... Italy honors international drug patents (evolves by 1990 as leading center for pill piracy business).

Business Events

Swedish computer consultant, Mats Gabrielsson acquires broke mini-computer distributor for symbolic one kroner and debts of creditors (after firing employees, selling inventory and paying creditors to clear $500,000, uses funds to set up computer distributorship for Commodore International, creates Datatronic as fast-growing collection of computer and electronic firms, after mastering several other turnabouts acquires ailing U.S.' Victor Technologies in 1984 to outbid British and West German rivals, revives business with low-priced IBM PC clones)... Consortium of businessmen, scientists form Biogen S.A. of Geneva as research-oriented firm (produces first gene-splicing Interferon in 1980)...

France's Peugeot-Citroen acquires European auto operations of Chrysler... Banque Rothschild changes from investment bank to holding company to manage interests in banking, industry... John De Lorean's 1974 De Lorean Motor Co. gets $144 million in grants and loans from Britain, Northern Ireland to build automobile-manufacturing plant in depressed Belfast (produces stainless-steel futuristic sports cars in 1981, is arrested in California in 1982 on smuggling cocaine to save bankrupt business, innocent)... Roger Monk starts Airship Industries, London (gets contract from Shell Oil to design airship, after Shell withdraws from project, is rescued in 1984 by Alan Bond to evolve as world's largest designer, builder and operator of blimps with new design, lightweight materials and guidance system, forms joint venture in 1987 with Westinghouse Electric to best Goodyear in winning U.S. Navy blimp contract, builds 16, including those for McDonald's, Fuji Film, Citibank and Resorts International, by 1989 for corporate advertising to compete with American Blimp, Aerotek))... After passage of U.S.' 200-mile limit to protect its fisheries, Soviet Ministry of Fisheries forms joint venture with U.S. enterprise to catch fish for its factory ships... Oland family sells its Canadian brewery to John Labatt Food Co. of London, Ontario (becomes Canada's No. 1 by 1989 as Molson, No. 2, seeks merger with Carling O'Keefe for U.S.-Canadian Free-Trade Market, as No. 6 exporter to U.S. and sales of $1 billion with ventures in film production and theatrical groups, enters U.S. market in 1987 with buy of Pennsylvania's Latrobe Brewery)... Renault invests in U.S.' American Motors, $645 million by 1987 for controlling interest (signs joint marketing agreement in 1979, with pressure from Communist-led unions and financial losses, sells out to Chrysler in 1987 for $235 million, bids $99 million for Mack Trucks in 1990)... Unicord Co. begins as food processor, uses equipment of U.S.' Bumble Bee, in Thailand to export canned tuna (by 1989 is largest supplier to Bumble Bee, Thailand passes Japan as world's No. 1 canned-tuna exporter, before acquiring Bumble Bee)..

After seeing simple camera in Miami pharmacy, Sonora Industrial of Brazil develops Love disposable camera... Samhura Co. is first South Korean footwear firm to invest in overseas plant as country becomes center for athletic shoes (leads to 1989 indictment of 18 people selling counterfeit South Korean shoes, fails to stop Itaewon, Seoul shopping strip, in hawking fake goods)... Former cabaret singer Silvio Berlusconi, $12.3 billion empire by 1990 as Gruppo Fininvest with interests in Standa department store chain, magazines, financial services, real estate and soccer team, discovers legal loophole in Italian laws to compete against state-owned TV (starts Italy's first private TV network in 1980, one year before court overturns government's monopoly, to get 63% of all ad revenues, some $1.5 billion, in 1989, launches France's first private TV channel in 1985 with Jerome Seydoux and others, wins rights in 1989 to sell Western commercials on Soviet TV, plans similar licenses with China, East Bloc nations)... Pichet Viraporn quits job at Thailand's Eli Lilly drug plant to import mag wheels for cars, by 1988 with sales of some $4 million and plans for $6 million in 1989...

European producers hold 16% of world's chip market, 9.7% in 1988 as chipmakers dwindle to Siemens, Philips and SGS-Thompson Eureka... De Benedetti pays $17 million for Olivetti, typewriter maker losing $8 million/month (as first major Italian firm to lay off large numbers of workers is target of Red Brigade terrorist group while transforming firm into one of Europe's leaders in office-automation, joins AT&T, gets access to EC, in 1983, for technology to make PCs - EC's No. 2 to IBM in PCs by 1988, forms joint venture in 1987 with Canon to enter copier market, drops AT&T venture in 1989, with profits, market shares sliding reorganizes in 1989 as three separate concerns: office equipment largest with sales of $2.5 billion, computers, software)... Jean-Louis Dumas is CEO of family's Hermes luxury business, founded 1837 as harness shop (by 1990 ups sales ninefold to $460 million, adds 80 shops for total of 238 - 30 planned, expands in U.S. and Far East, adds new products, British shoes and glass of 1767 Cristalleries de St. Louis, to sell some 30,000 items, and refuses to license name to maintain standards).

1979

General Events

China breaks up credit monopoly of People's Bank with specialized funding institutions... By 1986 some 250 new firms appear around Cambridge, makes area one of Britain's high-tech districts... China, U.S. resume (January 31) diplomatic relations... China introduces "agricultural responsibility system" (allows peasants to contract for sale of produce to state for fixed price, sell surplus on open market, and to form collectives on small economic units)... China International Trust & Investment is formed to obtain funds from foreign capital markets for profitable ventures, to find new ways to do business (creates four Special Economic Zones in coastal areas to attract foreign investment and foster export trade, develops Shenzhen, north of Hong Kong border, as high-tech industrial area - a district election in 1985, uses Sichuan Province to test traditional planned economy with free market - over 65,000 entrepreneurs use aggressive selling and mergers to eliminate unprofitable concerns, tries "shareholders" in factories to determine production plans, distribution of profits, and appointment, removal of managers)... Nigerian law allows payments by National Health Service to herbalists, "spirit mediums"... College of Cardinals holds first consistory in 400 years to consider Vatican's administration, finances... Khomeini returns (February 26) to Iran to establish Islamic Republic (supports stoning of adulterers, hacking off hands of thieves, men with multiple wives, sexual segregation in schools, and women in veils, forbids use of alcohol, lending of money at interest, dies in 1989 as economy slides into ruin)... China agrees (March 1) to pay 41 cents/dollar for U.S. assets seized 1949... First public demonstration of maglev train, uses magnetism to lift cars off track to reduce friction, is seen at Hamburg Transportation Fair... South Africa legalizes black labor unions, National Union of Mine Workers largest by 1986 with over 200,000 members... Conservative Party is elected (May 3) to govern Britain, Margaret Thatcher is first woman Prime Minister (-1990, during three elections fights inflation with tight money and strong currency - annual growth rate 2nd only to Japan by 1988, lifts foreign exchange controls - net overseas financial assets over $120 billion by 1988, lowers personal tax rate to increase middle class, privatizes 16 major state-owned enterprises by 1988, makes national unions financially responsible for actions of members, bans sympathy walkouts and secondary picketing of unions, forces unions to hold secret ballots before striking, crushes strikes of steelworkers in 1980, coal miners after one year in 1985 and teachers in 1986 - 29.5 million work days lost by strikes in 1979 to 3.7 million in 1988, posts interest rate of 13% and inflation rate of 7.9% in 1989, both highest in industrial countries, as economic gains erode)...

Deng Xiaoping launches economic reforms with Marxist central planning overseeing capitalist marketplace (opens coast area to foreign investment, 100% control to foreigners on priority projects, for export-oriented enterprises, reaches $25 billion, U.S. 2nd to Hong Kong with investment of $3.5 billion, for nearly 16,000 ventures until Beijing crackdown on student protests in 1989, causes drop in $2.2 billion/year tourist industry, launches "one-family, one-child" program to contain population growth with penalties, dismissal from government jobs and fines, and rewards, better housing and monthly stipend for child, evolves with two Chinas, prosperous coast and impoverished interior)... First elections are held (June 10) for European Parliament by nine EEC countries (orders majority of entertainment programs be produced in Europe by 1990, requires all new small cars use catalytic converters by 1991, seeks to ban chlorofluorocarbons, bans imports of $100 million worth of hormone-treated U.S. beef, rejects trade agreement with Israel over West Bank policies)... Spain's Communist Party rejects Marxism for pragmatic goals... Iran nationalizes (July 7) most heavy industry... China-U.S. trade agreement gives China most favored nation status (quadruples trade to $18 billion/year by 1990, is extended in 1990 despite attacks by Congress for violations in human rights)...

Marxist-oriented Sandinistas oust (July 27) Nicaraguan dictator Anastasio Samoza, family rule since 1933 (although promising better life leads to civil war, delivers hard times in late 1980s as hyperinflated economy collapses, introduces new cordoba in 1988 to cut inflation, as most people, Sandinista elite with special privileges, live by barter in underground economy, cuts national budget by nearly 50% in 1989, lays off nearly 35,000 government employees, including Army personnel and secret police, and swells unemployment to 30% of labor force, after 1990 democratic elections turns government over to Chamorro coalition to face foreign debt of $7 billion)... Nigeria nationalizes British oil interests... Vatican begins making its financial details public, deficit of $20 million to nearly $64 million in 1987 with largest outlays going to 2,325 employees, 880 retirees... China dismantles communes to give farmers more freedom to farm (in 1981-85 increases wheat production by 43%, meat by 39%, cotton by 40%)... Britain stops (September 10) making MG sportscars... U.S., Colombia sign treaty to extradite drug traffickers to U.S... Japan Railways tests prototype maglev train at 321 mph... Nicaragua nationalizes (October 17) insurance companies... Hernando de Soto, former CEO of Swiss consulting firm, returns to Peru to manage placer gold mine (forms Institute of Liberty and Democracy in 1980 to study underground economy, publishes The Other Path to urge legalization of hidden economy, perhaps 29% of Peru's GNP with Lima's food retailing dominated by some 90,000 illegal street vendors, to overcome poverty and combat

Maoist Shining Path terrorist group)... Britain is first country with public videotext service to provide computer data over telephone lines... Nicaragua nationalizes (November 3) mining industry... Venezuela finds (November 26) oil deposits equaling OPEC reserves... Hong Kong imports 521 tons of ivory, 290 in 1987, for City's traders, retailers, and carvers in scores of factories and some 300 shops, some 3,000 people in all dominated by 10 families or syndicates... After providing free labor for construction work from surplus of Guangdong Province, China Civil Construction Engineering is formed to provide unemployed Chinese for overseas projects to earn foreign exchange (by 1988 signs 4,700 labor contracts, $7.5 billion, to send 250,000 workers overseas)... Assn. of Vatican Lay Employees forms to present concerns to Vatican authority for consideration... Pakistan makes processing of opium illegal, replaced by other crops with U.S. funds... Libya raises (December 16) oil prices by $4 to $30/barrel... Japan has 14,000 women engineers, 62,000 in 1989... Second OPEC oil shock sends Japan's inflation to 18%... Sport of bungee jumping, copies rite of passage for New Guinea natives, begins when tuxedoed members of Oxford Dangerous Sports Club jump off Bristol bridge (spreads to New Zealand and U.S., $40 million industry in 1990s)... CP Rail, CN become all-freight lines after Canada forms Via Rail Canada to serve passengers.

Business Events

After competitive battle for survival, National Hockey League absorbs World Hockey Assn... Bu Xinsheng, former worker, is selected by textile industry officials in China to manage tiny, marginal Haiyan shirt factory near Shanghai with assets of some $10,000 and profits rarely over $2,300 (with authority to hire and fire, sets work rules and gives bonuses for good performance, revitalizes business as one of land's fastest-growing garment operations with 630 workers, assets of $817,000 and profits over $242,000 in 1983 with strict discipline, benefits, i.e., subsidized housing, and modern marketing methods)... West Germany's Philipp Holzmann AG, Europe's largest construction business, acquires U.S.' J.A. Jones Construction... Three Canadians design Trivial Pursuit's game in Toronto, sales over 11 million sets by 1984 as fad wanes in 1985... Minolta Camera, Sanki Engineering devise new manufacturing system with automated parts and supply systems, free-flow conveyor assembly for flexible production...

Samsung makes television sets for Sears... To expand their business interests despite losses from Belgian chain of stores, France's Willot brothers, convicted of fraud and forgery in 1974, acquire U.S.' pioneering Korvette discount chain, folds U.S. operation in two years... Lloyd's of London forms committee to study operations and make recommendations, last major revision of rules in 1871... Nippon Electric is first with personal computer for Japanese market... China's Xi Guan commune forms cooperative of 500 households, by 1987 is Bright Pearl with hospital, tourist hotel and trucking company... Canadian lawyer Garth Drabinski co-founds Cineplex with 18 theaters, 2nd-largest North American chain by 1988 with 1,752 screens to United Artists' 2,275 (buys complex of 14 Los Angeles theaters in 1982, after winning restraint of trade suit against rivals in 1983 buys Odeon chain, one of two ruling circuits with Famous Players to withhold first-run films from upstart, in 1984 for $17 million, buys U.S.' Plitt theaters in 1985 to operate 1,060 screens, fights for control in 1989 with financial problems from growth)...

U.S. retail chain of Tower Records enters Japanese market, sales of $36 million in 1988 (is joined by Toys 'R' Us in 1989 with plans for 100 large stores, attacked as unfair by thousands of mom-and-pop toy stores)... Lun Feng, one of some 1,000 Guangdong manufacturers in total of 10,000 along coast with over two million workers by 1989, is formed as joint venture by town of Kai Kong, nominal owner, and Hong Kong partner to make stuffed toys... Britain's Imperial Group acquires U.S.' Howard Johnson chain of 1,040 restaurants and 500 motor lodges, founded 1928, for $630 million, sold to Marriott in 1985, which sells bulk to Prime Motor Inns to retain some 400 restaurants... Fujitsu tops IBM as No. 1 in Japan's computer market, attacks IBM in 1989 with clone mainframes of U.S. affiliate Amdahl... Ceselsa, Spain's leading industrial in aviation systems and communications by 1989, is formed as agent for international technology producers, enters manufacturing field in 1980 to develop, make own high-tech equipment... With death of father, Shi

H. Huan returns from U.S. medical practice to take over (builds bicycle shop into one of Taiwan's leading auto and motorcycle makers, multi-billionaire by 1989)... When father-in-law dies in plane crash, Raul Gardini, farmer's son and university drop-out, takes over Ferruzzi grain-trading business (builds $25-30 billion conglomerate in agriculture, handles 20% of EC grain exports, financial services, trading and chemicals by 1989 with interests in host of firms, including European operation of U.S.' CPC International, giant maker of grocery products, wins control of Italy's 4th-largest industrial firm and chemical producer, Montedison, in 1987, merges chemical group with state-owned ENI in 1989 to form Enimont, world's 7th-largest chemical firm, denies wrongdoing to 1989 charges by Chicago Board of Trade in trying to corner U.S. soybean market, plans in 1989 for Soviet agribusiness project, fights government for control of Enimont, sales of $11 billion, in 1990)... Sony introduces Walkman audiocassette player, videocassette Video Walkman in 1988...

Britain's NatWest Bank, National Westminster is land's largest with assets of $170 billion, pays $430 million for NYC's National Bank of North America (gets First Jersey National Bank for $820 million in 1987, plans to spend up to $3 billion in bank takeovers by early 1990s)... Ichiro Takarabe starts famed Japanese training school, Kanrisha Yosei Gakko (exports harsh training methods to develop aggressive salesmen, managers to U.S. in 1987)... Frans Swarttouw heads sleepy Dutch aircraft manufacturer Fokker (revives business by introducing compact, efficient jet liners in 1987 with loans of $700 million from Holland, wins $3 billion contract from American Airlines in 1989 for 150 planes)... Al-Fayed buys Ritz Hotel (after remodeling, $150 million, plans haute cooking school in 1987)... Holland accounting group, Germany's 2nd ranking accounting firm and two U.S. accounting firms combine with others from Denmark, Canada, U.K. and Switzerland to form KMG (combines, world's largest in accounting, in 1987 with Peat, Marwick, Mitchell & Co-partners, began in 1897 with U.S.' Marwick, Mitchell & Co. and 1911 with U.K.'s Peat Marwick to merge in 1925 and form Peat Marwick International in 1978).

1980

General Events

Gold hits (January 21) high of $875 on world markets, $398.60 on January 4, 1990... Vatican lay workers threaten to strike over right to form a union, approved by John Paul II... West Germany plans synthetic-fuel program to convert coal into oil or gas... El Salvador nationalizes (March 7) banks, sugar and coffee in state of emergency... Transgene is formed in France with public, private funds as bioengineering business... "Sinking" supertanker, Salem, with oil cargo of $60.2 million is abandoned off Senegal by crew with packed suitcases (unloads oil later in South Africa with new name to avoid embargo)... Vredeling plan, requires disclosures by international corporations to employees and gives worker representatives right to consult with parent companies, is submitted to European Parliament, rejected 1982... Cousteau begins project to design revolutionary sailboat (develops 103-foot Alcyone with turbosails, vertical masts to capture wind, and computers to chart course and monitor boat's performance)...

After Tito dies (May 4), collective leadership, top positions rotate among six republics, is formed to govern Yugoslavia (evolves by 1989 with inflation of 170%, unemployment, social unrest and ethnic rivalries, faces disintegration in 1989-90 as Serbia threatens to cut all ties with rival Slovenia, land's most economically developed area on Austria border)... Britain's National Enterprise Board forms Celltech as biotechnology venture with exclusive rights for monoclonal antibody, follows DNA discoveries of Medical Research Council in 1975... Japanese tanker, Shin Aitoku Maru, uses sails for auxiliary power... Castro allows farmers' markets in Cuba to encourage farm output, reduce food shortages (are closed 1986 with discovery farmers, truckers, brokers make big money)... Two weeks of Swedish strikes end (May 11) with pay raise... Socialist Francois Mitterrand is new President of France (by 1986 nationalizes 39 banks, five major industries)... Israelis break (June 4) West Bank protest strike by forcing shops to open... OPEC raises (June 10) oil prices to $32/barrel... India is (July 18) 6th nation to orbit a satellite... Civilian government of Bolivia is overthrown by forces of General Luis Garcia Meza, "secretly" financed by Gomez (-1982, develops economy with government monopoly on cocaine trade, Gomez kingpin by giving funds to protect trade of some $3 billion/year)... Nigeria demands (August 8) return of oil from Gulf, Mobil, Royal Dutch Shell... In certain factories throughout Poland, elected representatives of workers, no Communists, are allowed to bargain with government on wages and food prices, key issue is self-government of trade unions (after labor turmoil over 17 days, grants workers most demands and allows, August 20-22, them to form own union, launches Solidarity movement of unemployed electrician Lech Walesa at Gdansk Lenin Shipyard, some 9.5 million members before suppression by martial law in 1981-82, is banned 1982 and becomes ineffective by 1986, is allowed to re-form by General Wojciech Jaruzelski in 1989, wins free elections as political party, first since 1947, and governs country as Communist Party takes minority role)... Marxist Shining Path guerilla group, formed by Peruvian philosophy professor Abimael Guzman in 1970, begins rural insurgency in highlands against business and industry, 2nd phase of Mao's strategy in China, to topple government and install peasant and worker regime, over 12,000 victims and $3 billion in economic damage by 1989 (forms alliance in 1987 with local drug lords to provide protection for funds)...

To protest Soviet invasion of Afghanistan, many nations boycott Moscow Summer Olympics... Unions at Fiat call strike to protest company's recovery plan to cut employment by over 30%, some 40,000 workers protest strike... MITI drops rule requiring non-Japanese firms be approved before opening subsidiaries in Japan, nearly 500 new U.S. enterprises by 1985... Iraq halts (September 26) oil exports due to Iranian bombing... Israel replaces (September 30) pound with new shekel... Arianespace is formed as consortium of 36 European aerospace firms, 11 European banks and French government agency (launches first commercial rocket in 1984, posts earnings in 1985 of $24.3 million on revenues of some $200 million, launches 16 missions, only three failures, by 1986, with orders for 45 satellites by 1991 gets business of downed U.S. space program)... Brazil's Amazon gold discovery (October 2) lures thousands... By 1990 some 3,520,000 South African Blacks lose jobs from divestments... Europe uses 28 commercial TV channels (U.K. with 3 stations, 8 in 1990, France with 3, 7, Spain with 2, 5, Italy with 4, 9, and West Germany with 3, 7 in 1990), 56 by 1990... Thailand's Prime Minister Prem Tinsulanond takes office (halts nationalization of private companies, keeps taxes and import duties low to stimulate economy - one of Asia's "Four Tigers" in 1988 with U.S. firms, AT&T largest with 20,000 workers, and Japanese, 250 firms making everything from cars to electronic components, to become world's leading exporter of canned pineapple and tuna while shipping over $2 billion in clothing, textiles and nearly $1 billion in polished gems, jewelry)...

France uses one golf course, 90 by 1990 as Europeans flock to sport... Former Viet Cong guerilla fighter, Nguyen Thi Thi takes over money-losing food department for Mekong Delta region (with government monopoly and capitalist principles, consolidates network of rice retailing shops, cuts staff, introduces new products, increases exports, and increases productivity of bureaucracy with incentive wages, as profitable success by 1987 plans small oil refinery with solar-powered system to keep factory running despite common shortages in electrical power)... Mexico ends (December 28) fishing pact with U.S... China requests William Dill, Dean of New York University's Graduate School of Business, to assemble management faculty, country's first real management program (forms The Chinese National Center for Industrial Science and Technology at Manchuria's Dalian Institute of Technology)... Japan is world's largest manufacturer of cars, trucks... China creates special economic zone for capitalist enterprises just north of Hong Kong border... France's PTT monopoly of communications starts electronic phone book project at St. Malo with 55 households (expands to 1,500 families in 1981 with Minitel terminals, grows as telephone-computer-directory-assistance service of two million units to supply some 4.5 million users with network for shopping, banking, reading and exchanging personal messages, adopts inexpensive pay-as-you-go policy in 1984, forms Intelmatique state agency to sell system overseas)... Saudi Arabia produces some 10 million barrels of oil/day, some 5 million/day in 1990... Spain grants Catalonia self-government, by 1990 produces 21% of land's GNP, over 25% of exports... Swiss counterespionage agents nab couple, Suchard employees, for trying to sell secret chocolate recipes to U.S.S.R., China...

By 1990 some 480 foreign plants, most in textiles, appear in Mauritius, attracted by government incentives, abundant labor and low wages (with economic success shows problems of industrialized society: labor shortages, pollution, loss of resources, high wages, inadequate infrastructure)... Iraq attacks Iran to seize oil-rich area of Khuzistan (-1990, spurs cronies of Saddam Hussein to buy privatized state companies during war as land uses oil revenues to build petrochemical and fertilizer industries, takes Kuwait in 1990 for its cash, oil resources, access to sea).

Business Events

Jean-Luc Bret starts Croissanterie as French fast-food chain to compete with 27 fast-food rivals, 180 including Mammy Croissante by 1982... Fortune: "Europe Outgrows Management American Style"... After years of financial losses and unending labor disputes, Times of London is sold... World's most valuable stamp, 1856 British Guiana one cent magenta, is auctioned for $850,000... After working for family's M.M. Rothschild & Sons in London since late 1950s (runs bank's first corporate finance department, plots $1 billion takeover of Watney Mann brewery in 1972), Jacob Rothschild is ousted from "gentlemen's" bank by cousin Evelyn for speculative ventures (builds Charterhouse J. Rothschild in 1983 to create new financial empire by seizing opportunities opened by financial deregulation)... Japan's Sharp produces first "talking wristwatch," made in Hong Kong... Some $90 million are invested in new U.S. businesses by foreign venture capital firms, such as Switzerland's Trans Venture and France's Elf Technologies... In this time, Western village theme park, styled after Knott's Berry Farm in Southern California, opens near Tokyo... Japan's Nippon Kokan launches wind-powered cargo ship, uses two rigid metal sails opening like pages of a book... 214 local businessmen are flogged in Zambia for over-charging customers on essential commodities... London's Midland Bank acquires California's Crocker National Bank, U.S.' 12th largest... London's Unlisted Securities Market trades venture capital stocks... Peter Lawrence: Managers and Management in West Germany (notes most managers not easily influenced by external information, not interested in modern planning and controlling techniques, and trained in science, engineering)...

Buxted Poultry, Britain's largest purveyor of table fowl, introduces Churkey, combines chicken and turkey... After decade of research, scientists at British milling and baking firm devise process to mass-produce "mycoprotean," food from fungus (follows development of Proteen, animal feed from dried bacteria, by ICI)... Britain's Redcoat Cargo Airlines contracts for delivery of four skyships in 1984 with top speed of 86 mph and ability to cross Atlantic in 2 1/2 days... Equipment makers form Japan Robot League, approved by MITI, to lease robotic devices to small factories... German-born American, Peter W. Schutz, former vice president of marketing and service for Cummins Engine, heads West Germany's Porsche... Japanese firms produce 26% of world's semiconductor market, 40% by 1984 as U.S. firms drop 61% to 51%... Vincent Bollore, Brittany native, leaves Paris bank job to run family's ailing producer of paper products for token payment of one franc (after switching into teabags and electronics, builds a conglomerate by 1987 with firms from financial services to tissue, his share is some $150 million)...

After serving as worldwide marketing head for Motorola's semiconductor division, Pasquale Pistorio, son of Sicilian farm cooperative worker, joins Italy's state-controlled semiconductor manufacturer (as one of many Italian enterprises moving into France, Spain, Germany and Britain, merges in 1987 with division of France's Thomson electronics to become 2nd only to Philips among European chipmakers)... After running glitzy Rhodes nightclub and exporting U.S. construction equipment to Europe, Middle East during oil-booming 1970s, Mohamed Hadid, descendent of Bedouin tradesman, leaves Middle East for U.S. (with real estate ventures, i.e., Ritz-Carlton hotels in NYC and Washington for $150 million and Aspen resort to trump Donald Trump, builds fortune of $100 million by 1989)... United Microelectronics pioneers Taiwan's chipmaking industry, Silicon Island follows California's Silicon Valley, Scotland's Silicon Glen and Oregon's Silicon Forest (is followed in 1985 by U.S.' C. Morris Chang to help launch Island's semiconductor industry and Texas Instruments joint venture with Acer in 1989 to build $250 million facility as Taiwan seeks to become world's No. 4 supplier in 1992 after Japan, U.S., and Korea)... Matsushita Electric is first Japanese firm to open Mexican maquiladora plant (leads to seven Japanese firms, Matsushita with 2,000 workers, in Tijuana by 1988)... Japanese firm buys Alaska's largest ski resort, later Japanese buy resorts of Steamboat and Breckenridge, CO., and Stratton Mountain, VT... Following work in mid-1960s by U.S.' Lofti Zadeh, Copenhagen's F.L. Smidth & Co. is world's first to market a commercial fuzzy expert system, computer program controls fuel-intake rate and gas flow of rotating kiln to make cement (is used in 1985 by Hitachi for Sendai's subway system, over 100 new applications by Japanese researchers by 1990 to outdistance world)... State-owned British Steel shows world's largest ever loss of some $4 billion, by 1988 is one of world's most profitable producers and more efficient than rival West German steelmakers... Christopher Hogg, Harvard MBA, is CEO of Courtaulds, a declining $3.5 billion-a-year textile business (reorganizes firm into six business sectors, measures performance by results and standards of best of competitors, shuts down all sales operations that can't perform, provides new funds for strategic operations to turn enterprise around, pretax profits for 1982-88 average 37%).... Mexico's Felix Gallardo moves tons of cocaine in early 1980s from South America to U.S. via Guadalajara, evolves as site for 18 major drug gangs in informal cartel... Black American Patrick Kelly reaches Paris, a hit peddling colorful buttons and little tube dresses on street (by 1985 is successful fashion designer with witty, sexy styles)... Facing bankruptcy Fiat lays off 23,000 workers to cut costs, drops 75,000 jobs by 1986 (invests $15 billion 1982-87 in automation, research and new models to double annual output to 29 cars/worker as Europe's lowest-cost carmaker and world's 6th largest)...

In this time posses appear in Jamaica to sell cocaine to raise political funds for elections, export drug activities to U.S. to challenge Columbia Cartel in major city markets... Swiss pharmaceutical giant, F. Hoffmann-La Roche, leads European biotech race in joint venture with U.S. pioneer Genentech (after six other ventures, loses $4.2 billion hostile takeover of U.S.' Sterling Drug in 1988, buys 60% of Genentech, needs funds for R & D, for some $2.1 billion to get U.S. biotech know-how as European drugmakers seek similar deals, 550 strategic alliances 1989-90)... Women's World Banking forms, NYC, to arrange loans for women with no collateral (grows by 1990 with 47 chapters on six continents with nearly $12 million outstanding in loans, only loses $35,000)... U.S.' Amway starts wholly-owned Japanese subsidiary (by 1990 uses 700,000 distributors, successful with religious zeal and family approach for 1989 sales of $524 million, to sell its 150 household products directly to consumers)... By 1990 overseas future exchanges snare 37% of market while U.S. exchanges drop from 100% to 63%... BAT forms Batus to run U.S. holdings (after selling Saks stores to Investcorp for $1.5 billion and Marshall Field chain to Dayton Hudson for $1.04 billion, closes Batus, as well as Batig unit in West Germany, in 1990)... After investing, 1960s, in oil and gas ventures, sold 1980 for $2.3 billion, Seagram loses battle for Conoco oil to Du Pont, gets 20% of Du Pont, largest interest, for its share of Conoco (in 1986 launches Golden Wine Cooler, tops all rivals by 1987 before market slumps, in 1987 buys Martell Cognac for $732 million, 60% of business overseas by 1989, in 1988 gets Tropicana Products for $1.2 billion to enter juice market, 22.5% share in 1991 to top Coca-Cola's Minute Maid, in 1989, after buying Oddbins, U.S. retail wine and spirits chain, and Germany's Mathers Muller, sparkling wine, adds American Natural Beverages, maker of Soho Natural Sodas, for $15 million, for sale in 1991, and goes after spirits division, sales of $600 million/year of U.K. conglomerate Whitbread, completes buy, 1990, of Premium beverages, realigns, 1991, from geographicals to spirits, non-spirits groups).

1981

General Events

Romania's Ceausescu launches "new agricultural revolution" to boost disappointing production of cereals, source of foreign exchange to reduce national debt (launches program in 1987 to raze villages, some 8,000 of 13,000, to create "agro-industrial centers" by 2000)... U.S.' solar-powered Challenger, designed by Paul MacCready, flies English Channel in 5 hours, 23 minutes... Poland gives (January 31) workers Saturdays off... Hungary's Danube Blue forms East Europe's first ecological group to oppose dam on river (evolves despite government opposition to protest industrial pollution)... Canadian, U.S. authorities nab four 13-year olds for breaking into computer systems, block access and destroy data, of several Canadian firms... New Polish Premier Jaruzelski seeks (February 12) no strikes for three months to halt economic crisis... China announces (February 28) new austerity plan (encourages private business, lets new entrepreneurs hire up to seven workers)... Zimbabwe Traditional Healers' Assn. starts research center to discover secrets of drugs used by herbalists... Twelve in Britain's Labor Party resign (March 2) to form new centrist Social Democrats... Canada adopts National Energy Program to increase Canadian ownership of energy firms doing business in country (forces U.S.' Conoco to sell 53% stake in Hudson's Bay Oil and Gas to Canada's Dome Petroleum and Atlantic Richfield Canada, Belgium's Petrofina Canada to sell to state-owned Petro-Canada)...

Poland's Solidarity holds (March 27) 4-hour nationwide strike... Shenzhen is sleepy fishing village on China's border with Hong Kong (in one of five special economic zones offering foreigners tax breaks and other incentives, evolves by 1989 as modern industrial city of 600,000 with skyscraper office buildings, Western luxury hotels and golf course to earn $2 billion/year on exports)... Hundreds of idled London youths riot (April 12) to protest unemployment and poverty, later in some 30 cities, towns... Polish farmers are allowed (April 17) to form Rural Solidarity union... Scandinavia is world's first area with international cellular telephone network using common standards, Britain in 1985... Poland, Solidarity compromise (lets union select enterprise managers in certain industries, grants union veto power in others)... East Bloc participates in five joint ventures with Western enterprises, 166 in 1987 with Hungary's 140 since 1970 as No. 1... Socialist Party, headed by Mitterrand, is elected (May 10) to govern France (adopts confiscatory income, wealth and inheritance taxes, doubles levies on yachts, power boats and business cars, decentralizes governmental powers, nationalizes 90% of all banking, 32% of industry for some $1 billion)... Government forms Singapore Investment Corp. to stimulate economic growth (hosts over 3,000 multinationals in 1990)...

Saudi Arabia awards contract, history's largest "fixed price" agreement, to French and U.S. construction firms to build new University of Riyadh... To maintain prices, EC orders (August 7) million tons of fruit destroyed... Mexico's 4th largest cash crop is marijuana, valued around $8.5 billion... Norway's Labor Government of 8 months is ousted (September 14) by conservatives, returns to power in 1986... Pope John Paul II: Laborum Exercens (exults dignity of toil, asserts "priority of labor" over impersonal factors of production, stresses right of workers to organize unions, participate in management and receive "just" family wages, condemns laissez-faire Capitalism, endorses strikes so long as use not abused, stresses women have right to work if not forced to abandon role as mothers, calls labor unions indispensable in struggle for social justice)... EC agrees to phase-out national subsidies to steel industry by 1985... Belize, Britain's last colony in Americas, wins (September 20) independence... TGV, France's high-speed train, begins (September 22) service from Paris to Lyons, handles 100 million passengers on two-hour, 168-mph trip (spurs other European countries to develop network of superfast trains for 1990s, to link with Britain in 1993 via Anglo-French Tunnel)...

Solidarity calls for free elections to challenge Communist government... Japan sponsors $136 million supercomputer research project, first introduced by U.S.' Cray in 1976 (leads to Fujitsu, NEC and Hitachi with 24% of market, U.S. 76%, by 1989)... Soviet troops maneuver (September 5) near Poland... Polish laws give (September 25) workers role in running plants... Some 9.1 million workers are unemployed in EC, 8.3% of labor force in 10 countries... Polish women occupy (October 14) textile mills to protest food shortages... OPEC sets (October 29) oil prices at $34/barrel (drops to $26 by January, 1986, dips below $10 in 1986 before slowly rising to around $17 by 1990)... Fortune: "Japan's Ominous Chip Victory" (notes land gaining 70% of world market in 64K random-access memory chips)... First Socialist Government of Greece is elected to office, Andreas Papandreau Prime Minister (-1989 when economic conditions sour, tries competitive socialism with committees of consumers, workers and management to set productivity guidelines for state-owned, private enterprises)... U.S.S.R. names Slava Zaitsev chief designer for new Moscow fashion house... Sweden devalues its krona... Brezhnev makes (November 16) food shortages No. 1 problem of U.S.S.R... Vietnam's Communist regime adopts incentive raises, bonuses to improve productivity, eliminate inefficiencies in work force... Heads of 22 countries meet in Cancun, Mexico, to discuss how industrialized nations can assist underdeveloped countries escape poverty... Britain sells state-owned British Aerospace to private interests (divests other state enterprises: Cable & Wireless, Amersham International, Britoil, Associated British Ports)... Poland declares (December 13) martial law after labor leaders call for national vote on future of government... Union members are killed (December 17) resisting Poland's martial law.... By 1989 60% of Hungary's restaurants, coffee houses are rented to managers as private businesses, true for many small stores... MITI starts fuel-cell power generation project (spends $20 million by 1991)... Britain transfers telecommunications from Port Office to new British Telecom Corp. (lets Mercury Communications, formed 1981 by Cable and Wireless, owns 100% in 1984, BP and Barclays, to compete, is privatized in 1984).

Business Events

Kawazaki Heavy Industries, Fujitsu Fanuc and Nippon Electric develop first generation of robots capable of assembling auto parts or electric motors... Holland's Fokker Aircraft, U.S.' McDonnell Douglas form joint venture to build new medium-range passenger jet liner... Wall Street guru Joseph Grandville advises English clients to sell (plunges value of stock traded on London Stock Exchange by over $3.9 billion, $10 billion in two days)... Group of restless talents, Milan, to redesign household items with irrelevant flair form Memphis (leads trend of architects designing personal objects)... SSIH, Switzerland's 2nd largest watchmaker with Omega and other brands, is saved from bankruptcy by banks to maintain land's prestige... Elf Aquitaine buys U.S.' Texasgulf for $2.7 billion... Yamazaki Machinery Works, Japan, operates computer-controlled plant to make component parts with robots for metal-working implements (needs only six employees for maintenance, security, and tourists)... Nomura Securities, Japan's largest investment firm and world's largest by 1986, buys first Japanese seat on New York Stock Exchange (is followed in 1982 by listing of Hitachi stock on NYSE)... Volkswagen, Nissan Motor form joint venture to make VW cars in Japan... Japan's automobile industry adopts "voluntary" 4-year limit on exports to U.S... Work begins to build 823-mile Northern Border Pipeline from Alberta, Canada, to Iowa (-1982 as largest privately-financed pipeline project)... Spain's Banco Central is first European bank to seek listing on NYSE... With unproductive workforce, lax management and poor service, state-owned British Airways loses nearly $1 billion (is revived by John King who reduces workforce from 59,000 to 36,000, sells surplus planes and real estate, and switches insurance and advertising agencies)...

Pinkerton's Detective Agency opens London office, employed by Bank of England in 1870 to solve $2 million robbery and used by Winston Churchill to protect Royal Family during 1911 coronation of George V... British businessman Tony James forms Sigue Sigue Sputniks "fantasy band" (markets group with image of "high-tech sex and designer violence," incorporates band as CEO to employ lawyers, agents and accountants, produces first album with ads between song tracks in 1986, starts forming subsidiaries for tours, merchandising products and diversifying into real estate, stock market)... Some 300 private enterprise agencies appear in Britain by 1988 to launch new firms, i.e., London Enterprise Agency sponsored by 15 major corporations (create thousands of new jobs)... Russian-born Ghermezian family, moved to Montreal in early 1950s to start carpet business, later U.S. chain, and to Edmonton in late 1960s to enter real estate business, opens West Edmonton Mall, world's largest shopping complex, $1.1 billion, by 1985 with 817 shops, 8 banks, 19 movie screens, amusement rides, skating rink, petting zoos, aquariums, water park and 110 eating spots over 110 acres (employs some 15,000 employees, provides 30,000 parking spaces)... After Socialists win election, Willot brothers, owners of Boussac-Saint Freres as France's biggest textile business, declare bankruptcy (leads to government attachments of holdings, such as Dior fashion business, Belgium's Galeries Anspach retail chain, and Bon Marche Paris department store, and liens on personal assets to hold them personally responsible for incompetence, dishonesty)...

N.V. Philips consolidates operations (closes 40 plants by 1986 to centralize decision-making in Eindhoven, forms strategic alliances with firms in other countries)... Cocaine retails for $115/gram in U.S., $88 in 1989 as Colombia Cartel supplies 100-200 tons/year in $500 billion global drug market with heroin from Golden Triangle in Southeast Asia... Eager for Soviet business Toshiba subsidiary gets MITI to approve export of machine tools to Soviet Union (leads to scandal in 1987 when discovered to have sold secret U.S. technology, ban on exports of Norway's Kongsberg by coordinating committee of free-world allies)... Esme Johnstone, Giles Clark buy two warehouses of bankrupt Majestic Wine Warehouses, chain of London wine marts (launch high-volume Liquor Barn chain, 21 wine stores by 1988, top 15 other bidders in 1987 to buy chain of 104 stores, CA and AZ, from Safeway for $334 million to enter U.S. market, face financial problems in 1988 by highly leveraged deals)...

Sony unveils prototype still camera to capture images on electronic sensors instead of film, sold in 1987 for $7,000 (re-introduced in 1989 by Sony and Canon for under $1,000)... Paris fashion designer Christian Lacroix, age 29, heads House of Patou, a hit with Spanish collection in 1985 (regains magic in 1988 by blending couture with pop culture breezy, sassy clothes, quits 1987 when blocked in doing ready-to-wear line, $13 million lawsuit follows, to start own house backed by Agache, after line of ready-to-wear to give women affordable styles plans menswear)... With $280,000, Wataru Ohashi starts Footwork as parcel-delivery service, by 1982 handles more parcels than all but two of Japan's other 41 delivery firms (sensing price war, finds new products for direct selling via 8,000-truck network - luxury items including fresh salmon, melons, caviar and furs, goes public in 1986, spends $49 million to open restaurants, shopping complexes, health clubs and condominiums for 1987 revenues of $115 million)... "Tiny" Rowland, owns 29.9% of House of Fraser - runs Harrods, seeks remaining shares, rebuffed on anti-trust grounds (sells most of holdings in retailing giant with 120 stores to Egyptian financier Mohamed Al-Fayed, brothers in 1984 for some $1 billion, leads to feud for control in 1985-1990 with charges by Rowland that brothers pilfered money from Mideast, Haiti and acted for Sultan of Brunei)...

Karlheinz Kaske is CEO of Siemens (transforms cash-rich giant into high-tech leader by spending $24 billion 1983-88 for acquisitions, joint ventures, i.e., semiconductors with Philips, and research - electronics business from 30% to 50% of sales by 1988 with plans for 75% by mid-1990, despite drop of earnings by 13.5% to $750 million in 1987, holds $13.5 billion in 1988, budgets $3.9 billion for R&D and $3 billion for investments and restructuring, after signing deals with Britain's Plessey, U.S.' Rolm and Bendix, Japan's Matsushita and France's Framatome buys control of ailing $3.3 billion Nixdorf for $350 million in 1990 to block non-German buyers)... After M-19 terrorist group grabs Martha Ochoa for ransom of several million dollars, brother Jorge Luis Ochoa summons 223 drug traffickers, process Bolivian and Peruvian cocaine for U.S. market, from Medellin, Colombia's 2nd largest City with industry and textiles as traditional economic base, Bogota, Cali, Letica, Cartagena and Barranquilla to deal with common enemy (leads to creation of Death to Kidnappers counter-terrorist group to rescue Martha after killing dozens associated with M-19 and other leftist groups and formation of cartels in Medellin, uses violence to dominate trade, and Cali, uses legal operations as cover for low market profile, to coordinate smuggling, payments to Panama's Noriega for protection, laundering money)...

Dior fashion house opens store in Beijing... Royal Dutch Shell reduces fleet of 35 tankers to 25, BP drops from 52 to 46 ships... Porsche begins selling engineering technology to other firms... Hanson Trust buys British Ever Ready, batteries (buys Allders retail business in 1983, wins hostile takeover, 1986, of SCM conglomerate, Smith-Corona office equipment, Glidden Paints and Durkee's foods, gets, 1987, Kaiser Cement for $250 million, sells six plants for $283 million, and Kidde, security systems, fire protection, and Jacuzzi, for $1.5 billion, in 1989 buys consolidated Gold Fields, includes 49% of Newmont Mining, and sells Kidde's fire protection, Allders, Hygrade, Lea & Perrins and 50% of Smith-Corona to public, in 1990 buys Peabody and sells Newmont share to Goldsmith's Cavenham Industries)... To block takeover of Robert Holmes a Court, Elders, Australian trading firm, merges with IXL, Tasmanian jam and food business (buys Wood Hall Trust, British trader, in 1982, acquires Carlton and United Breweries, threatened by takeover, in 1983-84 to make Elders IXL one of land's largest enterprises, fails to acquire U.K.'s Courage Breweries in 1986 for $3.5 billion, acquires Canada's Carling O'Keefe Breweries for $413 million in 1987 - joint venture with Molson in 1989, is reorganized in 1989 by $4.4 billion management takeover - named Foster's Brewing Group in 1990, swaps 50% in Courage Pubs in 1991 for Grant Met's brewing interests to top Bass as #1 in Britain's beer market).

1982

General Events

Business Week: "A Debate that Holds A Key to Japan's Future" (notes growth forecast of 3.2% by Foreign Ministry, 5.2% by MITI)... After India arrests 6,000 labor leaders, national strike is called (January 18)... Despite plea of U.S. to Allies to embargo material for U.S.S.R. natural gas pipeline from Siberia to Europe, France signs (January 23) contract with Soviet Union... Daniel Yergin: Global Insecurity: A Strategy for Energy and Renewal (warns energy crisis not over)... Canadian unemployment reaches high of some 1.2 million, 9.6% highest since 1930s... France nationalizes (February 14) 36 banks, including Banque Rothschild, and major firms in electrical, aluminum, synthetics and insurance (issues bonds to finance $8 billion in takeovers)... Gas prices drop (February 16) with global oil glut, Saudi light crude is $3.50 below official price... Canadian Chrysler plants are closed by some 10,000 workers refusing to grant contract concessions... To fight economic slide, Mexico devalues (February 18) peso 30% to fight inflation (requests 115 international banks to reschedule loan payments)... Denmark votes (February 23) to withdraw from EEC... Some 25-30% of world trade is handled by countertrade transactions (leads to some 30 U.S. firms with special departments, some 12 with separate trading organizations, for bartering)... Deposits of oil, natural gas are found in Georges Bank's in North Atlantic fishing area... OPEC cuts (March 20) production to maintain oil prices... EC proposes ESPRIT, European Strategic Program for Research and Information Technology, to coordinate efforts in microelectronics, robotics, artificial intelligence, software engineering... Some 4,000 black miners in West Rand gold mines riot over lower pay raises than given white workers, quelled by South African police... Pioneering micro-processor credit card, stores financial data to determine current balances and transfer funds, is test-marketed in France... Syria closes (April 8) border with Iraq, shuts pipeline carrying Iraqi oil to Mediterranean... Canadian dollar is valued at $0.77 U.S. (spurs production of U.S. movies in Canada)... British, U.S. scientists develop new man-made vaccine from synthetic chemicals...

Poland passes law, similar to laws against "social parasitism" passed by U.S.S.R. and East European nations, to require men between 18-45 unemployed over 90 days to register with local authorities (requires community work of those who fail to accept long-term employment)... EC denounces (August 12) U.S. for ban on aiding Soviet pipeline, lifted November 13... Weather patterns over 75% of globe are disrupted by El Nino effect in Pacific Ocean when unusually warm ocean current moves along the equator (-1983, causes over 88 deaths, $2-8 billion in damages)... Britain declares De Lorean Motor Co. in Northern Ireland as insolvent... Philippines eases restrictions on banks to encourage development of modern banking, reduce dependence on family conglomerates... Greenpeace boats block (August 28) dumping of atomic waste, Spain... Polish police break up (August 31) Solidarity rally... To fight debt crisis, $100 billion by 1989, Mexico nationalizes (September 1) private banks to block export of funds during crisis... Australia, U.S. sign pioneering executive agreement to resolve conflicting policies on anti-trust law... Canadian Labor Congress, some two million members, upholds policy not to accept government controls or concessionary bargaining... Under martial law, Gdansk workers end (October 13) 3-day strike... Eight of 13 OPEC countries are net borrowers... Japan's reform legislation provides jail terms for both corporate officials, sokaiya (are employed to represent either firms or stockholders at meetings to shout down, disrupt opposition) involved in payoffs, bypassed by 1986... Poland bans (October 26) Solidarity... Spain is governed (October 29) by Socialist Party, headed by Felipe Gonzalez (continues through 1989, reduces inflation rate of 14% to 9% by 1986 in luring investments from Europe, U.S. and Japan for low labor costs and large market, despite protests of leftists adopts pro-business, anti-labor policy to transform Spain as economic success, growth rate of 2.5% in 1985 to 5.3% in 1988 after joining EEC in 1986)... When threatened by sanctions on use of U.S. technology in building Soviet Union's 3,700-mile gas pipeline from Siberia to Europe, French firms, including U.S. subsidiaries, are ordered by France to fulfill contracts... After eight years of negotiations, Law of the Sea Convention for seabed mining is signed by some 118 nations with many European countries, including Soviet Bloc, and Japan abstaining and U.S., Turkey, Venezuela, Israel in opposition... West Germany scandal is exposed in consolidated union-owned housing company, evolved from early 1900s with interests in a bank, food store and insurance business... Italian authorities start campaign to arrest civil service employees for absenteeism... U.S.S.R. authorizes enterprises for deep-sea mining... Buddhist monk at Bangkok temple, founded 1830, uses computer program to provide astrology forecasts to public... Social Democratic Party of Olof Palme is re-elected (1969-76) to govern Sweden (establishes wage-earner funds, financed by payroll and excess-profits taxes, to buy corporations for workers)... Konstantin Simis: U.S.S.R.: The Corrupt Society (cites necessary use of corruption to make industrial system work, notes role of private production in unofficial economy)...

Employees of Amsterdam department store volunteer reductions in work week and wages to create 300 new jobs annually for workers under 27... Hungary joins IMF, follows membership of Romania... China forms Ministry of Television and Radio... Brazil, Mexico, Poland and Romania reveal inability to pay debts to world bankers... Advent Eurofund, European venture capital enterprise in high technology, is founded by universities of Oxford, Cambridge and St. Andrews with Imperial College, Boston University, U.S.' Monsanto... Argentina unilaterally converts some $5 billion in debt to world bankers into 5-year bonds at low interest rate... Chinese Communist Party approves "responsibility system" to permit growth of small businesses... National union of railwaymen calls strike in Britain (collapses when workers reject strike of leaders)... France plans to transform electronics industries into single integrated whole... Canadian Foreign Investment Review Agency eases rules to encourage job creation... Vietnam sends at least 10,000 workers to Soviet Union to work off loans to Hanoi... France's Socialist Government devalues franc... China reports plans for national incentive system... Vatican appoints international experts to audit operations of its bank (names council of 15 cardinals to seek more income, $50 million reserve of 1984 almost gone by 1987)...

Japan's foreign aid program loans C. Itoh, large trading firm, funds to build logging road into dense tropical rain forest of Sarawak, Malaysia (is attacked in 1989 for exploitation of natural resources, leads to Japan's first policy on environmental conservation)... France requires Chargeurs conglomerate to hire more workers... International Whaling Commission votes moratorium due to declining stocks... MITI begins project to develop field robots, spends $100 million by 1991 as leader in field... During abortive coup attempt in Kenya, looters raid mostly Asian shops, homes to steal or destroy some $100 million worth of goods... South Korea runs trade surplus of $287 million with U.S., $9 billion in 1987... Japan exports goods worth $138 billion, $211 billion in 1986... Only 9 megawatts of solar cells are sold worldwide, over 30 megawatts in 1987 as cells find myriad uses... With debt-plagued economy, Irish begin new wave of emigration, legal and illegal, to U.S... Number of Japanese women with managerial titles grows 50% by 1987... With lessons learned at Saint-Gobain's packaging division, Alain Gomez is CEO of state-controlled Thomson, France's first electronic conglomerate created in 1968 by merger of CSF and Thomson Brandt in consumer electronics, in technical bankruptcy (after ruthless restructuring, cuts costs and increases productivity, and ambitious acquisitions revives enterprise, wins major Pentagon contract in 1985 with GTE, in 1987 swaps $800 million in cash plus medical electronics group to GE for its RCA, U.S. maker of TV sets for 40 years, to become No. 2 in world in TVs after Philips, earns $350 million on sales of $12 billion, 41 plants in 17 countries, in 1988 in preparing to take on Matsushita, Siemens)... Temple is first U.S. university with branch, classes in English, in Japan, Dartmouth follows in 1988 with first English-language MBA program while over 40 other colleges make plans in 1989... Bulgarian Academy of Science Institute for Robotics and Cybernetics designs Pravetz 82 personal computer as Apple II clone, a hit in East Bloc and basis for joint venture with U.S.S.R. Academy of Sciences... MITI begins 10-year 5th-Generation Project, spends $45 million by 1991, to develop advanced computer, microelectronic technologies and artificial intelligence.

Business Events

Businessmen, opposed to Government's freeze on wages, prices and tax increase, explode smoke bombs in Paris Bourse... U.S.' Aetna Life & Casualty acquires 40% interest in one of Britain's largest merchant banks (shares control with Midland Bank Group, major owner of U.S.' Crocker National Bank and Thomas Cook travel business, German bank, English commercial finance firm, and English mortgage bank)... Britain's low-cost, no-frill Laker Airlines files for bankruptcy (sues nine international airlines for conspiring to force it out of business, reaches out-of-court settlement in 1985, Laker gets $8 million and airline some $48 million)... After investing over $1 billion since 1967 in developing Jari project on Amazon tributary to develop self-sustaining wood pulp operation, perhaps history's largest single entrepreneurial effort, Ludwig is forced to sell property to consortium of Brazil banks, insurance companies, and industrial groups... Willy Kork, West German and U.S. steel maker, develops new process to make pig iron without blast furnace... After developing first tape recorder and engineering breakthroughs in radio, radar and television to earn reputation for shoddy home appliances, AEG-Telefunken, West Germany's 2nd-largest electronics manufacturer and 8th-largest employer, declares insolvency with debts of $3.5 billion, loans guaranteed by Government... Italy's SGS-Ates, Toshiba start joint venture in computer-chip technology... When striking workers occupy Normandy cheese factory, owner heads commando raid to liberate plant, 39 tons of cheese...

After 133 years in original London location, Harrods plans boutiques for Tokyo, New York (opens first U.S. branch in 1990 on Queen Mary... After 107 years staging Gilbert and Sullivan operettas, D'Oyly Carte Opera Co. gives last performance... Western bankers, Polish representatives agree on terms for payment of nation's loans, Romania, Hungary, and East Germany other Communist debtors... Italian pizza parlor, first of 22-unit chain, opens in Moscow (joins other Western fads: jeans, T-shirts, sneakers, punk rock, skateboarding, hang gliders, sail boards)... Alliance is formed by Banque de Paris et de Pays-Bas, U.S.' Merrill Lynch, and Hong Kong financial interests of Fungking Hey, fled China in 1948 with several hundred dollars to amass fortune of some $300 million by 1980s... Britain's new Channel 4 Television shows weekly highlights of U.S.' National Football League games (boosts average audience from one million to over 4 million by 1985 in promoting U.S.-style football, leads to creation of British-American, Budweiser Leagues with total of 110 teams by 1985)... Five major Japanese banks extend $500 million in credit to Michigan so it can retain high credit rating for bond issue... Atlantic Richfield is first U.S. oil company to get drilling rights in China, follows Japan's National Oil, Elf Aquitaine in 1980... Club Med provides vacationers with computer workshops... Lawry's Foods, Los Angeles, starts Mexican-food factory in Dublin, first such in Europe, to prepare line of ethnic foods for continent... Canon introduces first "personal copier"...

China's first international hotel opens in Beijing... American-born Japanese businessman proposes "Partnership for Prosperity" whereby Japanese business would create fund of $10 billion to provide low-interest loans to revive U.S. economy... ASEA invades Japan's robot market... Brazil's Mendes Junior International, provides design, technology and capital, and China's Civil Engineering Construction Co., provides workers, form joint venture... Imitation Apple II computers are made in Taiwan, Hong Kong... Sony invades U.S. personal computer market... Business Week: "Europe's New Managers" (notes new focus in adopting U.S.' decentralization, Japanese competitive behavior)... London's Inter-Continental Hotels, U.S.' Comsat General plan first international TV-conference network... Loblaws, Canadian supermarket chain, introduces modern bulk buying from vats and bins, adopted by Safeway for some products in Los Angeles in 1983... Millie's Wholesale Center opens in Hong Kong, low markups and high turnover, as new discount operation with U.S. merchandising (offers daily price reductions, auctions)... Fujitsu Fanuc and unions agree that firm's robots will pay union dues, negated by Japan's Ministry of Labor... Nova-Park Elysees, world's most expensive hotel with 12-room Royal Suite at $5,000/night, opens in Paris... Mexican Government takes over Compania Mexicana de Aviacio, largest airline in Latin America, to avoid financial collapse... Seiko develops world's first wristwatch television... Japanese electronics firms, N.V. Philips introduce digital sound systems... ITT demonstrates prototype digital TV in West Germany (allows use of TV set as computer)... U.S.' Hewlett-Packard is first foreign firm to open computer plant in Mexico... U.S.' Corning Glass Works acquires Japanese firm to invade new market, buys three more by 1986... Confederation of Italian employers, Confindustria, revokes indexing of wages with inflation, suspended earlier in Belgium, Holland, Denmark... West German Dolch Logic Instruments, formed 1976, is acquired by its U.S. marketing subsidiary with funds from Japanese, European investors... Banco Ambrosiano of Milan, Italy's largest private banking group, declares bankruptcy after discovery it loaned $1.3 billion from other banks, including Vatican Bank, in unsecured loans to 10 dummy Panamanian corporations (leads to financial scandal, mysterious death in London of Robert Calvi, known as "God's Banker" for ties with Vatican)...

Compact-disk players, Sony, appear in market... Trained as an accountant, Britain's Antony Barry starts Blue Arrow Employment Agency with $500,000 (snaps up 21 firms in U.S. before bidding $1.2 billion for U.S.' Manpower, 1,337 offices in 33 countries, in 1987 to become world's No. 1)... A. Gary Klesch quits as CEO of Dean Witter Reynolds London subsidiary (starts Quadre to finance mergers with Arab backers, buys them out in 1987 for $120 million, builds financial and industrial empire, enters manufacturing field with two acquisitions in 1986 for stability, blocks British & Commonwealth Shipping's friendly bid in 1987 for Mercantile House Holdings, London's best-known in investment banking, compromise by carving up business)... After amassing over $15 million in real estate and other businesses by age of 40, Hong Kong-born Clifford Pang invests most of fortune in Canadian property and starts Lafe Holdings in high-tech manufacturing, sales of $22.4 million in 1987 (launches $12.8 million industrial project, eventually four factories with 8,000 workers, in family's ancestral village in Guangdong province, average monthly wage 15% of Hong Kong's, to make disk-drive heads, circuit boards later)... Former Paribas executives, Christian Moretti and Henri Balanchet, start Dynaction in Paris as vehicle to take over Beatrice's ailing Cryodiffusion (with strategy buys mid-sized firms, secure market shares but weak in capital and management, to form six subsidiaries, mostly in electronics or machine tools, for 1987 sales of $175 million, boosts sales to $360 million in 1988 with buy of Regma office equipment firm)... Italy's pro-baseball league forms, 18 teams by 1989 while 32 teams of Italian basketball league lure best U.S. players from colleges and NBA...

Klaus J. Jacobs' West German coffee business acquires Swiss chocolate maker Interfood, later U.S.' E.J. Bach candy, Italy's Du Lac, Belgium's Cote d'Or, Greece's Palvides, and Germany's Van Houten for $1 billion to capture 80% of Europe's confection market... Honda builds first Japanese automobile plant in U.S., Nissan in 1983, Toyota venture with GM in 1984, Mazda in 1987, Mitsubishi venture with Chrysler in 1988, Fuji venture with Isuzu in 1989, and Suzuki Motor with GM of Canada in 1989 (leads to some 2,000 Japanese firms in U.S. in 1990)... Spain's Farrutx opens in Majorca with collection of designer shoes for professional working women, sales of $21 million by 1989 from shoes for women, men plus leather apparel...

After exporting fruit from Turkish area of Cypress and branching into Turkey, Turkish Cypriot Asil Nadir builds London-based Polly Peck as major player, 1988 sales of $1.2 billion, in market of growing, packing, distributing fresh grapefruit, oranges and tropical fruit (opens Vestel electronics plant in 1984 when color TV hits Turkey, buys British home-appliance maker and Taiwanese electronics firm in 1987, gets NY produce importer in 1988, buys fresh produce unit of Campbell Soup in 1989, bids nearly $900 million in 1989 for Del Monte foods being sold in break up of RJR Nabisco, buys controlling interest of financially-troubled Sansui Electric, first foreign acquisition of major Japanese firm listed on Tokyo Stock Exchange, in 1989 for $110 million)... Armand Hammer's Occidental Petroleum signs contract with China for $750 million joint venture in open-pit mine project (loses steam by 1989 after bureaucratic obstacles)... Leaving family in Seattle, Tommy Quan, owner of two restaurants and ski resort, returns to China, left 1949 at age of 15, to become "orange king" of Guangdong's Taishan County on 300-acre farm, perhaps largest private landholding in China... Indian farmer Karan Singh gets $1,000 bank loan to build well near New Delhi for crop irrigation, quadruples income in two years to plan transportation business (shows country's rising middle class in social revolution)... Color TV appears in India, production of 70,000 sets/year to 1.3 million by 1989 (booms in 1984 when monopoly state television allows advertising)... Helmut Maucher is CEO of staid Nestle, one of first international firms (with series of acquisitions, i.e., U.S.' Carnation, MJB and Hills Bros. coffees in 1985, buys Rowntree confectioner in 1987 after fight with Swiss rival Suchard, builds firm for global market with plants in over 60 countries by 1989 to become world's No. 1 food business with sales of $6.5 billion, signs joint venture with General Mills in 1990 to distribute its cereals in Europe)... Jean Peyrelevade heads Compagnie Financiere de Suez bank after nationalization (later becomes head of privately owned Banque Stern and then CEO of huge, state-run Union des Assurances de Paris with plans in 1989 to build with state-owned Banque Nationale de Paris, Europe's largest commercial bank with assets over $150 billion, as French-style financial supermarket to compete with West Germany's Dresdner Bank with insurer Allianz and Britain's Abbey Life Group with Lloyds Bank)... Alcoa teams with Audi to design new manufacturing process to build cars with aluminum structural components... Olivetti introduces personal computer, a disappointment for not using IBM software (introduces IBM clone in 1984 to become Europe's 3rd largest in computer market)...

Some 15 firms, do $60 million in business, form Assn. of Outplacement Consulting Firms (in 1990 shows 55 U.S. members, 13 foreign with $350 million in total revenues)... Ryoei Saito resigns as CEO of family's Daishowa Paper Mfg. Co. to take responsibility for business slump (sells part of art collection to help business, returns in late 1980s with revival as de facto chief, buys two paintings, Van Gogh and Renoir, for some $160 million in 1990)... Nemir Kirdar, Arab investors form Investcorp (buys Tiffany & Co. in 1984 for $135 million, goes public in 1987 for profit of $100 million, after buying range of retailers, Cover Tile, U.S.' largest, Carvel ice cream chain and 50% of Gucci, buys Saks Fifth Avenue, 45 tony stores, from BAT in 1990 for $1.5 billion, over $500 million in cash to avoid debt burden)... After devising new spectrometer, Hungarian physicist, George Ferenczi, loses manufacturing deal with U.S. equipment maker when Hungarian bureaucrats take over six months to approve (peddles instruments to European labs in 1983 - viewed as outlaw scientist for business activities, forms Semilab, sales of $1 million in 1990, with 22 colleagues, capital of $700,000, and aid of West German firm)... At age of 39, Bernard Tapie, son of Paris pipe fitter, makes first million dollars by reviving troubled firms in key industries (posts sales of $1 billion in 1985, 116 factories in 28 countries in 1986, before trimming assets for sales of $180 million by 1990, wins National Assembly seat as Independent in 1988, bids for 80% of slipping Adidas, loses $72 million on 1989 sales of $2.8 billion, in 1990)... After creating eccentric furs and casual ready-to-wear for Fendi since 1964, Karl Lagerfeld is Chanel's new designer, revives moribund house by 1990 with fresh spin to classic line (begins own line of low-priced clothes in 1984)... ICI buys 100 companies by 1987 (expands in U.S. with Beatrice's chemical unit for $750 million in 1985, Glidden paints in 1986 for $580 million, and Stauffer Chemical in 1987 for $1.7 billion, all sold by 1991).

1983

General Events

Malaysia lets some 600 workers in free-trade zone unionize ITT electronics plant making semi-finished goods, follows unionization in mid-1970s of some Japanese firms making finished products... French court judges Leclerc stores as legal in setting prices under government minimums... China executes (January 18) official for economic crimes... Fortune: "Start-up Ventures Blossoms in Japan"... In first "labor reform" in U.S.S.R. since W.W. II, Law on Work Collectives, drafted in 1980 after rise of Solidarity, is adopted (lets shop-floor collectives participate in planning and management, provides incentives to increase collective output)... China Experimental University is formed in Shenzhen economic zone near Hong Kong to provide technical knowledge to attract Western high-tech industry... Nigeria breaks (February 19) with OPEC to drop oil prices by $5.50/barrel... Qingdao tries labor contract system to give workers freedom of employment, adopted by China in 1986... President of Argentina's central bank is arrested by district judge for making unconditional agreement with Morgan Guaranty Trust to roll over its debt in order to save country's airline (causes immediate suspension of foreign exchange, financing)... Soviet Union prepares reforms for economic system (grants some factories in key industries decentralized authority in 1984, plans in 1985 to decentralize economic decisions, purges hierarchy of some 10% of middle-level Communist Party officials and over 100 top-level economic policy makers)... To revive entrepreneurial spirit in China, small state-owned shops are leased as private enterprises to individuals, groups of workers... After eight years, Australia's conservative government loses (March 5) to Labor Party... Gdansk shipyard workers, Poland, demand (March 10) legal status for Solidarity... After two meetings, OPEC ministers fail to agree on petroleum prices, production levels (let price on spot markets continue at $30/barrel, $4 under "regulated" minimum)... Solidarity rallies clash (May 1) with police in 20 Polish cities...

Polish Communist Party officials, police order AWOL workers back to work... Greenpeace protests (July 18) Soviet whaling... Workweek for Belgian workers in food-processing, chemicals, non-ferrous metals, and paper industries drops to 37 hours... Betino Craxi is (August 4) first Socialist Prime Minister of Italy (-1986, launches capitalist renaissance, transforms state conglomerate, IRI operates 1,079 firms to lose some $2 billion/year, by selling all or part of 35 companies and holdings to realize $3 billion)... Japan's "sarakin regulation law" limits interest rates, some as high as 110%, of private collection agencies to 73%, 40% later, and limits use of threatening tactics sometimes ending in suicide... U.S.S.R. levels (August 7) harsh punishment for drinking at work... Japan's Yanmar Agricultural Equipment develops semi-automated rice combine, farmer only needs to control speed and make turns (tests prototype machine, Electro-X, without driver in 1985)...

Romanian police require all citizens to register typewriters... Britain grants permission to U.S.' People Express to provide no-frill flights between London, Newark, NJ, for $149 one way... Holland plans to reduce governmental influence, regulations over economy during 1984... When Hungarian Andras Nagy is unable to borrow money for business expansion from village farming cooperative, development bonds, first in Soviet Bloc, are issued by state-owned bank to raise money from investors... Oil is discovered in Celtic Sea off Ireland... Holland cuts social benefits, including unemployment payments, by 10-15%, echoes reductions in welfare programs by West Germany, Denmark... Britain drops 7-year-old monopoly suit against London Stock Exchange with its agreement to end fixed commissions in 1986 (spurs competitive revolution in financial market)... Jean-Francois Revel: How Democracies Perish (attacks Western societies for failing to recognize reality of Soviet Communism, for succumbing to Communist strategy)... Chinese Government forms audit administration (finds over $1.6 billion lost from fraud, waste, tax evasion in 1985)... Australian Prime Minster Hawke calls National Economic Summit Conference of labor, business and government leaders for consensus on resolving chronic economic problems... In opposition to Marxist leaders, English coal miners vote against national strike... Kakuei Tanaka, Japan's former Prime Minister, is convicted for accepting $2 million in bribes from Lockheed in early 1970s to persuade All Nippon Airways to buy its planes...

Soviet Union introduces first personal computer, copies Apple II... Ending military rule of eight years, Raul Alfonsin is President of Argentina (-1989, after establishing political stability pushes for economic reforms - blocked by Peronist-controlled Congress, is succeeded by Peronist Carlos Saul Menem to tackle economic collapse with hyperinflation, rate of 3,600%, foreign debt of $51 billion, and hyper-recession in 1990, restores stable economy with 90-day freeze on wages and prices, 116% devaluation of currency, privatization of most state-run enterprises losing $4 billion/year, ends many subsidies, increases levies on exports)... With Mexico in financial crisis from 1982 due to falling oil prices and recession, Miguel de la Madrid is new President, peso is 70/dollar and 2,700 in 1987 after October market crash (-1988, tries to stabilize economy by privatizing over 50% of state-owned 1,155 enterprises, sees,handicapped by inability to pay on foreign debt of $105 billion, rise of underground economy as Mexicans peddle whatever as illegal street vendors or seek illegal work in U.S.)... Venezuela forms Recadias government agency to sell

U.S. dollars to business importers at discount, multi-billion-dollar corruption scandal in 1989 with discovery importers sold cheap dollars on free market for premium prices... General Manuel Noriega, head of Panama Defense Forces, is de facto ruler of country (is indicted by U.S. grand juries in 1988 for conspiring with drug dealers to smuggle cocaine, marijuana to U.S., for accepting bribes over $4.6 million from Medellin Cartel to protect drug flights, and for laundering money, up to $200 million/month, through Panamanian banks, after 1989 U.S. overthrow faces Florida trial in 1990)... Japan has only one of world's top 10 banks, first five largest by 1988 and eight of top ten in 1990... Poland is first in Eastern Bloc with public opinion center, followed by Moscow, Czechoslovakia and Hungary in 1988... Canada sponsors, later private corporations foot 90% of $10 million annual budget, Le Cirque du Soleil with 28 virtuoso performers as theatrical, high-tech circus version of ancient-European street theater (makes U.S. debut in 1987)... Japan's net flow of capital is $17.7 billion, $49.7 billion in 1984 and $64.5 billion in 1985 as world's largest net creditor nation while U.S. becomes No. 1 debtor... To spur competition, EC campaigns against industrial subsidies, by 1989 orders $1.4 billion in paybacks in 26 cases... King, industrialist, confidant of Thatcher, and head of state-owned British Airways, hires Colin Marshall, former Avis executive, as CEO for marketing savvy to revive "Bloody Awful" (improves service with Danish program, as world's largest carrying 23 million passengers to 166 cities in 80 countries, sells 720 million shares to investors in 1987 for $1.4 billion, takes 26% share in new European computer reservation system in 1987)... Kuwait Petroleum buys Gulf's refining, marketing activities in Europe... Indonesian textile exports go from $150 million to projected $3 billion in 1990, foreign investment rises to record $4.7 billion in 1989 with booming economy... Many Israelis lose savings in stock market crash (blame banks for manipulating prices of their own shares to keep them artificially high).

Business Events

Theme park, licensed by Disney for 10% of gate and 5% of food and merchandise sales plus licensing fees, opens in Tokyo, 14 million visitors 1989-90... Some 500 agencies form International Gay Travel Assn... Occidental Petroleum gets drilling rights from China... 17 of Europe's top executives meet to organize private sector cooperation to fight invasions of market by U.S., Japanese, Soviet enterprises... Sotheby Parke Bernet, struggling auction house, rejects buy of two Americans as they were, after all, in manufacturing... Leaders of British Communist Party are outvoted by other stockholders of party paper, <u>Morning Star</u>, to achieve financial stability with commercial printing... Coldwell Banker arm of Sears opens London office to sell real estate, first new European office by major U.S. commercial firm... Clothing manufacturer opens Esprit apparel store, designed as high-tech disco, in Hong Kong, other stores later in San Francisco, Los Angeles, New Orleans (is copied by other clothing manufacturers to compete with fashion designers)... Hitachi, Fujitsu plan to export first Japanese supercomputers to U.S... Peugeot, France's private automaker, plans to eliminate 7,405 jobs, rejected by government but approves 1,905 layoffs in 1984 (leads to 2,905 layoffs, 4,500 early retirements later)... Thomson Group acquires bankrupted AEG-Telefunken to divide European electronics industry with Philips... World's first robot supermarket opens in Yokohama, Japan (uses 12 systems to operate unmanned transportation, storage)...

Japanese authorities license 78 managerial recruiting firms... NYC's Citicorp plans expansion to Europe (-1985, acquires banks in Spain, Belgium and France, purchases two leading stock brokerages and insurance business in London, opens investment offices in 14 European cities, develops branches in Britain, West Germany)... Atari is last U.S. consumer-electronics manufacturer to move U.S. plant operations to Far East... China's first supermarket opens in Beijing... Yamazaki operates flexible automation line, uses computer-controlled machine tools linked by fiber-optic cable (follows GM's flexible automated system in 1982)... Cardin, owner of Maxim's, opens Minim's in Paris to serve fast-food gourmet dishes... Stockholm Stock Exchange is silenced by computer malfunction, forces market to publish stock data in local business paper to continue operations... Restored Venice Simplon-Orient Express offers luxurious 32-hour trip from London for $770... Peter Vadasz, 12 partners start small software cooperative in Budapest with $3,000 for salaries, equipment... After seeing its world's share of watch production drop from 30% in 1974 to 9% from onslaught of Japanese quartz watches, consortium of watchmakers forms Societe Suisse de Microelectronique et Horlogerie (introduces trendy, low-price Swatches as fashion accessories for every occasion, 90% of sales of Swiss-made watches in 1988, leads to Le Clip watches, clip-on timepieces, in 1986 by small Swiss maker of watch straps and hand-wound Swatches in 1989 for export to Third World nations while Europeans buy clunky Soviet watches)... Canada's Sub Aquatic Development claims to pioneer tourist subs, popular in Barbados, St. Thomas and Hawaii in 1988...

London's Joanna Doniger opens evening-dress rental service, within year One Night Stand dresses a successful venture (opens NYC store in 1987)... After refueling Hong Kong property boom, John Mao, on paper one of world's richest running family's trading business, sees empire collapse after discovery of billion dollar check-kiting scheme (forces $500 million Hang Lung Bank to close and ruins deposit bank, gets 3-year jail term in 1985)... Sophie Mirman opens Sock Shop in London subway station, 118 outlets for trendy leg wear in Britain, Princess Diana most known customer, France, Belgium and U.S. (opens in NYC in 1988, closes U.S.' 17 stores in 1990 for high costs, faces bankruptcy in 1990)... James H. Ting starts Hong Kong business to make PCs for sale in U.S., Canada (shifts to Europe, Australia, Far East with 1984-85 computer bust, takes main company, Toronto-based International SemiTech Microelectronics, public in 1986, raises $40 million for expansion in 1987 by selling 49% of Hong Kong subsidiary, buys 89 Consumers Distributing Catalog retail stores in Eastern U.S. for $100 million and pays $220 million for old Singer Co., sewing machine outfit with 30,000 dealers in 100 countries, to sell consumer and durable goods bought from partners in China)...

Tom Padu quits lucrative sales job in Western Australia to develop first robot submarine <u>Down Under</u>, pioneers subsea industry... British marketer Tim Midgley's Euro-Gulf buys 800 square miles of Brazil's rain forest to produce wood by selective harvest for local craftsmen (after $14 million loss due to squeeze of lumbermen and officials clearcutting land, a cause celebre for conservationists in late 1980s, deeds land to local Indians)... ICI, world's 38th-largest industrial corporation in 1989 with annual sales of $21 billion from pharmaceuticals, film, polymers, agricultural chemicals, explosives and other products, abandons traditional country-by-country organization to establish worldwide units (while board is all British to 1982, evolves by 1989 with two Americans, Canadian, Japanese and German, 35% of 180 top people are non-British)... Professional women dart players hold first World Cup... As result of Japanese competition, Fiat abandons U.S. market (returns in 1989-90 to sell top-quality car with Chrysler as distributor)... Developer (begins in 1950 to build small stores, evolves as U.S.' largest builder of giant regional malls, buys department stores and real estate in 1980s to amass $3.7 billion by 1990s) A. Alfred Taubman, joined by Max M. Fisher, Milton Petrie and Leslie Wexner, buys Sotheby's for $139 million (recenters house in NYC for global market, offers financing to collectors, art as collateral, in 1984 - policy dropped in 1990 after art world furor, tops sales barrier in 1987 with $1.4 billion, Christie's with $1 billion, to reach nearly $3 billion in 1989, takes firm public in 1988 to make some $400 million)...

Japan's clothing giant, Itokin, buys Paris fashion house of Courreges (with costs out of control, suspends house's haute couture lines)... After four years of negotiations, U.S.' American Motors and China agree to jointly produce Jeeps in Beijing (makes 3,000 Cherokee Jeeps and Chinese Jeeps with U.S. part kits in 1987, leads to bureaucratic clashes, Beijing Automotive Works hoarding proceeds on sales of Chinese cars and hefty increases in duties on kits, ends with Tiananmen Square confrontation June, 1989)... After leaving France for U.S., builds Palm Beach condominiums, when Socialists came to power, Bernard Arnault returns to Paris when Socialists adopt conservative economic course (persuades government to sell him bankrupt Agache-Willot empire, textile maker Boussac-Saint Freres loses some $60 million/year, of retail stores to diaper firms, at bargain price, revamps textile business, fires over 8,000 employees including 90 at headquarters, to turn business around - sells most of parts for over $200 million by 1987, acquires Dior fashion house in 1984, in 1987 buys Celine line of ready-to-wear clothes, accessories and starts France's first new haute couture fashion house in decade with Lacroix)... Mitsui Petrochemical spawns Japan's bioengineering field with red dye for soaps, cosmetics (leads to six firms producing monoclonal antibodies in 1985, 300 biotech hopefuls in 1990)...Theodore Levitt: "The Globalization of Markets", Harvard Business Review (is utilized by Gillette to market new Sensor razor, Hyatt Hotels and Saatchi & Saatchi by 1990)... Lone Star Industries, U.S.' largest cement maker started in 1919, begins selling some $600 million in assets, most to foreign firms, in joint ventures to maintain profits and to slim down (puts up some $400 million of assets for sale in 1990 for survival while other producers, foreign and U.S., expand for rising demand)... Peter Laird and Kevin Eastman, struggling U. S. cartoonists, pen first "Teenage Mutant Ninja Turtles" comic book, world toy craze in 1988-90 with 1989 sales near $250 million from over 300 licensed products... American Express, in international banking since 1919, buys Geneva's Trade Development Bank of Lebanese financier Edmond J. Safra (opens new bank in 1988) for $550 million to join Swiss private banking (after fierce competition sells to Swiss private bank in 1990 for $1 billion, holds 20% of new business)... Australian-born pop singer Olivia Newton-John begins Koala Blue chain of stores, over 55 in U.S., Canada and Japan by 1990, to sell Australian-inspired clothing, accessories...

By 1989 loans of Japanese banks go from under $500 billion to $1.7 trillion, U.S. banks from over $600 billion to $675 billion, while nearly doubling its international market share to 40%, U.S. drops 27% to 15%... By 1990 U.S.' Monsanto funds Raymond Dwek's research at Oxford University with $11 million (forms business venture in 1989 with Oxford, its first, and Dwek to commercialize research, builds $4.8 million research facility at Oxford in 1990-91)... John A. Couri founds Duty Free International, 67 stores at North American airports and along U.S.-Canadian border for 1989 sales of $85.7 million (signs exclusive licensing pact with Harrods for airport outlets in 1990, plans to supply duty-free goods to cruise, merchant ships)... Allan Malachuck is president of U.S.' Royal Zenith, distributes presses of East Germany's state-owned efficient Planeta (leads to Planeta buying Royal in 1990)... After being blocked by France in buying minor Bordeaux vineyard in 1974, Suntory, world's 3rd largest beverage firm, buys run-down Chateau Lagrange vineyard in Medoc area (leads to Japanese food and real estate firms buying fine wine chateaux by 1988, Takashimaya department store business being blocked in 1988 in acquiring 33% of wine merchant with exclusive rights to sell Romanee Conti burgundy)... Bridgestone buys Firestone's Tennessee plant (tops , 1988, Pirelli to buy Firestone for $2.6 billion, Yokahama Rubber buys Mohawk Rubber in 1989 for $150 million as world industry consolidates, and, as GM drops Firestone as a supplier, compensates by selling tires via mass-market retailers, supplies, 1990, tires for GM's Saturn project, with Civil War in Liberia abandons, 1990, Firestone rubber plantation, 1 million acres leased in 1920s).

1984

General Events

When Britain's National Coal Board plans to close some 20 unprofitable mines and let go as many as 20,000 miners of industry's 182,000 in order to modernize nationalized coal industry, Marxist Arthur Scargill, head of National Union of Mine Workers, calls (March 12) strike (although some 25% of miners continue work, closes over 66% of mines with violence injuring over 160 pickets and 400 police, despite objection of Scargill ends by union vote, over 50% already back to work, on March 3,1985, after country's longest, most violent strike)... China's state-owned Fushan International Trust & Investment Corp. issues public stock offering, also used to raise money by Guizhou airline and Beijing department store... Soviet Union, China sign trade agreement... U.S.S.R. delivers first natural gas to France... The Cash Connection: Organized Crime, Financial Institutions and Money Laundering (cites Hong Kong as "a major financial center for Southwest Asia's drug trafficking")... Bolivia imports some $23 million in pesos, nation's 3rd-largest import after mining equipment and food, from Britain and Brazil to fight annual inflation rate of some 10,000%... Despite Labor Party's strong opposition, 50.2% of British Telecommunications is sold to public, largest stock transaction with some one million buyers... Poland, U.S.S.R. sign

(May 4) 15-year trade pact... Colombia's drug dealers, Marxist guerrillas swap protection of marijuana fields and cocaine factories for funds... Oxford University Press plans computerized publication of Oxford English Dictionary... Argentina submits (June 11) austerity plan to IMF... To prevent total collapse of London's Johnson Matthey Bankers, Bank of England takes over major gold trader with $545 million in commercial loans to eliminate inept management... Business Week: "Europe's Unions Are Losing Their Grip" (notes decline in membership as economies restructure with new industries)... Beijing workers are granted workday from 8 a.m. to 5 p.m., one hour for lunch instead of customary two hours... Discreet tax-free haven of Luxembourg lures $40 billion in bank deposits, over $100 billion in 1989 as money laundering becomes global industry with havens of Netherlands Antilles, Isle of Man, Switzerland (plans 1990 law to make laundering a crime), Vanuatu, Nauru and Truk Pacific islands and Hong Kong... Pope John Paul II: "The needs of the poor must take priority over the desires of the rich, and the rights of workers over maximization of profits"...

Melodia, Soviet record company, gets rights to issue records of Beatles... Fortune: "Crack in the Japanese Work Ethic"... MITI launches $48 million program to encourage joint research projects between companies (joins Education Ministry to fund joint industry-university research projects and research laboratories for business, 25 in 1983-84 and 15 in 1985)... Swedish Secretariat for Future Studies: Care and Welfare at the Crossroads (estimates 14% of Sweden's GNP in 1984 to go for public care and over 20% by 2000, projects taxes to pay for care costs to rise from 52% of GNP to 61% by 2000)... Japan's "The Mystery Man with 21 Faces" tries to extort money from candy manufacturers by poisoning their products, 2nd attempt in 1985... Nearly 4-year-old anti-trust suit by EC against IBM is settled by private negotiations, IBM to provide European computer firms with technical standards for compatibility... New Zealand Labor Party takes over (July 14) from Conservatives... After four years in development, University of Western Australia devises robotic sheep shearer... Business Week: "Europe's Escape from Inflation" (notes efforts to reduce governmental budgets, check monetary growth, lower labor costs, raise productivity, import goods from Third World)... Brazil law bans adoptions of children for profit...

Canada Post Co., Government's postal system, starts commercial mail-order business... Millions of French Government workers hold protest strike to denounce Socialist Government's refusal to grant wage increases... Business Week: "A Transatlantic Bidding War for the World's Savings"... West Germany bans (September 19) leaded gas... Britain, China announce (September 19) return of Hong Kong to China in 1997 (although promising Colony "high decree of autonomy," basic liberties with independent judiciary and elective legislature, and free economy to 2047, causes nearly $5 billion to leave by 1990 and troubled citizens to flee to Australia, some 9,500 visas in 1988, Canada, 22,000 visas, U.S., over 11,000 visas, and Singapore, leads to more unrest with 1989 military crushing of students in Beijing, sees Japanese invest some $8 billion by 1990)... Newsweek: "The Decline of Europe" (cites unemployment of EC at 12.5 million, countries going broke on high-cost social programs and low growth business)... Mitterrand plans to restructure French steel industry by eliminating some 25,000 of 90,000 jobs by 1987 (leads to riots, threats by workers with support of Communist Party)... IMF reduces (September 22) credit limits of debtor nations... Fortune: "The Trouble with Managing Japanese-Style"...

After working on string theory to explain interrelationships of basic forces of nature since 1979, physicists, Britain's Michael Green and U.S.' John Schwarz, present proof... IG Metall, West Germany's largest union of 3.7 million workers in automobile, metal-working, etc., strikes for 30-hour work week (agrees to 38.5 hours)... South Africa's new Constitution accepts non-whites in government for first time (dismantles Apartheid in 1990)... Beijing allows (September 30) Taiwan to retain capitalism if it reunites with China... Leonard Boff, Brazilian priest: Church: Charisma and Power (advocates use of class struggle, rhetoric to end political oppression, is investigated by Vatican for espousing liberation theology, is silenced by Vatican in 1985, reversed in 1986)... Newsweek: "Testing Moscow's Limits" (notes actions of East Bloc countries to assert political, economic independence from Soviet Union)... Swiss defeat referendum to provide more information on secret bank accounts... Chinese Government, party officials are required (October) to give up any direct role in running enterprises (makes factory managers responsible for profits, losses)... U.S. proposes talks with Japan to lower trade barriers, gets some concessions in 1990... Business Week: "Japan Is Buying Its Way Into U.S. University Labs" (notes trend from 1970s for Japanese firms to fund technological research at U.S. colleges)... Nigeria drops (October 18) price of oil to undercut other OPEC members (forces OPEC to cut January 30, 1985)... Britain's Chancellor of the Exchequer cancels half-penney, first minted 1270, as legal tender, production costs more than its value... Michael Voslensky: Nomenklatura: The Soviet Ruling Class (reports life of caste, some 3 million families, with major access by birth and sustained by personal favors of superiors, shows oppression, exploitation of bureaucratic elite created by Stalin)... World Court grants Canada 25% of fish-rich Georges Bank, U.S. 75%... Britain's National Oil Corp. lowers price of North Sea oil to $29.65/barrel, shocks petroleum industry... Nikolai Shchelokov, former Soviet interior minister, commits suicide when government probe uncovers his protection of illegal rackets... British Civil Aviation licenses Virgin Atlantic Airways for cut-rate transatlantic service... MITI proposes law to force foreign firms doing business in Japan to license their software to domestic firms, drops law after international uproar...

France approves first privately-owned TV station... Maciej Szczepanski, former head of Polish radio and television, goes to prison for eight years for blatant corruption (enriches himself with seven cars, two private jets, helicopter, yacht, mountain villa and 16-room palace with mistresses on call)... By 1989 average industrial wages of Asia's Four Tigers rise from 32% for Singapore to South Korea's 110%, plagued by labor disputes of radical union leaders... Carlos Salinas, Mexico's budget minister, ends longstanding practice of Pemex, national oil company, to award 40% of drilling contracts, 50% of other projects to petroleum union controlled by Galicia (in revenge tries to block Salinas' selection in 1987 as presidential candidate)... North Korean law allows joint ventures, domestic firms to hold 51%, with foreign concerns, some 100 by 1989 with firms of Hong Kong, Switzerland, Italy, Belgium, Australia, France, Japan with 70 and Thailand, about 20 from socialist countries)... Spain nabs leaders of Medellin, Cali drug cartels planning distribution networks for fast-growing European market (despite U.S. extradition papers returns two to Colombia in 1986 for trial)... Inspired by Holland's $9 million remodeling of Schipol airport, Emirate of Dubai opens duty-free store at its international airport, major Middle East refueling stop... India exports some $22 million in software (expects to exceed $300 million by 1990, spurs domestic production of hardware when Finance Ministry orders 40,000 branches of state-owned banks to computerize by 1986, adopts similar software policy in 1986)...

North Sea countries meet in Bremen to discuss pollution, pledge in 1987 to halt all dumping of industrial waste in sea by Jan. 1, 1990, and to reduce emissions of dangerous materials 70% by 1991... With pressure from World Bank and IMF Ghana begins economic reforms (by 1990 increases output of textiles, aluminum products to offset drop in prices of cocoa, its main export)... South Korean Sun Myung Moon, head of worldwide Unification Church, enters U.S. federal prison for tax evasion (-1985, by 1990 backs China's biggest foreign-investment project, Panda Motors, to build $1 billion auto complex, housing, university and resorts 50 miles north of Hong Kong, to make 100,000 cars/year by 1995)... After holding the application for 12 years, Japan (grants Nippon Steel, via MITI, $12 million to develop similar alloy, forms consortium of 33 firms to study commercial uses for its new alloy) grants patent to U.S.' Allied-Signal, spent 15 years and over $100 million in research, for Metglas, cuts energy losses in electrical transformers by 70% (is blocked in selling alloy to Japanese firms).

Business Events

Mazda plans to make cars in Michigan in 1987... U.S.' Hallmark acquires Britain's greeting card business of W.N. Sharpe Holdings... Daewoo Precision Industries, GM form joint venture to make automobile parts... 3M China, wholly-owned subsidiary of U.S.' Minnesota Mining and Manufacturing, is allowed to open facility in Shanghai without Chinese partners, first such contract since 1949... By vote of firm's officials, West German engineer is manager of Wuhan diesel-engine plant, China... Saint-Gobain forms special unit to assist small business in hiring its redundant workers, duplicated by Elf Aquitaine and others... U.S.' Standard & Poor's opens London office to provide rating service for European securities (plans Tokyo branch in 1986, is followed by Moody's Investors Service)... France's Bull, Britain's ICL, and West Germany's Siemens start joint research laboratory to work on artificial intelligence (is echoed by other European joint ventures: $3 billion research program by 12 European makers to adopt computer standards, Olivetti and AT&T, Bull with U.S.' Honeywell and Japan's NEC)... For enterprise in producing eggs, a net profit of some $17,000 for family business, Chinese chicken farmer is awarded personal car, used Toyota, by Government... China's first amusement park opens as part of Shenzhen Bay resort complex, managed by New World Hotels International... London's Daily Express closes after dispute of editors, publisher, reporters and print unions on who gets to say what is printed, echoed by debates at Times of London, Observer... First fast-food restaurant, called Righteousness and Profit with Disney's Donald Duck as symbol, opens in Beijing, planned by McDonald's franchise in Hong Kong... Joining GM, Ford and Fiat, Subaru develops new automatic transmission for cars without gears, based on technology of Holland's Van Doorne Transmissie after 25 years of research... Saatchi & Saatchi ad agency acquires 12 advertising agencies during year to serve accounts of some $3 billion, world's 3rd-largest in world behind Tokyo's Dentsu with $3.62 billion in billings and U.S.' Young & Rubicam with billings of $3.5 billion...

Al-Akaria modern shopping mall opens in Riyadh, Saudi Arabia, to compete with traditional souks in old city, later over six others... Nippon Kokan, Japan's 2nd-largest steel maker, acquires U.S.' National Steel... Over 3,400 are killed by toxic gas leak from Union Carbide's insecticide plant at Bhopal, India, one of largest industrial accidents in history with initial number of injured at some 150,000 (results in over 130 U.S. lawsuits and some 2,700 in India, settles in 1989 by paying $470 million to victims, India's new government demands $3 billion in 1990)... Colombia's Drug Cartel proposes truce to government (with cancellation of all arrest warrants and 1979 extradition treaty with U.S. promises to cease operations, pay off nation's entire foreign debt of $10.5 billion and make substantial contributions to health and educational programs, rejected although some 48% of public polled favor talks)... N.V. Philips begins to form joint research ventures with other firms, 60 by 1989... Diego Maradona, Argentine soccer great, is sold by Barcelona team to Naples for $7.5 million (signs $23 million, nine-year contract for villa, two cars, promotional fees and plane tickets to Argentina, to earn some $8 million/year with endorsements by 1990)... M. Kenneth Foreman, CEO of obscure British quarry firm of Atwoods, diversifies with Miami's Industrial Waste Services (after buying some 12 others, grows by 1989 as 4th-largest in U.S. in field of 10,000 with revenues of $97 million - Waste Management No. 1 with sales of $2.7 billion)... Hitachi is first in computer industry to try automating job of generating software... Chinese press hails Bu Xinsheng of Southern Zhejiang Province as "trailblazing entrepreneur" for transforming garment workshop into flourishing business (with business on verge of bankruptcy by 1989 is charged with incompetence for misjudging Chinese craze for Western-style suits)...

Khaled Bin Ibrahim and brother, brothers of King Fahd's favorite wife, make bundle representing Boeing in sale of ten 747s to Saudi national airline (after developing motels and gas stations, amass $1 billion by 1990)... After starting Quantum Fund in 1969 with $250,000 - $2.5 billion before losing $750 million in 1987 market crash, Hungarian-born George Soros, fortune of $300 million, sets up foundation in Budapest for charitable activities, by 1989 dispenses some $3.5 million/year (sets up similar foundations in Poland, China in 1988 and Moscow in 1989, plans communist world's first Western-style business school, East-West Center for Management and Business, for Budapest in 1989, starts $80 million First Hungary Fund in 1989 to spur business ventures)... With idea from New Zealand, Japan opens first maze, first popularized by England's King Henry VIII in 1509-47, for public amusement, 100 others by 1989 (appears in California in 1989 with adjustable partitions for changing labyrinth)... Schlumberger, Netherlands Antilles, buys U.S.' Sedco oil drilling firm for $970 million while Australia's Broken Hill gets Utah International for $2.4 billion... Benetton, Italian knitwear maker, launches "United Colors of Benetton" international ad campaign, features youths of divers nationalities... With Washington eager to lure foreign investors to help finance rising budget deficits, Japan's Big Four, Nomura Securities, Daiwa Securities, Nikko Securities, and Yamaichi Securities, begin expanding small U.S. branches to attract business with high volume and low mark-up, account for some 20% of long-term U.S. government bond trading market in 1987... As Germany's venture-capital industry's largest firm in 1988, Technoventure Management raises $100 million by 1989, invests some $60 million in 20 ventures... Matif opens as France's financial future exchange, 1988 scandal threatens its credibility... Britain privatizes Jaguar luxury car maker, is sold to Ford in 1990 for some $2.5 billion as GM backs off to get 50%, beats out Fiat, of Swedish automaker Saab-Scandia for some $700 million in 1989... Recruit, parent company of real estate firm called Recruit Cosmos, sells unlisted stock in subsidiary at bargain prices to politicians, journalists and business leaders (-1986, goes public in 1986 - value soars up to 400%, topples government with scandal in 1989)... By 1990, 481 Japanese firms establish bases in Europe (leads to Japan investing some $10 billion in EC in 1989)...

Japanese banks hold 20% of international banking assets, nearly 40% in 1990 with 14 of world's top 20 banks along with five European, France's Credit Agricole 10th, and one American... Daewoo, after entering aerospace field, inks contracts with Lockheed for $108 million and Dornier for $150 million, basis for ventures in Korean Air, Sammi Steel and Samsung Aerospace (loses, 1986, $156 million when U.S. Lines negates order for 12 container ships with bankruptcy, with $15.2 billion in sales from electronics, machinery, auto parts, shipbuilding, aerospace, trading and financial services in 1988 is land's 4th chaebol after Samsung, Hyundai and Lucky-Goldstar, seeks government aid in 1989 for near bankrupt shipyard, approved if four affiliates sold, and raises $225 million in own equity as state requires it to focus on only three core areas, in 1989 buys Leading Edge, U.S. PC marketer in bankruptcy, reveals plans in 1991 to make auto parts in U.S. as part of globalization strategy, and builds minicars with Suzuki license and runs Daewoo Securities, lands largest brokerage by 1991)... Hong Kong's Jardine Matheson relocates to Bermuda (in 1986 forms new organization to block takeovers).

1985

General Events

Industrial countries, World Bank pledge over one billion dollars for long-term economic assistance to African nations suffering famine, economic collapse... Canada, U.S. agree to study acid rain... In first strike of 12 years, some 320,000 are idled in Denmark... France suspends investments in South Africa... After year-long strike to protest closure of uneconomic mines, British coal miners return (March 3) to work... After disagreeing on official pricing policy for oil, OPEC allows individual members to strive for "their fair share in the world market" regardless of consequences, price/barrel under $15 in 1986... Chinese Communist Party meets (takes resignations from members of Politburo, Central Committee to promote new generation of technocrats)... Japan urges (April) its people to buy foreign goods... Britain evaluates its welfare program (proposes private plans to replace State earnings-related scheme, cuts in housing benefits, benefits for poor, and income-support benefits, no payments for death and maternity, new fund and safety net for poor, new benefits plan for working poor so that they will be better off than those on dole)... Japan agrees (April 15) to end commercial whaling in 1988...

Prime Minister Nakasone reveals 3-year program to open Japan to more foreign business (reduces tariffs on 1,850 items, eases some hidden barriers of standards, is attacked for not granting quotas on agricultural products)... U.S.S.R. starts (April) new campaign against alcoholism to improve productivity (closes vodka shops, ups drinking age from 18 to 21, cuts production of hard-liquor, ups fines for drunkenness, gives adults hard time in labor camp for causing children to drink)... Pacific island state, Kiribati, grants fishing licenses to Soviet trawlers for some $2 million... Bank of China's president is sacked for giving himself and other officials excessive pay hikes, similar actions taken to discipline officers of Fuzhou military reselling color TVs for profit and punish Manchurian party officials for reselling steel... Neil Kinnock, head of Britain's Labor Party, denounces far-left ideologues, union leaders for new party image... U.S. bans (May 1) all trade with Nicaragua (-1990, curbs exports by nearly 50%, is avoided by dummy firms in Panama and fishing licenses via Honduras, causes more damage by cutting off credit at World Bank, IMF)... Fortune: "British Unions Go Japanese" (cites labor contracts in 1980s of Japanese plants that wipe out traditional restrictive work rules)... Britain values pound at $1.11, $4.03 in 1949 and $2.41 in 1980... Italy's IRI starts $20 million land development in South Bronx, NYC, as industrial park for Italian firms... Japan invests nearly $2 billion in Europe, over 100% from 1982... Spain, Portugal agree (June 12) to terms for entering EC, join 1986... After repeated threats of U.S. sanctions (1976-), market share of foreign cigarettes goes from 2% to 14% in 1990 as tobacco monopoly allows competition... People's Republic holds China's first beauty pageant in Canton (shows acrobatics in 1986 with women in exercise tights, leotards)... Some 520 foreign businesses open offices in China, a total of 1,448 in 26 cities... Some 20,000 Swedish civil servants strike for higher wages, take minor raises after paralyzing Social Democrat Party's economy for 18 days (leads to austerity measures to reduce currency outflow)...

China drops price controls on 1,800 food items in 22 cities, provinces... After August political crisis, South Africa closes foreign-exchange and stock markets to stem capital flight of some $2 billion... Scientists from West Germany, Italy, France, Britain and Belgium form project to develop optical computers... Time: "European Labor In Retreat"... China finds multimillion-dollar scandal, involves members of Communist Party and Government, at duty-free port on Hainan Island... Japanese law asks employers to refrain from discriminatory hiring practices, no sanctions... Socialist Alan Garcia Perez is President of Peru (-1990, discharges 37 police generals, some with ties to drug lords, ousts head of military force fighting Shining Path guerrillas for harsh measures, withdraws oil-contracts of foreign companies, refuses to pay over 10% of Peru's export earnings for repayment of $14.3 billion foreign debt - loses credit, while denied funds from IMF in 1986 lowers annual inflation rate from 184% to 59% and increases wages by some 7% to offset rises in living costs to produce growth rate of 5.5%, after continual terrorism wipes out SAIS Cahuide, private co-op with 130,000 head of livestock, 800 workers, and 100 administrators and technical advisors in 1989, for peasant overthrow of government, faces inflation rate of 1,720% in 1988, possibly 10,000% in 1989, and polarization of society between extreme left and right, is succeeded by Alberto Fujimori in 1990, renounces "shock" therapy, would hurt poor, to face inflation rate near 2,500% and $17 billion foreign debt)...

In opposition to Japanese high-definition television, EEC sets own standards... As first of its kind, Japan makes $260 million in trade concessions, other measures to compensate U.S. for "unfair" trade practices (after U.S. firms sell $1.7 billion of Japanese assets in 1989, signs trade pact in 1990 with U.S., pledges to streamline retail sector to lessen power of tiny shops, adopt stiffer antitrust penalties, increase spending on public works, change tax laws for affordable housing, and reduce work week for government employees to 5 days)... France's Jacques Delors heads European Community's executive commission, output of $4.7 trillion in 1989 equals that of U.S. and greater than Japan and Asia's Four Tigers combined (sweeps away maze of nontariff barriers, goads bureaucracy to prepare standards, policies for single internal market, ratified 1988, in 1992 for 37% of world commerce with 324 million consumers)...

Vietnam introduces reforms to stimulate economy (sees Number One Frozen Seafood Export Co., Ho Chi Min City, reap $17 million in 1986 by shipping packaged products to Hong Kong, Japan, Singapore, Australia and Eastern Bloc, one of land's most successful enterprises)... EC Commissioner for Competition orders Alfa Romeo to return $420 million in state aid (in 1989 investigates France's action to forgive $1.8 billion in debts by state-owned Renault)... After allegedly issuing $2.3 billion in unauthorized loans and handling $66.8 million in check-kiting scheme, Hong Kong's Overseas Trust Bank closes with government takeover, Colony's "single biggest fraud"... Wall climbing sport is popular in France, U.S.' first rock gym in 1987... Paris-based Organization for Economic Cooperation and Development writes guidelines for environmental assessment of projects... Renault auto maker breaks strike of Confederation Generale du Travail, follows 1982 union defeat to French National Railways... Hong Kong secretly rescues Ka Wah Bank from dubious loans with $128 million in emergency credit... Backed by private interests and 19 European governments, $4.5 billion Eureka research program is launched to compete with U.S. and Japan (funds 302 projects, high-definition TV to computer-aided systems, for $10.3 billion by 1989)... China approves sale of public stock, first since 1949 (lets consumers buy on installment plan, encourages development of beauty parlors, tourist attractions, catering services, gymnasiums, etc.)... Small French brewery makes claim for instant beer syrup... Izvestia estimates moonlighting workers do 45% of all apartment repairs, 40% of car repairs and 30% of all technical repairs (suggests licenses, taxes for such illegal free-lancers)... China's first stockbroker, Shanghai, trades shares in some 10 local firms... U.S. banks lift (December) ban on lending to U.S.S.R., join British bank in $400 million loan... Mikhail S. Gorbachev is new leader of Soviet Union (-1991 with break-up of U.S.S.R., to make Socialism stronger initiates reforms of glasnost for open communications, demokratizatsiya to reshape political system with free elections, some in 1987, and perestroika to restructure failing economy, sputters to average 2% as lowest of industrial countries except Britain, by decentralizing economic decisions, improving productive efficiency and easing restrictions on small-scale free enterprise, introduces profit principle in state-owned industry - by 1987 several hundred of 48,000 on self-financing basis with worker-elected plant managers, creates system of factory inspectors to reject substandard work, allows new high-tech firms, most run by Academy of Sciences instead of ministries, to keep part of earned profits, lets private taxis compete with state-owned fleets, and allows collective farms to sell output through their own outlets, in 1989 retains central planning in new Five-Year plan, grants workers, over 90% in unions, right to strike, i.e., coal miners for economic demands, limits stoppages in public transportation, communications, power, defense and steelmaking, sees first U.S. cosmetic store, Estee Lauder, and first U.S. fast food, McDonald's, authorizes purchase, 5 million rubles, of foreign goods in 1989 to appease discontented consumers and reduce hoarding - 1,000 of 1,200 basic items hard to find, raises taxes on co-ops, basis for private business, from 5% to 35%, plans Novgorod as Free Economic Zone in 1989 to attract foreign investments, pressures cooperatives to lower prices and improve quality - over 100,000 co-ops by 1989 as illegal outlets in black market supply up to 84% of consumer goods with nearly 2.1% of labor force, sanctions restrictions and preferences in state loans and taxes for businesses selling goods, services at state-controlled prices to private business, adopts experimental program to pay foreign cash to growers on state farms for excess harvests, combines six agri-industrial ministries and equivalents in 15 republics into "lean superministry" to cut bureaucracy, thousands out of work get three months' pay with land's first unemployment benefits, lets entrepreneurs lease state-owned land, factories and equipment to develop private businesses, postpones decontrol of prices, wholesale and agricultural prices in 1990 and retail in 1992, adopts strong presidency and multi-party system in 1990, allows leasing of land, can be passed on to heirs, at state prices but bans sale of land, plans 5-year change over to market-economy in 1990, ingredients: to sell up to 60% of state assets, boost prices in 1991 - spurs near-panic hoarding, devalue ruble in 1991, protect pensioners, poor and students from high prices, set up unemployment insurance and wage-price indexing, levy "super-profit" tax on those who make over 30% on sales, boost interest rates, let foreigners own 100% of ventures, form free economic zones)...

Demand for OPEC oil is 17.5 million barrels/day, 23.6 million/day in 1989... Players' Union forms in Japan's professional baseball league (denounces strikes as unfair, sees bribery scandal in 1990)... 139 Japanese electronic firms in U.S. employ some 68,000, U.S. with 360 firms, over 72,000 workers, in Japan... State-owned Mexican firms employ nearly 1 million workers, accounts for some 75% of foreign-exchange earnings... Tokyo commercial land costs $1,735/square foot, $5,792 in 1989... Bolivia hires Harvard economist Jeffrey Sachs to advise on stemming annual hyperinflation of 24,000% (adopts shock treatment to freeze wages, raise prices, and cut state spending - inflation rate under 15% by 1987 and financial stability by 1989, advises Poland in 1989-90 on transformation to market capitalism)...

By 1990 Japanese sales of log cabins for rural living, city folk unable to own houses with high land prices, rises to some $450 million... Japan's travel deficit runs some $4 billion, perhaps $20 billion in 1989 with $7.7 billion spent in U.S... Soviet Garry Kasparov is World Chess Champion (pioneers game's promotional field with endorsements and manager, forms international Grandmasters' Assn. as trade union with corporate sponsorships to challenge International Chess

Federation)... Taiwan's per capita income is $3,000, $7,300 by 1990 (leads to some 4 million of 20 million playing stock market in 1989, average share changes hands 35 times/year in national obsession)... Jose Sarney is Brazil's new president (with bloated bureaucracy runs up Third World's largest foreign debt of $110 billion, leaves annual inflation rate over 5,000% for successor Fernando Collor de Mello in 1990, saddled with $115 billion foreign debt freezes financial assets worth $1,200 or more for 18 months to remove $85 billion from circulation and reduce 84% monthly inflation rate to under 13%, abolishes 24 state agencies, axes 100,000 government workers, and protects Amazon area from ranchers, settlers, miners and developers)... By 1990 U.S. dollar drops 43% against major currencies... China issues panda stamp, by 1990 is standard of value for all other stamps (with limited access to only two stock markets leads to some 25 million participating in informal, unauthorized stamp market).

Business Events

Mario Vazquez-Rana, wealthy Mexican newspaper owner, buys United Press International, started 1907 by newspaper owner Edward W. Scripps to fight wire service monopoly of Associated Press (in heyday employs 6,000 worldwide to serve 5,000 broadcast and newspaper clients, struggles in 1970s with two entrepreneurs after given $5 million to buy UP, with losses of $70 million is sold to Earl W. Bryan, former surgeon cum venture capitalist, in 1988 to deliver "Usefully Packaged Information" to business, non-media clients)... British Venture Capital Assn. invests $412 million in projects, $450-525 million in 1986... Murdoch's London-based News International forms venture with Groupe Bruxelles Lambert, Belgium's biggest financial and industrial holding company with interests in Europe's largest TV, radio station (gets position in Europe's TV market to complement U.S. interests)... Nissan acquires 25% of Yue Loong Motor Co., Taiwan's largest manufacturer of vehicles (leads to Mitsubishi's 25% share of Taiwan's China Motor in 1986)... Some 325 investors in syndicate rebuff Lloyd's of London by refusing to cover $80 million in losses, many allege fraud to avoid personal bankruptcy... France plans to open Euro Disneyland near Paris in 1992 while Busch Gardens plans Barcelona park for 1992, Marine World plans Paris park for 1993, Universal Studios, Florida park in 1990 with MCA to take on 1989 Disney-MGM park, plans Paris or London park for 1996, Disney MGM plans Paris park for 1996, and Battersea Park, Wonderworld, Magic Mountain, Andalusialand consider projects...

Institutional Networks installs equipment in London brokerage (allows 24-hour trading in U.S. stocks)... FCA International, world's largest debt collector founded 1926, in Montreal with some 25,000 clients, U.S. Government, American Express, and J.C. Penney, posts revenues of $50 million... Japan holds first official season of fashion shows (features 33 designers in 1986)... Cardin signs licensing agreement with U.S.S.R. to have Soviet clothing factories turn out designs for men, women and children (leads to Soviet contracts with French clothing makers in 1986 to upgrade 25 factories)... New short golf course, designed by Nicklaus, opens for play on Grand Cayman Island... Fortune: "Japan's Autocratic Managers"... Deutsche Bank acquires Flick family's industrial empire of steel, chemicals, and paper for some $2 billion, country's largest takeover, after its involvement in major scandal on secret political contributions... Goldsmith acquires San Francisco's Crown Zellerbach, 1.9 million acres of forests in Washington and Oregon, for $500 million...

Swiss-based International Forest & Leisure is exclusive agent, International Olympic Committee's first, to license Olympic emblem to international corporations for merchandising products... Fortune: "The Stock Market Upheaval in Europe" (notes changes in rise of global markets, predicts crystallization with centers at New York, London and Tokyo for three time zones)... Grand Met, $6.2-billion-a-year London food, beverage and hotel conglomerate, buys Pearle Health Services, some 1,276 optical convenience stores in 42 states and 5 countries, from U.S.' G.D. Searle drugs... Japan's four major breweries sell some 24 brands, 40 by 1989 in market war... Elaborate funeral of Masahisa Takenaka, Japan's most powerful underworld Yakuza boss with over some 10,400 mobsters, is attended by over 1,000 mourners... Edzard Reuter, CEO of Daimler-Benz, begins diversification in electronics, aerospace to ease firm's reliance on autos and trucks, $39 billion high-tech giant in 1989 with Deutsche Bank, nation's largest, as biggest stockholder with 28.5% (after acquiring German engine maker, MTV, airplane maker, Dornier, and electrical giant, AEG, in 1980s, pays $900 million for just over 50% of $3.7 billion aerospace conglomerate, Messerschmitt-Bolkow-Blohm - Blohm is Germany's No. 1 defense contractor and holds 37.9% share of Europe's Airbus consortium, in 1989 to build one of world's great global companies for integrated Europe's market, after pact with U.S.' United Technologies courts Mitsubishi, 28 core companies with sales of $200 billion, for cooperative deal)... British Petroleum forms BP Financial International as trading, banking subsidiary (posts profits of $32 million in first year)... In first known case, Paris civil court fines fashion designer Saint Laurent some $11,000 for plagiarizing design of another member of French Couturier Federation... David Bathearst, President of Christie's auction business in London and NYC, resigns after lying about selling two paintings at 1981 auction (spurs investigation of unregulated auction business by NYC Department of Consumer Affairs)...

Philip Morris introduces Ritz cigarettes, package designed by Saint Laurent... Elders IXL makes hostile bid of $2.6 billion for Britain's Allied-Lyons (to evade raid buys liquor business of Hiram Walker, acquired by Reichmann family via their Gulf Canada to block $2.9 billion bid of Trans Canada pipeline, for $1.9 billion to block Elders)... Holmes a Court tries hostile takeover of Broken Hill Proprietary, Australia's largest enterprise (is blocked when Elders IXL supports Broken Hill)... Whiz salesman Cuban-born Carlos I. Miro, after becoming Transit Casualty Insurance's largest producer under four years by writing over $100 million with dubious policies, leaves Dallas for partnership in London's Anglo-American Trust Group (begins insurance subsidiary in Dallas in 1986 - premiums of $60 million by 1988, after Louisiana investigation in 1988 is sued in 1989 for looting $28 million, after Transit and Anglo-American topple flees to London, gets $3 million in credit from British bank to pay off loan to Swiss bank to start Irish-based insurance firm)... As one of many in Ho Chi Min City, Nguyen Van Muoi Hai, son of Saigon shopkeepers, starts Vietnamese perfume business with under $1,000 in savings from selling jeans at street stall, by 1988 employs 19 regular workers, 200 others by contract, to become $1 million business... Harrods is first business to use international 880-number for customers...

C. Itoh & Co. forms consortium, CST Communications, with Suntory and Tokyo Broadcasting (pays $15 million to MGM/UA for stake in three films, leads to some 12 Tokyo-based firms with film divisions by 1989, spawns Japan's Apricot Entertainment, $50 million, and Victor Co., $100 million, of Japan in 1989 to produce films)... Siemens forms venture-capital subsidiary, spawns four high-tech enterprises by 1988... After averaging fewer than 20 acquisitions/year in early 1980s, Europe sees 40/year by 1989... Martin Sorrell, former financial director of Saatchi & Saatchi, buys Wire & Plastics Products, maker of supermarket carts (uses firm as base to acquire group of design houses in U.S., Britain in 1986, acquires U.S. advertising giant, J. Walter Thompson Group, 17 times size of WPT, in 1987 for $560 million, buys U.S. ad agency, Ogilvy Group, in 1989 for $864 million)... Nestle acquires U.S.' Carnation food giant for $2.9 billion (picks up candy maker, Rowntree, in 1988 for $4 billion while BSN, France's largest packaged-food and beverage group, buys European cookie and chips, sold to PepsiCo for $1.3 billion, business of RJR Nabisco in 1989 for $2.5 billion)...

After putting up shopping centers across Australia, Romanian-born George Herscu acquires L.J. Hooker as U.S. base (buys NYC's 1865 B. Altman and 1895 Bonwit Teller department stores in 1987 along with Merksamer jewelry chain, CA, Houston's Sakowitz and Birmingham-based Parisian, when Australian interest rates go over 20%, goes into liquidation, B. Altman closes 1989)... Nestle brings Lean Cuisine, acquired U.S.' Stouffer, which introduced line in 1981, in 1970, to Britain... Daimler-Benz starts working on pollution-free hydrogen engines for cars, unveils prototype in 1990... Volkswagen starts building engines in East Germany (plans to build cars in 1990 as two countries combine, East Germany's biggest restructuring target for free markets is 126 state-owned conglomerates producing 85% of GNP)... Fujitsu buys 45% of U.S.' Amdahl, No. 2 in global market for mainframe computers (with competitive battle leads to 1989 sale of National Advanced Systems of National Semiconductor to Hitachi, 80%, and GM, 20%, to challenge IBM and Amdahl in 1990, forces IBM to introduce new mainframe in 1990)... Flick Group sells its 26%, firm is largest shareholder, in W.R. Grace & Co. (borrows $600 million to keep shares from raiders, is forced on four-year crash plan to cut debt and restructure)... Britain's Tie Rack increases sales fifteenfold by 1989 with 242 shops, 41 in U.S., in 9 countries... Some 50 executive search firms operate in Tokyo, over 250 in 1990... Hachette, France's No. 1 publisher, enters U.S. market with Elle, joint venture with Murdock is instant hit (after Britain's Pearson buys U.S. publisher, Addison-Wesley, in 1990 for $283 million, puts up $1.2 billion for Grolier, publishes Encyclopedia America, to become world's No. 3 in books and for Diamandis, runs 12 magazines, to become world's No. 1 in magazines with 74 titles, sales of $1.9 billion)... Romeo Gigli, Italian fashion designer, shows first collection (pioneers softer, romantic silhouette for 1990s to replace hard modern wear)... Nikko, Japan Air Lines Co., buys NYC's Essex House to enter U.S. hotel market (instead of buying U.S. hotels as done by other Japanese chains, grows by building, four by 1991 for expected sales of $107 million)... Komatsu starts UK business to make construction equipment for European market (forms U.S. joint venture in 1988)... De Benedetti uses CIR group to buy 48% of Buitoni, global food conglomerate with 1986 sales of $1.1 billion (uses Italian holding company in 1989 to fight for Mondadori, Italy's largest newspaper and magazine publisher)... By 1991 Suntory, spirits giant, spends over $200 million buying seven U.S. bottled-water firms (buys Hawaiian resort, baseball team and restaurants)... Coca-Cola's share of Taiwan's soft-drink market is 6%, hits 40%, No. 1 with Pepsi at 4%, in 1990 with intensive service to retailers... Deutsche Bank underwrites public offering of Flick industrial group.

1986

General Events

European Court of Justice makes landmark ruling that Paris travel agency could sell airline tickets at prices less than those authorized by French Government (causes European prices for intra-country flights to decline)... Tokyo economic meeting, Canada, U.S., West Germany, Italy, France, Britain and Japan, adopts ambitious plan to control currencies by linking values directly to economic performance of participating countries... OPEC announces (February 18) price of petroleum is under $15/barrel... Twelve of OPEC's 13 price warring members agree to cut output by nearly 3 billion barrels/day to stabilize price of petroleum, fail... Newsweek: "Moscow Faces the New Age" (cites problems of closed society with computer revolution)... Israeli special commission censures 16 top banking, government officials for illegal manipulations in 1983 bank-stock crash... Rightist Jacques Chirac is (March 20) France's Prime Minister, plans to dismantle Mitterrand's Socialist programs by ending government subsidies, repealing labor laws requiring government approval of layoffs, eliminating most exchange and price controls (forms Denationalization Ministry to privatize 65 state enterprises, worth $23.5 billion, in banking, insurance and industry, including Renault, Saint-Gobain in glass and packaging, merchant bank Paribas, telecommunications giant CGE, AGF in insurance, and large commercial bank Societe Generale, by 1988)...

South Africa abolishes tax laws to restrict movements of blacks... U.S.S.R. puts unmanned cargo space craft into orbit, first of planned missions to build Mir space station... Poorly managed firms in China's industrial city of Shenyang are forced to declare bankruptcy... Switzerland's Belland develops new plastic material, tough and waterproof (dissolves under certain conditions)... U.S.S.R. reforms higher education to integrate sector with economy, conduct part of teaching process in work places... South Africa is (May 1) stymied by its biggest strike of 1.5 million blacks protesting Apartheid... Some 1,500 British scientists, including many Nobel Prize winners, urge government to "Save British Science" (leads to $160 million in research grants, fails to stop exodus of researchers going to U.S.)... Fortune: "Europe Starts to Create Jobs" (notes rise of employment from high-tech industries, service sector)... Belgium's Plant Genetic Systems develops strain of tobacco to kill insects praying on it... Poland arrests (May 31) Solidarity leader Zbigniew Bujak... Refurbished Musee d'Orsay, Gare d'Orsay railroad station 1898-1969, opens in Paris to showcase art in elegant surroundings... Time: "The Sun Also Sets" (notes rising Japanese unemployment from restructuring of industries, strong yen)... Bolivia, U.S. launch (July) joint raids on nation's cocaine labs... International bankers extend deadline for Mexico's repayment of loans... Business Week: "The Venture Communists Setting Up Shop in China" (cites formation of China Venturetech Investment, run by two U.S.-trained entrepreneurs, with $12.5 million in government money, bank credit of $15.6 million)... MITI plans villages overseas for Japanese retirees... Newsweek: "The Sheiks Rediscover Religion" (with falling oil revenues, block creditors with sharia, law of Islam, to ban payments of interest, previously hidden as "administrative fees" or "loan initiation discounts")... After years urging family program of "two is enough," Singapore promotes larger families to build labor force for export-oriented state... China allows (October 1) firms to dismiss employees... Moscow's Young Communist paper attacks high-stakes gambling as social ill... Time: "Sweet is Turning to Sour" (notes rise in bureaucratic difficulties of firms, some 1,448, doing business in China)... Holland opens (October 4) Europe's most advanced sea barrier... Rhine River is polluted by over 1,000 tons of toxic chemicals... South Africa declares state of emergency to prevent blacks honoring 1976 Soweto uprising (plunges rand by 17%)... Only 200 Poles attend Solidarity rally in Wroclaw... Japan allows foreign lawyers to practice law... Fortune: "Europe's New High Roller: The Little Guy" (cites rise of small investors in stock markets from tax incentives)...

China's first combination of U.S.-style laundromat, dry cleaning establishment opens in Tianjin... Business Week: "If You Can't Beat Them, Buy 'Em: Takeovers Arrive in Japan"... Soviet Union shows new Lada car, designed by Porsche and engineered by Fiat, at Belgian auto show, built by U.S.S.R.'s VAZ enterprise with financial and managerial autonomy (is allowed to retain profits and hard currency for plant modernization, to give incentive bonuses)... Brazil adopts radical inflation package to devalue currency by 300%, freeze wages and prices (establishes first unemployment compensation plan, reduces inflation of 250% to 25% by 1987)... Business Week: "The High Price Japanese Pay for Success" (cites rise of alcoholism, emotional breakdowns and suicides from work ethic)... For first time, value of Canadian dollar drops below $0.70/U.S. dollar... France, Denmark, West Germany, Switzerland, Britain and Austria dump thousands of gallons of adulterated Italian wine... Newsweek: "End of An Economic Miracle?" (notes slowdown of Japan's economy with declining GNP, rising unemployment, decreasing exports, and exporting jobs to other countries as value of yen soars)... U.S.' GM leaves (October) South Africa... Canadian entrepreneur Norman Gardner invents chemically-treated paper, Nocopi, that cannot be duplicated on photocopy machines...

Shenyang's Trust & Development Corp. opens China's first securities market to boost local stocks, attract capital... Fortune: "Japan's Comeback Plan" (slashes costs, buys finished goods from low-price countries like U.S., squeezes suppliers, and takes necessary losses to hold markets)... China seeks admission to GATT... Japan builds $300 million research center with technical university, biotechnology institute near Kumamoto... Newsweek: "Solving the Chinese Puzzle" (notes final mastery in translating language, over 50,000 characters, into computer program)... Newsweek: "The Economics of Relaxation" (shows easing of work, savings ethic of Japanese)... By 1987, China's Shekou, one example, sees 21 work stoppages and strikes, most from management's violations of contract regulations... Sweden's Space Media Network, Institute of International Affairs sell SPOT satellite pictures to firms, press, etc., while France focuses on selling such photos to governments... Business Week: "Europe and Japan are Catching Tax-Reform Fever (notes pressures on other countries to compete with lower tax rate of U.S., lowest of six major industrial nations at 40%)... With collapse of oil prices and rising debt, Labor Party's Dr. Gro Harlem Brundtland returns as Norway's Prime Minister, served in 1981 (caps wages, devalues krone, and clamps down on consumer credit to restore export markets, re-evaluates social programs taking over 50% of GNP, as Chairman of UN commission on environment releases report in 1987 to put issue of global responsibility on international agenda)... Ruble is officially valued at $1.47, $0.23 on black market, is $1.72, $0.21, in 1987, $1.64, $0.10, in 1988, and $1.63,and $0.07, in 1989 (forces people to buy whatever is available, leads to government crackdown on bribery, extortion causing food shortages)... In addition to voluntary curbs on exports of Japanese autos and steel, Japan and U.S. semi-conductor accord forces Japanese firms to stop dumping and abide by quotas (lets U.S. chipmakers get at least 20% of Japan's market by 1991)... Convention on International Trade in Endangered Species requires ivory-producing nations to adopt export quotas... Hungary's inflation rate is 5%, 17% in 1987 and over 22% in 1990... When most industrialized nations refuse new credits, Cuba suspends payment on foreign debt, $7 billion in 1990, despite getting $3-5 billion/year from U.S.S.R. (by 1990 owes U.S.S.R. $24.7 billion)... At 27th Communist Party Congress, Gorbachev attacks corruption, cronyism in inefficient bureaucracy blocking economic reforms (grants managers of factories, enterprises more authority)... Soviet Union breaks up organized-crime ring in Lenin factory, Michurinsk, trading in stolen merchandise... With Vietnam's economy in shambles, party chief Nguyen Van Lingh eases government controls of economy to encourage private enterprise, stimulate foreign trade and investment (leads to Hoang Viet Dung's electronics business, one of Hanoi's hottest capitalists in 1988, and some 3,000 private shops employing over 25,000 in Ho Chi Minh City in 1987)... Soviet law allows individuals, families to moonlight in 29 fields, auto repair, plumbing, tailoring, carpentry, tutoring and other jobs, with permits...

Britain's domestic securities market, including London Stock Exchange, are deregulated, eliminates fixed commissions and erases distinctions between selling brokers and trading jobbers (in upheaval, attracts Tokyo's Nomura Securities, U.S.' Merrill Lynch, and some 30 others as exchange members and international banks, i.e., Union Bank of Switzerland to seek brokerage partners, is global securities trading center by 1988)... China exports $1.2 billion in goods to U.S.S.R., $143 million in 1982, while Soviet exports to China rise $243 million to $1.4 billion... France's top business school, Ecole des Hautes Etudes Commerciales, offers management program in English... By 1991 wages in Sweden rise 28% and inflation rate hits 9% as opposition defeats painful plan of Social Democrats to cure economic woes... By 1990 Spain's National Organization for the Blind, blind Miguel Duran is CEO in 1986, invests some $150 million of tax-free profits from daily lotteries, grosses some $2.5 billion/year, in nearly 70 firms to become investment giant... Mexico joins GATT (grants observer status to China, U.S.S.R. in 1990)... Harvard checks trademark possibilities in Japan (by 1990 gets $130,000 from licensed menswear in Japan while Oxford, Cambridge seek non-academic revenues to bolster budgets)... By 1990 South Korean won rises 31% against U.S. dollar, wages soar 90%... Japan issues first gold coins since W.W. II, scandal in 1990 with counterfeiting scam... MITI funds space research project, $34 million by 1990, and laser ion beam project for machining, $18 million by 1990... U.S.S.R.'s first pedestrian street mall opens in Moscow, Copenhagen's in mid-1960s... Mexico's 16% budget deficit drops to 6.3% in 1989... U.K. sells shares in Rolls-Royce aerospace, nationalized 1971... Australians open hotel, early foreign investment in Vietnam after the war, in Ho Chi Minh... IRI sells Alfa Romeo to Fiat (with first losses in 12 years issues shares to public, after returning to profitability merges its chipmaking unit with Thomson CSF subsidiary in 1987, in 1988 restructures steel consolidation to trim losses, considers, 1990, merging two banks to form Italy's largest bank).

Business Events

Murdoch's News Corp. buys Metromedia, six TV stations, for $1.85 billion to get 21% of U.S. market (with his 20th Century-Fox movies forms Fox Network in 1986, first night prime-time shows in 1987 with 105 stations and national advertisers, after losses of $94 million shows first profits in 1989 while Paramount and MCA plan 5th TV network)... GM Europe, Britain's Vauxhall and Germany's Opel, move headquarters to Zurich (with corporate staff of 200 sees European market share of 8.4%, 1980, rise to 11%, 1989, while GM U.S.' share drops 46% to 35%)... Japan imports some 68,000 foreign cars, 182,000 in 1989, 4.5% of market with BMW, 120 outlets, selling 36,000 and Ford, via Mazda dealers, selling 75,000... After 23 years as management consultant Jean-Rene Fourton is CEO of Rhone-Poulenc, French state-owned profitless drug and chemical maker (after dumping 20 businesses, including textiles and fertilizers, and 35 acquisitions, including chemical units of U.S.' GAF, RTZ for $1.3 billion in 1988 and Canadian vaccine producer, restores $12.7 billion enterprise to acquire Rorer, U.S. drugmaker of Maalox, in 1990 for $3.2 billion after Beecham merges with financially-troubled Smith Kline Beekman, Contac cold medicine and Tagamet antiulcer drug, and Bristol-Myers buys Squibb in 1989, plans alliance with Heochst in 1990)... West Germany's Otto-Versand sells dresses in Japan via catalogs, sales of $72 million by 1990 (although other mail-order firms, The Sharper Image and Sears, were not successful, leads to Vernon H. Fraenke's Shop America distributing catalogs in 1990 via 7-Eleven's 4,000 stores to by-pass maze of middlemen to reach customers with prices under local shops)... Czechoslovakia's first VCR rental store opens in Prague... In strategy to build European banking network, Deutsche Bank, Europe's 6th largest, acquires Bank of America's Italian subsidiary (after buying financial institutions in Britain, Austria, Spain and Portugal, opens 100 new branches in East Germany in 1990 to cash in on currency union while Commerzbank and Dresdner Bank, once 162 branches in East, follow suit, in 1991 centralizes management and improves services to private clients)... Divers discover wreck of Nuestra Senora de la Maravilla, Vera Cruz ship sunk in 1656, in waters off of Bahamas with treasure of some $1.6 billion...

For first time London trader uses transatlantic computer link to buy stocks from NYC dealer... World's largest pilot plant to extract uranium from seawater operates at Nio, Japan... Business Week: "Film Makers Discover the Canadian Solution"... Brussels hosts Second World Whores Congress... Paris-based Club Med launches U.S. campaign to sell corporate clients recreational packages for employees... Fortune: "A New Dose of Capitalism Turns Italy Around"... After working for Britain's J. Sainsbury supermarket group, Peter J. Davis, CEO of Reed International publishing, buys Murdoch's travel information group, paid $340 million in 1984, for $825 million (becomes largest travel publisher in industry)... Fortune: "Networking: Japan's Latest Computer Craze" (notes linking of banks, dealers and suppliers with various automobile manufacturers into integrated systems)... Volvo, pharmaceutical producer Fermenta form $556 million venture to rule Sweden's biotech industry, negated on discovery Fermenta's El-Sayed did not have claimed U.S. doctorate (leads to fines by Stockholm Stock Exchange for violating securities trading rules in 1987 financial scandal)...

Amstrad introduces low-priced clone of IBM's PC, sales of $192 million by 1987 with mass-merchandising... Fortune: "Europe's New Managers" (cites youth movement with management training to operate without regard for borders, organizational hierarchies)... Mobile banks appear on Brazil beaches... Hungary hosts professional Formula I racing on new $2 million speedway... Business Week: "The Muscular Yen is Shoving Investment Abroad" (notes Japan's rise in foreign plants, 89 in Taiwan, South Korea and Southeast Asia, with higher value of yen)... London Stock Exchange and 1985 International Securities Regulatory Organization, group of 187 dealers in foreign securities, merge to form International Stock Exchange, prelude for 24-hour global marketplace for stocks... Barclays Bank sells interests in South Africa's 2nd-largest commercial bank... Newly privatized Nippon Telegraph & Telephone auctions shares, each for $7,500... Paris business sells blue jeans by vending machines... In defiance of traditional resistance of printing unions to new technology, Murdoch prints four papers with computerized technology, manned by members of other unions...

Tokyo Stock Exchange accepts four U.S. brokerage firms as full-fledged members... Club Med opens prototype "tropical space" center in Vienna to provide pseudo paradise for urban dwellers (plans centers for NYC, Paris, London, Tokyo)... Investors form Ali Motor Co., named after U.S. boxer Muhammed Ali, to build sports car for Middle East market in 1987... Elders IXL acquires Courage Brewing and 5,000 pubs, some 22,000 "tied houses" run by Allied-Lyons, Bass, Elders, Grand Metropolitan, Scottish and Newcastle, and Whitbread in 1989, for $2.1 billion, first foreigner to own major British brewer... Dai-Ichi Kangyo, assets of some $207 billion, replaces NYC's Citicorp, assets c. $176 billion, as world's No. 1 bank, makes 4 of top 5, including Fuji, Sumitomo and Mitsubishi banks, 5 of top 10 and 13 of top 25 from Japan... In declaring war on Colombia to avoid U.S. extradition, Drug Cartel's forces storm Palace of Justice to kill 11 supreme-court justices, some 170 judges and 87 journalists slain by 1989, in battle with army... Business Week: "Japan's Giants Goes Shopping for U.S. Startups" (notes entrance in capital venture market to acquire new technologies)... Olivetti, Europe's largest personal computer maker in world market, introduces computer software programs in 10 languages as other leading hardware makers go into software (starts joint venture with U.S.' Electronic Data Systems in 1987 to link computer systems for European manufacturers)... Gateway, Britain's 3rd-largest supermarket chain with 817 units in 1989, buys Herman's Sporting Goods from U.S.' W.R. Grace Co. for $414 million (with financial difficulties, attracts friendly $3 billion bid offer from U.S.' Great Atlantic & Tea, owned by West Germany's Tengelmann Group, in 1989 to avoid hostile bid, sign of LBOs in Britain)... C. Itoh & Co. is Japan's first private firm in satellite communications business... British Telecom buys 51% of Canadian maker of computerized phone exchanges for $251 million to go international (gets ITT Dialcom, leading U.S. electronic mail service, for some $35 million in 1986, U.S. national paging system, Metrocast, in 1988 for $28 million, 22% of U.S.' McCaw Cellular Communications, market leader in mobile phones, in 1989, for $1.5 billion and McDonnell Douglas data communications business for $355 million in 1989 after government allows more competition in 1990 spends over $106 million in 1991 to improve its image, service)... When FCC invokes rule prohibiting foreigners owning U.S. television stations, Mexican media baron of $1 billion empire with money machine Televisa as private monopoly, Emilio Azcarraga Milmo is forced to sell interests in Univision Holdings, U.S.' largest Spanish-language TV network with 10 stations, to Hallmark Cards for $620 million (fails to get copper mine and Mexican de Aviacion airline in 1988, launches U.S.' all-sports tabloid, The National, in 1989)... Skidmore, Owings & Merrill, U.S. architectural firm, opens London office to participate in developments to change city's skyline, 300 employees in 1989...

BSN's Riboud forms "shareholders club" of institutional investors who pledge to buy up to 30% of new BSN shares to block raids (swaps shares with Agnelli and buys bank to block unwanted takeovers, by 1989 inks deals of some $1 billion to chase Nestle's sales of $27 billion, Unilever's $14.5 billion)... Nissan makes cars in British plant for Europe (reveals 5-year, $400 million expansion in 1987), Toyota follows in 1989 with NEC, Fujitsu and Matsushita, its 15th, planning new plants... Bank of Tokyo, Sanwa Bank takeover California banks, spend $1.1 billion for others by 1988 with plans for Pacific Northwest, Midwest and Northeast in early 1990s... French holding company, Cerus, of De Beneditti pays $39 million for 37% of Saint Laurent fashion house (pays Squibb Corp. $631 million in 1986 for Charles of the Ritz Group holding rights to YSL perfumes, sells Ritz's mass-market lines to Revlon in 1987)... Hanson Trust acquires Imperial Group, cigarettes, Courage beer, food, hotels and restaurants (sells most of Imperial to keep tobacco unit for cash flow, prototype for Goldsmith's raid on BAT in 1989 as takeover fever grows (gobbles up $8 billion worth of European, U.S. firms by 1990 to seek others with $20 billion in cash, credit)... After investing $2-3 million in 1980-82 in emerging growth firms, Japanese firms start investing $200 million/year... Jean-Marc Aletti, Michel Vignon open Paris Arbitrage, biggest players with major clients on Matif futures exchange (flee investigation in 1988)... In Silicon Bavaria Ulrich Seng, $500,000 government grant and $1.2 million in venture capital, starts Spea Software in computer-aided design, sales of $3.2 million in 1987...

New Zealander Allan Hawkins, blossoms as corporate raider after floating shares in Australia for subsidiary of his Equiticorp Holdings, reorganizes as British-based financial services (with 1989 debt of $836 million and post-Crash shock, enters liquidation)... After disposing peripheral businesses since 1981, Guinness brewing giant beats rival, Argyll Group, to get Distillers Co. for $4.1 billion to build world's most profitable combine (is investigates by Britain for stock manipulation, fires 1981 CEO Ernest W. Saunders, faces 49 criminal charges in 1989 and is convicted in 1990, in 1987 while Jack Lyons and Gerald M. Ronson, CEO of Britain's No. 2 privately-held firm Heron International, are sentenced, 1990, for stealing millions in scandal)... Alfred Herrhausen is CEO of Deutsche Bank (buys nine commercial and investment banks, Europe to Australia, to become world's 20th-biggest with $168 billion in assets, pays record $1.5 billion in 1989 for London's Morgan Grenfell, blocks takeover by France's Indosuez, to strengthen role in East European financing, is slain by terrorists in 1989)... ITT sells European telecommunications business to French state-owned Compagnie Generale d'Electricite and partners, Spain's Telefonica National and Societe Generale de Belgique, for $1.5 billion and 37% interest in new venture, allows CGE to take on Sweden's Ericsson, Germany's Siemens, Japan's NEC, and AT&T so ITT can focus on U.S. hotel and insurance enterprises... After building first house in free time as factory foreman in 1949 (with $3,000 in profits, builds 40 more by 1950 and 20,000 around Ottawa in 1950s-60s for reputation as master builder, loses business in 1969 raising cash for expansion - buys back later for $38 million, moves to Toronto after blocked in buying old-line financial institution, Royal Trustco, for $413 million in 1980), eccentric Canadian developer Robert Campeau acquires U.S.' Allied Stores, 130 operations, for $3.6 billion (sheds 17 divisions including Brooks Bros., Bonwit Teller and Ann Taylor, of 21 for $2.2 billion and eliminates some 4,000 jobs to reduce debt)... Sumitomo Rubber buys Dunlop Tire for $80 million... Sumitomo Bank buys minority stake in NYC's Goldman, Sachs (leads to Yasuda, Japan's 5th largest in life insurance, buying 18% of Paine Webber, full-service financial firm with 285 offices worldwide, and Nippon Life buying 13% of American Express' Shearson Lehman in 1987)... By 1988 U.S. firms' funding of foreign R&D rises 33%, 6% gain in domestic R&D... Britain's David A. Quale buys money-losing video distributor (runs 730 Ritz video stores by 1990 for sales of $75 million)... Waterford Glass Group saves Wedgwood from clutches of London International Group, a condom maker (with falling U.S. crystal sales, launches cost-cutting program in 1988, tries to avoid takeover in 1989)... Ford opens plant in Hermosillo, Mexico (plans, as do other firms, $300 million expansion in 1990)... After introducing Prima, Europewide magazine for women, in 1980, Bertelsmann buys RCA Records for $222 million, Doubleday publishing for $475 million (by 1990 is world's No. 1 media giant with sales of $8.7 billion, $3.3 from publishing, $.5 from records, CDs and music videos, in 1990, after selling U.K. book club, buys East Berlin magazine, newspaper publisher with Maxwell and gets eastern Germany's largest book printer, forms record venture in 1991 with MCA, owned by Matsushita, prepares and spends $260 million on German pay-TV station, plans to spend some $4 billion by 1994 for expansion in Europe, U.S.)...

Saatchi & Saatchi buys Backer Spielvogel ad agency for $56 million and gets NYC's Ted Bates Worldwide, world's 3rd largest, for $450 million to become world's No. 1 with billings of $7.5 billion, tops 1986 merger of BBDO International, Doyle Dane Bernbach and Needham Harper Worldwide with billings of $5 billion (fails to acquire financially-troubled Midland Bank, one of world's largest, in 1987, uses team, psychologists and anthropologists, to aid clients to develop marketing strategies, adds 17 consulting firms in 1988, inks pact with U.S.S.R. in 1989 to package corporate sponsorships for first British-Soviet space mission in 1991, with falling profits hires Franc's Robert-Louis Dreyfus in 1989 to resolve its management problems, sells most of its consulting firms in 1990, with industry-wide slump from recession recapitalizes 1991, Jacob Rothschild, 12%, and Tisch family, 6%, as largest stockholders)...After merger talks with Ford in 1985, Fiat's truck operations and Ford's British truck business are combined (merge farm and construction equipment businesses in 1991)... Cadbury Schweppes buys Canada Dry and shares of Dr Pepper (sells non-candy, non-beverage firms, in 1987 forms U.K. joint venture with Coca-Cola, leaves, 1988, U.S. candy market after licensing Hershey's to handle products, in 1989 buys Orange Crush and Hires from P&G, in 1990 buys non-cola soft drinks units of Source Perrier)... Hanson Industries runs group of eight enterprises, $7.5 billion in revenues and over 35,000 employees (avoids 1987 October stock market crash to continue expansion with $6 billion war chest for acquisitions).

1987

General Events

December, 1986, strike, on pay restraints and merit promotions, of French rail workers, supported by Communist union of Confederation Generale du Travail and other transportation workers, is settled (January 13) to end protest of government reforms... Japan extends (January 27) voluntary curbs on U.S.auto exports (rejects higher quotas wanted by U.S. car makers in 1989)... Soviet Union seeks customers for space-launch facilities... Prague Exhibition of Electronics shows Ondra, personal computer from components of Warsaw Pact countries... Danish public-sector workers get work week, now 39 hours, of 37 by 1990... Bolivia issues new currency, drops 6 zeros from old money... Two of Britain's largest unions end year-long protest of Murdoch's new high-tech London printing plant... Brazil suspends interest payments on debt to foreign banks... Five Soviet ministries adopt new system of self-financing... China's Shenyang allows steel to be sold at market prices...

Taiwan eases travel restrictions (lets its manufacturers of labor-intensive products invade China's Fujian Province, ship dismantled factories to China via Hong Kong)... Yugoslavia freezes wages to fight 200% inflation rate, Europe's highest (causes 1,000 strikes by 1988, dinar to plunge 25% on world currency markets as land faces 15% unemployment, foreign debt of $19 billion)... Brazil ends (February 5) 12-month price freeze on some 2,000 products... Chile, Venezuela restructure debts to foreign banks... Liberia gets U.S. experts to revive debt-ridden economy... Tokyo judge rules Nomura Securities, world's biggest brokerage, guilty in making unauthorized, unnecessary trades to collect fees... For first time, Oman lets tourists visit Sultanate, 900 in 1st season and 6,000 in 2nd... Yugoslavia strikes end when Belgrade cuts prices... European Court of Justice rules 470-year-old German law, sets legal contents of beer, could not be used to bar foreign beers from West Germany's market of 1,250 breweries... Argentina adopts (February 25) 4-month freeze on wages, prices (devalues currency)...

Moscow's Sovintersport "lends" athletes to West European, U.S. clubs (signs venture, rights for 10 years for 10 Soviet fighters, in 1989 with U.S. boxing promoter)... China's Communist Party conservatives wage campaign against "bourgeois liberalization" caused by economic reforms... Australia replaces indexing of wages to inflation with two-tier system of wage increases... Japan reports (March 2) January unemployment rate of 3%, highest since 1953... IMF loans Nigeria $825 million to reschedule $20 billion foreign debt... Spain tries some 40 defendants for selling adulterated vegetable oil, perhaps killing some 600 in 1981-85... After administering China territory since 1976, Portugal agrees to restore Macao, mostly casinos, bars and message parlors for 4.2 million tourists, to China in 1999... Mexico, some 360 creditor banks arrange new loans up to $7.7 billion (by 1990 gets banks to lop $3.7 billion/year off payments on debt of $94.5 billion)... Japan, U.S. sign pact to open Japanese market to U.S. supercomputers, none sold by 1990 (agrees in 1990 to drop some barriers for government purchases)... Japan reports (March 17) lowest growth rate, 2.5%, in 12 years... Philippines restructures interest payments on foreign debt... Some 400,000 British teachers strike to protest pay, working conditions set by Conservative Government... Turkey, associate member, seeks full membership in European Community... Moscow officially registers 12,000 "individual laborers"...

Bank of China handles credit cards of Visa International, Mastercard International... Fortune: "Korea's Big Push Has Just Begun" (cites land's plan to become mini-West Germany)... All state banks in Russian federation form Bank of People's Earned Savings and Credit (lets depositors use first Soviet checks)... Widespread strikes occur in Spain to support wage increases in public sector... Vietnam unveils economic reforms (gives bonuses to encourage productivity, lets farmers and peasants earn up to 40% in profits, rids entrepreneurs of stifling regulations, removes road checkpoints for long-distance trading, uses actual market prices for economic decisions, legalizes moonlighting by doctors and teachers, lets factories form joint ventures with foreign firms)... Workers strike in Ecuador to protest austerity measures...

Japan approves $43 billion plan, includes $6.9 billion cut in income taxes, to stimulate economy slowed by strong yen... After firing 16,000 workers, South Africa crushes 6-week strike by black railway workers, 6 deaths... West Germany's IG Metall gets employers' group to reduce work week to 37 hours by 1990 to avert nationwide strike (wins 35 hours/week by 1995 in 1990 pact)... Some 5,000 workers, Bolivia, end 12-day hunger strike against Government's economic policies... Japan completes privatization of 115-year-old debt-ridden Japan National Railway system... U.S.S.R. authorizes some 10 ministries to form ventures with foreign partners... Wang Yachen is Mayor of Fuxin, China (with City of 700,000 almost broke, leases almost every City-owned grocery, department store, movie house and factory, i.e., Chen Zhiqin factory employee leases No. 2 Knitting Factory, founded 1966 to make nylon socks, with her savings of $3,000, revives business losing $118,000 in past two years)... Hungary, U.S. sign pact to establish International Management Center, opens 1989, in Budapest with assistance by American universities, convertible funds from Canadian, Reichmann family, and U.S. financiers, Armand Hammer and George Soros, and support from Hungarian Credit Bank, Hungarian Chamber of Commerce, Szenzor management consulting firm, Milan Chamber of Commerce, Sao Paolo Bank of Italy (is followed in 1989 by joint MBA program of Portland State University, OR, and Soviet Far East Khabarovsk Institute of National Economy)... U.S.S.R. legalizes underground economy, 137,000 enterprises with most in service sector from driving taxis to street artists, by July... Peruvian police strike for higher wages, demand 800% increase in danger money... Britain's new Thatcher Government, re-elected in wave of anti-union sentiment, plans to privatize 10 water authorities, prevent unions in disciplining striking members returning to work, end legal support for closed shop, require union leaders to stand for election or re-election, and withdraw supplementary benefits to anyone under 18 refusing Youth Training Scheme... As many countries no longer launder Drug Cartel's money, some $1.5 billion is returned to Colombia, makes cocaine foreign-exchange earner on par with leading coffee exports (raids across U.S., South America and England in 1989 by U.S. agents sever major billion-dollar laundering pipeline for drug money)... Brazil adopts anti-inflation plan... World Bank, Inter-American Development Bank suspend loans to Peru for overdue debt payments of $4.6 billion... Shenzhen Securities is formed to market shares of Chinese Government firms in zone... After 17 years of research Mexican ranchers, Jose Manuel Berruecos Villalobos and Angel Castrillon, develop miniature Brahman cattle, ultimate breed for Third World farmers... Nearly 50% of Japan's engineering students at top universities enter manufacturing sector, some 37% in 1988 while finance and real estate lure 26%, up from 13%...

Italian voters reject nuclear power in national referendum... OPEC limits daily production of members to 16.6 million barrels/day by end of 1987 to maintain prices at $18/barrel (avoids split between Iran, Libya and Algeria wanting lower output at higher prices and Saudi Arabia, Kuwait wanting to increase OPEC market share in world market)... Soviet Union requires local plant managers be elected by workers and state enterprises, 48,000, fund new and continuing operations from profits... Communist-led General Confederation of Peruvian Workers calls general strike to protest government's economic program as pro-business... U.S.S.R. cites failure of state-run building company in Leningrad, first such acknowledgement... With factories running at only 30% of capacity, prices in Peru rise 160%... China signs agreement with Twentieth Century Fox to televise 52 films with commercials... Gorbachev calls (June 25) for "radical reorganization of economic management" by end of 1980s (removes Gosplan, other central planning agencies from daily operations of economy to focus on long-range policies, grants more authority to state-run enterprises to manage own affairs in competing with one another for state contracts, demands new realistic pricing and new organizational structures to foster technological research)... Morocco plans to apply for membership in EC... State-owned British Coal calls for 6-day work week...

European Parliament abolishes internal trade barriers by 1992 (in 1989 orders majority of EC entertainment programming be European made, requires new small cars to use catalytic converters by 1991, bans imports of $100 million worth of U.S. hormone-treated beef, rejects trade pact with Israel for West Bank policies)... Moscow Sociological Research Institute's public opinion poll show workers support perestroika, wary of reforms... China, Australia form joint venture to develop new iron-ore mine in Western Australia... Bolivia buys back at discount almost $1 billion in debt of private creditors to commercial banks... Japan begins to deregulate oil industry, plans deregulation of financial markets... Canada probes Hyundai for dumping cars (clears South Korean firm in 1990)... Taiwan ends 38-year-old stringent foreign-exchange controls... Labor disputes appear at Daewoo Motor, Kia Industry, Lucky-Goldstar and Hyundai, land's largest conglomerate with sales of $14 billion and 150,000 employees... Hungary adopts austerity program raises prices on selected consumer goods, services... After opposition by U.S. commercial banks, Brazil scraps conversion plan to gain debt relief... Berlin demonstrates elevated light-rail train riding on cushion of air, first full-scale test of magnetic levitation technology... Gorbachev gives plant managers more say on wages, investments and products, implementation in 1988 blocked by ministry bureaucrats who load up factories with special state orders for up to 100% of production (orders ministries in 1989 to limit orders to mostly consumer and defense goods, transfers 600,000 bureaucrats to factories or institutes, disbands 60 ministries by 1989, and pushes for leasing of facilities to workers)... Argentina reschedules (August 1) foreign debt... U.S.S.R. holds first multi-candidate elections to select members of Communist Party soviets... Britain's National Union of Mine Workers supports industrial action against new British Coal code of conduct, a victory for Scargill... South African black miners, 230,000-340,000, strike (August 9) for higher wages, improved benefits (leads to arrest of 78 union officials by police, ends after three weeks with no wage gains after massive firings)... Canada's bill ends paralyzing national rail strike of Associated Railway Union, nine member unions, against CP Rail Canadian National, land's largest freight line, for wages, pensions, job security... General strike of Brazil's two largest trade union federations, 34 million members, to protest government's economic policy fizzles... IMF reports (August 14) West Germany is world's largest exporter with $243.3 billion in 1986, Japan 2nd with $210.8 billion while U.S. is No. 1 importer with $386 billion... With successful sale of state-owned Paz Oil, Israel's largest importer and marketer of crude oil and gasoline, Israel, burdened with $24 billion debt and 20% annual inflation rate , 445% in 1984, hires U.S.' First Boston, Shearson Lehman Brothers to sell some 200 state companies (starts selling 24 big state conglomerates in 1989, Jerusalem Economic Corp. goes for $53 million)...

India's National Institute of Fashion Technology opens... In biggest one-day drop in over a year, oil prices go (August 17) under $20/barrel with over-production by OPEC... With 48 hours the standard, Japan amends 40-year-old Labor Standards Law to make 40-hour work week official (tries to steer economy from exports to domestic consumption)... African nations consider freezing interest rates on combined foreign debt of $180 billion... After feuding over air rights, Canada and Britain sign (September 18) pact (gives Air Canada use of London for Europe, Asia flights and British carriers access, via Hong Kong, to U.S., Mexico, Caribbean, Hawaii, Pacific routes)... North Korea, 140 Western creditor banks reschedule land's unpaid foreign debt... Canadian Auto Workers Union ends two-day strike, gets pension indexed to inflation... After selling shares in 23 of 66 firms marked for privatization, France plans (September 24) to sell holdings in four more state-controlled companies, two insurance firms, deposit bank and industrial firm... Agrokomerc, state-owned food processing firm is one of Yugoslavia's largest, is found to have issued some $500 million in unbacked IOUs, pressured by local Communist chiefs, to 63 banks, other enterprises (causes land's vice president to resign, ruins banks and enterprises)...

With Cuba unable to meet Soviet demand for sugar, Dominican Republic, one of largest suppliers to U.S. until tightening of quota limits, signs export pact with U.S.S.R... To stem flow of capital, Peru nationalizes (September 29) 10 banks, 17 insurance firms and 6 finance companies... After one of longest strikes in history of Mexican auto industry, some 10,000 Volkswagen, Mexico's largest auto maker, workers return to work with 78% raise in pay... Japan's Private Sector Trade Union Confederation, 62 labor groups with 5.6 million workers, is land's largest union... Australia plans (October 7) airline deregulation by 1990 (uses military personnel to continue service during 1989 strike by pilots on domestic flights for higher wages)... With foreign debt of $34.5 billion, Poland unveils (October 10) program of sweeping reforms to revive stagnant economy: overhaul national system of wages and prices, reorganize government ministries, decentralize economic controls, dismiss up to 3,500 bureaucrats, give incentives for managers of state-owned enterprises, end government subsidies to unprofitable state enterprises, give more freedom to individuals to start businesses, create national bond market, overhaul banking system, form commercial banks, and lower government subsidies to families, is rejected by voters (with democratization in 1989 approves foreign joint ventures, adopts tough measures, lifts price controls, many shoppers buy goods in Berlin for resale at home, in 1990, to curb 900% hyperinflation, gets credit from IMF and World Bank, plans privatization of five state enterprises in 1990, several hundred in 1991)... Argentina takes (October 14) austerity measures, freezes wages and prices, devalues austral and raises public utility charges and import taxes, to curb inflation, reduce public debt, stimulate exports and attract private investments...

France sells state-owned financial combine, Compagnie Financiere de Suez, for $2.6 billion... Britain's Open College offers 50 job training courses on TV... Canada's jobless rate hits (October) 6-year low of 8.4%... Australia board rules employee could not be fired for refusing to join a union if union has substantial political affiliations... Britain's Labor Party offers $19 billion plan to cut unemployment: create jobs with government investment in ailing manufacturing sector, better job-training, improved social services... When New York Stock Exchange crashes (October 19) 508 points on Dow Jones Industrial Average (after topping 2900 level in 1990 breaks 3000 mark on July 13th), sharp declines in frantic selling appear in Taiwan, South Korea, Singapore, Sydney, Hong Kong, Tokyo and London exchanges (leads to smaller drops on Tokyo, London, Frankfort and Paris exchanges when NYSE drops 190.58 on Dow in 1989, October 13, when failed leveraged buyout of United Airlines shakes world markets, triggers coordinated response by industrial countries to minimize losses, stabilize markets)... Canada, U.S. plan free-trade treaty to lift all tariffs by 1999 between world's two largest trading partners with volume of $124 billion (form joint panel to resolve issues on dumping, subsidized exports)... By 1989, 16 U.S. states open trade offices in Taipei... Some 11,000 Yugoslav workers strike to protest frozen wages for public employees... Zhao Ziyang, Communist Party's new general secretary, outlines (October 25) plans to put China's economic reforms back on track while retaining orthodox Marx dogma (notes "State should regulate the market, and the market should guide enterprises," calls for establishment of civil service, specific tenures for political appointees, abolition of party cells at factories, price decontrols)... Beijing completes last section of subway line started in 1960s... Brazil ends 10-month payment moratorium on foreign debt, pays $357 million in overdue interest... Japan Air, nation's largest international carrier, is denationalized (ends 34 years of government control)... Australia voluntarily limits beef exports to U.S., its biggest market, when threatened by a quota... Thousands of Romanian workers in industrial city of Brasov, site of leading state enterprise making tractors and trucks, riot (November 15) over shortages...

Mexican peso drops (November 18) after central bank stops backing peso against U.S. dollar, goes from 1,715 (November 15) to 2,700 (November 18) in places (drops to 2,200 in 1989)... After opposing franchising of postal operations to private store owners to cut costs, Canadian Union of Postal Workers, 23,000 members, ends 17-day walk-out, 2nd in year, when indoor postal workers go to work after government passes back-to-work legislation... Canadian Communications Research Center, Ottawa, tests microwave beam to power experimental unmanned aircraft... Eight Latin American countries meet (November 26-29) to discuss region's foreign debt of almost $400 billion... Britain privatizes British Petroleum (sells 2.2 billion shares, 31.5% of equity, loses up to $1.7 billion on unsold shares)... Japanese direct investment in U.S. firms and real estate is $35.2 billion, $53.4 in 1988, while Britain goes from $79.7 billion to $109 (leads to Mitsubishi Estate's 50% buy of NYC's Rockefeller Center for $846 million, Mori Building Development's buy of Houston office center for $300 million in 1989)... Taiwan buys (November) large quantities of U.S. gold to reduce trade surplus with U.S... Following lead of Tiajin and Shanghai, Beijing begins (December 1) rationing pork... Japan blocks (December 3) GATT ruling ordering Tokyo to lift import quotas on 10 categories of agricultural products... Central banks of West Germany, six other European nations reduce (December 3) key interest rates to stem continuing fall in value of U.S. dollar...

After series of wildcat strikes by independent unions, some 12 million Italian workers, begins in public sector, stage 4-hour general walk-out, first in 3 years, to demand more money for health, education and less for defense (protest tighter economic policies)... EC transport ministers agree (December 7) to deregulate Europe's skies to create single air market by 1992... Brazil's federal court of appeals rules Autolatina, holding company of Ford and Volkswagen in Brazil with 55% of market and no profits since 1980, can raise prices above government limit... Despite production of 2 million barrels over market demand, OPEC extends (December 14) benchmark price of $18/barrel... By 1989 U.S.S.R. registers over 60,000 co-ops with 200,000 members... China's judicial system handles some 25,000 cases of profiteering, 37,000 in 1989 with over 100 embezzlers (gives bribe-takers death or life imprisonment)... Mexico, U.S. and NYC's Morgan Guaranty Trust ease (December 29) Mexican crisis by swapping up to $10 billion in discounted Mexican debts for U.S. Treasury bonds... Soviet-EC trade is some $25 billion, largest single source of Western technology for U.S.S.R. (sign sweeping 10-year accord, covers nuclear energy to banking, in 1989, first trade pact to support Soviet economic development)... U.S.S.R. merges Oil and Gas Ministries, by 1990 is split and re-merged as are other ministries (stymies foreign joint ventures, only 250 operating of some 1,400 registered in 1990)... Moscow registers 12,000 "individual laborers", over 650 "cooperatives"... Hanoi lets foreigners invest up to 99% in joint ventures (licenses 85 projects by 1990 for $832 million)... India begins program to encourage foreign investments (is listed in 1990 by U.S. as unfair for government monopoly of insurance, for restrictions on investments by outsiders)... Gold is found in Roraima state, Brazil (threatens existence of Yanomama Indians).

Business Events

Two law firms merge to form Clifford Chant, Britain's largest with over 160 partners... After buying first shares in 1970, BP gets remaining 45% of Standard Oil of Ohio, Sohio, for $7.9 billion to become world's 3rd-largest after Exxon, Royal Dutch/Shell... Japan's Otsuka Pharmaceutical Co. funds Seattle's Biomembrane Institute, a non-profit cancer research activity (gives firm access to University of Washington, echoed by 1989 with Hitachi at U.C. Irvine campus, Kobe Steel at North Carolina State and NEC at Princeton)... Hungary's five commercial banks begin competing for deposits of state-owned companies... Tokyo Stock Exchange admits 16 foreign institutions, including six from U.S., as members... Britain's Midland Bank quadruples its loan-loss reserve for Third World debt... Japanese firms in U.S. donate some $5 billion to United Way charities, $10 million in 1989... One-time peasant girl, Guan Guangmei, after leasing eight grocery stores in Northern town of Benxi to build chain, wrests control of distribution from local authorities by giving buyers good-quality, low-priced products (links salaries of 1,000 employees to sales to smash "iron rice bowl" guaranteeing wages regardless of contribution, demotes incompetent managers and pushes aside obstructionist Party shop stewards, is attacked in 1987 for exploiting workers and earning $11,892, 10 times pay of any top manager)... Jean-Marie Descarpentries, CEO of France's Carnaud in beverage cans, fruit jars and plastic containers before acquiring 28 packaging firms, mainly in Spain, Germany and Italy, to replace dozens of local suppliers to international food giants, i.e., Nestle, plans to achieve 1992 sales of $6 billion, 6-fold increase (merges with Britain's Metalbox in 1989 to form CMB Packaging in Brussels with sales of $4.4 billion, plans expansion to U.S., Asia by 2001)...

Japan's commercial trust banks stop giving loans for speculation in real estate... As co-chairman of cooperative, Andrei Fyodorov, former Metropol hotel food service director, opens Moscow's first free-enterprise restaurant, soon 61 others, with savings of $6,750, state bank loan of $75,000, interest-free for 5 years, and $15,000 credit at 3% for start-up costs (shows profit of 600,000 rubles on sales of 2 million rubles)... Combustion Engineering forms first U.S.-Soviet joint venture to build, run $2 billion petro-chemical complex in Western Siberia (leads to 365 ventures with Western nations in 1989, 1989 consortium by U.S. health care firms to form ventures with Health Ministry, 34 Soviet health care organizations)... Murdoch buys Australia's largest media enterprise (controls some 50% of land's newspapers)... Currency swindle costs Volkswagen some $259 million after schemers use forged VW documents to buy foreign currency... London newspapers, 11 major dailies, begin circulation war, biggest since 1950s... After U.S.opposition, Fujitsu drops buy of Fairchild Semiconductor, Silicon Valley pioneer... West Germany's Burda Moden, world's largest fashion monthly, is first capitalist fashion journal in Moscow... Right-wing publisher Robert Hersant, controls 30% of French press including Le Monde, wins concession to run France's private "Fifth Channel"...

Paris' Chaumet jewelers, supplier of luxury gems to elite for 200 years, is suspected of bilking creditors of nearly $300 million (sells assets for $17 million)... Spanish matador, Luis Reina, is first to wear advertising, A-K-A-I for Japanese electronics firm, on suit of lights, charges $16,000/appearance... Sony produces "digital audio tapes," threatens life of cassettes, records for recording, playing music... Unilever buys U.S.' Chesebrough-Ponds for $3.1 billion (gets tennis rackets, Vaseline, cold cream, spaghetti sauce and other consumer products, in 1989 buys Elizabeth Arden cosmetics along with Faberge for $1.5 billion and Calvin Klein Cosmetics for $306 million)... Zaitsev, Raisa Gorbachev's favorite fashion designer, makes U.S. debut, promoted by Intertorg, CA, with hopes to license Soviet cosmetics, jewelry and leather to U.S. manufacturer (licenses 30 designs/season to North Carolina apparel maker)... Kawasaki Steel plans 22% cut in work force in next two years... By 1989, speculation on Rio de Janeiro bourse rises nearly 400%

with Lebanese emigrant Naji Robert Nahas, fined $250,000 in 1986 by U.S. for manipulating silver prices, as leading bull trader, handles almost 50% of trades to 1989 until discovery of $31 million in bounced checks (forces Rio and Sao Paulo markets to close)... Honda enters U.S. luxury car market with Acura line, joined in 1989 by Toyota and Nissan... With economy in trouble from strong yen, Nippon Steel plans cutbacks, reduces blast furnaces from 12 to 8 and workforce by 29% (leads to 1989 merger of Japan Lines, Yamashita-Shinnihon Steamship to form one of world's largest shipping firms as Navix)... BAT Industries pays $5.148 billion for Farmers Group insurance, U.S.' 7th-largest in property, casualty and 3rd-largest in personal coverage, to diversify into financial services (tries to block hostile takeover of Goldsmith in 1989, abandoned in 1990 by ruling of California insurance regulators to deny his proposed sale of Farmers to French firm, restructures to spin off all units to focus on tobacco, financial services in 1991)...

Memorex acquires Telex computer terminals for $920 million... Medellin Drug Cartel uses mercenaries in all-out war with government (after bombings and killings throughout country in 1989, loses No. 2 leader, Jose Gonzalo Rodriguez Gacha, in gun battle with government forces)... Lladro, Spain's maker of fine porcelain since 1953, presents first collectible Christmas ornaments... After financing over 100 ventures since 1972, made $17 million on 4-year turnaround of Aunt Millie's sauces, James Niven, son of British actor, buys U.S.' rights for perfume and dusting powder business of J. Floris with $5 million from investors (plans 15 stores by 1994 with sales of $1 million each)...

Giuliano Tabacchi, brother take Safilo, Italy's top manufacturer in Padua, center of land's optical industry since Renaissance, of eyeglass frames from $75 plastic models to $450 designer frames, public (with sales of $133 million in 1988 and licenses from Gucci, Ferrari and Missoni, buys Optique du Monde for Polo-Ralph Lauren brand)... U.S.' National Football League sells some $45 million of licensed products in Britain, $23 million in Europe... To by-pass high costs of traditional middlemen, U.S.' Campbell Japan sells cookies via 7-Eleven Japan's chain of stores while V-8 juice uses Suntory's network... Michelin, some 110,000 employees worldwide, posts sales of some $8.8 billion (after manufacturing in U.S. in mid-1970s, acquires UniRoyal Goodrich Tire, merged 1986-88 as U.S.' 2nd-largest and world's 7th, for $1.5 billion in 1989 to top Goodyear as world's No. 1)... Swedish arms-dealer, Bofors, bribes Indian politicians, government officials to win $4.4 billion contract, discovery in 1989 topples government... Computer-maker Acer blazes trail for Taiwanese capital in Silicon Valley with buy of Counterpoint Computers, Island's biggest U.S. acquisition in 1989 with Continental Engineering buy of American Bridge for some $100 million (leads to business-government consortium with $170 million rescue of Wyse Technology, one of Valley's best-known makers of terminals, personal computers, in 1989 while Taiwan amasses capital, some $75 billion in foreign exchange as largest pool after Japan, to buy Girl Scout cookie maker, California real estate, Texas oil firms and savings and loans, and build huge petrochemical facilities in 1990)...

Sterling Airways sells $52.5 million of in-flight duty-free merchandise, highest of any airline... Japan's Aoki Group, U.S.' Robert N. Bass Group pay $1.4 billion for United Airline's Westin Hotel chain while All Nippon Airways buys San Francisco's Meridien Hotel for $100 million to compete with Japan Air managing 23 Nikko International Hotels... Hong Kong's Onwel Mfg. opens New York factory to avoid U.S. quota system while two other Hong Kong contractors for Liz Claiborne apparel open shops in NYC's Chinatown... Suchard, Swiss maker of Tobler chocolate, pays $73 million for Chicago's E.J. Brach candy business, follows with buy of Belgium's leading Cote D'Or to become world's third largest in coffee and confections (is bought in turn by Philip Morris in 1990 for $3.8 billion)... After Hawaiian acquisitions, Japanese investors buy La Costa Hotel and Spa in Carlsbad, CA, for $250 million and venerable Riviera Country Club, Los Angeles, for $108 million... SAS signs pact with Thai Airways for flights between Bangkok, Stockholm and Copenhagen (in 1989 forms alliances with All Nippon, Lan-Chile and Canadian Airlines International)... With loan of $27 million from Sotheby's, Alan Bond buys Van Gogh's "Irises" for record $53.9 million, topped by Ryoei Saito's buy of Van Gogh's "Portrait du Dr. Gachet" for $82.5 million in 1990 (with debt nearing $6 billion in 1990 gets Sotheby's to roll over loan)... Japan's Asahi Breweries introduces Super Dry beer, 20% of all beer consumed in 1989 (tops Sapporo Breweries as No. 2 in 1989 with 24.5%, follows Kirin Brewery, under 50%, with 15 kinds of beers for different market segments)... K.T. Wang, dean of Hong Kong ivory trade, ships 2,052 tusks worth $3.5 million to Japan, some 30,000 Japanese in market as traders, carvers, merchants... France's 2nd-biggest food-store chain, $5 billion/year Cora-Revillon Group, acquires rights to Karl Lagerfeld's designs... After buying 52% of Pierre Balmain fashion house and perfumes in 1986, Montreal real estate developer, Eric Fayer, tops Bernard Arnault to buy Ted Lapidus sporty clothes as high fashion becomes big business... Arabian-American Oil, Exxon, Mobil, Chevron and Texaco as Aramco, signs contract with Saudi Arabia to buy oil at $18/barrel, Saudi Arabia abandons maintaining $18 in 1989...

After draining over $100 million from U.S. operations for overseas deals, Khashoggi's U.S. flagship, Triad America, files for bankruptcy (is investigated in 1988 by France, Switzerland and U.S. for tax fraud, is extradited from Switzerland and jailed in NYC in 1989 for role in hiding assets of Philippine President Marcos, released 1990)... Kuwait buys shares in BP (after spending $1.9 billion by 1989 owns 21.6%, largest shareholder, as country builds $85 billion worldwide investment portfolio)... Guinness buys U.S.' Schenley Industries for $480 million... Robert Maxwell folds 5-month-old London Daily News, first to fail in British publishing revolution with direct-input technology... Geoffrey Collier, trader for London's Morgan Grenfell, pleads guilty to insider trading, first person prosecuted for 1985 company securities act... After selling television and major appliance firms to focus on lighting, records and video rentals, Britain's Thorn EMI buys U.S.' Rent-A-Center chain for $593.9 million... Murdoch, holds some 40% of Britain's newspaper market with Times of London, Sunday Times, Sun, and Sunday News of the World, buys Today paper for $60 million... Robert Holmes a Court is Australia's "first" billionaire, financial difficulties in 1988-89 (dies 1990)... Moet-Hennessy merges with Louis Vuitton, upscale maker of luggage and handbags, to create world's largest purveyor of luxury goods with 1988 sales of some $2.6 billion (merges most of distribution networks with Guinness in 1987, in 1988 sells control to Arnault, in charge, with Guinness, to block takeovers, acquires, 1988-89, 24.1% of Guinness while it gets 24.1% of LVMH)...Philips makes Jan D. Timmer head of core division, consumer electronics (by 1990 transforms, shuts plants and cuts 7,000 jobs, unit as world's No. 2 after Matsushita, is CEO in 1990 to restructure faltering $31 billion firm)... Hongkong & Shanghai bank buys 14.9% of London's Midland (proposes friendly merger in 1990 to create $237 billion global bank as insurance for China's 1997 takeover of Colony)...

Nissei Build Kogyo Co. enters market for high-rise car parks, makes 120 prefabricated, automated towers in 1989 for sales of $24 million... BUS Berzelivs Environmental Services, West Germany, devises new technology to process hazardous wastes cheaper (floats stock in 1990 to raise $130 million, stock jumps from $196 to $310 on first day, for expansion in rest of Europe)... U.S.' Marriott, Poland plan land's first Western-hotel (as first U.S. joint venture in land opens in Warsaw in 1990, trains Polish staff for hospitality)... Japanese carmakers snare 11.3% of European market... Japan's Canon introduces Color Laser Copier, over 50% of market by 1989 as Xerox loses lead and 3M, invented color copiers in 1967, leaves market... Balmy winters by 1990 put Europe's $3 billion ski industry in trouble, many of 90,000 Americans skiing in Europe/year ski snowy U.S. slopes... Philosopher Eite Veening opens business, Groningen, to treat anxieties of present with wisdom of ages... Japanese securities firms, control most of trading, keep Tokyo stock market losses on October Black Monday under 15% while Dow index drops 22.6% (fail to stem 1990's slide, 22% from all-time high December 29, 1989, from weak yen, outflow of cash to overseas investments, and political instability)... One-time waiter Giancarlo Parretti, Italian financier (buys three Sicilian hotels in 1970s, acquires sports club and Italian papers in 1980s, while avoiding jail, restructures European banks, insurance firms and joins Sasea, Swiss investment firm, in ventures from travel to real estate), pays $200 million for Cannon Group, faltering Hollywood ministudio, library and theaters, and adds French-held Pathe Cinema, 1,000 theaters, for $160 million later (with aid from Time Warner buys money-losing MGM/UA of Kirk Kerkorian for $1.3 billion in 1990)... Nippon Steel gets exclusive license from U.S. Space Camp Foundation to build facility in Japan (opens Space World theme park in 1990)... Printemps, tony

Paris department store, opens 1st U.S. branch in Denver (closes with area's recession)... After persuading, first to do so, U.S.S.R. to "lease" a factory to its workers, workers put up cash, government lends operating capital, to sell surplus bricks and boards to those building private houses and dachas (as market rises 50% by 1991, goes from needing a state subsidy to making a small profit)... De Beneditti uses Cerus, French holding firm, to take over Societe Generale de Belgique, sleeping holding company controlling over 30% of Belgium's $117 billion GDP with interests in 1,261 firms, some 100,000 employees, from banking, land's largest with assets of $66 billion, trading to mining, in an attempt to build super holding enterprise (after frenzied stock battle is forced to accept minority role with Compagnie Financiere de Suez, France's 2nd-largest merchant bank, the winner with 52% in 1988)... ASEA, Sweden's big electrical group with 23% owned by Wallenbergs, gets Brown Boveri & Co., barely profitable Swiss maker of transformers and generators with assets in West Germany (adds 60 firms, including turbine unit of AEG, and nuclear reactor joint venture with Siemens in 1988, joint venture with Italy's Finmeccanica, Westinghouse's power units, and 40% of Britain's leading railcar maker in 1989, U.S.' Combustion Engineering, majority share of Polish turbine maker, and Spanish electrical group in 1990, worth $3.6 billion to build $25 billion giant in 1990 to take on GE, Siemens and Hitachi, links with East German electrical equipment supplier in 1990)...

Wealthy Johannesburg pharmaceuticals entrepreneur, Solomon Krok, buys marketing rights to hair-removal appliance of Israeli kibbutz, Mepro (turns over rights to three daughters who launch Epilady in NYC, after building mini-empire with sales of $200 million, enter bankruptcy in 1990)... Delamare art gallery opens, Paris, to sell genuine copies of masterworks... Grand Met buys Heublein from RJR Nabisco for $1.2 billion, world's No. 1 seller of alcoholic beverages (fails to buy Martell Cognac in 1988 and bids $475 million for Irish Distillers, Ireland's only Whisky maker, acquires, U.K.'s largest takeover, Pillsbury, Burger King with 5,500 units, Haagen-Dazs ice cream and Green Giant foods, for $5.7 billion in hostile takeover, drops several brands for lack of international appeal, in 1989 buys 1970-year old Christian Brothers winery for some $150 million, in 1990 introduces new Alpo cat food to get 9% of market, sells U.K. brewing business to Foster's and forms venture with to own the pubs, will manage some)... Holland's Vendex International buys 50% of B. Dalton bookstores and 32% of Barnes & Noble College Book Stores (with financial problem in 1988 and Dreesmann's brain hemorrhage hires Arie Van der Zwan as CEO, is sacked after laying off 18% of staff, with return of Dreesmann, 1990, revamps by shedding money losers to focus on department stores)... Credit Lyonnaise forms investment arm (to raise capital in 1990 takes control of state-owned Thomson-CSF's finance operations and gives it a stake in the bank)... Nestle buys 52% of Vittel mineral water business (adds Buitoni, pasta and chocolate, in 1988 and Baby Ruth and Butterfinger from RJR Nabisco in 1990, forms, 1991, venture with Coca-Cola to market beverage concentrates via its 120-country distribution network).

1988

General Events

IMF posts replacement surplus for 1987... China re-imposes (January 19) price controls on most basic raw materials, services to restrain "widely" rising prices causing "market chaos"... New Soviet law, 11 decrees go into effect (force state-run factories and economic enterprises to pay own way by 1991, allow layoffs, concerns in debt to be liquidated, and firms to retain some profits, base wages on job performance or enterprise profitability)... Britain's savings rate falls to 29-year low of 5% in last quarter of 1987... Medellin Cartel slays (January 25) Colombia's Attorney General to fight extradition to U.S (kills presidential candidate in 1989)... Australia denounces Japan's beef quotas... Colombia orders arrest of Jorge Luis Ochoa Vasquez, four others of Medellin Cartel for extradition to U.S. for drug trafficking... Turkey shows 1987 inflation rate of 55.1%, highest in seven years... As one of few Latin American countries not to have rescheduled foreign debt, Colombia, over 100 of bank creditors sign $1 billion, 10-year loan to re-finance debt... Nigeria's commercial creditors approve rescheduling debt... Nurses, miners and seamen strike in Britain... For first time in five years, Japan's overall trade surplus drops in 1987 to $79.83

billion, down 3.5% from record high of $82.74 billion in 1986... Soviet press criticizes Gosplan, central agency for translating Communist Party economic policies into specific goals, as being too powerful over state enterprises... Soviet Union creates network of unemployment exchanges, system of unemployment benefits... Guangdong Province near Hong Kong is China's No. 1 exporting region, ships $5.5 billion in goods in 1987 (attracts $5.3 billion in foreign investment)...

After avoiding free-market medicine of IMF in early 1980s to devalue currency and reduce subsidies on staple foods, Zambia law allows seizure, no recourse to trial, of businesses in thriving black market (causes takeovers of many Asian shops, with $1.2 billion debt to World Bank and IMF adopts austerity measures in 1989, starts urban migration to villages with high prices)... Japan accepts (February 2) GATT ruling to remove import quotas on 10 categories of agricultural goods... Some 32,500 British workers of Ford close, first strike in decade, 22 plants to oppose extensive work-rule changes and productivity goals, intensified by Ford's "just-in-time" inventory system to compete with low-cost Japanese rivals (after 11 days, agree to consider Japanese-style assembly work teams for wage increases)... World Bank increases (February 22) capital to provide long-term development for Third World... Britain plans (February 25) to privatize state-owned electricity monopoly for $47 billion... Calgary Winter Olympics plans profit of $25.4 million on revenues of $279 million from TV rights, $71 million from sponsors and license fees, $32 million from ticket sales and $41 million from government grants... Romania drops (February 26) most-favored-nation trade status with U.S., granted 1975...

Some 60% of Soviet state enterprises go on self-financing basis, forced to focus on profits instead of subsidies... China's national tourist agency reports 26.9 million foreigners visit in 1987, up 17.9% from 1986... EC increases special funds for Spain, Portugal, Greece to even market advantages with industrialized North... Communist Party General Secretary, Zhao Ziyang, encourages economic development of coastal areas with 20% of population (rejects Mao's policy to develop interior areas)... With rising prices Poland devalues zloty 16%... Canada's Alberta signs contract with United Nurses of Alberta, ends 19-day illegal strike closing 104 hospitals in province... Gorbachev proposes (March 6) putting private business cooperatives on equal footing with state enterprises and letting private co-ops engage in foreign trade, hire workers laid off by state industries (suggests, March 8, progressive income tax on private ventures to penalize profiteers)... China gives (March 12) local jurisdictions, trading companies more control over imports, exports to spur foreign trade... Britain plans (March 15) sweeping tax reform with reductions in personal income taxes... Brazil holds (March 29) first debt conversion auction, creditors swap $186 million in debt for $150 million in cruzados for reinvestment in Brazil... After years of talks Japan opens (March 29) bidding on public works projects to U.S. contractors, stymied by traditional bid-rigging and collusion of Japanese contractors (ends quotas on beef, citrus by 1992)... China's National Automotive Industry Corp. buys $16 million assembly line from GM to make 150,000 small-truck engines/year...

Poland closes 4-year-old Warsaw business, core in network of firms in Europe and Middle East providing funds for terrorism, of Palestinian Abu Nidal, rumored under house arrest by Libya in 1989... With hyperinflation, Nicaragua revalues currency... Canada reports highest number of bankruptcies since 1984... Taiwan lowers tariffs on 3,500 items to open its markets, reduce nation's trade surplus... Muscovites crowd roving AstroPizza truck to buy first U.S. pizza in U.S.S.R.... Carlos Salinas de Gortari is Mexico's new President (takes office in 1989, to revive failing economy clamps down on union bosses, businessmen and drug dealers, drops trade and investment barriers, privatizes some 800 enterprises, including flagship carrier Aviacion Mexicana, truck maker, two copper mines and many sugar mills, by 1990, proclaims end of 10-year economic recession in November, 1989, spurs Cemex to spend over $800 million to buy cement firms in Mexico, Texas and California, Cementos Mexicanos, world's 4th-largest cement maker, to buy biggest rival for 66% of domestic market in 1989, and Vitro, Mexico's largest glass firm, to bid $920 million for U.S.' No. 2 glassmaker, Anchor Glass Container, lets foreigners invest up to $100 million in most areas without approval and own up to 100% of ventures, plans free-trade pact with U.S. in 1990)... Bank of England drops (April 8) commercial bank lending rate to 8%, lowest in

10 years... Seven leading industrial nations agree (April 13) to support the dollar... Canada's chartered banks up (April 21) prime interest rate to 10.25%, two-year high... Brazil reschedules foreign debt with major bank creditors... Soviet press notes strikes by workers in Nagorno-Karabakh Autonomous Region... IMF, World Bank take steps to ease burden of debtor nations... For first time in 25 years, Japan taxes interest on personal savings, $2.36 trillion in 1987... Mexico allows State airline, Aeromexico with 43 planes and 12,500 employees, to enter bankruptcy (sells business for $350 million)...

After ouster of 32-year Hungarian Communist Party head Janos Kadar, successor Karoly Grosz seeks reforms to revive sagging economy, slumping exports, stagnant manufacturing and high government spending pushing hard currency debt to $16 billion, highest/capita in East Bloc (spurs joint ventures with firms, i.e., Levi Strauss & Co. invests $1 million in project to produce denim jeans and jackets, $115 million glass factory by Guardian Industries, Ernst & Whinney joins Budapest's Bonitas in 1989 to provide accounting and business consulting and GM forms $150 million joint venture with state-owned truck-maker Raba, gets EC to cut quotas on Hungarian exports in 1989, leads to ad offices of Ogilvy & Mather Worldwide, venture with Mahir, Hungary's oldest, and Young & Rubicam, both open offices in Moscow, in 1989, and Suzuki planning $140 million plant in 1990 to make 15,000 small cars/year in 1992 for Europe, leads to political reforms and democratic elections, Communist Party, renamed Socialist, gets 11% of vote, in 1990, 1990 auction of 30% Ibusz travel agency, public outcry on 1990 sale of 50% of HungriHotels, 50 places, for $90 million to Swedish, Dutch investors as undervalued - rescinded, and plan for sale of 40,000 retail stores in 1990)... Some 70% of Chile's railway workers strike to protest government plans to privatize state-owned railroad... Britain sells troubled Rover Group car business to British Aerospace for $279 million... GATT rules Japan violated microchip accord... Swiss Banking Commission reprimands Bank Lev for role in Guinness scandal... With food prices up 40%, rent up 50%, gasoline up 60%, electricity up 100% and coal up 200% since February, new wave of strikes hit (May) Poland, worst unrest since 1981-82... For first time in over 50 years, U.S.S.R. allows (May) Western concerns to own up to 49% of a Soviet enterprise, over 35 ventures by June...

New Zealand plans (May 3) to deregulate oil (sells 70% of Petroleum Corp. of New Zealand to Fletcher Challenge, forestry and resources firm, for $517.7 million), broadcasting industries... With approval of IMF, Yugoslavia approves (May 15) austerity measures (with 2,000% inflation rate, unemployment rate of 15%, and foreign debt over $17 billion in 1989, seeks recovery by making economy more efficient, devaluating dinar, freezing wages and prices of raw materials and energy, and becoming more market oriented, backs democracy in 1989 before break-up of country in 1991-92)... Brazil starts (May 19) new industrial policy to ease restrictions on imports, exports... EC, U.S. compromise (May 19) to reduce farm subsidies... Mexico's 1987 economic solidarity pact by government, labor and business cuts May inflation rate to 1.9%, drops annual rate of 430% in January to 30%...

West Germany sells remaining 16% of Volkswagen, Europe's largest car maker, for $672 million... For first time, China takes bids of foreigners for long-term leases of land in Shanghai... Australia's High Court gives federal, state governments more power to regulate interstate trade... Marxist-led construction workers, auto mechanics hold hunger strike in Nicaragua to protest government's wage scales... Canada allows Japan's largest security firms, Nomura, Nikko, and Daiwa, to trade in country... British court rules members of International Tin Council are not liable to pay organization's debts... Colombian President Barco launches national crusade to eradicate drug trade supplying 80% of U.S. cocaine market (forces "The Extraditables" of Medellin and Cali cartels, handle 60-70% of trade, to declare "total and absolute war" in 1989 manifesto against all those in opposition)... When it lacks funds to join ventures, China grants foreigners 100% control on priority projects... Some two million black South Africans stage (June 6-8) massive strike to protest proposed labor law to ban union activity... Britain plans (June 7) privatization of Girobank, Post Office's banking subsidiary... EC ministers agree (June 13) to remove all restrictions on capital by 1992... Nicaragua lifts (June 14) wage, price controls and curbs on credit, imports to overcome annual inflation rate of 36,000%... West Germany's Bundesbank lifts (June 21) key refinancing rate to dampen rising U.S. dollar, check money supply growth and curb inflation... Hong Kong reports on role of its securities market in worldwide market crash in October, 1987 (pans market as private club, lax government regulations, and poor management, recommends new regulatory agency, new rules for members, and appointment of chief executive)... Australia, New Zealand agree (June 21) to drop all mutual tariffs (join with 10 leading Asian, North American nations in 1989 to form Asia Pacific Economic Cooperation to coordinate trade policy, boost Pacific-rim business)... Britain, West Germany, Italy and Spain launch $40 billion program to build new generation of fighter aircraft... Leftist rebels, Colombia, abduct 15 diplomats, journalists to protest foreign exploitation of oil resources... EC drops IBM anti-trust action... Mohawk Indians are accused of violating Canada's Customs and Excise Act by bringing U.S. cigarettes into land duty-free and selling them tax-free to non-Indians at reservation stores... Greek air traffic controllers walkout (July 12-13) to protest working conditions, disrupts European air travel... China's inflation hits (July 19) 40-year high with 19% rise in June retail prices... South Korea lifts (July 26) 3-year ban on beef imports...

Major industrial democracies in Toronto agree on measures to keep world economy growing (see power shift from U.S. to Japan, world's 2nd-largest economy, and European Community)... EC begins study to unify currencies of member nations... TUC, Britain's umbrella union confederation, gives dissident Electrical, Electronic, Telecommunications and Plumbing Union two weeks to comply with direction or face suspension over issues of single-union and no-strike contracts... Japan lowers restrictions on imports of Australian, U.S. beef... After dropping passenger service in 1969, Canada ends rail service in Newfoundland, only province without railway system... China forms Air China, replaces Civil Aviation Administration, to handle all international flights, 44 domestic routes... Canada, Newfoundland sign multi-billion-dollar agreement with energy consortium of five petroleum concerns to develop Hibernia offshore oil field by 1995... Bundesbank allows central bankers from 12 leading industrial nations to set minimum international requirements for banks... EC, U.S., Japan and Canada agree to strengthen copyright codes... China adopts (fall) austerity program to curb annual inflation rate of 30%... Poland struggles (August 15-26) with labor unrest... EC imposes (August 31) tough duties on VCRs from South Korea, Japan for dumping products, France blocked imports with bureaucratic red tape... Melbourne bus driver, a non-smoker, wins $57,000 in out-of-court settlement as compensation for lung cancer caused by smoking passengers...

Industrial Bank of Japan pans U.S. firms for loss of international competitiveness by ignoring long-term goals for short-term results, by focusing on domestic markets instead of foreign... European Court of Justice rules Italy must open its borders to pasta imports not meeting stringent standards for domestic makers... In rare strike, Hungarian miners protest new income-tax that will eliminate bonuses... Except for few basic commodities, China approves wage and price reforms (removes or liberalizes price controls for others, makes state enterprises responsible for profits, losses)... France, Britain balk at leveling of value-added tax rates among EC members... With strike of 14 days, their first national walkout in 17 years, British postal workers protest recruitment bonuses for new workers in London... UN Conference on Trade and Development urges (September 2) commercial banks to write off 30% of debt owed them by world's 15 most heavily indebted nations... With debt of $130 million, Rio de Janeiro declares (September 15) bankruptcy... French radio, television workers strike (September 21) to protest hiring of new anchorwoman by state-owned network with celebrity salary of $200,000/year, higher than those of senior journalists... Japan unveils (September 27) debt relief plan for Third World... China postpones (September 30) economic reforms, retains price controls to fight inflation... Argentina sells 40% of State's Aerolineas Argentinas to SAS for $240 million and 9% to employees... Venezuela's state-owned Carbozulia forms $586 million coal mine venture with two international firms... Brazil's new constitution nationalizes oil-and-mineral-mining rights, bars annual interest rates over 12%, cuts work week from 48 to 44 hours, and grants maturity and paternity leaves to working parents... Britain plans to privatize British Rail, British Coal... Brazil unveils environmental plan for Amazon Basin... Mexico cancels $910 million sale of state-owned copper concern (in 1990 plans sale of Conasupo, huge state commodities firm with 3,000 supermarkets, 9 food-processing plants and other assets)... Australian miners accept changes in work rules to improve productivity (agree to extend work week to six days, work longer hours, eliminate shut-downs during Christmas vacation and public holidays)... After paralyzing feeble economy, Burmese workers end two-month series of strikes for democratic reforms... China's constitution legalizes the private sector... French government workers strike (October 20) to protest pay policies of Socialist Government... Britain blocks (October 25) merger of Minoro S.A., Luxembourg-base enterprise owned by Anglo-American and De Beers of South Africa, with Consolidated Gold Fields, founded 1887 by Cecil Rhodes to become largest gold-mining firm outside South Africa, to prevent monopolistic control of world markets in diamonds, gold, titanium and other critical minerals for defense, aerospace industries...

Soviet Union discloses (October 27) budget deficit of $58 billion, 4% of GDP, for 1988... Burma's Trade Minister repeals (October 31) restrictions on foreign trade, investments... Peru's annual inflation rate tops (October) 1,000%... French state-owned metals conglomerate Pechiney buys U.S.' Triangle Industries, parent firm of American National Can and U.S.' largest with nearly 30% of market, for $1.26 billion (transforms world's 3rd-largest aluminum group into world's leading packaging concern ahead of France's CMB Packaging, formed by French and British interests in 1988, and Japan's Toyo Seikan Kasha)... Japan imports $2.8 billion in aerospace goods, exports $400 million... Britain loses 3.7 million work days from strikes, 29.5 million in 1979... U.S. adopts Trade Act, Super 301 Clause penalizes international trade violations (hits Japan in 1989, barriers to imports of U.S. supercomputers, satellites and lumber, India and Brazil, drops sanctions against Brazil, Japan in 1990)... Brazil signs "social pact" with unions, business to curb annual inflation rate of 900%, 27.25% in October... Soviet Union, first public admission, reveals (November 1) inflation rate of 0.9%-1.5%... Britain plans (November 7) to deregulate television, radio broadcasting... Some 18,000 Brazilian workers of state-controlled National Steel, land's largest, strike (November 7-23) to demand constitutionally mandated reduction in work hours and pay increases to offset inflation, quelled by army with three killed... Britain bares (November 25) record high payment deficit of $4.4 billion for October...

West Germany's health care reform bill puts (November 25) more costs on individuals... Britain plans to sell off water operations for $6 billion... OPEC, facing chronic over-production and depressed prices, agrees (November 28) on new production targets to push price of oil above $18/barrel by mid-1989 (tries for $21 in 1990 after pressure by Iraq on Kuwait, derailed by Iraq's invasion of Kuwait)... Workers' Party wins tight mayoral race in Sao Paulo, Brazil's financial hub... Britain sells British Steel to public for $4.6 billion... EC rate of unemployment shows largest year-to-year decline in September since 1983, 10.2% with 15.6 million idle... Bank of England successfully auctions first treasury bills denominated in European Currency Units... Britain closes 600-year-old Sunderland shipyard in Wearside area... Peru plans new austerity plan to devalue currency, eliminate government subsidies for food, and increase wages (spurs protest strikes)... At least 15 strikes occur during year in U.S.S.R., Leningrad police in 1989 to demand better working conditions... China posts (December) foreign trade of $82.6 billion... EC meets (December 2-3) to review progress on goal of open market for 1992... Mexico announces (December) new package of wage, price controls to keep inflation, 150% in 1986, 160% in 1987 and 52% in 1988, below 20%, drops to 17% by 1990 (reaches tentative agreement in 1989 with IMF to borrow $3.6 billion to lower debt payments of $14 billion, some 70% of land's exports)... U.S.S.R. plans (December 11) to devalue ruble 50% for domestic transactions on January 1 (requires public to turn in large ruble notes in 1991 to cut inflation, plans money exchanges in 1991 for trading in foreign currencies)... China shows (December) some 14.5 million small businesses, run by individuals or families in cities and countryside, and 18.8 million rural collectives, most owned by a village, township or county (with national crackdown on non-state enterprises in 1989, closes 2.2 million private concerns and one million rural industrial collectives, forces several hundred thousand rural collectives to halt production or shift to work for state needs, and cancels 10,000 rural development projects of $2.16 billion)... Some 8 million Spanish workers in two major union groups, over 50% of work force, stage (December 14) widest general strike since 1934 (protest Socialist

Government's allowing industry to hire young people under minimum wage, demand greater share in growing economy)... Some 250 foreign-owned plants of Japan, Korea, Europe and U.S. open during year in maquiladora industrial zone, six Mexican states with 16% of population generate 22% of GNP along U.S. border... EC approves (December 21) over $100 billion in subsidies by members to industry, agriculture, energy and transport... Interior China, 5.1% annual rate of industrial growth, accounts for 56% of total industrial output while Coastal China shows growth of 24% for 44% output...

Argentina's inflation rate hits (December) 388%, 3,500% in 1989 with some 10 million of total population of 32 million below poverty line of $100/month and 15 million more just above, while Brazil's rate is 934%, 1,600% in 1989... Israel halts (December 30) foreign currency trading to avoid panic from fears of possible austerity program... After political battle, Canada approves (December 30) free trade bill with U.S... EC bans U.S. meat imports of hormone-fed cattle... In late 1988 20% of China's factories close with austerity program, 5% unemployment highest since 1949 (sees high urban unemployment, official inflation rate near 20% in 1990)... Some 8.7 million workers belong to Britain's Trade Union Congress, 12.2 million in 1968... Business Week: "Laying the Foundation for A Great Wall of Europe" (notes EC planning "transitional" protection for such industries as automobiles, textiles, and footwear to prepare for one 1992 market)... To lure international travelers away from Amsterdam's Schipol's duty-free grand shopping area, Denmark spends $7 million to upgrade shopping arcade at Copenhagen's airport... Japanese women compose over 40% of labor force... Italian Space Agency forms...

Facing cutbacks in government funding, Britain's great national museums use admission fees, corporate sponsorships and advertising in new leisure industry... South Korea sees $11.6 million trade surplus (after $520 million deficit by July, 1989, declares economic crisis due to massive wage hikes, high interest rates and costly strikes)... West Germany's Federal Cartel Office cites 1,159 acquisitions of small, medium-sized concerns, up 30% over 1987, while some 1,200 mergers and acquisitions hit major firms throughout Europe... Productions spend nearly $300 million making 77 feature films, TV movies, and TV programs in Toronto, 3rd-largest film production center in North America after Los Angeles, NYC... Tourists to Kenya spend some $390 million, faces decline as poachers in illegal trade of ivory, rhinoceros horns, and pelts threaten existence of animals (with rampant corruption and excess of bureaucracy, sees foreign disinvestment in 1990)... After six years of negotiation, 20 nations agree to prohibit mining, drilling projects on Antarctica unless approved by all... Taiwan gains 11.4% share of world market in PCs, doubled in over 4 years...

East Germany spends over $5 billion, some 35% of investment budget, to bring technology up to Western standards (with 1990 unification uses West Germany's $3.5 billion to spawn small, medium-size businesses, struggles to restructure 220 unwieldy state enterprises controlling 85% of economy)... Ireland shows inflation rate of 2.1%, UK 5.75%, Portugal 9%, Spain 4.8%, Denmark 4.6%, Germany 1.2%, and Italy with 4.9%... Japan registers 40 million cars and 64 million bicycles, more than doubled since 1970 (leads to bicycle parking lots for up to 5,000 each, bicycle garages and rent-a-cycles)... EC raises $4.3 billion to finance expansions, LBOs, and turnabouts of small firms... Hungary's Innofinance, Middle Europe's first venture-capital enterprise, is privatized (after spending some $7.8 million in 10 years holds stakes in 40 firms in 1990)... Soviet Academy of Sciences, 162,000 scientists, forms 33 ventures with U.S. firms by 1990 (organizes 23 technical complexes to link research institutes, contracts with U.S. space services firm for space research in 1989, lets institutes start factories in 1990)... Moscow's Higher Commercial Management School begins teaching courses in free-market management... State-controlled Hungarian Credit Bank exchanges its $83 million debt of Tungsram, state-owned inefficient light bulb maker, for 91% of stock (sells 49% to consortium of Austrian banks, leads to GE buying 51% plus option for 20%, struggles in 1990 to raise 7% European market share, dominated by Siemens, 28%, and Philips, 39%)... MITI funds Laboratory for International Fuzzy Engineering Research with $70 million for five years, becomes world leader in smarter machines by 1991... MITI funds projects in superconductors, $33 million by 1997, and fine chemicals from marine organisms, $8 million by 1996 (starts projects in 1989: super/hypersonic propulsion, $10 million by 1996, high-performance materials for environment, $6 million by 1996, nonlinear photonics, $3 million by 1998)... Vietnam's foreign investment code allows wholly owned foreign ventures, 105 investment projects, Britain, France, Belgium, Holland, Australia, India, Hong Kong, Taiwan and Thailand, worth some $800 million by 1990... Thailand revokes all logging, blamed for over $120 million flood disaster (gets some 40 logging concessions from Burma, attacked in 1990 for depleting teak trees to get foreign exchange)... Private investment in Mexico rises 10.1%, federal spending down 2.7%... Aided by University of Tennessee Budapest's Karl Marx University plans MBA program... SAS inks marketing pact with Continental, ownership goes from 10% to 16.8% in 1990 (takes stake in Texas Air for link with Continental at Newark, buys 24.9% of British Holdings for link at London'a Heathrow Airport, leases Continental's, in financial woes, airport space for $50 million in 1989, helps buyout of Continental's Frank Lorenzo for $30 million in 1990, Continental declares bankruptcy in 1990).

Business Events

Ford scraps plant for Dundee, Scotland, after 11 unions at other 21 plants oppose one overall union for Dundee... Bolivia nabs drug baron Roberto Gomez, with five ranches is world's biggest cocaine producer (is extradited to U.S. for 15-year sentence)... BP wins hostile takeover of Britoil, independent oil producer in Glasgow, for $4.42 billion, sells most of mineral business to RTZ (in 1989 sells $1.3 billion of oil properties to Oryx while U.K. forces Kuwait to reduce its 21.6% in BP to 9.9%, buys Metromed, Spain's 3rd largest refiner, in 1991)... After losing some $1 billion in October 1987 global stock market crash, selling assets for $140 million, and losing $260 million on sale of 28% in Broken Hill, Holmes a Court needs to sell most of core Bell Group, once controlled assets of $4.55 billion, for $252 million to Perth rival Alan Bond when three key firms post heavy losses... Japanese sales of imported cars, BMW, Volkswagen and Mercedes-Benz with 74% of 1986 market of 73,924 cars, rises 41.1% in fiscal 1987... Pirelli, Italy's tiremaker, buys U.S.' Armstrong Rubber for $190 million... London's International Cocoa Cartel fails to stop slide in worldwide prices... Total Compagnie Francaise des Petroles buys Houston-based CDX Oil & Gas for $612 million... AEG buys Gould's U.S. industrial automation unit for $290 million... Royal Bank of Scotland Group buys U.S.' Citizens Financial Group for $440 million... Saatchi & Saatchi buys share of Seoul-based ad agency... International Coffee Organization clears Mexico of violating cartel's rules... Lazard Partners, jointly owned by Lazard Bros. of London and Lazard Freres of NYC and Paris, extends partnership for 21 years...

U.S.' IBM, Digital Equip., Hewlett-Packard, and Apollo Computer join Siemens, Nixdorf Computer and Groupe Bull to challenge alliance of AT&T, Sun Microsystems... For first time ever, European venture capital funds raise more money for new starts than does U.S. in 1987, Britain largest venture capital market in Europe with France, Belgium and Holland following... After media rival, Robert Maxwell, unveils plans to expand into satellite television broadcasting, Murdoch plans satellite Sky Television with four TV channels to cover Britain and Europe in 1989 (loses $3 million/week, 1.1 million viewers, in 1990 while British Satellite Broadcasting, backed by British media groups, Granada and Chargeurs, uses $1.5 billion to begin five-channel service in 1990, both merge to form British Sky Broadcasting)... After bid of Jacobs Suchard, Swiss worldwide confectionery and coffee maker, Rowntree takes Nestle's $4.5 billion offer (challenges U.S.' Mars in world market)... South Korea's four leading automakers, Hyundai, Daewoo, Kia and Ssangyong, plan to double production to 3.4 million cars/year by 1993... Colombia drug cartels, Medellin's headed by Pablo Escobar Gaviria and Cali's by Gilberto Rodriguez Orejuela, wage violent battle for NYC market (distribute cocaine via wholesale network of some 200-300 cells in U.S., most on U.S. coastline and Mexican border, and Canada, New Brunswick new route in 1989, copies Prohibition bootleggers, as U.S. improves interdiction methods)... News Corp., 200-odd holdings, buys U.S.' Triangle Publications, TV Guide, Seventeen and Daily Racing Form, for $2.8 billion, largest deal in publishing industry to become one of world's largest media firms with over 150 properties on four continents (sees financial difficulties in 1989 to service debt of almost $9 billion, buys, 1989, Scott, Foreman textbook publisher and, 1990, two Hungarian dailies and 50%

of Germany's Borda printing, sells, 1990, 49% of Hong Kong's <u>South China Morning Post</u>, bought 1986, and <u>Star</u> tabloid, bought 1974, to Enquirer publisher, 80% stake of merger sold to public in 1991, for $200 million, in 1991 agrees to sell <u>Daily Racing Form</u> and all U.S. magazines, except <u>Mirabella</u> and <u>TV Guide</u>, and U.K. magazines to reduce debt)... Spain's two largest private banks, Banco Espanol de Credito and Banco Central, merge in $48.39 billion deal, followed by Algemene Bank Nederland and Amsterdam - Rotterdam Bank to form Europe's 6th largest and world's 19th largest bank with assets of $184 billion in 1990...

Dai-Ichi Kangyo Bank is world's largest with deposits of $312 billion, followed by Sumitomo, $296 billion, Fuji Bank, $284 billion, Mitsubishi Bank and Sanwa Bank, $269 billion, Industrial Bank of Japan, $215 billion, Norinchukin Trust, $212 billion and Mitsubishi Trust at $186 billion, for first time in 31 years, no U.S. bank in top 25 - Citibank 28th at $104.9 billion... First Boston merges with London-based affiliate Credit Suisse First Boston, extends influence of Swiss-based bank over one of Wall Street's leading houses (is only commercial bank with major U.S. securities house)... Nippon Mining buys U.S.' Gould electronics for $1.1 billion... Nomura Securities, world's largest, pays $100 million for 25% of U.S.' acquisitions and mergers firm of Wasserstein Perella & Co... Seibu Saison Group, $23 billion empire of department stores, supermarkets and service firms, buys Inter-Continental hotels, 105 worldwide, from Grand Met for $2.15 billion (sells 40% to SAS, one of competing bidders in 1989)... Groupe Michelin buys aircraft tire business of B.F. Goodrich...

Bayer buys medical technology of U.S.' Cooper Technicon for $500 million, is world's 2nd-largest diagnostic business after Abbott Laboratories... Heidelberger Druckmaschinen, world's largest maker of printing presses and leading printing machinery firm in West Germany, buys NYC's Webb Press Group for $300 million, its first foreign acquisition... Nestle, breaking tradition of Swiss multinational firms, lets foreigners buy stock... Grand Met acquires two European restaurant chains, Spaghetti Factory with 5 units in Switzerland and Wienerwald with 231 units in West Germany, for some $36 million... Allied Irish Bank of Dublin acquires rest of First Maryland Bancorp for $340 million... Owing $800 million, Koor Industries, Israel's largest industrial conglomerate, gets month extension to settle debts with Israeli, U.S. banks... After suing eldest son to block takeover of his Toronto-based real estate development business, Robert Campeau buys Federated Department Stores, 14 divisions, for $6.6 billion after two-month battle with R.H. Macy (runs 382 stores as largest U.S. department store business and 4th-largest retailer after Sears, K Mart and Wal-Mart, to reduce debt of $11.7 billion, cuts some 5,000 jobs and sells Bullock's and I. Magnin to R.H. Macy, Filene's and Foley's fashion stores to May Department Stores, and Brooks Bros. to keep five chains, Bloomingdale's, Lazarus, Abraham & Straus, Burdines and Rich/Goldsmith's, with empire near bankruptcy in 1989 from over-extension, junk bond financing, Drexel Burnham Lambert collapse in 1990, and retail slump, borrows $260 million from Reichmann's and puts up Bloomingdale's tony 17-store chain for sale, declares Chapter 11 bankruptcy, largest in retailing, in 1990 when unable to service debt, is dropped from board in 1990...

Sergei Olevsky founds Iskatel, cooperative makes controls to link Soviet-made personal computers with automated factory machines (with makeshift work force, mostly 250 moonlighters in three shops, plans to make 8,000/year with factory, full-time workers by 1990)... Some 630,000 private businesses in Poland, most in agriculture, employ over 1.5 million, 8.6% of work force, to produce some 30% of nation's output, 20% in 1986... French police arrest Thomas F. Quinn, former New York stock broker, for masterminding 1984 stock-promotion scheme in Europe (bilks investors for some $250 million using high-pressure brokers to tout unknown U.S. penny-stock issues)... Hong Kong hosts offices of 114 foreign banks, 23 of U.S., as financial Capitol of Far East... After spending $14.8 billion on research in past four years, Siemens, telecommunications and electronics giant with sales of $33 billion, goes on $2 billion acquisitions spree to challenge IBM, AT&T and GE in global market (with $13 billion in cash, seeks new targets in 1989)... Ukraina Kolkhoz, one of U.S.S.R.'s most profitable collective farms with over 7,000 people working 12,000 acres near Romanian border, shows profit of some $4.7 million on sales of cattle, corn, sugar beets, wheat, other products... Accion International, U.S. group helping small businesses in Latin America, divides $14.4 million in loans among 27,000 entrepreneurs, default rate for 16 years is under 2%... Japanese banks provide $5.8 billion in loans for Kohlberg Kravis Roberts leveraged buyout of RJR Nabisco... After losing an average of $4 million for several years, Los Angeles King's hockey franchise shows first profitable year in 22-year history with gross over $9 million for 1987-88 after signing Canadian hockey great, Wayne Gretzky, for $15 million and salary of $2 million/year (rings up additional $3.46 million from attendance, spurs $150 million from licensing and merchandising, up 50%, for NHL)... Britain's TVS Entertainment pays $320 million for U.S.' MTM Entertainment to get fresh programs for overseas markets... Japanese investors develop 41 overseas resorts, 3 in 1984 and 21 in first 5 months of 1989... Swiss-Argentine firm, Nucal de Mexico, purchases avocado-packing plant in Uruapan, Mexico's chief source of avocados (after massive exports to Europe, is attacked by local exporters as Israeli plot to maintain control, 80%, over European market)...

IBM Japan's powerful computer, SHALT, translates English into Japanese... In total investment of $14 billion, Japanese spend some $12.7 billion buying 75 U.S. firms (run 2,000 in 1990)... IBM is top PC seller in European market with 26.6%, Olivetti 8.7%, Apple Computer 7.4%, Compaq Computer 7.1%, Hewlett-Packard 3.2%, Tandem 3% and Toshiba 2.6%, first entered market in 1985... Carlton Communication, Britain's largest processor of video cassettes, buys privately-owned Technicolor Holdings, founded 1915 to pioneer color film, for $780 million (is itself bought by U.S.' Paramount Communications in 1989, also buys 49% of Britain's Zenith, Europe's leading TV independent programmer)... UK publisher Pearson buys Addison-Wesley Publishing, 9th largest in U.S. educational market, for $283 million as takeover fever hits Britain... Marks & Spencer retailer acquires U.S.' Brooks Bros. (with falling profits, changes conservative line of 171-year-old institution of impeccable taste to attract younger customers with designer labels, trendy clothes)... Zantac antiulcer drug, introduced 1983, aids Glaxo to become world's No. 2 in prescription-drug industry behind Merck with sales of $4 billion (spends $500 million annually to find new drugs)...

Lured by border trade, Mexico City's Bancomer, $10 billion bank holding company, buys San Antonio's Executive National Bank, TX (spurs other Mexican acquisitions of U.S. banks)... After buying two other candy firms and selling Friendly Ice Cream stores in 1987, Hershey buys Peter Paul Almond Joy, Mounds and York Peppermint brands from Cadbury Schweppes for 20.5% share of U.S. candy market, Mars 18.5%, Jacobs Suchard 6.7%, Nestle 6.7%, and Leaf 5.6%... Lev Modell, Soviet emigre, George Carroll, multimillionaire entrepreneur, and Jay Chiat start Torg International as joint venture with Soviet trading firm to import Zhiguli beer, Georgian mineral water (leads to New York bakery chain selling Moscow-baked pumpernickel in 1989)... State-owned Thai International airline acquires land's domestic carrier... Two of biggest Paris stock brokers, Puget and Buscher, are fined $90,000 each for irregular trading in takeover of French retailer, La Redoute... French spend $2.8 billion for U.S. assets, doubled since 1985... After Kosaido printing group buys British golf course, Old Thorns, in 1984 and Tokyo's Nitto Kogyo golf-management firm, manages 26 golf courses in Japan, buys Scotland's Classic Turnberry Hotel and Golf courses in 1987 for $25 million, Seibu Saison acquires part of Old Course Hotel at St. Andrews, Mecca of golf... Le Cong Thanh starts business in Ho Chi Minh City to produce furniture, ceramics, hand-generated-powered flashlights, machines to make and bottle soft drinks and strip paint.... US West consortium lands world's largest cable television franchise to serve 1.5 million homes in Hong Kong... U.S.' ESPN Cable Network pays $8.25 million to increase its stake in British-based pan-European cable network, Screensport, from 5% to 25% (provides much of programming for Japan Sports Channel, joint venture with C. Itoh & Co. and others, in 1990)... South Korean conglomerates, chaebol with nearly 15% of GNP, spend $37 million on foreign acquisitions, rises by 1990 as labor-intensive work moves to low-wage Thailand and Philippines... Japan's Big Four, Nomura Securities, Daiwa, Nikko and Yamaichi, start using hedging strategies in investments, blamed for March market dive in 1990... After losing costly takeover of Harcourt Brace Jovanovich in 1987, Maxwell gets Macmillan publishing for $2.558 billion after six-month battle to enter U.S. market (buys U.S' Dun & Bradstreet airline guide in 1988 for $750 million, is blocked by public outcry in buying Melbourne paper in 1988, sponsors international management school, Bulgaria's first, in 1989, empire in ruins after curious death in 1992)... French record producers promote, merchandise Brazil's lambada dance, dates to 1920s, fad with records, videos and movies to create 1990 craze (fails to catch on with public... France's airline UTA bids for Air Inter to get foreign routes, blocked by state's Air France (sells 54% to Air France, 17% to Alitalia in 1990 while Lufthansa, Air France agree to share routes, Sabena links with KLM and British Airways, SAS with Finnair and Swissair, United with British Airways, Northwest with KLM, America West with Australia's Ansett, American with Qantas, and SAS with Chile's state line)... Crown Communications, Britain, is formed by merger of London radio franchise, TV production outfit (shows meteoric success by 1990 with plans to get new channel, BBC production work and European radio stations)... South Korean Tae Kwong Industrial Co., makes athletic shoes, forms joint venture with Jakarta firm... Publicis forms first big Franco-U.S. advertising alliance with Chicago's Foote, Cone & Belding, joint billings of $4.6 billion (leads to Eurocom with Della Femina McNamee and others for $3.4 billion, Boulet Dru Dupuy Petit with Wells, Rich, Green for $1.6 billion)...

Masato Mizuno succeeds father as CEO of Japan's largest sporting-goods maker in financial trouble (installs automation to cut costs, pushes marketing to get 30% share of Japan's 1989 $1.3 billion market in golf, baseball equipment, with 35,000 products in 1990 invades U.S., other countries)... ICL, British electronics giant, forms joint venture, Furnel International, with six Polish partners to make computers and furniture, Furnel exports furniture to Western stores for currency to buy parts to assemble computers for Polish buyers... Top ten oil companies are Saudi Aramco, Royal Dutch/Shell, Exxon, Venezuela's PDVSA, Pemex, Iran's NIOC, Chevron, Mobil, BP and Texaco, follows 1980's list of Exxon, Royal Dutch/Shell, Pemex, Texaco, Mobil, PDVSA, BP, Chevron, NIOC and Amoco... Maxwell reveals plan for Continental newspaper, appears 1990 (buys 50% of two Hungarian papers in 1990 and stake in Moscow News, plans to invest over $1 billion in East Bloc ventures in 1990)... Sotheby's holds first international auction in U.S.S.R. and first sale by Western auction house in China (begins auctioning non-art items in 1989, after expanding sales in Germany, Israel and Austria stages Japan's first big auction in 1990 and opens Korean office)... Foreign firms invest $3 billion in Mexico, $3.5 billion in 1989... Sony buys CBS Records for $2 billion, drops 84% of sales from electronics to 60% (pays $4.9 billion in 1989 to Coca-Cola for its Columbia Pictures to get library, over 3,000 films and some 2,600 TV shows, and 820-screen Loews movie theater chain, pays $200 million to buy Guber-Peters Entertainment for successful production team, settles $1 billion civil suit of Warner Bros. for inducing two to break contracts by paying $400-600 million extra, signs, 1991, superstar Michael Jackson to mega-bucks contract, largest ever in industry... Provincial Russian, "Egger", goes to Moscow to seek fortune (after seeing scalpers peddling tickets for Bolshoi shows to foreigners, starts own black market business, by 1990 hires 10 hustlers, makes "$1,000/day" buying services, tickets, hotel rooms, etc., with rubles for resale to tourists and Intourist, stashes "$100,000" in London bank for future Soviet investments).

Selected Bibliography

Baines, John and Jaromir Malek. <u>Atlas of Ancient Egypt</u>, New York: Facts on File Publications, 1980

Blake, Robert (ed.). <u>World History</u> (Volume 4), Oxford: Oxford University Press, 1988.

Boorstin, Daniel J. <u>The Discoverers</u>, New York: Random House, 1983.

Braudel, Fernand. <u>Civilization & Capitalism in 15th-18th Century</u> (3 Volumes), New York: Harper & Row, 1981.

Brown, Archie (ed.). <u>Cambridge Encyclopedia of Russia and the Soviet Union</u>, Cambridge: Cambridge University Press, 1982.

Burke, James. <u>Connections</u>, Boston: Little, Brown & Co., 1978.

Bursk, Edward (ed.). <u>The World of Business</u> (4 Volumes), New York: Simon and Schuster, 1962.

Carus-Wilson, E. M. <u>Medieval Merchant Venturers</u>, London: Methuen & Co., 1984.

Collier, Simon (ed.). <u>Cambridge Encyclopedia of Latin America</u>, Cambridge: Cambridge University Press, 1985.

Constable, George (ed.). <u>Time Frame</u> (16 Volumes), Alexandria: Time-Life Books, 1989.

Cornell, Tim and John Matthews. <u>Atlas of the Roman World</u>, Oxford: Phaidon Press, 1982.

Cotterel, Arthur (ed.). <u>The Encyclopedia of Ancient Civilizations</u>, New York: Mayflower Books, 1980.

Daniel, Clifton (ed.). <u>Chronicle of the 20th Century</u>, Mount Kisco, New York: Chronicle Publications, 1987.

d'Estaing, Valerie-Anne Giscard. <u>World Almanac Book of Inventions</u>, New York: World Almanac Publications, 1985.

438   **Selected Bibliography**

Dupuy, R. Ernest and Trevor N. Dupuy. The Encyclopedia of Military History, New York: Harper and Row, 1970.

Durant, Will and Ariel Durant. The Story of Civilization (10 volumes), New York: Simon and Schuster, 1954-1967.

George, Clause S., Jr. The History of Management Thought (2nd Ed.), Englewood Cliffs: Prentice-Hall, 1972.

Gernet, Jacques. A History of Chinese Civilization, Cambridge: Cambridge University Press, 1982.

Gimpel, Jean. The Medieval Machine, New York: Penguin Books, 1977.

Goerlitz, Walter. History of The German General Staff, Boulder, Colorado: Westview Press, 1985.

Grun, Bernard. The Timetables of History, New York: Simon and Schuster, 1975.

Hellemans, Alexander and Bryan Bunch. Timetables of Science, New York: Simon and Schuster, 1988.

Hibbert, Christopher. The English, New York: W. W. Norton & Co., 1987.

Hoover, Gary, et al (ed.). Hoover's Handbook of World Business 1992, Austin, Texas: The Reference Press.

Hucker, Charles O. China's Imperial Past, Stanford: Stanford University Press, 1975.

Hudson, Kenneth. The Archeology of the Consumer Society, Cranbury: Fairleigh Dickinson University Press, 1983.

Jeremy, David J. (ed.). Dictionary of Business Biography (5 Volumes), London: Butterworths, 1984.

Judge, Harry (ed.). World History (Volume 3), Oxford: Oxford University Press, 1988.

Kennedy, Paul. The Rise and Fall of the Great Powers, New York: Random House, 1987.

Korn, Jerry (ed.). Great Ages of Man (21 Volumes), Alexandria, Virginia: Time-Life Books, 1967.

Landes, David S. Revolution in Time, Cambridge: Belknap Press, 1983.

Langer, William L. An Encyclopedia of World History (5th Edition), Boston: Houghton Mifflin Co., 1972.

Levi, Peter. Atlas of the Greek World, New York: Facts on File Publications, 1980.

Lopez, Robert S. The Commercial Revolution of the Middle Ages, 950-1350, Englewood Cliffs: Prentice-Hall, 1971.

Matthew, Donald. Atlas of Medieval Europe, New York: Facts on File Publications, 1983.

McEvedy, Colin. The Macmillan World History Factfinder, New York: Macmillan Publishing, 1985.

Murray, Jocelyn (ed.). Cultural Atlas of Africa, New York: Facts on File Publications, 1981.

Platt, Colin. The Atlas of Medieval Man, New York: St. Martin's Press, 1979.

Pollard, Sidney. The Genesis of Modern Management, Cambridge: Harvard University Press, 1965.

Raff, Diether. A History of Germany, Hamburg: Berg Publishers, 1988.

Reynolds, Terry S. Stronger Than A Hundred Men, Baltimore: Johns Hopkins University Press, 1983.

Robinson, Francis. Atlas of The Islamic World, New York: Facts on File Publications, 1982.

Steinberg, S. H. Historical Tables, New York: St. Martin's Press, 1979.

Temple, Robert. The Genius of China, New York: Simon and Schuster, 1986.

Thrupp, Sylvia L. The Merchant Class of Medieval London, Ann Arbor: University of Michigan Press, 1948.

Van Creveld, Martin. Command in War, Cambridge, Massachusetts: Harvard University Press, 1985.

Veblen, Thorstein. Imperial Germany, Ann Arbor: University of Michigan Press, 1966.

Weinreb, Ben and Christopher Hibbert (ed.). The London Encyclopedia, London: Macmillan, 1983.

Williams, Trevor I. The History of Invention, New York: Facts on File Publications, 1987.

Wren, Daniel A. The Evolution of Management Thought, New York: Ronald Press, 1972.

Introduction to the Indexes

Three indexes follow, listing names, places and subjects, to aid in finding desired data. The indexes record each item by page, followed by the year in parentheses.

The Index of Names organizes each letter group into sections on Business Enterprises, Individuals/Families, Labor Organizations and Other Events to simplify the research process.

The Index of Places lists the geographical locations where the recorded events - mostly those identified in the chronology's General Events sections - occurred.

The Index of Subjects is organized by major categories, such as Accounting Activities and Advertising Practices. These major categories list entries by country or geographical area represented. When the specific location was not cited in the original reference, the item is recorded under the subentry Unknown. Items in the Index of Subjects provide access primarily to the material recorded in the chronology's Business Events sections. The entries in these sections are not intended to represent separate comprehensive historical calendars. Perhaps, as research continues, such individual timetables will be formulated.

Index of Names

Allied Suppliers, 358 (1959)
All Nippon Airways, 425 (1987), 426 (1987)
Almack's Assembly Room, 183 (1765)
Aluminum Co. of Canada, Alcan, 280 (1900)
Amazon Steam Navigation Company, 232 (1950s)
Amdahl computers, 413 (1985), 414 (1985)
American Express, Switzerland, 405 (1983)
American Motors, China, 404 (1983)
American Telephone & Telegraph, AT&T, 433 (1988), 435 (1988)
American Tobacco, 229 (1846), 238 (1857), 243 (1862) 281 (1901), 282 (1902)
Amicable Contributorship, 159 (1696)
Amstel beer, 244 (1864), 250 (1870)
Amsterdam Exchange, 122 (1585), 131 (1613)
Amsterdam-Rotterdam Bank, 434 (1988)
Amstrad, 371 (1968)
Amtorg Trading Corp., 318 (1928)
Amway, Japan, 393 (1980)
Anglo-American business, 286 (1905), 302 (1917), 431 (1988)
Anglo-American Oil, 267 (1888), 431 (1988)
Anglo-Iranian Company, 347 (1951)
Anglo-Mexican Petroleum Co., 281 (1901)
Anglo-Persian Oil, 265 (1886), 284 (1904) 296 (1912), 298 (1914), 311 (1922), 324 (1932)
Anglo-Swedish Nordenfeldt, 261 (1881)
Antskog Iron Works, 137 (1630)
Aoki Group, 425 (1987)
Apothecaries' Society, London, 133 (1617)
Apricot Entertainment, Japan, 413 (1985)
Aquascutum retailing, 234 (251)
Aramco, 326 (1933), 346 (1950), 347 (1951), 426 (1987)
Ariel Cycle Company, 277 (1898), 293 (1910)
Armani fashions, 381 (1974)
Armourers, 80 (1322)
Armstrong business, 228 (1845), 229 (1846), 287 (1906), 292 (1909), 317 (1927)
Armstrong Tire, 252 (1872)
Arte della Lania, 63 (1182)
Arte di Calimala, 63 (1182), 96 (1453)
Arthur Andersen accounting, 297 (1912)
Arundel textiles, Britain, 367 (1965)
Asahi Breweries, Japan, 368 (1966), 426 (1987)
ASEA, Switzerland, 262 (1883), 366 (1964), 399 (1982), 427 (1987)
Ashanti Goldfields Corp., 275 (1896)
Ashley fashions, 351 (1953)
Asiatic Petroleum, 269 (1890)
Asiento Guinea Company, 161 (1702)
"As Is" cartel, 298 (1914)

Assn. of Manufacturers, Denmark, 264 (1885)
Assn. of Netherlands Employers, 278 (1899)
Assn. of Outplacement Consulting Firms, 401 (1982)
Assn. of Surfing Professionals, 384 (1976)
Assn. of Tennis Professionals, 370 (1967)
Assn. of Wholesale Merchants, 199 (1797)
Aston Martin cars, 310 (1921)
Atari consumer electronics, 403 (1984)
Atlantic Richfield, 399 (1982)
Atochem chemicals, 339 (1946)
Atwoods business, 408 (1984)
Audi cars, 292 (1909), 301 (1916), 411 (1982)
Aulo de Commercio, 177 (1750)
Austin Motor Company, 286 (1905), 297 (1912)
Austrian East India Company, 168 (1722)
Auto Union, 292 (1909), 301 (1916), 332 (1938)
Avon Japan, 373 (1969)

Individuals/Families

Abbas the Great, 123 (1588)
Abbe, Ernest, 229 (1846), 267 (1888), 286 (1905)
Abedi, Agha Hassan, 379 (1973)
Abegglen, James C., 370 (1967)
Accum, Frederick, 211 (1820)
Acontius, 117 (1563)
Adamiecki, Karol, 275 (1896)
Adams, Will, 125 (1598)
Addison, Joseph, 163 (1709)
Adler, Clement, 269 (1890), 276 (1897)
Africanus, Julius, 29 (275)
Agnelli family, 280 (1900), 369 (1966), 418 (1986)
Ahmad, Muhammad ibn, 49 (976)
Aiken, William Maxwell, 287 (1906)
Akbar, 115 (1556)
Alberti, Leon Battista, 95 (1452)
Albrecht family, 338 (1945)
Albuquerque, Afonso de, 105 (1509), 106 (1511)
Alcock, J.W., 304 (1919)
Al-Din, Hasan, 137 (1631)
Aldrecht, Karl, 309 (1920)
Aleotti, Gian-Battista, 133 (1618)
Alestree, Richard, 145 (1660)
Aletti, Jean-Marc, 418 (1986)
Alexander I, Russia, 202 (1802), 212 (1823)
Alexander II, Russia, 236 (1855)
Alexander the Great, 14 (336), 15 (331, 329)
Al-Fayed, Mohamed, 390 (1979), 396 (1981)

Alfonsin, Raul, 402 (1983)
Alfonso the Wise, 73 (1270, 1276)
Alfred the Great, 45 (871)
Al-Ghussein, Jaweed, 343 (1948)
Al-Haitham, Ibn, 52 (1028)
Al-Kindi, 45 (860)
Allais, Maurice, 335 (1943)
Allcraft, John D., 229 (1846)
Allen, J., 157 (1690)
Allende, Salvador, 374 (1970), 378 (1973)
Allhusen, A.H., 251 (1871)
Al-Mamun, 43 (813)
Al-Mansur, 40 (765)
Al-Masri, Munib, 359 (1959)
Almeida, Francisco de, 105 (1507, 1509)
al-Mulk, Nizam, 55 (1092)
Al-Mulk, Nizam, 157 (1690)
Al-Qaddafi, Muammar, 372 (1969), 378 (1973)
Al Rajhi, Suliman Abdul-Aziz, 311 (1922)
Al-Rashid, Haroun, 41 (786)
Al Sulaiman, Abdul-Aziz, 333 (1939)
Alstromer, Jonas, 169 (1723)
Amalrik, Andrei, 374 (1970)
Amenhotep, IV, 6 (1385)
Amin, Idi, 377 (1972)
Ammar, Tarak Ben, 382 (1975)
Ammenemes III, 5 (1844)
Amundsen, Roald, 283 (1903)
Andersen, H.N., 276 (1987)
Anderson, John, 226 (1842)
Andre, George, 257 (1877)
Angus, Robert, 252 (1872)
Anushirwan the Just, 34 (531)
Aoki, Yunosuke, 329 (1935)
Apel, Fritz von, 320 (1929)
Appert, Nicholas, 198 (1795), 206 (1811)
Appleton, Edward, 266 (1887), 313 (1924)
Aquinas, Thomas, 73 (1273)
Arafat, Yasir, 358 (1959)
Arana, Martin de, 135 (1625), 136 (1627)
Archer, Frederick Scott, 233 (1851)
Archer, Thomas, 134 (1622)
Archimedes, 18 (212), 115 (1556), 184 (1768)
Argand, Aime, 192 (1784)
Aristarchus of Samos, 15 (310)
Aristotle, 15 (335), 16 (280)
Arkwright, Richard, 173 (1738), 184 (1768), 185 (1769), 186 (1771, 1772), 189 (1779), 192 (1784), 193 (1785)
Armstrong, W.G., 223 (1839)
Arnault, Bernard, 404 (1983), 426 (1987)
Arnim, Bettina von, 227 (1843)
Arnold of Villanova, 75 (1285)
Arrieta, Avelino, 333 (1940)

Artevelde, Jacques van, 82 (1345)
Aryan, Izzedin, 364 (1963)
Ashcroft, Michael, 373 (1969)
Asoka, 16 (269)
Aspdin, Joseph, 213 (1824)
Astley, Philip, 187 (1773)
Athelstan, 47 (925)
Attlee, Clement, 336 (1945)
Augustulus, Romulus, 33 (476)
Aurelius, Marcus, 24 (30), 28 (121)
Austin, Herbert, 266 (1887)
Ayukawa, Y., 296 (1912)
Azcarraga, Emilio, 418 (1986)

Labor Organizations

All-India Trade Union Congress, 307 (1920)
Amalgamated Engineer Union, Britain, 308 (1920)
Amalgamated Society of Carpenters and Joiners, Britain, 224 (1841)
Amalgamated Society of Engineers, Britain, 224 (1841), 233 (1850)
Assn. of Handicraft Apprentices, Germany, 229 (1846)
Assn. of Vatican Lay Employees, 389 (1979), 390 (1980)

Other Events

Academia Secretorum Naturae, Naples, 116 (1560)
Academie des Exercises, France, 128 (1606)
Academie Royale des Operas, France, 149 (1669)
Academie Royale des Sciences, France, 148 (1666)
Academy of Sciences, U.S.S.R., 411 (1985), 432 (1988)
Accadema del Cimento, Florence, 145 (1657)
Accademia dei Lineei, Rome, 127 (1603)
Adulteration Act, Britain, 252 (1872)
Aero Club of France, 277 (1898)
Agrarian Reform Act, Chile, 370 (1967)
African National Conference, 296 (1912)
AIESEC, 342 (1948)
Al-Akaria mall, Riyadh, 408 (1984)
Alexandria Library, 98 (1472)
Almagest, 28 (129), 40 (765), 44 (828), 62 (1175), 74 (1276)
American Highway, 317 (1928)
Amoco Cadiz, oil spill, 386 (1978)
Amsterdam Park, 154 (1682)
Anasazi Society, 52 (1050)
Apothecaries Act, Britain, 207 (1815)

Brown Boveri & Co., 271 (1891), 427 (1987)

Brunner & Mond, 253 (1873), 268 (1889), 280 (1900)

BSN, France, 370 (1967), 413 (1985), 418 (1986) 323 (1931), 405 (1983)

Budapest Stock Exchange, 344 (1948)

Buenos Aires-Valpariso Railroad, 294 (1911)

Building Society, Birmingham, 191 (1781)

Bunge & Born traders, 209 (1817)

Burmah Oil, 265 (1886), 281 (1901)

BUS Berzelivs Environmental Services, 426 (1987)

Buscher brokerage, Paris, 435 (1988)

Bushmills, 129 (1608)

Butchers' Company, 128 (1605)

Butlin camps, 310 (1921)

Butterfield & Swire, 246 (1866), 258 (1879), 344 (1948)

"Butterships", 384 (1977)

Buxted Poultry, Britain, 392 (1980)

Individuals/Families

Babbage, Charles, 206 (1812), 211 (1822), 218 (1831, 1832), 233 (1851)

Bacon, Anthony, 183 (1765)

Bacon, Francis, 125 (1597), 133 (1620)

Bacon, Roger, 72 (1264, 1265, 1266, 1267, 1268), 185 (1769)

Bader, Ernest, 343 (1948)

Baffin, William, 132 (1615)

Bailey, Captain, 138 (1635)

Baille, Pierre, 154 (1682)

Bain, 227 (1844)

Bainbridge, Emerson, 222 (1838)

Baird, Charles, 241 (1860)

Baird, John L., 263 (1884), 313 (1924), 317 (1928), 324 (1932)

Baker, Roger, 197 (1793)

Baker, William G., 289 (1907)

Balanchet, Henri, 400 (1982)

Balboa, Vasco Nunez de, 105 (1508), 106 (1514)

Balsamo, Joseph "Cagliostro", 174 (1743)

Barbarigo, Andrea, 92 (1418)

Barbon, Nicholas, 149 (1667), 156 (1686)

Bardas, 45 (856)

Barham, George, 234 (1851)

Barker, John, 250 (1870)

Barker, R., 194 (1787)

Barnack, Oskar, 315 (1925)

Barnov, Alexander, 195 (1790)

Barnum, P.T., 239 (1858)

Baron, Bernhard, 270 (1890)

Barrans, John, 240 (259)

Barratt, Thomas J., 270 (1891)

Barry, Antony, 400 (1982)

Bartlett, Charles, J., 308 (1920)

Bastiat, Frederic, 231 (1848)

Bate, John, 138 (1634)

Bathearst, David, 413 (1985)

Battuta, Ibn, 80 (1325), 81 (1331)

Bauer, George, 115 (1556)

Bauer, Melchior, 182 (1764)

Baugh, Benjamin, 239 (1859)

Bauwens, Lievin, 200 (1798)

Baxter, Richard 147 (1664)

Baylis, Lilian, 296 (1912)

Beach, Sylvia, 305 (1919)

Beale, John E., 261 (1881)

Beauchesne, Jean de, 118 (1570)

Beauvillers, 191 (1782)

Beauvoir, Simone de, 344 (1949)

Bebel, August, 248 (1869)

Becquerel, Antoine, 222 (1839)

Beeton, Samuel, 234 (1852)

Begin, Jean, 130 (1610)

Behaim, Martin, 101 (1490)

Behn brothers, 299 (1914)

Behring, Emile von, 269 (1890)

Beighton, Henry, 166 (1717)

Beisheim, Otto, 360 (1960)

Beit, Alfred, 251 (1871), 259 (1880)

Bejart, Joseph, 141 (1643)

Belidor, Bernard Forest de, 159 (1697), 170 (1730)

Bell, Alexander Graham, 291 (1909)

Bell, Henry, 191 (1783), 206 (1812)

Bellisario, Marisa, 360 (1960)

Belzberg family, 305 (1919)

Benedict XIV, 174 (1742)

Benjamin of Tudela, 60 (1158)

Benn, John, 280 (1900)

Benson, Samuel H., 272 (1893)

Bentham, Samuel, 197 (1794)

Benz, Karl, 257 (1878), 272 (1893)

Berger, Rheinhold, 269 (1890)

Bergman, 185 (1770)

Berguis, Fredrich, 298 (1913), 309 (1921)

Bering, Vitus, 169 (1725)

Berliner, Emile, 277 (1898)

Berlusconi, Silvio, 387 (1978)

Berry, William E., 281 (1901)

Berthier, Marshal, 196 (1792), 207 (1813)

Berthollet, Claude-Louis, 187 (1774), 193 (1785)

Berthoud, Ferdinand, 174 (1741)

Bessemer, Henry, 226 (1842), 235 (1854), 238 (1858), 243 (1863)

Bettman, Siegfried, 264 (1885)

Buessing, Heinrich, 284 (1904)
Buffon, George Louis de, 173 (1739)
Bulganin, N.A., 353 (1955)
Bullock, William, 205 (1809)
Bulow, Bernhard von, 279 (1900)
Bundy, William, 205 (1809)
Bunsen, R.W., 233 (1850)
Buonsignori family, 66 (1209)
Burbage, James, 120 (1576)
Burberry, Thomas, 238 (1856)
Burbidge, Richard, 268 (1889)
Burda, Franz, 320 (1929)
Burn, Kit, 240 (1860s)
Burns, John, 268 (1889)
Burns, Tom, 362 (1961)
Burton, Montague M., 284 (1904)
Busch, Hans, 326 (1933)
Butler, Edward, 254 (1874)
Byung-Chull, Lee, 329 (1936)

Labor Organizations

Bakewell Hall, 65 (1200)
Butchers' Guild, 104 (1501)

Other Events

Baedeker's travel guide, 215 (1827)
Banking Act, Japan, 252 (1872)
Banking Act, Switzerland, 327 (1934)
Basic Agreement, Sweden, 339 (1946)
Battle of Courtrai, 77 (1302)
Battle of Grandson, 99 (1476)
"Battle of Midway", 334 (1942)
Battle of Poitiers, 84 (1356)
"Battle of the Bulge", 336 (1944)
Battle of Tours, 39 (732)
Bayreuth Festival, Germany, 255 (1876)
Benedictine Order, 34 (529), 35 (597), 63 (1182), 64 (1198)
Benelux, 340 (1947), 357 (1958
Berlin Airlift, 342 (1948)
Berlin Conference for Africa, 263 (1884)
Berlin Handelsgesellschaft, 235 (1853)
Berlin International Monetary Conference, 283 (1903)
Berlin University, 205 (1809)
Berlin Wall, 361 (1961)
Bhopal disaster, India, 408 (1984)
Binational Industrial Research & Development, Israel, 385 (1977)
Blackheath FC, 235 (1835)
Blue Cross, 256 (1877)
Blue Train, South Africa, 377 (1972)
Board of Longitude, Britain, 165 (1714)

Bocconi University, Milan, 377 (1972)
Boer War, 278 (1899)
Bologna University, 57 (1119), 59 (1150)
Boodle's Club, 182 (1762)
Book of Rules, England, 114 (1553)
Book of the Perfect, 46 (886)
Boxers Society, China, 277 (1898), 279 (1900)
Briare Canal, 129 (1609)
Bright Pearl cooperative, China, 389 (1974)
British Broadcasting Company, 304 (1919), 309 (1921), 317 (1927), 324 (1932), 329 (1936), 331 (1938), 352 (1954)
British Football (soccer) Assn., 243 (1863)
British Management Research Group, 316 (1926)
British Post Office, 295 (1911)
Brotherhood of St. Thomas à Becket, 69 (1248)
Bruges-Dunkirk Canal, 134 (1622)
Bubonic Plague, 81 (1332), 82 (1341), 83 (1347, 1348, 1351), 86 (1374), 87 (1381)
Building Societies Act, Britain, 273 (1894)
Bullet Train, Japan, 364 (1964)
Bundespost, Germany (1876)
Burlington Arcade, London, 210 (1819)
Business Research Institute, Sweden, 318 (1928)
Butchart Gardens, Canada, 339 (1946)
Byzantine Empire, 34 (527), 35 (565), 39 (717), 48 (963), 54 (1081, 1082), 61 (1171), 64 (1198), 80 (1326), 96 (1453)

C

Business Enterprises

Cabaret Uberbretti, Berlin, 281 (1901)
Cable & Wireless, 320 (1929), 395 (1981)
Cadbury confectionery, 192 (1783), 213 (1824), 264 (1885), 419 (1986), 435 (1988)
Cafe Procope, 146 (1660)
Caisse d'Escompte, 188 (1776)
Caisse de Depot de Placement, Canada, 368 (1966)
Caledonian Airways, 319 (1928), 362 (1961)
Cali Cartel, 396 (1981), 407 (1984), 429 (1988), 433 (1988)
Calixto Valenti goldsmith firm, 160 (1700)
Camorra, 92 (1417)
Campari wine, 271 (1892)
Campbell's Soup, 382 (1975), 425 (1987)
Canada Company, 136 (1628)
Canada Dry ginger ale, 285 (1904)
Canada Post Company, 406 (1984)
Canadian Bank of Commerce, 247 (1867)
Canadian National Railroad, 312 (1923), 384

(1977), 389 (1979)

Canadian Pacific Railway, CP, 260 (1881), 261 (1881), 267 (1888), 291 (1908), 334 (1942), 384 (1977), 389 (1979)

Canadian Pacific Air, 334 (1942)

Cancun resort, Mexico, 380 (1974)

Canon business, 330 (1937), 382 (1975), 396 (1981), 399 (1982), 426 (1987)

Cape-Johannesburg Railroad, 271 (1892)

Caracas Company, 165 (1714), 170 (1728)

Cardin fashions, 355 (1956), 345 (1964), 371 (1968), 412 (1985)

Caribbean Lines, 369 (1966)

Carl Linstrom Company, 284 (1904)

Carling beer, 225 (1841)

Carlsberg Brewery, 230 (1847), 274 (1895), 375 (1970)

Carlton and United Breweries, 267 (1888), 396 (1981)

Carlton Communication, Britain, 435 (1988)

Carpenters' Company, 81 (1333)

Carr biscuits, 218 (1831)

Carrefour stores, 384 (1976)

Carron Iron Works, 181 (1760), 182 (1762)

Cartier jewelry, 230 (1847), 289 (1907), 374 (1970)

Casa da Mina, 104 (1505)

Casa de la Contratacion, 104 (1503)

Casa de las Indies, 104 (1501), 105 (1508)

Casa di San Giorgio, 90 (1407)

Casio Computer, 335 (1942)

Caspian & Black Sea Company, 259 (1880)

Castle & Cooke, Hawaii, 234 (1851)

Catalan Company, 74 (1282)

Cathago Films, Tunisia, 382 (1975)

Cathay Construction, 315 (1925)

Cathay Life Insurance, 315 (1925)

Cathay Pacific Airways, 340 (1947), 344 (1948)

C. Brewer & Co., 216 (1827)

CBS Records, 436 (1988)

Celltech, Britain, 390 (1980)

Cepsa petroleum, 322 (1930)

Ceselsa, Spain, 389 (1979)

Chanel fashions, 299 (1914), 311 (1922), 401 (1982)

Charles of the Ritz cosmetics, 305 (1919), 418 (1986)

Charly Records, 381 (1974)

Charterhouse J. Rothschild, 392 (1980)

Chat Noir cabaret, Paris, 260 (1881)

Chateau Frontenac, Canada, 271 (1892)

Chateau Lafite, 191 (1781)

Chateau Masar, Lebanon, 385 (1977)

Chatelain's, London, 149 (1668)

Chaumet jewelers, Paris, 424 (1987)

Cheung Kong plastics, 335 (1942)

Chevalier Holdings, 349 (1952)

China Company, 166 (1717)

China International Trust & Investment, 387 (1979)

China Merchants' Steam Navigation Co., 253 (1873)

Chivas Scotch, 201 (1801)

Chivers & Sons jams, 253 (1873)

Christie's auction house, 183 (1766), 404 (1983), 413 (1985)

Ciba-Geigy business, 241 (1860), 265 (1886)

Cie Internationale des Wagon-Lits, 256 (1876)

Cineplex theaters, 389 (1979)

Cinzano distillery, 179 (1757)

Citicorp bank, 403 (1983)

Citizen Watch Company, 322 (1930)

C. Itoh & Company, 413 (1985), 418 (1986)

Citroen cars, 296 (1912), 300 (1915), 305 (1919), 371 (1968), 384 (1976), 386 (1978)

Civil Service Stores, Britain, 243 (1864)

C.J. Hambro & Son banking, 223 (1839)

Clarendon Press, 151 (1672), 191 (1781)

Claridges Hotel, 236 (1855)

Clark shoes, 214 (1825)

Clayton & Shettleworth Company, 226 (1842)

Clifford Chant law firm, Britain, 424 (1987)

Clifford's Inn, 82 (1345)

Clinique La Prairie, 323 (1931)

Clockmakers' Company, 137 (1631), 145 (1658), 161 (1704), 162 (1704), 224 (1840s)

Cloth Workers Company, 171 (1732)

Clouston Foods, Quebec, 370 (1967)

Club Mediterranee, 346 (1950), 399 (1982), 417 (1986)

CMB Packaging, Brussels, 424 (1987), 431 (1988)

Coal, Oil and Gas Corp., South Africa, 354 (1955)

Cobb & Company, 247 (1867)

Coca-Cola, 414 (1985), 436 (1988)

Cockpit theater, 130 (1609)

Codornio wine, 114 (1551)

Co-Hong Company, 167 (1720)

Coldwell Banker, London, 403 (1983)

Cole retailing, 300 (1914)

Cologne Hanse, 85 (1367)

Columbia Pictures, 436 (1988)

Columbia records, 287 (1906)

Comau robots, Italy, 382 (1975)

Combustion Engineering, Siberia, 424 (1987)

Commercial Company, 142 (1649), 155 (1684)

Commercial Trademark Services, 374 (1970)

Commerzbank, Germany, 235 (1853), 417 (1986)

Commission des Operations de Bourse, 370 (1967)

Compagnia dell' Arte della lana, 87 (1383)

Compagnie de la Louisiane, 166 (1717)

Compagnie de Saint-Gobain, 148 (1665), 158 (1695), 407 (1984), 414 (1986)

Compagnie des Iles d'Amerique, 135 (1625)

Compagnie des Messageries Maritime, 234 (1851)

Compagnie du Nord, 150 (1669)

Compagnie Financiere de Suez, 401 (1982), 422 (1987), 427 (1987)

Compagnie Generale d'Electricite, 277 (1898), 418 (1986)

Compagnie Generale des Eaux, 383 (1976)

Companie Mexicana de Aviacio, 399 (1982)

Company Le Bazacle, 62 (1177)

Company of Drapers, 132 (1616)

Company of Far Lands, 124 (1594, 1595), 125 (1598)

Company of Gotland Travelers, 50 (1000), 60 (1150), 68 (1237)

Company of Leathersellers, 139 (1638)

Company of London Bricklayers and Tylers, 118 (1568)

Company of Mastersingers, 81 (1332)

Company of Merchants of London, 131 (1612)

Company of Musicians, 128 (1604)

Company of Nail Makers, 175 (1743)

Company of Printers, 146 (1660)

Company of Royal Adventurers into Africa, 147 (1663)

Company of Saltmakers, 139 (1636)

Company of Santo Domingo, 166 (1717)

Company of St. Christopher, 135 (1625)

Company of the Indies, 166 (1717)

Company of the Merchants of the Staple, 85 (1362)

Concession Oil Syndicate, 265 (1886)

Confcummerico, Italy, 306 (1919)

Confindustria, Italy, 305 (1919), 400 (1982)

Consolidated Contractors, Aden, 349 (1952)

Consolidated Goldfields, 265 (1886), 286 (1905), 431 (1988)

Consolidated Zinc, 286 (1905)

Continental Grain Co., 207 (1813)

Continental Telegraph, 232 (1849)

Cook travel agency, 225 (1841), 234 (1851), 256 (1876), 317 (1927), 399 (1982)

Cooper beer, 242 (1862)

Cooperative de Productes de Mola, 363 (1963)

Co-operative Wholesale Society, 244 (1864)

Coopers & Lybrand accounting, 352 (1957)

Coopers Company, 104 (1501)

Cordwainers' Company, 73 (1272)

Corning Glass, U.S. 408 (1982)

Corporacion de Fomento de la Production, Chile, 319 (1929)

Corporation of Coachmen, 139 (1639)

Coupon Clearing Service, Mexico, 374 (1970)

Courreges fashions, 404 (1983)

Courtauld textiles, 209 (1816), 270 (1891), 285 (1904), 301 (1916), 393 (1980)

Coutts & Co., 157 (1692)

Crawford advertising, 299 (1914), 317 (1927)

Credit Agricole, France, 308 (1920)

Credit Anstalt, Vienna, 322 (1931)

Credit Foncier, 240 (1859)

Credit Lyonnaise, 243 (1863), 427 (1987)

Credit Mobilier, 234 (1852), 240 (1859)

Credit Suisse, 237 (1856), 434 (1988)

Creditanstalt, Vienna, 236 (1855)

Cristalleries de St. Louis, 387 (1978)

Croissanterie, France, 392 (1980)

Crossair, 382 (1975)

Crosse & Blackwell foods, 205 (1809)

Crossley Bros., 249 (1869)

Crown Communication, Britain, 436 (1988)

CST Communications, 413 (1985)

Cunard Line, 222 (1838), 223 (1839), 224 (1840), 229 (1846), 231 (1848), 236 (1855), 251 (1871), 284 (1904), 295 (1911), 311 (1922), 328 (1934), 332 (1938), 368 (1966), 370 (1967), 371 (1968)

Cuper's Garden, London, 141 (1643)

Cutlers' Company, 91 (1416)

C.Z. sherry, 143 (1650)

Individuals/Families

Cabet, Etienne, 224 (1840)

Cabot family, 102 (1496, 1498), 105 (1508), 114 (1553)

Cabral, Pedro, 103 (1500)

Cadbury, Edward, 296 (1912)

Caesar, Augustus, 23 (50), 144 (1653)

Caesar, Julius, 10 (578), 22 (60, 52) 23 (46)

Calvi, Robert, 376 (1971), 400 (1982)

Calvin, John, 111 (1536)

Campeau, Robert 419 (1986), 434 (1988)

Cantillon, Richard, 170 (1730), 179 (1755)

Caprivi, Graf von Leo, 269 (1890)

Cardano, Geronimo, 113 (1545)

Cardano, Girolamo, 104 (1501)

Carletti, F., 124 (1591)

Carlier, Francois, 245 (1866)

Carras, John M., 301 (1916)

Chartres Cathedral, 64 (1194)
Chelsea Water Works Company, 168 (1723)
Cheops Pyramid, 3 (2600)
China Civil Construction Engineering, 389 (1979), 399 (1982)
China Venturetech Investment, 415 (1986)
Chinese Center for Industrial Science, 391 (1980)
Chinese Immigrants Act, 260 (1881)
Chinese Labor Corps, 307 (1920)
Chou Dynasty, 7 (1122)
Christian-Social Workers' Party, 257 (1878)
Cistersian Order, 55 (1098), 56 (1100), 57 (1115)
Club of Rome, 377 (1972), 380 (1974), 386 (1978)
Coal Mines Act, Britain, 321 (1930)
Code of Justinian, 34 (529, 533)
Collective Agreements Act, Sweden, 318 (1928)
Collegium Indicum, Holland, 134 (1623)
Cologne Carnival, 212 (1823)
Cologne Confederation, 72 (1267)
Cologne University, 88 (1388)
Colon Free Zone, 344 (1948)
Colosseum, Rome, 26 (75)
Combination Law, Britain, 213 (1824)
Comecon, 344 (1949), 374 (1970)
Comedie-Francaise, 153 (1680)
Cominform, 339 (1946)
Commedia dell' arte, 123 (1590), 150 (1670)
Commercial Code, Japan, 345 (1950)
Common Market, Africa, 362 (1962)
"Communist Manifesto", 231 (1848)
Communist Party, Britain, 307 (1920)
Communist Party, China, 310 (1921)
Communist Party, France, 386 (1978)
Communist Party, Germany, 304 (1919)
Communist Party, Hungary, 304 (1919), 429 (1988)
Communist Party, India, 311 (1923)
Communist Party, Italy, 381 (1975)
Companies Act, Britain, 227 (1844)
Companies Act, Canada, 327 (1934)
Companies Act, France, 246 (1867)
Companies Act, Germany, 307 (1920s)
Companies Act, India, 238 (1857)
Conciliation Act, Britain, 275 (1896)
Conciliation Society, Japan, 315 (1925)
Concorde SST, 362 (1962), 383 (1976)
Congres Internationaux d'Architecture Moderne, 318 (1928)
Congress of Co-operative Societies, London, 234 (1852)
Congress of Vienna, 208 (1815)
Contingency Management, 361 (1961)

Convention on International Trade in Endangered Species, 416 (1986)
Cooke Committee, Switzerland, 381 (1975)
Coordinating Committee for Multilateral Export Controls, COCOM, 344 (1949)
Copenhagen School of Economics and Business, 302 (1917)
Cordoba University, 48 (968)
Corn Laws, England, 156 (1689), 229 (1846)
Cornelian Laws, Rome, 22 (81)
Corps des Ponts et Chaussees, 165 (1716)
Council of Churchmen, 44 (825)
Council of Europe, 344 (1949)
Council of Nicaea, 31 (325)
Council of Trade, England, 142 (1650)
Court of Augmentation, England, 111 (1536)
Covent Garden Market, London, 144 (1656)
Covent Garden Opera House, London, 171 (1732)
Cox's Museum, London, 186 (1772)
Craftsmen's Educational Society, 230 (1847)
Crockford's house, 216 (1828)
Crusades, 55 (1096, 1097), 56 (1099), 57 (1102), 59 (1147), 63 (1189), 65 (1202), 67 (1218, 1228), 69 (1248), 72 (1270)
Crystal Palace, London, 233 (1850, 1851)
Cultural Revolution, China, 368 (1966), 383 (1976)
Currency Act, England, 163

D

Business Enterprises

Daehnseldt seeds, Denmark, 203 (1804)
Daewoo Group, 371 (1967), 407 (1984), 409 (1984), 421 (1987), 433 (1988)
DAF vehicles, 318 (1928)
Daiei retailing, 356 (1957)
Dai-Ichi Kangyo Bank, 253 (1873), 376 (1971), 379 (1973), 417 (1986), 434 (1988)
Daily Express paper, London, 408 (1984)
Daimaru stores, 167 (1720)
Daimler Airway, 301 (1916), 311 (1922), 313 (1924)
Daimler-Benz, 230 (1847), 250 (1870), 262 (1883), 264 (1885), 266 (1887), 280 (1900), 316 (1926), 354 (1955), 380 (1974), 412, 413 (1985)
Daimler Motor Co., Britain, 275 (1896), 293 (1910), 350 (1952)
Daiwa Securities, 429 (1988), 436 (1988)
Danat Bank, 322 (1931)
Danfoss refrigeration, 326 (1933)

Danieli steel, 295 (1911)
Danish Asiatic Company, 171 (1732)
Danish East India Company, 132 (1614)
Danish Employers' Confederation, 275 (1896)
Danish West India Company, 135 (1625)
Danish West India-Guinea Company, 151 (1672)
Darmstadt Bank, 235 (1853)
Datatronic, Sweden, 386 (1978)
David Lewis retailing, 308 (1920)
Day and Martin blacking, 186 (1770)
DeBeers Consolidated Mines, 203 (1805), 250 (1870), 251 (1871), 259, 260 (1880), 267 (1880), 286 (1905), 324 (1932), 358 (1959), 431 (1988)
Debenham stores, 346 (1950)
Decca Dulcephone, 219 (1832)
Decca Records, 319 (1928)
De Havilland Aircraft, 291 (1908), 344 (1949), 349 (1952), 350 (1953)
Delamare art gallery, Paris, 427 (1987)
Delhi Cloth & General Mills Company, 268 (1889), 296 (1912)
De Lorean Motor Company, 386 (1978), 397 (1982)
Den Fujita, 376 (1971)
Dennis bicycles/vehicles, 274 (1895)
Dentsu advertising, 282 (1901), 329 (1936), 408 (1984)
Deruluft, 310 (1921)
Deutsche Aero Lloyd, 315 (1925)
Deutsche Bank, 235 (1853), 250 (1870), 357 (1957), 412, 413, 414 (1985), 417, 418 (1986)
Deutsche Lufthansa, 316 (1926), 353 (1955)
Deutsche Reichsbank, 254 ((1875)
Dewar whisky, 229 (1846)
Didot St. Leger, 200 (1799)
Dillingham business, 267 (1888)
Dinky toys, 281 (1901), 326 (1933)
Dior fashions, 341 (1947), 356 (1957), 370 (1967), 395, 396 (1981), 404 (1983)
Distillers' Company, 139 (1638)
Dolch Logic Instruments, Germany, 400 (1982)
D'Oyly Carte Opera Co., 399 (1982)
Dom Perignon wine, 149 (1668), 156 (1688), 175 (1743)
Dorchester Hotel, London, 384 (1976)
Dorland advertising, 286 (1905), 302 (1917)
Doulton china, 208 (1815)
Douro Wine Company, 179 (1756)
Doyukai, 340 (1947)
Drambuie liquor, 287 (1906)
Drapers' Company, 85 (1364)

Dresdner Bank, 235 (1853), 347 (1950), 401 (1982), 417 (1986)
Dublin Exchange, 200 (1799)
Dubonnet wine, 229 (1846)
Dunlop tires, 228 (1845), 252 (1872), 267 (1888), 268 (1889), 320 (1929), 376 (1971), 419 (1986)
Du Pont, 316 (1926), 332 (1938), 334 (1941), 350 (1952), 393 (1980)
Dutch East India Co., 127 (1602), 130 (1610), 132 (1615), 133 (1619), 134 (1621), 136 (1628), 140 (1641), 143 (1652), 170 (1729), 189 (1778)
Dutch West Africa Company, 133 (1618)
Dutch West India Company, 130 (1610), 134 (1621)
Duty Free International shops, 405 (1983)
Duty-Free Shoppers, 341 (1947), 360 (1960)
Dyers' Company, 98 (1471)
Dynaction, Pris, 400 (1982)

Individuals/Families

D'Abbans, Claude de Jouffroy, 191 (1783)
Dafforne, Richard, 137 (1630)
Dagobert I, 36 (630)
Daguerre, Jacques M., 212 (1823), 216 (1829), 222 (1838), 223 (1839)
Daimachus, 14 (340)
Daimler, Gottlieb, 246 (1867), 254 (1874), 255 (1876), 261 (1881), 262 (1883)
Dalziel, Davison A., 261 (1882), 287 (1906)
D'Amarto, Salvino, 75 (1290)
Daniell, John F., 221 (1836)
Dannevig, A., 358 (1959)
Darakananda, Damri, 362 (1961)
Darby family, 161 (1704), 163 (1707, 1709), 178 (1754), 184 (1767), 190 (1779), 201 (1800)
D'Arcy, William Knox, 265 (1886), 281 (1901)
Darius I, 11 (521, 518), 12 (513)
Darracq, A., 287 (1906)
D'Arsonval, Arsene, 287 (1906)
Dassler, Adi, 308 (1920)
Datini, Francesco, 85 (1363)
Davey, Edmund, 221 (1836)
David, Christian, 377 (1972)
David-Weil, Michel, 367 (1965)
Davis, John, 82 (1342), 116 (1558), 122 (1585, 1586), 124 (1594, 1595)
Davis, Peter J., 417 (1986)
Davy, Humphrey, 201 (1801, 1802), 203 (1806), 204 (1808), 206 (1813), 207 (1815), 208 (1816), 210 (1820)
De Benedetti, Carlo, 384 (1976), 387 (1978),

Labor Organizations

Other Events

Elliott, John D., 376 (1971)
Ellul, Jacques, 364 (1964)
El-Sayed, Refaat, 379 (1973)
Elzevir family, 121 (1503)
Engels, Friedrich, 227 (1844), 228 (1845), 231 (1848)
Eno, James C., 234 (1852)
Epicurus, 15 (306)
Erathosthenes, 17 (240)
Ercker, Lazarus, 119 (1574)
Erhard, Ludwig, 340 (1947), 344 (1949), 363 (1963)
Ericsson, John, 214 (1826)
Ericsson, Leif, 50 (1001)
Erland, A.K., 302 (1917)
Esch, Horst-Dieter, 364 (1964)
Escoffier, Auguste, 268 (1889), 277 (1898)
Esposito, Raffaelo, 268 (1889)
Esslinger, Hartmut, 373 (1969)
Euclid, 16 (300), 41 (774)
Euler, Leonhard, 172 (1736)
Eupalinus, 11 (530)
Evans, William, 264 (1885)
Eyre, Charles, 160 (1700)

Other Events

Earth Day, 372 (1969)
East-West Center for Management, Budapest, 408 (1984)
Ecole des Hautes Etudes Commerciales, 416 (1986)
Economist, 227 (1843)
Edict of Milan, 31 (313)
Edict of Nantes, 116 (1562), 125 (1598), 155 (1685)
Edict of Peking, 198 (1796)
Electricity Supply Act, Britain, 304 (1919)
Elektroprojekt, Yuguslavia, 347 (1951)
El Nino weather, 397 (1982)
Employers' Liability Act, Britain, 259 (1880)
Employment of Children Act, Britain, 283 (1903)
Enfield Arsenal, 235 (1854)
Engineering & Development Group, 359 (1959)
Enterprise Zones, 383 (1976)
Eshunna, 5 (1900)
ESPRIT project, 397 (1982)
Eureka project, 410 (1985)
European Aeronautical Society, 328 (1934)
European Assn. of Personnel Management, 385 (1977)
European Coal and Steel Community, 347 (1951)
European Conference on Personnel

Administration, 358 (1959)
European Common Market, EC, 356 (1957), 361 (1961), 363 (1963), 364 (1964), 366 (1965), 368 (1966), 374 (1970), 375 (1971), 377 (1972), 381 (1975), 388 (1979), 394 (1981), 397 (1982), 406 (1984), 410 (1985), 420 (1987), 421 (1987), 428 (1988), 429 (1988), 430 (1988), 431 (1988), 432 (1988)
European Free Trade Assn., 360 (1960)
European Payments Union, 345 (1950)
European Space Agency, 381 (1975)
European Steel Cartel, 315 (1926)
European Systems Research Institute, 370 (1967)
European Union, 353 (1955)
Eurotunnel, 381 (1975), 394 (1981)
Eurovision, 350 (1953)
Exchequer, England, 57 (1102), 58 (1130), 60 (1154), 61 (1172), 151 (1672), 194 (1788)
Exeter Change, 152 (1676)
Exxon Valdez oil spill, 386 (1978)

F

Business Enterprises

Faberge jewelry, 226 (1842), 264 (1885)
Fairey Aviation, 300 (1915)
Falkland Islands Company, 234 (1851)
Farman aircraft, 312 (1923)
Farrutx fashions, Majorca, 400 (1982)
FCA International, Montreal, 412 (1985)
Federacao das Industrias, Brazil, 351 (1953)
Federation of Employers Assn., Japan, 343 (1948)
Federation of Swedish Industries, 324 (1932), 342 (1948)
Fendi fashions, 321 (1930), 401 (1982)
Ferme generale, France, 169 (1726)
Fermenta, Sweden, 379 (1973), 417 (1986)
Ferrari cars, 320 (1929), 341 (1947), 373 (1969)
Ferre fashions, 380 (1973)
F. Hoffmann-La Roche, 273 (1894), 393 (1980)
F. International, 363 (1962)
Fiat cars, 280 (1900), 291 (1908), 323 (1931), 329 (1936), 356 (1957), 360 (1960), 369 (1966), 371 (1968), 373 (1969), 382 (1975), 384 (1976), 391 (1980), 393 (1980), 404 (1983), 408 (1984), 416 (1986), 419 (1986)
Financial Times, Britain, 267 (1888)
Finisterra Hotel, Baja, California, 350 (1952)
Finch's Grotto Gardens, England, 181 (1760)

Individuals/Families

Labor Organizations

Other Events

G

Business Enterprises

Individuals/Families

Labor Organizations

Other Events

Grand Trunk Canal, Britain, 181 (1761), 183 (1766)
Grandmasters' Assn., 411 (1985)
Great Contract, England, 127 (1603)
"Great Depression", Britain, 253 (1873)
Great Exhibition, London, 233 (1850, 1851)
Great Fire, London, 148 (1666), 149 (1667)
Great Plague, London, 148 (1665)
Great Tea Race, 246 (1866)
Great Wall, China, 13 (400), 17 (250)
Greenpeace, 375 (1971), 397 (1982), 402 (1983)
Guildhall Library, London, 92 (1423)
Gupta Dynasty, India, 31 (320, 379)

H

Business Enterprises

Haberdashers' Company, 95 (1448)
Habitat home furnishings, 365 (1964)
Hachette publishing, 215 (1826), 338 (1945), 414 (1985)
Haig & Haig whisky, 136 (1627)
Hallmark cards, 250 (1870), 407 (1984), 418 (1986)
Hamburg-American Line, 230 (1847), 279 (1900), 297 (1912)
Hamley toys, London, 181 (1760)
Hancock rubber, 227 (1843)
Hang Seng Bank, 326 (1933)
Hanson Group, 342 (1948), 364 (1963), 380 (1973), 396 (1981), 418 (1986), 419 (1986)
Haranbee Savings & Credit, Kenya, 383 (1976)
Hard Rock Cafe, London, 376 (1971)
Hardy Amies clothes, 365 (1964)
Harris Tweed Assn., 383 (1976)
Harrods Department Store, 232 (1849), 268 (1889), 380 (1974), 396 (1981), 399 (1982)
Harry's Bars, 295 (1911)
Hartley jams, 243 (1862)
Hawker-Siddeley aircraft, 281 (1901), 360 (1960)
Hawley Group, 373 (1969)
Haurie bodega, Spain, 187 (1772)
Haut-Brion wine, 146 (1660)
Havana Company, 165 (1714)
Haviland china, 185 (1770), 226 (1842)
Heering liquors, Copenhagen, 210 (1818)
Heidelberger Druckmaschinen, 434 (1988)
Heineken beer, 244 (1864), 375 (1970)
Heinkel aircraft, 327 (1934), 333 (1939)
Henkel soap business, 255 (1876), 345 (1949)

Hennessy Cognac, 165 (1715)
Herend porcelain, Budapest, 223 (1839)
Hermes leather goods, 258 (1879), 387 (1978)
Hertie Waren-und Kaufhaus, 261 (1882)
Hewlett-Packard, U.S., 400 (1982)
Higham advertising, 309 (1920)
Highbury Barn, England, 185 (1770)
Hitachi, 294 (1910), 361 (1961), 393 (1980), 394 (1981), 403 (1983), 408 (1984), 413 (1985), 424 (1987)
Hoare & Company, 151 (1672), 152 (1676)
Hoechst business, 237 (1856), 243 (1863), 285 (1904), 298 (1913), 306 (1919), 315 (1925), 417 (1986)
Holland & Holland gunsmiths, 220 (1835)
Holzschuher Company, 78 (1304)
Home and Colonial stores, 210 (1819), 257 (1878), 281 (1901), 300 (1914), 358 (1959)
Honda vehicles, 330 (1937), 343 (1948), 361 (1961), 365 (1964), 400 (1982), 425 (1987)
Honduras Company, 165 (1714)
Hong Kong Exchange, 373 (1969)
Hongkong & Shanghai Bank, 245 (1865), 268 (1889), 326 (1933), 426 (1987)
Hoover vacuums, 306 (1919)
Horch cars, 301 (1916)
Hotel des Louvre, 236 (1855)
Hotel Pupp, Bohemia, 161 (1701)
House of Bruges, 89 (1399)
House of Konoike, 144 (1656)
Hudson's Bay Company, 150 (1670), 157 (1690), 186 (1772), 210 (1819), 211 (1821), 214 (1825), 229 (1846), 322 (1930), 323 (1931)
Humber cars, 248 (1868)
Hungarian Credit Bank, 432 (1988)
Huntley biscuits, 219 (1832)
Hutchison Whampoa, 242 (1861), 260 (1880), 335 (1942), 357 (1957)
Hyatt Regency Hotel, Singapore, 376 (1971)
Hydrogen Syndicate Corp., Berlin, 306 (1919)
Hyundai Engineering & Construction, 341 (1947), 409 (1984), 421 (1987), 433 (1988)

Individuals/Families

Haavelmo, Trygve, 334 (1941)
Haber, Fritz, 298 (1913)
Hadfield, Robert A., 262 (1883)
Hadid, Mohamed, 392 (1980)
Hadley, John, 171 (1731)
Hadrian, 28 (117)

Hogg, Ralph, 118 (1567)
Hohenlohe, Prince, 273 (1894)
Holden, William, 358 (1959)
Holding, Thomas H., 281 (1901), 290 (1908)
Holkes, John, 178 (1751)
Holloway, Thomas, 222 (1837)
Holmes, Burton, 254 (1875)
Holmes, Frederick, 238 (1857)
Honnecourt, Villard le, 68 (1235)
Hooke, Robert, 144 (1655), 145 (1658, 1660), 149 (1667), 152 (1675, 1676)
Horace, 23 (38)
Horch, August, 292 (1909)
Hornblower, Jonathan, 190 (1781)
Hornly, Frank, 281 (1901)
Horsely, John C., 229 (1846)
Hotzhausen, August Friedrich Wilhelm, 198 (1794)
Houghton, John, 157 (1692)
Houdry, Emile, 314 (1925)
Houqua, 227 (1843)
Howe, William, 187 (1774)
Hoyle, Edmund, 174 (1742)
Hsu, Y.Z., 337 (1945)
Hu, Wan, 103 (1500)
Huan, Shi H., 390 (1979)
Huang-ti, 3 (2700)
Hudson, George, 228 (1845)
Hudson, Henry, 129 (1607), 130 (1610)
Hugenberg, Alfred, 292 (1909), 323 (1931)
Hughes, David, 236 (1855), 257 (1878)
Huishen, 32 (400)
Hull, T.T., 324 (1932)
Hulls, Jonathan, 157 (1690), 172 (1736)
Huntsman, Benjamin, 174 (1740), 176 (1748)
Hussein, Saddam, 392 (1980)
Hutchison, John, 260 (1880)
Huxley, Aldous, 324 (1932)
Huygens, Christiaan, 73 (1270), 137 (1630), 139 (1637), 145 (1658), 148 (1666), 151 (1673), 152 (1675)
Hyatt, J.W., 7 (1200)
Hyde, Robert R., 306 (1919)

Labor Organizations

Harmonization Society, Japan, 307 (1920s)
Histadrut, Israel, 308 (1920), 313 (1924)

Other Events

Halafian Society, 2 (5000)
Halles Centrales, Paris, 233 (1851)
Han Dynasty, 18 (202), 20 (141), 24 (04), 25 (09, 25), 29 (220)

Handelshockschule, Berlin, 287 (1906)
Hanlin Academy, China, 40 (750)
Hanseatic League, 50 (1000), 65 (1201), 69 (1241), 70 (1255), 72 (1265), 76 (1293, 1294), 83 (1347), 84 (1358, 1360, 1361), 85 (1369), 86 (1377), 87 (1381), 88 (1388, 1392), 89 (1400), 90 (1401), 92 (1417), 94 (1438, 1441, 1443), 95 (1450, 1451), 98 (1474), 99 (1478), 100 (1484, 1487), 101 (1494), 108 (1523), 111 (1537), 113 (1545), 115 (1553), 118 (1567), 120 (1579, 125 (1597, 1598), 149 (1669)
Harappans, 4 (2300)
Harvard University, 416 (1986)
Hassuna Society, 2 (6000)
Haymarket Opera House, London, 166 (1718)
Health and Morals Act, Britain, 202 (1802)
Heavenly Clockwork, China, 55 (1086, 1094)
Heidelberg University, 87 (1386)
Hendon airport, London, 293 (1910)
Highway Act, 174 (1741)
Hittites, 5 (2000), 6 (1300)
Hofkammer, Austria, 101 (1493)
Holy Roman Empire, 48 (962), 86 (1370, 1378), 92 (1423), 103 (1500), 107 (1519), 108 (1520), 110 (1530), 112 (1540), 116 (1559), 125 (1731), 201 (1800), 203 (1805)
"Honourable Artillery Company", England, 111 (1537)
Honourable Company of Edinburgh Golfers, 115 (1744)
Honshu-Hokkaido Tunnel, Japan, 364 (1964)
House of Wisdom, Baghdad, 43 (813)
Huguenots, France, 116 (1562), 119 (1572), 125 (1598), 131 (1612), 136 (1629), 143 (1652), 155 (1685), 156 (1687)
Human Rights Act, Canada, 386 (1978)
Humiliation Order, 68 (1239)
Hundred Years War, 81 (1337), 96 (1453)

I

Business Enterprises

Iceberg Transport International, 385 (1977)
IG Farben, 180 (1758), 241 (1861), 243 (1863), 283 (1903), 285 (1904), 315 (1925), 316 (1926), 320 (1929), 323 (1931), 332 (1938), 333 (1939)
Igibi Bank, 10 (575)
IKEA retailing, 335 (1943)
Impa engineering, Sicily, 382 (1975)
Imperial Airways, 305 (1919), 306 (1919), 308

Individuals/Families

Labor Organizations

Other Events

J

Business Enterprises

Jameson whiskey, 190 (1780)

Japan Air Lines, 312 (1923), 348 (1951), 414 (1985), 425 (1987)

Japan Credit Bureau, 362 (1961)

Japan Export Overseas Pearl Producers' Assn., 365 (1964)

Japan Iron & Steel, 281 (1901)

Japan Lines, 425 (1987)

Japan Robot League, 392 (1980)

Jardine & Matheson, 219 (1832), 258 (1879), 409 (1984)

Jersey Standard, 245 (1866), 248 (1869), 326 (1933)

Johannesburg Stock Exchange, 277 (1898)

John Labatt Food Co., 387 (1978)

John Lee Benham & Sons stoves, 213 (1824)

John Lewis retailing, 244 (1864)

Joiners' Company, 119 (1571)

Jonathan's Coffee House, 168 (1722)

Joseph E. Seagram & Sons, 314 (1924), 317 (1927), 335 (1942), 393 (1980)

Jules Porges et Cie, 251 (1871)

Jumberca textile machinery, 343 (1948)

Junkers aircraft, 302 (1917), 306 (1919), 316 (1926), 318 (1928)

Individuals/Families

J. Arthur Rank, 350 (1952)

Jabir, 41 (782)

Jackson, John, 256 (1876)

Jacobi, M.H., 223 (1839)

Jacobi, N.H. von, 220 (1834)

Jacquard, Joseph Marie, 174 (1741), 201 (1801)

Jacques, Elliot, 347 (1951), 383 (1976)

James, Tony, 395 (1981)

James I, England, 127 (1603), 129 (1608), 132 (1615), 133 (1618)

Janszoom, Willem, 128 (1605)

Japy, Fredric, 186 (1770)

Jaray, Paul, 309 (1921)

Jaruzelski, Wojciech, 391 (1980), 394 (1981)

Jay, Antony, 370 (1967)

Jay, John, 99 (1480)

Jeebehoy, Jamsitjee, 192 (1783)

Jefferson, Thomas, 193 (1785)

Jellinek, Emil, 280 (1900)

Jenkenson, Anthony, 116 (1558), 121 (1583)

Jensen, Nickolas, 99 (1480)

Jessup, 193 (1785)

Jesus of Nazareth, 24 (04)

Jevons, W.S., 251 (1871), 257 (1878)

Joffre, Joseph J.C., 294 (1911)

John, England, 64 (1199)

John XXIII, 361 (1961), 362 (1962), 363 (1963)

John of Calabria, 89 (1400)

John of Seville, 58 (1135)

John Paul II, 386 (1978), 394 (1981), 406 (1984)

Johnson, Amy, 321 (1930)

Johnson, Richard, 124 (1592)

Johnson, Samuel, 180 (1759)

Johnston, John L., 254 (1874)

Johnstone, Esme, 396 (1981)

Jolly, Jean Baptiste, 213 (1825)

Jomini, Antoine Henri, 218 (1832)

Jonchere, De la, 167 (1720)

Jones, Inigo, 132 (1615)

Jones, Samuel, 216 (1828)

Jonual, 224 (1841)

Joseph, Maxwell, 343 (1948)

Jovan, William S., 248 (1869)

Julius II, 104 (1503)

Junghans, G., 244 (1864)

Jurgens family, 239 (1858), 252 (1872), 320 (1929)

Justinian the Great, 34 (527, 529), 35 (541, 552, 565)

Ju-Yung, Chung 341 (1947)

Other Events

January Agreement, Finland, 333 (1940)

Japan National Railroad, 252 (1872), 420 (1987)

Japanese Productivity Center, 354 (1955)

Jerusalem Economics Corp., 422 (1987)

Jockey Club, Britain, 177 (1750)

Jockey Club, Hong Kong, 263 (1884)

Joint-Stock Companies Act, Britain, 237 (1856)

Juni-i-Shapur College, Persia, 34 (531)

K

Business Enterprises

Kanebo textiles, Japan, 348 (1951)

Ka Wah Bank, Hong Kong, 410 (1985)

Kawazaki Heavy Industries, 395 (1981), 434 (1987)

Kelly fashions, 393 (1980)

Kennecott Copper, 286 (1905)

Kentucky Fried Chicken, Hong Kong, 382 (1975)

Kentucky Fried Chicken, Japan, 374 (1970)

Kenzo fashions, 377 (1972)

Kia automotive, Korea, 433 (1988)

Kikkoman soy sauce, 146 (1661), 222 (1838), 266 (1887), 303 (1918), 337 (1945)

Killian lager, 244 (1864)

Kinetic Chemical, 323 (1931)

Individuals/Families

Other Events

L

Business Enterprises

Individuals/Families

(1666), 157 (1690, 1691), 197 (1793)
Louis XV, France, 166 (1718), 174 (1743)
Louis XVI, France, 194 (1787)
Louis-Dreyfus, Leopold, 234 (1852)
Lovelock, James, 374 (1970)
Lowe, Thaddeaus, 245 (1865)
Loyola, Ignatius de, 111 (1534)
Luca, G.B., Cardinale di, 151 (1673)
Luciano, Lucky, 339 (1946)
Luderitz, Adolf, 262 (1883)
Ludwig, Daniel, 370 (1967), 399 (1982)
Lully, Jean Baptiste, 151 (1672)
Lumiere brothers, 274 (1895), 275 (1896), 288 (1907)
Luther, Martin, 107 (1517), 108 (1523), 109 (1524)
Luxembourg, Rosa, 272 (1893), 304 (1914)
Lyons, William, 311 (1922)

Labor Organizations

Labor Federation, Japan, 309 (1921)
Labor Front, Germany, 326 (1933), 327 (1934)
Labor Party, Australia, 269 (1890), 284 (1904)
Labor Party, Belgium, 264 (1885)
Labor Party, Britain, 266 (1887), 272 (1893), 279 (1900), 303 (1918), 312 (1924), 336 (1945), 338 (1946), 376 (1971), 394 (1981), 409 (1985), 422 (1987)
Labor Party, Germany, 301 (1917)
Labor Party, Holland, 272 (1894)
Labor Party, New Zealand, 293 (1910)
Labor Party, Norway, 394 (1981)
Labor Union Confederation, France, 305 (1919)
La Fraternidad, Argentina, 265 (1886)
League of Labor Unions, Japan, 308 (1920)
London Carmen, 149 (1668)

Other Events

Labor Charter, Italy, 316 (1916)
Land Enclosures, England, 100 (1488), 105 (1509), 108 (1523), 113 (1549), 133 (1620), 163 (1709), 170 (1730), 181 (1760)
Latin American Free Trade Assn., 361 (1961)
Latin Monetary Union, 244 (1865)
La Varenne, Paris, 382 (1975)
Law of Debts, 33 (500)
Law of Lubeck, 72 (1265)
Law of Magdeburg, 102 (1498)
Law of the Sea Convention, 398 (1982)
Law on Work Collectives, U.S.S.R., 401 (1983)
Laws of Manu, India, 27 (100)
Leadenhall Market, London, 86 (1377), 148

(1666)
League of Cambrai, 105 (1508)
League of Communists, Germany, 230 (1847)
League of Nations, 308 (1920), 327 (1934)
League of Time, U.S.S.R., 303 (1918)
Le Cirque du Soleil, Canada, 403 (1983)
Le Cordon Bleu, 273 (1895)
Leipzig University, 91 (1409)
Leningrad Institute for Social Research, 364 (1963)
Liberation Theology, 371 (1968), 378 (1973), 406 (1984)
Liberty Democratic Party, Japan, 353 (1958)
Licensing Act, England, 158 (1695)
Limited Liability Act, Britain, 242 (1862)
Lisbon University, 75 (1290)
Little Ice Age, 78 (1306)
Livonian Brothers, 64 (1198), 65 (1201)
Lombard League, Italy, 61 (1167)
London Automobile Assn., 286 (1905)
London Business School, 366 (1965)
London Co-Operative Society, 211 (1821)
London Guildhall, 91 (1411)
London Institute of Actuaries, 231 (1848)
London Opera House, 293 (1910)
London Passenger Transport Board, 326 (1833)
London School of Economics, 274 (1895)
London Statistical Society, 220 (1834)
London Symphony Orchestra, 284 (1904)
London Tailors Act, 184 (1768)
Longleat House, Britain, 345 (1949)
L'Opera-Comique, 165 (1715)
Lords of the Salt Privilege, England, 118 (1566)
Lowther Arcade, London, 217 (1830)
Luddites, Britain, 206 (1811, 1812)

M

Business Enterprises

Macintosh waterproofing, 212 (1823), 230 (1847)
Mack Trucks, U.S., 375 (1971)
Mackintosh toffee, 271 (1891)
Macmillan publishing, 247 (1867)
Mafia, 74 (1282), 360 (1960)
Magasin Du Nord, Copenhagen, 328 (1934), 346 (1950)
Maggs dairy business, 251 (1871)
Magna Societas, 87 (1380), 103 (1500
Magna Tavola, 76 (1298)
Mahona Co., 50 (1000)
Main Company of Russian Railways, 238 (1856)
Mainbocher fashions, 321 (1930)
Makers of Playing Cards' Company, 136 (1628)

Mannlicher Arms, 257 (1878)
Manon chocolates, 280 (1900)
Manufacture Royale des Meubles de la
    Couronne, 149 (1667)
Manufacturers' Loan Fund, 169 (1726)
Maquet envelopes, 225 (1841)
Maranhao Company, 154 (1682)
Marbella Club, Costa del Sol, 347 (1950)
Marks and Spencer, 263 (1884), 292 (1909),
    302 (1917), 356 (1956), 435 (1988)
Marriott Hotels, Warsaw, 426 (1987)
Mars confectionery, 324 (1932)
Martell Cognac, 165 (1715)
Martini and Rossi vermouth, 244 (1864)
Marui Company, 360 (1960)
Marylebone Garden, 143 (1650)
Maserati cars, 383 (1976)
Masius advertising, 341 (1947)
Massey-Ferguson, 230 (1847), 288 (1907), 295
    (1911)
Matif Exchange, France, 409 (1984), 418 (1986)
Matsushita business, 303 (1918), 325 (1932),
    350 (1952), 358 (1959), 385 (1977),
    393 (1980), 418 (1986), 419 (1986),
    426 (1987)
Maudslay Motor Company, 282 (1902)
Maus Freres retailing, 322 (1930)
Maxim's Bistro, 273 (1894), 355 (1956), 403
    (1983)
Maypole dairy products, 210 (1819), 300
    (1914), 358 (1959)
Mazda cars, 309 (1920), 382 (1975), 416 (1986)
McCaw Cellular Communications, U.S., 418
    (1986)
McDonald's restaurants, 376 (1971), 384
    (1976), 408 (1984), 411 (1985)
Medellin Cartel, 379 (1973), 381 (1975), 384
    (1976), 396 (1981), 403 (1983), 406
    (1984), 407 (1984), 408 (1984), 417
    (1986), 421 (1987), 425 (1987), 427
    (1988), 428 (1988), 429 (1988), 433
    (1988)
Meecano toys, 281 (1901)
Meissen porcelain, 163 (1708), 167 (1719), 177
    (1751), 184 (1768)
Melitta-Worke Benz & Sohn, 291 (1908)
Melodia records, U.S.S.R., 406 (1984)
Memphis designs, Milan, 395 (1981)
Mendes Junior International, Brazil, 399 (1982)
Mercantile Discount Company, 240 (1859)
Mercers' Company, 88 (1394), 114 (1551)
Merchant Adventurers, 90 (1407), 97 (1467),
    101 (1493), 102 (1497), 103 (1500),
    104 (1505), 105 (1509), 117 (1564),
    131 (1611), 132 (1614)

Merchant Adventures, London, 98 (1475)
Merchant Bank, St. Petersburg, 178 (1754), 193
    (1785)
Merchant Taylor's Company, 80 (1327)
Messerschmitt aircraft, 312 (1923), 327 (1934),
    333 (1939), 413 (1985)
Metal Box, Britain, 320 (1929)
Metra International, 358 (1959)
Mexican Petroleum, 279 (1900)
Mexican Telephone & Telegraph, 283 (1903)
MG cars, 388 (1979)
M. Guggenheim & Sons, 271 (1892), 286
    (1905)
Michelin tires, 219 (1832), 266 (1886), 274
    (1895), 280 (1900), 330 (1937), 345
    (1949), 371 (1968), 425 (1987), 434
    (1988)
Midland Bank, London, 392 (1980), 399 (1982),
    424 (1987), 426 (1987)
Midland Counties Dairy, 278 (1899)
Mikimoto pearls, 290 (1908)
Millie's Wholesale Center, 399 (1982)
Minas Gerais, Brazil, 354 (1955)
Mineral and Battery Works, 117 (1565), 118
    (1568)
Minolta cameras, 319 (1928), 382 (1975), 389
    (1979)
Minton china, 197 (1793)
Mitsubishi Group, 250 (1870), 262 (1882), 269
    (1890s), 302 (1917), 339 (1946), 353
    (1954), 354 (1955), 370 (1967), 373
    (1969), 377 (1972), 379 (1973), 400
    (1982), 412 (1985), 417 (1986), 434
    (1988)
MMG Patricof Group, 385 (1977)
Mobard Odier & Cie, 200 (1798)
Moet champagne, 166 (1716), 174 (1743), 376
    (1971)
Moet-Hennessy, 376 (1971), 379 (1973), 426
    (1987)
Molson brewery, 193 (1786), 231 (1847), 387
    (1978), 397 (1981)
Mombasa-Lake Victoria Railway, 281 (1901)
Mond Nickel, 280 (1900)
Mondi fashions, 382 (1975)
Monte Carlo Casino, 242 (1862), 351 (1953)
Montedison, 368 (1966), 390 (1979)
Moreau confectionery, 262 (1882)
Morning Star paper, 403 (1983)
Morris cars, 296 (1912), 327 (1934), 350 (1952)
Morson pharmaceuticals, 310 (1921)
Moscow Merchants' Society of Mutual Credit,
    249 (1869)
Moscow Woolen Manufacture, 155 (1684)
Moulin Rouge, 267 (1888)

Individuals/Families

(1923), 312 (1924), 314 (1925), 315 (1926)

"Mystery Man With 21 Faces", Japan, 406 (1984)

Labor Organizations

Miners' Assn of Great Britain and Ireland, 224 (1841)

Miners' Federation of Great Britain, 267 (1888)

Musicians' Union, Britain, 309 (1921)

Other Events

Madre de Deus, 124 (1592)

Magic Canal, China, 17 (250)

Maginot Line, France, 372 (1969)

Magna Carta, England, 66 (1215)

Manchu Dynasty, China, 141 (1644, 1645), 294 (1911)

Manufacturing College, Russia, 169 (1724)

Marriage Act, Britain, 178 (1754)

Marshall Plan, 340 (1947), 342 (1948), 361 (1961)

Masonic Grand Lodge, England, 166 (1717)

Maya Society, 9 (600), 19 (150), 32 (397)

Mechanics Institute, London, 212 (1823)

Medical Precision Engineering Institute, Japan, 366 (1965)

Meiji Dynasty, Japan, 247 (1868)

Mepro kibbutz, Israel, 427 (1987)

Mercantilism, 131 (1612), 149 (1669), 150 (1671), 113 (1549), 121 (1581), 212 (1823)

Merchants' Volunteer Corps, China, 307 (1920s)

Metropolitan Streets Act, London, 246 (1867)

Ming Dynasty, China, 85 (1368), 90 (1405), 92 (1420, 1421), 93 (1431, 1432), 94 (1436), 141 (1644)

Ministry of Fisheries, U.S.S.R., 387 (1978)

Ministry of International Trade and Industry, MITI, Japan, 314 (1925), 345 (1950), 355 (1956), 358 (1959), 364 (1964), 365 (1964), 374 (1970), 380 (1974), 383 (1976), 391 (1980), 392 (1980), 395 (1981), 396 (1981), 397 (1982), 398 (1982), 406 (1984), 407 (1984), 415 (1986), 416 (1986), 433 (1988)

Ministry of Labor, Britain, 301 (1917)

Ministry of Science & Technology, Britain, 368 (1966)

Mississippi Bubble, England, 166 (1718)

Mogul Empire, India, 109 (1526), 115 (1556), 129 (1608), 131 (1612), 136 (1628), 162 (1707), 166 (1717)

Mogul v. McGregor, Britain, 268 (1889)

Mohawk Indians, Canada, 430 (1988)

Monroe Doctrine, U.S., 211 (1821)

Montier-en-Der Monastery, 44 (845)

Montmor Academy, France, 145 (1657)

Moscow Eye Clinic, 378 (1973)

Municipal Corporations Act, Britain, 220 (1835)

N

Business Enterprises

Nafta-B, Belgium, 371 (1968)

Nag's Head Tavern, 155 (1683)

Nakajima pachinko machines, 337 (1945)

Namco video games, 381 (1974)

Napier automobiles, 274 (1895)

Narodny Bank, Moscow, 305 (1919)

National Bank, Denmark, 210 (1818)

National Cash Register, 345 (1950)

National Commercial Bank, Saudi Arabia, 353 (1954)

National Confederation of Employers' Organization, Britain, 275 (1896)

National Federation of Associated Employers, Britain, 252 (1872)

National Football Assn., Japan, 373 (1969)

National Football League, Britain, 399 (1982), 425 (1985)

National Hockey League, 293 (1910), 389 (1979)

National Semiconductor, U.S., 376 (1971), 413 (1985)

National Westminster Bank, 390 (1979)

Nestle foods, 246 (1866), 247 (1867), 329 (1936), 330 (1937), 341 (1947), 356 (1957), 384 (1977), 401 (1982), 413 (1985), 418 (1986), 427 (1987), 433 (1988), 434 (1988), 435 (1988)

Neuhaus confectionery, 238 (1857)

New Guinea Company, 264 (1884)

New Lanark mills, 192 (1784)

New Zealand Airline, 336 (1945)

Newcastle Chemical Works, 251 (1871)

Newfoundland Company, 130 (1610)

News Corp., 348 (1951), 350 (1952), 381 (1974), 412 (1985), 414 (1985), 416 (1986), 417 (1986), 419 (1987), 424 (1987), 426 (1987), 433 (1988), 434 (1988)

Niger Company, 278 (1899)

Nike athletic shoes, 385 (1977)

Nikko Hotels, 414 (1985), 425 (1987)

Nikon cameras, 302 (1917)

Individuals/Families

Labor Organizations

National Assn. for Protection of Labor, Britain, 217 (1830s)

National Christian Federation of Trade Unions, 291 (1909)

National Union of Agricultural Workers, Britain, 252 (1872)

National Union of Elementary Teachers, Britain, 250 (1870)

National Union of Mine Workers, Britain, 421 (1987)

National Union of Mine Workers, South Africa, 388 (1979)

National Union of Russian Workers, 257 (1878)

National Union of Working Classes, Britain, 218 (1831)

Netherlands Federation of Trade Unions, 285 (1905)

Norwegian Federation of Labor, 278 (1899)

Other Events

"Napier's Bones", 132 (1617), 148 (1666)

National Automotive Industry Corp., 428 (1988)

National Board for Efficiency, Germany, 309 (1921)

National Cocoa Enterprise, Peru, 361 (1961)

National Copper Corp., Chile, 368 (1966)

National Economic Summit, Australia, 402 (1983)

National Energy Program, Canada, 394 (1984)

National Enterprise Board, Britain, 390 (1980)

National Front, France, 377 (1972)

National Health Service, Nigeria, 388 (1979)

National Health Services, Britain, 342 (1948)

National Institute for Industrial Psychology, London, 310 (1921)

National Oil Corp., Britain, 407 (1984)

National Organization for the Blind, Spain, 416 (1986)

National Social League, Germany, 275 (1896)

National Socialist Party, Germany, 304 (1919), 307 (1920), 308 (1920), 310 (1921), 314 (1925), 323 (1931)

Navigation Acts, England, 87 (1381), 143 (1651), 146 (1660), 231 (1849)

New Zealand Colonization Company, 214 (1825)

New Zealand Company, 223 (1839)

Nizhnyi fair, Russia, 279 (1900)

Nootka Convention, Canada, 195 (1790)

Nordic Council, 353 (1955)

North Atlantic Treaty Organization, NATO, 344 (1949), 352 (1954)

Northern Border Pipeline, Canada, 395 (1981)

Notre Dame Cathedral, 61 (1163)

Nuremberg Trials, Germany, 338 (1946)

O

Business Enterprises

Occidental Petroleum, U.S., 400 (1982), 403 (1983)

Odeon theater, Paris, 199 (1797)

Oki Electric Company, 261 (1881)

Oland brewery, 387 (1978)

Old Curiosity Shop, London, 118 (1567)

Olde Wine Shades, London, 147 (1663)

Olivetti typewriters, 291 (1908), 360 (1960), 387 (1978), 401 (1982), 408 (1984), 417 (1986)

Olympia Press, Paris, 351 (1953)

Olympic Airways, 323 (1931)

Omega timepieces, 273 (1894), 395 (1981)

One Night Stand stores, 404 (1983)

Onnel Mfg., Hong Kong, 425 (1987)

Opel cars, 242 (1862), 320 (1929), 416 (1986)

Orford & Canadian Copper, 263 (1884), 283 (1902)

Orient Express, 256 (1876), 385 (1977), 403 (1983)

Oriental Company, 167 (1719)

Oriental Spinning & Weaving, 239 (1858)

Orrefors glass, Sweden, 174 (1742)

Osaka Spinning, 262 (1882)

Osram lamp business, 306 (1919)

Ostend Company, 171 (1731)

Ostrer Bros. Merchant Bank, 310 (1921)

Otani Hotels, 365 (1964)

Otto-Versand mail order, 346 (1950), 417 (1986)

Overseas Trading Corporation, 186 (1772)

Overseas Trust Bank, Hong Kong, 410 (1985)

Owen Owen retailing, 247 (1867)

Individuals/Families

Oakes, Harry, 295 (1911)

Obrecht, Georg, 119 (1575)

Ochoa, Fabio, 381 (1975)

Octavius, Caius, 23 (30)

Oden, Svante, 370 (1967)

Odoacer, 33 (476)

Offa, 40 (757), 41 (787)

Oersted, Hans C., 210 (1819), 213 (1825), 216 (1829)

Oetker family, 337 (1945)

Ohain, Hans von, 327 (1934)

Ohashi, Wataru, 396 (1981)

Ohligs, W., 238 (1858)

Other Events

P

Business Enterprises

Pilkington glass, 214 (1826), 336 (1944)
Pininfarina cars, 322 (1930)
Pinkerton's Detective Agency, London, 395 (1981)
Pinmakers' Company, 128 (1605)
Pioneer products, Japan, 325 (1932)
Pirelli tires, 252 (1872), 291 (1908), 360 (1960), 376 (1971), 433 (1988)
Pittsburgh Steel, 368 (1966)
Planeta, East Germany, 405 (1983)
Plant Genetic Systems, Belgium, 414 (1986)
Player cigarettes, 243 (1862)
Plaza-Athenee Hotel, Paris, 247 (1867)
Plumbers' Company, 131 (1611)
Plymouth Company, 128 (1605)
Polly Peck business, 400 (1982)
Porsche cars, 326 (1933), 342 (1948), 392 (1980), 396 (1981)
Portsea Inland Mutual Co-operative Society, 343 (1948)
POSCO, South Korea, 372 (1968)
Prada leather, Milan, 298 (1913)
Premier Electric Heaters, 289 (1907)
Price Waterhouse accounting, 241 (1861)
Printemps store, 245 (1865), 427 (1987)
Proprietary Articles Trade Assn., Britain, 275 (1896)
Prudential Mutual Insurance, Britain, 232 (1849)
Prussian Herring Company, 185 (1769)
Publicis advertising, 436 (1988)
Pucci fashions, 340 (1947), 368 (1965)
Puget brokerage, Paris, 435 (1988)
Puig perfumes, 299 (1914)
Puma athletic shoes, 343 (1948)
Punch, 225 (1841)

Individuals/Families

Pachomius, 31 (325)
Pacinotti, A., 240 (1860)
Pacioli, Luca, 101 (1494), 113 (1544)
Packer, Kerry, 348 (1951), 351 (1953), 381 (1974)
Pacquier, Claude Innocent du, 167 (1619)
Padu, Tom, 404 (1983)
Paganini, Niccol, 196 (1791)
Pahlavi, Reza, 334 (1941), 351 (1953), 386 (1978)
Palme, Olof, 398 (1982)
Pamplin, Terence, 366 (1965)
Pang, Clifford, 400 (1982)
Panhard, Rene, 266 (1887)
Pankhurst, Emmeline, 283 (1903)
Pao, Y.K., 354 (1955)
Papandreau, Andreas, 394 (1981)

Papin, Denis, 153 (1679), 157 (1690), 158 (1695), 162 (1707), 163 (1708)
Pappus of Alexandria, 30 (285)
Pareto, Vilfredo, 282 (1902)
Paris, John, 214 (1825)
Parissot, Pierre, 213 (1824)
Parkes, Alexander, 242 (1862)
Parkinson, C. Northcote, 356 (1957)
Parmelle, D.D., 233 (1850)
Parretti, Giancarlo, 426 (1987)
Parsons, Charles, 263 (1884), 276 (1897)
Pascal, Blaise, 140 (1642), 144 (1654, 1655), 146 (1661), 211 (1822)
Pasch, Gustaf, 227 (1844)
Pasteur, Louis, 237 (1856), 245 (1865)
Patteson, John, 197 (1793)
Paul, Lewis, 173 (1738), 176 (1748)
Paul, Vincent de, 138 (1633)
Paxton, Joseph, 233 (1850)
Peabody, George, 222 (1837)
Peale, Robert, 187 (1773), 202 (1802)
Pearson, Weetman, 281 (1901)
Peisistratus, 11 (560, 534)
Pelisson, Gerard, 370 (1967)
Pelletier, Pierre J., 210 (1820)
Penaud, Alphonse, 199 (1796), 255 (1876)
Penteado, Sebastiao Ferraz De Camargo, 332 (1938)
Penty, J.J., 287 (1906)
Percival, Thomas, 130 (1611)
Pereire brothers, 234 (1852)
Perez, Alan Garcia, 410 (1985)
Perez, Carlos Andres, 380 (1974)
Pericles, 12 (461)
Perier, 142 (1648)
Perkin, William, 237 (1856), 247 (1868)
Perky, Henry, 291 (1908)
Peron, Evita, 339 (1946)
Peron, Juan, 335 (1943), 336 (1945), 338 (1946), 353 (1955)
Perrelet, A.L., 188 (1775)
Perrin, Pierre, 149 (1669)
Perry, Ralph B., 315 (1926)
Peter of St. Omer, 73 (1270)
Peter the Great, 121 (1581), 154 (1682), 159 (1696, 1697), 160 (1700), 161 (1703, 1704), 162 (1706), 163 (1708), 164 (1711), 165 (1714, 1716), 166 (1718), 167 (1719), 168 (1722), 169 (1724, 1725)
Peter the Pilgrim, 72 (1269)
Petler brothers, 274 (1895)
Petri, Carl A., 362 (1962)
Petty, William, 137 (1631), 152 (1676), 153 (1679), 154 (1682), 157 (1691)

Labor Organizations

Other Events

Public Health Act, Britain, 231 (1848)
Public Health Act, France, 282 (1902)
Pulp Cartel case, Germany, 276 (1897)
Punic Wars, 16 (264), 17 (218)

Q

Business Enterprises

Qantas airline, 310 (1921), 331 (1937), 336 (1945), 340 (1947), 436 (1988)
Qintex, Australia, 379 (1973)
Quadre financing, 400 (1982)
Quant fashions, 354 (1955), 357 (1958)
Quantum Fund, 408 (1908)
Queen's Company of Players, 122 (1583)
Quelle mail-order, 335 (1942)

Individuals/Families

Quale, David A., 419 (1986)
Quan, Tommy, 400 (1982)
Quesada, Gonzalo Jimenez de, 111 (1536)
Quesnay, Francois, 180 (1758), 184 (1767)
Quetelet, Lambert A.J., 224 (1841)
Quinn, Thomas F., 434 (1988)

R

Business Enterprises

Radio Caroline, 365 (1964), 369 (1967)
Radio Normandy, 321 (1930)
Raffles Hotel, 245 (1865), 300 (1915)
Raleigh Cycle Company, 259 (1880s)
Railway Clearing House, 226 (1842)
Rank Organization, 310 (1921), 314 (1925), 328 (1934), 341 (1947), 354 (1952)
Recruit business, Japan, 409 (1984)
Redcoat Cargo Airlines, 392 (1980)
Redouly & Cie, 222 (1838)
Reebok shoes, 274 (1895)
Reed & Sons outfitters, 280 (1900)
Reed International, 284 (1903), 417 (1986)
Regine's disco club, Paris, 381 (1974)
Remy Martin Cognac, 367 (1965)
Renault cars, 277 (1898), 282 (1902), 285 (1904), 293 (1910), 296 (1912), 336 (1945), 364 (1963), 387 (1978), 410 (1985), 414 (1986)
Reuters news agency, 220 (1835), 232 (1849), 298 (1913), 365 (1964), 379 (1973)
Rhone-Poulenc chemicals, 306 (1919), 416 (1986)
Ricoh Electronics, Japan, 379 (1973)

Rio Tinto mining, RT2, 169 (1725), 253 (1873), 286 (1905), 416 (1986), 433 (1988)
Ritz video stores, 419 (1986)
Ritz Hotel, London, 285 (1904)
Ritz Hotel, Paris, 247 (1867), 277 (1898), 390 (1979)
Robertson marmalades, 238 (1857)
Roger & Gallet perfumes, 204 (1806)
Rolex timepieces, 285 (1904), 299 (1914)
Rolling Stones, 363 (1962)
Rolls-Royce business, 284 (1904), 354 (1955), 374 (1970), 376 (1971)
Roneo duplicating, 278 (1899)
Rootes Group, 302 (1917), 331 (1937)
Rorer pharmaceuticals, 416 (1986)
Rowntree confectionery, 242 (1862) 249 (1869), 268 (1889), 276 (1897), 305 (1919), 308 (1920), 310 (1921), 413 (1985), 433 (1988)
Royal Africa Company, 146 (1660), 147 (1663), 148 (1665), 151 (1672), 159 (1696), 165 (1713)
Royal Bagnio, 153 (1679)
Royal Bank of Canada, 244 (1864)
Royal Bank of Scotland, 158 (1695), 433 (1988)
Royal Circus, London, 191 (1782)
Royal Copenhagen porcelain, 188 (1775)
Royal Dutch Airline, KLM, 307 (1919), 353 (1954), 377 (1972), 436 (1988)
Royal Dutch Shell, 201 (1800), 245 (1866), 248 (1869), 250 (1870), 269 (1890), 282 (1901), 290 (1907), 296 (1912), 367 (1965), 368 (1966), 396 (1981)
Royal Exchange, London, 118 (1566)
Royal Mail Shipping Company, 278 (1900s)
Royal Monceau Hotel, Paris, 318 (1928)
Royal Netherlands Yeast and Spirits, 250 (1870), 278 (1900s)
Royal Niger Company, 265 (1886)
Royal Stafford china, 228 (1845)
Royal Vienna porcelain, 167 (1719)
Royal Worcester porcelain, 178 (1751), 186 (1770)
Rubinstein cosmetics, 282 (1902), 289 (1907)
Ruiz Casa, 114 (1550)
Runtinger Company, 87 (1383)
Russian-American Fur Company, 192 (1784), 195 (1790), 203 (1805)

Individuals/Families

Radisson, Pierre, 144 (1654), 150 (1670)
Raffles, Thomas, 198 (1795)
Rahere, 58 (1133)
Raiffeisen, F.W., 232 (1849)

Rutherford, Ernest, 274 (1895)
Ruysbroecke, William, 70 (1253)

Labor Organizations

Rural Solidarity, Poland, 394 (1981)

Other Events

Railway Act, Britain, 309 (1921)
Recadias agency, Venezuela, 402 (1983)
Red Cross, 242 (1862)
Red Flag Act, Britain, 244 (1865)
Re'formatori, Siena, 87 (1385)
Regulation Act, Britain, 187 (1773)
Reign of Terror, Paris, 197 (1793)
Renaissance, 78 (1306)
Reparation Recovery Act, Germany, 309 (1921)
Rhenish League, 70 (1254)
Rhine River pollution, 415 (1986)
Rialto Bridge, Venice, 123 (1588)
Rice Institute, Philippines, 359 (1960)
Riga Polytechnical Institute, 285 (1905)
Rochdale Society of Equitable Pioneers, 228 (1844)
Rome University, 77 (1303)
Royal Academy of Music, France, 151 (1672)
Royal Institution, England, 200 (1799)
Royal Iron Works, Prussia, 178 (1753)
Royal Laboratory, England, 158 (1694)
Royal Observatory, England, 152 (1675)
Royal Ordinance of Labourers, England, 83 (1349)
Royal Society, England, 120 (1579), 133 (1620), 141 (1645), 146 (1660), 149 (1667), 163 (1708), 180 (1758), 206 (1811), 218 (1831)
Royal Warehouse, Prussia, 173 (1740)
Russian Academy of Science, 169 (1725)
Ryukoku University, Japan, 139 (1639)

S

Business Enterprises

S.A. Matarazzo Reunidas, 296 (1912)
Saab-Scandia, 282 (1901), 325 (1932), 330 (1937), 409 (1984)
Saatchi & Saatchi advertising, 375 (1970), 408 (1984), 419 (1986), 433 (1988)
Sabena airline, 308 (1920), 314 (1925), 377 (1972), 436 (1988)
Sacilor Steel, France, 386 (1978)
Saddlers' Company, 89 (1395)
Sadler Wells Company, 153 (1680)

Sadler Wells Theater, 296 (1912)
Safilo eyeglass frames, Italy, 425 (1987)
Sainsbury stores, 238 (1858)
Salters, 88 (1394)
Samhura Company, South Korea, 387 (1978)
Samininati firm, 143 (1652)
Sammi Steel, 409 (1984)
Samsung Group, Korea, 329 (1936), 341 (1947), 389 (1979), 409 (1984)
Sandoz business, 265 (1886)
Sanki Engineering, Japan, 389 (1979)
Sanko steamship line, Japan, 328 (1934)
San Miguel beer, Philippines, 270 (1890)
Sanofi business, 379 (1973)
Sant' Ambrogio Bank, 124 (1593)
Santo Domingo Company, 165 (1714)
Sanwa Bank, Japan, 379 (1973), 418 (1986), 434 (1988)
Sanyo electrical business, 346 (1950)
Savoy Hotel, London, 268 (1889)
SCADTA airline, 309 (1921)
Scandinavia Airline System, SAS, 307 (1920), 339 (1946), 349 (1952), 353 (1954), 426 (1987), 430 (1988), 433 (1988), 434 (1988)
Schaaffhausensche Bankverin, 231 (1848)
Schlumberger oil business, 305 (1919), 408 (1989)
Schneider et Cie, 248 (1868)
Schroders bank, 203 (1804), 210 (1818)
Schweppes, 192 (1783), 213 (1824), 349 (1952), 419 (1986)
Scottish Africa Company, 158 (1694)
Seafarers Guild, Seville, 131 (1613)
Sears Roebuck, 340 (1947)
Seat cars, Spain, 346 (1950)
Seibu Saison Group, 343 (1948), 365 (1964), 379 (1973), 434 (1988), 435 (1988)
Seiko timepieces, 261 (1881), 365 (1964), 371 (1968), 400 (1982)
Selenia, 360 (1960)
Selfridge & Company, 287 (1906), 308 (1920)
Semilab, 401 (1982)
Senegal Company, 136 (1628)
Servico Nacional de Aprendizagem Commercial, Brazil, 340 (1947)
Servico Nacional de Aprendizagem Industrial, Brazil, 334 (1941)
7-Eleven stores, Japan, 380 (1973), 425 (1987)
Sevres porcelain, 173 (1738), 184 (1768)
Shakespeare & Company, 305 (1919)
Shanghai Electricity Company, 261 (1882)
Sharp business, Japan, 297 (1912), 392 (1980)
S.H. Benson advertising, 357 (1958)
Shell Transport & Trading, 201 (1800), 258

Individuals/Families

Shao, Liu, 29 (240)
Shaw, George Bernard, 263 (1884)
Shayne, Peter, 376 (1971)
Sheldon, Oliver, 308 (1920), 312 (1923)
Sheng, Bi, 52 (1041)
Shepherd, Alan, 361 (1961)
Sheridan, Richard Brinsley, 189 (1779)
Sherwood, James, 385 (1977)
Shibusawa, Eiichi, 253 (1873), 254 (1874)
Shih, Stan, 382 (1975)
Shih, Tu, 30 (290)
Shino, Rinj, 292 (1909)
Shippam, Charles, 234 (1852)
Shirley, Steve, 363 (1962)
Shoman, Abdul Majeed, 320 (1929)
Shultz, J.F.E., 243 (1864)
Shun, China, 4 (2255)
Siemens family, 225 (1842), 226 (1842), 227
    (1844), 230 (1847), 240 (1860s), 246
    (1866), 261 (1882)
Siddeley, John D., 281 (1901)
Sieff, Israel M., 292 (1909)
Sikorsky, Igor, 288 (1907), 297 (1913)
Simis, Konstantin, 398 (1982)
Simms, Frederick R., 268 (1889)
Sinclair, Michael J., 375 (1970)
Sindona, Michele, 357 (1958), 372 (1969), 376
    (1971)
Singer, A.R.E., 374 (1970)
Singh, Karan, 400 (1982)
Skaladenowsky brothers, 274 (1895)
Skase, Chris, 379 (1973)
Smanton, John, 178 (1754), 181 (1761), 183
    (1765), 186 (1771)
Smiles, Samuel, 239 (1859)
Smith, Adam, 189 (1776)
Smith, Francis Pettit, 222 (1838)
Smith, Frank, 299 (1914)
Smith, Frederick, 218 (1832)
Smith, G.A., 290 (1908)
Smith, James, 196 (1792)
Smith, Thomas, 113 (1549), 122 (1583)
Smith, W.H., 196 (1792)
Smith, William, 243 (1863)
Smuts, Jan Christian, 315 (1926)
Solaro, Ascanio, 229 (1847)
Solinus, Gaius Julius, 28 (200)
Solon, 10 (594)
Sombert, Werner, 282 (1902), 287 (1906),
    298 (1913), 300 (1915)
Somerset, Edward, 147 (1663)
Sommelier, Germain, 241 (1861)
Soranzo brothers, 91 (1410)
Sorby, Henry C., 243 (1863)
Sorel, Georges, 290 (1908)

Soros, George, 408 (1984), 420 (1987)
Sorrell, Martin, 413 (1985)
Soto, Hernando de, 388 (1979)
Soubirous, Bernadette, 238 (1858)
Sousa, Maurico de, 357 (1958)
Spartacus, 22 (73)
Spencer, Herbert, 233 (1850), 240 (1859), 253
    (1873)
Spencer, Oswald, 322 (1931)
Spengler, Oswald, 303 (1918)
Spilsbury, John, 177 (1750)
Spiltler, Adolph, 276 (1897)
Spratt, James, 241 (1860)
Ssu-Mo, Sun, 37 (650)
St. Augustine, 35 (597)
St. Clement, 27 (92)
St. Fergil, 40 (748)
Staite, W.E., 230 (1847)
Stalker, G.M., 362 (1961)
Stalin, Joseph, 309 (1921), 311 (1923), 312
    (1924), 313 (1924), 316 (1927), 321
    (1930), 322 (1931), 324 (1932), 327
    (1934)
Stearn, W.H., 283 (1903)
Steele, Richard, 163 (1709)
Steiff, Margarete, 259 (1880)
Stein, Baron Von, 173 (1740)
Steinmetz, Charles P., 292 (1910)
Stel, Simon van der, 155 (1685)
Stephens, Henry, 218 (1832)
Stephenson, George, 207 (1813, 1814), 211
    (1821), 212 (1822), 230 (1847)
Stephenson, Robert, 216 (1828)
Stephenson, William, 276 (1897), 292 (1909)
Sterns, Abel, 215 (1827)
Steuart, James, 184 (1767)
Stirling, Robert, 208 (1816)
Stinnes, Hugo, 272 (1893), 303 (1918), 309
    (1920)
Stoddard, J.L., 254 (1875)
Stohl, Oswald, 260 (1880)
Stoke, Roger de, 79 (1321)
Stolt-Nielsen, Jacob, 358 (1959)
Strafford, William, 121 (1581)
Strassman, Fritz, 331 (1938)
Strauss, Johann, 246 (1867)
Street, John, 197 (1793)
Stringer, Axel, 352 (1948)
Strutt, Jedediah, 123 (1589), 180 (1758)
Stumpe, W., 112 (1543)
Sturtevant, Simon, 131 (1612)
Sugar, Alan, 371 (1968)
Suk-Won, Kim, 382 (1975)
Suleyman the Magnificent, 108 (1520)
Sulieman, 44 (840, 851)

Sully, Duke of, 125 (1597)
Sumichrast, Michael, 344 (1948)
Sung, Su, 55 (1086)
Sung-Hak, Baik, 359 (1959)
Sussmilch, Johann, 181 (1761)
Suter, Moritz, 382 (1975)
Sutter, John, 223 (1839)
Sutton, John, 204 (1806)
Sutton, Thomas, 119 (1570)
Suud, Khaled Abu, 380 (1974)
Swan, Joseph, 226 (1842), 252 (1872), 262 (1883)
Swarttouw, Frans, 390 (1979)
Swing, Captain, 217 (1830s)
Sy Cip, Washington, 339 (1946)
Szekely, Alex, 333 (1940)

Labor Organizations

Scandinavian Labor Congress, 265 (1886)
Society of Musicians, London, 261 (1882)
Solidarity, Poland, 391 (1980), 394 (1981), 397 (1982), 402 (1983), 414 (1986), 415 (1986)
Steel Labor Union, Japan, 276 (1897)

Other Events

Safeguarding of Industries Act, Britain, 309 (1921)
Sailors' Home, Liverpool, 229 (1846)
Saint-Sauduer Monastery, 49 (987)
Salerno University, 44 (850)
Salvation Army, 245 (1865)
Salzburg Music Festival, 301 (1917)
Sankey Canal, Britain, 179 (1755)
Santa Maria Technical University, Chile, 324 (1932)
Sassanid Empire, 29 (226)
Saudi Arabian Monetary Agency, 349 (1952)
Saville Row, London, 230 (1847)
Schemmitz Mining Academy, 172 (1733)
Schonbrunn Palace, Austria, 158 (1696)
School of Bridges and Highways, France, 176 (1747)
Scottish Convention, 125 (1599)
Sea Beggars, Holland, 118 (1566), 127 (1602)
Second International Workingmen's Assn., 268 (1889)
Seven Years War, 179 (1756)
"Seventeen Towns", 65 (1200)
Seveso disaster, Italy, 383 (1976)
Shang Dynasty, China, 5 (1766)
Shannon Airport, 340 (1947), 341 (1947)
Shenzhen Securities, China, 421 (1987)

Shining Path guerillas, Peru, 391 (1980), 410 (1985)
Siberia Pipeline, 397 (1982), 398 (1982), 405 (1982)
Silk Road, 3 (2700), 20 (138, 121), 21 (100), 32 (400), 36 (600), 39 (712)
Singapore Investment Corp., 394 (1981)
Six Day War, 369 (1967)
Smithfield Market, London, 62 (1173)
Social Darwinism, 253 (1873)
Social Democratic Assn., 257 (1878)
Social Democratic Party, Finland, 283 (1903)
Social-Democratic Party, Poland, 272 (1893)
Social Democratic Party, Romania, 293 (1910)
Social Democratic Party, Russia, 277 (1898), 283 (1903)
Social Democrat Party, Sweden, 267 (1888), 268 (1889)
Socialist League, Britain, 263 (1884)
Society for Regulation of Street Music, London, 259 (1880)
Society for Scientific Management in Agriculture, Finland, 313 (1924)
Society for the Encouragement of Arts Manufacturers and Commerce, Britain, 178 (1754)
Society of Blackheath Golfers, 129 (1608)
Society of Friends, England, 142 (1648)
Society of Mines, England, 118 (1568)
Society of St. Andrews Golfers, 114 (1552), 178 (1754), 240 (1860)
Society of St. Vincent de Paul, Paris, 219 (1833)
Solvay process, 241 (1861), 251 (1871), 253 (1873), 299 (1914), 316 (1926), 332 (1938)
South American Common Market, 372 (1969)
South Sea Bubble, 164 (1711), 167 (1720), 168 (1722)
Southwark Fair, England, 90 (1401)
Sovintersport, Moscow, 420 (1987)
Spa, Belgium, 103 (1500)
Spanish Armada, 123 (1588)
Special Economic Zones, China, 387 (1979), 391 (1980), 394 (1981), 428 (1988)
Speenhamland Law, Britain, 198 (1795)
Spitalfields Act, Britain, 187 (1773)
Spitalfields Market, London, 154 (1682)
Springfield Armory, U.S., 235 (1854)
St. Andrews University, 91 (1411)
St. Denis Abbey, France, 36 (600)
St. Gaul Monastery, 34 (520), 43 (820), 46 (890)
St. James Club, London, 240 (1859)
St. Lawrence Seaway, 358 (1959)

Urwick, Lyndall F., 308 (1920), 317 (1927), 318 (1928), 326 (1933), 328 (1934)

Labor Organizations

Union of Diamond Cutters, 246 (1866)

Other Events

Ubaidians, 2 (4000)
Ukraina Kolkhoz collective farm, 435 (1988)
United Nations, 338 (1946), 360 (1960), 361 (1961), 369 (1967), 376 (1971), 384 (1977), 415 (1986), 430 (1988)
University of Bologna, 119 (1572)
University of Copenhagen, 99 (1479)
University of Edinburgh, 121 (1582), 236 (1855)
University of Leyden, 119 (1575)
University of Oxford, 61 (1167), 70 (1250), 72 (1264)
University of Padua, 67 (1222)
University of Paris, 53 (1070), 59 (1150), 66 (1210), 68 (1231), 81 (1336)
University of Sydney, 233 (1850)

V

Business Enterprises

Vacheron & Constantin, 216 (1827)
Valentino fashions, 360 (1960)
Van den Burgh family, 239 (1858) 252, (1870), 281 (1901), 320 (1929)
Van Doorne brothers, 318 (1928), 408 (1984)
VARIG airline, 317 (1927)
Vauxhall cars, 238 (1857), 308 (1920), 322 (1930), 416 (1986)
Vauxhall Gardens, London, 146 (1660)
Veleda S.A., 385 (1977)
Vendex International, 427 (1987)
Venice Company, 124 (1592)
Vespa motor scooters, 339 (1946)
Vickers armaments, 243 (1863), 267 (1888), 287 (1906), 297 (1913), 317 (1927), 354 (1955), 376 (1971)
Victor Company, Japan, 413 (1985)
Victoria Wine Company, 245 (1865)
Vienna Bourse, 178 (1753)
Villa d'Este, 253 (1873)
Ville de Paris, 228 (1844)
Vintners' Company, 77 (1302)
Vionnet fashions, 304 (1918)
Virgin Atlantic Airline, 373 (1969), 407 (1984)
Virgin Records, 373 (1969)

Virginia Company, 128 (1605), 133 (1619), 135 (1624)
Vittel Mineral Water Company, 373 (1969)
Volkswagen, 230 (1847), 292 (1909), 326 (1933), 332 (1938), 345 (1949), 346 (1950), 358 (1959), 364 (1964), 384 (1976), 395 (1981), 413 (1985), 422 (1987), 423 (1987), 424 (1987), 429 (1988)
Volvo, 373 (1969), 376 (1971), 417 (1986)
Vuitton leather, 236 (1854), 291 (1908), 426 (1987)

Individuals/Families

Vadasz, Peter, 403 (1983
Valazquez, Diego, 104 (1504), 105 (1508)
Vancouver, George, 196 (1791, 1792)
Vanderbilt Cornelius, 237 (1856)
Varennes, Pierre de Gaultier, 170 (1727)
Varro, Marcus Terentius, 23 (36)
Vaucanson, Jacques de, 169 (1725), 173 (1738), 174 (1741), 185 (1770), 201 (1801)
Vaughan, Philip, 176 (1749)
Vaughn, Roland, 130 (1610)
Vazquez-Rana, Mario, 412 (1985)
Veblen, Thorstein, 284 (1904)
Veening, Eite, 426 (1987)
Vega, Joseph de la, 156 (1688)
Venerable Bede, 39 (731)
Venturi, Giovanni Battista, 199 (1797)
Vereniging family, 275 (1896)
Vergerio, Pier Paolo, 90 (1404)
Vernier, P., 137 (1631)
Verrazano, Giovanni de, 109 (1524)
Vespucci, Amerigo, 101 (1492), 102 (1497), 103 (1499), 104 (1501, 1502, 1504), 105 (1508)
Vestey, Samuel, 256 (1876)
Vico, Giambattista, 169 (1725)
Viegerano, Guido da, 81 (1335)
Vierkotter, Paul, 314 (1925)
Vignon, Michel, 418 (1986)
Villalobos, Jose Manuel Berruecos, 421 (1987)
Villani, Giovanni, 77 (1300)
Vinci, Leonardo da, 100 (1494), 101 (1492), 102 (1494, 1496), 103 (1500), 108 (1519), 137 (1630), 185 (1769)
Vinogradov, Oleg, 385 (1977)
Vinturinus, Georg, 190 (1780)
Viraporn, Pichet, 387 (1978)
Visunsin, Admiral, 125 (1596)
Vitellius, 26 (69)
Vitruvius, Marius, 21 (90)
Vivaldi brothers, 75 (1291)

Labor Organizations

Other Events

Workman's Combination Bill, Britain, 200 (1799)
Workmen's Compensation Act, Britain, 276 (1897)
Works Constitution Act, West Germany, 349 (1952)
World War I, 298 (1914), 303 (1918)
World War II, 332 (1939), 336 (1945)
Wu Dynasty, China, 29 (222)

X

Individuals/Families

Xenophon, 13 (400)
Xerxes, 12 (480)
Xiaoping, Deng, 386 (1978), 388 (1979)
Xinsheng, Bu, 389 (1979), 408 (1984)

Y

Business Enterprises

Yakuza, 126 (1600)
Yamaha business, 264 (1885)
Yamazaki Machinery Works, 395 (1981), 403 (1983)
Yanmar Agricultural Equipment Co., 402 (1983)
Yasuda insurance, 260 (1880)
Yawata Works, Japan, 281 (1901), 371 (1968)
Yeovil Motor Car & Cycle Co., 274 (1895)
Yodoya merchant house, 162 (1705)
Yokohama Specie Bank, 260 (1880)
Yujiang Carved Wood Factory, 377 (1972)

Individuals/Families

Yachen, Wang, 420 (1987)
Yale, Elihu, 156 (1687), 168 (1721)
Yamani, Ahmed Zaki, 363 (1962)
Yao, 4 (2350)
Yat-sen, Sun, 141 (1644), 285 (1905), 294 (1911), 313 (1924)
Yen, Jimmy, 359 (1960)
Yerex, Lowell, 324 (1932)
Yergin, Daniel, 397 (1982)
Yew, Lee Kuan, 366 (1965)
Ympyrn, Jan, 113 (1544)
Yorinao, Hosokawa, 198 (1796)
Young, James, 224 (1840), 231 (1848)
Yu, Ko, 24 (01)
Yuan-Hung, Li, 39 (721)
Yunus, Muhammad, 383 (1976)

Other Events

Yom Kippur War, 378 (1973)
Young Men's Christian Assn., 227 (1844)

Z

Business Enterprises

Zaitsev fashions, 395 (1981), 424 (1987)
Zeiss optical instruments, 229 (1846), 267 (1888), 286 (1905)
Zeppelin airships, 254 (1874), 277 (1898), 279 (1900), 287 (1906), 290 (1908), 291 (1909), 298 (1913), 302 (1917), 309 (1921), 318 (1928), 319 (1929), 324 (1932)

Individuals/Families

Zaccaria, Benedetto, 69 (1240)
Zadeh, Lofti, 393 (1980)
Zaharoff, Basil, 261 (1881)
Zamorensis, Rodericus, 99 (1475)
Zander, Jonas G.W., 244 (1865)
Zede, G., 266 (1887)
Zeno, 15 (301)
Zeno, Nicolo, 116 (1558)
Zenobia of Palmyra, 29 (260)
Zhivkov, Todor, 352 (1954)
Zias, Dinis, 95 (1445)
Zimmerman, M.M., 346 (1950)
Zosimas of Alexandria, 30 (300)
Zouch, Edward, 130 (1611)
Zuiken, Kawamura, 133 (1618)
Zuse, Konrad, 322 (1931), 328 (1935)
Zwan, Arie Van der, 427 (1987)
Zwingli, Ulrich, 108 (1519), 109 (1525)

Other Events

Zollverein, Germany, 210 (1819), 238 (1857), 244 (1865

Index of Places

406 (1984)

Israel, 7 (1000), 66 (1215), 75 (1290), 78 (1306), 83 (1348), 87 (1382), 92 (1420), 101 (1492), 102 (1494), 130 (1610), 206 (1812), 293 (1910), 336 (1945), 342 (1948), 353 (1955), 355 (1956), 369 (1967), 370 (1967), 390 (1980), 403 (1983), 414 (1986), 432 (1988)

Istanbul, see also Constantinople

Italy, 7 (800), 234 (1852), 277 (1898), 311 (1922), 314 (1925), 316 (1927), 328 (1935), 335 (1943), 345 (1950), 381 (1975), 386 (1978), 402 (1983)

J

Jamaica, 105 (1509), 138 (1635), 144 (1655), 228 (1845), 363 (1962), 365 (1964), 393 (1980)

Japan, 17 (250), 38 (710), 42 (794), 46 (894), 60 (1156), 63 (1185), 81 (1336), 97 (1467), 112 (1542), 119 (1570, 1573), 120 (1576), 121 (1582, 1583), 122 (1585), 125 (1598), 126 (1599, 1600, 1601), 127 (1602), 130 (1609), 132 (1616), 136 (1672), 138 (1633), 139 (1636, 1639), 156 (1688), 169 (1726), 206 (1811), 207 (1813), 224 (1841), 227 (1844), 235 (1854), 237 (1856), 246 (1867), 247 (1868), 249 (1869, 1870), 251 (1871), 259 (1880s), 269 (1890s, 1890), 275 (1896), 276 (1897), 277 (1898), 279 (1900), 300 (1915, 1916), 321 (1930), 324 (1932), 330 (1937), 334 (1941), 337 (1945), 397 (1982), 398 (1982), 403 (1983), 407 (1984), 409 (1985), 415 (1986), 420 (1987), 428 (1988)

Java, Indonesia, 106 (1511), 124 (1595), 125 (1597), 136 (1628), 155 (1684)

Jerico, 1 (8000)

Jerusalem, Israel, 7 (1000), 37 (633)

K

K'ai-feng, China, 48 (960)

Kenya, 275 (1896), 364 (1963), 384 (1977), 398 (1982), 432 (1988)

Kiev, Russia, 42 (800), 46 (882), 49 (988), 57 (1113)

Kilwa, Congo, 49 (976), 81 (1331), 104 (1505)

Kiribati Islands, 409 (1985)

Konigsberg, Germany, 70 (1255)

Korea (North, South), 80 (1329), 81 (1337), 86 (1370), 88 (1392), 90 (1403), 255 (1876), 293 (1910), 345 (1950), 351 (1953), 368 (1966), 398 (1982), 407 (1984), 416 (1986), 420 (1987), 422 (1987), 432 (1988)

Kroton, Italy, 10 (588)

Kuwait, 339 (1946), 361 (1961), 380 (1974), 381 (1975), 392 (1980), 426 (1987), 433 (1988)

Kyoto, Japan, 42 (794), 127 (1601), 134 (1622)

L

Latvia, 305 (1919), 333 (1940)

Lazise, Italy, 49 (983)

Lebanon, 315 (1926), 377 (1972), 382 (1975)

Leeds, England, 66 (1207)

Leipzig, Germany, 80 (1328), 218 (1831), 264 (1885)

Leon, France, 51 (1020)

Levant, 7 (1200), 86 (1378), see also Lebanon

Leyden, Holland, 140 (1640), 147 (1663), 160 (1701)

Liberia, 420 (1987)

Libya, 358 (1959), 372 (1969), 374 (1970), 375 (1971), 376 (1971), 377 (1972), 378 (1973), 380 (1974), 384 (1976), 389 (1979)

Liechtenstein, 327 (1934), 331 (1938)

Liege, Belgium, 65 (1200), 83 (1348), 87 (1384), 95 (1450), 100 (1487), 101 (1492), 174 (1740), 189 (1777)

Lisbon, Portugal, 59 (1147), 179 (1755)

Lithuania, 305 (1919), 333 (1940)

Liverpool, England, 64 (1199), 227 (1844), 230 (1847)

London, England, 26 (43), 54 (1079), 56 (1100), 58 (1132), 62 (1180), 63 (1191), 79 (1318), 84 (1358), 91 (1416), 121 (1580), 148 (1665, 1666), 155 (1684), 158 (1694, 182 (1764), 183 (1766), 190 (1781), 192 (1784), 199 (1798), 204 (1806), 206 (1812, 1813), 210 (1820), 212 (1823), 216 (1829), 217 (1830), 219 (1833), 221 (1837), 222 (1839), 228 (1845), 241 (1861), 242 (1862), 245 (1865), 254 (1875), 257 (1878), 263 (1884), 275 (1897), 293 (1910), 328 (1935), 357 (1958), 394 (1981)

Louvain, Belgium, 99 (1477)

Lubeck, Germany, 59 (1143), 68 (1230), 69 (1241), 70 (1252, 1253), 71 (1259), 72 (1265), 74 (1282), 76 (1293, 1298)

Lucca, Italy, 57 (1111), 89 (1400)

Index of Subjects

Arms Industry

Automotive Industry

Spain, 346 (1950)
Sweden, 282 (1901), 370 (1967), 376 (1971)
Switzerland, 193 (1785)
Taiwan, 390 (1979)
United States, 274 (1895)
U.S.S.R., 311 (1922), 318 (1928), 319 (1929),
321 (1930), 324 (1932), 375 (1971),
415 (1986)

Aviation/Space Industry

Argentina, 430 (1988)
Australia, 273 (1894), 310 (1921), 318 (1928),
321 (1930), 327 (1934), 340 (1947),
422 (1987)
Austria, 267 (1888), 277 (1898)
Belgium, 308 (1920), 314 (1925), 351 (1953)
Brazil, 317 (1927), 372 (1969)
Canada, 305 (1919), 316 (1927), 332 (1939),
334 (1942), 336 (1944), 345 (1950),
422 (1987), 423 (1987)
China, 103 (1500), 374 (1970), 430 (1988)
Colombia, 309 (1921)
Cuba, 358 (1959)
Czechoslovakia, 313 (1924)
Denmark, 295 (1912), 307 (1920), 331 (1938),
339 (1946), 353 (1954), 432 (1988),
433 (1988)
Dubai, 407 (1984)
Europe, 150 (1670), 226 (1842), 244 (1864),
249 (1870s), 296 (1912), 320 (1929),
322 (1931), 391 (1980), 423 (1987)
Flanders, 80 (1325)
France, 143 (1650), 153 (1678), 184 (1768),
190 (1781), 191, 1783), 192 (1784),
193 (1785), 197 (1794), 234 (1852),
237 (1856), 238 (1857), 249 (1870),
255 (1876), 262 (1883), 263 (1884),
265 (1886), 269 (1890s), 276 (1897),
277 (1898), 282 (1902), 286 (1905),
287 (1906), 288 (1907), 289 (1907),
290 (1908), 291 (1909), 292 (1909),
293 (1910), 295 (1912), 296 (1912),
298 (1913), 303 (1918), 304 (1918),
312 (1923), 315 (1925), 319 (1929),
321 (1930), 326 (1933), 361 (1961),
362 (1962), 366 (1965), 383 (1976),
414 (1986), 426 (1988)
Gabon, 380 (1974)
Germany, 90 (1405), 108 (1522), 182 (1764),
252 (1872), 254 (1874), 266 (1887),
270 (1891), 274 (1895), 276 (1897),
277 (1898), 287 (1906), 290 (1908),
291 (1909), 292 (1909), 293 (1910),
298 (1913), 302 (1917), 302 (1918),

304 (1919), 310 (1921), 312 (1923),
313 (1924), 315 (1926), 317 (1927),
318 (1928), 319 (1929), 320 (1929),
321 (1930), 322 (1931), 324 (1932),
327 (1934), 329 (1936), 330 (1937),
333 (1939), 336 (1944), 342 (1948),
373 (1969)
Great Britain, 72 (1268), 142 (1648), 144
(1655), 192 (1784), 193 (1785), 198
(1796), 208 (1816), 209 (1817), 221
(1836), 227 (1843), 231 (1848, 1849),
235 (1853), 246 (1866), 247 (1868),
251 (1871), 255 (1876), 272 (1894),
273 (1894), 274 (1895), 278 (1899),
270 (1900), 287 (1906), 288 (1907),
291 (1908), 293 (1910), 294 (1911),
297 (1913), 300 (1915), 301 (1916),
303 (1918), 304 (1919), 305 (1919),
306 (1919), 308 (1920), 311 (1923),
321 (1930), 322 (1931), 324 (1932),
328 (1934), 329 (1935), 334 (1941),
336 (1944), 337 (1945), 338 (1946),
344 (1949), 349 (1952), 350 (1953),
354 (1955, 1956), 357 (1958), 360
(1960), 362 (1961), 368 (1966), 377
(1972), 386 (1978), 392 (1980), 399
(1982), 407 (1984), 422 (1987), 425
(1987), 430 (1988)
Greece, 323 (1931), 430 (1988)
Holland, 151 (1673), 305 (1919), 353 (1954),
373 (1969), 390 (1979), 395 (1981)
Hong Kong, 340 (1947)
India, 294 (1911)
Italy, 30 (300s), 98 (1470), 101 (1492), 102
(1499), 111 (1536), 150 (1670), 153
(1680), 255 (1876), 294 (1911), 295
(1912), 305 (1919), 318 (1928), 334
(1941), 372 (1969), 430 (1988)
Japan, 293 (1910), 312 (1923), 348 (1951), 350
(1952), 363 (1962), 402 (1983), 414
(1985), 423 (1987), 426 (1987), 431
(1988)
Malaysia, 331 (1937)
Mexico, 294 (1911), 318 (1928), 399 (1982),
429 (1988)
New Zealand, 336 (1945)
Norway, 331 (1938), 339 (1946), 353 (1954),
433 (1988)
Peru, 340 (1947)
Poland, 311 (1923)
Portugal, 163 (1709)
Russia, 274 (1895), 283 (1903), 291 (1909), 297
(1913), 298 (1914)
Singapore, 331 (1937)
Spain, 45 (875), 307 (1920), 389 (1979), 390

(1980), 430 (1988)

Sweden, 165 (1716), 330 (1937), 331 (1938), 335 (1943), 339 (1946), 353 (1954), 433 (1988)

Switzerland, 306 (1919), 316 (1926), 323 (1931), 358 (1959), 382 (1975)

Thailand, 295 (1912), 425 (1987)

United States, 333 (1939), 338 (1945), 384 (1976), 393 (1981)

U.S.S.R., 310 (1921), 313 (1924), 316 (1927), 356 (1957), 361 (1961), 366 (1965), 371 (1968), 375 (1971), 419 (1987)

B

Beer Industry

Australia, 242 (1862), 267 (1888)

Belgium, 99 (1477), 114 (1552), 115 (1554)

Canada, 193 (1786), 225 (1841), 231 (1847), 387 (1978)

China, 2 (6000)

Czechoslovakia, 86 (1378), 224 (1840)

Denmark, 230 (1847), 253 (1873), 274 (1895), 282 (1902), 375 (1970)

Egypt, 6 (1500)

Europe, 41 (768)

France, 43 (812), 237 (1856), 411 (1985)

Germany, 74 (1283), 86 (1376), 87 (1383), 107 (1516), 227 (1843), 258 (1879), 259 (1880s), 420 (1987)

Great Britain, 100 (1486), 118 (1568), 172 (1736), 176 (1748), 177 (1750), 191 (1781), 197 (1793), 228 (1845), 302 (1917), 362 (1961), 417 (1986)

Holland, 244 (1864), 250 (1870), 375 (1970)

Ireland, 180 (1759), 242 (1862), 244 (1864), 248 (1868), 269 (1890), 354 (1955)

Japan, 255 (1876), 289 (1907), 312 (1985), 426 (1987)

Kenya, 311 (1922)

Mesopotamia, 2 (6000), 6 (1728)

Philippines, 270 (1890)

Spain, 112 (1542)

Switzerland, 34 (520), 43 (820), 368 (1966)

U.S.S.R., 435 (1988)

Behavioral Sciences

China, 29 (240)

Europe, 257 (1878), 320 (1929)

France, 220 (1835), 223 (1839), 272 (1893), 285 (1905)

Germany, 227 (1843, 1844), 254 (1874), 270 (1891), 288 (1907), 334 (1941)

Great Britain, 165 (1714), 176 (1749), 199 (1797), 207 (1813), 208 (1815), 218 (1831), 227 (1844), 244 (1844), 253 (1873), 258 (1879), 262 (1883), 285 (1905), 324 (1932)

Greece, 15 (335)

Poland, 403 (1983)

Russia, 184 (1767), 285 (1905)

U.S.S.R., 363 (1963), 374 (1970), 421 (1987)

Beverage Industry

Brazil, 170 (1727), 217 (1830s), 323 (1931), 384 (1977)

Canada, 285 (1904), 293 (1980)

Ceylon, 216 (1892), 217 (1830s), 326 (1933)

China, 24 (01), 29 (222), 34 (525)

Ethiopia, 50 (1000s)

Europe, 106 (1515)

France, 139 (1636), 150 (1669), 201 (1802), 225 (1841), 339 (1947), 373 (1969), 385 (1977)

Germany, 190 (1781), 290 (1908), 291 (1908)

Great Britain, 143 (1650), 144 (1652), 145 (1657), 162 (1706), 182 (1765), 186 (1772, 1773), 192 (1783), 210 (1819), 221 (1836), 224 (1840), 234 (1851), 251 (1871), 253 (1873), 264 (1885), 265 (1886), 274 (1895), 275 (1896), 278 (1898), 281 (1901), 349 (1952), 351 (1953), 419 (1986)

Holland, 130 (1610), 164 (1711), 322 (1930)

India, 217 (1830s), 223 (1839), 326 (1933)

Italy, 121 (1580), 338 (1946)

Japan, 63 (1191), 356 (1957), 414 (1985)

Mocha, 95 (1450)

Surinam, 166 (1718)

Sweden, 185 (1770), 236 (1854)

Switzerland, 284 (1904)

Taiwan, 414 (1985)

Turkey, 115 (1554)

U.S.S.R., 358 (1959)

Venezuela, 170 (1728)

See Also Beer Industry; Spirits Industry; Wine Industry

Bicycle Industry

Egypt, 7 (1292)

Europe, 49 (976), 248 (1869), 280 (1901)

France, 195 (1790), 247 (1867, 1868), 248 (1869), 267 (1888), 283 (1903)

Germany, 208 (1816), 257 (1878)

Great Britain, 223 (1839), 248 (1868), 254 (1874), 256 (1876), 257 (1878), 259

(1880s, 1880), 260 (1880), 264 (1885), 266 (1887), 271 (1891), 274 (1895), 278 (1898)

Japan, 432 (1988)

See Also Automotive Industry (for motorcycles)

Business Conglomerates

Argentina, 217 (1830s), 290 (1908), 382 (1975)

Australia, 348 (1951), 376 (1971), 379 (1973), 381 (1975), 396 (1981)

Belgium, 212 (1822)

Brazil, 296 (1912), 303 (1918)

Canada, 159 (1670), 297 (1912), 335 (1942)

Finland, 245 (1865)

France, 370 (1967), 383 (1976), 392 (1980), 398 (1982), 401 (1982), 404 (1983), 424 (1987)

Germany, 250 (1870), 272 (1893), 316 (1926), 412 (1985)

Great Britain, 278 (1900s), 351 (1953), 356 (1957), 364 (1963), 378 (1972), 380 (1973), 396 (1981), 401 (1982), 418 (1986), 419 (1986)

Hong Kong, 219 (1832)

India, 268 (1889), 296 (1912)

Ireland, 354 (1955)

Israel, 308 (1920)

Italy, 257 (1877), 326 (1933), 349 (1952), 363 (1962), 384 (1976), 387 (1978), 390 (1979), 414 (1985)

Japan, 151 (1673), 249 (1870s), 250 (1870), 252 (1872), 256 (1877), 257 (1877), 259 (1880), 264 (1885), 296 (1912), 303 (1918), 355 (1956), 370 (1967), 385 (1977), 396 (1981)

Korea, 329 (1936), 341 (1947), 371 (1967), 382 (1975), 409 (1984)

Mexico, 361 (1960), 393 (1980)

New Zealand, 242 (1865), 362 (1961), 418 (1986)

Spain, 322 (1930s), 334 (1941), 416 (1986)

Sweden, 75 (1288), 325 (1932)

Switzerland, 401 (1982)

Taiwan, 325 (1932)

Turkey, 368 (1966), 400 (1982)

United States, 401 (1982)

Yugoslavia, 369 (1967)

Zimbabwe, 362 (1961)

Business Development

Afghanistan, 335 (1943)

Africa, 364 (1963)

Albania, 344 (1949)

Argentina, 325 (1933), 338 (1946)

Athens, 10 (594), 11 (560), 12 (461)

Austria, 185 (1770), 327 (1934)

Babylonia, 5 (1728)

Brazil, 429 (1988), 430 (1988)

Bulgaria, 344 (1949)

California, 219 (1833)

Canada, 117 (1565), 370 (1967), 378 (1973), 397 (1982), 398 (1982)

Cayman Islands, 368 (1966)

Chile, 319 (1929), 332 (1939), 379 (1973)

China, 141 (1644), 239 (1859), 249 (1870), 253 (1873), 277 (1898), 283 (1903), 350 (1953), 357 (1958), 358 (1959), 368 (1966), 387 (1979), 388 (1979), 389 (1979), 394 (1981), 398 (1982), 402 (1983), 407 (1984), 408 (1984), 410 (1985), 415 (1986), 420 (1987), 428 (1988), 430 (1988), 431 (1988), 432 (1988)

Colombia, 360 (1960)

Czechoslovakia, 344 (1949)

Denmark, 192 (1784), 222 (1838), 227 (1844), 246 (1866)

Egypt, 5 (1844)

Ekron, 9 (603)

Europe, 385 (1977), 428 (1988), 432 (1988)

Finland, 173 (1738)

France, 123 (1589), 147 (1662, 1664), 167 (1720), 182 (1763), 187 (1774), 193 (1785), 203 (1806), 217 (1830), 338 (1946), 340 (1947), 407 (1984), 435 (1988)

Germany, 109 (1527), 155 (1683), 173 (1740), 186 (1772), 190 (1780), 194 (1789), 211 (1821), 221 (1836), 269 (1890), 326 (1933), 327 (1934), 329 (1936), 331 (1938), 340 (1947), 342 (1948), 344 (1949), 347 (1951), 363 (1963), 409 (1984), 413 (1985), 418 (1986)

Great Britain, 73 (1271), 75 (1285), 77 (1300s), 78 (1303), 113 (1547), 116 (1558), 117 (1563, 1564), 121 (1581), 130 (1610), 133 (1619), 142 (1649), 156 (1689), 159 (1696), 160 (1701), 161 (1704), 171 (1733), 178 (1754), 188 (1774), 192 (1783), 234 (1851), 237 (1856), 275 (1896), 282 (1902), 304 (1919), 305 (1919), 328 (1934), 337 (1945), 383 (1976), 390 (1980), 395 (1981), 398 (1982), 412 (1985), 433 (1988)

Greece, 340 (1947)

Hawaii, 220 (1835)

Holland, 131 (1612), 170 (1728), 398 (1982)

Hong Kong, 344 (1949)

Business Education

Business Ethics

333 (1940)
New Zealand, 242 (1861), 362 (1961)
Nigeria, 318 (1928)
Norway, 286 (1905), 339 (1946)
Philippines, 270 (1890)
Puerto Rico, 242 (1862)
Saudi Arabia, 333 (1940)
South Africa, 251 (1871)
Spain, 229 (1846)
Sweden, 146 (1661), 262 (1883), 273 (1894),
    286 (1905), 289 (1907), 294 (1910),
    328 (1934), 330 (1937), 339 (1946),
    366 (1964)
Switzerland, 180 (1758), 247 (1867), 265
    (1886), 271 (1891), 273 (1894), 274
    (1895), 297 (1912), 341 (1947), 365
    (1964)
Taiwan, 325 (1932), 382 (1975)
Turkey, 316 (1926), 343 (1948)
United Arab Emirates, 343 (1948)
United States, 271 (1892), 360 (1960)
U.S.S.R., 378 (1973)
Vietnam, 391 (1980), 413 (1985)
Yugoslavia, 347 (1951)

Business Publications

Denmark, 180 (1759), 366 (1965)
Europe, 205 (1810), 320 (1929)
France, 152 (1675), 168 (1723), 171 (1730),
    177 (1751), 179 (1755), 181 (1762),
    209 (1817), 211 (1823), 213 (1825).
    218 (1831), 335 (1943), 370 (1967),
    402 (1983)
Germany, 78 (1305), 103 (1500s), 224 (1841),
    284 (1904), 294 (1911), 298 (1913),
    300 (1915), 301 (1917), 329 (1936),
    332 (1939), 334 (1942), 381 (1975)
Great Britain, 123 (1589), 124 (1592), 127
    (1601), 131 (1611, 1612), 139 (1638),
    153 (1679), 154 (1681), 157 (1691,
    1692), 159 (1696), 160 (1701), 169
    (1726), 170 (1727, 1730), 175 (1745),
    206 (1811), 207 (1815),209 (1817), 218
    (1832), 227 (1843), 233 (1850), 234
    (1852), 239 (1859), 242 (1862), 251
    (1871), 253 (1873), 267 (1888), 269
    (1890), 271 (1892), 275 (1896), 310
    (1922), 311 (1923), 315 (1926), 317
    (1927), 324 (1932), 326 (1933), 329
    (1936), 336 (1944), 347 (1951), 356
    (1957), 363 (1963), 378 (1973)
Holland, 156 (1688)
Italy, 27 (77), 125 (1597)
Japan, 155 (1685)

Peru, 388 (1979)
Spain, 184 (1767)
Syria, 44 (850)
United States, 374 (1970), 405 (1983)
Yugoslavia, 96 (1458)

Business Regulations

Argentina, 342 (1862)
Australia, 377 (1972)
Brazil, 406 (1984)
Byzantium, 31 (326), 34 (527, 533), 35 (565),
    39 (717), 46 (886)
Canada, 327 (1934), 377 (1972)
China, 20 (144), 198 (1796), 431 (1988)
Europe, 86 (1370)
France, 33 (481), 42 (801), 65 (1205), 73
    (1274), 88 (1393), 89 (1396), 164
    (1710), 237 (1856), 315 (1926)
Germany, 90 (1401), 92 (1417), 106 (1512),
    107 (1516), 232 (1849), 241 (1861),
    245 (1865), 248 (1869), 258 (1879),
    268 (1889), 275 (1896), 276 (1897),
    327 (1934)
Great Britain, 60 (1157), 64 (1197), 66 (1215),
    75 (1285), 78 (1311), 83 (1345), 87
    (1381), 88 (1392), 100 (1484), 104
    (1504), 113 (1545), 114 (1552), 115
    (1555, 1557), 120 (1576), 135 (1623,
    1624), 136 (1627), 143 (1651), 146
    (1660, 1662), 148 (1666), 150 (1669,
    1671), 156 (1689), 159 (1699), 160
    (1700), 177 (1750), 187 (1773), 214
    (1826), 229 (1846), 231 (1849), 242
    (1862)
Holland, 129 (1609), 261 (1882)
India, 33 (500s)
Italy, 12 (450), 14 (367), 18 (210), 24 (30), 28
    (117), 28 (121, 193), 59 (1148), (1396),
    114 (1552), 151 (1673)
Japan, 181 (1761), 340 (1947), 345 (1950), 410
    (1985)
Nicaea, 31 (325)
Norway, 73 (1274)
Oleron, 60 (1152)
Russia, 168 (1722), 171 (1732)
Spain, 92 (1423), 103 (1500), 104 (1501), 112
    (1541), 325 (1933)
Sweden, 121 (1580), 377 (1972)
Switzerland, 406 (1984)
See Also Work Regulations

C

1627), 193 (1636, 1638), 139 (1639), 161 (1701, 1703), 197 (1793), 234 (1851)
Holland, 80 (1328)
Huy, 53 (1066)
Italy, 23 (46), 51 (1015)
Russia, 155 (1684)
Spain, 35 (569), 51 (1020), 114 (1552)
Sweden, 141 (1644)

Charts/Maps

Akkadia, 4 (2360)
Ardres, 59 (1119)
Babylonia, 4 (2500)
Brazil, 95 (1448)
China, 60 (1155)
Egypt, 28 (170)
Europe, 118 (1568, 1569, 1570)
France, 137 (1632), 175 (1744), 177 (1750), 179 (1756), 183 (1765)
Germany, 100 (1490), 106 (1511), 111 (1538)
Great Britain, 72 (1266), 73 (1275), 120 (1579), 236 (1855), 288 (1907)
Holland, 122 (1584)
Italy, 24 (30), 73 (1275), 77 (1300s), 116 (1558)
Mallus, 20 (140)
Miletus, 11 (549)
New World, 104 (1502), 105 (1506, 1507)
Portugal, 104 (1504)
Spain, 36 (624), 54 (1081), 86 (1375), 105 (1508), 106 (1511), 107 (1519)
Sweden, 415 (1986)
Unknown, 68 (1230), 73 (1270)
See Also Navigation

Chemical Industry

Asia, 6 (1500)
Belgium, 232 (1849), 241 (1861)
China, 7 (1200), 20 (141, 140), 21 (98), 24 (01)
Egypt, 28 (180), 30 (300s)
Europe, 103 (1500), 106 (1515), 112 (1540), 198 (1796), 258 (1879), 276 (1897)
France, 191 (1783), 194 (1789), 196 (1791), 213 (1825), 265 (1886), 274 (1895), 290 (1908), 306 (1919), 314 (1925)
Germany, 110 (1533), 149 (1669), 176 (1747), 213 (1824), 214 (1826), 216 (1828), 217 (1830), 220 (1834), 221 (1837), 227 (1843), 228 (1845), 241 (1861), 242 (1862), 243 (1863), 247 (1868), 248 (1868), 255 (1876), 257 (1878), 263 (1884), 283 (1903), 285 (1904),

286 (1905), 296 (1912), 298 (1913), 314 (1925), 315 (1925)
Great Britain, 146 (1661), 175 (1746), 179 (1755), 183 (1766), 186 (1772), 187 (1774), 188 (1775), 203 (1806), 206 (1813), 212 (1823), 214 (1825), 221 (1836), 228 (1845), 230 (1847), 232 (1849), 237 (1856), 242 (1862), 251 (1871), 253 (1873), 262 (1883), 270 (1891), 280 (1900), 284 (1904), 316 (1926), 327 (1933)
Holland, 281 (1901), 290 (1908)
Italy, 22 (50), 25 (10), 31 (369), 60 (1150), 61 (1167), 78 (1307), 79 (1317), 97 (1461), 99 (1480), 352 (1954)
Japan, 191 (1781), 374 (1970)
Middle East, 39 (720), 41 (782), 46 (880), 64 (1200s)
Phoenicia, 7 (1000)
Spain, 39 (711), 75 (1287)
St. Omer, 73 (1270)
Sweden, 187 (1774)
Switzerland, 180 (1758), 241 (1860), 265 (1886), 294 (1911), 318 (1928), 332 (1939), 414 (1986)
United States, 7 (1200)

Civil Administration

Austria, 109 (1527)
Bursa, 80 (1326)
Canada, 290 (1908)
China, 7 (1122), 10 (600), 17 (230), 19 (165), 20 (124, 141), 29 (219), 40 (733), 48 (969, 973), 53 (1065, 1068), 139 (1638), 141 (1644), 170 (1729), 281 (1901), 415 (1986)
Egypt, 2 (5000), 3 (2800), 4 (2500), 6 (1385), 349 (1952)
Europe, 122 (1585)
France, 86 (1378), 116 (1560), 125 (1597), 146 (1661), 167 (1720), 200 (1799), 430 (1988)
Germany, 168 (1722), 170 (1728), 202 (1804)
Great Britain, 52 (1042), 56 (1100), 60 (1154, 1155), 61 (1172), 62 (1172), 67 (1216), 71 (1256), 73 (1275), 74 (1279), 76 (1298), 79 (1315), 99 (1479), 100 (1485), 122 (1583), 137 (1630), 143 (1651), 152 (1674), 171 (1733), 202 (1816), 220 (1835), 235 (1853, 1854), 249 (1870), 301 (1917)
Greece, 347 (1951)
India, 115 (1555), 160 (1700), 185 (1769), 186 (1772), 192 (1784), 197 (1793), 219

Coal Industry

Communications

Computer Industry

D

Demographics

Department Stores

Disasters

Drinking Places

Educational Sector

Festivals/Carnivals

Financial Failures

Financial Institutions

Financial Instruments

Financing

Glass Industry

Government Nationalizations

Government Organization

Government Privatizations

Germany, 255 (1876), 358 (1959), 429 (1988)

Great Britain, 298 (1914), 320 (1929), 395 (1981), 416 (1986), 421 (1987), 423 (1987), 428 (1988), 429 (1988), 430 (1988)

Hungary, 431 (1988)

Iraq, 392 (1980)

Israel, 422 (1987)

Italy, 402 (1983), 416 (1986)

Japan, 252 (1872), 259 (1880), 417 (1986), 420 (1987), 423 (1987)

Mexico, 397 (1982), 402 (1983), 428 (1988), 429 (1988)

New Zealand, 429 (1988)

U.S.S.R., 428 (1988)

Guilds

Babylonia, 5 (2000)

Belgium, 65 (1200s), 74 (1282), 78 (1304, 1308), 93 (1428), 104 (1501), 125 (1598), 192 (1784)

Byzantium, 46 (886), 48 (963)

China, 24 (04), 307 (1920s)

Denmark, 131 (1613), 181 (1761), 200 (1800), 232 (1849), 238 (1857), 242 (1862)

Europe, 67 (1227), 171 (1731)

France, 28 (200s), 36 (630), 50 (1000s), 65 (1200s), 66 (1210), 71 (1258, 1261), 76 (1295), 81 (1330, 1332), 83 (1351), 111 (1534), 113 (1544), 123 (1589), 135 (1625), 147 (1662), 151 (1673), 156 (1686), 165 (1717), 183(1765), 187 (1774), 196 (1791)

Germany, 46 (900s), 56 (1099), 57 (1106), 58 (1128), 85 (1363, 1368), 96 (1459), 102 (1496), 109 (1527), 117 (1565), 124 (1590), 171 (1732), 195 (1790), 206 (1811), 218 (1831), 228 (1845), 231 (1849)

Great Britain, 33 (500s), 37 (688), 53 (1066), 55 (1093), 56 (1100), 58 (1130), 62 (1180), 63 (1191), 65 (1200s), 72 (1267, 1268), 78 (1307, 1311), 80 (1322, 1327), 81 (1333, 1337), 82 (1339), 84 (1356), 85 (1364, 1369), 87 (1384), 88 (1389), 93 (1428, 1431), 88 (1394), 91 (1411, 1416), 97 (1461, 1463), 100 (1484, 1486), 104 (1501, 1504), 106 (1514), 110 (1528), 111 (1537), 113 (1545, 1547, 1548), 116 (1562), 117 (1563, 1565), 118 (1565), 119 (1571), 128 (1605), 129 (1606), 132 (1615, 1616), 135 (1624), 136 (1629), 137 (1631), 139 (1638), 145

(1658), 147 (1663), 160 (1700s), 161 (1704), 166 (1717), 176 (1747), 189 (1779), 224 (1839), 257 (1878), 287 (1906)

Holland 146 (1661)

India, 31 (379), 75 (1290)

Iran, 34 (531)

Ireland, 65 (1200s)

Italy, 8 (715), 21 (100), 22 (50), 24 (30), 25 (41), 28 (121, 200s), 29 (222), 30 (284), 31 (372), 32 (395), 33 (500s), 36 (600s), 37 (636), 53 (1052), 57 (1119), 60 (1151), 63 (1182), 65 (1200s, 1204), 67 (1222), 70 (1250), 74 (1282), 76 (1293, 1294), 82 (1343), 88 (1389), 93 (1427), 94 (1434), 96 (1453, 1460), 112 (1539)

Japan, 81 (1336), 119 (1573), 130 (1609), 133 (1617), 146 (1661), 168 (1721)

Mexico, 30 (300s)

Russia, 198 (1795), 205 (1808)

Spain, 77 (1301), 102 (1494), 131 (1613), 136 (1629)

Sweden, 229 (1846)

Switzerland, 184 (1768)

Syria, 5 (2000)

Turkey, 108 (1520)

H

Hotels/Lodgings

Australia, 262 (1883)

Austria, 219 (1832)

Cambodia, 63 (1181)

Canada, 261 (1881), 267 (1888), 271 (1892), 291 (1909)

China, 15 (329), 389 (1979), 399 (1982)

Czechoslovakia, 161 (1701)

Europe, 318 (1928)

France, 121 (1582), 162 (1705), 236 (1855), 247 (1867), 277 (1898), 317 (1927), 318 (1928), 327 (1934), 360 (1966), 370 (1967), 375 (1970), 377 (1972), 399 (1982)

Germany, 297 (1912), 298 (1914)

Great Britain, 82 (1345), 106 (1514), 205 (1808), 221 (1837), 236 (1855), 240 (1859), 244 (1864), 251 (1871), 268 (1889), 283 (1903), 285 (1904), 293 (1910), 328 (1934), 332 (1938), 348 (1948), 351 (1953), 359 (1959), 364 (1963), 368 (1966), 375 (1970), 384 (1976)

Hong Kong, 318 (1928)

India, 16 (269)
Italy, 39 (727), 253 (1873)
Japan, 365 (1964), 414 (1985), 425 (1987), 434 (1988)
Mexico, 350 (1952)
Poland, 426 (1987)
Singapore, 245 (1865), 300 (1915), 376 (1971)
South Africa, 377 (1972)
Spain, 58 (1130)
Switzerland, 255 (1874), 275 (1896)
United States, 392 (1980)

Household Conveniences

China, 10 (598), 17 (230), 30 (300s), 35 (577)
Crete, 5 (2000)
Egypt, 2 (5000), 3 (3500)
Europe, 51 (1025), 89 (1400s), 160 (1700s)
France, 40 (750), 189 (1777), 200 (1799)
Germany, 40 (750), 193 (1786), 264 (1885), 314 (1925)
Great Britain, 62 (1180), 63 (1185), 70 (1252, 1254), 114 (1552), 146 (1660), 157 (1691), 161 (1701), 167 (1720), 175 (1745), 176 (1748), 178 (1754), 188 (1775), 191 (1781), 192 (1784), 193 (1786), 196 (1792), 203 (1804), 213 (1824, 1825), 218 (1831), 224 (1840), 230 (1847), 241 (1861), 244 (1864), 251 (1871), 259 (1880), 271 (1892), 278 (1900s), 289 (1907), 365 (1964)
Greece, 13 (400), 17 (230)
Italy, 13 (400), 21 (100), 26 (50)
Middle East, 1 (7000), 2 (5000), 3 (3000)
Unknown, 3 (3500), 167 (1720), 218 (1831)

I

Industrial/Commercial Areas

Belgium, 171 (1730), 200 (1798)
China, 50 (1000s), 197 (1793), 391 (1980), 394 (1981), 428 (1988)
Ekron, 9 (603)
France, 198 (1795)
Germany, 194 (1789), 259 (1880s), 347 (1950)
Great Britain, 183 (1765), 196 (1792), 212 (1823), 226 (1842), 239 (1858), 387 (1979), 392 (1980)
India, 239 (1858)
Italy, 57 (1104)
Japan, 262 (1882)
Mexico, 366 (1965), 393 (1980)
Russia, 167 (1720), 221 (1837), 263 (1884)
Singapore, 359 (1960), 366 (1965)

Spain, 177 (1750), 196 (1792)
Taiwan, 392 (1980)

Industrial Espionage

Austria, 167 (1719)
Brazil, 245 (1866), 253 (1873), 256 (1877)
Byzantium, 35 (552)
France, 178 (1754), 184)1768)
Germany, 241 (1861), 322 (1931)
Great Britain, 134 (1621), 158 (1695), 159 (1699), 166 (1716), 171 (1731), 212 (1823), 187 (1774), 195 (1790), 210 (1820), 212 (1823)
Holland, 124 (1592)
Italy, 51 (1024), 74 (1281), 113 (1549)
Japan, 255 (1875), 396 (1981)
Russia, 113 (1547)
Sweden, 169 (1723)
Switzerland, 391 (1980)

Insurance Industry

Australia, 258 (1879), 290 (1908)
Babylonia, 6 (1728)
Belgium, 56 (1100s), 78 (1310), 279 (1900), 298 (1914)
Byzantium, 35 (565)
Canada, 328 (1935)
Denmark, 270 (1891)
France, 80 (1328), 144 (1656), 233 (1850), 262 (1883), 292 (1910), 293 (1910), 307 (1920), 321 (1930), 338 (1946), 401 (1982)
Germany, 262 (1883), 279 (1900), 294 (1911), 315 (1926), 316 (1927), 347 (1950)
Great Britain, 115 (1555), 121 (1583), 127 (1601),149 (1667), 154 (1681), 155 (1683), 156 (1687, 1688), 159 (1696, 1698), 160 (1699), 162 (1706), 182 (1762), 191 (1782), 197 (1793), 198 (1794), 220 (1834), 221 (1835), 227 (1843), 231 (1848), 232 (1849), 236 (1854), 258 (1879), 259 (1880), 262 (1883), 276 (1897), 279 (1900), 287 (1907), 290 (1908), 291 (1909), 296 (1912), 301 (1916), 307 (1920), 314 (1925), 327 (1934), 334 (1942), 336 (1944), 371 (1968), 412 (1985), 413 (1985)
Holland, 124 (1592), 125 (1598), 135 (1623), 136 (1629), 297 (1913)
Iceland, 60 (1151)
Italy, 18 (200), 79 (1318), 91 (1408, 1426), 108 (1523), 109 (1525), 294 (1911), 353

Labor Unrest

Language

Leather Industry

Licenses/Franchises

Lotteries

M

Markets

Metallurgy

Military Administration

Monopolies

Motion Picture Industry

Music Industry

N

Navigation

P

Paper Industry

Patents/Asientos

Personnel Practices

(1818), 211 (1820), 226 (1842), 229 (1846), 235 (1852, 1853), 236 (1855), 239 (1859), 241 (1860), 243 (1862), 245 (1865), 249 (1870), 251 (1871), 260 (1881), 263 (1884), 264 (1885), 267 (1888), 268 (1889), 276 (1897), 285 (1905), 292 (1909), 296 (1912), 298 (1913), 301 (1916), 303 (1918), 307 (1920s), 310 (1921), 319 (1928), 331 (1938), 371 (1968)
Greece, 13 (400)
Holland, 189 (1778), 250 (1870), 272 (1893), 278 (1900s), 280 (1900), 296 (1912), 321 (1930), 337 (1945), 360 (1960)
Hong Kong, 280 (1900)
India, 32 (379), 257 (1877), 294 (1910)
Israel, 347 (1951)
Italy, 75 (1289), 89 (1400s), 93 (1427), 330 (1937), 398 (1982)
Japan, 222 (1838), 303 (1918), 323 (1931), 332 (1938), 382 (1975), 403 (1983), 410 (1985), 414 (1985)
Luxembourg, 231 (1848)
Poland, 397 (1982)
Rhodes, 7 (1167)
Russia, 206 (1811)
South Africa, 240 (1860)
Spain, 104 (1503), 105 (1508), 129 (1607), 136 (1629)
Sweden, 313 (1924), 324 (1932), 328 (1935), 330 (1937), 336 (1944), 349 (1952), 354 (1956), 373 (1969)
Switzerland, 257 (1878), 365 (1964)
Unknown, 401 (1982)
U.S.S.R., 302 (1918), 303 (1918), 309 (1921)

Pharmaceutical Industry

China, 237 (1856), 287 (1906)
Egypt, 311 (1923)
Europe, 110 (1530), 269 (1890)
France, 210 (1820), 216 (1829), 239 (1858), 253 (1873), 330 (1937), 379 (1973), 390 (1980), 416 (1986)
Germany, 77 (1300s), 207 (1814), 242 (1862), 243 (1863), 272 (1893), 277 (1898), 324 (1932), 361 (1961)
Great Britain, 129 (1606), 187 (1773), 222 (1837), 224 (1841), 230 (1847), 231 (1847, 1848), 254 (1874), 257 (1878), 260 (1880), 264 (1885), 287 (1906), 310 (1921), 314 (1924), 318 (1928), 390 (1980), 397 (1982)
Italy, 329 (1935), 386 (1978)
Japan, 307 (1920), 405 (1983)

New Zealand, 291 (1909), 435 (1988)
Palestine, 364 (1963)
Peru, 361 (1961)
Spain, 103 (1500s)
Switzerland, 265 (1886), 273 (1894), 386 (1978), 393 (1980)
Turkey, 343 (1948)
United States, 397 (1982)
Unknown, 137 (1630), 203 (1805), 262 (1883)
Vietnam, 242 (1862)
Zimbabwe, 394 (1981)

Photography Industry

Austria, 315 (1925)
Brazil, 387 (1978)
France, 208 (1816), 211 (1822), 215 (1827), 216 (1829), 222 (1838), 223 (1839), 224 (1840), 288 (1907)
Germany, 141 (1645), 170 (1722), 247 (1867), 314 (1925), 315 (1925)
Great Britain, 138 (1634), 206 (1813), 219 (1833), 220 (1835), 223 (1839), 233 (1851), 263 (1884), 264 (1885), 340 (1947)
Italy, 100 (1484), 116 (1558, 1560)
Japan, 302 (1917), 319 (1928), 328 (1934), 330 (1937), 382 (1975), 396 (1981)
Unknown, 253 (1873)

Planning Activities

Argentina, 338 (1946)
China, 15 (300), 36 (618), 71 (1260)
Egypt, 4 (2600), 6 (1600)
Europe, 110 (1531)
France, 92 (1417), 98 (1474), 340 (1947)
Germany, 246 (1867), 326 (1933), 329 (1936)
Great Britain, 45 (871), 66 (1213), 94 (1435), 156 (1689), 160 (1701), 161 (1701), 198 (1794), 211 (1821), 220 (1835), 235 (1852), 309 (1921), 353 (1955), 357 (1958), 369 (1967)
Greece, 13 (400)
Holland, 396 (1981)
Hungary, 371 (1968)
India, 347 (1951)
Iran, 11 (550, 521), 344 (1949)
Italy, 18 (200), 70 (1255), 72 (1265), 73 (1274), 109 (1526), 345 (1950)
Japan, 127 (1603), 325 (1932), 346 (1950), 358 (1959)
Peru, 65 (1200s)
Portugal, 104 (1504)
Russia, 164 (1710)

Publishing Industry

Q

Quality Control

R

Radio Industry

Railroad Industry

Research Activities

Resorts

Retailing

Rubber Industry

S

Science

Securities Markets

Shipbuilding Industry

Shopping Areas

Slave Trade/Serfdom

Social Values

Spirits Industry

Sports Industry

Steam Power

See Also Railroad Industry

T

Taxes/Tariffs

Technology

Time

Time Industry

Trade Alliances

Trade Conflicts

Trademarks/Copyrights/Brands

V

Vessels

W

Weather

Weights and Standards

Wholesaling

Wine Industry

Women

About the Compiler

RICHARD ROBINSON is a retired Professor of Business and taught most recently at Portland State University. He is also the compiler of *United States Business History, 1602-1988: A Chronology* (Greenwood, 1990).